ORGANIZATIONAL BEHAVIOR

FIFTH EDITION

ORGANIZATIONAL BEHAVIOR

Concepts, Controversies, and Applications

STEPHEN P. ROBBINS

San Diego State University

PRENTICE HALL
Englewood Cliffs, N.J. 07632

Library of Congress Cataloging-in-Publication Data

Robbins, Stephen P. (date)
    Organizational behavior: concepts, controversies, and
applications/Stephen P. Robbins.—5th ed.
        p.   cm.
    Includes bibliographical references and indexes.
    ISBN 0-13-643438-X
    1. Organizational behavior.   I. Title.
HD58.7.R62   1991
302.3'5—dc20   90-25936
                                                     CIP

Editorial/production supervision: Barbara Grasso
Acquisitions editor: Alison Reeves
Interior design: Suzanne Behnke
Cover design and cover art: Suzanne Behnke
Photo research: Anita Duncan and Teri Stratford
Photo editor: Lori Morris-Nantz
Prepress buyer: Trudy Pisciotti
Manufacturing buyer: Robert Anderson

 © 1991, 1989, 1986, 1983, 1979 by Prentice-Hall, Inc.
A Division of Simon & Schuster
Englewood Cliffs, New Jersey 07632

Printed in the United States of America
10 9 8 7 6 5 4 3 2

ISBN 0-13-643438-X

Prentice-Hall International (UK) Limited, *London*
Prentice-Hall of Australia Pty. Limited, *Sydney*
Prentice-Hall Canada Inc., *Toronto*
Prentice-Hall Hispanoamericana, S.A., *Mexico*
Prentice-Hall of India Private Limited, *New Delhi*
Prentice-Hall of Japan, Inc., *Tokyo*
Simon & Schuster Asia Pte. Ltd., *Singapore*
Editora Prentice-Hall do Brasil, Ltda., *Rio de Janeiro*

For My Friends in OBTS,
Who Continually Provide Me
with New Ideas on How to Improve
the Teaching of Organizational Behavior

OVERVIEW

CONTENTS

PART II THE INDIVIDUAL

6   Values, Attitudes, and Job Satisfaction   155

7   Basic Motivation Concepts   189

PART III   THE GROUP

10 Communication and Group Decision Making   313

11 Leadership   351

15 Organization Design 485

16 Human Resource Policies and Practices 529

17 Organizational Culture 569

20 Organizational Development 659

PREFACE TO THE STUDENT

Did you ever notice that most textbooks are boring? Me, too! Maybe that's the way it has to be in subjects like calculus or geology. But it certainly doesn't have to be true in a textbook on organizational behavior. Why? Because organizational behavior (OB) is concerned with understanding the behavior of people at work. Since almost all of us are interested in human behavior and expect to work at least part of our adult lives, OB has the potential to be a very interesting and relevant subject.

When the first edition of this text came to life, in the late 1970s, I was determined to write a book that would capture the excitement of the OB discipline. Based on responses from students to that first and subsequent editions, I think I've achieved those objectives. In the following pages, I'll tell you a bit about this book and why I think you'll find it interesting and relevant. Let me begin by explaining to you why it's organized as it is.

ORGANIZATION OF THE TEXT

If a textbook is to be an effective learning device, it has to be more than merely 15 or 20 topics, each called a "chapter," randomly shuffled together. It needs integration. It must provide some logical framework that can guide readers through its maze of topics.

I was particularly sensitive to this need for integration when I began planning the first edition. What I came up with at that time was a building block model of OB. This model describes OB as focusing on three levels—the individual, the group, and the organization system—with each level adding increased complexity. This model has stood the test of time. It has proven to be an effective structure for overviewing the field of organizational behavior and for helping students to integrate concepts. In Chapter 2, the builidng block model is introduced, as well as the key topics that make up OB and the interrelationships between them. This model, then, becomes the framework upon which the rest of the text is built. Specifically, Parts II, III, and IV focus on the individual, the group, and the organization system, respectively.

KEEPING YOUR INTEREST

OB is a serious and intellectually rigorous discipline. That, however, should not preclude a textbook on the subject from being interesting. What have I done in this book to help sustain your interest? Two things! First, I have worked very hard to create a lively writing style. Second, I've made sure that I've included a healthy dose of provocative topics and issues.

Writing Style

You can almost take for granted today that any textbook will be well-written. By that I mean that explanations will be clear, concise, and logical. But I don't think that's enough. I wanted this book to be more. So I concentrated on developing detailed and focused explanations, using lots of examples, and creating a conversational writing style.

In order to cover a large number of concepts, many textbook authors end up creating cursory "laundry lists." Their books are more like 700 page outlines. You'll find that I take the time to carefully explain every concept so that it can be readily grasped. Ideas are developed, explained, and linked. The result is that this text teaches rather than outlines.

The best content, of course, means little if a book can't hold your attention. Years ago I decided to mold my writing style to the way people talk. I use contractions. I ask questions which I then answer. And I use other techniques to create an informal, lively style. Some of my friends tell me that when they read my books they hear me talking. I take that as a compliment since that's my goal.

Provocative Issues

The second thing that I've done to make this book interesting is to emphasize stimulating and thought-provoking ideas.

One of the best things about OB is that there is no shortage of provocative issues. Let me give you a sampling. The following statements, each of which is discussed in this book, are essentially true although they run counter to what many people would intuitively think:

- Happier workers are not necessarily more productive workers.
- Between 70 and 80 percent of American workers report that they are satisfied with their jobs.
- Intelligence is strongly and positively correlated with performance on most jobs.
- Voluntary employee turnover is often functional for an organization.
- Interviews are generally poor selection devices.
- Organizations engage in brainwashing-like practices to shape new hires into good employees.
- The "average" employee rates his or her performance at about the seventy-fifth percentile.
- Much of what is often described as poor communication in organizations is purposeful.

- Money doesn't motivate most employees today.
- Conflict can enhance group performance.

I think you'll find that this book offers enough surprises and provocative ideas to stimulate your continued interest in reading further.

MAKING OB RELEVANT

As a group, today's students are increasingly seeking relevance in their course work. You want realism, applications, and useful knowledge. I've sought to make the concepts in this book relevant by means of several features.

First, there are lots of examples. Wherever possible, I use examples to illustrate concepts. Some of these come from the corporate world—IBM, General Motors, Walt Disney, Sony, and the like. But I've also found that, since we've all shared the college experience, the classroom and campus often offer excellent illustrations of concepts with which we can all readily identify.

Second, I've updated this book's content to address current issues. In North America, for instance, managers are finding themselves increasingly overseeing a more diverse work force. These same managers are also facing a coming labor shortage. These are examples of important issues of the 1990s and I address a number of them here. On a more macro level, you'd have had to have been in a cave for the past couple of years to have missed the globalization trend in business. The global economy is effectively breaking down traditional national boundaries. Chapter 3 introduces the idea of viewing OB in a global context. Each of the following chapters then reinforce this viewpoint by applying OB concepts in diverse cultural settings.

Third, each chapter ends with a case incident and exercise that offers you an opportunity to apply the knowledge you've gained from that chapter. Most of the exercises are of the self-assessment variety. You'll get the chance, for instance, to test how current you are on the changing global economy, to learn your basic leadership style, and to determine how power-oriented you are. In addition, there are half-a-dozen group exercises that will allow you to experience with some of your classmates, first hand, a number of OB concepts.

ACKNOWLEDGMENTS

Textbooks are a team project. While my name is on the cover, there are literally hundreds of people who have contributed to this book and its previous editions.

Several dozen colleagues throughout North America have been kind enough to review all or part of this book over the years. There isn't the space to name and thank them all. But I can say unequivocally that this is a whole lot better book because of their insights and suggestions.

My students have also been a rich source of ideas over the years. Many have been quick to point out concepts that they found difficult to understand or in need of better examples. This revision includes dozens of their ideas. Again, as with the comments made by colleagues, this is certainly a better book as a result of the feedback they've provided me.

Several people at San Diego State University were particularly helpful during this revision. Dean Alan Bailey; department chair Penny Wright; and Ken Marino, acting department chair for spring 1990, provided the support resources that helped minimize the hassles one confronts when working on a textbook during the school year. My graduate assistant during the 1989-90 school year, Joyce Falk (now at Point Loma College), was also of great help. And special thanks to Mark Butler who, in addition to writing the annotated instructor's edition of this book, was a valuable source of feedback as the revision progressed.

Regardless of how good the manuscript is that I turn in, it's only a tall pile of paper until my friends at Prentice Hall swing into action. Then P-H's crack team of editors, production personnel, designers, marketing specialists, and sales representatives turn that pile of paper into a bound textbook and see to it that it gets into faculty and students' hands. My thanks on this project go to Alison Reeves, Dennis Hogan, Barbara Grasso, Lori Morris, Anita Duncan, Lioux Brun, Caroline Ruddle, Sandy Steiner, and Belen Hoyt.

Finally, I want to acknowledge my gratitude to the hundreds of members of the Organizational Behavior Teaching Society who share their thoughtful and creative teaching ideas at the Society's annual conference and through publication in the *Organizational Behavior Teaching Review*. The people in this group demonstrate amazing commitment to their teaching. Additionally, they are not afraid to experiment, to take risks, and to share both their classroom successes and failures with their colleagues. A number of ideas in this revision, especially the exercises, came from members of this group.

Oh yes. One last point. I'm always looking for suggestions on how I can improve this book. If you have some ideas and would like to share them with me, please drop me a line. My address is: Department of Management; College of Business Administration; San Diego State University; San Diego, CA 92182.

Stephen P. Robbins
Del Mar, California

WHAT IS ORGANIZATIONAL BEHAVIOR?

LEARNING OBJECTIVES

After studying this chapter, you should be able to:

1. *Define organizational behavior (OB)*
2. *Describe what managers do*
3. *Explain the value of the systematic study of OB*
4. *Identify the contributions made by major behavioral science disciplines to OB*
5. *Describe why managers require a knowledge of OB*
6. *Explain the need for a contingency approach to the study of OB*

Patricia Carrigan has become one of General Motors' most highly rated managers predominantly because of her ability to work with people. Her secret, she says, is in creating "an environment where people who make the parts can make them right the first time . . . at a competitive cost—and can do so with some sense of responsibility and pride in what they're doing." John Hillery/Black Star.

I'm not smart. I try to observe. Millions saw the apple fall but Newton was the one who asked why.

B. BARUCH

Meet Patricia Carrigan.[1] A clinical psychologist by training, she joined General Motors in 1976, working in employee relations. Six years later, at the age of fifty-three, she was named manager of GM's Lakewood assembly plant in Atlanta.

The Lakewood plant was famous throughout GM for its history of labor strife. But, using her finely-honed interpersonal skills, Carrigan broke down the traditionally antagonistic relationship between plant management and the unions. She got union members involved in operating and design decisions and achieved new standards of productivity and quality. Carrigan now manages an engine and transmission parts plant for GM in Bay City, Michigan.

Carrigan's record at Bay City clearly demonstrates that her previous successes were no flukes. The Bay City plant was over seventy years old and inefficient. Yet in her first year at the plant, she succeeded in cutting rejects by forty-four percent and increasing productivity by forty percent. As one union leader put it, she "saved it from the wrecking ball."

During her first year at the Bay City plant, Carrigan reorganized workers into voluntary teams and gave team members freedom they had never experienced before at GM. One worker described her as "about the unbossiest boss you can have." Further, Carrigan instructed her entire management staff on the importance of trusting workers and letting them have control. As her track record shows, GM employees seem to flourish in the work environment she creates.

Technical skills are a necessary, but not sufficient, requirement to succeed in management. Pat Carrigan, for instance, obviously needs to have some technical knowledge about manufacturing automobile parts. But in today's increasingly competitive and demanding workplace, managers can't succeed on their technical abilities alone. Like Pat Carrigan, they've also got to have good "people skills." This book is designed to help both managers and potential managers develop their people skills.

WHAT MANAGERS DO

Let's begin by briefly defining the terms *manager* and the place where managers work—the *organization*. Then, let's look at the manager's job; specifically, what do managers do?

Managers Individuals who achieve goals through other people.

Organization A consciously coordinated social unit, composed of two or more people, that functions on a relatively continuous basis to achieve a common goal or set of goals.

Managers get things done through other people. They make decisions, allocate resources, and direct the activities of others to attain goals. Managers do their work in an **organization.** This is a consciously coordinated social unit, composed of two or more people, that functions on a relatively continuous basis to achieve a common goal or set of goals. Based on this definition, manufacturing and service firms are organizations and so are schools, hospitals, churches, military units, retail stores, police departments, and local, state, and federal government agencies. The people who oversee the activities of others and who are responsible for attaining goals in these organizations are their managers (although they're sometimes called *administrators,* especially in not-for-profit organizations).

Management Functions

In the early part of this century, a French industrialist by the name of Henri Fayol wrote that all managers perform five management functions: they plan, organize, command, coordinate, and control.[2] Today, we've condensed these down to four: planning, organizing, leading, and controlling.

If you don't know where you're going, any road will get you there. Since organizations exist to achieve goals, someone has to define these goals and the means by which they can be achieved. Management is that someone. The **planning** function encompasses defining an organization's goals, establishing an overall strategy for achieving these goals, and developing a comprehensive hierarchy of plans to integrate and coordinate activities.

Planning Includes defining goals, establishing strategy, and developing plans to coordinate activities.

Managers are also responsible for designing an organization's structure. We call this function **organizing.** It includes the determination of what tasks are to be done, who is to do them, how the tasks are to be grouped, who reports to whom, and where decisions are to be made.

Organizing Determining what tasks are to be done, who is to do them, how the tasks are to be grouped, who reports to whom, and where decisions are to be made.

Every organization contains people, and it is management's job to direct and coordinate these people. This is the **leading** function. When managers motivate subordinates, direct the activities of others, select the most effective communication channel, or resolve conflicts among members, they are engaging in leading.

Leading Includes motivating subordinates, directing others, selecting the most effective communication channels, and resolving conflicts.

The final function managers perform is **controlling.** After the goals are set; the plans formulated; the structural arrangements delineated; and the people hired, trained, and motivated, there is still the possibility that something may go amiss. To ensure that things are going as they should, management must monitor the organization's performance. Actual performance must be compared with the previously set goals. If there are any significant deviations, it is management's job to get the organization back on track. This monitoring, comparing, and potential correcting is what is meant by the controlling function.

Controlling Monitoring activities to ensure they are being accomplished as planned and correcting any significant deviations.

So using the functional approach, the answer to the question, what do managers do? is that they plan, organize, lead, and control.

Management Roles

In the late 1960s, a graduate student at MIT, Henry Mintzberg, undertook a careful study of five executives to determine what these managers did on their jobs. Based on his observations of these managers, Mintzberg concluded that managers perform ten different, highly interrelated roles, or sets of behaviors attributable to their jobs.[3] As shown in Table 1–1, these ten roles can be grouped as being primarily concerned with interpersonal relationships, the transfer of information, and decision making.

TABLE 1–1   Mintzberg's Managerial Roles

Role	Description	Identifiable Activities
Interpersonal		
Figurehead	Symbolic head; obliged to perform a number of routine duties of a legal or social nature	Ceremony, status requests, solicitations
Leader	Responsible for the motivation and activation of subordinates; responsible for staffing, training, and associated duties	Virtually all managerial activities involving subordinates
Liaison	Maintains self-developed network of outside contacts and informers who provide favors and information	Acknowledgements of mail; external board work; other activities involving outsiders
Informational		
Monitor	Seeks and receives wide variety of special information (much of it current) to develop thorough understanding of organization and environment; emerges as nerve center of internal and external information of the organization	Handling all mail and contacts categorized as concerned primarily with receiving information (e.g., periodical news, observational tours)
Disseminator	Transmits information received from outsiders or from other subordinates to members of the organization; some information factual, some involving interpretation and integration of diverse value positions of organizational influencers	Forwarding mail into organization for informational purposes; verbal contacts involving information flow to subordinates (e.g., review sessions, instant communication flows)
Spokesperson	Transmits information to outsiders on organization's plans, policies, actions, results, etc.; serves as expert on organization's industry	Board meetings; handling mail and contacts involving transmission of information to outsiders
Decisional		
Entrepreneur	Searches organization and its environment for opportunities and initiates "improvement projects" to bring about change; supervises design of certain projects as well	Strategy and review sessions involving initiation or design of improvement projects
Disturbance handler	Responsible for corrective action when organization faces important, unexpected disturbances	Strategy and review sessions involving disturbances and crises
Resource allocator	Responsible for the allocation of organizational resources of all kinds—in effect the making or approval of all significant organizational decisions	Scheduling; requests for authorization; any activity involving budgeting and the programming of subordinates' work
Negotiator	Responsible for representing the organization at major negotiations	Negotiation

Source: Table from *The Nature of Managerial Work* by Henry Mintzberg. Copyright © 1973 by Henry Mintzberg. Reprinted by permission of Harper & Row, Publishers, Inc.

Interpersonal Roles Roles that include figurehead, leadership, and liaison activities.

INTERPERSONAL ROLES   All managers are required to perform duties that are ceremonial and symbolic in nature. When the president of a college hands out diplomas at commencement or a factory supervisor gives a group of high school students a tour of the plant, he or she is acting in a *figurehead* role. All managers have a *leadership* role. This role includes hiring, training, motivating, and disciplining employees. The third role within the interpersonal grouping is the *liaison* role. Mintzberg described this activity as contacting outsiders who provide the manager with information. These may be individuals or groups inside or outside the organization. The sales manager who obtains information from the personnel manager in his or her own company has an internal liaison relationship. When that sales manager has contacts with other sales executives through a marketing trade association, he or she has an outside liaison relationship.

Informational Roles Roles that include monitoring, disseminating, and spokesperson activities.

INFORMATIONAL ROLES   All managers will, to some degree, receive and collect information from organizations and institutions outside their own. Typically this is done through reading magazines and talking with others to learn of changes in the public's tastes, what competitors may be planning, and the like. Mintzberg called this the *monitor* role. Managers also act as a conduit to transmit information to organizational members. This is the *disseminator* role. Managers additionally perform a *spokesperson* role when they represent the organization to outsiders.

Decisional Roles Roles that include those of entrepreneur, disturbance handler, resource allocator, and negotiator.

DECISIONAL ROLES   Finally, Mintzberg identified four roles that revolve around the making of choices. In the *entrepreneur* role, managers initiate and oversee new projects that will improve their organization's performance. As *disturbance handlers,* managers take corrective action in response to previously unforeseen problems. As *resource allocators,* managers are responsible for allocating human, physical, and monetary resources. Lastly, managers perform a *negotiator* role, in which they discuss and bargain with other units to gain advantages for their own unit.

Management Skills

Still another way of considering what managers do is to look at the skills or competencies they need to successfully achieve their goals. Robert Katz has identified three essential management skills: technical, human, and conceptual.[4]

Technical Skills The ability to apply specialized knowledge or expertise.

TECHNICAL SKILLS   **Technical skills** encompass the ability to apply specialized knowledge or expertise. When you think of the skills held by professionals such as civil engineers, tax accountants, or oral surgeons, you typically focus on their technical skills. Through extensive formal education, they have learned the special knowledge and practices of their field. Of course, professionals don't have a monopoly on technical skills and these skills don't have to be learned in schools or formal training programs. All jobs require some specialized expertise and many people develop their technical skills on the job.

Katz recognized that few managers perform purely managerial functions. Relating back to our chapter opening, while Pat Carrigan plans,

Diana Slumskie (center) fulfills interpersonal, informational, and decisional roles in managing her California motorcycle dealership.   Alan Levenson.

organizes, leads, and controls, she also undertakes these activities in a parts manufacturing plant. It is this technical aspect of managerial work that often limits the transferability of managerial skills between diverse organizations or even specialized departments within organizations. As good as Pat Carrigan is at running manufacturing operations for General Motors, she would have to develop some new technical skills to perform equally effectively as head of the news division for a major television network.

Human Skills The ability to work with, understand, and motivate other people, both individually and in groups.

HUMAN SKILLS   The ability to work with, understand, and motivate other people, both individually and in groups, describes **human skills.** Many people are technically proficient but interpersonally incompetent. They might, for example, be poor listeners, unable to understand the needs of others, or have difficulty managing conflicts. Since managers get things done through other people, they must have good human skills to communicate, motivate, and delegate.

Conceptual Skills The mental ability to analyze and diagnose complex situations.

CONCEPTUAL SKILLS   Managers must have the mental ability to analyze and diagnose complex situations. These are **conceptual skills.** Decision making, for instance, requires managers to spot problems, identify alternatives that can correct them, evaluate these alternatives, and select the best one. Managers can be technically and interpersonally competent yet still fail because of the inability to rationally process and interpret information.

FIGURE 1–1
Source: Reprinted by permission of United Feature Syndicate, Inc.

A Review of the Manager's Job

One common thread runs through the functions, roles, and skills approaches to management. Each recognizes the paramount importance of managing people. Whether it is called the leading function, interpersonal roles, or human skills, it is clear that the successful manager needs to develop his or her people skills.

Recent studies add additional support to the above conclusions. For instance, it has been found that, regardless of a manager's level in the organization, human skills are rated most important for his or her success.[5] Moreover, when managers with MBAs have been asked what skills, knowledge, and abilities they would consider most important in selecting someone to fill their current jobs, interpersonal skills and communication skills finished first and second out of a list of 17 items.[6]

ENTER ORGANIZATIONAL BEHAVIOR

We've made the case for the importance of people skills. But neither this book nor the discipline upon which it rests are called *People Skills*. The term that is widely used to describe the discipline is called *Organizational Behavior*.

Organizational behavior (frequently abbreviated as OB) is *a field of study that investigates the impact that individuals, groups, and structure have on behavior within organizations, for the purpose of applying such knowledge toward improving an organization's effectiveness.* That's a lot of words, so let's break it down.

Organizational behavior is a field of study. This means that it is a distinct area of expertise with a common body of knowledge. What does it study? It studies three determinants of behavior in organizations: individuals, groups, and structure. Additionally, OB is an applied field. It applies the

The closing of plants, like the American Bridge Co. (owned by USX Corp.) factory in Ambridge, PA, resulted in tens of thousands of workers losing their jobs during the 1980s. But these layoffs were not restricted to old-line industries like steel. Almost all of the largest U.S. corporations—including such established names as AT&T, CBS, Ford, Motorola, and Du Pont—cut thousands of workers from their payrolls.
Bill Campbell/Picture Group.

People Skills: A Primary Deficiency of Today's Business School Graduates

A recent study prepared by the major accrediting body of collegiate business schools reported that a primary deficiency of business school graduates is not their inability to write, perform analytical studies, or make decisions. It's their people or interpersonal skills.[7]

Schools of business are preparing tomorrow's managers. But managers fail more often because they lack solid interpersonal skills than because of inadequate technical competencies. Successful managers must be able to lead, motivate, communicate, work as part of a team, resolve conflicts, and engage in similar interpersonal activities. Unfortunately, until very recently, courses in organizational behavior, interpersonal processes, human relations, and applied psychology have taken a back seat to those in finance, accounting, and quantitative techniques. However, now that this weakness in the preparation of business students has been identified, actions are being planned to correct the problem. Colleges will be expanding their courses in the applied behavioral sciences, and making more of these courses required. Business, too, will respond by ensuring that current managers, and those with management potential, receive training to improve their interpersonal skills. Some companies will send employees to workshops offered by universities and training firms. Others will offer in-house programs for employees.

knowledge gained about individuals, groups, and the effect of structure on behavior in order to make organizations work more effectively.

To sum up our definition, OB is concerned with the study of what people do in an organization and how that behavior affects the performance of the organization. And because OB is specifically concerned with employment-related environments, you should not be surprised to find that it emphasizes behavior as related to jobs, work, absenteeism, employment turnover, productivity, human performance, and management.

There is increasing agreement as to the components or topics that comprise the subject area of OB. While there continues to be considerable debate as to the relative importance of each, there appears to be general agreement that OB includes the core topics of motivation, leader behavior and power, interpersonal communication, group structure and process, learning, attitude development and perception, change processes, conflict, job design, and work stress.[8]

REPLACING INTUITION WITH SYSTEMATIC STUDY

Each of us is a student of behavior. Since our earliest years, we have watched the actions of others and have attempted to interpret what we see. Whether or not you have explicitly thought about it before, you have been "reading" people

An OB Challenge for the 1990s

The changing world of work will present a unique OB challenge for managers in the 1990s: How to respond to the loss of employee loyalty resulting from the restructuring decisions and massive layoffs made in the 1980s.[9]

Loyal corporate employees used to believe that their employers would reward good work with job security, full benefits, and increased pay. But in the 1980s, when, in response to global competition, unfriendly takeovers, and the like, corporations discarded traditional notions about job security, seniority, and compensation, that loyalty eroded. Corporations sought to become "lean and mean" by closing factories, moving operations overseas, selling off and closing up less profitable businesses, and eliminating entire levels of management. This has resulted in a sharp decline in employee loyalty. In one recent survey of workers, for instance, fifty-seven percent said companies are less loyal to employees today than they were a decade ago.[10] So, as corporations have shown less commitment to employees, employees have responded in kind.

An OB challenge will be for managers to devise ways to motivate workers who feel less commited to their employers, while at the same time maintaining the organization's global competitiveness.

almost all your life. You watch what others do and try to explain why they have engaged in their behavior. Additionally, you've attempted to predict what they might do under different sets of conditions.

Generalizations About Behavior

You have already developed some generalizations that you find helpful in explaining and predicting what people do and will do. But how did you arrive at these generalizations? You did so by observing, sensing, asking, listening, and reading. That is, your understanding comes either directly from your own experience with things in the environment, or secondhand, through the experience of others.

How accurate are the generalizations that you hold? Some may represent extremely sophisticated appraisals of behavior and may prove highly effective in explaining and predicting the behavior of others. However, most of us also carry with us a number of beliefs that frequently fail to explain why people do what they do.[11] To illustrate, consider the following statements about work-related behavior:

1. Happy workers are productive workers.
2. All individuals are most productive when their boss is friendly, trusting, and approachable.
3. Interviews are effective selection devices for separating job applicants who would be high-performing employees from those who would be low performers.

4. Everyone wants a challenging job.

5. You have to scare people a little to get them to do their jobs.

6. Everyone is motivated by money.

7. Most people are much more concerned with the size of their own salaries than with others'.

8. The most effective work groups are devoid of conflict.

How many of these statements are true? For the most part, they are all false, and we shall touch on each later in this text. But whether these statements are true or false is not really important at this time. What is important is to be aware that many of the views you hold concerning human behavior are based on intuition rather than fact. As a result, a systematic approach to the study of behavior can improve your explanatory and predictive abilities.

Consistency Versus Individual Differences

Casual or commonsense approaches for obtaining knowledge about human behavior are inadequate. In reading this text you will discover that a systematic approach will uncover important facts and relationships, and provide a base from which more accurate predictions of behavior can be made.

Caused Behavior Behavior that is directed toward some end; not random.

Underlying this systematic approach is the belief that **behavior** is not random. It is **caused** and directed toward some end that the individual believes, rightly or wrongly, is in his or her best interest.

Behavior generally is predictable if we know how the person perceived the situation and what is important to him or her. While people's behavior may not appear to be rational to an outsider, there is reason to believe it usually is *intended* to be rational and it is seen as rational by them. An observer often sees behavior as nonrational because the observer does not have access to the same information or does not perceive the environment in the same way.[12]

Certainly there are differences between individuals. Placed in similar situations, all people do not act alike. However, there are certain fundamental consistencies underlying the behavior of all individuals that can be identified and then modified to reflect individual differences.

These fundamental consistencies are very important. Why? Because they allow predictability. When you get into your car, you make some definite and usually highly accurate predictions about how other people will behave. You predict that other drivers will stop at stop signs and red lights, drive on the right side of the street, pass on your left, and not cross the solid double line on mountain roads. Notice that your predictions about the behavior of people behind the wheels of their cars is almost always correct. Obviously, the rules of driving make predictions about driving behavior fairly easy. What may be less obvious is that there are rules (written and unwritten) in every setting. Therefore, it can be argued that it is possible to predict behavior (obviously, not always with 100 percent accuracy) in supermarkets, classrooms, doctors' offices, elevators, and in most structured situations. To illustrate further, do you turn around and face the doors when you get into an elevator? Almost everyone does, yet did you ever read that you're supposed to do this? Probably

Systematic Study Looking at relationships, attempting to attribute causes and effects, and drawing conclusions based on scientific evidence.

Intuition A feeling not necessarily supported by research.

not! Just as I make predictions about automobile drivers (where there are definite rules of the road), I can make predictions about the behavior of people in elevators (where there are few written rules). In a class of sixty students, if you wanted to ask a question of the instructor, I would predict that you would raise your hand. Why don't you clap, stand up, raise your leg, cough, or yell "Hey, over here!"? The reason is that you have learned that raising your hand is appropriate behavior in school. These examples support a major contention in this text: Behavior is generally predictable, and the **systematic study** of behavior is a means to making reasonably accurate predictions.

When we use the phrase "systematic study," we mean looking at relationships, attempting to attribute causes and effects, and basing our conclusions on scientific evidence; that is, on data gathered under controlled conditions and measured and interpreted in a reasonably rigorous manner.

Systematic study replaces **intuition** or those "gut feelings" about "why I do what I do" and "what makes others tick." Of course, a systematic approach does not mean that those things you have come to believe in an unsystematic way are necessarily incorrect. Some of the conclusions we make in this text, based on reasonably substantive research findings, will only support what you always knew was true. But you will also be exposed to research evidence that runs counter to what you may have thought was common sense. In fact, one of the challenges to teaching a subject like organizational behavior is to overcome the notion, held by many, that "it's *all* common sense."[13] You will find that many of the so-called "commonsense" views you hold about human behavior are, on closer examination, wrong. Moreover, what one person considers "common sense" frequently runs counter to another's version of "common sense." Are leaders born or made? Is conflict in a group always a bad sign, or can conflict increase group performance? You probably have answers to such questions, and individuals who have not reviewed the research are likely to differ on their answers. Our point is that one of the objectives of this text is to encourage you to move away from your intuitive views of behavior toward a systematic analysis, in the belief that the latter will enhance your effectiveness in accurately explaining and predicting behavior.

IS OB WORTH STUDYING?

So far, we have only *assumed* that there is value in being able to explain and predict behavior in an organizational setting. Therefore, we need to consider some specific reasons why the study of OB deserves your attention and effort.

Many people are interested in learning about OB for the sake of curiosity alone. They seek to understand behavior. They have no intention of ever applying their knowledge; rather, they merely seek an answer to why people behave the way they do in organizations with which they are familiar.

Beyond this understanding lies a desire to be able to predict what others will do. You may want to develop your skills to make valid predictions; that is, if *X,* then *Y.* The study of OB will help you to develop this predictive skill as it relates to behavior within organizations.

Probably the most popular reason for studying OB is that the reader is interested in pursuing a career in management and wants to learn how to predict behavior and apply it in some meaningful way to make organizations more effective. As we made clear at the opening of this chapter, having good "people skills" is a vital requirement if you are going to succeed as a manager.

Our final reason for studying OB may not be very exciting, but it is pragmatic—it may be a requirement for a particular degree or certificate you are seeking. In other words, you may be a captive in a required course, and learning OB in your opinion may offer no obvious end that has value to you. In that case, studying OB is only a means toward getting a degree or certificate. I hope that one of our first three reasons holds more relevance to *you*.

CONTRIBUTING DISCIPLINES TO THE OB FIELD

Organizational behavior is an applied behavioral science and, as a result, is built upon contributions from a number of behavioral disciplines. The predominant areas are psychology, sociology, social psychology, anthropology, and political science.[14] As we shall learn, contributions of the psychologists have been mainly at the individual or micro level of analysis, while the latter disciplines have contributed to our understanding of macro concepts—group processes and organization. Figure 1–2 overviews the major contributions to the study of organizational behavior.

Psychology

Psychology is the science that seeks to measure, explain, and sometimes change the behavior of humans and other animals. Psychologists concern themselves with studying and attempting to understand *individual* behavior. Those who have contributed and continue to add to the knowledge of OB are learning theorists, personality theorists, counseling psychologists, and, most important, industrial and organizational psychologists.

Early industrial psychologists concerned themselves with problems of fatigue, boredom, and any other factor relevant to working conditions that could impede efficient work performance. More recently, their contributions have been expanded to include learning, perception, personality, training, leadership effectiveness, needs and motivational forces, job satisfaction, decision-making processes, performance appraisals, attitude measurement, employee selection techniques, job design, and work stress.

Sociology

Whereas psychologists focus their attention on the individual, sociologists study the social system in which individuals fill their roles; that is, sociology studies people in relation to their fellow human beings. Specifically, sociologists have made their greatest contribution to OB through their study of group behavior in organizations, particularly formal and complex organizations. Some of the areas within OB that have received valuable input from sociologists include group dynamics, organizational culture, formal organization theory and structure, organizational technology, bureaucracy, communications, power, conflict, and intergroup behavior.

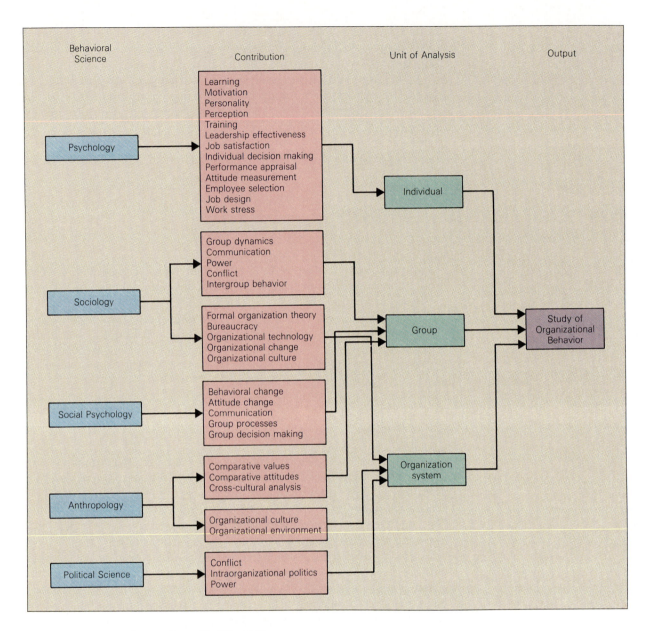

FIGURE 1–2   Toward an OB Discipline

Social Psychology

Social psychology is an area within psychology, but blends concepts from both psychology and sociology. It focuses on the influence of people on one another. One of the major areas receiving considerable investigation from social psychologists has been *change*—how to implement it and how to reduce barriers to its acceptance. Additionally, we find social psychologists making significant contributions in measuring, understanding, and changing attitudes, communication patterns, the ways in which group activities can satisfy individual needs, and group decision-making processes.

Anthropology

Anthropologists study societies to learn about human beings and their activities. Their work on cultures and environments, for instance, has helped us understand differences in fundamental values, attitudes, and behavior between people in different countries and within different organizations. Much of our current understanding of organizational culture, organizational environments, and differences between national cultures is the result of the work of anthropologists or those using their methodologies.

Political Science

Although frequently overlooked, the contributions of political scientists are significant to the understanding of behavior in organizations. Political scientists study the behavior of individuals and groups within a political environment. Specific topics of concern here include structuring of conflict, allocation of power, and how people manipulate power for individual self-interest.

Twenty-five years ago, little of what political scientists were studying was of interest to students of organizational behavior. But times have changed. We have become increasingly aware that organizations are political entities; if we are to be able to accurately explain and predict the behavior of people in organizations, we need to bring a political perspective to our analysis.

THERE ARE FEW ABSOLUTES IN OB

Contingency Variables Those variables that moderate the relationship between the independent and dependent variables and improve the correlation.

There are few, if any, simple and universal principles that explain organizational behavior. There are laws in the physical sciences—chemistry, astronomy, physics—that are consistent and apply in a wide range of situations. They allow scientists to generalize about the pull of gravity, or confidently to send astronauts into space to repair satellites. But as one noted behavioral researcher aptly concluded, "God gave all the *easy* problems to the physicists." Human beings are very complex. They are not alike, which limits the ability to make simple, accurate, and sweeping generalizations. Two people often act very differently in the same situation, and the same person's behavior changes in different situations. For instance, not everyone is motivated by money, and you behave differently at church on Sunday than you did at the beer party the night before.

That doesn't mean, of course, that we can't offer reasonably accurate explanations of human behavior or make valid predictions. It does mean, however, that OB concepts must reflect situational or contingency conditions. We can say that x leads to y, but only under conditions specified in z (the **contingency variables**). The science of OB was developed by using general concepts, and then altering their application to the particular situation. So, for example, OB scholars would avoid stating that effective leaders should always seek the ideas of their subordinates before making a decision. Rather, we shall find that in some situations a participative style is clearly superior, but in other situations, an autocratic decision style is more effective. In other words, the effectiveness of a particular leadership style is *contingent* upon the situation in which it is utilized.

Viewing a Common Event Through Dissimilar Eyes

The diversity of training, interests, and perspective among members of the various behavioral disciplines has contributed to divergent approaches to the study of many OB topics. To illustrate, take the issue of conflict within organizations. If an industrial psychologist and an organizational sociologist look at the same conflict situation, they rarely see it in the same way. Psychologists tend to see the cause of most conflicts as lying in the motives and personalities of the parties involved. In contrast, sociologists tend to see the source of the conflict as the roles and structure that define the relationships between the parties. As a result, the psychologist's solution to conflict focuses on changing people, whereas the sociologist's solution is more likely to emphasize restructuring relationships.

This illustration dramatizes two important points that you should keep in mind as you read this text: The field of OB has clearly been broadened by the diverse insights brought to it by psychologists, sociologists, social psychologists, anthropologists, and political scientists. However, each discipline molds issues of interest to fit into the perspective with which that discipline views the world.

As you proceed through this text, you'll encounter a wealth of research-based theories about how people behave in organizations. But don't expect to find a lot of straightforward cause–effect relationships. There aren't many! Organizational behavior theories mirror the subject matter with which they deal. People are complex and complicated, and so too must be the theories developed to explain their actions.

Consistent with the contingency philosophy, you'll find point–counterpoint debates at the conclusion of each chapter. These debates are included to reinforce that within the OB field there are many issues over which there is significant disagreement. By directly addressing some of the more controversial issues, using the point–counterpoint format, you get the opportunity to explore different points of view, discover how diverse perspectives complement and oppose each other, and gain insight into some of the debates currently taking place within the OB field.[15]

So, at the end of one chapter, you'll find an argument that projects leadership as playing an important role in an organization attaining its goals, followed by the argument that there is little evidence to support this claim. Similarly, at the end of other chapters, you'll read both sides of the debate on whether money is a motivator, clear communication is always desirable, bureaucracies have become obsolete, and the like. These arguments are meant to demonstrate that OB, like many disciplines, has disagreements over specific findings, methods, and theories. Some of the point–counterpoint arguments are more provocative than others, but each makes some valid points that you should find thought-provoking. The key is to be able to decipher under what conditions each argument may be right or wrong.

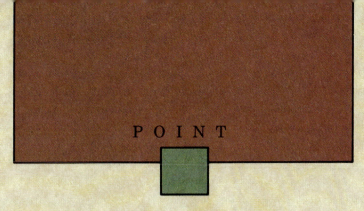

OB Is a Social Science

OB has grown out of at least two older fields in business schools: human relations and management. It also includes significant ideas from psychology and sociology, although other social sciences such as economics, anthropology, and political science have certainly contributed to OB's development. In the past twenty years, OB has received substantial inputs from a younger generation of scholars who have received their training in business schools either under the label of Organizational Behavior itself or under some related term. If one, however, were required to select a single discipline that has most influenced the content of OB and its research methodologies, there is little disagreement over the answer: psychology. In second place, and closing slowly on the leader, is sociology.

Any study of the OB field would be generally acknowledged as incomplete without a discussion of the following ten topics: attitudes, job satisfaction, personality, perception, motivation, learning, job design, leadership, communication, and group dynamics. With the exception of the last two, the major work on each of these topics has been done by individuals whose primary training has been in psychology. The study of groups has belonged to the social psychologist and the sociologist. The interest in the past fifteen years in power and conflict in organizations has also generally been furthered by individuals with sociological training. But the topics of power, conflict, and other interests of sociologists —including organizational culture and structure—

suffer in contrast to the previously mentioned psychologically-based concepts by failing to achieve unanimity among OB scholars as to their legitimacy.

Based on contributions from researchers in psychology, sociology, and other social sciences, we have made substantial progress in our search to be able to explain and predict the behavior of people at work. We have, for example, identified a number of factors that contribute to employees voluntarily quitting their jobs. More important, we have also developed models that show how these factors interact.

Does this imply that we now have a science of OB that can consistently and perfectly predict behavior? No! We have made substantial progress, but our knowledge is far from complete. There are many questions that remain unanswered. There is also considerable research that is inconsistent and, in some cases, even contradictory. Unfortunately, understanding human behavior is not as simple as the understanding of, say, polio. The latter led to a vaccine that effectively eliminated polio in North America. Further research on polio is not necessary. The understanding of human behavior, in contrast, will never be fully understood. Research will continue, leading old theories to be replaced with new ones. We have come a great distance in our understanding of human behavior, but the road is long and we still have considerable distance to cover.

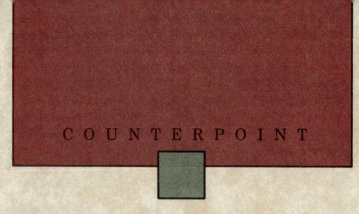

Behavior Is Genetically Determined

Harvard zoologist Edward O. Wilson has, for nearly two decades, been developing his argument that social behavior is substantially biologically based. He would claim that the study of human behavior is not the sole province of social scientists. Human beings are not born with a blank slate as social scientists claim, with their behavior being totally a response to their environment. Wilson views a large part of human behavior—why we organize ourselves as we do, act as we do, and perhaps even think as we do—as a result of a gene-culture coevolution. Genetic makeup helps to guide and create culture, whereas culture in turn operates directly on the genes. Wilson believes that the future of understanding and changing behavior may lie in sociobiology—the study of the biological basis of social behavior.

Sociobiology began innocently enough as an attempt to understand the social behavior of animals, particularly insects. Wilson focused on their population structure, castes, and communication, together with all the physiology underlying the social adaptations. For instance, he found that the incest taboo, which prohibits sexual relations between close relatives, has been strengthened in the animal world by natural selection. In some animal social systems, males are programmed to leave home and find a new colony or herd when they reach puberty. And in a specialized form of programmed learning known as "imprinting," many young animals, birds as well as mammals, memorize the appearance, voice, or odor of their siblings and parents and use the resulting image to make later mating decisions. They will go to great lengths in adulthood to avoid mating with a sibling with whom they have been raised.

Of course, it is one thing to talk about insects and another to talk about human beings. Not surprisingly, it's been Wilson's extension of sociobiolog-ical concepts to humans that has generated the most discussion and criticism. He is suggesting some interesting ideas—such as the possibility of social engineering—that touch the deepest level of human motivation and moral reasoning. By selectively controlling the gene makeup in our society, we could significantly increase SAT scores, produce employees with high internal motivation, and eradicate racial divisiveness and wars.

Is this such a preposterous notion? Not really. In the spring of 1989, scientists at the National Institute of Health initiated a $3 billion project that seeks, by the year 2005, to map the chromosomes and decipher the complete instructions for making a human being. Encoded in an infant's forty-six chromosomes are instructions that affect not only structure, size, coloring and other physical attributes, but also intelligence, susceptibility to disease, life-span, and some aspects of behavior. The ultimate goal of the NIH project is to read and understand those instructions. This project might well lead to scientists being able to read the entire genetic message and even, perhaps, to alter it.

Keep in mind that Wilson and his followers are not proposing that sociobiology will replace the social sciences. Rather, they see disciplines such as psychology and sociology in some future time— probably 100 or more years from now—being encompassed within the physical sciences. The study of topics like stress, perception, learning, and creativity would then be analyzed in physiological terms. Stress would be evaluated in terms of the neurophysiological perturbations and their relaxation times. Perception would be translated into brain circuitry. Learning and creativity would be defined as the alteration of specific portions of the cognitive machinery regulated by input from the motive centers.

FOR DISCUSSION

1. Contrast an intuitive approach to studying behavior with a systematic approach. Is intuition always inaccurate?

2. What does the phrase "behavior is caused" mean?

3. Define organizational behavior. How does this compare with management?

4. What is an organization? Is the family unit an organization?

5. Give four reasons for studying OB.

6. In what areas has psychology contributed to OB? Sociology? Social psychology? Anthropology? Political science? What other academic disciplines may have contributed to OB?

7. "The best way to view OB is through a contingency approach." Build an argument to support this statement.

8. "Since behavior is generally predictable, there is no need to formally study OB." Why is this statement wrong?

9. Some authors have defined the purpose of OB as being "to explain, predict, and *control* behavior." Do you agree or disagree? Discuss.

10. Why do you think the subject of OB might be criticized as being "only common sense," when one would rarely hear such a criticism of a course in physics or statistics?

11. Can the behavioral sciences such as psychology, sociology, and organizational behavior ever reach the precision of predictability that exists in the physical sciences? Support your position.

12. Give some examples of problems a manager might face for which a knowledge of organizational behavior might prove beneficial for finding solutions.

FOR FURTHER READING

BOONE, L. E., and D. D. BOWEN, *The Great Writings in Management and Organizational Behavior,* 2nd edition. New York: Random House, 1987. Presents classic articles and essays by major names in management and organizational behavior.

BROCKNER, J., "The Effects of Work Layoff on Survivors: Research, Theory, and Practice," in B. M. Staw and L. L. Cummings (eds.), *Research in Organizational Behavior,* Vol. 10. Greenwich, Conn.: JAI Press, 1988, pp. 213–55. This article elaborates on the challenge of motivating employees after restructuring by exploring the effects of layoffs on the work behaviors and attitudes of the employees who are not laid off.

ILGEN, D. R., and H. J. KLEIN, "Organizational Behavior," in M. R. Rosenzweig and L. W. Porter (eds.), *Annual Review of Psychology,* Vol. 40. Palo Alto, CA.: Annual Reviews, Inc., 1989, pp. 327–51. Reviews recent contributions to OB using a cognitive perspective.

LORSCH, J. W. (ed.), *Handbook of Organizational Behavior.* Englewood Cliffs, NJ: Prentice Hall, 1987. A collection of twenty-seven essays covering the history of OB, its underlying disciplines, methodologies, analysis at various systems levels, managerial issues, and applications in nonbusiness settings.

MOHR, L., *Explaining Organizational Behavior.* San Francisco: Jossey-Bass, 1982. Offers a critical appraisal of efforts to develop explanatory theories about organizational behavior.

WHYTE, W. F., "From Human Relations to Organizational Behavior: Reflections on the Changing Scene," *Industrial and Labor Relations Review,* July 1987, pp. 487–500. Interprets the last fifty years of behavioral science research in industry.

What Do You Know About Human Behavior?

Much of what we "know" about the world is based on intuition. We have opinions, biases, hunches, and misinformation that we use both in making statements about others and in deciding what we do. The following twenty questions are designed to provide you with some feedback regarding what you "know" about human behavior. Read each statement and mark T (true) or F (false).

True or False?

_____ **1.** People who graduate in the upper third of their college class tend to make more money during their careers than do average students.

_____ **2.** Exceptionally intelligent people tend to be physically weak and frail.

_____ **3.** Most great athletes are of below average intelligence.

_____ **4.** All people in America are born equal in capacity for achievement.

_____ **5.** On the average, women are slightly more intelligent than men.

_____ **6.** People are definitely either introverted or extroverted.

_____ **7.** After you learn something, you forget more of it in the next few hours than in the next several days.

_____ **8.** In small doses, alcohol facilitates learning.

_____ **9.** Women are more intuitive than men.

_____ **10.** Smokers take more sick days per year than do nonsmokers.

_____ **11.** Forty-year-old people are more intelligent than twenty-year-olds.

_____ **12.** If you have to reprimand someone for a misdeed, it is best to do so immediately after the mistake occurs.

_____ **13.** People who do poorly in academic work are superior in mechanical ability.

_____ **14.** High-achieving people are high risk-takers.

_____ **15.** Highly cohesive groups are also highly productive.

_____ **16.** When people are frustrated, they frequently become aggressive.

_____ **17.** Experiences as an infant tend to determine behavior in later life.

_____ **18.** Successful top managers have a greater need for money than for power.

_____ **19.** Most people who work for the federal government are low risk-takers.

_____ **20.** Most managers are highly democratic in the way that they supervise their people.

Turn to page 687 for scoring directions and key.

Source: Adapted from *Organizational Behavior: Theory and Practice* by S. Altman, E. Valenzi, and R. M. Hodgetts, © 1985 by Harcourt Brace Jovanovich, Inc. Reprinted by permission of the publisher.

When Harry Met Stacey

Stacey Friedman has been a literary agent with one of the largest literary agencies in New York for four years. Her job entails matching up authors and their manuscripts with book publishers. She has about two dozen established authors whom she represents in negotiations with the publishing houses. Stacey also regularly reviews manuscripts of new or less established authors who want her firm to represent them.

"I live and breathe this job. I'm up at 5:30 in the morning and in the office by 7:00. I either skip lunch or use lunch as an excuse to meet with publishing editors, with one of my established authors, or to talk with a prospective client. I'm never out of the office before 7:30 P.M., and it's usually closer to 9:00. When I get home, I spend a couple of hours lying in bed reading manuscripts. I only wish I could find another five hours a day so I could squeeze in more things."

Stacey approaches her work almost compulsively. In college, she was in a sorority, played on her school's soccer team, and dated regularly. But Stacey's job is now her whole life. She hasn't taken more than five or six vacation days in four years. She hasn't been on a date in five months, although she has had several dozen offers. She has no social life, except for that which rotates around her work.

"My house is a total mess. I haven't dusted in six weeks. But I don't care. Every morning I pop out of bed and just thank the Lord for having a job that makes me so happy. I'd rather be working than doing anything else."

Stacey Friedman's enthusiasm appears to have had a very positive impact on her job performance. Her boss says she is the best young agent in the office.

Now consider Harry Nelson. Harry is an acquisitions editor with one of the publishing houses with whom Stacey negotiates. Harry is about the same age as Stacey but that is about all they have in common.

"I've known Stacey for about three years," relates Harry. "She's a first-rate agent. She knows her clients. She knows her projects. She's a tough negotiator. But Stacey takes her job and herself far too seriously. When we have a business lunch, all she wants to do is talk business. She's even called me at home, as late as midnight, to discuss one of her client's projects.

"Quite frankly, I don't understand Stacey. She lives and breathes her job. To me, my job is just a job. It provides me a good living. It's relatively secure. There isn't too much stress. I get to travel a few days a month—and the company provides me with a generous expense account. Oh, and the benefits are great. Five weeks of vacation after I'm here only five years, a good profit-sharing plan, and I'll be able to retire in my late fifties on a pension that pays me nearly 90 percent of my top salary.

"I've got a wife and a small child. I really value the time I can spend at home with them. Now don't get me wrong. I do a very good job. My book list is one of the largest and most profitable in the company. But my life is balanced. I put in my forty hours a week and go home. I never take work back to the house with me. When I close my office door at night, I leave my problems behind."

QUESTIONS

1. Why do you think Stacey is so motivated and Harry isn't?

2. If you were to learn that Stacey and Harry made $22,000 and $48,000 a year, respectively, would you be surprised? Explain.

3. As a manager, who would you prefer to have working for you—Harry or Stacey? Why?

NOTES

[1]Based on L. Korteez, "GM Critic Praises GM Manager," *Automotive News,* July 25, 1988, p. 34; and "Women in Management," *Business Month,* April 1989, p. 40.

[2]H. Fayol, *Industrial and General Administration* (Paris: Dunod, 1916).

[3]H. Mintzberg, *The Nature of Managerial Work* (New York: Harper & Row, 1973).

[4]R. L. Katz, "Skills of an Effective Administrator," *Harvard Business Review,* September–October 1974, pp. 90–102.

[5]C. M. Pavett and A. W. Lau, "Managerial Work: The Influence of Hierarchical Level and Functional Specialty," *Academy of Management Journal,* March 1983, pp. 170–77.

[6]S. A. Waddock, "Educating Managers for the Future Not the Past," in W. A. Ward and E. G. Gomolka (eds.), *Managing for Improved Performance.* Proceedings of the Eastern Academy of Management; Portland, Maine; May 1989, pp. 71–73.

[7]L. W. Porter and L. E. McKibbin, *Future of Management Education and Development: Drift or Thrust into the 21st Century?* (New York: McGraw-Hill, 1988).

[8]See, for instance, J. E. Garcia and K. S. Keleman, "What Is Organizational Behavior Anyhow?" Paper presented at the Organizational Behavior Teaching Conference; Columbia, Missouri; June 1989.

[9]See, for instance, J. Castro, "Where Did the Gung-Ho Go?" *Time,* September 11, 1989, pp. 52–56; and Alan Farnham, "Trust Gap," *Fortune,* December 4, 1989, pp. 56–78.

[10]J. Castro, "Where Did the Gung-Ho Go?" p. 53.

[11]See, for instance, A. Kohn, "You Know What They Say . . ." *Psychology Today,* April 1988, pp. 36–41.

[12]E. E. Lawler III and J. G. Rhode, *Information and Control in Organizations* (Pacific Palisades, CA: Goodyear, 1976), p. 22.

[13]R. Weinberg and W. Nord, "Coping with 'It's All Common Sense,'" *Exchange,* Vol. VII, No. 2 (1982), pp. 29–33; R. P. Vecchio, "Some Popular (But Misguided) Criticisms of the Organizational Sciences," *Organizational Behavior Teaching Review,* Vol. 10, No. 1 (1986–87), pp. 28–34; and M. L. Lynn, "Organizational Behavior and Common Sense: Philosophical Implications for Teaching and Thinking." Paper presented at the 14th Annual Organizational Behavior Teaching Conference; Waltham, MA; May 1987.

[14]See, for example, M. J. Driver, "Cognitive Psychology: An Interactionist View;" R. H. Hall, "Organizational Behavior: A Sociological Perspective;" and C. Hardy, "The Contribution of Political Science to Organizational Behavior," all in J. W. Lorsch (ed.), *Handbook of Organizational Behavior* (Englewood Cliffs, NJ: Prentice Hall, 1987), pp. 62–108.

[15]D. Tjosvold, "Controversy for Learning Organizational Behavior," *Organizational Behavior Teaching Review,* Vol. XI, No. 3 (1986–87), pp. 51–59; and L. F. Moore, D. C. Limerick, and P. J. Frost, "Debating the Issue: Increasing Understanding of the 'Close Calls' in Organizational Decision Making," *Organizational Behavior Teaching Review,* Vol. XIV, No. 1 (1989–90), pp. 37–43.

TOWARD EXPLAINING AND PREDICTING BEHAVIOR

LEARNING OBJECTIVES

After studying this chapter, you should be able to:

1. Describe the purpose of research

2. Summarize the criteria used to evaluate research

3. Identify the research designs most used by OB researchers

4. List the individual advantages of laboratory and field settings

5. Define the three levels of analysis in OB

6. Describe the four key dependent variables in OB

Kenn Ricci found excessive turnover was undermining his business. To attract and keep high performing pilots, he came up with a package of pay and benefits that he believes is tailored to their interests. Bruce Zake.

Get your facts first, and then you can distort them as much as you please.

M. Twain

*T*here's an old adage that "there's nothing wrong with employee turnover, as long as the right people are turning over." But what if the people you most want to keep are the ones leaving? What can management do? That was the dilemma faced by Kenn Ricci, president of Corporate Wings, Inc., an air-charter firm based in Cleveland, Ohio.[1]

When Corporate Wings was founded in 1978, it had no trouble hiring pilots. The war in Vietnam was over and the airlines were fully staffed, so there was a pilot surplus. Corporate Wings could hire experienced pilots and pay them substandard wages—starting at about $24,000 a year. Of course, as openings occurred at the major airlines, Ricci accepted the fact that his pilots would desert his firm for their higher wages and greater prestige and stability. Pilots stuck around Corporate Wings for about fourteen months and then left. As Ricci put it, "We were programmed for turnover."

This revolving-door policy worked fine for several years. Then regular customers began to complain about flying with new people all the time. In late 1986, two of the company's biggest clients severed their ties with Corporate Wings. Between October 1986 and March 1987, the company lost about a third of its business, almost all directly due to the high turnover among its pilots. Ricci realized that it was time to change the way his firm handled its pilots. He needed to continue to attract good people but he also had to do something to keep them.

Ricci knew he couldn't pay his pilots the $100,000-plus yearly salaries that they could earn with the commercial airlines and still keep his firm profitable. What he decided to do was to create a two-tiered personnel system similar to that found in law firms. Ricci created a new rank called senior flight captain, reserved for only thirty percent of the company's pilots. Attaining this position was the equivalent of making partner in a law firm, and it was allocated only to the best of the company's pilots. Senior flight captains made fifteen to twenty percent more than the company's other senior pilots and these top-tiered jobs were secure as long as pilots maintained safety, health, and personal-conduct standards. They also got more health and life insurance, more paid vacation time, deferred compensation payable at retirement, and a greater say in scheduling their flying assignments.

After its first year of operation, the new program seems to be working. Corporate Wings had been losing about six or seven pilots a year but lost only two during the first twelve months of the new program. Additionally, Ricci is pleased to find that the caliber of applicants for pilot positions has significantly improved.

The Corporate Wings story illustrates a widespread concern of managers: How do you keep turnover down? In this chapter, we'll show you that employee turnover is one of four primary concerns that OB addresses, and we'll give you an overview of the factors that influence an employee's decision to leave an organization. Later in the chapter, we'll present a model that demonstrates how topics within OB fit together and how they can help you to predict outcomes such as employee turnover.

First, however, we want to briefly discuss the research upon which this book is built. This text will introduce hundreds of research studies in support of a number of behavioral theories. But theories are only as good as the research presented to support them. How do you, as a consumer of OB theories, evaluate the individual research studies presented in this text? We'll begin to answer that in the next section.

So this chapter addresses two concerns: research methodology, and the structuring of the topics within OB into an integrative whole. These two concerns may, at first glance, seem somewhat unrelated. However, by the time you get to the end of this chapter, it should become obvious that these two issues form the foundation for building an integrative framework for explaining and predicting behavior.

RESEARCH IN ORGANIZATIONAL BEHAVIOR

A few years back, a friend was all excited because he had read about the findings from a research study that finally, once and for all, resolved the question of what it takes to make it to the top in a large corporation. I doubted there was any simple answer to this question but, not wanting to dampen his enthusiasm, I asked him to tell me what he had read. The answer, according to my friend, was: *participation in college athletics*. To say I was skeptical of his claim is a gross understatement, so I asked him to tell me more.

The study encompassed 1,700 successful senior executives at the 500 largest U.S. corporations. The researchers found that half of these executives had played varsity-level college sports.[2] My friend, who happens to be good with statistics, informed me that since fewer than two percent of all college students participate in intercollegiate athletics, the probability of this finding occurring by mere chance is less than one in 10,000,000! He concluded his analysis by telling me that, based on this research, I should encourage my management students to get into shape and to make one of the varsity teams.

My friend was somewhat perturbed when I suggested that his conclusions were likely to be flawed. These executives were all males who attended college in the 1940s and 1950s. Would his advice be meaningful to females in the 1990s? These executives also weren't your typical college students. For the most part, they attended small, private colleges, where a large proportion of the student body participates in intercollegiate sports. Moreover, maybe the researchers had confused the direction of causality. That is, maybe individuals with the motivation and ability to make it to the top of a large corporation are drawn to competitive activities like college athletics.

My friend was guilty of misusing research data. Of course, he is not alone. We are all continually bombarded with reports of experiments that link certain substances to cancer in mice, and surveys that show changing attitudes toward sex among college students, for example. Many of these studies are carefully designed, with great caution taken to note the implications and limitations of the findings. But some studies are poorly designed,

Research is concerned with the systematic gathering of information and is undertaken in a wide range of settings. These laundresses at Procter & Gamble's Cincinnati research center test detergents in waters and washing machines from different countries.   Louis Psihoyos/ Matrix.

making their conclusions at best suspect, and at worst meaningless.

Rather than attempting to make you a researcher, the purpose of this section is to increase your awareness as a consumer of behavioral research. A knowledge of research methods allows you to appreciate more fully the care in data collection that underlies the information and conclusions that will be presented in this text. Moreover, an understanding of research methods will make you a more skilled evaluator of those OB studies you will encounter in business and professional journals. So an appreciation of behavioral research is important because (1) it is the foundation upon which the theories in this text are built, and (2) it will benefit you in future years when you read reports of research and attempt to assess their value.

Purpose of Research

Research The systematic gathering of information.

Research is concerned with the systematic gathering of information. Its purpose is to help us in our search for the truth. While we will never find ultimate truth—in our case, that would be to know precisely how any person would behave in any organizational context—ongoing research adds to our body of OB knowledge by supporting some theories, contradicting others, and suggesting new theories to replace those that fail to gain support.

Research Terminology

Researchers have their own vocabulary for communicating among themselves and with outsiders. The following briefly defines some of the more popular terms you're likely to encounter in behavioral science studies.[3]

Variable Any general characteristic that can be measured and that changes in either amplitude, intensity, or both.

VARIABLE   A **variable** is any general characteristic that can be measured and that changes in either amplitude, intensity, or both. Some examples of OB variables you'll find in this text are job satisfaction, employee productivity, work stress, ability, personality, and group norms.

Hypothesis A tentative explanation about the relationship between two or more variables.

HYPOTHESIS   A tentative explanation about the relationship between two or more variables is called a **hypothesis.** My friend's statement that participation in college athletics leads to a top executive position in a large corporation is an example of a hypothesis. Until confirmed by empirical research, a hypothesis remains only a *tentative* explanation.

Dependent Variable A response that is affected by an independent variable.

DEPENDENT VARIABLE   A **dependent variable** is a response that is affected by an independent variable. In terms of the hypothesis, it is the variable that the researcher is interested in explaining. Referring back to the previous example, the dependent variable in my friend's hypothesis was executive succession. In organizational behavior research, the most popular dependent variables are productivity, absenteeism, turnover, job satisfaction, and organizational commitment.[4]

Independent Variable The presumed cause of some change in the dependent variable.

INDEPENDENT VARIABLE   An **independent variable** is the presumed cause of some change in the dependent variable. Participating in varsity athletics was the independent variable in my friend's hypothesis. Popular independent variables studied by OB researchers include intelligence, personality, job satisfaction, experience, motivation, reinforcement patterns, leadership style, reward allocations, selection methods, and organization design. We have said that job satisfaction is frequently used by OB researchers as both a dependent and independent variable. This is not an error. It merely reflects that the label given to a variable depends on its place in the hypothesis. In the statement "Increases in job satisfaction lead to reduced turnover," job satisfaction is an independent variable. However, in the statement, "Increases in money lead to higher job satisfaction," job satisfaction becomes a dependent variable.

Moderating Variable Abates the effect of the independent variable on the dependent variable; also known as contingency variable.

MODERATING VARIABLE   A **moderating variable** abates the effect of the independent variable on the dependent variable. It might also be thought of as the contingency variable: If X (independent variable), then Y (dependent variable) will occur, but only under conditions Z (moderating variable). To translate this into a real-life example, we might say that if we increase the amount of direct supervision in the work area (X), then there will be a change in worker productivity (Y), but this effect will be moderated by the complexity of the tasks being performed (Z).

Causality The implication that the independent variable causes the dependent variable.

CAUSALITY   A hypothesis, by definition, implies a relationship. That is, it implies a presumed cause and effect. This direction of cause and effect is called **causality.** Changes in the independent variable are assumed to *cause* changes in the dependent variable. However, in behavioral research, even though relationships may be found, it is possible to make an incorrect assumption of causality. For example, as we'll show in a later chapter, early behavioral scientists found a relationship between employee satisfaction and productivity. They concluded that a happy worker was a productive worker. Follow-up research has supported the relationship, but disconfirmed the direction of the arrow. The evidence more correctly suggests that high productivity leads to satisfaction, rather than the other way around.

Correlation Coefficient Indicates the strength of a relationship between two or more variables.

CORRELATION COEFFICIENT   It is one thing to know that there is a relationship between two or more variables. It is another to know the *strength* of that relationship. The term **correlation coefficient** is used to indicate that strength, and is expressed as a number between -1.00 (a perfect negative relationship) to $+1.00$ (a perfect positive correlation).

When two variables vary directly with one another, the correlation will be expressed as a positive number. When they vary inversely—that is, one increases as the other decreases—the correlation will be expressed as a negative number. If the two variables vary independently of each other, we say that the correlation between them is zero.

For example, a researcher might survey a group of employees to determine the satisfaction of each with his or her job. Then, using company absenteeism reports, the researcher could correlate the job satisfaction scores against individual attendance records to determine whether employees who are more satisfied with their jobs have better attendance records than their counterparts who indicated lower job satisfaction. Let's suppose the researcher found a correlation coefficient between satisfaction and attendance of +0.50. Would that be a strong association? There is, unfortunately, no precise numerical cutoff separating strong and weak relationships. A standard statistical test would need to be applied to determine whether or not the relationship was a significant one.

A final point needs to be made before we move on: A correlation coefficient measures only the strength of association between two variables. A high value does *not* imply causality. The length of women's skirts and stock market prices, for instance, have long been noted to be highly correlated, but one should be careful not to infer that a causal relationship between the two exists. In this instance, the high correlation is more happenstance than predictive.

THEORY   The final term we'll introduce in this section is **theory.** Theory describes a set of systematically interrelated concepts or hypotheses that purport to explain and predict phenomena. In OB, theories are also frequently referred to as *models*. We'll use the two terms interchangeably.

There are no shortages of theories in OB. For instance, we have theories to describe what motivates people, the most effective leadership styles, the best way to resolve conflicts, and how people acquire power. In some cases, we have half-a-dozen or more separate theories that purport to explain and predict a given phenomenon. In such cases, is one right and the others wrong? No! They tend to reflect science at work—researchers testing previous theories, modifying them, and, when appropriate, proposing new models that may prove to have higher explanatory and predictive powers. Multiple theories attempting to explain common phenomena merely attest that OB is an active discipline, still growing and evolving.

As we proceed through this text, we'll introduce and describe a great many theories. We'll also review the research evidence underlying them. In this way you'll see the present state of the field, and assess which theories, at least at the current time, provide the best explanations of OB phenomena.

Evaluating Research

As a potential consumer of behavioral research, you should follow the dictum of *caveat emptor*—let the buyer beware! In evaluating any research study, you need to ask three questions.[5]

Is it valid? Is the study actually measuring what it claims to be measuring? Many psychological tests have been discarded by employers in recent years because they have not been found to be valid measures of the applicants' ability to successfully do a given job. But the **validity** issue is

Theory A set of systematically interrelated concepts or hypotheses that purport to explain and predict phenomena.

Validity The degree to which a

research study is actually measuring what it claims to be measuring.

Reliability Consistency of measurement.

Generalizability The degree to which results of a research study are applicable to groups of individuals other than those who participate in the original study.

relevant to all research studies. So, if you find a study that links cohesive work groups with higher productivity, you want to know how each of these variables were measured and whether they are actually measuring what they are supposed to be measuring.

Is it reliable? **Reliability** refers to consistency of measurement. If you were to have your height measured every day with a wooden yardstick, you would get highly reliable results. On the other hand, if you were measured each day by an elastic tape measure, there would probably be considerable disparity between your height measurements from one day to the next. Your height, of course, does not change from day to day. The variability is due to the unreliability of the measuring device. Reliable measurement procedures are free from systematic sources of error.

Is it generalizable? Are the results of the research study **generalizable** to groups of individuals other than those who participated in the original study? Be aware, for example, of the limitations that might exist in research that uses college students as subjects. Are the findings in such studies generalizable to full-time employees in real jobs? Similarly, how generalizable to the overall work population are the results from a study that assesses job stress among ten nuclear power plant engineers in the hamlet of Mahone Bay, Nova Scotia?

Research Design

Doing research is an exercise in trade-offs. Richness of information typically comes with reduced generalizability. The more a researcher seeks to control for confounding variables, the less realistic his or her results are likely to be. High precision, generalizability, and control almost always translate into higher costs. When researchers make choices about who they'll study, where their research will be done, the methods they'll use to collect data, and so on, they must make some concessions. Good research designs are not perfect, but they are chosen to carefully reflect the questions being addressed. Keep these facts in mind as we review the strengths and weaknesses of five popular research designs: case studies, field surveys, laboratory experiments, field experiments, and aggregate quantitative reviews.

CASE STUDY You pick up a copy of Lee Iacocca's autobiography. In it he describes how he moved up the management ladder at Ford Motor Co., eventually became president, was fired, took over as head of Chrysler Corp., and, in one of the most dramatic turnarounds in U.S. corporate history, took Chrysler from the brink of bankruptcy to billions in profits. Or, you're in a business class and the instructor distributes a fifty-page handout covering two companies: Apple Computer and Control Data Corporation. The handout details the two firms' histories, describes their product lines, production facilities, management philosophy, marketing strategies, and includes copies of recent balance sheets and income statements from each. The instructor asks the class members to read the handout, analyze the data, and determine why Apple has been more successful in recent years than CDC.

Case Study An in-depth analysis of one setting.

Lee Iacocca's autobiography and the Apple and CDC handouts are **case studies.** Drawn from real-life situations, case studies represent an in-depth analysis of one setting. They are thorough descriptions, rich in details about an individual, group, or organization. The primary source of information in case studies is obtained through observation, occasionally backed up by interviews and a review of records and documents.

Case studies have their drawbacks. They're open to the perceptual bias and subjective interpretations of the observer. The reader of a case is captive to what the observer/case writer chooses to include and exclude. Cases also trade off generalizability for depth of information and richness of detail. Since it's always dangerous to generalize from a sample of one, case studies make it difficult to prove or reject a hypothesis. On the other hand, you can't ignore the in-depth analysis that cases often provide. They are an excellent device for initial exploratory research and for evaluating real-life problems in organizations.

FIELD SURVEY   A questionnaire was made up of approximately a dozen items, and sought to examine the content of supervisory training programs in billion-dollar corporations. Copies of the questionnaire, with a cover letter explaining the nature of the study, were mailed to the corporate training officers at 250 corporations randomly selected from the *Fortune 500* list; 155 officers responded to it. The results of this survey found, among other things, that the most common training topic was providing performance evaluation feedback to employees (92 percent of the surveyed companies selected this topic as the most common aspect of their program). This was closely followed by developing effective delegation skills (90 percent) and listening skills (83 percent).[6]

Field Survey Questionnaire or interview responses are collected from a sample, analyzed, and then inferences are made about the larger population from which the sample is representative.

The preceding study illustrates a typical **field survey.** A sample of respondents (in this case, 250 corporate training officers) were selected to represent a larger group which was under examination (corporate training officers in *Fortune 500* firms). The respondents were then surveyed using a questionnaire or interviewed to collect data on particular characteristics (the content of supervisory training programs) of interest to the researcher. The standardization of response items allows for data to be easily quantified,

Some of the most widely recognized field surveys are done by the Gallup Polls. Using a carefully selected sample of less than 1500 people, they are able to obtain extremely accurate estimates of the attitudes held by millions of people on many diverse issues.

Bohdan Hrynewych/Stock, Boston.

analyzed, and summarized, and for the researcher to make inferences about the larger population from the representative sample.

The field survey provides economies for doing research. It's less costly to sample a population than to obtain data from every member of that population. Moreover, as the supervisory training program example illustrated, field surveys provide an efficient way to find how people feel about issues or how they say they behave. These data can then be easily quantified. But the field survey has a number of potential weaknesses. First, mailed questionnaires rarely obtain one hundred percent returns. Low response rates call into question whether conclusions based on respondents' answers are generalizable to nonrespondents. Second, the format is better at tapping respondents' attitudes and perceptions than behaviors. Third, responses can suffer from social desirability; that is, people saying what they think the researcher wants to hear. Fourth, since field surveys are designed to focus on specific issues, they're a relatively poor means of acquiring depth of information. Finally, the quality of the generalizations is largely a factor of the population chosen. Responses from executives at *Fortune 500* firms, for instance, tell us nothing about small- or medium-sized firms or not-for-profit organizations. In summary, even a well-designed field survey trades off depth of information for breadth, generalizability, and economic efficiencies.

LABORATORY EXPERIMENT   The following study is a classic example of the **laboratory experiment:** A researcher wondered how far individuals would go in following commands. If subjects were placed in the role of a teacher in a learning experiment and told by an experimenter to administer a shock to a learner each time that learner made a mistake, would the subjects follow the commands of the experimenter? Would their willingness to comply decrease as the intensity of the shock was increased?

To test these hypotheses, the researcher hired a set of subjects. Each was led to believe that the experiment was to investigate the effect of punishment on memory. Their job was to act as a teacher, and administer punishment whenever the learner made a mistake on the learning test.

Punishment was administered by an electric shock. The subject sat in front of a shock generator with thirty levels of shock—beginning at zero and progressing in fifteen-volt increments to a high of 450 volts. The demarcations of these positions ranged from "Slight Shock" at fifteen volts to "Danger: Severe Shock" at 450 volts. To increase the realism of the experiment, the subjects received a sample shock of forty-five volts and saw the learner—a pleasant, mild-mannered man, about fifty years old—strapped into an "electric chair" in an adjacent room. Of course, the learner was an actor, and the electric shocks were phony, but the subjects didn't know this.

Taking his seat in front of the shock generator, the subject was directed to begin at the lowest shock level and to increase the shock intensity to the next level each time the learner made a mistake or failed to respond.

When the test began, the shock intensity rose rapidly because the learner made many errors. The subject got verbal feedback from the learner: at seventy-five volts the learner began to grunt and moan; at 150 volts he demanded to be released from the experiment; at 180 volts he cried out that he could no longer stand the pain; and at 300 volts he insisted that he be let out, yelled about his heart condition, screamed, and then failed to respond to further questions.

Most subjects protested and, fearful they might kill the learner if the increased shocks were to bring on a heart attack, insisted they could not go on

Laboratory Experiment In an artificial environment, the researcher manipulates an independent variable under controlled conditions, and then concludes that any change in the dependent variable is due to the manipulation or change imposed on the independent variable.

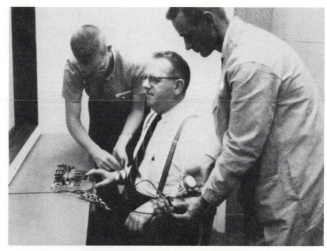
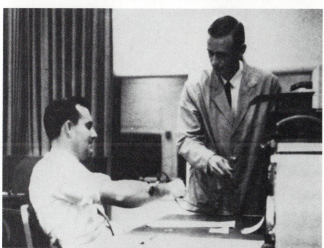
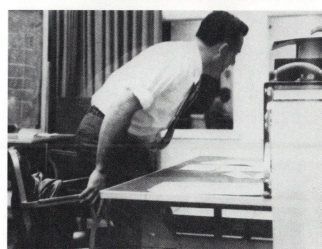

How far would you go in following orders? That was the question proposed by Yale social psychologist, Stanley Milgram. His research results—which indicated that a majority of subjects would follow commands that they found personally objectionable—created much discussion among behavioral scientists who were greatly surprised by Milgram's findings.   Copyright 1965 by Stanley Milgram. From the film *OBEDIENCE,* distributed by the New York University Film Library.

with their job. Hesitations or protests by the subject were met by the experimenter's statement, "You have no choice, you must go on! Your job is to punish the learner's mistakes." Of course, the subjects did have a choice. All they had to do was stand up and walk out.

The majority of the subjects dissented. But dissension isn't synonymous with disobedience. Sixty-two percent of the subjects increased the shock level to the maximum of 450 volts. The average level of shock administered by the remaining thirty-eight percent was nearly 370 volts.[7]

In a laboratory experiment, an artificial environment is created by the researcher. Then, the researcher manipulates an independent variable under controlled conditions. Finally, since all other things are held equal, the researcher is able to conclude that any change in the dependent variable is due to the manipulation or change imposed on the independent variable. Note that, because of the controlled conditions, the researcher is able to imply causation between the independent and dependent variables.

The laboratory experiment trades off realism and generalizability for precision and control. It provides a high degree of control over variables and precise measurement of those variables. But findings from laboratory studies are often difficult to generalize to the real world of work. This is because the artificial laboratory rarely duplicates the intricacies and nuances of real organizations. Additionally, many laboratory experiments deal with phenomena that cannot be reproduced or applied to real-life situations.

Field Experiment A controlled experiment conducted in a real organization.

FIELD EXPERIMENT   The following is an example of a **field experiment:** The management of a large company is interested in determining the impact that a four-day workweek would have on employee absenteeism. To be more specific, they want to know if employees working four ten-hour days have lower absence rates than similar employees working the traditional five-day week of eight hours each day. Because the company is large, it has a number of manufacturing plants that employ essentially similar work forces. Two of these are chosen for the experiment, both located in the greater Cleveland area. Obviously, it would not be appropriate to compare two similar-sized plants if one is in rural Mississippi and the other is in downtown Boston. Factors such as transportation and weather, in comparison, might more likely explain any differences found than changes in the number of days worked per week.

In one plant, the experiment was put into place—workers began the four-day week. At the other plant, which became the control group, no changes were made in the employees' five-day week. Absence data was gathered from the company's records at both locations for a period of eighteen months. This extended time period lessened the possibility that any results would be distorted by the mere novelty of changes being implemented in the experimental plant. After eighteen months, management found that absenteeism had dropped by forty percent at the experimental plant, and only by six percent in the control plant. Because of the design of this study, management believed that the larger drop in absences at the experimental plant was due to the introduction of the compressed work week.

The field experiment is similar to the laboratory experiment, except it is conducted in a real organization. The natural setting is more realistic than the laboratory setting. Additionally, unless control groups are maintained, there can be a loss of control if extraneous forces intervene—for example, an employee strike, a major layoff, or a corporate restructuring. Maybe the greatest concern with field studies has to do with organizational selection bias. Not all organizations are going to allow outside researchers to come in and study their employees and operations. This is especially true of organizations that have serious problems. Therefore, since most published studies in OB are done by outside researchers, the selection bias might work toward publication of studies conducted almost exclusively at successful and well-managed organizations.

Our general conclusion is that, of the four research designs we've discussed, the field experiment typically provides the most valid and generalizable findings and, except for its high cost, trades off the least to get the most. (See Table 2–1.)

AGGREGATE QUANTITATIVE REVIEWS   What relationship, if any, is there between the sex of employees and occupational stress? There have been a

Is OB the "Science of the College Sophomore"?

A major determinant of the generalizability of any laboratory experiment is the characteristics of the study's subjects. If the subjects are all male managers, between the ages of forty-five and sixty, working in large corporations like General Motors and IBM, conclusions based on the study's findings need to be limited to reflect this.

This recognition of limiting generalizability to reflect characteristics of the subjects would not be a problem in OB if laboratory experiments tended to include all sizes, shapes, and kinds of subjects. After all, organizations come in all types, and so do their employees. But it has long been observed that the behavioral studies which compose a large part of the OB research literature rely heavily upon college students as experimental subjects.[8] Generations of college students have toiled in university laboratories solving problems they didn't create, working at "jobs" that only hours before they knew nothing about, selecting applicants for hire in nonexistent organizations, and the like. The results of these experiments then find their way into the behavioral literature and form the basis for current theories as well as suggestions for improved practices. For instance, approximately seventy-five percent of published research in social psychology has involved college students.

Why has this occurred? The best answer is: Convenience. College students are a readily available resource to faculty researchers and a low-cost alternative to investigating full-time employees in work organizations.

Does this wide use of college students invalidate OB theories? This question is not easily answered. On one hand, clearly college students are not representative of the general work population. This is especially true where subjects are young college undergraduates with little or no substantive work experience. On the other hand, for many research objectives, students are not unlike nonstudents. For example, studies dealing with perception, attitude change, learning processes, or communication are likely to be as generalizable with college students as with any other population. Additionally, *any* research population can be argued to be atypical. Homogeneously defined groups of subjects—be they college-educated, white-collar professionals, employees in high-tech industries, *or* college students—require the researcher to qualify his or her findings. And since no group can fully represent the complete diversity of employees in all types of organizations, in all countries of the world, all studies will have some limitations to their generalizability. The key is understanding what those limitations are.

TABLE 2–1   Comparing Four Research Designs

Variable	Research Designs			
	Case Studies	Field Surveys	Laboratory Experiments	Field Experiments
Generalizability	Low	Moderate	Low	High
Realism	High	High	Low	Moderate-to-high
Precision	Low	Low	High	High
Control	Low	Moderate	High	Moderate-to-high
Cost	Moderate	Moderate	Low	High

and innovation as dependent variables.[11] In defense of innovation, he argues, "As a greater percentage of work becomes highly skilled and professionalized, the criteria of performance will likely become more ambiguous and subject to change. Therefore, questions of [employee] productivity may become translated into inquiries about working smarter rather than harder. . . . Where there is rapid change or competition is fierce, innovation may be the organization's most important outcome variable."[12] The fact remains, however, that productivity, absenteeism, turnover, and job satisfaction currently dominate the field. So let's review these terms to ensure that we understand what they mean and why they have achieved the distinction of being OB's primary dependent variables.

PRODUCTIVITY   An organization is productive if it achieves its goals, and does so by transferring inputs to outputs at the lowest cost. As such, **productivity** implies a concern for both **effectiveness** and **efficiency.**

Productivity A performance measure including effectiveness and efficiency.

Effectiveness Achievement of goals.

Efficiency The ratio of effective output to the input required to achieve it.

A hospital, for example, is *effective* when it successfully meets the needs of its clientele. It is *efficient* when it can do this at a low cost. If a hospital manages to achieve higher output from its present staff by reducing the average number of days a patient is confined to a bed or by increasing the number of staff-patient contacts per day, we can say that the hospital has gained productive efficiency. Similarly, a school may be effective when a certain percentage of students achieve a specified score on standardized achievement tests. The school can improve its efficiency if these higher test scores can be secured by a smaller teaching and support staff. A business firm is effective when it attains its sales or market share goals, but its productivity also depends on achieving these goals efficiently. Measures of such efficiency may include return on investment, profit per dollar of sales, and output per hour of labor.

We can also look at productivity from the perspective of the individual employee. Take the cases of Mike and Al, who are both long-distance truckers. If Mike is supposed to haul his fully loaded rig from New York to its destination in Los Angeles in seventy-five hours or less, he is effective if he makes the three-thousand-mile trip within this time period. But measures of productivity must take into account the costs incurred in reaching the goal. That is where efficiency comes in. Let us assume that Mike made the New York to Los Angeles run in sixty-eight hours and averaged seven miles per gallon. Al, on the other hand, made the trip in sixty-eight hours also but averaged nine miles per gallon (rigs and loads are identical). Both Mike and Al were effective— they accomplished their goal—but Al was more efficient than Mike because his rig consumed less gas and, therefore, he achieved his goal at a lower cost.

In summary, one of OB's major concerns is productivity. We want to know what factors will influence the effectiveness and efficiency of individuals, of groups, and of the overall organization.

ABSENTEEISM   The annual cost of **absenteeism** to U.S. organizations has been estimated at nearly forty billion dollars a year. At the job level, a one-day absence by a clerical worker can cost an employer up to one hundred dollars in reduced efficiency and increased supervisory workload.[13] These figures indicate the importance to an organization of keeping absenteeism low.

Absenteeism Failure to report to work.

It is obviously difficult for an organization to operate smoothly and to attain its objectives if employees fail to report to their jobs. The work flow is disrupted, and often important decisions must be delayed. In organizations that rely heavily upon assembly-line technology, absenteeism can be considerably more than a disruption—it can result in a drastic reduction in quality of output, or, in some cases, it can bring about a complete shutdown of the production facility. Examples abound, for example, of the problems that the major U.S. automobile manufacturers have with alarmingly large increases in absences on Mondays and Fridays, especially in summer months and at the onset of the hunting and fishing seasons. Certainly, levels of absenteeism beyond the normal range have a direct impact on an organization's effectiveness and efficiency.

Are *all* absences bad? Probably not! While most absences impact negatively on the organization, we can conceive of situations where the organization may benefit by an employee voluntarily choosing not to come to work. For instance, fatigue or excess stress can significantly decrease an employee's productivity. In jobs where an employee needs to be alert—surgeons and airline pilots are obvious examples—it may well be better for the organization if the employee does not report to work rather than show up and perform poorly. The cost of an accident in such jobs could be prohibitive. Even in managerial jobs, where mistakes are less spectacular, performance may be improved when incumbents absent themselves from work rather than make a poor decision under stress. But these examples are clearly atypical. For the most part, we can assume that organizations benefit when employee absenteeism is reduced.

Turnover Voluntary and involuntary permanent withdrawal from the organization.

TURNOVER   A high rate of **turnover** in an organization means increased recruiting, selection, and training costs. It can also mean a disruption in the efficient running of an organization when knowledgeable and experienced personnel leave and replacements must be found and prepared to assume positions of responsibility. All organizations, of course, have some turnover. If the right people are leaving the organization—the marginal and submarginal employees—turnover can be positive. It may create the opportunity to replace an individual with someone with higher skills or motivation, open up increased opportunities for promotions, and add new and fresh ideas to the organization.[14] But turnover often means the loss of people who the organization doesn't want to lose. For instance, a recent study covering nine hundred employees who had resigned their jobs found that ninety-two percent earned performance ratings of "satisfactory" or better from their superiors.[15] So when turnover is excessive, or when it involves valuable performers, it can be a disruptive factor, hindering the organization's effectiveness.

Job Satisfaction A general attitude toward one's job; the difference between the amount of rewards workers receive and the amount they believe they should receive.

JOB SATISFACTION   The final dependent variable we will look at is **job satisfaction,** which we'll define simply, at this point, as the difference between the amount of rewards workers receive and the amount they believe they should receive. (We'll expand considerably on this definition in Chapter 6.) Unlike the previous three variables, job satisfaction is unique because it represents an attitude rather than a behavior. Why is it then that it has become a primary dependent variable? This is probably due to its demonstrated relationship to performance factors, and the value preferences held by many OB researchers.

The belief that satisfied employees are more productive than dissatisfied employees has been a basic tenet among managers for years. While evidence questions this assumed causal relationship, it can be argued that advanced societies should not only be concerned with the quantity of life, but also with improving its quality. Those researchers with strong humanistic values argue that satisfaction should be a legitimate objective of an organization. Not only is satisfaction negatively related to absenteeism and turnover, but, they argue, organizations have a responsibility that goes beyond dollars and cents to provide employees with jobs that are challenging and intrinsically rewarding. Therefore, although job satisfaction represents an attitude rather than a behavior, OB researchers typically consider job satisfaction an important dependent variable.

The Independent Variables

What are the major determinants of productivity, absenteeism, turnover, and job satisfaction? Our answer to that question brings us to the independent variables. Consistent with our belief that organizational behavior can best be understood when viewed essentially as a set of increasingly complex building blocks, the base or first level of our model lies in understanding individual behavior.

INDIVIDUAL-LEVEL VARIABLES   It has been said that "managers, unlike parents, must work with used, not new, human beings—human beings whom others have gotten to first."[16] When individuals enter an organization, they're a bit like used cars. Each is different. Some are "low mileage"—they have been treated carefully and have limited exposure to the realities of the elements. Others are "well worn," having experienced a number of rough roads. This metaphor indicates that people enter organizations with certain characteristics that will influence their behavior at work. The more obvious of these are personal or biographical characteristics such as one's age, sex, and marital status; one's personality characteristics; one's values and attitudes; and one's basic ability levels. These characteristics are essentially intact when an individual enters the work force, and, for the most part, there is little management can do to alter them. Yet, they have a very real impact on employee behavior. Therefore, each of these factors—biographical characteristics, personality, values and attitudes, and ability—will be discussed as independent variables in Chapters 4 and 6.

There are four other individual-level variables that have been shown to affect employee behavior: perception, individual decision making, learning, and motivation. These topics will be introduced and discussed in Chapters 4, 5, 7, and 8.

Figure 2–2 describes the individual level in our OB model. Note the dotted line around biographical characteristics, personality, values and attitudes, and ability. This is to dramatize that these variables, for the most part, are already in place when an employee joins an organization. The individual variables shown in Figure 2–2 are the subject matter of Chapters 4 through 8.

GROUP-LEVEL VARIABLES   The behavior of people in groups is more than the sum total of each individual acting in his or her own way. The complexity of our model is increased when we acknowledge that people's behavior when they are in groups is different from their behavior when they are alone. Therefore, the next step in the development of an understanding of OB is the study of group behavior.

Chapter 9 lays the foundation for an understanding of the dynamics of group behavior. This chapter discusses how individuals in groups are influ-

Organizational behavior addresses three levels of analysis. It looks at individual-level variables (top left), group-level variables (bottom left), and organization system-level variables (top right). Top left and bottom left, Hewlett Packard; top right, Superstock.

enced by the patterns of behavior they are expected to exhibit, what the group considers to be acceptable standards of behavior, and the degree to which group members are attracted to each other. Chapters 10 through 13 demonstrate how communication patterns, group decision making processes, leadership styles, power and politics, intergroup relations, and levels of conflict affect group behavior. Figure 2–3 describes how these concepts interact and form the group level in our OB model.

ORGANIZATION SYSTEM-LEVEL VARIABLES Organizational behavior reaches its highest level of sophistication when we add formal structure to our

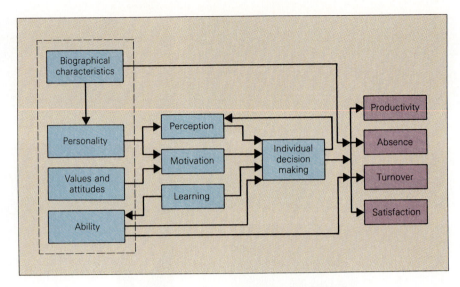

FIGURE 2–2   The Individual Level in the OB Model

previous knowledge of individual and group behavior. Just as groups are more than the sum of their individual members, organizations are not necessarily merely the summation of the behavior of a number of groups. The structural design of the formal organization, the organization's human resource policies and practices (that is, selection processes, training programs, performance appraisal methods), levels of work stress, and the organization's internal culture all have an impact on the dependent variables.

Figure 2–4 describes the organization system-level variables in our model. These are discussed in detail in Chapters 14 through 18.

FIGURE 2–3   The Group Level in the OB Model

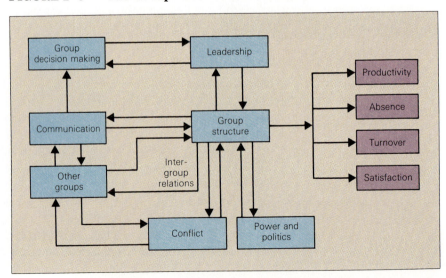

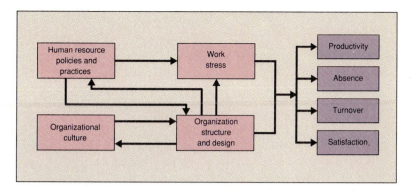

FIGURE 2–4   The Organization System Level in the OB Model

Toward a Contingency OB Model

Our final model is shown in Figure 2–5. It shows the four key dependent variables and a large number of independent variables that research suggests have varying impacts on them. Of course, the model does not do justice to the complexity of the OB subject matter, but it should prove valuable in helping to explain and predict behavior.

For the most part, our model does not explicitly identify the vast number of moderating variables because of the tremendous complexity that would be involved in such a diagram. Rather, throughout this text we shall introduce important moderating variables that will improve the explanatory linkage between the independent and dependent variables in our OB model. One exception is the specific inclusion of *national culture* as a variable that effects all levels of analysis.

We need to look at OB from a global perspective. Why? Because organizational behavior is different in different countries and these differences affect all the independent variables. Moreover, organizations are no longer constrained by national boundaries. General Motors, for instance, makes cars in a dozen or more countries outside the United States. Honda, a so-called Japanese firm, now makes more cars in the United States than does Chrysler. Our point is that you need to be able to explain and predict behavior in a global context. The next chapter introduces this theme; and it is reinforced throughout the text by inclusion of "OB in a Global Context"—boxes that show you how concepts and practices must be altered to reflect differences across national cultures.

Also note that we've added the concepts of change and development to Figure 2–5, acknowledging the dynamics of behavior and recognizing that there are ways for change agents or managers to modify many of the independent variables if they are having a negative impact on the key dependent variables. Specifically, in Chapters 19 and 20 we'll discuss the change process and techniques for changing employee attitudes, improving communication processes, modifying organization structures, and the like.

Finally, Figure 2–5 includes linkages between the three levels of analysis. For instance, organization structure is linked to leadership. This is meant to convey that authority and leadership are related—management exerts its influence on group behavior through leadership. Similarly, communication is the means by which individuals transmit information; thus, it is the link between individual and group behavior.

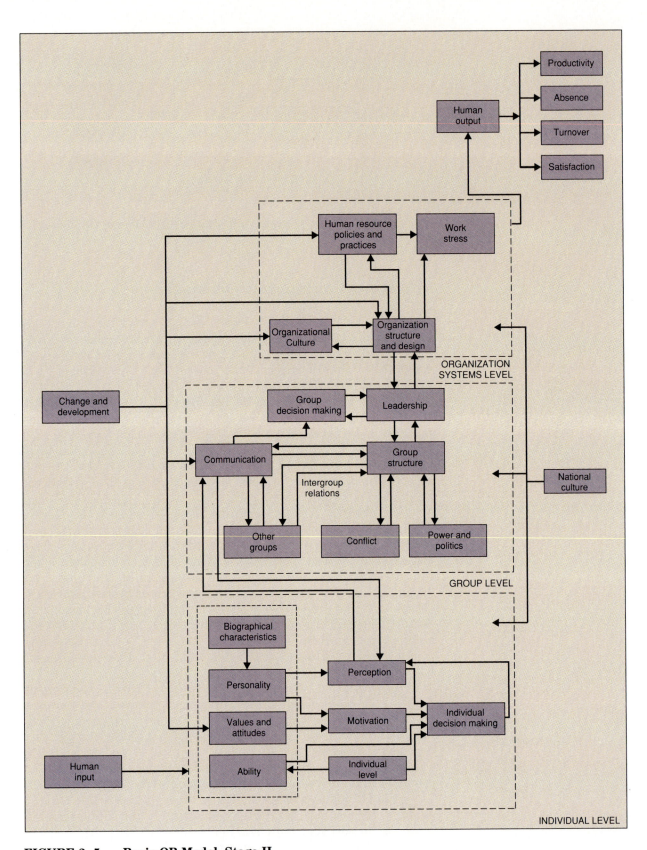

FIGURE 2–5 Basic OB Model, Stage II

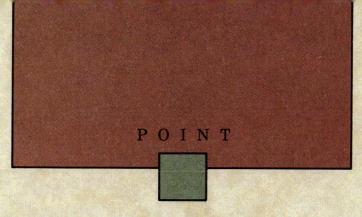

Employee Turnover Is Dysfunctional to an Organization

This text presents employee turnover as one of the four primary dependent variables in OB. This is consistent with the view—held by executives, personnel managers, and researchers in OB—that turnover has negative consequences for organizational performance.

When an employee quits and has to be replaced, the organization incurs some very real and tangible costs. These can range from a few hundred dollars to train a counter clerk at McDonald's, to several hundred thousand dollars for a nuclear power engineer or Air Force fighter pilot. Turnover costs to a firm for a typical job is probably at least several thousand dollars, as evidenced by research in a bank that found every instance of turnover by a teller costing approximately $2,800.

Every turnover incidence includes both direct and indirect costs. A review of these costs goes a long way in explaining why management should be concerned with minimizing employee turnover.

When an employee leaves, a replacement needs to be found. If inadequate notice is given, management will not have time to find and train the replacement, and a temporary employee will need to fill in. The result in this case is typically a drop in productivity. Where sufficient notice is given, the organization incurs the costs of recruiting, selecting, and training the replacement. In many cases, there may be a period of a few weeks or months where two people are on the payroll to do one job—the departing employee staying on to train his or her replacement.

The recruitment and training costs for almost any job quickly amount to a sizable dollar figure. These costs include advertisements, maintaining a college recruitment staff, employment agency fees, travel and accommodation expenses for recruits, screening tests, background investigations, and the time spent by executives in interviewing. The departure of a middle-level manager may result in replacement costs exceeding $80,000, as the following suggests:

Search fees and expenses	$30,000
Interviewing time and expenses	5,000
Administrative costs (reference checks, psychological tests, medical exams)	5,000
Reimbursement associated with selling old home and purchasing new one	25,000
Travel and temporary living expenses	10,000
Moving expenses	10,000
	$85,000

This list considers only the direct costs attributable to employee turnover. To these we must add indirect costs such as training the replacement, loss in productivity incurred while the replacement develops his or her proficiency, loss in work group cohesiveness and morale, and the general organizational disruption caused by turnover (such as scheduling difficulties).

Given the direct and indirect costs associated with turnover, it is obvious that a management team that is concerned with maintaining effectiveness and efficiency will want to keep employee turnover to a minimum.

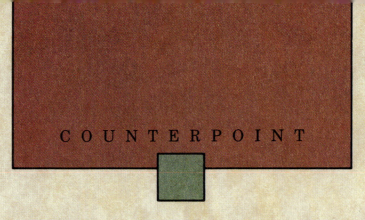

Employee Turnover Can Be Functional

All turnover is not bad for an organization. Discussions on the subject tend to stress the costs side of the ledger. But turnover also provides benefits to the organization. In fact, healthy levels of employee turnover may be a virtual windfall—in hard dollar terms—for the organization.

To consider all turnover negatively overstates its impact. Why? Well, first we need to look only at voluntary turnover. Involuntary turnover—where management initiates the departure—is functional, if we assume the decision is for a cause. Second, there are people who voluntarily leave the organization and in so doing benefit it. They may have been poor or, at best, marginal performers. But because of institutionalized employment security (labor unions, appeal boards, etc.), sympathetic bosses, the desire to maintain group morale, or similar factors, these people are not terminated. Finally, all voluntary quits are not controllable by management. That is, there are situations in which no reasonable action by management could have prevented it. It's a waste of organizational resources to try to reduce this element of turnover. In summary, any discussion of turnover should be concerned only with voluntary quits, and from that number we need to subtract all functional turnover plus the portion that, while dysfunctional, is unavoidable.

Now let's turn to a neglected issue: Turnover has a positive "dollar and cents" impact on the organization. In support of this position, we need to recognize that turnover may be reduced, but at a cost that exceeds its benefits, and new hires are not as costly to maintain in terms of salary and fringe benefits as are more senior employees.

A number of jobs have characteristically high levels of turnover—for instance, waitresses and bank clerks—that could be significantly reduced by merely raising their wage rates. But management has chosen not to pay the wages that would be necessary to keep these people. In cost-effectiveness terms, management's strategy has been to trade off higher turnover for lower labor costs.

An overlooked fact in organizations is that there are a number of jobs where wage rates increase with time, but there is no comparable increase in productivity. For instance, at one public utility, entry-level employees receive $7.82 per hour and then move through the wage progression to $15.45 in their fifth year. The job remains the same, but the hourly wage cost nearly doubles. While employee productivity will increase over this five-year period, the increase is more likely to be in the ten to twenty percent range. Additionally, given that fringe benefit costs tend to be a percentage of direct labor costs, these too go up significantly as employee seniority increases. The result: Recent hires cost the organization less.

There are relatively large economies to be realized by employee turnover. To the extent that turnover is not excessive, that is, its costs do not exceed its benefits, a large amount of money might be saved each year by reasonable levels of turnover. Vigorous programs by organizations to reduce the incidence of employee turnover may be thoroughly shortsighted. This caveat may be particularly appropriate for organizations in which training requirements are minimal and experience may not lead to appreciably higher levels of performance.

Based on D. R. Dalton, W. D. Todor, and D. M. Krackhardt, "Turnover Overstated: The Functional Taxonomy," *Academy of Management Review*, January 1982, pp. 117–23; Dalton and Todor, "Turnover: A Lucrative Hard Dollar Phenomenon," *Academy of Management Review*, April 1982, pp. 212–18; and J. R. Hollenbeck and C. R. Williams, "Turnover Functionality Versus Turnover Frequency: A Note on Work Attitudes and Organizational Effectiveness," *Journal of Applied Psychology*, November 1986, pp. 606–11.

FOR DISCUSSION

1. Why should students of OB spend time to develop an elementary understanding of research design?

2. What factors might reduce the generalizability of a research study?

3. What are the advantages and disadvantages of a (a) case study, (b) field survey, (c) laboratory experiment, and (d) field experiment?

4. What is reliability? Validity? What is the relevance of each to research?

5. Define *independent, dependent,* and *moderating variables.* Explain their relationship.

6. It is well-documented that married men and women live longer than their unmarried counterparts. Does marriage cause longer life? Explain.

7. Statistics clearly show that college graduates earn substantially more money during their working lives than do individuals who have not attended college. Does the college experience cause higher earnings? Explain.

8. What are the three levels of analysis in our OB model? Are they related? If so, how?

9. If job satisfaction is not a behavior, why is it considered as an important dependent variable?

10. What are "effectiveness" and "efficiency," and how are they related to organizational behavior?

11. What are the four dependent variables in the OB model? Why have they been chosen over, for instance, percent return-on-investment?

12. Why are individual-, group-, and organization system-level behaviors each described as increasingly more complex?

FOR FURTHER READING

BACHARACH, S. B., "Organizational Theories: Some Criteria for Evaluation," *Academy of Management Review,* October 1989, pp. 496–515. Proposes a set of ground rules and a vocabulary to facilitate focused discussion about the structure of organization and management theories.

EISENHARDT, K. M., "Building Theories from Case Study Research," *Academy of Management Review,* October 1989, pp. 532–50. Provides a framework for building theories from case study research and puts theory building from case studies into the larger context of social science research.

LOCKE, E. A. (ed.), *Generalizing from Laboratory to Field Setting.* Lexington, MA: Lexington Books, 1986. Presents behavioral research findings and seeks to answer the question of the generalizability of lab studies to real-life settings.

McGUIRE, J. B., "Management and Research Methodology," *Journal of Management,* Spring 1986, pp. 5–17. Discusses the generalizability of the literature on research methodology to linking theory and management practice.

NAUGHTON, T. J., "Levels of Analysis and Organizational Behavior: A Suggested Cognitive Framework for Educational Use," *Organizational Behavior Teaching Review,* Vol. XII, No. 2, 1987–88. Proposes a general cognitive framework that views organizational problems and solutions in terms of multiple levels of analysis.

PODSAKOFF, P. M., and D. R. DALTON, "Research Methodology in Organizational Studies," *Journal of Management,* Summer 1987, pp. 419–41. A content analysis of articles in key OB journals finds that a relatively limited set of research strategies and analytical procedures dominate the organizational sciences.

How Do You Feel About Your Present Job?

Some jobs are more interesting and satisfying than others. This exercise contains eighteen statements about jobs. Check the response next to each statement which best describes how you feel about your present job. There are no right or wrong answers.

	Strongly Agree	Agree	Undecided	Disagree	Strongly Disagree
1. My job is like a hobby to me.	___	___	___	___	___
2. My job is usually interesting enough to keep me from getting bored.	___	___	___	___	___
3. It seems that my friends are more interested in their jobs.	___	___	___	___	___
4. I consider my job rather unpleasant.	___	___	___	___	___
5. I enjoy my work more than my leisure time.	___	___	___	___	___
6. I am often bored with my job.	___	___	___	___	___
7. I feel fairly well satisfied with my present job.	___	___	___	___	___
8. Most of the time I have to force myself to go to work.	___	___	___	___	___
9. I am satisfied with my job for the time being.	___	___	___	___	___
10. I feel that my job is no more interesting than others I could get.	___	___	___	___	___
11. I definitely dislike my work.	___	___	___	___	___
12. I feel that I am happier in my work than most other people.	___	___	___	___	___
13. Most days I am enthusiastic about my work.	___	___	___	___	___
14. Each day of work seems like it will never end.	___	___	___	___	___
15. I like my job better than the average worker does.	___	___	___	___	___
16. My job is pretty uninteresting.	___	___	___	___	___
17. I find real enjoyment in my work.	___	___	___	___	___
18. I am disappointed that I ever took this job.	___	___	___	___	___

Turn to page 687 for scoring directions and key.

Source: Adapted from A. H. Brayfield and H. F. Rothe, "An Index of Job Satisfaction," *Journal of Applied Psychology,* October 1951, pp. 307–11.

Evaluating "In Search of Excellence"

Tom Peters and Robert Waterman's *In Search of Excellence* (Harper & Row, 1982), with sales in excess of 5,000,000 copies, has become one of the largest selling and most often quoted books in the popular management literature. The book describes what the authors have found to be the distinct cultural traits that lead to excellence in a company. Based on Peters and Waterman's research, they propose that there are eight cultural characteristics (the independent variables) that predict companies' excellence as defined in terms of financial performance and innovation (the dependent variables).

The authors make no mention of how their original population of firms was chosen. Nevertheless, they identified seventy-five firms which appeared, on the surface, to be excellent companies. Most or all of the European firms were eliminated to bring the sample down to sixty-two. These firms were then screened on the basis of seven criteria. Six criteria were measures of financial performance: compound asset growth, compound equity growth, ratio of market value to book value, average return on total capital, average return on equity, and average return on sales. If a firm was in the top half of its industry on at least four of these six financial criteria for each year over a twenty-year period, the authors considered them excellent and kept them in the research set. The seventh selection criterion was innovation. An informal group of businessmen, consultants, members of the press, and business academics were used to judge the remaining companies on the basis of innovativeness. This was a subjective assessment.

The result was a set of forty-three "excellent" firms. These companies became the primary focus of

Peters and Waterman's study. Some of the companies that were described as excellent included Avon, Boeing, Disney Productions, Dow Chemical, IBM, Johnson & Johnson, K-mart, 3M Co., Marriot, Procter & Gamble, Texas Instruments, and Wang Labs. A few of the firms that didn't "make the cut" included General Electric, General Foods, Lockheed, Polaroid, and Xerox. The authors had extensive interviews in twenty-one of the firms, and briefer interviews in the remaining twenty-two. The description in the book of the structure and substance of the interviews is not clearly revealed.

The major conclusion from *In Search of Excellence* is that there is a strong link between culture and business performance. More specifically, excellent companies share eight common cultural characteristics: (1) a bias for action; (2) keeping close to the customer; (3) autonomy and entrepreneurship; (4) productivity through people; (5) hands-on, value driven; (6) sticking to what the organization knows; (7) a simple form, lean staff; and (8) maintaining simultaneous loose-tight properties. It should be noted, however, that Peters and Waterman do not tell us if all forty-three firms had all eight characteristics or whether some had only six or seven.

QUESTIONS

1. What flaws can you find in the research upon which this book is based?

2. How generalizable do you think this study's findings are?

3. How do you explain the tremendous popularity of this book, given its questionable research base?

NOTES

[1]Based on B. G. Posner, "To Have and To Hold," *INC.,* October 1988, pp. 130–32.

[2]J. A. Byrne, "Executive Sweat," *Forbes,* May 20, 1985, pp. 198–200.

[3]This discussion is based on material presented in E. Stone, *Research Methods in Organizational Behavior* (Santa Monica, CA: Goodyear, 1978).

[4]B. M. Staw and G. R. Oldham, "Reconsidering Our Dependent Variables: A Critique and Empirical Study," *Academy of Management Journal,* December 1978, pp. 539–59; and B. M. Staw, "Organizational Behavior: A Review and Reformulation of the Field's Outcome Variables," in M. R. Rosenzweig and L. W. Porter (eds.), *Annual Review of Psychology,* Vol. 35 (Palo Alto, CA: Annual Reviews, 1984), pp. 627–66.

[5]R. S. Blackburn, "Experimental Design in Organizational Settings," in J. W. Lorsch (ed.), *Handbook of Organizational Behavior* (Englewood Cliffs, NJ: Prentice Hall, 1987), pp. 127–28.

[6]G. G. Alpander, "Supervisory Training Programmes in Major U.S. Corporations," *Journal of Management Development,* Vol. 5, No. 5, 1986, pp. 3–22.

[7]S. Milgram, *Obedience to Authority* (New York: Harper & Row, 1974).

[8]This box is based on M. E. Gordon, L. A. Slade, and N. Schmitt, "The 'Science of the Sophomore' Revisited: From Conjecture to Empiricism," *Academy of Management Review,* January 1986, pp. 191–207; J. Greenberg, "The College Sophomore as Guinea Pig: Setting the Record Straight," *Academy of Management Review,* January 1987, pp. 157–59; and E. A. Locke (ed.), *Generalizing from Laboratory to Field Settings: Research Findings from Industrial— Organizational Psychology, Organizational Behavior, and Human Resource Management* (Lexington, MA: Lexington Books, 1986).

[9]J. J. Martocchio and A. M. O'Leary, "Sex Differences in Occupational Stress: A Meta-Analytic Review," *Journal of Applied Psychology,* June 1989, pp. 495–501.

[10]See, for example, R. A. Guzzo, S. E. Jackson, and R. A. Katzell, "Meta-Analysis Analysis," in L. L. Cummings and B. M. Staw (eds.), *Research in Organizational Behavior,* Vol. 9 (Greenwich, Conn.: JAI Press, 1987), pp. 407–42.

[11]B. M. Staw, "Organizational Behavior: A Review and Reformulation."

[12]Ibid, pp. 655–56.

[13]Cited in "Expensive Absenteeism," *Wall Street Journal,* July 29, 1986, p. 1.

[14]See, for example, D. R. Dalton and W. D. Todor, "Functional Turnover: An Empirical Assessment," *Journal of Applied Psychology,* December 1981, pp. 716–21; and G. M. McEvoy and W. F. Cascio, "Do Good or Poor Performers Leave? A Meta-Analysis of the Relationship Between Performance and Turnover," *Academy of Management Journal,* December 1987, pp. 744–62.

[15]Cited in "You Often Lose the Ones You Love," *Industry Week,* November 21, 1988, p. 5.

[16]H. J. Leavitt, *Managerial Psychology,* rev. ed. (Chicago: University of Chicago Press, 1964), p. 3.

ORGANIZATIONAL BEHAVIOR IN A GLOBAL CONTEXT

LEARNING OBJECTIVES

After studying this chapter, you should be able to:

1. *Define a multinational corporation*
2. *Describe the effect of regional cooperative arrangements on managing global enterprises*
3. *Explain how American cultural values permeate the organizational behavior literature*
4. *List six basic cultural dimensions in which cultures vary*
5. *Describe Hofstede's four cultural dimensions*
6. *Explain the four distinct stages that individuals go through in adjusting to a foreign country*

Europe will be getting their "Chez Mickey Mouse" in 1992. However, Disneyland and Walt Disney World reflect the cultural norms and practices of the United States. Will Disney's practices transfer to Europe or will they have to be modified to fit into another culture? M. Stevens/Gamma-Liaison.

Japanese and American management is ninety-five percent the same, and differs in all important respects.

S. HONDA

I t is scheduled for opening in 1992, and it is going to cost more than $2.5 billion. While the corporation that is developing it has an almost unbroken string of successes, this new project may end up being the most visible and expensive flop in the company's history. The project we're talking about is Euro Disneyland and the corporation that's developing it is the Walt Disney Co.[1]

Disney, of course, has had unparalleled success with its two theme parks in California and Florida. Why should Euro Disneyland, rising twenty miles east of Paris, be any different? If Disney could successfully transfer its Magic Kingdom mystique from Anaheim to Orlando, why not to Paris? Consider a few of the challenges that Euro Disneyland presents that Disney has never encountered before:

1. In contrast to Americans, the French have little previous exposure to theme parks. The idea of paying just to walk inside the gate is foreign to them.

2. The French reserve one day and only one day a week—Sunday—for family outings. Going out with the family on a Saturday or weekday isn't something they're used to doing.

3. The French vacation *en masse*. In August, everything closes up and everyone goes on holiday. Demand at the theme park is unlikely, therefore, to be as spread out as it is in the United States.

4. The French have long had an aversion to meeting strangers. The idea of being welcomed by strangers with buoyant smiles and a lighthearted greeting is not appreciated.

5. In the United States, fifty percent of Disney visitors eat fast food at the parks. Most French, however, don't snack. Should Euro Disneyland have as many eating places as the American parks do? If they do, will they be empty?

6. The French insist on eating lunch at exactly 12:30. How will the restaurants at Euro Disneyland handle 30,000 or more people, all queuing up for lunch at the same time?

7. The French are impatient. They are not comfortable waiting in long lines. Americans seem to accept waits of half an hour or more for the more popular rides. Will this limit attendance and be the "kiss of death" to the new park?

8. The French adore their dogs. They take them everywhere—inside most French resorts and even fine restaurants. Dogs, however, have always been banned from Disney parks.

9. Disney employees wearing badges identifying them by their first names only work well in the United States, where informality is well accepted. Such a practice is an un-French way of doing business.

10. French workers don't like to obey orders. They are not likely to take kindly to management's demands that they not smoke, chew gum, or converse with their co-workers.

The previous facts illustrate that the French are different from Americans and managing a theme park in France will require some very different practices, if it is to succeed, than those followed in the United States. If Disney's management fails to fully comprehend the unique qualities of the French culture and to adapt its operations to that culture, it may find itself having built the better "mousetrap" and still being ignored.

The Euro Disneyland example illustrates a problem that managers are increasingly likely to face in the 1990s and beyond: What changes, if any, do you need to make in your management style when managing in a different country?

THE GLOBAL ECONOMY

Corporations that you typically think of as "All-American"—companies such as Exxon, Gillette, Colgate-Palmolive, IBM, and Coca-Cola—today receive more than half their revenues from operations outside the United States.[2] Other "All-American" companies—CBS Records, General Tire, Macmillan Publishers, and Pillsbury, for example—aren't American at all anymore. They're foreign-owned. And, of course, foreign firms like Sony, Honda, Mitsubishi, Seagrams, and Nestlé each employ thousands of people in the United States. In the 1950s or 60s, national boundaries represented real barriers to trade. That is no longer the case.[3] Today's world is truly a global village. This may be best demonstrated by looking at the growing impact of multinational corporations and the rise of regional cooperative arrangements between countries.

Multinational Corporations

Multinational Corporations
Companies that maintain significant operations in two or more countries simultaneously.

Most of the firms currently listed in the *Fortune* 500 are **multinational corporations.** They are companies that maintain significant operations in two or more countries simultaneously.

While international businesses have been around for centuries, multinationals are a relatively recent phenomenon. They are a natural outcome of a global economy. For instance, Ford focuses on building a "world car"—a standardized vehicle that can be manufactured and sold around the globe. Multinationals use their worldwide operations to develop global strategies. Rather than confining themselves to their domestic borders, they are scanning the world for competitive advantages. The result? Manufacturing, assembly, sales, and other functions are being strategically located to give firms advantages in the marketplace. A photocopying machine, for instance, might be designed in Toronto, have its microprocessing chips made in Taiwan, its physical case manufactured in Japan, be assembled in South Korea, and then be sold out of warehouses located in Melbourne, London, and Los Angeles.

How big are multinationals? It's hard to overstate their size and influence. If nations and industrial firms are ranked by gross national product and total sales, respectively, thirty-seven of the first one hundred on the list would be industrial corporations.[4] Exxon's sales, as a case in point, exceed the GNPs of countries such as Indonesia, Nigeria, Argentina, and Denmark.

Managers of multinationals confront a wealth of challenges. They face diverse political systems, laws, and customs. But these differences create both problems and opportunities. It's obviously more difficult to manage an operation that spans fifteen thousand miles and whose employees speak five different languages than one located under a single roof where a common language is spoken. Differences create opportunities and that has been the primary motivation for corporations to expand their worldwide operations.

Regional Cooperative Arrangements

National boundaries are also being blurred by the creation of regional cooperative arrangements. The most notable of these, so far, is the European Community, made up of twelve West European countries. But the United States and Mexico have established border zones to stimulate low-cost manufacturing and the United States and Canada have negotiated an agreement to reduce trade barriers. Maybe the most potentially far-reaching cooperative efforts, however, will be coming in the near future among the Eastern European countries that have recently thrown off the shackles of communism.

THE EUROPEAN COMMUNITY   December 31, 1992, is the target date. It marks the creation of a United States of Europe.[5] There are 320 million people in the twelve nations—France, Denmark, Belgium, Greece, Ireland, Italy, Luxembourg, the Netherlands, Portugal, Spain, the United Kingdom, and West Germany—that make up the European Community. Separated by borders, they have border controls, border taxes, border subsidies, nationalistic policies, and protected industries. But by the end of 1992, they will become a single market. Gone will be national barriers to travel, employment, investment, and trade. There will be a free flow of money, workers, goods, and services. A driver hauling cargo from Amsterdam to Lisbon will be able to clear four border crossings and five countries by showing a single piece of paper. In 1991, that same driver needed two pounds of documents.

The primary motivation for these 12 nations to unite was to reassert their position against the industrial might of the United States and Japan. As separate countries, creating barriers against one another, European industries were unable to develop the economies of scale enjoyed by the United States and Japan. The new European Community, however, will allow European firms to tap into what will become the world's single richest market. This reduction in trade barriers will also encourage non-Western European companies to invest in these countries to take advantage of new opportunities. Finally, European multinationals will have new clout in attacking American, Japanese, and other world-wide markets.

Maquiladoras Assembly plants operating along the Mexican side of the border from Texas to California.

UNITED STATES–MEXICO BORDER ZONES   It's called **maquiladoras** and an estimated 1400 firms—including General Motors, GE, Zenith, Honeywell, Hitachi, and Sanyo—are doing it. What they're doing is operating assembly plants along the Mexican side of the border from Texas to California with minimal trade restrictions.[6]

The maquiladoras concept was devised by the Mexican and American governments in 1965 to help develop both sides of the impoverished border region. But it was the massive devaluation of the peso, which occurred in 1982,

Traffic on this bridge across the Rio Grande reflects the increasing trade taking place between the United States and Mexico.
Barbara Laing/Black Star.

that initiated a virtual explosion of maquiladoras. Since 1982, the number of these assembly plants has nearly tripled. They're in Ciudad Juaréz, Nogales, Tijuana, Mexicali, and other northern Mexican cities. One estimate indicates that these cross-border plants could employ as many as three million workers by the year 2000.

Mexican wages are now equal to, or even less than, those paid in many Asian countries. With a Mexican minimum wage of around forty cents an hour, at current exchange rates, companies producing for North American markets no longer have to go to the Far East to find low cost labor.

U.S.–CANADA ALLIANCE   Another set of national barriers are coming down between the United States and Canada.[7] These two countries are already the world's largest trading partners—they do at least $150 billion worth of business a year with each other. The recent signing of the United States–Canadian Free Trade Agreement means increased competition for firms and expanded opportunities in each country.

The Free Trade Agreement, in effect, seeks to create a unified North America. It phases out tariffs on most goods trading between the two countries. It also is triggering a wave of consolidations as Canadian companies merge among themselves or with American companies to form single giant firms.

THE NEW EASTERN EUROPE   In early 1989, Romania, Poland, Hungary, and East Germany were Communist countries. East Germans, for instance, literally put their lives on the line to sneak into West Germany. Who at that time would have believed that only a year later East Germans would stroll across the border into West Germany, or that the Berlin Wall would be little more than a tourist attraction? By 1990, United States–Soviet relations were stronger than they had been in forty years. Concern over a world war between these countries had almost completely faded. West and East Germany were rapidly moving toward reunification. A new concern, ironically, was over the political, military, and economic threats that a unified Germany created for the rest of Europe.[8]

Just when Europeans had assimilated the dramatic implications that a twelve-nation Economic Community would have on world trade and economics, Eastern Europe changed the rules again. Will, for example, a unified Germany dominate Europe?

A free Eastern Europe creates almost unlimited opportunities for multinationals. It opens up new markets with huge growth potentials. It also creates a new supply of highly skilled, low-cost labor. More than any other event in recent times, the fall of communism in Eastern Europe appears to signal the creation of a true global economy.

FACING THE INTERNATIONAL CHALLENGE

National Cultures The primary values and practices that characterize particular countries.

A global economy presents challenges to managers that they never had to confront when their operations were constrained within national borders. They face different legal and political systems. They confront different economic climates and tax policies. But they also must deal with varying **national cultures**—the primary values and practices that characterize particular countries—many of which are nothing like those in which they have spent their entire lives.

If this were an economics text, we could carefully dissect the economic implications on managers of a global economy. But this book is about organizational behavior and understanding people at work. Therefore, let's look at why managers, especially those born and raised in the United States, often find managing people in foreign lands so difficult.

Parochialism A narrow view of the world; an inability to recognize differences between people.

PAROCHIALISM   Americans have been singled out as suffering particularly from **parochialism;** that is, they view the world solely through their own eyes and perspective.[9] People with a parochial perspective do not recognize that other people have different ways of living and working. We see this most explicitly in Americans' knowledge of foreign languages. While it is not uncommon for Europeans to speak three or four languages, Americans are almost entirely monolingual. The reasons probably reflect the huge domestic market in the United States, the geographical separation of the United States from Europe and Asia, and the reality that English has become the international business language in many parts of the world.

Managing across national borders provides new challenges. For instance, Malaysia's ethnic mix shows up in this Hewlett-Packard microchip factory.
Munshi Ahmed.

Ethnocentric Views The belief that one's cultural values and customs are superior to all others.

Americans have also been frequently criticized for holding **ethnocentric views**.[10] They believe that their cultural values and customs are superior to all others. This may offer another explanation for why Americans don't learn foreign languages. Many think their language is superior and that it's the rest of the world's responsibility to learn English.

There is no shortage of stories illustrating the problems created when American managers failed to understand cultural differences. Consider the following examples:

> An American manager recently transferred to Saudi Arabia successfully obtained a million-dollar contract from a Saudi manufacturer. The manufacturer's representative had arrived at the meeting several hours late, but the American executive considered it unimportant. The American was certainly surprised and frustrated to learn later that the Saudi had no intention of honoring the contract. He had signed it only to be polite after showing up late for the appointment.
>
> An American executive operating in Peru was viewed by Peruvian managers as cold and unworthy of trust because, in face-to-face discussions, the American kept backing up. He did not understand that, in Peru, the custom is to stand quite close to the person with whom you are speaking.
>
> An American manager in Japan offended a high-ranking Japanese executive by failing to give him the respect his position deserved. The American was introduced to the Japanese executive in the latter's office. The American assumed that the executive was a low-level manager and paid him little attention because of the small and sparsely furnished office he occupied. The American didn't realize that the offices of top Japanese executives do not flaunt the status symbols of their American counterparts.[11]

FOREIGNERS IN AMERICA   Don't assume that Americans are alone in blundering on foreign soil. Cultural ignorance goes two ways. Foreign owners now control more than twelve percent of all American manufacturing assets and employ over three million American workers. In one recent year alone, foreign investors acquired nearly four hundred American businesses, worth a total of sixty billion dollars.[12] However, these foreign owners are facing the same challenges and making many of the same mistakes that American executives have long made overseas.[13]

Americans, for instance, are used to stability. The high uncertainty created by new owners with different management styles is threatening to American workers, yet is often ignored by foreign managers. Some foreign owners, especially those from relatively homogeneous cultures, have the outmoded, stereotypical attitudes toward women and minorities that builds ill will. Many American employees complain that they feel left out of the established personal networks that already exist in traditional European and Asian corporations when they acquire American firms. Japanese managers, as a case in point, work ten- to twelve-hour days and then socialize until midnight. A lot of important business is done at these social gatherings, but American managers are excluded, and this exclusion creates feelings of hurt and distrust. The Japanese way of dealing with people also confounds Americans. Communication, for example, is often more difficult. Americans value directness. They tend to say exactly what they mean. The Japanese are more subtle and see this directness as rude and abrasive. The Japanese emphasis on group consensus is another practice that doesn't fit well in the United States. Americans, used to making decisions fast, get frustrated by what they interpret as unnecessary delays.[14]

UNDERSTANDING A COUNTRY'S NATIONAL CULTURE

American children are taught early the values of individuality and uniqueness. In contrast, Japanese children are indoctrinated to be "team players," to work within the group, and to conform. A significant part of an American student's education is to learn to think, to analyze, and to question. Their Japanese counterparts are rewarded for recounting facts. These different socialization practices reflect different cultures and, not surprisingly, result in different types of employees. The average American worker is more competitive and self-focused than is the Japanese worker. Predictions of employee behavior, based on samples of American workers, are likely to be off target when they are applied to a population of employees—like the Japanese—who prefer and perform better in standardized tasks, as part of a work team, with group-based decisions and rewards.

It's relatively easy to get a reading of the Japanese culture—dozens of books and hundreds of articles have been written on the subject. But how do you gain an understanding of Venezuela or Denmark's national culture? A popular notion is that you should talk with people from those countries. Evidence suggests, however, that this rarely works.[15] Why? Because people born and raised in a country are fully programmed in the ways of its culture by the time they're adults. They understand how things are done and can work comfortably within their country's unwritten norms, but they *can't* explain their culture to someone else. It is pervasive, but it is hidden. Most people are unaware of just how their culture has shaped them. Culture is to people as water is to fish. It's there all the time but the fish are oblivious to it. So one of the frustrations of moving into a different culture is that the "natives" are often the least capable of explaining its unique characteristics to an outsider.

To illustrate the difficulty of accurately describing the unique qualities of one's own culture, if you're an American, raised in the United States, ask yourself: What are Americans like? Think about it for a moment and then see how many of the points in Table 3–1 you identified correctly.

Although foreign cultures are difficult to fathom from what its natives tell you, there is an expanding body of research that can tell us how cultures vary, and give us key differences between, say, the United States and Venezuela. We will look at this research in the next two sections.

HOW CULTURES VARY

One of the most widely referenced frameworks for analyzing variations among cultures identifies six basic cultural dimensions: a person's relationship to nature, and to others; the culture's orientation to time, and to activity; the nature of the culture's people, and the conception of space.[17] In this section, we'll review each.

TABLE 3–1   What Are Americans Like?

Americans are very *informal*. They don't tend to treat people differently even when there are great differences in age or social standing.

Americans are *direct*. They don't talk around things. To some foreigners, this may appear as abrupt or even rude behavior.

Americans are *competitive*. Some foreigners may find Americans assertive or overbearing.

Americans are *achievers*. They like to keep score, whether at work or at play. They emphasize accomplishments.

Americans are *independent* and *individualistic*. They place a high value on freedom and believe that individuals can shape and control their own destinies.

Americans are *questioners*. They ask a lot of questions, even to someone they have just met. Many of these questions may seem pointless ("How ya doing?") or personal ("What kind of work do you do?").

Americans dislike *silence*. They would rather talk about the weather than deal with silence in a conversation.

Americans value *punctuality*. They keep appointment calendars and live according to schedules and clocks.

Americans value *cleanliness*. They often seem obsessed with bathing, eliminating body odors, and wearing clean clothes.

Source: Based on M. Ernest, ed., *Predeparture Orientation Handbook: For Foreign Students and Scholars Planning to Study in the United States* (Washington, D.C.: U.S. Information Agency, Bureau of Cultural Affairs, 1984), pp. 103–5; A. Bennett, "American Culture Is Often a Puzzle for Foreign Managers in the U.S.," *Wall Street Journal*, February 12, 1986, p. 29; "Don't Think Our Way's The Only Way," *The Pryor Report*, February 1988, p. 9; and B. J. Wattenberg, "The Attitudes Behind American Exceptionalism," *U.S. News & World Report*, August 7, 1989, p. 25.

People's Relationships to Nature

Are people *subjugated* to their environment, in *harmony* with it, or able to *dominate* it? In many Middle Eastern countries, people see life as essentially preordained. When things happen, they tend to see it as God's will. In contrast, Americans and Canadians believe that they can control nature. They're willing to spend billions of dollars each year on cancer research, for example, because they think that cancer's cause can be identified, a cure can be found, and it eventually can be eradicated.

In between these two extreme positions is a more moderate view. This one seeks harmony with nature. In many Far Eastern countries, the way to deal with nature is to work around it.

You should expect these different perspectives toward nature to have some influence on organizational practices. Take the setting of goals as an example. In a subjugation society, goal-setting is not likely to be very popular. Why set goals if you believe people can't do much toward achieving them? In a harmony society, goals are likely to be used but deviations will be expected and penalties for failing to reach the goals are likely to be minimal. In a domination society, goals will be widely applied, people will be expected to achieve their goals, and the penalties for failure will tend to be quite high.

Time Orientation

Does the culture focus on the *past, present,* or *future?* Societies differ on the value they place on time. For instance, Western cultures perceive time as a scarce resource. "Time is money," and must be used efficiently. Americans focus on the present and the near future. You see evidence of this in the short-term orientation of performance appraisals. In the typical North American organization, people are evaluated every six or twelve months. The

Aren't Canadians Just Like Their Neighbors to the South?

Most Americans don't see much difference between themselves and Canadians. Yet many Canadians resent the assumption by Americans that they're just like their southern neighbors.[16] For example, in a recent survey, seventy-nine percent of Canadians polled stated that they consider themselves to be different from Americans. However, there was no consensus among those respondents as to what exactly makes Canadians unique.

Studies indicate that Canadians *perceive* themselves as more collective, traditional, and readier to accept government authority with passivity than Americans. Canadians see Americans as more aggressive, individualistic, and violent. In contrast, Canadians see themselves as more concerned about the environment and the poor than their southerly neighbors. They also see themselves as more honest and fair.

But perceptions can be erroneous. For instance, a number of Canadian companies, run by Canadians, are highly fierce competitors in the American market. These would include Olympia & York Development Ltd., Seagrams, and Cineplex Odeon Corporation. Many of the executives at these firms are as or more aggressive than their American counterparts.

On close examination of the research, the most meaningful conclusion that can be drawn is that Canada is a more regionalized nation than the United States and that English-speaking Canadians (anglophones) and Americans seem to be more alike in their styles of communication and influence than anglophones and French-speaking Canadians. Research evidence indicates, for instance, that francophones take a more competitive approach to negotiations than do either Americans or anglophone Canadians.

If Canadians are unique from Americans, then the differences are more nebulous than substantive. In fact, the differences between French-speaking and English-speaking Canadians are probably more significant than the difference between English-speaking Canadians and Americans.

Japanese, in contrast, take a longer-term view and this is reflected in their performance appraisal methods. Japanese workers are often given ten years or more to prove their worth.

Some cultures have still another approach to time: They focus on the past. Italians, for instance, follow traditions and seek to preserve historical practices.

Knowledge of a culture's time orientation can provide you with insights into the importance of deadlines, whether long-term planning is widely practiced, the length of job assignments, and what constitutes lateness. It can explain, for example, the fascination Americans have with making and keeping appointments.

Nature of People

Does a culture view people as *good, evil,* or some *mix* of these two? In many Third World countries, people see themselves as basically honest and trust-

TABLE 3–2   Variations in Value Dimensions

Value Dimension	Variations		
People's Relationships to Nature	Domination	Harmony	Subjugation
Time Orientation	Past	Present	Future
Nature of People	Good	Mixed	Evil
Activity Orientation	Being	Controlling	Doing
People's Relationships to Others	Individualistic	Group	Hierarchical
Conception of Space	Private	Mixed	Public

ed a limited number of countries or analyzed different companies in different countries, Hofstede surveyed 160,000 employees in sixty countries, all of whom worked for a single multinational corporation. This database eliminated any differences that might be attributable to varying practices and policies in different companies, so any variations that he found between countries could reliably be attributed to national culture.

What did Hofstede find? His huge database confirmed that national culture had a major impact on employees' work-related values and attitudes. In fact, it explained more of the differences than did age, sex, profession, or position in the organization. More important, Hofstede found that managers and employees vary on four dimensions of national culture: (1) individualism versus collectivism; (2) power distance; (3) uncertainty avoidance; and (4) masculinity versus femininity.

Individualism vs. Collectivism

Individualism A national culture attribute describing a loosely knit social framework in which people emphasize only the care of themselves and their immediate family.

Collectivism A national culture attribute that describes a tight social framework in which people expect others in groups of which they are a part to look after them and protect them.

Individualism refers to a loosely knit social framework in which people are supposed to look after their own interests and those of their immediate family. This is made possible because of the large amount of freedom that such a society allows individuals. Its opposite is **collectivism,** which is characterized by a tight social framework in which people expect others in groups of which they are a part (such as an organization) to look after them and protect them when they are in trouble. In exchange for this, they feel they owe absolute loyalty to the group.

Hofstede found that the degree of individualism in a country is closely related to that country's wealth. Rich countries like the United States, Great Britain, and the Netherlands are very individualistic. Poor countries like Colombia, Pakistan, and Taiwan are very collectivist.

Power Distance

Power Distance A national culture attribute describing the extent to which a society accepts that power in institutions and organizations is distributed unequally.

People naturally vary in terms of physical and intellectual abilities. This, in turn, creates differences in wealth and power. How does a society deal with these inequalities? Hofstede used the term **power distance** as a measure of the extent to which a society accepts the fact that power in institutions and organizations is distributed unequally. A high power distance society accepts wide differences in power in organizations. Employees show a great deal of respect for those in authority. Titles, rank, and status carry a lot of weight. When negotiating in high power distance countries, companies find that it helps to send representatives with titles at least as high as those with whom they're bargaining. Countries high in power distance include the Philippines, Venezuela, and India. In contrast, a low power distance society plays down inequalities as much as possible. Superiors still have authority, but employees are not fearful or in awe of the boss. Denmark, Israel, and Austria are examples of countries with low power distance scores.

Uncertainty Avoidance

Uncertainty Avoidance A national culture attribute describing the extent to which a society feels threatened by uncertain and ambiguous situations and tries to avoid them.

We live in a world of uncertainty. The future is largely unknown and always will be. Societies respond to this uncertainty in different ways. Some socialize their members into accepting it with equanimity. People in such societies are more or less comfortable with risks. They're also relatively tolerant of behavior and opinions that differ from their own because they don't feel threatened by them. Hofstede describes such societies as having low **uncertainty avoidance.** That is, people feel relatively secure. Countries that fall into this category include Singapore and Denmark.

A society high in uncertainty avoidance is characterized by an increased level of anxiety among its people, which manifests itself in greater nervousness, stress, and aggressiveness. Because people feel threatened by uncertainty and ambiguity in these societies, mechanisms are created to provide security and reduce risk. Their organizations are likely to have more formal rules, there will be less tolerance for deviant ideas and behaviors, and members will strive to believe in absolute truths. Not surprisingly, in organizations in countries with high uncertainty avoidance, employees demonstrate relatively low job mobility, and lifetime employment is a widely practiced policy. Countries in this category include Japan, Portugal, and Greece.

Masculinity vs. Femininity

The fourth dimension, like individualism and collectivism, represents a dichotomy. Hofstede called it masculinity versus femininity. Though his choice of terms is unfortunate (as you'll see, he gives them a strong sexist connotation), to maintain the integrity of his work we'll use his labels.

Masculinity A national culture attribute describing the extent to which the dominant societal values are characterized by assertiveness, acquisition of money and things, and not caring for others or for the quality of life.

Femininity A national culture attribute that emphasizes relationships, concern for others, and the overall quality of life.

According to Hofstede, some societies allow both men and women to take many different roles. Others insist that people behave according to rigid sex roles. When societies make a sharp division between male and female activities, Hofstede claims "the distribution is always such that men take more assertive and dominant roles and women the more service-oriented and caring roles."[19] Under the category **masculinity** he puts societies that emphasize assertiveness and the acquisition of money and material things, while deemphasizing caring for others. In contrast, under the category **femininity** he puts societies that emphasize relationships, concern for others, and the overall quality of life. Where femininity dominates, members put human relationships before money and are concerned with the quality of life, preserving the environment, and helping others.

Hofstede found Japan to be the most masculine country. In Japan, almost all women are expected to stay home and take care of children. At the other extreme, he found the Nordic countries and the Netherlands to be the most feminine. There it's common to see men staying home as househusbands while their wives work, and working men are offered paternity leave to take care of newborn children.

Contrasting the United States and Other Countries

Comparing the sixty countries on the four dimensions, Hofstede found the U.S. culture to rank as follows:

- Individualism/collectivism = Highest among all countries on individualism
- Power distance = Below average
- Uncertainty avoidance = Well below average
- Masculinity/femininity = Well above average on masculinity

The results are not inconsistent with the world image of the United States. The below-average score on power distance aligns with what one might expect from a representative type of government with democratic ideals. In this category, the United States would rate below nations with a small ruling class and a large, powerless set of subjects, and above those nations with very strong commitments to egalitarian values. The well-below-average ranking on uncertainty avoidance is also consistent with a representative type of government, having democratic ideals. Americans perceive themselves as being relatively free from threats of uncertainty. The individualistic ethic is one of the most frequently used stereotypes to describe Americans, and, based on

TABLE 3–3   Examples of Cultural Differences Among World Nations

Individualism	Collectivism
United States	Colombia
Australia	Venezuela
Great Britain	Pakistan
Canada	Peru
High Power Distance	**Low Power Distance**
Philippines	Austria
Mexico	Israel
Venezuela	Denmark
Yugoslavia	New Zealand
High Uncertainty Avoidance	**Low Uncertainty Avoidance**
Greece	Singapore
Portugal	Denmark
Belgium	Sweden
Japan	Hong Kong
High Masculinity	**High Femininity**
Japan	Sweden
Austria	Norway
Venezuela	Yugoslavia
Italy	Denmark

Hofstede's research, the stereotype seems well founded. The United States was ranked as the single most individualistic country in his entire set. Finally, the well-above-average score on masculinity is no surprise. Capitalism—which values aggressiveness and materialism—is consistent with Hofstede's "masculine" characteristics.

We haven't the space to review the results Hofstede obtained for each of the sixty countries, although some examples of extreme scores are presented in Table 3–3. Since our concern is essentially with identifying similarities and differences among cultures, let's briefly identify those countries that are most like and least like the United States on the four dimensions.

The United States is strongly individualistic but low on power distance. This same pattern was exhibited by Great Britain, Australia, Canada, the Netherlands, and New Zealand. Those least similar to the United States on these dimensions were Venezuela, Colombia, Pakistan, Singapore, and the Philippines.

The United States scored low on uncertainty avoidance and high on masculinity. The same pattern was shown by Ireland, Great Britain, the Philippines, Canada, New Zealand, Australia, India, and South Africa. Those least similar to the United States on these dimensions were Chile, Yugoslavia, and Portugal.

A person's rank and position in his or her company is very important in Japan. It allows executives to know how much deference to show others. As a result, the exchange of business cards is a widely-followed custom and the cards always clearly state a person's title. Dennis Brack/ Black Star.

THE REALITY OF CULTURE SHOCK

Culture Shock Confusion, disorientation, and emotional upheaval caused by being immersed in a new culture.

Any move from one country to another will create a certain amount of confusion, disorientation, and emotional upheaval. We call this **culture shock.** The transfer of an executive from the United States to Canada, for example, would require about as little adjustment as one could possibly make. Why? Because the United States and Canada look very much alike in terms of Hofstede's four cultural dimensions. But there would still be some cultural shock. The executive would still have to adjust to differences that would include the form of representative government (Canadians have a parlimentary system, much like the one in Great Britain), language (Canada is a bilingual—English- and French-speaking—country), and even holidays (Canadian Thanksgiving is in early October). However, culture shock will obviously be more severe when individuals move to cultures that are most unlike their old environment.

The adjustment to a foreign country has been found to follow a U-shaped curve that contains four distinct stages.[21] This is shown in Figure 3–1.

The initial stage, I, is one of novelty. The newcomer is excited and optimistic. His or her mood is high. For the temporary visitor to a foreign country, this stage is all that is experienced. A person who spends a week or two on vacation in a strange land considers cultural differences to be interesting, even educational. However, the employee who makes a permanent, or relatively permanent, move experiences euphoria and then disillusionment. In this stage, II, the "quaint" quickly becomes "obsolete," and the "traditional," "inefficient." The opportunity to learn a new language turns into the reality of struggling to communicate. After a few months, the newcomer hits bottom. At this stage, III, any and all of the culture's differences have become blatantly clear. The newcomer's basic interpretation system, which worked fine at home, now no longer functions. He or she is bombarded by millions of sights, sounds, and other cues, that are uninterpretable. Frustration and confusion are highest and mood lowest in Stage III. Finally, the newcomer begins to adapt, and the negative responses related to culture shock dissipate. In this stage, IV, the newcomer has learned what is important and what can be ignored.

What are the implications of this model? There are at least two. First, if you're a newcomer in a foreign land or you are managing a newcomer, expect culture shock. It's not abnormal. To some degree everyone goes through it. Second, culture shock follows a relatively predictable pattern. Expect early euphoria, followed by depression and frustration. However, after about four to

FIGURE 3–1   Culture Shock Cycle

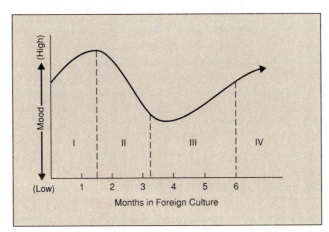

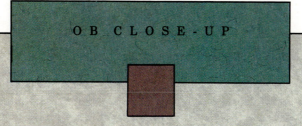

What's It Really Like Working in Japan?

No foreign country has received more attention in the last decade from students of management than Japan. Japanese organizations are routinely described as models of efficiency, and Japanese workers are depicted as loyal and hard-working partners in the production process. But is this the way it really is? Research tells us that Japanese workers *are* loyal and hardworking,[20] yet theirs is a life many North Americans might not opt for.

For example, Japanese employees put in very long hours. It is not uncommon for them to spend several hours a day commuting to and from work. After work, employees regularly go out drinking and socializing together. The end result is that—including commuting and socializing time—the typical Japanese worker is away from home sixty to seventy hours a week.

In addition to long hours, loyalty and dedication to the organization is a must in Japan. It's not an option. Japanese organizations have a strong seniority system with strict adherence to order, rank, and authority. For the most part, new recruits have their salaries fixed for the first

six years. Only after they have demonstrated a capacity for hard work and respect for their boss—which typically takes a dozen years—can employees begin to move up the ranks. And then promotions tend to be in small, incremental steps. Japanese organizations, in contrast to their American counterparts, tend to have more steps in the career ladder, but the steps are smaller. Inequality in status and rewards between top management and production rank-and-file in Japan is also typically much less than in the United States.

Yes, the Japanese are loyal and hardworking. Surprisingly, however, research shows that Japanese workers are no more committed to their organizations than are American workers. Maybe even more surprising, American employees appear to be much more satisfied with their jobs than are the Japanese. In fact, surveys contrasting Japanese and Western work attitudes regularly find that work satisfaction is lowest among the Japanese.

six months most people adjust to their new culture. What was previously different and strange becomes understandable.

KEEPING OB IN A GLOBAL CONTEXT

Most of the concepts that currently make up the body of knowledge we call *organizational behavior* have been developed by Americans, using American subjects, within domestic contexts. A comprehensive study, for instance, of more than 11,000 articles published in twenty-four management and organizational behavior journals over a ten-year period revealed that approximately eighty percent of the studies were done in the United States and had been conducted by Americans.[22] What this means is that not all the concepts that you'll read about in future chapters may be universally applicable to managing people around the world.

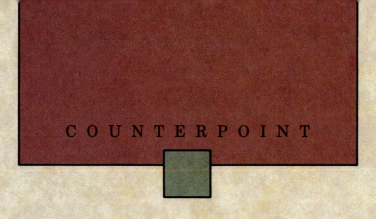

Cross-Cultural Training Is Effective

Yes, it's true that most corporations don't provide cross-cultural training. And that's a mistake! Clearly, the ability to adapt to the cultural differences in a foreign assignment is important to managerial success. Moreover, contrary to what many managers believe, cross-cultural training is very effective. Let's elaborate on this second point.

A comprehensive review of studies that specifically looked at the effectiveness of cross-cultural training shows overwhelming evidence that this training fosters the development of cross-cultural skills and leads to higher performance. Training has been shown to improve an individual's relationships with host nationals, to allow that person to adjust more rapidly to a new culture, and to improve his or her work performance.

While the above results are impressive, they don't say anything about the type of training the employee received. Does that make a difference?

There are a variety of training techniques available to prepare people for foreign work assignments. They range from documentary programs that merely expose people to a new culture through written materials on the country's sociopolitical history, geography, economics, and cultural institutions, to intense interpersonal-experience training, where individuals participate in role-playing exercises, simulated social settings, and similar experiences to "feel" the differences in a new culture.

A recent research study looked at the effectiveness of these two approaches on a group of American managers. These managers, who worked for an electronic products firm, were sent on assignment to Seoul, South Korea. Twenty of them received no training, twenty got only the documentary program, and twenty received only interpersonal-experience training. The training activities were all completed in a three-day period. All participants, no matter which group they were in, received some language training, briefings covering company operations in South Korea, and a cursory three-page background description of the country.

The results of this study confirmed the earlier evidence that cross-cultural training works. Specifically, the study found that managers who received either form of training were better performers and perceived less need to adjust to the new culture than those who received no such training. Additionally, no one training method proved superior to the other.

The evidence in this argument is drawn from J. S. Black and M. Mendenhall, "Cross-Cultural Training Effectiveness: A Review and a Theoretical Framework for Future Research," *Academy of Management Review,* January 1990, pp. 113–36; and P. C. Earley, "Intercultural Training for Managers: A Comparison of Documentary and Interpersonal Methods," *Academy of Management Journal,* December 1987, pp. 685–98.

1. What are the challenges facing the managers of multinational corporations?

2. Why is December 1992 an important date for managers of global enterprises?

3. What are *maquiladoras?* What advantages do they provide management?

4. How does American parochialism hinder effectiveness in international business?

5. Why is a country's national culture so hard to identify and understand?

6. What are Americans like?

7. Describe the United States in terms of the American's relationship to nature, time orientation, activity orientation, and conception of space.

8. Describe American culture in terms of Hofstede's four major criteria.

9. How could you use Hofstede's research if you were an American manager transferred to Mexico?

10. In which country are employees *most* like those in the United States? *Least* like those in the United States?

11. Contrast Japanese organizations with American organizations.

12. What is *culture shock?* How could you use the four-stage culture-shock model to better understand employee behavior?

FOR FURTHER READING

ADLER, N. J., *International Dimensions of Organizational Behavior,* 2nd ed. Boston: Kent Publishing, 1991. Discusses the impact of culture on organizations, managing cultural diversity, and managing international transitions.

CHILD, J., "Culture, Contingency, and Capitalism in the Cross-National Study of Organizations," in L. L. Cummings and B. M. Staw (eds.), *Research in Organizational Behavior,* Vol. 3. Greenwich, CT: JAI Press, 1981, pp. 303–56. Examines the contribution which culture, contingency, and capitalism make toward developing a framework of analysis for cross-national studies.

LANE, H. W., and J. J. DISTEFANO, *International Management Behavior.* Scarborough, Ontario: Nelson, 1988. Reviews the influence of national culture on management behavior.

OVERMAN, S., "Shaping the Global Workplace," *Personnel Administrator,* October 1989, pp. 41–44. Discusses the trend toward globalization of business operations on international human resource professionals.

PHATAK, A. V., *International Dimensions of Management,* 2nd ed. Boston: Kent Publishing, 1989. Reviews the cultural environment of international management and how it impacts on management activities of planning, organizing, staffing, and controlling.

RONEN, S., and O. SHENKAR, "Clustering Countries on Attitudinal Dimensions: A Review and Synthesis," *Academy of Management Review,* July 1985, pp. 435–54. Reviews research that grouped similar countries together into clusters that allows for generalizing about attitudes within clusters.

Are You Keeping Up on the Changing Global Economy?

As pointed out at the beginning of this chapter, where primary ownership of a corporation lies is not clear anymore. To see how well you've been keeping up with current international business events, take the following quiz. Next to each company, indicate in the space provided which country you think the primary owners reside.

1. Brooks Brothers (clothing) _____
2. Carnation (food) _____
3. Columbia Pictures (motion pictures) _____
4. Du Pont (chemicals) _____
5. Farmers Group (insurance) _____
6. Firestone Tire & Rubber (tires) _____
7. Irving Bank & Trust (banking) _____
8. K-mart (retailing) _____
9. Maserati (sports cars) _____
10. Miles Laboratories (pharmaceuticals) _____
11. Motel 6 (travel motels) _____
12. Spalding (sporting goods) _____
13. Thermos (insulated containers) _____
14. Wilson (sporting goods) _____

Turn to page 688 for scoring directions and key.

NEC Corp.'s Boot Camp

Listening in, from outside the conference room you can hear statements such as "Don't preach," "Be more logical," "People don't identify with the company 100% in America." Once inside the conference room, you will find a group of "students" listening to a lecture by Mr. Iwashita. This scenario is typical of what many Japanese companies are doing to prepare their managers for overseas assignments.

As NEC Corp. expands its presence in the computer and communications market worldwide, there is an increasing need to prepare managers for overseas assignment. While the company has over 500 Japanese managers outside Japan, it expects that number to rise 60 percent in the next few years. In an effort to help Japanese managers adapt to a different culture, NEC has developed an in-house training camp for those managers being assigned outside of Japan. In the camp these managers are taught the English language, table manners, the art of negotiating with non-Japanese overseas partners, and the nuances of different cultures. One of the more popular topics in the camp is "cross cultural adaptation."

Mr. Iwashita, a Japanese consultant, teaches his students about American individualism and the potential conflict it can create with the Japanese inclination for group decision making and what Westerners too often perceive as a slow decision-making process.

In the art of negotiation the Japanese managers are taught among other things, the need to say no and yes directly which is very un-Japanese. They also learn some American negotiating slang such as, "going in cold, shooting from the hip, and beating around the bush."

As NEC Japanese managers go outside of Japan they face an increasingly complex multinational and multi-cultural work place and work force. As pointed out by Mr. Yoneyama, a Japanese manager at NEC America Inc. in New York, not only does he have more diverse responsibilities since he moved to America, he also has to contend with a legal system that is very different from the Japanese system. Coming from a society where large trading companies are commonplace, it was difficult for Mr. Yoneyama to understand the rationale behind anti-trust laws in the United States.

In addition to training managers chosen for overseas assignment, NEC also offers classes for the spouses of these managers. The spouses are trained in how to live in foreign countries as expatriates. They are trained on how to participate in the life of an American community. Attempts are made to alleviate fears about their future and the education of their children.

The efforts made by NEC to ease the transition of its managers to another culture are now considered imperative by many multinational companies to improve their managers' chances of success abroad.

QUESTIONS

1. With the increasing level of foreign direct investment in North America, what role will culture play in understanding organizational behavior and applying management theories in the work place?

2. Using Hofstede's cultural dimensions of values, how can you explain the differences between Japanese and American approaches to the art of negotiations?

3. Why can it be misleading to have a course on "American Culture?"

This case is contributed by S. Kim Sokoya, Middle Tennessee State University and is based on "Japanese Executives Going Overseas Take Anti-Shock Courses," *Wall Street Journal,* January 12, 1987.

NOTES

[1]Based on R. Tempest, "No Magic in These Kingdoms," *Los Angeles Times,* October 21, 1989, p. A1.

[2]"The 100 Largest U.S. Multinationals," *Forbes,* July 23 1990, pp. 363–64.

[3]See, for example, K. Ohmae, "Managing in a Borderless World," *Harvard Business Review,* May-June 1989, pp. 152–61.

[4]World Bank, *World Development Report: 1986* (Washington, D.C., 1986); and "International 150," *Business Week,* April 18, 1986, p. 290.

[5]See, for example, "Reshaping Europe: 1992 and Beyond," *Business Week,* December 12, 1988, pp. 48–51; and J. S. McClehahen, "Europe 1992: The Challenge to the U.S.," *Industry Week,* April 3, 1989, pp. 78–85.

[6]See, for example, "The Magnet of Growth in Mexico's North," *Business Week,* June 6, 1988, pp. 48–50.

[7]C. Hawkins and W. J. Holstein, "The North American Shakeout Arrives Ahead of Schedule," *Business Week,* April 17, 1989, pp. 34–35.

[8]B. W. Nelan, "Anything to Fear?" *Time,* March 26, 1990, pp. 32–47.

[9]N. J. Adler, *International Dimensions of Organizational Behavior* (Boston: Kent Publishing, 1986), p. 5.

[10]R. Knotts, "Cross-Cultural Management: Transformations and Adaptations," *Business Horizons,* January-February 1989, p. 32.

[11]See D. A. Ricks, M. Y. C. Fu, and J. S. Arpas, *International Business Blunders* (Columbus, Ohio: Grid, 1974); A. Bennett, "American Culture Is Often a Puzzle for Foreign Managers in the U.S.," *Wall Street Journal,* February 12, 1986; and C. F. Valentine, "Blunders Abroad," *Nation's Business,* March 1989, p. 54.

[12]W. McWhirter, "I Came, I Saw, I Blundered," *Time,* October 9, 1989, p. 72.

[13]*Ibid,* pp. 72–77.

[14]*Ibid.*

[15]H. W. Lane and J. J. DiStefano, *International Management Behavior* (Scarborough, Ontario, Canada: Nelson Canada, 1988), pp. 4–5.

[16]This box is based on K. Freed, "Canadians New Pride in Own Identity," *Los Angeles Times,* January 22, 1986, p. 1; M. McDonald, "Pride and Patriotism," *Maclean's,* July 7, 1986, pp. 10–13; N. J. Adler and J. L. Graham, "Business Negotiations: Canadians Are Not Just Like Americans," *Canadian Journal of Administrative Sciences,* September 1987, pp. 211–38; and A. Phillips, "Defining Identity," *Maclean's,* January 4, 1988, pp. 44–45.

[17]F. Kluckhohn and F. L. Strodtbeck, *Variations in Value Orientations* (Evanston, IL: Row, Peterson, 1961).

[18]G. Hofstede, *Culture's Consequences: International Differences in Work-Related Values* (Beverly Hills, CA: Sage Publications, 1980); and G. Hofstede, "The Cultural Relativity of Organizational Practices and Theories," *Journal of International Business Studies,* Fall 1983, pp. 75–89.

[19]Hofstede, "The Cultural Relativity of Organizational Practices and Theories," p. 85.

[20]See J. R. Lincoln, "Employee Work Attitudes and Management Practice in the U.S. and Japan: Evidence From a Large Comparative Survey," *California Management Review,* Fall 1989, pp. 89–106; and B. D. Cooney, "Japan and America: Culture Counts," *Training and Development Journal,* August 1989, pp. 58–61.

[21]This section is based on the work of J. T. Gullahorn and J. E. Gullahorn, "An Extension of the U-Curve Hypothesis," *Journal of Social Sciences,* January 1963, pp. 34–47.

[22]N. J. Adler, "Cross-Cultural Management Research: The Ostrich and the Trend," *Academy of Management Review,* April 1983, pp. 226–32.

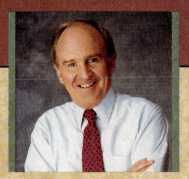

FOUNDATIONS OF INDIVIDUAL BEHAVIOR

LEARNING OBJECTIVES

After studying this chapter, you should be able to:

1. *Define the key biographical characteristics*
2. *Identify two types of ability*
3. *Explain the factors that determine an individual's personality*
4. *Describe the impact of job typology on the personality–job performance relationship*
5. *Summarize how learning theories provide insights into changing behavior*
6. *Distinguish between the four schedules of reinforcement*
7. *Clarify the role of punishment in learning*

Today's GE reflects its chairman's no-nonsense personality. Jack Welch has succeeded in transforming GE into an organization that emphasizes winning in the marketplace.
Courtesy General Electric Co.

I ain't much, baby—but I'm all I've got.

J. LAIR

H is detractors often refer to him as "Neutron Jack."[1] Since becoming chief executive of General Electric in 1981, John F. Welch, Jr. has totally restructured GE, including the elimination of well over 100,000 jobs through layoffs, attrition, and the sale of businesses. Although he is widely regarded as one of the world's toughest managers, you can't argue with his success.

Jack Welch joined GE right out of graduate school and quickly rose through the ranks. His appointment to the CEO job, when he was only 45, made him the youngest chief executive in the company's history. Since taking the top spot, he has bought companies worth sixteen billion dollars, notably RCA and investment banker Kidder Peabody, and sold operations worth nine billion. He has refocused GE's product lines, trimmed corporate staff by forty percent, and turned America's largest diversified corporation into a growth machine. In the 1980s, GE's annual revenues went from under twenty-five billion dollars to more than fifty billion. Its return on equity and earnings per share far outpaced most *Fortune* 500 firms.

But what makes Jack Welch the kind of executive he is? Here are some clues. He was an only child whose main source of inspiration was his dominant mother. "She always felt I could do anything. It was my mother who trained me, taught me the facts of life. She wanted me to be independent. Control your own destiny—she always had that idea. Saw reality. No mincing words. Whenever I got out of line she would whack me one. But always positive. Always constructive. Always uplifting." Jack Welch's philosophy of business was also strongly influenced by his mother's values: Face reality, even when doing so is uncomfortable, and communicate candidly, even when doing so may sting. These are necessary means to achieve that all-important end—controlling your own destiny. If you don't control your destiny, someone else will control it for you.

Jack Welch's determination to control his own life is a personality characteristic that he developed at an early age. His mother instilled in him the idea that assertive behavior was acceptable, even desirable. And she shaped his behavior through encouragement and physical punishment.

Jack Welch is not unique. *All* our behavior is somewhat shaped by our personalities and the learning experiences we've encountered. In this chapter, we'll look at four individual-level variables—biographical characteristics, ability, personality, and learning—and consider their effect on employee performance and satisfaction.

BIOGRAPHICAL CHARACTERISTICS

Biographical Characteristics
Personal characteristics—such as age, sex, and marital status—that are objective and easily obtained from personnel records.

As discussed in Chapter 2, this text is essentially concerned with finding and analyzing those variables that have an impact on employee productivity, absence, turnover, and satisfaction. The list of these variables—as shown in Figure 2–5—is long and contains a number of complicated concepts. Many of these concepts—motivation level, say, or power relations, or organizational culture—are hard to assess. It might be valuable, then, to begin by looking at factors that are easily definable and readily available; data that can be obtained, for the most part, simply from information available in an employee's personnel file. What factors would this include? Obvious characteristics would be an employee's age, sex, marital status, number of dependents, and length of service with an organization. Fortunately, there is a sizable amount of research that has specifically analyzed many of these **biographical characteristics.**

Age

The relationship between age and job performance is likely to be an issue of increasing importance during the next decade. Why? There are at least three reasons. First, there is a widespread belief that job performance declines with increasing age. Regardless of whether it's true or not, a lot of people believe it and act on it. Second is the reality that the work force is aging. For instance, between the years 1985 and 2000, the number of workers between the ages of forty-five and sixty-five will grow by forty-one percent.[2] The third reason is recent American legislation which, for all intents and purposes, outlaws mandatory retirement. Most workers today no longer have to retire at the age of seventy.

Now let's take a look at the evidence. What affect does age actually have on turnover, absenteeism, productivity, and satisfaction?

The older you get, the less likely you are to quit your job. That is the overwhelming conclusion based on studies of the age–turnover relationship.[3] Of course, this conclusion should not be too surprising. As workers get older they have fewer alternative job opportunities. In addition, older workers are less likely to resign because their longer tenure tends to provide them with higher wage rates, longer paid vacations, and more attractive pension benefits.

It's tempting to assume that age would also be inversely related to absenteeism. After all, if older workers are less likely to quit, wouldn't they also demonstrate higher stability by coming to work more regularly? Not necessarily! Most studies *do* show an inverse relationship, but closer examination finds that the age-absence relationship is partially a function of whether the absence is avoidable or unavoidable.[4] Generally, older employees have lower rates of avoidable absence than do younger employees. However, they have higher rates of unavoidable absence. This is probably due to poorer health associated with aging and the longer recovery period that older workers need when injured.

How does age affect productivity? There is a widespread belief that productivity declines with age. It is often assumed that an individual's skills—particularly speed, agility, strength, and coordination—decay over time, and that prolonged job boredom and lack of intellectual stimulation all contribute to reduced productivity. The evidence, however, contradicts these beliefs and assumptions. A recent meta-analysis of the literature found that age and job performance were unrelated.[5] Moreover, this seems to be true for all types of jobs, professional and nonprofessional. The natural conclusion is that the demands of most jobs, even those with heavy manual labor requirements, are not extreme enough for potential declines in physical skill levels due to age to have an impact on productivity; or, even if there is some decay due to age, it is offset by gains due to experience.

Our final concern is the relationship between age and job satisfaction. There is overwhelming evidence indicating a positive association between age and satisfaction, at least up to age sixty.[6] However, current changes taking place in technology may alter this. In jobs where workers are subject to dramatic changes causing their skills to become obsolete, such as those affected by the computer, the satisfaction of older workers is likely to be lower than that of younger employees.

Sex

Few issues initiate more debates, myths, and unsupported opinions than whether females perform as well on jobs as do males. In this section, we want to review the research on this issue.

The evidence suggests that the best place to begin is with the recognition that there are few, if any, important differences between males and females that will affect their job performance. There are, for instance, no consistent male–female differences in problem-solving ability, analytical skills, competitive drive, motivation, leadership, sociability, or learning ability.[7] While psychological studies[8] have found that women are more willing to conform to authority, and that men are more aggressive and more likely than women to have expectations of success, these differences are minor. Given the significant changes that have taken place in the last twenty years in terms of increasing female participation rates in the work force and rethinking what constitutes male and female roles, you should operate from the assumption that there is no significant difference in job productivity between males and females. Similarly, there is no evidence indicating that an employee's sex affects job satisfaction.[9]

But what about absence and turnover rates? Are females less stable employees than males? First, on the question of turnover, the evidence is mixed.[10] Some have found females to have higher turnover rates, while others have found no difference. There doesn't appear to be enough information from which to draw meaningful conclusions. The research on absence, however, is a different story. The evidence consistently indicates that women have higher rates of absenteeism than do men.[11] The most logical explanation for this finding is that our society has historically placed home and family responsibilities on the female. When a child is ill or someone needs to stay home to await the plumber, it has been the woman who has traditionally taken time off work. However, this research is undoubtedly time-bound. The historical role of the woman in child caring and as secondary breadwinner has definitely changed in the past decade; and a large proportion of men, nowadays, are as interested in day-care and the problems associated with child care in general as are women.

Marital Status

There are not enough studies to draw any conclusions as to the effect of marital status on productivity. But consistent research indicates that married employees have fewer absences, undergo less turnover, and are more satisfied with their jobs than their unmarried coworkers.[12]

Marriage imposes increased responsibilities that may make a steady job more valuable and important. Of course, the results represent correlational studies; therefore, the causation issue is not clear. It may very well be that conscientious and satisfied employees are more likely to be married. Another offshoot of this issue is that research has not pursued other statuses besides single or married. Does being divorced have an impact on an employee's performance and satisfaction? What about couples who live together without being married? These are questions in need of investigation.

Number of Dependents

Again, we don't have enough information relating to employee productivity, but quite a bit of research has been done on the relationship between the number of dependents an employee has and absence, turnover, and satisfaction.

There is very strong evidence that the number of children an employee has is positively correlated with absence, especially among females.[14] Similarly, the evidence seems to point to a positive relationship between number of dependents and job satisfaction.[15] In contrast, studies relating number of dependents and turnover produce a mixed bag of results.[16] Some indicate that children increase turnover, while others show that they result in lower turnover. At this point, the evidence regarding turnover is just too contradictory to permit us to draw conclusions.

The CEO of the public relations firm of Hill & Knowlton, with his 4-year old son, combines parental and job responsibilities. Here he handles correspondence on Easter morning, using the company's electronic mail system that is networked to his home.   Rob Kinmonth.

Are Married Men Really More Productive?

Many studies have reported that married men get anywhere from 10 to 50 percent higher wages than single men of comparable age, race, education, and the like.[13] But why? Are they more productive?

One theory is that productivity has little to do with it. Rather, higher-paid men are more desirable marriage partners and so are more likely to be "selected" into marriage. Another theory is that employers discriminate in favor of married men, either sympathizing with their family needs or regarding them as more stable workers. Recent research, however, suggests that neither of these theories may be on target.

A recent large-scale study covering the fifteen-year employment history of a sample of young men found that married men *actually are* more productive than their single counterparts. The researchers found that the wages of married men in their sample outstripped those of comparable single men by a gap that steadily widened over the first ten to twenty years of marriage, indicating more than simple discrimination at work. Examination of supervisors' performance ratings of managers and professionals in a large manufacturing company found that the married men were consistent in drawing higher performance ratings than comparable single men and were far more likely to be promoted into higher-paying jobs.

While generalizing from only two studies is dangerous, these studies do indicate that the "selection" into marriage and discrimination theories explain little of the wage difference. Rather, they suggest that marriage wage premiums are due to a productivity effect of marriage.

Even if this is true, an important point of caution needs to be made. Employers must be wary of stigmatizing and discriminating against single men. Demographic statistics indicate that, because of a trend towards later marriages and a heightened divorce rate, there has been an increase in the number of unmarried adults. Labeling all single males as less productive than married males—thus reducing promotion and salary increase opportunities—would certainly have adverse consequences for an increasingly large segment of the work force. The research relates to the marital status of a group, not to any specific individual. Marital status *alone* should never be a determinant of rewards or opportunities in an organization.

Tenure

The last biographical characteristic we'll look at is tenure. With the exception of the concern about male-female differences, there is probably no other issue that is more subject to myths and speculations than the impact of seniority on job performance.

Extensive reviews of the seniority-productivity relationship have been conducted.[17] While past performance tends to be related to output in a new position, seniority by itself is not a good predictor of productivity. In other words, holding all other things equal, there is no reason to believe that people who have been on a job longer are more productive than are those with less seniority.

The research relating tenure with absence is quite straightforward. Studies consistently demonstrate seniority to be negatively related to absenteeism.[18] In fact, in terms of both absence frequency and total days lost at work, tenure is the single most important explanatory variable.[19]

As with absence, tenure is also a potent variable in explaining turnover. "Tenure has consistently been found to be negatively related to turnover and has been suggested as one of the single best predictors of turnover."[20] Moreover, consistent with research that suggests that past behavior is the best predictor of future behavior,[21] evidence indicates that tenure on an employee's previous job is a powerful predictor of future employee turnover.[22]

ABILITY

Contrary to what we were taught in grade school, we weren't all created equal. Most of us are to the left of the median on some normally distributed ability curve. Regardless of how motivated you are, it is unlikely that you can write as well as Stephen King, run as fast as Carl Lewis, act as well as Meryl Streep, or do improvisation as well as Robin Williams. Of course, just because we aren't all equal in abilities does not imply that some individuals are generally inferior to others. What we're acknowledging is that everyone has strengths and weaknesses in terms of ability that make him or her relatively superior or inferior to others in performing certain tasks or activities.[23] From management's standpoint, the issue isn't whether or not people differ in terms of their abilities. They do! The issue is knowing *how* people differ in abilities and *using* that knowledge to increase the likelihood that an employee will perform his or her job well.

Ability An individual's capacity to perform the various tasks in a job.

What does **ability** mean? As we'll use the term, ability refers to an individual's capacity to perform the various tasks in a job. It is a current assessment of what one *can* do. An individual's overall abilities are essentially madeup of two sets of skills: intellectual and physical.

Intellectual Abilities

Intellectual Ability That required to do mental activities.

Intellectual abilities are those needed to perform mental activities. IQ tests, for example, are designed to ascertain one's intellectual abilities. So, too, are popular college admission tests like the SAT and ACT and graduate admission tests in business (GMAT), law (LSAT), and medicine (MCAT). Some of the more relevant dimensions making up intellectual abilities include number aptitude, verbal comprehension, perceptual speed, and inductive reasoning. Table 4–1 describes these dimensions.

Jobs differ in the demands they place on incumbents to use their intellectual abilities. Generally speaking, the higher an individual rises in an organization's hierarchy, the more general intelligence and verbal abilities will be necessary to perform the job successfully. A high IQ, for example, may not be a prerequisite for all jobs. In fact, for many jobs—where employee behavior is highly routine and there are little or no opportunities to exercise discretion—a high IQ may be unrelated to performance. On the other hand, a careful review of the evidence demonstrates that tests that assess verbal, numerical, spatial, and perceptual abilities are valid predictors of job proficiency across all levels of jobs.[24] So tests that measure specific dimensions of intelligence have been found to be strong predictors of job performance.

TABLE 4–1   Dimensions of Intellectual Ability

Dimension	Description	Job Example
Number aptitude	Ability to do speedy and accurate arithmetic computations	Accountant: Determining the sales tax on a set of items
Verbal comprehension	Ability to understand what is read or heard and the relationship of words to each other	Plant Manager: Following corporate policies
Perceptual speed	Ability visually to identify similarities and differences quickly and accurately	Fire Investigator: Identifying clues to support a charge of arson
Inductive reasoning	Ability to identify a logical sequence in a problem and then solve the problem	Market Researcher: Forecasting demand for a product in the next time period

The major dilemma faced by employers who use mental ability tests for selection, promotion, training, and similar personnel decisions is that they have a negative impact on racial and ethnic groups.[25] The evidence indicates that some minority groups score, on the average, as much as one standard deviation lower than whites on verbal, numerical, and spatial ability tests. The negative impact from these tests can be eliminated by either avoiding these types of tests or seeking racial and ethnic balance by hiring and promoting on

FIGURE 4–1

School for the Mechanically Declined

the basis of ability within each ethnic group separately. This latter suggestion, incidentally, underlies legal efforts by the courts to eliminate employment discrimination through the use of targets and goals.

Physical Abilities

Physical Ability That required to do tasks demanding stamina, dexterity, strength, and similar skills.

To the same degree that intellectual abilities play a larger role in performance as individuals move up the organizational hierarchy, specific **physical abilities** gain importance for successfully doing less skilled and more standardized jobs in the lower part of the organization. Jobs where success demands stamina, manual dexterity, leg strength, or similar talents require management to identify an employee's physical capabilities.

Research on the requirements needed in hundreds of jobs has identified nine basic abilities involved in the performance of physical tasks.[26] These are described in Table 4–2. Individuals differ in the amount to which they hold each of these abilities. Not surprisingly, there is also little relationship between them: A high score on one is no assurance of a high score on others. High employee performance is likely to be achieved when management has ascertained the extent to which a job requires each of the nine abilities and then ensures that employees in that job have those abilities.

The Ability–Job Fit

Our concern is with explaining and predicting the behavior of people at work. In this section, we have demonstrated that jobs make differing demands on people and that people differ in the abilities they possess. Employee performance, therefore, is enhanced when there is a high ability–job fit.

The specific intellectual or physical abilities required for adequate job

TABLE 4–2   Nine Basic Physical Abilities

Strength Factors

1. Dynamic strength	Ability to exert muscular force repeatedly or continuously over time
2. Trunk strength	Ability to exert muscular strength using the trunk (particularly abdominal) muscles
3. Static strength	Ability to exert force against external objects
4. Explosive strength	Ability to expend a maximum of energy in one or a series of explosive acts

Flexibility Factors

5. Extent flexibility	Ability to move the trunk and back muscles as far as possible
6. Dynamic flexibility	Ability to make rapid, repeated flexing movements

Other Factors

7. Body coordination	Ability to coordinate the simultaneous actions of different parts of the body
8. Balance	Ability to maintain equilibrium despite forces pulling off balance
9. Stamina	Ability to continue maximum effort requiring prolonged effort over time

Source: Reprinted from the June 1979 issue of *Personnel Administrator,* copyright 1979, The American Society for Personnel Administration; 606 North Washington Street; Alexandria, Virginia 22314, pp. 82–92.

performance depend on the ability requirements of the job. Directing attention at only the employee's abilities or the ability requirements of the job ignores that employee performance depends on the interaction of the two.

What predictions can we make when the fit is poor? As alluded to previously, if employees lack the required abilities, they are likely to fail. If you're hired as a typist and you can't meet the job's basic typing requirements, your performance is going to be poor irrespective of your positive attitude or your high level of motivation. When the ability–job fit is out of sync because the employee has abilities that far exceed the requirements of the job, our predictions would be very different. Job performance is likely to be adequate, but there will be organizational inefficiencies and possible declines in employee satisfaction. Given that employee pay tends to reflect the highest skill level that they possess, if an employee's abilities far exceed those necessary to do the job, management will be paying more than they need to. Abilities significantly above those required can also reduce the employee's job satisfaction when the employee's desire to use his or her ability is particularly strong but that desire is frustrated by the limitations of the job.

PERSONALITY

Why are some people quiet and passive, while others are loud and aggressive? Are certain personality types better adapted for certain job types? What do we know from theories of personality that can help us to explain and predict the behavior of individuals in organizations? In this section we will attempt to answer such questions.

Employees have different backgrounds and personalities. Hewlett-Packard's King-Ming Young manages her company's diversity programs which use videotapes on cultural issues to help H-P employees learn to understand and appreciate differences.   Doug Menuez.

What Is Personality?

When we talk of personality, we do not mean that a person has charm, a positive attitude toward life, a smiling face, or is a finalist for "Happiest and Friendliest" in this year's Miss America contest. When psychologists talk of personality, they mean a dynamic concept describing the growth and development of a person's whole psychological system. Rather than looking at parts of the person, personality looks at some aggregate whole that is greater than the sum of the parts.

The most frequently used definition of personality was produced by Gordon Allport more than fifty years ago. He said personality is "the dynamic organization within the individual of those psychophysical systems that determine his unique adjustments to his environment."[27] For our purposes, you should think of **personality** as the sum total of ways in which an individual reacts and interacts with others. This is most often described in terms of measurable personality traits that a person exhibits.

Personality The sum total of ways in which an individual reacts and interacts with others.

Personality Determinants

An early argument in personality research was whether an individual's personality was the result of heredity or environment. Was the personality predetermined at birth, or was it the result of the individual's interaction with his or her environment? Clearly, there is no simple, black or white answer. Personality appears to be a result of both influences. Additionally, there has recently been an increased interest in a third factor—the situation. Thus, an adult's personality is now generally considered to be made up of both hereditary and environmental factors, moderated by situational conditions.

HEREDITY   Heredity refers to those factors that were determined at conception. Physical stature, facial attractiveness, sex, temperament, muscle composition and reflexes, energy level, and biological rhythms are characteristics that are generally considered to be either completely or substantially influenced by who your parents were; that is, by their biological, physiological, and inherent psychological makeup. The heredity approach argues that the ultimate explanation of an individual's personality is the molecular structure of the genes, located in the chromosomes. "In fact, much of the early work in personality could be subsumed under the series: Heredity is transmitted through the genes; the genes determine the hormone balance; hormone balance determines physique; and physique shapes personality."[28]

The heredity argument can be used to explain why Veronica's nose looks like her father's or why her chin resembles her mother's. It may explain why Diane is a gifted athlete when both her parents were similarly gifted. More controversy would surround the conclusion, by those who advocate the heredity approach, that Michael is lethargic as a result of inheriting this characteristic from his parents.

If all personality characteristics were completely dictated by heredity, they would be fixed at birth and no amount of experience could alter them. If you were relaxed and easygoing, for example, that would be the result of your genes, and it would not be possible for you to change these characteristics. While this approach may be appealing to the bigots of the world, it is an inadequate explanation of personality.

ENVIRONMENT   Among the factors that exert pressures on our personality formation are the culture in which we are raised, our early conditioning, the norms among our family, friends, and social groups, and other influences that we experience. The environment we are exposed to plays a critical role in shaping our personalities.

For example, culture establishes the norms, attitudes, and values that are passed along from one generation to the next and create consistencies over time. An ideology that is fostered in one culture may have only moderate influence in another. For instance, we in North America have had the themes of industriousness, success, competition, independence, and Protestant ethic constantly instilled in us through books, the school system, family, and friends. North Americans, as a result, tend to be ambitious and aggressive relative to individuals raised in cultures that have emphasized getting along with others, cooperation, and the priority of family over work and career.

An interesting area of research linking environmental factors and personality has focused on the influence of birth order. It has been argued that sibling position is an important psychological variable "because it represents a microcosm of the significant social experiences of adolescence and adulthood."[29] Those who see birth order as a predictive variable propose that while personality differences between children are frequently attributed to heredity, the environment in which the children are raised is really the critical factor that creates the differences. And the environment that a firstborn child is exposed to is different from that of later-born children.

The research indicates that firstborns are more prone to schizophrenia, more susceptible to social pressure, and more dependent than the later-born.[30] The firstborn are also more likely to experience the world as more orderly, predictable, and rational than later-born children. Of course, there is much debate as to the differing characteristics of first- versus later-born children, but the evidence does indicate that firstborns of the same sex "should be more concerned with social acceptance and rejection, less likely to break the rules imposed by authority, more ambitious and hard-working, more cooperative, more prone to guilt and anxiety, and less openly aggressive."[31]

Careful consideration of the arguments favoring either heredity or environment as the primary determinant of personality forces the conclusion that both are important. Heredity sets the parameters or outer limits, but an individual's full potential will be determined by how well he or she adjusts to the demands and requirements of the environment.

SITUATION   A third factor, the situation, further influences the effects of heredity and environment on personality. An individual's personality, while generally stable and consistent, does change in different situations. Different demands in different situations call forth different aspects of one's personality. We should not, therefore, look at personality patterns in isolation.

While it seems only logical to suppose that situations will influence an individual's personality, a neat classification scheme that would tell us the impact of various types of situations has so far eluded us. "Apparently we are not yet close to developing a system for clarifying situations so that they might be systematically studied."[32] However, we do know that certain situations are more relevant than others in influencing personality.

> What is of interest taxonomically is that situations seem to differ substantially in the constraints they impose on behavior, with some situations—e.g. church, an employment interview—constraining many

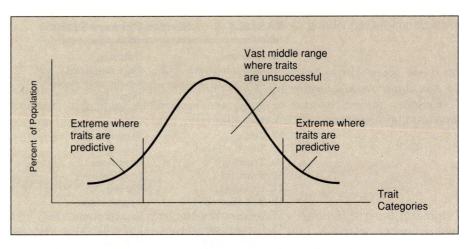

FIGURE 4–4   Predictive Validity of Personality Traits

to where one perceives the locus of control in one's life. The others are achievement orientation, authoritarianism, Machiavellianism, self-esteem, self-monitoring, and propensity for risk taking. In this section, we shall briefly introduce these attributes and summarize what we know as to their ability to explain and predict employee behavior.

LOCUS OF CONTROL   Some people believe that they are masters of their own fate. Other people see themselves as pawns of fate, believing that what happens to them in their lives is due to luck or chance. The first type, those who believe that they control their destinies, have been labeled **internals,** whereas the latter, who see their lives as being controlled by outside forces, have been called **externals.**[40]

A large amount of research comparing internals with externals has consistently shown that individuals who rate high in externality are less satisfied with their jobs, have higher absenteeism rates, are more alienated from the work setting, and are less involved on their jobs than are internals.[41]

Why are externals more dissatisfied? The answer is probably because they perceive themselves as having little control over those organizational outcomes that are important to them. Internals, facing the same situation, attribute organizational outcomes to their own actions. If the situation is unattractive, they believe that they have no one else to blame but themselves. Also, the dissatisfied internal is more likely to quit a dissatisfying job.

The impact of **locus of control** on absence is an interesting one. Internals believe that health is substantially under their own control through proper habits, so they take more responsibility for their health and have better health habits. This leads to lower incidences of sickness and, hence, lower absenteeism.[42]

We shouldn't expect any clear relationship between locus of control and turnover. The reason is that there are opposing forces at work. "On the one hand, internals tend to take action and thus might be expected to quit jobs more readily. On the other hand, they tend to be more successful on the job and more satisfied, factors associated with less individual turnover."[43]

The overall evidence indicates that internals generally perform better on their jobs, but that conclusion should be moderated to reflect differences in

Internals Individuals who believe that they control what happens to them.

Externals Individuals who believe that what happens to them is controlled by outside forces such as luck or chance.

Locus of Control The degree to which people believe they are masters of their own fate.

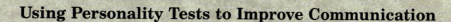
Using Personality Tests to Improve Communication

The Myers-Briggs Type Indicator (MBTI) is a 100-question personality test that asks people how they usually feel or act in particular situations.[39] It is one of the most widely used personality tests in the U.S.—in one recent year alone, some twenty million people took it. Organizations using the MBTI include Allied-Signal, Apple Computer, AT&T, Citicorp, Exxon, GE, Honeywell, 3M Co., plus many hospitals, educational institutions, and even the U.S. Armed Forces.

The test labels people as extroverted or introverted (E or I), sensing or intuitive (S or N), thinking or feeling (T or F), and perceiving or judging (P or J). These are then combined into sixteen personality types. (These are different from the sixteen primary traits in Table 4–3.) To illustrate, let's take several examples. INTJ's are visionaries. They usually have original minds and great drive for their own ideas and purposes. They're characterized as skeptical, critical, independent, determined, and often stubborn. ESTJ's are organizers. They're practical, realistic,

matter-of-fact, with a natural head for business or mechanics. They like to organize and run activities. The ENTP-type is a conceptualizer. He or she is quick, ingenious, and good at many things. This person tends to be resourceful in solving challenging problems, but may neglect routine assignments.

Users of MBTI aren't using the test to screen job applicants. Rather, it is being used to improve employee self-awareness, and in management development programs to help executives understand how they come across to others who may see things differently. For instance, some users report that the results help explain behaviors of colleagues that have puzzled them for years. Proponents argue that when people are aware of their own and their coworkers' types, communication improves, and with it productivity. Whether the use of MBTI actually improves employee productivity is problematic. But the growing popularity of MBTI in organizations can't be ignored.

jobs. Internals search more actively for information before making a decision, are more motivated to achieve, and make a greater attempt to control their environment. Externals, however, are more compliant and willing to follow directions. Therefore, internals do well on sophisticated tasks—which includes most managerial and professional jobs—that require complex information processing and learning. Additionally, internals are more suited to jobs that require initiative and independence of action. In contrast, externals should do well on jobs that are well structured and routine and where success depends heavily on complying with the direction of others.

ACHIEVEMENT ORIENTATION   We have noted that internals are motivated to achieve. This achievement orientation has also been singled out as a personality characteristic that varies among employees and that can be used to predict certain behaviors.

nAch Need to achieve or strive continually to do things better.

Research has centered around the need to achieve **(nAch).** People with a high need to achieve can be described as continually striving to do things better. They want to overcome obstacles, but they want to feel that their success (or failure) is due to their own actions. This means they like tasks of intermediate difficulty. If a task is very easy, it will lack challenge. High achievers receive no feeling of accomplishment from doing tasks that fail to challenge their abilities. Similarly, they avoid tasks that are so difficult that the probability of success is very low. Even if they succeed, it is more apt to be due to luck than ability. Given the high achiever's propensity for tasks where the outcome can be attributed directly to his or her efforts, the high-*nAch* person looks for challenges having approximately a 50–50 chance of success.

What can we say about high achievers on the job? In jobs that provide intermediate difficulty, rapid performance feedback, and allow the employee control over his or her results, the high *nAch* individual will perform well.[44] This implies, though, that high achievers will do better in sales, professional sports, or in management than on an assembly line or in clerical tasks. That is, those individuals with a high *nAch* will not always outperform those who are low or intermediate in this characteristic. The tasks that high achievers undertake must provide the challenge, feedback, and responsibility they look for if the high-*nAch* personality is to be positively related to job performance.

AUTHORITARIANISM   There is evidence that there is such a thing as an authoritarian personality, but its relevance to job behavior is more speculation than fact. With that qualification, let us examine **authoritarianism** and consider how it might be related to employee performance.

Authoritarianism refers to a belief that there should be status and power differences among people in organizations.[45] The extremely high-authoritarian personality is intellectually rigid, judgmental of others, deferential to those above and exploitative of those below, distrustful, and resistant to change. Of course, few people are extreme authoritarians, so conclusions must be guarded. It seems reasonable to postulate, however, that possessing a high-authoritarian personality would be related negatively to performance where the job demanded sensitivity to the feelings of others, tact, and the ability to adapt to complex and changing situations.[46] On the other hand, where jobs are highly structured and success depends on close conformance to rules and regulations, the high-authoritarian employee should perform quite well.

MACHIAVELLIANISM   Closely related to authoritarianism is the characteristic of **Machiavellianism** (Mach), named after Niccolo Machiavelli who wrote in the sixteenth century on how to gain and manipulate power. An individual high in Machiavellianism is pragmatic, maintains emotional distance, and believes that ends can justify means. "If it works, use it" is consistent with a high-Mach perspective.

A considerable amount of research has been directed toward relating high- and low-Mach personalities to certain behavioral outcomes.[47] High Machs manipulate more, win more, are persuaded less, and persuade others more than do low Machs.[48] Yet these high-Mach outcomes are moderated by situational factors. It has been found that high Machs flourish (1) when they interact face to face with others rather than indirectly; (2) when the situation has a minimum number of rules and regulations, thus allowing latitude for improvisation; and (3) where emotional involvement with details irrelevant to winning distracts low Machs.[49]

Should we conclude that high Machs make good employees? That answer depends on the type of job and whether you consider ethical implications in evaluating performance. In jobs that require bargaining skills (such as labor negotiation) or where there are substantial rewards for winning (as in commissioned sales), high Machs will be productive. But if ends can't justify

Authoritarianism The belief that there should be status and power differences among people in organizations.

Machiavellianism Degree to which an individual is pragmatic, maintains emotional distance, and believes that ends can justify means.

Dominant Personality Attributes Should Vary Across National Cultures

There are certainly no common personality types for a given country. You can, for instance, find high and low risk-takers in almost any culture. Yet a country's culture should influence the dominant personality characteristics of its population. Let's build this case by looking at three personality attributes—locus of control, achievement orientation, and authoritarianism.

In Chapter 3 we introduced a "person's relationship to nature" as a value dimension that separates national cultures. We noted that North Americans believe that they can dominate nature while other societies, such as Middle Eastern countries, believe that life is essentially preordained. Notice the close parallel to internal and external locus of control. We should expect a larger proportion of internals in the American and Canadian workforce than in Saudi Arabia or Iran.

The U.S. is well known for its emphasis on individualism and achievement. Managers in the United States, in contrast to, say, Third World nations, should expect to find more employees with a high achievement focus.

Authoritarianism is closely related to the concept of power–distance. In high power–distance societies, such as Mexico or Venezuela, there should be a large proportion of individuals with authoritarian personalities, especially among the ruling class. In contrast, since the United States rates below average on this dimension, we'd predict that authoritarian personalities would be less prevalent than in the high power–distance countries.

the means, if there are *absolute* standards of behavior, or if the three situational factors noted in the previous paragraph are not in evidence, our ability to predict a high Mach's performance will be severely curtailed.

Self-esteem An individual's degree of like or dislike for him or herself.

SELF-ESTEEM   People differ in the degree to which they like or dislike themselves. This trait is called **self-esteem**.[50]

The research on self-esteem (SE) offers some interesting insights into organizational behavior. For example, self-esteem is directly related to expectations for success. High SEs believe that they possess more of the ability they need in order to succeed at work. Individuals with high SEs will take more risks in job selection and are more likely to choose unconventional jobs than people with low SEs.

The most generalizable finding on self-esteem is that low SEs are more susceptible to external influence than are high SEs. Low SEs are dependent on the receipt of positive evaluations from others. As a result, they are more likely to seek approval from others and more prone to conform to the beliefs and behaviors of those they respect than are high SEs. In managerial positions, low SEs will tend to be concerned with pleasing others and, therefore, less likely to take unpopular stands than are high SEs.

Not surprisingly, self-esteem has also been found to be related to job satisfaction. A number of studies confirm that high SEs are more satisfied with their jobs than low SEs.

Self-monitoring A personality trait that measures an individual's ability to adjust his or her behavior to external situational factors.

SELF-MONITORING   Another personality trait that has recently received increased attention is called **self-monitoring**.[51] It refers to an individual's ability to adjust his or her behavior to external, situational factors.

Individuals high in self-monitoring can show considerable adaptability in adjusting their behavior to external, situational factors. They are highly sensitive to external cues and can behave differently in different situations. High self-monitors are capable of presenting striking contradictions between their public persona and their private selves. Low self-monitors can't deviate their behavior. They tend to display their true dispositions and attitudes in every situation; hence there is high behavioral consistency between who they are and what they do.

The research on self-monitoring is in its infancy so predictions must be guarded. However, preliminary evidence suggests that high self-monitors tend to pay closer attention to the behavior of others and are more capable of conforming than are low self-monitors.[52] We might also hypothesize that high self-monitors will be more successful in managerial positions where individuals are required to play multiple, and even contradicting, roles. The high self-monitor is capable of putting on different "faces" for different audiences.

RISK TAKING   People differ in their willingness to take chances. This propensity to assume or avoid risk has been shown to have an impact on how long it takes managers to make a decision and how much information they require before making their choice. For instance, seventy-nine managers worked on simulated personnel exercises that required them to make hiring decisions.[53] High-risk-taking managers made more rapid decisions and used less information in making their choices than did the low-risk-taking managers. Interestingly, the decision accuracy was the same for both groups.

While it is generally correct to conclude that managers in organizations are risk aversive,[54] there are still individual differences on this dimension.[55] As a result, it makes sense to recognize these differences and even to consider aligning risk-taking propensity with specific job demands. For instance, a high-risk-taking propensity may lead to more effective performance for a stock trader in a brokerage firm. This type of job demands rapid decision making. On the other hand, this personality characteristic might prove a major obstacle to accountants performing auditing activities. This latter job might be better filled by someone with a low-risk-taking propensity.

Matching Personality and Jobs

In the previous discussion of personality attributes, our conclusions were often qualified to recognize that the requirements of the job moderated the relationship between possession of the personality characteristic and job performance. This concern with matching the job requirements with personality characteristics has recently received increased attention. It is best articulated in John Holland's personality–job fit theory.[56] The theory is based on the notion of fit between a person's interests (taken to be an expression of personality) and his or her occupational environment. Holland presents six personality types and proposes that satisfaction and the propensity to leave a job depends on the degree to which individuals successfully match their personalities with a congruent occupational environment.

Each one of the six personality types has a matching occupational environment. Listed next is a description of the six types and examples of congruent occupations:

Type	Occupations
1. *Realistic*—involves aggressive behavior, physical activities requiring skill, strength, and coordination	Forestry, farming
2. *Investigative*—involves activities requiring thinking, organizing, and understanding rather than feeling or emotion	Biology, mathematics, news reporting
3. *Social*—involves interpersonal rather than intellectual or physical activities	Foreign service, social work, clinical psychology
4. *Conventional*—involves rule-regulated activities and sublimation of personal needs to an organization or person of power and status	Accounting, finance, corporate management
5. *Enterprising*—involves verbal activities to influence others, to attain power and status	Law, public relations, small-business management
6. *Artistic*—involves self-expression, artistic creation, or emotional activities	Art, music, writing

Holland has developed a Vocational Preference Inventory questionnaire that contains 160 occupational titles. Respondents indicate which of these occupations they like or dislike, and these answers are used to form personality profiles. Utilizing this procedure, research strongly supports the hexagonal diagram in Figure 4–5.[57] This figure shows that the closer two fields or orientations are in the hexagon, the more compatible they are. Adjacent categories are quite similar, while those diagonally opposite are highly dissimilar.

What does all this mean? The theory argues that satisfaction is highest and turnover lowest where personality and occupation are in agreement. Social individuals should be in social jobs, conventional people in conventional jobs, and so forth. A realistic person in a realistic job is in a more congruent situation than is a realistic person in an investigative job. A realistic person in a social job is in the most incongruent situation possible. The key points of this model are that (1) there do appear to be intrinsic differences in personality among individuals, (2) there are different types of jobs, and (3) people in job environments congruent with their personality types should be more satisfied and less likely to voluntarily resign than should people in incongruent jobs.

LEARNING

The last topic we will introduce in this chapter is learning. It is included for the obvious reason that almost all complex behavior is learned. If we want to explain and predict behavior, we need to understand how people learn.

A Definition of Learning

Learning Any relatively permanent change in behavior that occurs as a result of experience.

What is **learning?** A psychologist's definition is considerably broader than the layperson's view that "it's what we did when we went to school." In

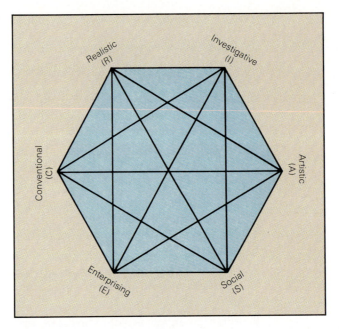

**FIGURE 4–5   Relationships Among Occupational
Personality Types**

Source: J. L. Holland, *Making Vocational Choices: A Theory of Vocational
Personalities and Work Environments,* 2nd ed. (Englewood Cliffs, NJ:
Prentice Hall, 1985). Used by permission. This model originally appeared
in J. L. Holland et al., "An Empirical Occupational Classification Derived
from a Theory of Personality and Intended for Practice and Research," ACT
Research Report No. 29 (Iowa City: The American College Testing Program, 1969).

actuality, each of us is continuously going "to school." Learning occurs all of
the time. A generally accepted definition of learning is, therefore, *any
relatively permanent change in behavior that occurs as a result of experience.*
Ironically, we can say that changes in behavior indicate that learning has
taken place and that learning is a change in behavior.

Obviously, the foregoing definition suggests that we shall never see
someone "learning." We can see changes, but not the learning itself. The
concept is theoretical and hence not directly observable:

> You have seen people in the process of learning, you have seen people who
> behave in a particular way as a result of learning and some of you (in fact,
> I guess the majority of you) have "learned" at some time in your life. In
> other words, we infer that learning has taken place if an individual
> behaves, reacts, responds as a result of experience in a manner different
> from the way he formerly behaved.[58]

Our definition has several components that deserve clarification. First,
learning involves change. This may be good or bad from an organizational
point of view. People can learn unfavorable behaviors—to hold prejudices or to
restrict their output, for example—as well as favorable behaviors. Second, the
change must be relatively permanent. Temporary changes may be only
reflexive and fail to represent any learning. Therefore, this requirement rules
out behavioral changes caused by fatigue or temporary adaptations. Third, our

definition is concerned with behavior. Learning takes place where there is a change in actions. A change in an individual's thought processes or attitudes, if accompanied by no change in behavior, would not be learning. Finally, some form of experience is necessary for learning. This may be acquired directly through observation or practice. Or it may result from indirect experiences, such as that acquired through reading. The crucial test still remains: Does this experience result in a relatively permanent change in behavior? If the answer is "Yes," we can say that learning has taken place.

Theories of Learning

How do we learn? Three theories have been offered to explain the process by which we acquire patterns of behavior. These are classical conditioning, operant conditioning, and social learning.

Classical Conditioning A type of conditioning where an individual responds to some stimulus that would not invariably produce such a response.

CLASSICAL CONDITIONING   **Classical conditioning** grew out of experiments to teach dogs to salivate in response to the ringing of a bell, conducted at the turn of the century by a Russian physiologist, Ivan Pavlov.[59]

A simple surgical procedure allowed Pavlov to measure accurately the amount of saliva secreted by a dog. When Pavlov presented the dog with a piece of meat, the dog exhibited a noticeable increase in salivation. Then Pavlov withheld the presentation of meat and merely rang a bell, the dog had no salivation. Then, Pavlov proceeded to link the meat and the ringing of the bell. After repeatedly hearing the bell before getting the food, the dog began to salivate as soon as the bell rang. After a while, the dog would salivate merely at the sound of the bell, even if no food was offered. In effect, the dog had learned to respond—that is, to salivate—to the bell. Let's review this experiment to introduce the key concepts in classical conditioning.

The meat was an *unconditioned stimulus;* it invariably caused the dog to react in a specific way. The reaction that took place whenever the unconditioned stimulus occurred was called the *unconditioned response* (or the noticeable increase in salivation, in this case). The bell was an artificial stimulus, or what we call the *conditioned stimulus*. While it was originally neutral, when the bell was paired with the meat (an unconditioned stimulus), it eventually produced a response when presented alone. The last key concept is the *conditioned response*. This describes the behavior of the dog salivating in reaction to the bell alone.

Using these concepts, we can summarize classical conditioning. Essentially, learning a conditioned response involves building up an association between a conditioned stimulus and an unconditioned stimulus. Using the paired stimuli, one compelling and the other one neutral, the neutral one becomes a conditioned stimulus and, hence, takes on the properties of the unconditioned stimulus.

Classical conditioning can be used to explain why Christmas carols often bring back pleasant memories of childhood—the songs being associated with the festive Christmas spirit and initiating fond memories and feelings of euphoria. In an organizational setting, we can also see classical conditioning operating. For example, at one manufacturing plant, every time the top executives from the head office would make a visit the plant management would clean up the administrative offices and wash the windows. This went on for years. Eventually, employees would turn on their best behavior and look prim and proper whenever the windows were cleaned—even in those occasional instances when the cleaning was not paired with the visit from the top brass. People had learned to associate the cleaning of the windows with the visit from the head office.

Classical conditioning is passive. Something happens and we react in a specific way. It is elicited in response to a specific, identifiable event. As such it can explain simple reflexive behaviors. But most behavior—particularly the complex behavior of individuals in organizations—is emitted rather than elicited. It is voluntary rather than reflexive. For example, employees choose to arrive at work on time, ask their boss for help with problems, or "goof off" when no one is watching. The learning of these behaviors is better understood by looking at operant conditioning.

Operant Conditioning A type of conditioning in which desired voluntary behavior leads to a reward or prevents a punishment.

OPERANT CONDITIONING　　**Operant conditioning** argues that behavior is a function of its consequences. People learn to behave to get something they want or avoid something they don't want. Operant behavior means voluntary or learned behavior in contrast to reflexive or unlearned behavior. The tendency to repeat such behavior is influenced as a result of the reinforcement or lack of reinforcement brought about by the consequences of the behavior. Reinforcement, therefore, strengthens a behavior and increases the likelihood that it will be repeated.

What Pavlov did for classical conditioning, noted Harvard psychologist B. F. Skinner has done for operant conditioning.[60] Building on earlier work in the field, Skinner's research has extensively expanded our knowledge of operant conditioning. Even his staunchest critics, who represent a sizable group, admit that his operant concepts work.

Behavior is assumed to be determined from without—that is, learned—rather than from within—reflexive or unlearned. Skinner argues that by creating pleasing consequences to follow specific forms of behavior, the frequency of that behavior will increase. People will most likely engage in desired behaviors if they are positively reinforced for doing so. Rewards, for example, are most effective if they immediately follow the desired response. Additionally, behavior that is not rewarded, or is punished, is less likely to be repeated.

You see illustrations of operant conditioning everywhere. For example, any situation in which it is either explicitly stated or implicitly suggested that reinforcements are contingent on some action on your part involves the use of operant learning. Your instructor says that if you want a high grade in the course you must supply correct answers on the test. A commissioned salesperson wanting to earn a sizable income finds that this is contingent on generating high sales in her territory. Of course, the linkage can also work to teach the individual to engage in behaviors that work against the best interests of the organization. Assume your boss tells you that if you will work overtime during the next three-week busy season, you will be compensated for it at the next performance appraisal. However, when performance appraisal time comes, you find that you are given no positive reinforcement for your overtime work. The next time your boss asks you to work overtime, what will you do? You will probably decline! Your behavior can be explained by operant conditioning: If a behavior fails to be positively reinforced, the probability that the behavior will be repeated declines.

SOCIAL LEARNING　　Individuals can also learn by observing what happens to other people and just by being told about something, as well as by direct experiences. So, for example, much of what we have learned comes from watching models—parents, teachers, peers, motion picture and television performers, bosses, and so forth. This view that we can learn both through observation and direct experience has been called **social learning theory.**[61]

While social learning theory is an extension of operant conditioning, that is, it assumes that behavior is a function of consequences, it also acknowledges the existence of observational learning and the importance of perception in learning. People respond to how they perceive and define consequences, not to the objective consequences themselves.

The influence of models is central to the social learning viewpoint. Four processes have been found to determine the influence that a model will have on an individual. As we'll show later in this chapter, the inclusion of the following processes when management sets up employee training programs will significantly improve the likelihood that the programs will be successful:

1. *Attentional processes.* People only learn from a model when they recognize and pay attention to its critical features. We tend to be most influenced by models that are attractive, repeatedly available, we think are important, or we see as similar to us.

2. *Retention processes.* A model's influence will depend on how well the individual remembers the model's action, even after the model is no longer readily available.

3. *Motor reproduction processes.* After a person has seen a new behavior by observing the model, the watching must be converted to doing. This process then demonstrates that the individual can perform the modeled activities.

4. *Reinforcement processes.* Individuals will be motivated to exhibit the modeled behavior if positive incentives or rewards are provided. Behaviors that are reinforced will be given more attention, learned better, and performed more often.

Shaping: A Managerial Tool

Because learning takes place on the job as well as prior to it, managers will be concerned with how they can teach employees to behave in ways that most benefit the organization. When we attempt to mold individuals by guiding their learning in graduated steps, we are **shaping behavior.**

Consider the situation in which an employee's behavior is significantly different from that sought by management. If management only reinforced the individual when he or she showed desirable responses, there might be very little reinforcement taking place. In such a case, shaping offers a logical approach toward achieving the desired behavior.

We *shape* behavior by systematically reinforcing each successive step that moves the individual closer to the desired response. If an employee who has been chronically a half-hour late for work comes in only twenty minutes late, we can reinforce this improvement. Reinforcement would increase as responses more closely approximate the desired behavior.

METHODS OF SHAPING BEHAVIOR There are four ways in which to shape behavior: through positive reinforcement, negative reinforcement, punishment, or extinction. When a response is followed with something pleasant, it is called *positive reinforcement.* This would describe, for instance, the boss who

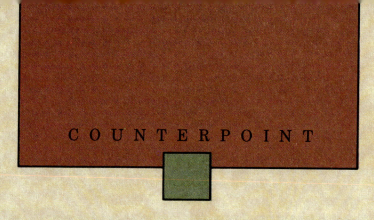

IQ Tests Are the Single Best Predictor of Worker Productivity

The validity of IQ tests is an emotionally-packed issue. A few well-substantiated results regarding these tests can illustrate why. The average gap in IQ scores between black and white Americans is fifteen points, while Japanese, Chinese, and Korean scores are between four and nine points higher than those of white Americans. Women have less variability than men on IQ scores, which results in men out-numbering women by a ratio of 7 to 5 at 140 IQ and above. If this were not incendiary enough, the evidence demonstrates that hereditary factors ac-count for at least sixty percent of the variability in IQ and may explain up to eighty percent of differenc-es. Moreover, like it or not, we should know that the following facts are well supported by research findings: Not all people are equally intelligent; general intelligence represents real and fundamen-tal differences in how well individuals perform cog-nitive tasks; and the evidence demonstrates a high correlation between cognitive ability and perfor-mance on *all* jobs. The observable hierarchy in occupational status in North America is, in essence, an intelligence hierarchy. Only about ten to twenty percent of the population has the intelligence to perform minimally as a doctor, but about eighty percent could make it as a licensed practical nurse. A recent survey of 120 corporate chief executive officers, reported in the *Wall Street Journal,* found that these executives averaged 121 on an intelli-gence test. That would place them, as a group, among the top four percent of the population.

A review of the massive evidence from hun-dreds of studies on intelligence shows unquestion-ably that general cognitive ability predicts perfor-mance on all jobs, including the so-called "manual" jobs as well as "mental" jobs. The path, too, is fairly straightforward. The correlation between general cognitive ability and job knowledge is 0.80. Similar-ly, job knowledge is correlated 0.80 with job perfor-mance as measured by objective work sample perfor-mance. So general cognitive ability predicts job performance in large part because it predicts learn-ing and job mastery. Ability is highly correlated with job knowledge, and job knowledge is highly correlated with job performance. At the aggregate level, cognitive ability predicts performance with a correlation of 0.75. No other predictor is currently known to have similar validity. This means that tests of general cognitive ability (which is essential-ly what IQ tests are) are the single best predictor of worker productivity. They are better than tests that seek to measure specific job skills or motivation.

Why does cognitive ability correlate with per-formance in all jobs? One answer is that even simple jobs require far more learning than is evident to outsiders. Planning, judgment, and memory—all major cognitive processes—are used in day-to-day performance on all jobs. Since learning the job is the key to job performance, and general cognitive ability predicts learning, it is to be expected that general cognitive ability will be the key predictor of job performance. High ability workers are faster at cognitive operations on the job, are better able to prioritize between conflicting rules, are better able to adapt old procedures to altered situations, are better able to innovate to meet unexpected prob-lems, and are better able to learn new procedures quickly as the job changes over time.

The evidence in this argument is drawn from J. E. Hunter, "Cognitive Ability, Cognitive Aptitudes, Job Knowledge, and Job Performance," *Journal of Vocational Behavior,* December 1986, pp. 340–62; L. S. Gottfredson, "Societal Consequences of the g Factor in Employment," *Journal of Vocational Behavior,* December 1986, pp. 379–410; and S. Itzkoff, *Why Humans Vary in Intelligence* (New York: Paideia, 1987).

1. Which biographical characteristics best predict *productivity? Absenteeism? Turnover? Satisfaction?*

2. Describe the specific steps you would take to ensure that an individual has the appropriate abilities to satisfactorily do a given job.

3. How does *heredity* influence personality? *Environment? The situation?*

4. What constrains the ability of personality traits to predict behavior?

5. What behavioral predictions might you make if you knew that an employee had (a) an external locus of control? (b) a high *nAch?* (c) a low Mach score? (d) low self-esteem?

6. "The type of job an employee does moderates the relationship between personality and job productivity." Do you agree or disagree with this statement? Discuss.

7. One day your boss comes in and he's nervous, edgy, and argumentative. The next day he is calm and relaxed. Does this suggest that personality traits aren't consistent from day to day?

8. "Everyone is a trait theorist. If one really believed that situations determined behavior, then there would be no reason to test or interview prospective employees for jobs—it would only be necessary to structure the situation properly." Do you agree or disagree? Discuss.

9. Contrast classical conditioning, operant conditioning, and social learning.

10. "Managers should never use discipline with a problem employee." Do you agree or disagree? Discuss.

11. Learning theory can be used to *explain* behavior and to *control* behavior. Can you distinguish between the two objectives? Can you give any ethical or moral arguments why managers should not seek control over others' behavior? How valid do you think these arguments are?

12. What have you learned about "learning" that could help you to explain the behavior of students in a classroom if (a) the instructor gives only one test—a final examination at the end of the course? (b) the instructor gives four exams during the term, all of which are announced on the first day of class? (c) the student's grade is based on the results of numerous exams, none of which are announced by the instructor ahead of time?

FOR FURTHER READING

ADLER, S. and H. M. WEISS, "Recent Developments in the Study of Personality and Organizational Behavior," in C.L. Cooper and I. Robertson (eds.), *International Review of Industrial and Organizational Psychology 1988* (Chichester, England: Wiley, 1988), pp. 307–30. Argues for the value of personality in predicting a wide range of behaviors, especially in less structured work settings that permit the expression of individual differences.

DAVIS-BLAKE, A. and J. PFEFFER, "Just a Mirage: The Search for Dispositional Effects in Organizational Research," *Academy of Management Review,* July 1989, pp.

Predicting Performance

Alix Maher is the new admissions director at a small, highly selective New England college. She has a bachelor's degree in education and a recent M.A. in Educational Administration. But she has no prior experience in college admissions.

Alix's predecessor, in conjunction with the college's admissions committee (made up of five faculty members), had given the following weights to student selection criteria: high school grades (40 percent); Scholastic Aptitude Test (SAT) scores (40 percent); extra-curricular activities and achievements (10 percent); and the quality and creativity of a written theme submitted with the application (10 percent).

Alix had serious reservations about using SAT scores. In their defense, she recognized that the quality of high schools varies greatly. The level of student performance that receives an "A" in American History at one school might earn only a "C" at a far more demanding school. And Alix is aware that the people who design the SATs, the Educational Testing Service, argue forcibly that these test scores are valid predictors of how well a person will do in college. Yet, Alix has several concerns:

1. The pressure of the SAT exam is very great and many students suffer from test anxiety. The results, therefore, may not be truly reflective of what a student knows.

2. There is evidence that coaching improves scores from between 40 to 150 points. Test scores, therefore, may adversely affect the chances of acceptance for students who cannot afford the $500 or $600 to take test-coaching courses.

3. Are SAT's really valid? Do they discriminate against minorities, the poor, and those who have had limited access to cultural growth experiences?

As Alix ponders whether she wants to recommend changing the college's selection criteria and weights, she is reminded of a recent conversation she had with a friend who is an industrial psychologist with a *Fortune* 100 company. He had told her that his company regularly uses intelligence tests to help select from among job applicants. For instance, after the company's recruiters interview graduating seniors on college campuses and identify possible hirees, they give the applicants a standardized intelligence test. Those who fail to score at least in the 80th percentile are eliminated from the applicant pool.

Alix thought that if intelligence tests are used by billion-dollar corporations to screen job applicants, why shouldn't colleges? Moreover, since one of the objectives of a college should be to get its graduates placed into good jobs, maybe SAT scores should be given even higher weight than 40 percent in the selection decision. After all, she wondered, if SATs tap intelligence and employers want intelligent job applicants, why not make college selection decisions predominantly on the basis of SAT scores?

QUESTIONS

1. What do *you* think SATs measure: aptitude, innate ability, achievement potential, intelligence, ability to take tests, or something else?

2. If the best predictor of future behavior is past behavior, what should college admissions directors use to identify the most qualified applicants?

3. If you were Alix, what would you do? Why?

NOTES

[1]Based on S. P. Sherman, "Inside the Mind of Jack Welch," *Fortune,* March 27, 1989, pp. 38–50.

[2]Reported in W.B. Johnston, *Workforce 2000: Work and Workers for the 21st Century* (Indianapolis: Hudson Institute, 1987).

[3]L. W. Porter and R. Steers, "Organizational, Work and Personal Factors in Employee Turnover and Absenteeism," *Psychological Bulletin,* January 1973, pp. 151–76; W. H. Mobley, R. W. Griffeth, H. H. Hand, and B. M. Meglino, "Review and Conceptual Analysis of the Employee Turnover Process," *Psychological Bulletin,* May 1979, pp. 493–522; and S. R. Rhodes, "Age-Related Differences in Work Attitudes and Behavior: A Review and Conceptual Analysis," *Psychological Bulletin,* March 1983, pp. 328–67.

[4]Rhodes, "Age-Related Differences," pp. 347–49.

[5]G. M. McEvoy and W. F. Cascio, "Cumulative Evidence of the Relationship Between Employee Age and Job Performance," *Journal of Applied Psychology,* February 1989, pp. 11–17.

[6]A. L. Kalleberg and K. A. Loscocco, "Aging, Values, and Rewards: Explaining Age Differences in Job Satisfaction," *American Sociological Review,* February 1983, pp. 78–90; and R. Lee and E. R. Wilbur, "Age, Education, Job Tenure, Salary, Job Characteristics, and Job Satisfaction: A Multivariate Analysis," *Human Relations,* August 1985, pp. 781–91.

[7]See, for example, G. N. Powell, *Women and Men in Management* (Beverly Hills, CA: Sage Publications, 1988); and P. Chance, "Biology, Destiny, and All That," *Across the Board,* July/August 1988, pp. 19–23.

[8]E. Maccoby and C. Nagy Jacklin, *The Psychology of Sex Differences* (Stanford, CA: Stanford University Press, 1974), pp. 154, 211.

[9]R. P. Quinn, G. L. Staines, and M. R. McCullough, *Job Satisfaction: Is There a Trend?* (Washington, D.C.: U.S. Government Printing Office, Document 2900–00195, 1974).

[10]T. W. Mangione, "Turnover—Some Psychological and Demographic Correlates," in R. P. Quinn and T. W. Mangione (eds.), *The 1969–70 Survey of Working Conditions* (Ann Arbor: University of Michigan, Survey Research Center, 1973); and R. Marsh and H. Mannari, "Organizational Commitment and Turnover: A Predictive Study," *Administrative Science Quarterly,* March 1977, pp. 57–75.

[11]R. J. Flanagan, G. Strauss, and L. Ulman, "Worker Discontent and Work Place Behavior," *Industrial Relations,* May 1974, pp. 101–23; K. R. Garrison and P. M. Muchinsky, "Attitudinal and Biographical Predictors of Incidental Absenteeism," *Journal of Vocational Behavior,* April 1977, pp. 221–30; G. Johns, "Attitudinal and Nonattitudinal Predictors of Two Forms of Absence from Work," *Organizational Behavior and Human Performance,* December 1978, pp. 431–44; and R. T. Keller, "Predicting Absenteeism from Prior Absenteeism, Attitudinal Factors, and Nonattitudinal Factors," *Journal of Applied Psychology,* August 1983, pp. 536–40.

[12]Garrison and Muchinsky, "Attitudinal and Biographical Predictors"; C. J. Watson, "An Evaluation and Some Aspects of the Steers and Rhodes Model of Employee Attendance," *Journal of Applied Psychology,* June 1981, pp. 385–89; Keller, "Predicting Absenteeism"; J. M. Federico, P. Federico, and G. W. Lundquist, "Predicting Women's Turnover as a Function of Extent of Met Salary Expectations and Biodemographic Data," *Personnel Psychology,* Winter 1976, pp. 559–66; Marsh and Mannari, "Organizational Commitment;" and D. R. Austrom, T. Baldwin, and G. J. Macy, "The Single Worker: An Empirical Exploration of Attitudes, Behavior, and Well-Being," *Canadian Journal of Administrative Sciences,* December 1988, pp. 22–29.

[13]Based on "Men, Here's the Secret to Greater Productivity," *Wall Street Journal,* September 16, 1988, p. 19.

[14]Porter and Steers, "Organizational, Work, and Personal Factors"; N. Nicholson and P. M. Goodge, "The Influence of Social, Organizational and Biographical Factors on Female Absence," *Journal of Management Studies,* October 1976, pp. 234–54; P. M. Muchinsky, "Employee Absenteeism: A Review of the Literature," *Journal of Vocational Behavior,* June 1977, pp. 316–40; and R. M. Steers and S. R. Rhodes, "Major Influences on Employee Attendance: A Process Model," *Journal of Applied Psychology,* August 1978, pp. 391–407.

[15]Porter and Steers, "Organizational, Work, and Personal Factors"; Federico, Federico, and Lundquist, "Predicting Women's Turnover"; and Marsh and Mannari, "Organizational Commitment."

[16]A. S. Gechman and Y. Wiener, "Job Involvement and Satisfaction as Related to Mental Health and Personal Time Devoted to Work," *Journal of Applied Psychology,* August 1975, pp. 521–23.

[17]M. E. Gordon and W. J. Fitzgibbons, "Empirical Test of the Validity of Seniority as a Factor in Staffing Decisions," *Journal of Applied Psychology,* June 1982, pp. 311–19; and M. E. Gordon and W. A. Johnson, "Seniority: A Review of Its Legal and Scientific Standing," *Personnel Psychology,* Summer 1982, pp. 255–80.

[18]Garrison and Muchinsky, "Attitudinal and Biographical Predictors"; N. Nicholson, C. A. Brown, and J. K. Chadwick-Jones, "Absence from Work and Personal Characteristics," *Journal of Applied Psychology,* June 1977, pp. 319–27; and Keller, "Predicting Absenteeism."

[19]P. O. Popp and J. A. Belohlav, "Absenteeism in a Low Status Work Environment," *Academy of Management Journal,* September 1982, p. 681.

PERCEPTION AND INDIVIDUAL DECISION MAKING

LEARNING OBJECTIVES

After studying this chapter, you should be able to:

1. *Distinguish between perception and reality in determining behavior*
2. *Explain how two people can see the same thing and interpret it differently*
3. *List the three determinants of attribution*
4. *Describe how shortcuts can assist in or distort our judgment of others*
5. *Explain how perception affects the decision-making process*
6. *Outline the six steps in the optimizing decision process*
7. *List the assumptions of the optimizing model*
8. *Explain how individuals satisfice*
9. *Describe the implicit favorite model of decision making*

Attribution Theory When individuals observe behavior, they attempt to determine whether it is internally or externally caused.

ment of a person's actions, therefore, will be significantly influenced by the assumptions we make about the person's internal state.

Attribution theory has been proposed to develop explanations of the ways in which we judge people differently depending on what meaning we attribute to a given behavior.[2] Basically, the theory suggests that when we observe an individual's behavior, we attempt to determine whether it was internally or externally caused. That determination, however, depends largely on three factors: (1) distinctiveness, (2) consensus, and (3) consistency. First, let's clarify the differences between internal and external causation and then elaborate on each of the three determining factors.

Internally caused behaviors are those that are believed to be under the personal control of the individual. Externally caused behavior is seen as resulting from outside causes; that is, the person is seen as forced into the behavior by the situation. If one of your employees were late for work, you might attribute his lateness to his partying into the wee hours of the morning and then oversleeping. This would be an internal interpretation. But if you attributed his arriving late to a major automobile accident that tied up traffic on the road that your employee regularly uses, then you are making an external attribution.

Distinctiveness refers to whether an individual displays different behaviors in different situations. Is the employee who arrives late today also the source of complaints by co-workers for being a "goof-off"? What we want to know is if this behavior is unusual or not. If it is, the observer is likely to give the behavior an external attribution. If this action is not unique, it will probably be judged as internal.

If everyone who is faced with a similar situation responds in the same way, we can say the behavior shows *consensus*. Our late employee's behavior would meet this criterion if all employees who took the same route to work were also late. From an attribution perspective, if consensus is high you would be expected to give an external attribution to the employee's tardiness, whereas if other employees who took the same route made it into work on time, your conclusion as to causation would be internal.

Finally, an observer looks for *consistency* in a person's actions. Does the person respond the same way over time? Coming in ten minutes late for work is not perceived in the same way if for one employee it represents an unusual case (she hasn't been late for several months), while for another it is part of a routine pattern (she is regularly late two or three times a week). The more consistent the behavior, the more the observer is inclined to attribute it to internal causes.

Figure 5–3 summarizes the key elements in attribution theory. It would tell us, for instance, that if an employee—let's call her Ms. Smith—generally performs at about the same level on other related tasks as she does on her current task (low distinctiveness), if other employees frequently perform differently—better or worse—than Ms. Smith does on that current task (low consensus), and if Ms. Smith's performance on this current task is consistent over time (high consistency), her manager or anyone else who is judging Ms. Smith's work is likely to hold her primarily responsible for her task performance (internal attribution).

One of the more interesting findings from attribution theory is that there are errors or biases that distort attributions. For instance, there is substantial evidence to support that when we make judgments about the behavior of other people, we have a tendency to underestimate the influence of external factors and overestimate the influence of internal or personal factors.[3] This is called

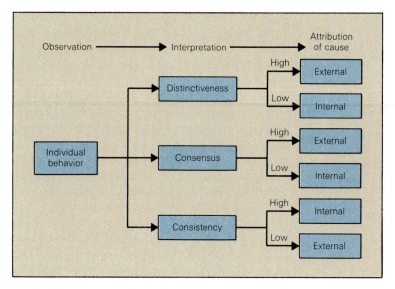

FIGURE 5-3   Attribution Theory

the **fundamental attribution error** and can explain why a sales manager may be prone to attribute the poor performance of her sales agents to laziness rather than the innovative product line introduced by a competitor. There is also a tendency for individuals to attribute *their own* successes to internal factors like ability or effort while putting the blame for failure on external factors like luck. This is called the **self-serving bias** and suggests that feedback provided to employees in performance reviews will be predictably distorted by recipients depending on whether it is positive or negative.

Frequently Used Shortcuts in Judging Others

We use a number of shortcuts when we judge others. Perceiving and interpreting what others do is burdensome. As a result, individuals develop techniques for making the task more manageable. These techniques are frequently valuable—they allow us to make accurate perceptions rapidly and provide valid data for making predictions. However, they are not foolproof. They can and do get us into trouble: An understanding of these shortcuts can be helpful toward recognizing when they can result in significant distortions.

SELECTIVE PERCEPTION   Any characteristic that makes a person, object, or event stand out will increase the probability that it will be perceived. Why? Because it is impossible for us to assimilate everything we see—only certain stimuli can be taken in. This explains why, as we noted earlier, you're more likely to notice cars like your own or why some people may be reprimanded by their boss for doing something that when done by another employee goes unnoticed. Since we can't observe everything going on about us, we engage in **selective perception.** A classic example shows how vested interests can significantly influence what problems we see.

Dearborn and Simon[4] performed a perceptual study in which twenty-three business executives read a comprehensive case describing the organization and activities of a steel company. Six of the twenty-three executives were in the sales function, five in production, four in accounting, and eight in miscellaneous functions. Each manager was asked to write down the most important problem he found in the case. Eighty-three percent of the sales executives rated sales important, while only twenty-nine percent of the others did so. This, along with other results of the study, led the researchers to conclude that the participants perceived aspects in a situation that related specifically to the activities and goals of the unit to which they were attached. A group's perception of organizational activities is selectively altered to align with the vested interests they represent. In other words, where the stimuli are ambiguous, as in the steel company case, perception tends to be influenced more by an individual's base of interpretation (that is, attitudes, interests, and background) than by the stimulus itself.

But how does selectivity work as a shortcut in judging other people? Simply, since we cannot assimilate all that we observe, we take in bits and pieces. But these bits and pieces are not chosen randomly; rather, they are selectively chosen depending on the interests, background, experience, and attitudes of the observer. Selective perception allows us to "speed read" others, but not without the risk of drawing an inaccurate picture. Because we see what we want to see, we can draw unwarranted conclusions from an ambiguous situation. If there is a rumor going around the office that your company's sales are down and that large layoffs may be coming, a routine visit by a senior executive from headquarters might be interpreted as the first step in management's identification of people to be fired, when in reality such an action may be the farthest thing from the mind of the senior executive.

PROJECTION   It is easy to judge others if we assume they are similar to us. For instance, if you want challenge and responsibility in your job, you assume

FIGURE 5–4
Source: Drawing by William Steig; © 1987 The New Yorker Magazine, Inc.

"I do not hate you. You're projecting."

Projection Attributing one's own characteristics to other people.

that others want the same. This tendency to attribute one's own characteristics to other people—which is called **projection**—can distort perceptions made about others. When managers engage in projection, they compromise their ability to respond to individual differences. They tend to see people as more homogeneous than they really are.

What this means in practice is that among people who engage in projection, their perception of others is influenced more by what the observer is like than by what the person being observed is like. When observing others who actually are like them, these observers are quite accurate—not because they are more perceptive, but only because they judge people as being similar to themselves, so when they finally find someone who is, they are naturally correct.

Stereotyping Judging someone on the basis of the perception of the group to which that person belongs.

STEREOTYPING   When we judge someone on the basis of our perception of the group to which he or she belongs, we are using the shortcut called **stereotyping.** William Faulkner engaged in stereotyping in his reported conversation with Ernest Hemingway, when he said, "The rich are different from you and me." Hemingway's reply, "Yes, they have more money," indicated that other than the required difference (you need money to be rich), he refused to stereotype or generalize characteristics about people based on their wealth.

Generalizations, of course, are not without their advantages. It makes assimilating easier since it permits us to maintain consistency. It is less difficult to deal with an unmanageable number of stimuli if we use stereotypes. But the problem occurs when we inaccurately stereotype. All accountants are *not* quiet and introspective just as all salespeople are *not* aggressive and outgoing.

In an organizational context, we frequently hear comments that represent stereotyped representation of certain groups: "Managers don't give a damn about their people, only getting the work out"; or "Union people expect something for nothing." Clearly, these phrases represent stereotypes, but if people expect these perceptions, that is what they will see, whether it represents reality or not.

Obviously, one of the problems of stereotypes is that they are so widespread, despite the fact that they may not contain a shred of truth, or may be irrelevant. Their being widespread may only mean that many people are making the same inaccurate perception based on a false premise about a group.

Halo Effect Drawing a general impression about an individual based on a single characteristic.

HALO EFFECT   When we draw a general impression about an individual based on a single characteristic, such as intelligence, sociability, or appearance, a **halo effect** is operating. This phenomenon frequently occurs when students appraise their classroom instructor. Students may isolate a single trait such as enthusiasm and allow their entire evaluation to be tainted by how they judge the instructor on this one trait. Thus, an instructor may be quiet, assured, knowledgeable, and highly qualified, but if his style lacks zeal, he will be rated lower on a number of other characteristics.

The reality of the halo effect was confirmed in a classic study where subjects were given a list of traits like intelligent, skillful, practical, industrious, determined, and warm and asked to evaluate the person to whom these traits applied.[6] Based on these traits, the person was judged to be wise, humorous, popular, and imaginative. When the same list was modified to substitute cold for warm in the trait list, a completely different set of

The Pervasiveness of Sex-Role Stereotypes

Tim Ganter received a report from the corporate engineering research office. The report was signed by the office's director, Dr. L. L. Stockton. Tim has never met Dr. Stockton, but had a question about the report. So he called Stockton's office. The phone rang. A woman answered, "Engineering research. Can I help you?" Tim replied, "Yes, I'm trying to reach Dr. Stockton. Are you his secretary?" The voice replied, "No, I'm Dr. Stockton!"

Tim Ganter had made a mistake. He was embarrassed, and rightly so. He was guilty of sex-role stereotyping. Managers are not all males; nor are all engineers with doctoral degrees. Yet sex-role stereotypes are widespread in organizations. This is especially true for women managers. Studies indicate that male and female managers alike hold negative stereotypes about the ability of women to manage effectively.[5] Successful managers—whether male or female—tend to be perceived as having personality traits and skills associated with men. But, unfortunately, the same aggressive behavior that is judged positively when exhibited by a male manager is often appraised negatively when exhibited by a female manager. As one female executive confided, "When I'm forceful and direct, I'm accused of being too aggressive. When I'm thoughtful or considerate, I'm told that I'm too weak. No matter what I do, I can't win!" Such negative stereotypes create conflicts for women in, and aspiring to, managerial positions. And, of course, they suboptimize the organization's effectiveness when they prevent the selection or promotion of the most qualified applicant.

perceptions was obtained. Clearly, the subjects were allowing a single trait to influence their overall impression of the person being judged.

The propensity for the halo effect to operate is not random. Research suggests that it is likely to be most extreme when the traits to be perceived are ambiguous or unclear in behavioral terms, when the traits have moral overtones, and when the perceiver is judging traits with which he or she has had limited experience.[7]

Specific Applications in Organizations

People in organizations are always judging each other. Managers must appraise their subordinates' performances. We evaluate how much effort our co-workers are putting into their jobs. When a new person joins a department, he or she is immediately "sized up" by the other department members. In many cases, these judgments have important consequences for the organization. Let us briefly look at a few of the more obvious applications.

EMPLOYMENT INTERVIEW   A major input into who is hired or rejected is the employment interview. It's fair to say that few people are hired without an interview. But the evidence indicates that interviewers make perceptual judgments that are often inaccurate. Additionally, interrater agreement among interviewers is often poor; that is, different interviewers see different things in the same candidate and thus arrive at different conclusions about the applicant.

Interviewers generally draw early impressions that become very quickly entrenched. If negative information is exposed early in the interview, it tends to be more heavily weighted than if that same information were conveyed later.[8] Studies indicate that most interviewers' decisions change very little after the first four or five minutes of the interview. As a result, information elicited early in the interview carries greater weight than does information elicited later, and a "good applicant" is probably characterized more by the absence of unfavorable characteristics than by the presence of favorable characteristics.

Importantly, who you think is a good candidate and who I think is one may differ markedly. Because interviews usually have so little consistent structure and interviewers vary in terms of what they consider a good candidate, judgments of the same candidate can vary widely. If the employment interview is an important input into the hiring decision, and it usually is, you should recognize that perceptual factors influence who is hired and eventually the quality of an organization's labor force.

PERFORMANCE EVALUATION Although the impact of performance evaluations on behavior will be discussed fully in Chapter 16, it should be pointed out here that an employee's performance appraisal is very much dependent on the perceptual process. An employee's future is closely tied to his or her appraisal—promotions, pay raises, and continuation of employment are among the most obvious outcomes. The performance appraisal represents an assessment of an employee's work. While this can be objective (for example, a

The global economy has added another dimension to evaluating an employee: the ability to perform one'e job at odd hours. This photo depicts Citicorp traders at 1 a.m. in New York, where foreign exchange lines are open 24 hours each day. Traders who can perform well only during normal business hours aren't likely to succeed in these jobs.   Claudio Edinger/ Gamma-Liaison.

salesperson is appraised on how many dollars of sales she generates in her territory), many jobs are evaluated in subjective terms. Subjective measures are easier to implement, they provide managers with greater discretion, and many jobs do not readily lend themselves to objective measures. Subjective measures are, by definition, judgmental. The evaluator forms a general impression of an employee's work. To the degree that managers use subjective measures in appraising employees, what the evaluator perceives to be "good" or "bad" employee characteristics/behaviors will significantly influence the appraisal outcome.

EMPLOYEE EFFORT   An individual's future in an organization is usually not dependent on performance alone. In many organizations, the level of an employee's effort is given high importance. Just as teachers frequently consider how hard you try in a course as well as how you perform on examinations, so often do managers. And assessment of an individual's effort is a subjective judgment susceptible to perceptual distortions and bias. If it is true, as some claim, that "more workers are fired for poor attitudes and lack of discipline than for lack of ability,"[9] then appraisal of an employee's effort may be a primary influence on his or her future in the organization.

EMPLOYEE LOYALTY   Another important judgment that managers make about employees is whether they are loyal to the organization. Few organizations appreciate employees, especially those in the managerial ranks, disparaging the firm. Further, in some organizations, if the word gets around that an employee is looking at other employment opportunities outside the firm, that employee may be labeled as disloyal, cutting off all future advancement opportunities. The issue is not whether organizations are right in demanding loyalty, but that many do, and that assessment of an employee's loyalty or commitment is highly judgmental. What is perceived as loyalty by one decision maker may be seen as excessive conformity by another. An employee who questions a top management decision may be seen as disloyal by some, yet caring and concerned by others. When evaluating a person's attitude, as in loyalty assessment, we must recognize that we are again involved with person perception.

THE LINK BETWEEN PERCEPTION AND INDIVIDUAL DECISION MAKING

Individuals in organizations make decisions. That is, they make choices from among two or more alternatives. Top managers, for instance, determine their organization's goals, what products or services to offer, how best to organize corporate headquarters, or where to locate a new manufacturing plant. Middle- and lower-level managers determine production schedules, select new employees, and decide how pay raises are to be allocated. Of course, making decisions is not the sole province of managers. Nonmanagerial employees also make decisions that affect their jobs and the organizations they work for. The more obvious of these decisions might include whether to come to work or not on any given day, how much effort to put forward once at work, and whether to comply with a request made by the boss. Individual decision making, therefore, is an important part of organizational behavior. But how individuals in organizations make decisions, and the quality of their final choices, are largely influenced by their perceptions.

Decision making occurs as a reaction to a problem. There is a discrepancy between some *current* state of affairs and some *desired* state, requiring consideration of alternative courses of action. So, if your car breaks down and you rely on it to get to school, you have a problem that requires a decision on your part. Unfortunately, most problems don't come neatly packaged with a label "problem" clearly displayed on them. One person's *problem* is another person's *satisfactory state of affairs*. One manager may view her division's two percent increase in quarterly sales to be a serious problem requiring immediate action on her part. In contrast, her counterpart in another division of the same company, who also had a two percent sales increase, may consider that quite satisfactory. So the awareness that a problem exists and that a decision needs to be made is a perceptual issue.

Moreover, every decision requires interpretation and evaluation of information. Data is typically received from multiple sources and it needs to be screened, processed, and interpreted. What data, for instance, is relevant to the decision and what isn't? The perceptions of the decision maker will answer this question. Alternatives will be developed and the strengths and weaknesses of each will need to be evaluated. Again, because alternatives don't come with "red flags" identifying themselves as such or with their strengths and weaknesses clearly marked, the individual decision maker's perceptual process will have a large bearing on the final outcome.

THE OPTIMIZING DECISION-MAKING MODEL

Optimizing Model A decision-making model that describes how individuals should behave in order to maximize some outcome.

Let's begin by describing how individuals should behave in order to maximize some outcome. We will call this the **optimizing model** of decision making.[10]

Steps in the Optimizing Model

Table 5–1 outlines the six steps an individual should follow, either explicitly or implicitly, when making a decision.

STEP 1: ASCERTAIN THE NEED FOR A DECISION   The first step requires recognition that a decision needs to be made. The existence of a problem, or as we stated previously, a disparity between some desired state and the actual condition, brings about this recognition. If you calculate your monthly expenses and find that you're spending fifty dollars more than you allocated in your budget, you have ascertained the need for a decision. There is a disparity between your desired expenditure level and what you're actually spending.

TABLE 5–1   Steps in the Optimizing Decision Model

1. Ascertain the need for a decision
2. Identify the decision criteria
3. Allocate weights to the criteria
4. Develop the alternatives
5. Evaluate the alternatives
6. Select the best alternative

STEP 2: IDENTIFY THE DECISION CRITERIA   Once an individual has determined the need for a decision, the criteria that will be important in making the decision must be identified. For illustration purposes, let's consider the case of a high school senior confronting the problem of choosing a college. The concepts derived from this example may be generalized to any decision a person might confront.

For the sake of simplicity, let's assume that our high school senior has already chosen to attend college (versus other noncollege options). We know that the need for a decision is precipitated by graduation. Once she has recognized this need for a decision, the student should begin to list the criteria or factors that will be relevant to her decision. For our example, let's assume she has identified the following criteria about the school: annual cost, availability of financial aid, admission requirements, status or reputation, size, geographic location, curricula offering, male–female ratio, quality of social life, and the physical attractiveness of the campus. These criteria represent what the decision maker thinks is relevant to her decision. Note that, in this step, what is *not* listed is as important as what *is*. For example, our high school senior did not consider factors such as where her friends were going to school, availability of part-time employment, or whether freshmen are required to reside on campus. To someone else making a college selection decision, the criteria used might be considerably different.

This second step is important because it identifies only those criteria that the decision maker considers relevant. If a criterion is omitted from this list, we treat it as irrelevant to the decision maker.

STEP 3: ALLOCATE WEIGHTS TO THE CRITERIA   The criteria listed in the previous step are not all equally important. It's necessary, therefore, to weight the factors listed in Step 2 in order to prioritize their importance in the decision. All the criteria are relevant, but some are more relevant than others.

How does the decision maker weight criteria? A simple approach would merely be to give *the* most important criteria a number—say ten—and then assign weights to the rest of the criteria against this standard. So the result of Steps 2 and 3 is to allow decision makers to use their personal preferences both to prioritize the relevant criteria and to indicate their relative degree of importance by assigning a weight to each. Table 5–2 lists the criteria and weights our high school senior is using in her college decision.

STEP 4: DEVELOP THE ALTERNATIVES   The fourth step requires the decision maker to list all the viable alternatives that could possibly succeed in resolving the problem. No attempt is made in this step to appraise the alternatives; only to list them. To return to our example, let us assume that our high schooler has identified eight potential colleges—Alpha, Beta, Delta, Gamma, Iota, Omega, Phi, and Sigma.

STEP 5: EVALUATE THE ALTERNATIVES   Once the alternatives have been identified, the decision maker must critically evaluate each one. The strengths and weaknesses of each alternative will become evident when they are compared against the criteria and weights established in Steps 2 and 3.

The evaluation of each alternative is done by appraising it against the weighted criteria. In our example, the high school senior would evaluate each college using every one of the criteria. To keep our example simple we'll assume that a ten means that the college is rated as "most favorable" on that criterion. The results from evaluating the various alternative colleges are shown in Table 5–3.

TABLE 5–2   Criteria and Weights in Selection of a College

Criteria	Weights
• Availability of financial aid	10
• School's reputation	10
• Annual cost	8
• Curricula offering	7
• Geographic location	6
• Admission requirements	5
• Quality of social life	4
• School size	3
• Male–female ratio	2
• Physical attractiveness of the campus	2

Keep in mind that the ratings given the eight colleges shown in Table 5–3 are based on the assessment made by the decision maker. Some assessments can be made in a relatively objective fashion. If our decision maker prefers a small school, one with an enrollment of 1,000 is obviously superior to one with 10,000 students. Similarly, if a high male–female ratio is sought, 3:1 is clearly higher than 1.2:1. But the assessment of criteria such as reputation, quality of social life, or the physical attractiveness of the campus reflects the decision maker's values. The point is that most decisions contain judgments. They are reflected in the criteria chosen in Step 2, the weights given to these criteria, and the evaluation of alternatives. This explains why two people faced with a similar problem—such as selecting a college—may look at two totally different sets of alternatives or even look at the same alternatives but rate them very differently.

Table 5–3 represents an evaluation of only eight alternatives against the decision criteria. It does not reflect the weighting done in Step 3. If one choice had scored ten on every criterion, there would be no need to consider the weights. Similarly, if the weights were all equal, you could evaluate each

TABLE 5–3   Evaluation of Eight Alternatives Against the Decision Criteria*

Criteria	ALTERNATIVES							
	Alpha College	Beta College	Delta College	Gamma College	Iota College	Omega College	Phi College	Sigma College
Availability of financial aid	5	4	10	7	7	8	3	7
School's reputation	10	6	6	6	9	5	9	6
Annual cost (low cost preferred)	5	7	8	8	5	10	5	8
Curricula offering	6	10	8	9	8	8	9	8
Geographic location	6	7	10	10	6	9	10	7
Admission requirements (in terms of likelihood of acceptance)	7	10	10	10	8	10	8	10
Quality of social life	10	5	7	7	3	7	10	8
School size	10	7	7	7	9	7	9	4
Male–female ratio	2	2	8	8	8	10	2	8
Physical attractiveness of the campus	8	10	6	3	4	10	5	9

*The colleges that achieved the highest rating for a criterion are given ten points.

alternative merely by summing up the appropriate column in Table 5–3. For instance, Omega College would be highest, with a total score of eighty-four. But our high school senior needs to multiply each alternative against its weight. The result of this process is shown in Table 5–4. The summation of these scores represents an evaluation of each college against the previously established criteria and weights.

STEP 6: SELECT THE BEST ALTERNATIVE   The final step in the optimizing decision model is the selection of the best alternative from among those enumerated and evaluated. Since best is defined in terms of highest total score, the selection is quite simple. The decision maker merely chooses the alternative that generated the largest total score in Step 5. For our high school senior, that means Delta College. Based on the criteria identified, the weights given to the criteria, and the decision maker's evaluation of each college on each of the criteria, Delta College scored highest and thus becomes the best.

Assumptions of the Optimizing Model

The steps in the optimizing model contain a number of assumptions. It is important to understand these assumptions if we are to determine how accurately the optimizing model describes actual individual decision making.

Rationality Choices that are consistent and value-maximizing.

The assumptions of the optimizing model are the same as those that underly the concept of **rationality.** Rationality refers to choices that are consistent and value-maximizing. Rational decision making, therefore, implies that the decision maker can be fully objective and logical. The individual is assumed to have a clear goal, and all of the six steps in the optimizing model are assumed to lead toward the selection of the alternative that will maximize that goal. Let's take a closer look at the assumptions inherent in rationality and, hence, the optimizing model.

GOAL-ORIENTED   The optimizing model assumes that there is no conflict over the goal. Whether the decision involves selecting a college to attend, determining whether or not to go to work today, or choosing the right applicant

TABLE 5–4   Evaluation of College Alternatives

Criteria (and weight)	ALTERNATIVES							
	Alpha College	Beta College	Delta College	Gamma College	Iota College	Omega College	Phi College	Sigma College
Availability of financial aid (10)	50	40	100	70	70	80	30	70
School's reputation (10)	100	60	60	60	90	50	90	60
Annual cost (8)	40	56	64	64	40	80	40	64
Curricula offering (7)	42	70	56	63	56	56	63	56
Geographic location (6)	36	42	60	60	36	54	60	42
Admission requirements (5)	35	50	50	50	40	50	40	50
Quality of social life (4)	40	20	28	28	12	28	40	32
School size (3)	30	21	21	21	27	21	27	12
Male–female ratio (2)	4	4	16	16	16	20	4	16
Physical attractiveness of the campus (2)	16	20	12	6	8	20	10	18
Totals	393	373	467	438	395	459	404	420

to fill a job vacancy, it is assumed that the decision maker has a single, well-defined goal that he or she is trying to maximize.

ALL OPTIONS ARE KNOWN   It is assumed that the decision maker can identify *all* the relevant criteria and can list *all* viable alternatives. The optimizing model portrays the decision maker as fully comprehensive in his or her ability to assess criteria and alternatives.

PREFERENCES ARE CLEAR   Rationality assumes that the criteria and alternatives can be assigned numerical values and ranked in a preferential order.

PREFERENCES ARE CONSTANT   The same criteria and alternatives should be obtained every time because, in addition to the goal and preferences being clear, it is assumed that the specific decision criteria are constant and the weights assigned to them are stable over time.

FINAL CHOICE WILL MAXIMIZE THE OUTCOME   The rational decision maker, following the optimizing model, will choose the alternative that rates highest. This most preferred solution will, based on Step 6 of the process, give the maximum benefits.

Predictions from the Optimizing Model

Using the preceding assumptions, we would predict that the individual decision maker would have a clear and specific goal; a fully comprehensive set of criteria that determine the relevant factors in the decision; a precise ranking of the criteria, which will be stable over time; and that the decision maker will select the alternative that scores highest after all options have been evaluated. (See Figure 5–5.)

FIGURE 5–5   The Optimizing Model

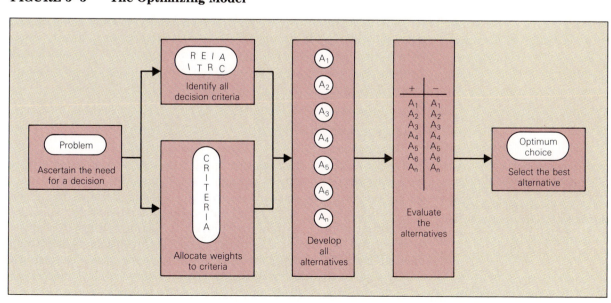

In terms of the college selection decision introduced earlier, the optimizing model would predict that the high school student could identify every factor that might be important in her decision. Each of these factors would be weighted in terms of importance. All of the colleges that could possibly be viable options would be identified and evaluated against the criteria. Remember, because all alternatives are assumed to be considered, our decision maker might be looking at hundreds of colleges. Also, even if this activity took six months to complete, the criteria and weights would not vary over time. If the college's reputation was most important in September, it would still be so in March. Further, if Beta College was given a score of six on this criterion in September, six months later the assessment would be the same. Finally, since every factor that is important in the decision has been considered and given its proper weight, and since every alternative has been identified and evaluated against the criteria, the decision maker can be assured that the college that scores highest in the evaluation is the best choice. There are no regrets because all information has been obtained and evaluated in a logical and consistent manner.

ALTERNATIVE DECISION-MAKING MODELS

Do individuals actually make their decisions the way the optimizing model predicts? Sometimes. When decision makers are faced with a simple problem having few alternative courses of action, and when the cost to search out and evaluate alternatives is low, the optimizing model provides a fairly accurate description of the decision process.[11] Buying a pair of shoes or a new personal computer might be examples of decisions where the optimizing model would apply. But many decisions, particularly important and difficult ones—the kind a person hasn't encountered before and for which there are no standardized or programmed rules to provide guidance—don't involve simple and well-structured problems. Rather, they're characterized by complexity, relatively high uncertainty (all the alternatives, for example, are unlikely to be known), and goals and preferences that are neither clear nor consistent. This latter category would include choosing a spouse, considering whether to accept a new job offer in a different city, selecting among job applicants for a vacancy in your department, developing a marketing strategy for a new product, deciding where to build an additional manufacturing plant, or determining the proper time to take your small company public by selling stock in it. In this section, we'll review two alternatives to the optimizing model: the satisficing or bounded rationality model and the implicit favorite model.

The Satisficing Model

Satisficing Model A decision-making model where a decision maker chooses the first solution that is "good enough"; that is, satisfactory and sufficient.

The essence of the **satisficing model** is that, when faced with complex problems, decision makers respond by reducing the problems to a level at which they can be readily understood. This is because the information-processing capability of human beings makes it impossible to assimilate and understand all the information necessary to optimize. Since the capacity of the human mind for formulating and solving complex problems is far too small to meet all the requirements for full rationality, individuals operate within the confines of **bounded rationality.** They construct simplified models that

Bounded Rationality
Individuals make decisions by constructing simplified models that extract the essential features from problems without capturing all their complexity.

extract the essential features from problems without capturing all their complexity.[12] Individuals can then behave rationally within the limits of the simple model.

How does bounded rationality work for the typical individual? Once a problem is identified, the search for criteria and alternatives begins. But the list of criteria is likely to be far from exhaustive. The decision maker will identify a limited list made up of the more conspicuous choices. These are the choices that are easy to find and which tend to be highly visible. In most cases, they will represent familiar criteria and the tried and true solutions. Once this limited set of alternatives is identified, the decision maker will begin reviewing them. But the review will not be comprehensive. That is, not all the alternatives will be carefully evaluated. Instead, the decision maker will begin with alternatives that differ only in a relatively small degree from the choice currently in effect. Following along familiar and well-worn paths, the decision maker proceeds to review alternatives only until he or she identifies an alternative that satisfices—one that is satisfactory and sufficient. So the satisficer settles for the first solution that is "good enough," rather than continuing to search for the optimum. The first alternative to meet the "good enough" criteria ends the search, and the decision maker can then proceed toward implementing this acceptable course of action. This is illustrated in Figure 5–6.

One of the more interesting aspects of the satisficing model is that the order in which alternatives are considered is critical in determining which alternative is selected. If the decision maker were optimizing, all alternatives would eventually be listed in a hierarchy of preferred order. Since all the alternatives would be considered, the initial order in which they would be evaluated is irrelevant. Every potential solution would get a full and complete evaluation. But this is not the case with satisficing. Assuming that a problem has more than one potential solution, the satisficing choice will be the first acceptable one the decision maker encounters. Since decision makers use simple and limited models, they typically begin by identifying alternatives that are obvious, ones with which they are familiar, and those not too far from the status quo. Those solutions that depart least from the status quo and meet the decision criteria are most likely to be selected. This may help to explain why many decisions that people make don't result in the selection of solutions radically different from those they have made before. A unique alternative may present an optimizing solution to the problem; however, it will rarely be chosen. An acceptable solution will be identified well before the decision maker is required to search very far beyond the status quo.

Using the satisficing model, how might we predict that the high school senior introduced earlier would make her college choice? Obviously, she will not consider all of the more than 2,000 colleges in the United States or the multitude of others in foreign countries. Based on schools that she's heard about from friends and relatives, plus possibly a quick look through a guide to colleges, she would typically select a half-a-dozen or a dozen colleges to which she will send for catalogs, brochures, and applications. Based on a cursory appraisal of the materials she receives from the colleges, and using her rough decision criteria, she will look for a school that meets her minimal requirements. When she finds one, the decision search will be over. If none of the colleges in this initial set meet the "good enough" standards, she will expand her search to include more diverse colleges. But even following this extended search, the first college she uncovers that meets her minimal requirements will become the alternative of choice.

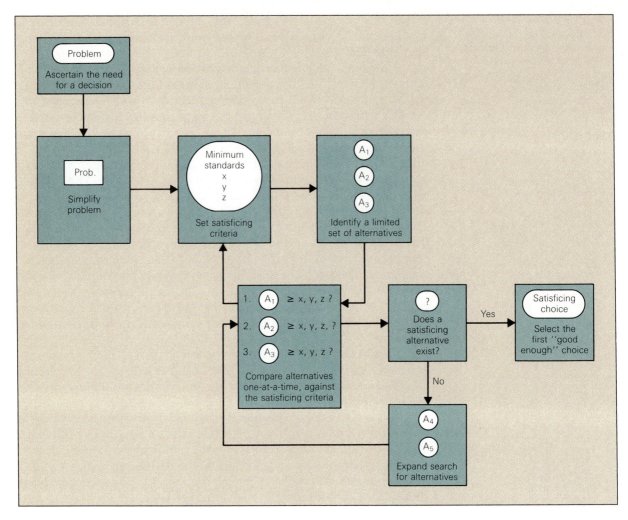

FIGURE 5–6   The Satisficing Model

The Implicit Favorite Model

Implicit Favorite Model A decision making model where the decision maker implicitly selects a preferred alternative early in the decision process and biases the evaluation of all other choices.

Another model designed to deal with complex and nonroutine decisions is the **implicit favorite model.**[13] Like the satisficing model, it argues that individuals solve complex problems by simplifying the process. However, simplification in the implicit favorite model means not entering into the difficult "evaluation of alternatives" stage of decision making until one of the alternatives can be identified as an implicit "favorite." In other words, the decision maker is neither rational nor objective. Instead, early in the decision process, he or she implicitly selects a preferred alternative. Then the rest of the decision process is essentially a decision confirmation exercise, where the decision maker makes sure that his or her implicit favorite is indeed the "right" choice.

The implicit favorite model evolved from research on job decisions by graduate management students at the Massachusetts Institute of Technology. Clearly, these students knew and understood the optimizing model. They had spent several years repeatedly using it for solving problems and analyzing cases in accounting, finance, management, marketing, and quantitative methods courses. Moreover, the job choice decision was an important one. If there was a decision where the optimizing model should be used, and a group experienced in using it, this should be it. But the researcher found that the optimizing model was not followed. Rather, the implicit favorite model provided an accurate description of the actual decision process.

The implicit favorite model is outlined in Figure 5–7. Once a problem is identified, the decision maker implicitly identifies an early favorite alternative. But the decision maker doesn't end the search at this point. In fact, the decision maker is often unaware that he or she has already identified an implicit favorite and that the rest of the process is really an exercise in prejudice. So more alternatives will be generated. This is important, for it gives the appearance of objectivity. Then the confirmation process begins. The alternative set will be reduced to two—the choice candidate and a confirmation candidate. If the choice candidate is the only viable option, the decision maker will try to obtain another acceptable alternative to become the confirmation candidate, and so he or she will have something to compare against. At this point, the decision maker establishes the decision criteria and weights. A great deal of perceptual and interpretational distortion is taking place, with the selection of criteria and their weight being "shaped" to ensure victory for the favored choice. And, of course, that's exactly what transpires. The evaluation demonstrates unequivocally the superiority of the choice candidate over the confirmation candidate.

If the implicit favorite model is at work, the search for new alternatives ends well before the decision maker is willing to admit having made his or her decision. In the job search with MIT students, the researcher found that he

FIGURE 5–7   The Implicit Favorite Model

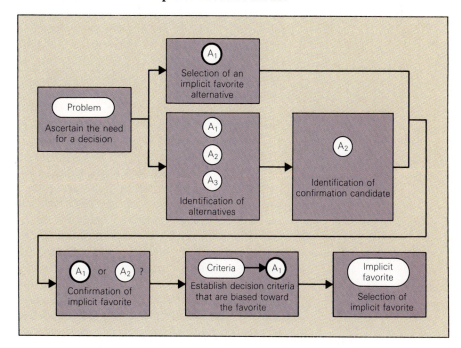

was able to accurately predict eighty-seven percent of the career jobs taken two to eight weeks before the students would admit that they had reached a decision.[14] This points to a decision process that is influenced a lot more by intuitive feelings than by rational objectivity.

Using the implicit favorite model, let's look at how our high school senior might go about choosing which college to attend. Early on in the process, she will find that one of the colleges seems intuitively right for her. However, she may not reveal this to others, nor be aware of it herself. She'll review catalogs and brochures on a number of schools, but eventually reduce the set to two. One of these two, of course, will be her implied favorite. She'll then focus in on the relevant factors in her decision. Which college has the best reputation? Where will she have the better social life? Which campus is more attractive? Her evaluation of criteria such as these are subjective judgments. Her assessment, though, won't be fair and impartial. Rather, she'll distort her judgments to align with her intuitive preference. Since "the race is fixed," the winner is a foregone conclusion. Our high school student won't necessarily choose the optimum alternative, nor can we say that her choice will satisfice. Remember, she distorted her evaluations to get the results she wanted, so there is no guarantee that her final selection will reflect the assumptions of bounded rationality. What we can say is that, if she follows the implicit favorite model, she'll choose the college that was her early preference, regardless of any relevant facts that may have surfaced later in the decision process.

IMPLICATIONS FOR PERFORMANCE AND SATISFACTION

Perception

Individuals behave in a given way based not on the way their external environment actually is but, rather, on what they see or believe it to be. Because individuals act on their interpretations of reality rather than reality itself, it is clear that perception must be a critical determinant of our dependent variables.

An organization may spend millions of dollars to create a pleasant work environment for its employees. However, in spite of these expenditures, if an employee believes that his or her job is lousy, he or she will behave accordingly. It is the employee's perception of a situation that becomes the basis on which he or she behaves. The employee who perceives his or her supervisor as a hurdle-reducer and an aid to help him or her do a better job and the employee who sees the same supervisor as "big brother, closely monitoring every motion, to ensure that I keep working" will differ in their behavioral responses to their supervisor. The difference has nothing to do with the reality of the supervisor's role; the difference in behavior is due to different perceptions.

The evidence suggests that what individuals *perceive* from their work situation will influence their productivity more than will the situation itself. Whether a job is actually interesting or challenging is irrelevant. Whether a manager successfully plans and organizes the work of his or her subordinates and actually helps them to structure their work more efficiently and effectively is far less important than how subordinates perceive his or her efforts. Similarly, issues like fair pay for work performed, the validity of performance

Decision Making in Different Cultures

Who makes a decision, when it is made, and the importance placed on rationality vary in organizations around the world.[15]

Our knowledge of power-distance differences, for example, tells us that in high power–distance cultures, such as India, only very senior-level managers make decisions. But in low power–distance cultures, such as Sweden, low-ranking employees expect to make most of their own decisions about day-to-day operations. Our knowledge that cultures vary in terms of time orientation helps us understand why managers in Egypt will make decisions at a much slower and more deliberate pace than their American counterparts. Even the assumption of rationality is culturally biased. A North American manager might make an important decision intuitively, but he or she knows that it is important to appear to proceed in a rational fashion. This explains why, in the implicit favorite model, the decision maker develops a confirmation candidate. It reassures the decision maker that he or she is seeking to be rational and objective by reviewing alternative options. In countries such as Iran, where rationality is not deified, efforts to appear rational are not necessary.

We can also assess cultural influences in terms of the six steps in the optimizing decision model. To illustrate, let's look at just two of those steps: ascertaining the need for a decision and developing alternatives.

Based on a society's activity orientation, some cultures emphasize solving problems while others focus on accepting situations as they are. The United States falls in the former category, while Thailand and Indonesia are examples of cultures that fall into the latter. Because problem-solving managers believe they can and should change situations to their own benefit, American managers might identify a problem long before their Thai or Indonesian counterparts would choose to recognize it as such. We can also use differences in time orientation to project the type of alternatives that decision makers might develop. Because Italians value the past and traditions, managers in that culture will tend to rely on tried-and-proven alternatives to problems. In contrast, the United States and Australia are more aggressive and now-oriented; managers in these countries are more likely to propose unique and creative solutions to their problems.

appraisals, and the adequacy of working conditions are not judged by employees in a way that assures common perceptions, nor can we be assured that individuals will interpret conditions about their jobs in a favorable light. Therefore, to be able to influence productivity, it is necessary to assess how workers perceive their jobs.

It is unacceptable for a sales manager to argue that "John should be selling far more of our products in his territory. His territory is a gold mine. It has unlimited potential." When John is interviewed, we find that he believes he is getting as much as possible out of his territory. Whether the salesman is right or wrong is irrelevant. He *perceives his view to be right*. If the manager hopes to improve sales in John's territory, he or she must first succeed in changing John's perceptions.

As with productivity, absenteeism, turnover, and job satisfaction are reactions to the individual's perceptions. Dissatisfaction with working conditions or the belief that there is a lack of promotion opportunities in the organization are judgments based on attempts to make some meaning out of one's job. Since there can be no such thing as a "bad job," only the perception that the job is bad, managers must spend time to understand how each individual interprets reality and, where there is a significant difference between what is seen and what exists, try to eliminate the distortions. Failure to deal with the differences when individuals perceive the job in negative terms will result in increased absenteeism and turnover and lower job satisfaction.

Individual Decision Making

Individuals think and reason before they act. It is because of this that an understanding of how people make decisions can be helpful if we are to explain and predict their behavior.

Under some decision situations, people follow the optimizing model. But for most people, and most nonroutine decisions, this is probably more the exception than the rule. Few important decisions are simple or unambiguous enough for the optimizing model's assumptions to apply. So we find individuals looking for solutions that satisfice rather than optimize, and injecting biases and prejudices into the decision process.

The alternative decision models we presented can help us explain and predict behaviors that would appear irrational or arbitrary if viewed under optimizing assumptions. Let's look at a couple of examples.

Employment interviews are complex decision activities. The interviewer finds himself or herself inundated with information. Research indicates that interviewers respond by simplifying the process.[16] Most interviewers' decisions change very little after the first four or five minutes of the interview. In a half-hour interview, the decision maker tends to make a decision about the suitability of the candidate in the first few minutes and then uses the rest of the interview time to select information that supports the early decision. In so doing, interviewers reduce the probability of identifying the highest performing candidate. They bias their decision toward individuals who make favorable first impressions.

Evaluating an employee's performance is a complex activity. Decision makers simplify the process by focusing on visible and easy to measure criteria.[17] This may explain why factors such as neatness, promptness, enthusiasm, and a positive attitude are often related to good evaluations. It also explains why quantity measures typically override quality measures. The former category is easier to appraise. This effort at satisficing encourages individuals to take on visible problems rather than important ones.

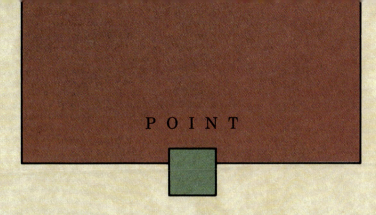

When Hiring New Employees: Emphasize the Positive

Hiring new employees requires managers to become salespeople. They have to emphasize the positive, even if it means failing to mention the negative aspects in the job. While there is a real risk of setting unrealistic expectations about the organization and about the specific job, that's a risk managers have to take. As in dealing with any salesperson, it is the job applicant's responsibility to follow the dictum of *caveat emptor*—let the buyer beware!

Why should managers emphasize the positive when discussing a job with a prospective candidate? They have no choice! First, there is a dwindling supply of applicants; and second, this approach is necessary to meet the competition.

The supply of qualified applicants for almost any job today is increasingly limited. In contrast to a generation ago, when there was a rising number of young workers entering the labor force, the 1990s are a different time. Beginning in the late 1960s, the baby boom has turned into the baby bust. Since the early 1970s, birthrates have dropped significantly. For instance, an average of only 1.3 million people will enter the labor force every year throughout the 1990s compared to 3 million a year

during the 1970s. This slower-growing population is creating a labor shortage that is likely to last throughout the 1990s; this shortage is compounded by a widening gap between the skills workers have and the skills employers need. In the 1990s labor market, managers must *sell* jobs to the limited pool of applicants. This means presenting the job and the organization in the most favorable light possible.

In addition to the dwindling supply of qualified candidates, management is forced to emphasize the positive with job candidates because that's what the competition will be doing. Other employers also face a limited applicant pool. As a result, to get people to join their organizations, they are forced to put a positive "spin" on their descriptions of their organizations and the jobs they seek to fill. In this competitive environment, any employer who presents jobs realistically to applicants—that is, openly provides the negative aspects of a job along with the positive —risks losing most or all of his or her most desirable candidates.

Some of the facts in this argument are from L. S. Richman, "The Coming World Labor Shortage," *Fortune,* April 9, 1990, pp. 70–77.

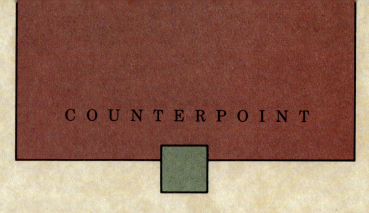

When Hiring Employees: Balance the Positive with the Negative

Regardless of the changing labor market, managers who treat the recruiting and hiring of candidates as if the applicants must be *sold* on the job and exposed to only positive aspects set themselves up to have a workforce that is dissatisfied and prone to high turnover.

Every applicant acquires, during the selection process, a set of expectations about the organization and about the specific job he or she hopes to be offered. When the information an applicant receives is excessively inflated, a number of things happen that have potentially negative effects on the organization. First, mismatched applicants who would probably become dissatisfied with the job and soon quit are less likely to select themselves out of the search process. Second, the absence of negative information builds unrealistic expectations. If hired, the new employee is likely to become quickly disappointed. And inaccurate perceptions lead to premature resignations. Third, new hires are prone to become disillusioned and less committed to the organization when they come face-to-face with the negatives in the job. Employees who feel they were tricked or misled during the hiring process are unlikely to be satisfied workers.

To increase job satisfaction among employees and reduce turnover, applicants should be given a realistic job preview, with both unfavorable and favorable information, before an offer is made. For example, in addition to positive comments, the candidate might be told that there are limited opportunities to talk with co-workers during work hours, or that erratic fluctuations in work load creates considerable stress on employees during rush periods.

Research indicates that applicants who have been given a realistic job preview hold lower and more realistic expectations about the job they'll be doing and are better prepared for coping with the job and its frustrating elements. The result is fewer unexpected resignations by new employees. In a tight labor market, retaining people is as critical as hiring them in the first place. Presenting only the positive aspects of a job to a recruit may initially entice him or her to join the organization but it may be a marriage that both parties will quickly regret.

Information in this argument came from J. A. Breaugh, "Realistic Job Previews: A Critical Appraisal and Future Research Directions," *Academy of Management Review,* October 1983, pp. 612–19; S. L. Premack and J. P. Wanous, "A Meta-Analysis of Realistic Job Preview Experiments," *Journal of Applied Psychology,* November 1985, pp. 706–20; and B. M. Meglino, A. S. DeNisi, S. A. Youngblood, and K. J. Williams, "Effects of Realistic Job Previews: A Comparison Using an Enhancement and a Reduction Preview," *Journal of Applied Psychology,* May 1988, pp. 259–66.

FOR DISCUSSION

1. Define perception.

2. "That you and I agree on what we see suggests we have similar backgrounds and experiences." Do you agree or disagree? Discuss.

3. What is attribution theory? What are its implications for explaining organizational behavior?

4. What factors do you think might create the fundamental attribution error?

5. How might perceptual factors be involved when an employee receives a poor performance appraisal?

6. How does selectivity affect perception? Give an example of how selectivity can create perceptual distortion.

7. What is stereotyping? Give an example of how stereotyping can create perceptual distortion.

8. Give some positive results from using shortcuts when judging others.

9. What is the optimizing decision making model? Under what conditions is it applicable?

10. Explain the satisficing model. How widely applicable do you think this model is?

11. Contrast the implicit favorite model to the satisficing model.

12. "For the most part, individual decision making in organizations is an irrational process." Do you agree or disagree? Discuss.

FOR FURTHER READING

ASHFORD, S. J., "Self-Assessments in Organizations: A Literature Review and Integrative Model," in L. L. Cummings and B. M. Staw (eds.), *Research in Organizational Behavior,* Vol. 11 (Greenwich, Conn.: JAI Press, 1989), pp. 133–74. To regulate their behavior and, ultimately, to succeed in organizations, individuals must make a variety of self-assessments concerning their past performances, skills, and potential.

BAZERMAN, M. H., *Judgment in Managerial Decision Making,* 2nd ed. (New York: John Wiley & Sons, 1990). Reviews the judgmental aspects of decision making, including biases in the human thinking process.

DUGAN, K. W., "Ability and Effort Attributions: Do They Affect How Managers Communicate Performance Feedback Information?," *Academy of Management Journal,* March 1989, pp. 87–114. When providing feedback on poor performance, managers follow a script. Managers' initial attributions of effort or ability influence both how they define their roles within the script and the flow of interaction.

JANIS, I. L., and L. MANN, *Decision Making: A Psychological Analysis of Conflict, Choice and Commitment.* New York: The Free Press, 1977. Excellent analysis of psychological properties that limit applicability of the optimizing model.

MCK. AGNEW, N., and J. L. BROWN, "Bounded Rationality: Fallible Decisions in Unbounded Decision Space," *Behavioral Science,* July 1986, pp. 148–61. Reviews assumptions of the satisficing model.

ROWE, A. J., J. D. BOULGARIDES, and M. R. MCGRATH, *Managerial Decision Making.* Chicago: Science Research Associates, Inc., 1984. Reviews the decision making process, with particular attention given to the role of decision "style" on decision outcomes.

NOTES

[1]D. C. McClelland and J. W. Atkinson, "The Projective Expression of Needs: The Effect of Different Intensities of the Hunger Drive on Perception," *Journal of Psychology,* Vol. 25 (1948), pp. 205–22.

[2]H. H. Kelley, "Attribution in Social Interaction," in E. Jones et al. (eds.), *Attribution: Perceiving the Causes of Behavior* (Morristown, NJ: General Learning Press, 1972).

[3]See L. Ross, "The Intuitive Psychologist and His Shortcomings," in L. Berkowitz (ed.), *Advances in Experimental Social Psychology,* Vol. 10 (Orlando, FL.: Academic Press, 1977), pp. 174–220; and A. G. Miller and T. Lawson, "The Effect of an Informational Option on the Fundamental Attribution Error," *Personality and Social Psychology Bulletin,* June 1989, pp. 194–204.

[4]D. C. Dearborn and H. A. Simon, "Selective Perception: A Note on the Departmental Identification of Executives," *Sociometry,* June 1958, pp. 140–44. Some of the conclusions in this classic study have recently been challenged in J. P. Walsh, "Selectivity and Selective Perception: An Investigation of Managers' Belief Structures and Information Processing," *Academy of Management Journal,* December 1988, pp. 873–96.

[5]See, for example, G. E. Stephens and A. S. Denisi, "Women as Managers: Attitudes and Attributions for Performance by Men and Women," *Academy of Management Journal,* June 1980, pp. 355–61; and A. S. Baron and K. Abrahamsen, "Will He—Or Won't He—Work with a Female Manager?" *Management Review,* November 1981, pp. 48–53.

[6]S. E. Asch, "Forming Impressions of Personality," *Journal of Abnormal and Social Psychology,* July 1946, pp. 258–90.

[7]J. S. Bruner and R. Tagiuri, "The Perception of People," in E. Lindzey (ed.), *Handbook of Social Psychology* (Reading, MA: Addison-Wesley, 1954), p. 641.

[8]See, for example, E. C. Webster, *Decision Making in the Employment Interview* (Montreal: McGill University, Industrial Relations Center, 1964).

[9]D. Kipnis, *The Powerholders* (Chicago: University of Chicago Press, 1976).

[10]For a comprehensive review of the optimizing model and its assumptions, see E. F. Harrison, *The Managerial Decision-Making Process,* 2nd ed. (Boston: Houghton Mifflin, 1981), pp. 53–57 and 81–93.

[11]D. L. Rados, "Selection and Evaluation of Alternatives in Repetitive Decision Making," *Administrative Science Quarterly,* June 1972, pp. 196–206.

[12]See H. A. Simon, *Administrative Behavior,* 3rd ed. (New York: Free Press, 1976); and J. Forester, "Bounded Rationality and the Politics of Muddling Through," *Public Administration Review,* January–February 1984, pp. 23–31.

[13]See P. O. Soelberg, "Unprogrammed Decision Making," *Industrial Management Review,* Spring 1967, pp. 19–29; and D. J. Power and R. J. Aldag, "Soelberg's Job Search and Choice Model: A Clarification, Review, and Critique," *Academy of Management Review,* January 1985, pp. 48–58.

[14]Soelberg, "Unprogrammed Decision Making."

[15]A number of the ideas in this box are based on N. J. Adler, *International Dimensions of Organizational Behavior* (Boston: Kent Publishing, 1986), pp. 135–40.

[16]E. C. Mayfield in N. Schmitt's "Social and Situational Determinants of Interview Decisions: Implications for Employment Interviews," *Personnel Psychology,* Spring 1976, p. 81.

[17]G. P. Huber, *Managerial Decision Making* (Glenview, IL: Scott, Foresman, 1980), p. 215.

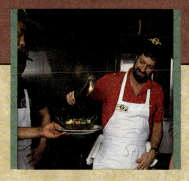

VALUES, ATTITUDES, AND JOB SATISFACTION

LEARNING OBJECTIVES

After studying this chapter, you should be able to:

1. *Explain the source of an individual's value system*
2. *List the dominant values in today's work force*
3. *Describe the three primary job-related attitudes*
4. *Summarize the relationship between attitudes and behavior*
5. *Identify the role consistency plays in attitudes*
6. *Clarify how individuals reconcile inconsistencies*
7. *Explain what determines job satisfaction*
8. *State the relationship between job satisfaction and behavior*
9. *Describe the current level of job satisfaction among Americans in the workplace*
10. *Identify four employee responses to dissatisfaction*

Keith Dunn tried to make his restaurants employee-oriented by "buying employees off" with benefits and the like. He treated them like nagging children, writing checks to keep them out of his hair. It was only when he began to listen to their real concerns that he was able to improve employee performance and his restaurants' profitability.

Photograph © Herb Snitzer.

*When you prevent me from doing anything I want to
do, that is persecution; but when I prevent you from
doing anything you want to do, that is law, order and morals.*

G. B. SHAW

*I*t was 1983, and Keith Dunn opened his first McGuffey's restaurant in Asheville, North Carolina.[1] He started the business out of frustration over all the abuse *he* had suffered personally while working at big restaurant chains such as TGI Friday's and Bennigan's. His restaurant would be different. He was going to be authentically employee-oriented.

Dunn's Asheville restaurant was an immediate success. He soon opened another in a nearby city. It too started fast. Faithful to his original intentions, Dunn sought to make his employees feel appreciated. He gave them a free drink and a meal at the end of every shift, let them give away appetizers and desserts, and provided them with health and dental insurance plus a week of paid vacation each year.

Dunn was convinced that he had created a people-oriented business and a highly satisfied group of employees. He was aware that sales had plateaued and then declined a bit at each of his restaurants a few months after each opened, but he had all kinds of external rationalizations to explain this occurrence.

In 1986, Dunn was feeling a bit wary. He needed a shot of confidence. He knew how his 230 employees felt about him, but he wanted to hear it from them. That's why he decided to send them an attitude survey. He wanted to see their satisfaction in writing. One day he gathered up the anonymous questionnaires, sat down in his small office with one of his partners by his side, and began to open the envelopes. His eyes zoomed directly to the question where employees were asked to rate the owners' performance on a scale of one to ten. He couldn't believe what he was reading: "Zero," "Zero," "Two," "Zero," "One" . . . The written comments, too, said similar things: "Your nose is in the air;" "You never say hello;" "You're never around." How could his employees be so ungrateful, Dunn wondered. Why weren't they as thrilled as he was with the chain's growth and expansion? Out of curiosity, Dunn called in an assistant and asked him a favor. Can you calculate our annual turnover rate? Came the reply: "220%, sir."

Dunn realized that he had lost sight of the original reason why he had started McGuffey's. He had gotten more involved with impressing his bankers than in listening to his employees. He didn't know his employees' real needs and concerns. They felt ignored, resentful, and abandoned. In response, the rest rooms weren't getting scrubbed as thoroughly, the food wasn't arriving quite piping hot, the servers weren't smiling as often. And sales declined!

Dunn got the message. He began to listen to his employees and make the changes *they* felt were important. For example, employees now participate much more in decision making. They're helping to design new restaurants as well as their compensation programs. Today, McGuffey's is again a fun place for his employees to work. Turnover is below sixty percent—roughly one-quarter the industry average. Sales and profits are at record levels. And the employees don't hate Keith Dunn anymore.

People at work have opinions, and you don't have to undertake a formal attitude survey to get at them. They're voiced all the time: "Managers should never socialize with their employees." "A little conflict in this place is good—it keeps everyone on their toes." "I don't think there's any justification for the president of this company making a million dollars a year." "To me, the best boss is one who just leaves me alone!"

Importantly, these opinions—which we call values and attitudes—are not meaningless. As Keith Dunn saw, they are often related to behavior. In this chapter, we will discuss values and attitudes and then look closely at the topic of job satisfaction.

VALUES

Values Basic convictions that a specific mode of conduct or end-state of existence is personally or socially preferable to an opposite or converse mode of conduct or end-state of existence.

Value System A ranking of individual values according to their relative importance.

Is capital punishment right or wrong? How about engaging in sexual relations before marriage—is it right or wrong? If a person likes power, is that good or bad? The answers to these questions are value laden. Some might argue, for example, that capital punishment is right because it is an appropriate retribution for crimes like murder or treason. However, others may argue, just as strongly, that no government has the right to take anyone's life.

Values represent basic convictions that "a specific mode of conduct or end-state of existence is personally or socially preferable to an opposite or converse mode of conduct or end-state of existence."[2] They contain a judgmental element in that they carry an individual's ideas as to what is right, good, or desirable. Values have both content and intensity attributes. The content attribute says that a mode of conduct or end-state of existence is *important*. The intensity attribute specifies *how important* it is. When we rank an individual's values in terms of their intensity, we obtain that person's **value system**. All of us have a hierarchy of values that forms our value system. This system is identified by the relative importance we assign to such objects of values as freedom, pleasure, self-respect, honesty, obedience, equality, and so forth.

Importance of Values

Values are important to the study of organizational behavior because they lay the foundation for the understanding of attitudes and motivation as well as influencing our perceptions. Individuals enter an organization with preconceived notions of what "ought" and what "ought not" to be. Of course, these notions are not value free. On the contrary, they contain interpretations of right and wrong. Further, they imply that certain behaviors or outcomes are preferred over others. As a result, values cloud objectivity and rationality.

Values generally influence attitudes and behavior.[3] Suppose that you enter an organization with the view that allocating pay on the basis of performance is right, whereas allocating pay on the basis of seniority is wrong or inferior. How are you going to react if you find that the organization you have just joined rewards seniority and not performance? You're likely to be disappointed—and this can lead to job dissatisfaction and the decision not to exert a high level of effort since "it's probably not going to lead to more money, anyway." Would your attitudes and behavior be different if your values aligned with the organization's pay policies? Most likely.

Sources of Our Value Systems

When we were children, why did many of our mothers tell us "you should always clean your dinner plate"? Why is it that, at least historically in our society, achievement has been considered good and being lazy has been considered bad? The answer is that, in our culture, certain values have developed over time and are continuously reinforced. Achievement, peace, cooperation, equity, and democracy are societal values that are considered desirable in North America. These values are not fixed, but when they change, they do so very slowly.

The values we hold are essentially established in our early years—from parents, teachers, friends, and others. Your early ideas of what is right and wrong were probably formulated from the views expressed by your parents. Think back to your early views on such topics as education, sex, and politics. For the most part, they were the same as those expressed by your parents. As you grew up, and were exposed to other value systems, you may have altered a number of your values. For example, in high school, if you desired to be a member of a social club whose values included the conviction that "every person should carry a knife," there is a good probability that you changed your value system to align with members of the club, even if it meant rejecting your parents' value that "only hoodlums carry knives, and hoodlums are bad."

Interestingly, values are relatively stable and enduring.[4] This has been explained as a result of the way in which they are originally learned.[5] As children, we are told that a certain behavior or outcome is *always* desirable or *always* undesirable. There are no gray areas. You were told, for example, that you should be honest and responsible. You were never taught to be just a little bit honest or a little bit responsible. It is this absolute or "black-or-white" learning of values that more or less assures their stability and endurance.

The process of questioning our values, of course, may result in a change. We may decide that these underlying convictions are no longer acceptable. More often, our questioning merely acts to reinforce those values we hold.

Types of Values

At this point, we might rightfully inquire if it is possible to identify certain value "types." The most important early work in categorizing values was done by Allport and his associates.[6] They identified six types of values:

1. *Theoretical*—places high importance on the discovery of truth through a critical and rational approach
2. *Economic*—emphasizes the useful and practical

3. *Aesthetic*—places the highest value on form and harmony

4. *Social*—assigns the highest value to the love of people

5. *Political*—places emphasis on acquisition of power and influence

6. *Religious*—is concerned with the unity of experience and understanding of the cosmos as a whole

Allport and his associates developed a questionnaire that describes a number of different situations and asks respondents to preference rank a fixed set of answers. Based on the respondents' replies, the researchers can rank individuals in terms of the importance they give to each of the six types of values. The result is a value system for a specific individual.

Using this approach, it has been found, not surprisingly, that people in different occupations place different importance on the six value types.

Table 6–1 shows the responses from ministers, purchasing agents, and industrial scientists. As expected, religious leaders consider religious values most important and economic values least important. Economic values, on the other hand, are of highest importance to the purchasing executives.

More recent research suggests that there is a hierarchy of levels that are descriptive of personal values and life-styles. One such study identified seven levels:[7]

Reactive Values Individuals who value basic physiological needs and are unaware of themselves or others as human beings.

Tribalistic Values The belief in tradition and power exerted by authority figures.

Egocentric Values The belief in rugged individualism and selfishness.

Conforming Values A low tolerance for ambiguity, having difficulty in accepting people with different values, and a desire that others accept one's values.

Manipulative Values The striving to achieve goals by manipulating things and people.

Level 1. Reactive. These individuals are unaware of themselves or others as human beings, and react to basic physiological needs. Such individuals are rarely found in organizations. This is most descriptive of newborn babies.

Level 2. Tribalistic. These individuals are characterized by high dependence. They are strongly influenced by tradition and the power exerted by authority figures.

Level 3. Egocentric. These persons believe in rugged individualism. They are aggressive and selfish. They respond primarily to power.

Level 4. Conforming. These individuals have a low tolerance for ambiguity, have difficulty in accepting people whose values differ from their own, and desire that others accept their values.

Level 5. Manipulative. These individuals are characterized by striving to achieve their goals by manipulating things and people. They are materialistic and actively seek higher status and recognition.

Level 6. Sociocentric. These individuals consider it more important to be liked and to get along with others than to get ahead. They are repulsed by materialism, manipulation, and conformity.

TABLE 6–1   Ranking of Values by Importance Among Three Groups

Ministers	Purchasing Executives	Scientists in Industry
1. Religious	1. Economic	1. Theoretical
2. Social	2. Theoretical	2. Political
3. Aesthetic	3. Political	3. Economic
4. Political	4. Religious	4. Aesthetic
5. Theoretical	5. Aesthetic	5. Religious
6. Economic	6. Social	6. Social

Source: R. Tagiuri, "Purchasing Executive: General Manager or Specialist?" *Journal of Purchasing*, August 1967, pp. 16–21.

TABLE 6–2   Dominant Values in Today's Work Force

Stage	Category	Entered the Work Force	Approximate Current Age	Dominant Work Values	Level in the Value Hierarchy
I.	Protestant Work Ethic	1940s–1950s	50–70	Hard work. Conservative. Loyal to the organization.	Levels 2 and 4
II.	Existentialism	1960s–1970s	30–50	Quality of life. Nonconforming. Seeks autonomy. Loyal to self.	Levels 6 and 7
III.	Pragmatism	1980s–1990s	Under 30	Success. Achievement. Ambition. Hard work. Loyal to career.	Level 5

Sociocentric Values The belief that it is more important to be liked and to get along with others than to get ahead.

Existential Values A high tolerance for ambiguity and individuals with differing values.

Level 7. Existential. These individuals have a high tolerance for ambiguity and people with differing values. They are outspoken on inflexible systems, restrictive policies, status symbols, and arbitrary use of authority.

This value hierarchy can be used to analyze the problem of disparate values in organizations. Table 6–2 proposes that employees can be segmented by the era in which they entered the work force. Because most people start work between the ages of eighteen and twenty-three, the eras also correlate closely with the chronological age of employees.[8]

Workers who grew up during the Great Depression and World War II entered the work force in the 1940s and 1950s, believing in the Protestant Work Ethic. Once hired, they tended to be loyal to their employers. Levels 2 and 4 in the value hierarchy characterize these older workers in today's work force.

Employees who entered the work force during the 1960s and 1970s brought with them a large measure of the "Hippie ethic" and existential philosophy. They were more concerned with the quality of life than with the

Work values can be seen in characters from past television shows. Ward Cleaver, the father on "Leave It To Beaver," represented the era when Protestant Work Ethics' values dominated. The elder Keatons from "Family Ties" espoused existential values, while their son, Alex, typified pragmatism.   Both photos courtesy of Photofest.

material quantity of money and possessions. Their desire for autonomy directed their loyalty toward themselves rather than any organization that employed them. These values align well with levels 6 and 7.

Finally, individuals who entered the work force since 1980 reflect a return to more traditional values, but with far greater emphasis on achievement and material success. Today's younger worker is a pragmatist. He or she believes that ends can justify means. These workers see the organizations that employ them merely as vehicles that will propel their careers. The manipulative values of level 5 appear to most closely match this group of employees.

An understanding that people's values differ but tend to reflect the times and societal values of when they grew up can be a valuable aid for explaining and predicting behavior. Employees in their twenties and sixties, for instance, are more likely to be conservative and accepting of authority than their existential peers. Yet, when workers under thirty perceive that their contributions are not being immediately rewarded by their employer, they are more likely to quit their jobs and seek bigger and quicker payoffs somewhere else.

ATTITUDES

Attitudes Evaluative statements or judgments concerning objects, people, or events.

Attitudes are evaluative statements—either favorable or unfavorable—concerning objects, people, or events. They reflect how one feels about something. When I say "I like my job," I am expressing my attitude about work.

Attitudes are not the same as values. Values are the broader and more encompassing concept, so attitudes are more specific than values. Values also contain a moral flavor of rightness or desirability. The statement that "discrimination is bad" reflects one's values. "I favor the implementation of an affirmative action program to recruit and develop women for managerial positions in our organization" is an attitude.

While attitudes and values are different, they are closely related. One comprehensive study took a cross section of heterogeneous value issues—including rights of blacks and the poor, family security, salvation, cleanliness, imaginativeness, obedience—and found values and attitudes to be significantly correlated.[9] The researcher concluded that virtually any attitude will be significantly associated with some value set. The evidence allows us to say that the values people hold can explain their attitudes and, in many cases, the behaviors they engage in, but unfortunately, we cannot yet say which values underlie which attitudes and behaviors.

Sources of Attitudes

Attitudes, like values, are acquired from parents, teachers, and peer group members. In our early years, we begin modeling our attitudes after those we admire, respect, or maybe even fear. We observe the way family and friends behave, and we shape our attitudes and behavior to align with theirs. People imitate the attitudes of popular individuals or those they admire and respect. If the "right thing" is to favor eating at McDonald's, you are likely to hold that attitude.

In contrast to values, your attitudes are less stable. Advertising messages, for example, attempt to alter your attitudes toward a certain product or

Attitudes shape behavior. For example, IBM physicist Philip Seiden's attitude toward work had always been to do what made him happy. After achieving a senior management position at IBM in the mid-1970s, and realizing that he wasn't content, Seiden opted out of management to concentrate exclusively on research into such matters as galactic structures. "If you haven't made it in society's eyes, who cares? Have you made it in your own eyes? That's what really matters." Seiden says he doesn't regret the move back to research a bit. Andy Freeberg.

service: If the people at Ford can get you to hold a favorable opinion toward their cars, that attitude may lead to a desirable behavior (for them)—the purchase of a Ford product.

In organizations, attitudes are important because they affect job behavior. If workers believe, for example, that supervisors, auditors, bosses, and time and motion engineers are all in conspiracy to make the employee work harder for the same or less money, then it makes sense to try to understand how these attitudes were formed, their relationship to actual job behavior, and how they can be made more favorable.

Types of Attitudes

A person can have thousands of attitudes, but OB focuses our attention on a very limited number of job-related attitudes. These job-related attitudes tap positive or negative evaluations that employees hold about aspects of their work environment. Most of the research in OB has been concerned with three attitudes: job satisfaction, job involvement, and organizational commitment.[10]

JOB SATISFACTION   The term job satisfaction refers to an individual's general attitude toward his or her job. A person with a high level of job satisfaction holds positive attitudes toward the job, while a person who is dissatisfied with his or her job holds negative attitudes about the job. When people speak of employee attitudes, more often than not they mean job satisfaction. In fact, the two are frequently used interchangebly. Because of the high importance OB researchers have given to job satisfaction, we'll review this attitude in considerable detail later in this chapter.

Job Involvement The degree to which a person identifies with his or her job, actively participates in it, and considers his or her performance important to his or her sense of self-worth.

Organizational Commitment An individual's orientation toward the organization in terms of loyalty, identification and involvement.

JOB INVOLVEMENT   The term **job involvement** is a more recent addition to the OB literature.[11] While there is no complete agreement over what the term means, a workable definition states that job involvement measures the degree to which a person identifies psychologically with his or her job and considers his or her perceived performance level important to his or her self-worth.[12] Employees with a high level of job involvement strongly identify with and really care about the kind of work they do on their job.

High levels of job involvement have been found to be related to fewer absences and lower resignation rates.[13] However, it seems to more consistently predict turnover than absenteeism, accounting for as much as sixteen percent of the variance in the former.[14]

ORGANIZATIONAL COMMITMENT   The third job attitude we shall discuss is **organizational commitment.** It's defined as a state in which an employee identifies with a particular organization and its goals, and wishes to maintain membership in the organization.[15] So, high *job involvement* means identifying with one's specific job, while high *organizational commitment* means identifying with one's employing organization.

As with job involvement, the research evidence demonstrates negative relationships between organizational commitment and both absenteeism and turnover.[16] In fact, studies demonstrate that an individual's level of organizational commitment is a better indicator of turnover than the far more frequently used job satisfaction predictor, explaining as much as thirty-four percent of the variance.[17] Organizational commitment is probably a better predictor because it is a more global and enduring response to the organization as a whole than is job satisfaction.[18] An employee may be dissatisfied with his or her particular job, consider it a temporary condition, and not be dissatisfied with the organization as a whole. But when dissatisfaction spreads to the organization itself, individuals are more likely to consider resigning.

Attitudes and Consistency

Did you ever notice how people change what they say so it doesn't contradict what they do? Perhaps a friend of yours has consistently argued that American cars are poorly built and that he'd never own anything but a foreign import. But his dad gives him a late-model American-made car, and suddenly they're not so bad. Or, when going through sorority rush, a new freshman believes that sororities are good and that pledging a sorority is important. If she fails to make a sorority, however, she may say: "I recognized that sorority life isn't all it's cracked up to be, anyway!"

Research has generally concluded that people seek consistency among their attitudes and between their attitudes and behavior. This means that individuals seek to reconcile divergent attitudes and align their attitudes and behavior so they appear rational and consistent. When there is an inconsistency, forces are initiated to return the individual to an equilibrium state where attitudes and behavior are again consistent. This can be done by altering either the attitudes or the behavior or by developing a rationalization for the discrepancy.

For example, a recruiter for the ABC Company, whose job it is to visit college campuses, identify qualified job candidates, and sell them on the advantages of ABC as a place to work, would be in conflict if he personally believes the ABC Company has poor working conditions and few opportunities for new college graduates. This recruiter could, over time, find his attitudes toward the ABC Company becoming more positive. He may, in effect, brainwash himself by continually articulating the merits of working for ABC. Another alternative would be for the recruiter to become overtly negative about ABC and the opportunities within the firm for prospective candidates. The original enthusiasm that the recruiter may have shown would dwindle, probably to be replaced by open cynicism toward the company. Finally, the recruiter might acknowledge that ABC is an undesirable place to work, but as a professional recruiter his obligation is to present the positive side of working for the company. He might further rationalize that no place is perfect to work at; therefore, his job is not to present both sides of the issue, but rather to present a rosy picture of the company.

Cognitive Dissonance Theory

Can we additionally assume from this consistency principle that an individual's behavior can always be predicted if we know his or her attitude on a subject? If Mr. Jones views the company's pay level as too low, will a substantial increase in his pay change his behavior; that is, make him work harder? The answer to this question is, unfortunately, more complex than merely a "Yes" or "No."

Cognitive Dissonance Any incompatibility between two or more attitudes or between behavior and attitudes.

Leon Festinger, in the late 1950s, proposed the theory of **cognitive dissonance**.[20] This theory sought to explain the linkage between attitudes and behavior. Dissonance means an inconsistency. Cognitive dissonance refers to any incompatibility that an individual might perceive between two or more of his or her attitudes, or between his or her behavior and attitudes. Festinger argued that any form of inconsistency is uncomfortable and that individuals will attempt to reduce the dissonance and, hence, the discomfort. Therefore, individuals will seek a stable state where there is a minimum of dissonance.

Of course, no individual can completely avoid dissonance. You know that cheating on your income tax is wrong, but you "fudge" the numbers a bit every year, and hope you're not audited. Or you tell your children to brush after every meal, but *you* don't. So how do people cope? Festinger would propose that the desire to reduce dissonance would be determined by the importance of the elements creating the dissonance, the degree of influence the individual believes he or she has over the elements, and the rewards that may be involved in dissonance.

If the elements creating the dissonance are relatively unimportant, the pressure to correct this imbalance will be low. However, say that a corporate manager—Mrs. Smith—believes strongly that no company should pollute the air or water. Unfortunately, Mrs. Smith, because of the requirements of her job, is placed in the position of having to make decisions that would trade off her company's profitability against her attitudes on pollution. She knows that dumping the company's sewage into the local river (which we shall assume is legal) is in the best economic interest of her firm. What will she do? Clearly, Mrs. Smith is experiencing a high degree of cognitive dissonance. Because of the importance of the elements in this example, we cannot expect Mrs. Smith to ignore the inconsistency. There are several paths that she can follow to deal with her dilemma. She can change her behavior (stop polluting the river). Or she can reduce dissonance by concluding that the dissonant behavior is not so important after all ("I've got to make a living, and in my role as a corporate

Attitudes on Social Issues: Students vs. Executives

In the spring of 1990, Louis Harris & Associates surveyed the attitudes of 585 executives from major American corporations and 83 MBA students.[19] The results indicated that business school students were more concerned with social issues than were the practicing managers.

When asked: "Should corporations become more directly involved in solving such social problems as substance abuse, homelessness, health care, and education?", both groups thought that corporations should become more involved, although the students were more in agreement—eighty-nine percent vs. the executives' sixty-nine percent.

Two issues where executives' and students'

attitudes seemed to vary greatly related to testing and equal opportunity. Fifty-nine percent of the executives thought that corporations should routinely test new employees for AIDS and drug use. Only thirty-two percent of the students agreed. Forty-four percent of the executives thought that women and minority group members have the same opportunities to advance in American business as do white men. Only nineteen percent of the students agreed.

Do students hold more idealistic attitudes on social issues than practicing executives? Will the attitudes of these students change once they become part of the corporate establishment? What do *you* think?

decision maker, I often have to place the good of my company above that of the environment or society"). A third alternative would be for Mrs. Smith to change her attitude ("There is nothing wrong in polluting the river"). Still another choice would be to seek out more consonant elements to outweigh the dissonant ones ("The benefits to society from our manufacturing our products more than offset the cost to society of the resulting water pollution").

The degree of influence that individuals believe they have over the elements will have an impact on how they will react to the dissonance. If they perceive the dissonance to be an uncontrollable result—something over which they have no choice—they are less likely to be receptive to attitude change. If, for example, the dissonance-producing behavior was required as a result of the boss's directive, the pressure to reduce dissonance would be less than if the behavior was performed voluntarily. While dissonance exists, it can be rationalized and justified.

Rewards also influence the degree to which individuals are motivated to reduce dissonance. High dissonance, when accompanied by high rewards, tends to reduce the tension inherent in the dissonance. The reward acts to reduce dissonance by increasing the consistency side of the individual's balance sheet.

These moderating factors suggest that just because individuals experience dissonance they will not necessarily move directly toward consistency; that is, toward reduction of this dissonance. If the issues underlying the dissonance are of minimal importance, if an individual perceives that the dissonance is externally imposed and is substantially uncontrollable by him or her, or if rewards are significant enough to offset the dissonance, the

Employees can cope with more dissonance at work than they can at home because organizations give them pay, titles, authority, impressive offices, attractive benefit plans, and similar rewards. These act to reduce the tension inherent in the dissonance. Rob Kinmonth.

individual will not be under great tension to reduce the dissonance.

What are the organizational implications of the theory of cognitive dissonance? It can help to predict the propensity to engage in attitude and behavioral change. If individuals are required, for example, by the demands of their job to say or do things that contradict their personal attitude, they will tend to modify their attitudes in order to make it compatible with the cognition of what they have said or done. Additionally, the greater the dissonance—after it has been moderated by importance, choice, and reward factors—the greater the pressures to reduce it.

Measuring the A–B Relationship

We have maintained throughout this chapter that attitudes affect behavior. The early research work on attitudes assumed that they were casually related to behavior; that is, the attitudes that people hold determine what they do. Common sense, too, suggests a relationship. Is it not logical that people watch television programs that they say they like or that employees try to avoid assignments they find distasteful?

However, in the late 1960s this assumed relationship between attitudes and behavior (A–B) was challenged by a review of the research.[22] Based on an evaluation of a number of studies that investigated the A–B relationship, the reviewer concluded that attitudes were unrelated to behavior or, at best, only slightly related.[23] More recent research has demonstrated that the A–B relationship can be improved by taking moderating contingency variables into consideration.

When Consistency Is Dysfunctional

Cognitive dissonance theory argues that an individual's motivation to change his or her attitudes is based on his or her desire to appear consistent to himself or herself. Put in terms of the optimizing model presented in the previous chapter, individuals seek to appear rational.

But this desire for consistency isn't always a positive attribute in decision makers because consistency can lead to inflexibility. If conditions change so that previous solutions no longer work, but the decision maker digs in his or her heels and refuses to acknowledge this fact, then this search for consistency can be counter-productive for the organization.

The desire to reduce dissonance has been shown to be dysfunctional when it leads to an *escalation of commitment;* that is, an increased commitment to a previous decision in spite of negative information. This is the proverbial situation where one "throws good money after bad." It

has been well documented that individuals escalate commitment to a failing course of action when they view themselves as responsible for the failure.[21] Congruent with cognitive dissonance theory, they want to demonstrate that the initial decision was not wrong.

Maybe the most frequently cited example of the escalation of commitment phenomenon was President Lyndon Johnson's decisions regarding the Vietnam War. Despite continued information that bombing North Vietnam was not bringing the war any closer to conclusion, his solution was to increase the tonnage of bombs dropped. Of course, escalation of commitment doesn't apply only to presidential decisions. Many business firms have suffered large losses as a result of managers who were determined to prove their original decisions were right by continuing to commit resources to what was a lost cause from the beginning.

MODERATING VARIABLES   One thing that improves our chances of finding significant A–B relationships is the use of both specific attitudes and specific behaviors.[24] It is one thing to talk about a person's attitude toward "preserving the environment" and another to speak of his or her attitude toward recycling. The more specific the attitude we are measuring, and the more specific we are in identifying a related behavior, the greater the probability that we can show a relationship between A and B. If you ask people today whether they are concerned about preserving the environment, most will probably say "yes." That doesn't mean, however, that they separate out recyclable items from their garbage. The correlation between a question that asks about concern-for-protecting-the-environment and recycling may be only +.20 or so. But as you make the question more specific—by asking, for example, about the degree of personal obligation one feels to separating recyclable items—the A–B relationship is likely to reach +.50 or higher.

Another moderator is social constraints on behavior. Discrepancies between attitudes and behavior may occur because the social pressures on the individual to behave in a certain way may hold exceptional power.[25] Group pressures, for instance, may explain why an employee who holds strong anti-union attitudes attends pro-union organizing meetings.

Still another moderating variable is experience with the attitude in question.[26] The A–B relationship is likely to be much stronger if the attitude being evaluated refers to something with which the individual has experience. For instance, most of us will respond to a questionnaire on almost any issue. But is my attitude toward starving fish in the Amazon any indication of whether I'd donate to a fund to save these fish? Probably not! Asking college students, with no work experience, their views on job factors that are important in determining whether they would stay put in a job is an example of an attitude response that is unlikely to predict much in terms of actual turnover behavior.

SELF-PERCEPTION THEORY   While most A–B studies yield positive results[27]—that attitudes do influence behavior—the relationship tends to be weak before adjustments are made for moderating variables. But requiring specificity, an absence of social constraints, and experience in order to get a meaningful correlation imposes severe limitations on making generalizations about the A–B relationship. This has prompted some researchers to take another direction—to look at whether behavior influences attitudes. This view, called **self-perception theory,** has generated some encouraging findings.[28] Let's briefly review the theory.

When asked about an attitude toward some object, individuals recall their behavior relevant to that object and then infer their attitude from the past behavior. So if an employee were asked about her feelings about being a payroll clerk at Exxon, she would likely think, "I've had this same job at Exxon as a payroll clerk for ten years, so I must like it!" Self-perception theory, therefore, argues that attitudes are used, after the fact, to make sense out of the action that has already occurred rather than as devices that precede and guide action.

Self-perception theory has been well supported.[29] While the traditional attitude-behavior relationship is generally positive, it is also weak. In contrast, the behavior-attitude relationship is quite strong. So what can we conclude? It seems that we are very good at finding reasons for what we do, but not so good at doing what we find reasons for.[30]

An Application: Attitude Surveys

The preceding review should not discourage us from using attitudes to predict behavior. In an organizational context, most of the attitudes management would seek to inquire about would be ones with which employees have some experience. If the attitudes in question are specifically stated, management should obtain information that can be valuable in guiding their decisions relative to these employees. But how does management get information about employee attitudes? The most popular method is through the use of **attitude surveys.**[31]

Table 6–3 illustrates what an attitude survey might look like. Typically, attitude surveys present the employee with a set of statements or questions. Ideally, the items will be tailor-made to obtain the specific information that management desires. An attitude score is achieved by summing up responses to individual questionnaire items. These scores can then be averaged for job groups, departments, divisions, or the organization as a whole.

As Keith Dunn of McGuffey's found in the opening case at the beginning of this chapter, results from attitude surveys frequently surprise management. Consistent with our discussion of perceptions in the previous chapter,

Self-Perception Theory
Attitudes are used, after the fact, to make sense out of action that has already occurred.

Attitude Surveys Eliciting responses from employees through questionnaires about how they feel about their jobs, work groups, supervisors, and/or the organization.

TABLE 6–3   Sample Attitude Survey

Please answer each of the following statements using the following rating scale:

    5 = Strongly agree
    4 = Agree
    3 = Undecided
    2 = Disagree
    1 = Strongly disagree

Statement	Rating
1. This company is a pretty good place to work.	———
2. I can get ahead in this company if I make the effort.	———
3. This company's wage rates are competitive with those of other companies.	———
4. Employee promotion decisions are handled fairly.	———
5. I understand the various fringe benefits the company offers.	———
6. My job makes the best use of my abilities.	———
7. My work load is challenging but not burdensome.	———
8. I have trust and confidence in my boss.	———
9. I feel free to tell my boss what I think.	———
10. I know what my boss expects of me.	———

the policies and practices that management views as objective and fair may be seen as inequitable by employees in general or among certain groups of employees. That these distorted perceptions have led to negative attitudes about the job and organization should be important to management. This is because employee behaviors are based on perceptions, not reality. Remember, the employee who quits because she believes she is underpaid—when in fact management has objective data to support that her salary is highly competitive—is just as gone as if she had actually been underpaid. The use of regular attitude surveys can alert management to potential problems and employees' intentions early so that action can be taken to prevent repercussions.[32]

JOB SATISFACTION

We have already discussed job satisfaction briefly—earlier in this chapter as well as in Chapter 2. In this section we want to dissect the concept more carefully. How do we measure job satisfaction? Are most workers today satisfied with their jobs? What determines job satisfaction? What is its effect on employee productivity, absenteeism, and turnover rates? We'll answer each of these questions in this section.

Measuring Job Satisfaction

We've previously defined job satisfaction as an individual's general attitude toward his or her job. This definition is clearly a very broad one. Yet this is inherent in the concept. Remember, a person's job is more than just the obvious activities of shuffling papers, waiting on customers, or driving a truck. Jobs require interaction with co-workers and bosses, following organizational rules and policies, meeting performance standards, living with working conditions that are often less than ideal, and the like.[33] This means that an employee's assessment of how satisfied or dissatisfied he or she is with his or

Penny Ward Moser is a staff writer for *Fortune* magazine. But she is also a farmer. On a 26-acre parcel of land she inherited from her father, she plants oats. Farming provides Moser with satisfaction that her writing doesn't. Steve Leonard/ Black Star.

her job is a complex summation of a number of discrete job elements. So how then do we measure the concept?

The two most widely used approaches are a single global rating and a summation score made up of a number of job facets. The single global rating method is nothing more than asking individuals to respond to one question, such as "All things considered, how satisfied are you with your job?" Respondents then reply by circling a number between one and five that corresponds with answers from "Highly Satisfied" to "Highly Dissatisfied." The other approach—a summation of job facets—is more sophisticated. It identifies key elements in a job and asks for the employee's feelings about each. Typical factors that would be included are the nature of the work, supervision, present pay, promotion opportunities, and relations with co-workers.[34] These factors are rated on a standardized scale and then added up to create an overall job satisfaction score.

Is one of the foregoing approaches superior to the other? Intuitively, it would seem that summing up responses to a number of job factors would achieve a more accurate evaluation of job satisfaction. The research, however, doesn't support such intuition.[35] This is one of those rare instances in which simplicity wins out over complexity. Comparisons of one-question global ratings with the more lengthy summation of job factors method indicate that the former is more valid. The best explanation for this outcome is that the concept of job satisfaction is inherently so broad that the single question actually becomes a more inclusive measure.

Job Satisfaction as a Dependent Variable

We now turn to considering job satisfaction as a dependent variable. That is, we seek an answer to the question: *What* work-related variables determine job satisfaction? An extensive review of the literature indicates that the more important factors conducive to job satisfaction include mentally challenging work, equitable rewards, supportive working conditions, and supportive colleagues.[36]

MENTALLY CHALLENGING WORK   Employees tend to prefer jobs that give them opportunities to use their skills and abilities and offer a variety of tasks, freedom, and feedback on how well they are doing. These characteristics make work mentally challenging. Jobs that have too little challenge create boredom, but too much challenge creates frustration and feelings of failure. Under conditions of moderate challenge, most employees will experience pleasure and satisfaction.

EQUITABLE REWARDS   Employees want pay systems and promotion policies that they perceive as being just, unambiguous, and in line with their expectations. When pay is seen as fair based on job demands, individual skill level, and community pay standards, satisfaction is likely to result. Of course, not everyone seeks money. Many people willingly accept less money to work in a preferred location or in a less demanding job or to have greater discretion in the work they do and the hours they work. But the key in linking pay to satisfaction is not the absolute amount one is paid; rather, it is the perception of fairness. Similarly, employees seek fair promotion policies and practices. Promotions provide opportunities for personal growth, more responsibilities, and increased social status. Individuals who perceive that promotion decisions are made in a fair and just manner, therefore, are likely to experience satisfaction from their jobs.

SUPPORTIVE WORKING CONDITIONS   Employees are concerned with their work environment for both personal comfort and facilitating doing a good job. Studies demonstrate that employees prefer physical surroundings that are not dangerous or uncomfortable. Temperature, light, noise, and other environmental factors should not be at either extreme—for example, having too much heat or too little light. Additionally, most employees prefer working relatively close to home, in clean and relatively modern facilities, and with adequate tools and equipment.

SUPPORTIVE COLLEAGUES   People get more out of work than merely money or tangible achievements. For most employees, work also fills the need for social interaction. Not surprisingly, therefore, having friendly and supportive co-workers leads to increased job satisfaction. The behavior of one's boss also is a major determinant of satisfaction. Studies generally find that employee satisfaction is increased when the immediate supervisor is understanding and friendly, offers praise for good performance, listens to the employee's opinions, and shows a personal interest in his or her employees.

DON'T FORGET THE PERSONALITY-JOB FIT!   In Chapter 4, we presented Holland's personality-job fit theory. As you remember, one of Holland's conclusions was that high agreement between an employee's personality and occupation results in a more satisfied individual. His logic was essentially this: People with personality types congruent with their chosen vocations should find that they have the right talents and abilities to meet the demands of their jobs; are thus more likely to be successful on those jobs; and, because of this success, have a greater probability of achieving high satisfaction from their work. Studies to replicate Holland's conclusions have been almost universally supportive.[37] It's important, therefore, to add this to our list of factors that determine job satisfaction.

Job Satisfaction in the Workplace Today

Are American workers satisfied with their jobs? The answer to this question, based on numerous studies, is a resounding "Yes!" Moreover, the numbers are surprisingly constant over time. Let's take a closer look at what we know.

Regardless of what studies you choose to look at, when employees are asked if they are satisfied with their jobs, the results tend to be very similar: Between seventy and eighty percent of American workers report they are satisfied with their jobs.[38] Older workers report the highest satisfaction (ninety-two percent for those age sixty-five and over), but even young people— under age twenty-five—report high levels of satisfaction (seventy-three percent).[39]

While there was some concern in the late 1970s that satisfaction was declining across almost all occupational groups,[40] recent reinterpretations of these data and additional longitudinal studies indicate that job satisfaction levels have held steady for decades—through economic recessions as well as prosperous times.[41]

How does one explain these results? Taken literally, we can say that whatever it is that people want from their jobs, they seem to be getting it and have been for quite some time, at least if we believe what people say in job satisfaction surveys. But if we dig a little deeper, we might question this literal interpretation. For instance, based on our knowledge of cognitive dissonance theory, we might expect employees to resolve inconsistencies between dissatisfaction with their jobs and their staying with those jobs by not reporting the dissatisfaction. Also, when employees are asked whether they would again choose the same work or whether they would want their children to follow in their footsteps, typically less than half answer in the affirmative.[42] So maybe employees aren't as satisfied with their jobs as the numbers would suggest.

An interesting explanation has also been proposed for the stability of job satisfaction findings over time. Satisfaction may lie more in the employee's personality than in the job.[43] Analysis of satisfaction data for a selected sample of individuals over a fifty-year period found that individual results were consistently stable over time, even when these people changed the employer for whom they worked and their occupation. It may well be that many of the work-related variables that we think *cause* job satisfaction aren't that important. Rather, most individuals' disposition toward life—positive or negative—is established by adolescence, holds over time, carries over into their disposition toward work, and —at least among Americans—is generally upbeat.

Job Satisfaction as an Independent Variable

Managers' interest in job satisfaction tends to center on its effect on employee performance. Researchers have recognized this interest, so we find a large number of studies that have been designed to assess the impact of job satisfaction on employee productivity, absenteeism, and turnover. Let's look at the current state of our knowledge.

SATISFACTION AND PRODUCTIVITY A number of reviews were done in the 1950s and 1960s, covering dozens of studies that sought to establish the relationship between satisfaction and productivity.[44] These reviews could find

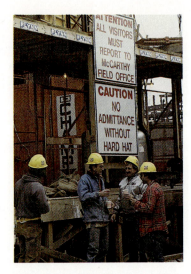

One of the greatest myths held by managers is that the happier a worker is, the more he or she will produce. Research tells us that positive emotions don't cause productivity. It is more likely that high productivity leads to satisfaction. Management may have to do specific things to increase productivity, and separate things to improve satisfaction, and the things may not be all that related.   Left, Roy Morsch/The Stock Market; right, John Coletti/Stock, Boston.

no consistent relationship. In the early 1990s, though the studies are far from unambiguous, we can make some sense out of the evidence.

The early views on the satisfaction–performance relationship can be essentially summarized in the statement "a happy worker is a productive worker." Much of the paternalism shown by managers in the 1930s, 1940s, and 1950s—forming company bowling teams and credit unions, having company picnics, providing counseling services for employees, training supervisors to be sensitive to the concerns of subordinates—was done to make workers happy. But belief in the happy worker thesis was based more on wishful thinking than hard evidence. A careful review of the research indicates that if there is a positive relationship between satisfaction and productivity, the correlations are consistently low—in the vicinity of 0.14.[45] However, introduction of moderating variables has improved the relationship.[46] For example, the relationship is stronger when the employee's behavior is not constrained or controlled by outside factors. An employee's productivity on machine-paced jobs, for instance, is going to be much more influenced by the speed of the machine than his or her level of satisfaction. Similarly, a stockbroker's productivity is largely constrained by the general movement of the stock market. When the market is moving up and volume is high, both satisfied and dissatisfied brokers are going to ring up lots of commissions. Conversely, when the market is in the doldrums, the level of broker satisfaction is not likely to mean much. Job level also seems to be an important moderating variable. The satisfaction–performance correlations are stronger for higher-level employees. Thus, we might expect the relationship to be more relevant for individuals in professional, supervisory, and managerial positions.

Another point of concern in the satisfaction–productivity issue is the direction of the causal arrow. Most of the studies on the relationship used research designs that could not prove cause and effect. Studies that have controlled for this possibility indicate that the more valid conclusion is that productivity leads to satisfaction rather than the other way around.[47] If you do a good job, you intrinsically feel good about it. Additionally, assuming that the organization rewards productivity, your higher productivity should increase verbal recognition, your pay level, and probabilities for promotion. These rewards, in turn, increase your level of satisfaction with the job.

SATISFACTION AND ABSENTEEISM   We find a consistent negative relationship between satisfaction and absenteeism, but the correlation isn't high—usually less than 0.40.[48] While it certainly makes sense that dissatisfied employees are more likely to miss work, other factors have an impact on the relationship and reduce the correlation coefficient. For example, remember our discussion of sick pay versus well pay in Chapter 4. Organizations that provide liberal sick leave benefits are encouraging all their employees—including those who are highly satisfied—to take days off. Assuming that you have a reasonable number of varied interests, you can find work satisfying and yet still take off work to enjoy a three-day weekend, tan yourself on a warm summer day, or watch the World Series on television if those days come free with no penalties. Also, as with productivity, outside factors can act to reduce the correlation.

An excellent illustration of how satisfaction directly leads to attendance, where there is a minimum impact from other factors, is a study done at Sears, Roebuck.[49] Satisfaction data were available on employees at Sears' two headquarters in Chicago and New York. Additionally, it is important to note that Sears' policy was not to permit employees to be absent from work for avoidable reasons without penalty. The occurrence of a freak April 2 snowstorm in Chicago created the opportunity to compare employee attendance at the Chicago office with New York, where the weather was quite nice. The interesting dimension in this study is that the snowstorm gave the Chicago employees a built-in excuse not to come to work. The storm crippled the city's transportation, and individuals knew they could miss work this day with no penalty. This natural experiment permitted the comparison of attendance records for satisfied and dissatisfied employees at two locations—one where you were expected to be at work (with normal pressures for attendance) and the other where you were free to choose with no penalty involved. If satisfaction leads to attendance, where there is an absence of outside factors, the more satisfied employees should have come to work in Chicago, while dissatisfied employees should have stayed home. The study found that, on this April 2 day, absenteeism rates in New York (the control group) were just as high for satisfied groups of workers as for dissatisfied groups. But in Chicago, the workers with high satisfaction scores had much higher attendance than did those with lower satisfaction levels. These findings are exactly what we would have expected if satisfaction is negatively correlated with absenteeism.

SATISFACTION AND TURNOVER   Satisfaction is also negatively related to turnover, but the correlation is stronger than what we found for absenteeism.[50] Yet, again, other factors such as labor market conditions, expectations about alternative job opportunities, and length of tenure with the organization are important constraints on the actual decision to leave one's current job.[51]

Evidence indicates that an important moderating variable on the satisfaction–turnover relationship is the employee's level of performance.[52] Specifically, level of satisfaction is less important in predicting turnover for superior performers. Why? The organization typically makes considerable efforts to keep these people. They get pay raises, praise, recognition, increased promotional opportunities, and so forth. Just the opposite tends to apply to poor performers. Few attempts are made by the organization to retain them. There may even be subtle pressures to encourage them to quit. We would expect, therefore, that job satisfaction is more important in influencing poor performers to stay than superior performers. Regardless of level of satisfaction, the latter are more likely to remain with the organization because the receipt of recognition, praise, and other rewards gives them more reasons for staying.

How Employees Can Express Dissatisfaction

One final point before we leave the issue of job satisfaction: Employee dissatisfaction can be expressed in a number of ways. For example, employees can choose to complain rather than quit. Figure 6–1 offers four responses that differ from one another along two dimensions: constructiveness/destructiveness and activity/passivity. They are defined as follows:[56]

Exit Dissatisfaction expressed through behavior directed toward leaving the organization.

Voice Dissatisfaction expressed through active and constructive attempts to improve conditions.

Loyalty Dissatisfaction expressed by passively waiting for conditions to improve.

Neglect Dissatisfaction expressed through allowing conditions to worsen.

- **Exit** - Behavior directed toward leaving the organization. Includes looking for a new position as well as resigning.
- **Voice** - Actively and constructively attempting to improve conditions. Includes suggesting improvements, discussing problems with superiors, and some forms of union activity.
- **Loyalty** - Passively but optimistically waiting for conditions to improve. Includes speaking up for the organization in the face of external criticism and trusting the organization and its management to "do the right thing."
- **Neglect** - Passively allowing conditions to worsen. Includes chronic absenteeism or lateness, reduced effort, and increased error rate.

FIGURE 6–1   Responses to Job Dissatisfaction
Source: C. Rusbult and D. Lowery, "When Bureaucrats Get the Blues," *Journal of Applied Social Psychology*, Vol. 15, No. 1, 1985, p. 83. With permission.

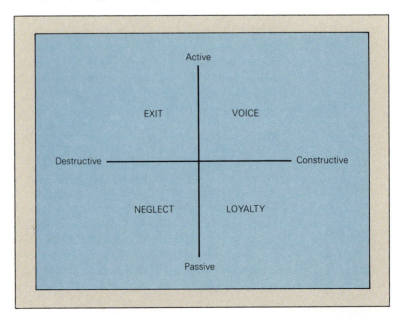

A Cross-Cultural Look at Values and Job Satisfaction

A country's national culture shapes the values of its citizens. As noted earlier in this chapter, American culture reinforces values such as achievement, equity, and democracy. You should not, however, assume these values to be universally held.

On the assumption that today's students become tomorrow's managers, two Canadian researchers developed a comparative study of job values of business students in France and English Canada.[53] Their findings support the theory that the diversity of cultural values has shaped the values held by students in each country. For instance, English Canadians placed a higher value on competition, achievement, independence, and pragmatism than did their French counterparts. The French Canadian students, on the other hand, placed a greater value on spiritual and society-oriented outcomes.

Another study on values, this one comparing American and Japanese managers, confirmed the value-divergence thesis and upheld many of the stereotypes held of Americans and Japanese.[54] American managers placed greater importance on ambition, competence, and independence. The Japanese managers placed more value on self-respect, helpfulness, and forgiveness.

The level of job satisfaction also appears to vary from country to country. This is clearly dramatized by data from Japanese workers. You'll remember that seventy to eighty percent of American workers described themselves as satisfied with their jobs. A survey of Japanese workers found a dismal fourteen percent of their younger workers to be satisfied![55] Is there any explanation for such a low rate? The answer seems to have to do with Japanese organizations' widespread practice of assigning employees and managers to jobs regardless of their interests. In contrast, most American firms take considerable care in identifying differences among new employees' personalities and preferences, and then using this information in making hiring and placement decisions.

Exit and neglect behaviors encompass our performance variables—productivity, absenteeism, and turnover. But this model expands employee response to include voice and loyalty—constructive behaviors that allow individuals to tolerate unpleasant situations or to revive satisfactory working conditions. It helps us to understand situations, such as those sometimes found among unionized workers, where low job satisfaction is coupled with low turnover.[57] Union members often express dissatisfaction through the grievance procedure or through formal contract negotiations. These voice mechanisms allow the union members to continue in their jobs while convincing themselves that they are acting to improve the situation.

IMPLICATIONS FOR PERFORMANCE AND SATISFACTION

What is the importance of knowing about an individual's values? Although they don't have a direct impact on behavior, values strongly influence a

One of the most overt indicators of job dissatisfaction by union workers is to engage in a strike. A recent strike by mine workers against Pittston Coal in West Virginia began with peaceful sit-ins and polite picketing. But animosity toward the company and other mine operators intensified, culminating in nearly 300 strikers being arrested for blocking the road to a nonunion mine.   AP/Wide World Photos.

person's attitudes. So knowledge of an individual's value system can provide insight into his or her attitudes.

Given that people's values differ, managers can use the seven-level hierarchy to characterize potential employees and determine if their values align with the dominant values of the organization. An employee's performance and satisfaction are likely to be higher if his or her values fit well with the organization. For instance, the egocentric individualist is poorly matched with an organization that seeks conformity from its employees. Managers are more likely to appreciate, evaluate positively, and allocate rewards to employees who "fit in," and employees are more likely to be satisfied if they perceive that they do fit. This argues for management to pay close attention during the selection of new employees to not only find job candidates with the ability, experience, and motivation to perform—but also with a value system that is compatible with the organization's.

Managers should be interested in their employees' attitudes because attitudes give warnings of potential problems and because they influence behavior. Satisfied and committed employees, for instance, have lower rates of turnover and absenteeism. Given that managers want to keep resignations and absences down—especially among their more productive employees—they will want to do those things that will generate positive job attitudes.

Managers should also be aware that employees will try to reduce cognitive dissonance. More important, dissonance can be managed. If employees are required to engage in activities that appear inconsistent to them or that are at odds with their attitudes, the pressures to reduce the resulting dissonance are lessened when the employee perceives that the dissonance is externally imposed and is beyond his or her control or if the rewards are significant enough to offset the dissonance.

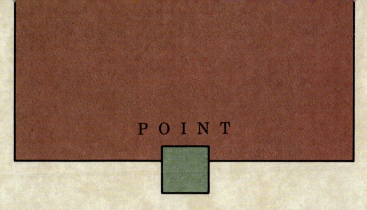

POINT

The Importance of High Job Satisfaction

The importance of job satisfaction is obvious. Managers should be concerned with the level of job satisfaction in their organizations for at least three reasons: (1) there is clear evidence that dissatisfied employees skip work more often and are more likely to resign; (2) it has been demonstrated that satisfied employees have better health and live longer; and (3) satisfaction on the job carries over to the employee's life outside the job.

We reviewed the evidence between satisfaction and withdrawal behaviors in this chapter. That evidence was fairly clear: Satisfied employees have lower rates of both turnover and absenteeism. If we consider the two withdrawal behaviors separately, however, we can be more confident about the influence of satisfaction on turnover. Specifically, satisfaction is strongly and consistently negatively related to an employee's decision to leave the organization. Although satisfaction and absence are also negatively related, conclusions regarding the relationship should be more guarded.

An often-overlooked dimension of job satisfaction is its relationship to employee health. Several studies have shown that employees who are dissatisfied with their jobs are prone to health setbacks, ranging from headaches to heart disease. Some research even indicates that job satisfaction is a better predictor of length of life than is physical condition or tobacco use. These studies suggest that dissatisfaction is not solely a psychological phenomenon. The stress that results from dissatisfaction apparently increases one's susceptibility to heart attacks and the like. For managers, this means that even if satisfaction didn't lead to less voluntary turnover and absence, the goal of a satisfied work force might be justifiable because it would reduce medical costs and the premature loss of valued employees by way of heart disease or strokes.

Our final point in support of job satisfaction's importance is the spin-off effect that job satisfaction has for society as a whole. When employees are happy with their jobs, it improves their lives off the job. In contrast, the dissatisfied employee carries that negative attitude home. In wealthy countries, such as the United States, doesn't management have a responsibility to provide jobs from which employees can receive high satisfaction? There are benefits, after all, that accrue to every citizen in our society. Satisfied employees contribute toward being satisfied citizens. These people will hold a more positive attitude toward life in general and make for a society of more psychologically healthy people.

The evidence is impressive. Job satisfaction is important. For management, a satisfied work force translates into higher productivity due to fewer disruptions caused by absenteeism or good employees quitting and lower medical and life insurance costs. Additionally, there are benefits for society in general. Satisfaction on the job carries over to the employee's off-the-job hours. So the goal of high job satisfaction for employees can be defended in terms of both dollars and cents and social responsibility.

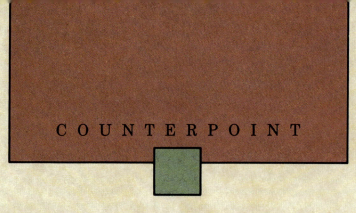

Job Satisfaction Has Been Overemphasized

Few issues have been more blown out of proportion than the importance of job satisfaction at work. Let's look closely at the evidence.

There is no consistent relationship indicating that satisfaction leads to productivity. And, after all, isn't productivity the name of the game? Organizations are not altruistic institutions. Management's obligation is to use efficiently the resources that it has available. It has no obligation to create a satisfied work force if the costs exceed the benefits. As one executive put it, "I don't care if my people are happy or not! Do they produce?"

It would be naive to assume that satisfaction alone would be a major impact on employee behavior. As a case in point, consider the issue of turnover. Certainly there are a number of other factors that have an equal or greater impact on whether an employee decides to remain with an organization or take a job somewhere else—length of time on the job, one's financial situation, availability of other jobs, and so on. If I'm fifty-five years old, have been with my company twenty-five years, perceive few other opportunities in the job market, and have no other source of income other than my job, does my unhappiness have much impact on my decision to stay with the organization? No!

Did you ever notice who seems to be most concerned with improving employee job satisfaction? It's usually college professors and researchers! They've chosen careers that provide them considerable freedom and opportunities for personal growth. They place a very high value on job satisfaction. The problem is that they also impose their values on others. Because job satisfaction is important to them, they suppose that it's important to everyone. To a lot of people, a job is merely a means by which to get the money they want to do the things they desire during their nonworking hours. Assuming you work forty hours a week and sleep eight hours a night, you still have seventy hours or more a week to achieve fulfillment and satisfaction in off-the-job activities. So the importance of job satisfaction may be oversold when you recognize that there are other sources—outside the job—where the dissatisfied employee can find satisfaction.

A final point against overemphasizing job satisfaction is to consider the issue in a contingency framework. Even if satisfaction were significantly related to performance, it is unlikely that the relationship would hold consistently across all segments of the work force. In fact, evidence demonstrates that people differ in terms of the importance that work plays in their lives. To some, the job is their central life interest. But for the majority of people, their primary interests are off the job. Nonjob-oriented people tend not to be emotionally involved with their work. This relative indifference allows them to accept frustrating conditions at work more willingly. Importantly, the majority of the work force probably falls into this nonjob-oriented category. So while job satisfaction might be important to lawyers, surgeons, and other professionals, it may be irrelevant to the average worker because he or she is generally apathetic toward the job's frustrating elements.

1. "Thirty-five years ago, young employees we hired were ambitious, conscientious, hard-working, and honest. Today's young workers don't have the same values." Do you agree or disagree with this manager's comments? Support your position.

2. "Job candidates for a sales position are more likely to be successful if they hold egocentric values." Discuss.

3. Do you think there might be any positive and significant relationship between the possession of certain personal values and successful career progression in organizations like Merrill Lynch, the AFL-CIO, or the City of Cleveland's Police Department? Discuss.

4. What is cognitive dissonance and how is it related to attitudes?

5. What is self-perception theory? Does it increase our ability to predict behavior?

6. What contingency factors can improve the statistical relationship between attitudes and behavior?

7. Why does job satisfaction receive so much attention by OB researchers? Do you think this interest is shared by practicing managers?

8. What determines job satisfaction?

9. What is the relationship between job satisfaction and productivity?

10. What is the relationship between job satisfaction and *absenteeism? Turnover?* Which is the stronger relationship?

11. What actions might management take if it wanted to change a specific employee attitude—for example, a negative view toward introduction of a new information system that requires many of the office personnel to make significant changes in the forms they use and the reports they fill out?

12. Contrast exit, voice, loyalty, and neglect as employee responses to job dissatisfaction.

■ *FOR FURTHER READING*

ASHFORD, S. J., C. LEE, and P. BOBKO, "Content, Causes, and Consequences of Job Insecurity: A Theory-Based Measure and Substantive Test," *Academy of Management Journal*, December 1989, pp. 803–29. Found that personal, job, and organizational realities associated with a perceived lack of control were associated with job insecurity, and job insecurity leads to the desire to quit, reduced commitment, and reduced satisfaction.

BERGER, C. J., C. A. OLSON, and J. W. BOUDREAU, "Effects of Unions on Job Satisfaction: The Role of Work-Related Values and Perceived Rewards," *Organizational Behavior and Human Performance*, December 1983, pp. 289–324. Examines the effects of unions on five facets of job satisfaction.

LEE, J. A., "Changes in Managerial Values, 1965–86," *Business Horizons*, July-August 1988, pp. 29–37. A twenty-one–year study of management values found that they did not change dramatically over time.

NORD, W. R., A. P. BRIEF, J. M. ATIEH, and E. M. DOHERTY, "Work Values and the Conduct of Organizational Behavior," in B. M. Staw and L. L. Cummings (eds.), *Research in Organizational Behavior*, Vol. 10 (Greenwich, Conn.: JAI Press, 1988), pp. 1–42. Reviews and critiques perspectives on work values, then presents a framework for classifying and analyzing conceptions of work values.

ORGAN, D. W., "A Restatement of the Satisfaction–Performance Hypothesis," *Journal of Management,* December 1988, pp. 547–57. Argues that satisfaction more generally correlates with organizational prosocial or citizenship-type behaviors than with traditional productivity variables.

RAVLIN, E. C., and B. M. MEGLINO, "Effect of Values on Perception and Decision Making: A Study of Alternative Work Values Measures," *Journal of Applied Psychology,* November 1987, pp. 666–73. Values were found to affect perceptual organization and act as a guide to decision making.

The Job Feelings Scale

This questionnaire has a list of five different aspects of your job. For each aspect there are a number of scales for you to indicate your feelings about your job. Indicate your response by circling the number that best represents your feelings on the dimension given.

WORK

Complex	5	4	3	2	1	Simple
Creative	5	4	3	2	1	Routine
Fascinating	5	4	3	2	1	Boring
Good	5	4	3	2	1	Bad
Satisfying	5	4	3	2	1	Unsatisfying
Respected	5	4	3	2	1	Not respected
Useful	5	4	3	2	1	Worthless
Pleasant	5	4	3	2	1	Unpleasant
Healthful	5	4	3	2	1	Tiresome
Gives sense of accomplishment	5	4	3	2	1	Endless

SUPERVISOR

Competent	5	4	3	2	1	Incompetent
Intelligent	5	4	3	2	1	Stupid
Around when needed	5	4	3	2	1	Doesn't supervise enough
Tactful	5	4	3	2	1	Impolite
Praises good work	5	4	3	2	1	Hard to please
Even-tempered	5	4	3	2	1	Quick-tempered
Flexible	5	4	3	2	1	Stubborn
Good	5	4	3	2	1	Bad
Leaves me on my own	5	4	3	2	1	Meddlesome
Tells me where I stand	5	4	3	2	1	Gives no feedback

COWORKERS

Stimulating	5	4	3	2	1	Boring
Loyal	5	4	3	2	1	Treacherous
Fast	5	4	3	2	1	Slow
Responsible	5	4	3	2	1	Irresponsible
Smart	5	4	3	2	1	Stupid
Active	5	4	3	2	1	Lazy
Respect my privacy	5	4	3	2	1	Gives no privacy
Pleasant	5	4	3	2	1	Unpleasant
Friendly	5	4	3	2	1	Hard to meet
Broad interests	5	4	3	2	1	Narrow interests

PROMOTIONS

Fair	5	4	3	2	1	Unfair
Regular	5	4	3	2	1	Intermittent
Frequent	5	4	3	2	1	Infrequent
Promotion on ability	5	4	3	2	1	Arbitrary
Good opportunity for advancement	5	4	3	2	1	Limited opportunity for advancement

PAY

Good	5	4	3	2	1	Bad
Secure	5	4	3	2	1	Insecure
Highly paid	5	4	3	2	1	Underpaid
Adequate for normal expenses	5	4	3	2	1	Barely live on income
What I deserve	5	4	3	2	1	Less than I deserve
Income provides luxuries	5	4	3	2	1	Income provides necessities only

Turn to page 688 for scoring directions and key.

Source: Courtesy of Professors J. Wysocki and G. M. Kromm.

Whose Career Do We Follow?

Jeff and Ginny Mason are a two-career family who have worked hard to achieve the life style that they currently enjoy. Having met in college, they married during the summer following their graduation from Louisiana State University.

Ginny graduated with a degree in accounting and started working for a large regional firm in New Orleans while Jeff entered law school. Over the next three years, Ginny worked her way up in the firm, gaining more and more experience and assuming greater responsibilities. Jeff was able to pursue his law school studies on a full-time basis due to Ginny's financial support. Upon graduation from law school, Jeff joined a well established firm, McCloskey and Dennery, in the same city as Ginny's accounting firm.

Jeff and Ginny have both progressed rapidly in their respective firms. Jeff has recently been approached by a corporate client, Reich-Hold Chemicals, Inc., with an offer of a new job. The job would require that Jeff leave the law practice in which he is currently a junior partner, and join the legal department of the corporation. He is being offered the position of chief legal counsel due to the retirement of the present head of the corporate legal department. Jeff is very excited by this offer. His specialty is corporate law and he has always enjoyed a good working relationship with the corporation. Jeff sees this as an excellent opportunity to engage in corporate law and enjoy the benefits of focusing all of one's energies on the problems of one client, rather than being spread thin over several different clients. Accepting the position will mean a move to the client's corporate headquarters in Houston, Texas, approximately 350 miles away.

Ginny, while pleased for Jeff, is faced with the situation of leaving a regional firm in which she is due a promotion. Her many years of hard work are about to be rewarded by being promoted to the level of partner. For Jeff to take the corporate position, Ginny will have to resign from the accounting firm. Her particular firm is regional in the sense that it services clients within a one-hundred mile radius. There would be no opportunity for Ginny to continue working for the firm with which she is now associated. However, there are several large regional firms located in Houston. Such a move would likely result in Ginny losing her seniority, taking a pay cut, and having to reestablish herself in a new organization.

DISCUSSION QUESTIONS

1. Is Ginny experiencing cognitive dissonance? Explain.
2. What problems do you foresee for Ginny in making the move to the new locality?
3. Assume that Ginny agrees to the move because of its impact on Jeff's career. Using Allport's value types, which values would you say describe Ginny's decision making? Jeff's decision making?
4. If Jeff and Ginny decide not to make the move, what problems might Jeff face?

This case contributed by Dr. Sarah Dawkins, Middle Tennessee State University. Used with permission.

NOTES

[1]This is based on J. Hyatt, "The Odyssey of an 'Excellent' Man," *INC.*, February 1989, pp. 63–69.

[2]M. Rokeach, *The Nature of Human Values* (New York: Free Press, 1973), p. 5.

[3]See, for instance, J. H. Barnett and M. J. Karson, "Personal Values and Business Decisions: An Exploratory Investigation," *Journal of Business Ethics,* July 1987, pp. 371–82.

[4]M. Rokeach and S. J. Ball-Rokeach, "Stability and Change in American Value Priorities, 1968–1981," *American Psychologist,* May 1989, pp. 775–84.

[5]M. Rokeach, *The Nature of Human Values,* p. 6.

[6]G. W. Allport, P. E. Vernon, and G. Lindzey, *Study of Values* (Boston: Houghton Mifflin, 1951).

[7]C. W. Graves, "Levels of Existence: An Open Systems Theory of Values," *Journal of Humanistic Psychology,* Fall 1970, pp. 131–55; and M. S. Myers and S. S. Myers, "Toward Understanding the Changing Work Ethic," *California Management Review,* Spring 1974, pp. 7–19.

[8]This three-stage chronological model of values is based on ideas presented in R. J. Aldag and A. P. Brief, "Some Correlates of Work Values," *Journal of Applied Psychology,* December 1975, pp. 757–60; D. J. Cherrington, S. J. Condie, and J. L. England, "Age and Work Values," *Academy of Management Journal,* September 1979, pp. 617–23; T. Carson, "Fast-Track Kids," *Business Week,* November 10, 1986, pp. 90–92; and J. A. Raelin, "The '60s Kids in the Corporation: More Than Just 'Daydream Believers,'" *Academy of Management Executive,* February 1987, pp. 21–30.

[9]Rokeach, *Human Values,* pp. 95–121.

[10]P. P. Brooke Jr., D. W. Russell, and J. L. Price, "Discriminant Validation of Measures of Job Satisfaction, Job Involvement, and Organizational Commitment," *Journal of Applied Psychology,* May 1988, pp. 139–45.

[11]See, for example, S. Rabinowitz and D. T. Hall, "Organizational Research in Job Involvement," *Psychological Bulletin,* March 1977, pp. 265–88; G. J. Blau, "A Multiple Study Investigation of the Dimensionality of Job Involvement," *Journal of Vocational Behavior,* August 1985, pp. 19–36; and N. A. Jans, "Organizational Factors and Work Involvement," *Organizational Behavior and Human Decision Processes,* June 1985, pp. 382–96.

[12]Based on G. J. Blau and K. R. Boal, "Conceptualizing How Job Involvement and Organizational Commitment Affect Turnover and Absenteeism," *Academy of Management Review,* April 1987, p. 290.

[13]G. J. Blau, "Job Involvement and Organizational Commitment as Interactive Predictors of Tardiness and Absenteeism," *Journal of Management,* Winter 1986, pp. 577–84; and K. Boal and R. Cidambi, "Attitudinal Correlates of Turnover and Absenteeism: A Meta Analysis." Paper presented at the meeting of the American Psychological Association; Toronto, Canada, 1984.

[14]G. Farris, "A Predictive Study of Turnover," *Personnel Psychology,* Summer 1971, pp. 311–28.

[15]Blau and Boal, "Conceptualizing," p. 290.

[16]See, for instance, P. W. Hom, R. Katerberg, and C. L. Hulin, "Comparative Examination of Three Approaches to the Prediction of Turnover," *Journal of Applied Psychology,* June 1979, pp. 280–90; H. Angle and J. Perry, "Organizational Commitment: Individual and Organizational Influence," *Work and Occupations,* May 1983, pp. 123–46; and J. L. Pierce and R. B. Dunham, "Organizational Commitment: Pre-Employment Propensity and Initial Work Experiences," *Journal of Management,* Spring 1987, pp. 163–78.

[17]P. W. Hom, R. Katerberg, and C. L. Hulin, "Comparative Examination"; and R. T. Mowday, L. W. Porter, and R. M. Steers, *Employee Organization Linkages: The Psychology of Commitment, Absenteeism, and Turnover* (New York: Academic Press, 1982).

[18]L. W. Porter, R. M. Steers, R. T. Mowday, and P. V. Boulian, "Organizational Commitment, Job Satisfaction, and Turnover Among Psychiatric Technicians," *Journal of Applied Psychology,* October 1974, pp. 603–09.

[19]"A Kinder, Gentler Generation of Executives?" *Business Week,* April 23, 1990, pp. 86–87.

[20]L. Festinger, *A Theory of Cognitive Dissonance* (Stanford, CA: Stanford University Press, 1957).

[21]B. M. Staw, "The Escalation of Commitment to a Course of Action," *Academy of Management Review,* October 1981, pp. 577–87.

[22]A. W. Wicker, "Attitude Versus Action: The Relationship of Verbal and Overt Behavioral Responses to Attitude Objects," *Journal of Social Issues,* Autumn 1969, pp. 41–78.

[23]Ibid., p. 65.

[24]T. A. Heberlein and J. S. Black, "Attitudinal Specificity and the Prediction of Behavior in a Field Setting," *Journal of Personality and Social Psychology,* April 1976, pp. 474–79.

[25]H. Schuman and M. P. Johnson, "Attitudes and Behavior," in A. Inkeles (ed.), *Annual Review of Sociology,* (Palo Alto, CA: Annual Reviews, 1976), pp. 161–207.

[26]R. H. Fazio and M. P. Zanna, "Direct Experience and Attitude-Behavior Consistency," in L. Berkowitz (ed.), *Advances in Experimental Social Psychology,* (New York: Academic Press, 1981), pp. 161–202.

[27]L. R. Kahle and H. J. Berman, "Attitudes Cause Behaviors: A Cross-Lagged Panel Analysis," *Journal of Personality and Social Psychology,* March 1979, pp. 315–21; and C. L. Kleinke, "Two Models for Conceptualizing the Attitude-Behavior Relationship," *Human Relations,* April 1984, pp. 333–50.

[28]D. J. Bem, "Self-Perception Theory," in L. Berkowitz (ed.), *Advances in Experimental Social Psychology,* Vol. 6 (New York: Academic Press, 1972), pp. 1–62.

[29]See, for example, C. A. Kiesler, R. E. Nisbett, and M. P. Zanna, "On Inferring One's Belief from One's Behavior," *Journal of Personality and Social Psychology,* April 1969, pp. 321–27.

[30]R. Abelson, "Are Attitudes Necessary?" in B. T. King and E. McGinnies (eds.), *Attitudes, Conflicts, and Social Change* (New York: Academic Press, 1972), p. 25.

[31]See, for example, G. E. Lyne, "How to Measure Employee Attitudes," *Training and Development Journal,* December 1989, pp. 40–43.

[32]G. Gallup, "Employee Research: From Nice to Know to Need to Know," *Personnel Journal,* August 1988, pp. 42–43.

[33]The Wyatt Company's 1989 national WorkAmerica study identified twelve dimensions of satisfaction: work organization, working conditions, communications, job performances and performance review, co-workers, supervision, company management, pay, benefits, career development and training, job content and satisfaction, and company image and change.

[34]See J. L. Price and C. W. Mueller, *Handbook of Organizational Measurement* (Marshfield, MA: Pitman Publishing, 1986), pp. 223–27.

[35]V. Scarpello and J. P. Campbell, "Job Satisfaction: Are All the Parts There?," *Personnel Psychology,* Autumn 1983, pp. 577–600.

[36]E. A. Locke, "The Nature and Causes of Job Satisfaction," in M. D. Dunnette (ed.), *Handbook of Industrial and Organizational Psychology* (Chicago: Rand McNally, 1976), pp. 1319–28.

[37]See, for example, D. C. Feldman and H. J. Arnold, "Personality Types and Career Patterns: Some Empirical Evidence on Holland's Model," *Canadian Journal of Administrative Science,* June 1985, pp. 192–210.

[38]See, for instance, studies cited in A. F. Chelte, J. Wright, and C. Tausky, "Did Job Satisfaction Really Drop During the 1970s?," *Monthly Labor Review,* November 1982, pp. 33–36; "Job Satisfaction High in America, Says Conference Board Study," *Monthly Labor Review,* February 1985, p. 52; and C. Hartman and S. Pearlstein, "The Joy of Working," *Inc.,* November 1987, pp. 61–66. See also "Wyatt WorkAmerica," published by The Wyatt Company, 1990.

[39]"Job Satisfaction High in America," p. 52.

[40]G. L. Staines and R. P. Quinn, "American Workers Evaluate the Quality of Their Jobs," *Monthly Labor Review,* January 1979, pp. 3–12.

[41]Chelte, Wright, Tausky, "Did Job Satisfaction Really Drop?" and B. M. Staw, N. E. Bell, and J. A. Clausen, "The Dispositional Approach to Job Attitudes: A Lifetime Longitudinal Test," *Administrative Science Quarterly,* March 1986, pp. 56–77.

[42]R. L. Kahn, "The Meaning of Work: Interpretation and Proposals of Measurement," in A. Campbell and P. E. Converse (eds.), *The Human Meaning of Social Change* (New York: Russell Sage Foundation, 1972).

[43]Staw, Bell, and Clausen, "The Dispositional Approach to Job Attitudes;" and R. D. Arvey, T. J. Bouchard, Jr., N. L. Segal, and L. M. Abraham, "Job Satisfaction: Environmental and Genetic Components," *Journal of Applied Psychology,* April 1989, pp. 187–92. These conclusions, however, have been challenged in B. Gerhart, "How Important Are Dispositional Factors as Determinants of Job Satisfaction? Implications for Job Design and Other Personnel Programs," *Journal of Applied Psychology,* August 1987, pp. 366–73; and A. Davis-Blake and J. Pfeffer, "Just a Mirage: The Search for Dispositional Effects in Organizational Research," *Academy of Management Review,* July 1989, pp. 385–400.

[44]A. H. Brayfield and W. H. Crockett, "Employee Attitudes and Employee Performance," *Psychological Bulletin,* September 1955, pp. 396–428; F. Herzberg, B. Mausner, R. O. Peterson, and D. F. Capwell, *Job Attitudes: Review of Research and Opinion* (Pittsburgh: Psychological Service of Pittsburgh, 1957); V. H. Vroom, *Work and Motivation* (New York: John Wiley, 1964); G. P. Fournet, M. K. Distefano, Jr., and M. W. Pryer, "Job Satisfaction: Issues and Problems," *Personnel Psychology,* Summer 1966, pp. 165–83.

[45]Vroom, *Work and Motivation;* and M. T. Iaffaldano and P. M. Muchinsky, "Job Satisfaction and Job Performance: A Meta-Analysis," *Psychological Bulletin,* March 1985, pp. 251–73.

[46]See, for example, J. B. Herman, "Are Situational Contingencies Limiting Job Attitude–Job Performance Relationship?," *Organizational Behavior and Human Performance,* October 1973, pp. 208–24; and M. M. Petty, G. W. McGee, and J. W. Cavender, "A Meta-Analysis of the Relationship Between Individual Job Satisfaction and Individual Performance," *Academy of Management Review,* October 1984, pp. 712–21.

[47]C. N. Greene, "The Satisfaction-Performance Controversy," *Business Horizons,* February 1972, pp. 31–41; E. E. Lawler III, *Motivation in Organizations* (Monterey, CA: Brooks/Cole, 1973); and Petty, McGee, and Cavender, "A Meta-Analysis of the Relationship Between Individual Job Satisfaction and Individual Performance."

48Locke, "The Nature and Causes of Job Satisfaction," p. 1331; S. L. McShane, "Job Satisfaction and Absenteeism: A Meta-Analytic Re-Examination," *Canadian Journal of Administrative Science,* June 1984, pp. 61–77; R. D. Hackett and R. M. Guion, "A Reevaluation of the Absenteeism-Job Satisfaction Relationship," *Organizational Behavior and Human Decision Processes,* June 1985, pp. 340–81; K. D. Scott and G. S. Taylor, "An Examination of Conflicting Findings on the Relationship Between Job Satisfaction and Absenteeism: A Meta-Analysis," *Academy of Management Journal,* September 1985, pp. 599–612; and R. D. Hackett, "Work Attitudes and Employee Absenteeism: A Synthesis of the Literature," paper presented at 1988 National Academy of Management Conference; Anaheim, Calif., August 1988.

49F. J. Smith, "Work Attitudes as Predictors of Attendance on a Specific Day," *Journal of Applied Psychology,* February 1977, pp. 16–19.

50Brayfield and Crockett, "Employee Attitudes"; Vroom, *Work and Motivation;* J. Price, *The Study of Turnover* (Ames: Iowa State University Press, 1977); and W. H. Mobley, R. W. Griffeth, H. H. Hand, and B. M. Meglino, "Review and Conceptual Analysis of the Employee Turnover Process," *Psychological Bulletin,* May 1979, pp. 493–522.

51See, for example, C. L. Hulin, M. Roznowski, and D. Hachiya, "Alternative Opportunities and Withdrawal Decisions: Empirical and Theoretical Discrepancies and an Integration," *Psychological Bulletin,* July 1985, pp. 233–50; and J. M. Carsten and P. E. Spector, "Unemployment, Job Satisfaction, and Employee Turnover: A Meta-Analytic Test of the Muchinsky Model," *Journal of Applied Psychology,* August 1987, pp. 374–81.

52D. G. Spencer and R. M. Steers, "Performance as a Moderator of the Job Satisfaction-Turnover Relationship," *Journal of Applied Psychology,* August 1981, pp. 511–14.

53S. A. Ahmed and J. Jabes, "A Comparative Study of Job Values of Business Students in France and English Canada," *Canadian Journal of Administrative Sciences,* June 1988, pp. 51–59.

54A. Howard, K. Shudo, and M. Umeshima, "Motivation and Values Among Japanese and American Managers," *Personnel Psychology,* Winter 1983, pp. 886–98.

55Cited in L. Smith, "Cracks in the Japanese Work Ethic," *Fortune,* May 14, 1984, pp. 162–68.

56See D. Farrell, "Exit, Voice, Loyalty, and Neglect as Responses to Job Dissatisfaction: A Multidimensional Scaling Study," *Academy of Management Journal,* December 1983, pp. 596–606; C. E. Rusbult, D. Farrell, G. Rogers, and A. G. Mainous III, "Impact of Exchange Variables on Exit, Voice, Loyalty, and Neglect: An Integrative Model of Responses to Declining Job Satisfaction," *Academy of Management Journal,* September 1988, pp. 599–627; and M. J. Withey and W. H. Cooper, "Predicting Exit, Voice, Loyalty, and Neglect," *Administrative Science Quarterly,* December 1989, pp. 521–39.

57R. B. Freeman, "Job Satisfaction as an Economic Variable."

BASIC MOTIVATION CONCEPTS

LEARNING OBJECTIVES

After studying this chapter, you should be able to:

1. *Outline the motivation process*

2. *Describe Maslow's need hierarchy*

3. *Contrast Theory X and Theory Y*

4. *Differentiate motivators from hygiene factors*

5. *List the characteristics that high achievers prefer in a job*

6. *Explain the job characteristics model*

7. *Summarize the types of goals that increase performance*

8. *State the impact of underrewarding employees*

9. *Clarify the key relationships in expectancy theory*

Some of the factory workers at Lincoln Electric earn more than $100,000 a year. In recent years, the average Lincoln Electric employee earned about $44,000 a year; this is more than double the average for U.S. manufacturing workers. Courtesy The Lincoln Electric Company.

Money is what you'd get on beautifully without if only other people weren't so crazy about it.

M. C. HARRIMAN

Lincoln Electric is a Cleveland-based firm that employs about 2400 people and generates ninety percent of its sales from manufacturing arc-welding equipment and supplies. Founded in 1895, the company's legendary profit-sharing incentive system and resultant productivity record are the envy of the manufacturing world.[1]

Factory workers at Lincoln receive piece-rate wages with no guaranteed minimum hourly pay. After working for the firm for two years, employees begin to participate in the year-end bonus plan. Determined by a formula that considers the company's gross profits, the employees' base piece rate, and merit rating, it may be the most lucrative bonus system for factory workers in American manufacturing. The *average* size of the bonus over the past fifty-five years has been 95.5 percent of base wages!

The company has a guaranteed-employment policy, which it put in place in 1958. Since that time, it has not laid off a single worker. In return for job security, however, employees agree to several things. During slow times, they will accept reduced work periods. They also agree to accept work transfers, even to lower-paid jobs, if that is necessary to maintain a minimum of thirty hours of work per week.

You'd think the Lincoln Electric system would attract quality people, and it does. For instance, the company recently hired four Harvard M.B.A.s to fill future management slots. But, consistent with company tradition, they started out, like everyone else, doing piecework on the assembly line.

Lincoln Electric's profit-sharing incentive system has provided positive benefits for the company as well as for its employees. One company executive estimates that Lincoln's overall productivity is about double that of its domestic competitors. The company has earned a profit every year since the depths of the 1930s depression and has never missed a quarterly dividend. And Lincoln has one of the lowest employee turnover rates in United States industry.

Lincoln Electric has successfully integrated employment security, financial incentives, job flexibility, and high productivity standards into a system that motivates its employees. Most organizations haven't been so successful. This may explain why the concept of motivation is probably the most researched and discussed topic in the organizational sciences.

A cursory look at most organizations quickly suggests that some people work harder than others. Who among us, for instance, hasn't seen an individual with outstanding abilities outperformed by someone with obviously inferior talents? Why do some people appear to be "highly motivated," while others are not? We'll try to answer this latter question in this and the following chapter.

WHAT IS MOTIVATION?

Maybe the place to begin is to say what motivation isn't. Many people incorrectly view motivation as a personal trait—that is, some have it and others don't. In practice, some managers label employees who seem to lack motivation as lazy. Such a label assumes that an individual is always lazy or is lacking in motivation. Our knowledge of motivation tells us that this just isn't true. What we know is that motivation is the result of the interaction of the individual and the situation. Certainly, individuals differ in their basic motivational drive. But the same employee who is quickly bored when pulling the lever on his drill press may pull the lever on a slot machine in Las Vegas for hours on end without the slightest hint of boredom. You may read a complete novel at one sitting, yet find it difficult to stay with a textbook for more than twenty minutes. It's not necessarily you—it's the situation. So as we analyze the concept of motivation, keep in mind that level of motivation varies both between individuals and within individuals at different times.

We'll define **motivation** as the willingness to exert high levels of effort toward organizational goals, conditioned by the effort's ability to satisfy some individual need. While general motivation is concerned with effort toward *any* goal, we'll narrow the focus to *organizational* goals in order to reflect our singular interest in work-related behavior. The three key elements in our definition are effort, organizational goals, and needs.

The effort element is a measure of intensity. When someone is motivated, he or she tries hard. But high levels of effort are unlikely to lead to favorable job performance outcomes unless the effort is channeled in a direction that benefits the organization.[2] Therefore, we must consider the quality of the effort as well as its intensity. Effort that is directed toward, and consistent with, the organization's goals is the kind of effort that we should be seeking. Finally, we will treat motivation as a need-satisfying process. This is depicted in Figure 7–1.

A **need,** in our terminology, means some internal state that makes certain outcomes appear attractive. An unsatisfied need creates tension that stimulates drives within the individual. These drives generate a search behavior to find particular goals that, if attained, will satisfy the need and lead to the reduction of tension.

Motivation The willingness to exert high levels of effort toward organizational goals, conditioned by the effort's ability to satisfy some individual need.

Need Some internal state that makes certain outcomes appear attractive.

FIGURE 7–1   **The Motivation Process**

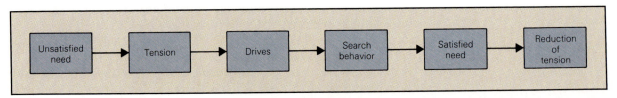

Unsatisfied need → Tension → Drives → Search behavior → Satisfied need → Reduction of tension

So we can say that motivated employees are in a state of tension. To relieve this tension, they exert effort. The greater the tension, the higher the effort level. If this effort successfully leads to the satisfaction of the need, tension is reduced. But since we are interested in work behavior, this tension-reduction effort must also be directed toward organizational goals. Therefore, inherent in our definition of motivation is the requirement that the individual's needs are compatible and consistent with the organization's goals. Where this does not occur, we can have individuals exerting high levels of effort that actually run counter to the interests of the organization. This, incidentally, is not so unusual. For example, some employees regularly spend a lot of time talking with friends at work in order to satisfy their social needs. There is a high level of effort, only it's being unproductively directed.

EARLY THEORIES OF MOTIVATION

The 1950s were a fruitful period in the development of motivation concepts. Three specific theories were formulated during this period, which, though heavily attacked and now questionable in terms of validity, are probably the best known explanations for employee motivation. These are the hierarchy of needs theory, Theories X and Y, and the motivation-hygiene theory. As you'll see later in this chapter, we have since developed more valid explanations of motivation, but you should know these early theories for at least two reasons: (1) they represent a foundation from which contemporary theories have grown, and (2) practicing managers regularly use these theories and their terminology in explaining employee motivation.

Hierarchy of Needs Theory

Hierarchy of Needs Theory
There is a hierarchy of five needs—physiological, safety, social, esteem, and self-actualization—and as each need is sequentially satisfied, the next need becomes dominant.

It's probably safe to say that the most well-known theory of motivation is Abraham Maslow's **hierarchy of needs.**[3] He hypothesized that within every human being there exists a hierarchy of five needs. These needs are:

1. *Physiological*—includes hunger, thirst, shelter, sex, and other bodily needs
2. *Safety*—includes security and protection from physical and emotional harm
3. *Social*—includes affection, belongingness, acceptance, and friendship
4. *Esteem*—includes internal esteem factors such as self-respect, autonomy, and achievement; and external esteem factors such as status, recognition, and attention
5. *Self-actualization*—is represented by the drive to become what one is capable of becoming; includes growth, achieving one's potential, and self-fulfillment

Self-actualization The drive to become what one is capable of becoming.

As each of these needs becomes substantially satisfied, the next need becomes dominant. In terms of Figure 7–2, the individual moves up the hierarchy. From the standpoint of motivation, the theory would say that although no need is ever fully gratified, a substantially satisfied need no longer motivates. So if you want to motivate someone, according to Maslow,

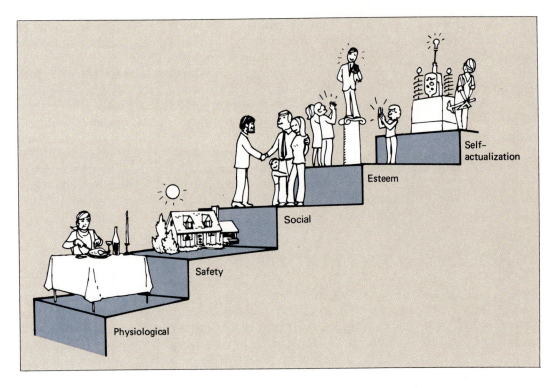

FIGURE 7–2   Maslow's Hierarchy of Needs
Source: By permission of the Modular Project of Organizational Behavior and Instructional Communications Centre. McGill University, Montreal, Canada.

Lower-order Needs Needs that are satisfied externally; physiological and safety needs.

Higher-order Needs Needs that are satisfied internally; needs for social, esteem, and self-actualization.

you need to understand where that person currently is on the hierarchy and focus on satisfying those needs at or above that level.

Maslow separated the five needs into higher and lower levels. Physiological and safety needs were described as **lower-order** and social, esteem, and self-actualization as **higher-order** needs. The differentiation between the two orders was made on the premise that higher-order needs are satisfied internally to the person, whereas lower-order needs are predominantly satisfied externally (by such things as money wages, union contracts, and tenure). In fact, the natural conclusion to be drawn from Maslow's classification is that in times of economic plenty, almost all permanently employed workers have their lower-order needs substantially met.

Maslow's need theory has received wide recognition, particularly among practicing managers. This can be attributed to the theory's intuitive logic and ease of understanding. Unfortunately, however, research does not generally validate the theory. Maslow provided no empirical substantiation, and several studies that sought to validate the theory found no support.[4]

Old theories, especially ones that are intuitively logical, apparently die hard. One researcher reviewed the evidence and concluded that "although of great societal popularity, need hierarchy as a theory continues to receive little empirical support."[5] Further, the researcher stated that the "available research should certainly generate a reluctance to accept unconditionally the implication of Maslow's hierarchy."[6] Another review came to the same conclusion.[7] Little support was found for the prediction that need structures are organized along the dimensions proposed by Maslow, that unsatisfied needs motivate, or that a satisfied need activates movement to a new need level.

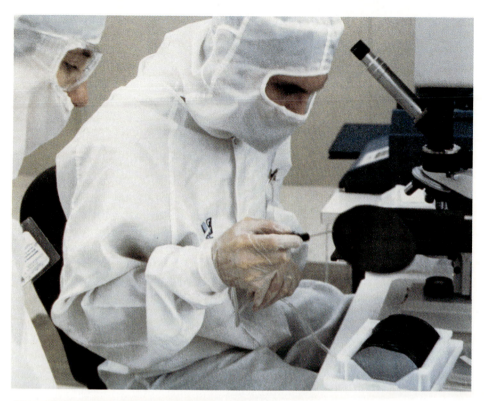

Motorola, Inc. is concerned with satisfying its employees' security needs. It is committed to steady employment. For instance, during a recent slump in its semiconductor business, it needed to respond to a 10 percent drop in demand. Rather than laying off 10 percent of its work force, it got its reduction by instituting a four-day workweek every other week. The work-sharing program allowed Motorola to keep many thousands of regular employees who otherwise would have been laid off. The result: Motorola workers feel a sense of job security and skilled workers are more likely to stay with the firm.   Courtesy Motorola, Inc.

Theory X and Theory Y

Theory X Assumes that employees dislike work, are lazy, dislike responsibility, and must be coerced to perform.

Theory Y Assumes that employees like work, are creative, seek responsibility, and can exercise self-direction.

Douglas McGregor proposed two distinct views of human beings: one basically negative, labeled **Theory X,** and the other basically positive, labeled **Theory Y.**[8] After viewing the way in which managers dealt with employees, McGregor concluded that a manager's view of the nature of human beings is based on a certain grouping of assumptions and that he or she tends to mold his or her behavior toward subordinates according to these assumptions.

Under Theory X, the four assumptions held by managers are:

1. Employees inherently dislike work and, whenever possible, will attempt to avoid it.

2. Since employees dislike work, they must be coerced, controlled, or threatened with punishment to achieve goals.

3. Employees will shirk responsibilities and seek formal direction whenever possible.

4. Most workers place security above all other factors associated with work and will display little ambition.

In contrast to these negative views toward the nature of human beings, McGregor listed four other positive assumptions that he called Theory Y:

1. Employees can view work as being as natural as rest or play.
2. People will exercise self-direction and self-control if they are committed to the objectives.
3. The average person can learn to accept, even seek, responsibility.
4. The ability to make innovative decisions is widely dispersed throughout the population and is not necessarily the sole province of those in management positions.

What are the motivational implications if you accept McGregor's analysis? The answer is best expressed in the framework presented by Maslow. Theory X assumes that lower-order needs dominate individuals. Theory Y assumes that higher-order needs dominate individuals. McGregor, himself, held to the belief that Theory Y assumptions were more valid than Theory X. Therefore, he proposed such ideas as participation in decision making, responsible and challenging jobs, and good group relations as approaches that would maximize an employee's job motivation.

Unfortunately, there is no evidence to confirm that either set of assumptions is valid or that accepting Theory Y assumptions and altering one's actions accordingly will lead to more motivated workers. As will become evident later in this chapter, either Theory X or Theory Y assumptions may be appropriate in a particular situation.

Motivation-Hygiene Theory

Motivation-Hygiene Theory
Intrinsic factors are related to job satisfaction, while extrinsic factors are associated with dissatisfaction.

The **motivation-hygiene theory** was proposed by psychologist Frederick Herzberg.[9] In the belief that an individual's relation to his or her work is a basic one and that his or her attitude toward this work can very well determine the individual's success or failure, Herzberg investigated the question, "What do people want from their jobs?" He asked people to describe, in detail, situations when they felt exceptionally *good* and *bad* about their jobs. These responses were tabulated and categorized. Factors affecting job attitudes as reported in twelve investigations conducted by Herzberg are illustrated in Figure 7–3.

From the categorized responses, Herzberg concluded that the replies people gave when they felt good about their jobs were significantly different from the replies given when they felt bad. As seen in Figure 6–3, certain characteristics tend to be consistently related to job satisfaction (factors on the right side of the figure), and others to job dissatisfaction (the left side of the figure). Intrinsic factors, such as achievement, recognition, the work itself, responsibility, advancement, and growth seem to be related to job satisfaction. When those questioned felt good about their work, they tended to attribute these characteristics to themselves. On the other hand, when they were dissatisfied, they tended to cite extrinsic factors, such as company policy and administration, supervision, interpersonal relations, and working conditions.

The data suggest, says Herzberg, that the opposite of satisfaction is not dissatisfaction, as was traditionally believed. Removing dissatisfying characteristics from a job does not necessarily make the job satisfying. As illustrated in Figure 7–4, Herzberg proposes that his findings indicate the existence of a dual continuum: The opposite of "Satisfaction" is "No Satisfaction," and the opposite of "Dissatisfaction" is "No Dissatisfaction."

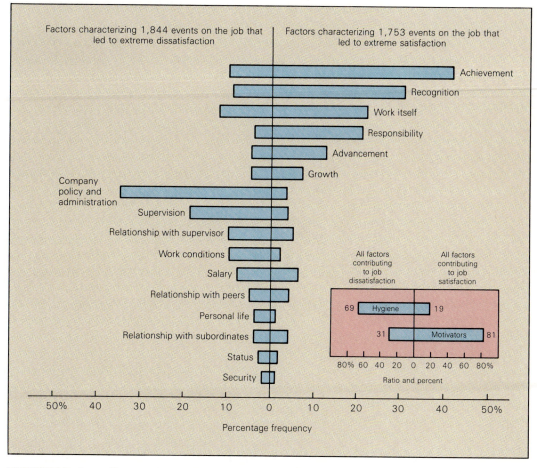

FIGURE 7–3   Comparison of Satisfiers and Dissatisfiers

Source: Reprinted by permission of *Harvard Business Review*. An exhibit from "One More Time: How Do You Motivate Employees?" by Frederick Herzberg, September/October 1987. Copyright © 1987 by the President and Fellows of Harvard College; all rights reserved.

Hygiene Factors Those factors—such as company policy and administration, supervision, and salary—that, when present in a job, placate workers. When these factors are present, people will not be dissatisfied.

According to Herzberg, the factors leading to job satisfaction are separate and distinct from those that lead to job dissatisfaction. Therefore, managers who seek to eliminate factors that create job dissatisfaction can bring about peace, but not necessarily motivation. They will be placating their work force rather than motivating them. As a result, such characteristics as company policy and administration, supervision, interpersonal relations, working conditions, and salary have been characterized by Herzberg as **hygiene factors.** When they are adequate, people will not be dissatisfied; however, neither will they be satisfied. If we want to motivate people on their jobs, Herzberg suggests emphasizing achievement, recognition, the work itself, responsibility, and growth. These are the characteristics that people find intrinsically rewarding.

The motivation-hygiene theory is not without its detractors. The criticisms of the theory include the following:

1. The procedure that Herzberg used is limited by its methodology. When things are going well, people tend to take credit themselves. Contrarily, they blame failure on the extrinsic environment.

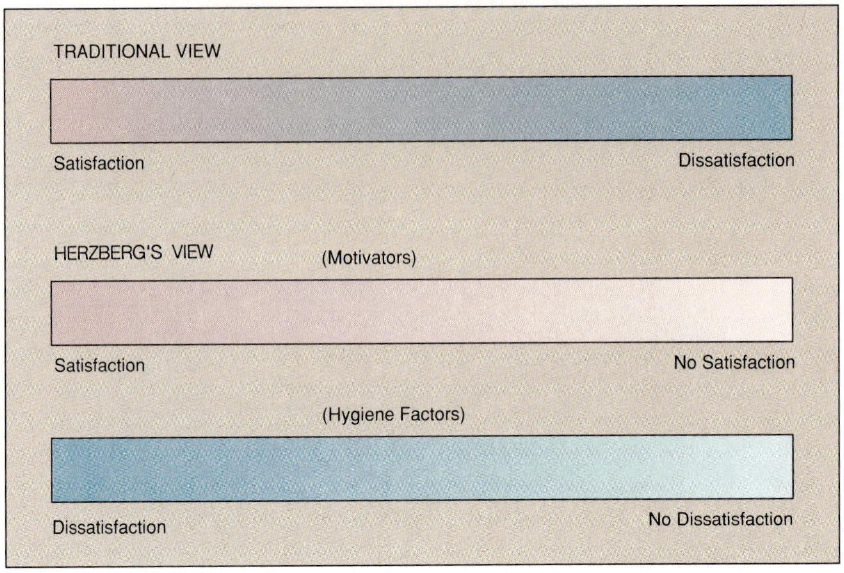

FIGURE 7-4   **Contrasting Views of Satisfaction-Dissatisfaction**

2. The reliability of Herzberg's methodology is questioned. Since raters have to make interpretations, it is possible that they may contaminate the findings by interpreting one response in one manner while treating another similar response differently.

3. The theory, to the degree that it is valid, provides an explanation of job satisfaction. It is not really a theory of motivation.

4. No overall measure of satisfaction was utilized. In other words, a person may dislike part of his or her job, yet still think the job is acceptable.

5. The theory is inconsistent with previous research. The motivation-hygiene theory ignores situational variables.

6. Herzberg assumes that there is a relationship between satisfaction and productivity. But the research methodology he used looked only at satisfaction, not at productivity. To make such research relevant, one must assume a high relationship between satisfaction and productivity.[10]

Regardless of criticisms, Herzberg's theory has been widely read and few managers are unfamiliar with his recommendations. The increased popularity since the mid-1960s of vertically expanding jobs to allow workers greater responsibility in planning and controlling their work can probably be largely attributed to Herzberg's findings and recommendations.

CONTEMPORARY THEORIES OF MOTIVATION

The previous theories are well known but, unfortunately, have not held up well under close examination. However, all is not lost.[13] There are a number of contemporary theories that have one thing in common—each has a reasonable

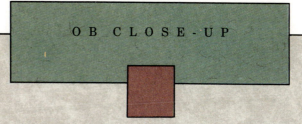

OB CLOSE-UP

What Do People Want from Their Jobs?

Regardless of the criticism leveled at Herzberg's research and conclusions, his findings appear to be consistent with surveys of the workforce in general and managers in particular.

Nationwide polls conducted by the National Opinion Research Center indicate that "more than half of the white, male work force in the United States believes that the most important characteristic of a job is that it involves work that is important and provides a sense of accomplishment."[11] Meaningful work is rated "most important" three times more frequently than "high income" and seven times more frequently than is the desire for "shorter work hours and much free time."

A recent survey of middle- and top-level managers by the American Productivity and Quality Center found similar results.[12] For instance, ninety percent or more of the respondents rated challenging work, participation in decision making, and recognition for their accomplishments as important or very important.

These studies support Herzberg's conclusion that employees value factors like achievement, recognition, and challenging work more than things like pay or security. But just because many people rate motivators above hygiene factors is no guarantee that the former's existence in jobs will actually increase work motivation for all employees. These findings may not be generalizable to the entire population. Moreover, it may only result in increasing employee satisfaction and have no affect on productivity.

degree of valid supporting documentation. Of course, this doesn't mean that the theories we are about to introduce are unquestionably "right." What they do represent is the current "state of the art" in explaining employee motivation.

ERG Theory

ERG Theory There are three groups of core needs: existence, relatedness, and growth.

Clayton Alderfer of Yale University has reworked Maslow's need hierarchy to align it more closely with the empirical research. His revised need hierarchy is labeled **ERG theory.**[14]

Alderfer argues that there are three groups of core needs—existence, relatedness, and growth—hence the label: ERG theory. The existence group is concerned with providing our basic material existence requirements. They include the items that Maslow considered as physiological and safety needs. The second group of needs are those of relatedness—the desire we have for maintaining important interpersonal relationships. These social and status desires require interaction with others if they are to be satisfied, and they align with Maslow's social need and the external component of Maslow's esteem classification. Finally, Alderfer isolates growth needs—an intrinsic desire for personal development. These include the intrinsic component from Maslow's esteem category and the characteristics included under self-actualization.

Besides substituting three needs for five, how does Alderfer's ERG theory differ from Maslow? In contrast to Maslow, the ERG theory demonstrates that (1) more than one need may be operative at the same time and (2) if the gratification of a higher-level need is stifled, the desire to satisfy a lower-level need increases.

Maslow's need hierarchy is a rigid steplike progression. ERG theory does not assume that there exists a rigid hierarchy where a lower need must be substantially gratified before one can move on. A person can, for instance, be working on growth even though existence or relatedness needs are unsatisfied; or all three need categories could be operating at the same time.

ERG theory also contains a frustration–regression dimension. Maslow, you'll remember, argued that an individual would stay at a certain need level until that need was satisfied. ERG theory counters by noting that when a higher-order need level is frustrated, the individual's desire to increase a lower-level need takes place. Inability to satisfy a need for social interaction, for instance, might increase the desire for more money or better working conditions. So frustration can lead to a regression to a lower need.

In summary, ERG theory argues, like Maslow, that satisfied lower-order needs lead to the desire to satisfy higher-order needs; but multiple needs can be operating as motivators at the same time, and frustration in attempting to satisfy a higher-level need can result in regression to a lower-level need.

ERG theory is more consistent with our knowledge of individual differences among people. Variables such as education, family background, and cultural environment can alter the importance or driving force that a group of needs holds for a particular individual. The evidence demonstrating that people in other cultures rank the need categories differently—for instance, natives of Spain and Japan place social needs before their physiological requirements[15]—would be consistent with the ERG theory. Several studies have supported the ERG theory,[16] but there is also evidence that it doesn't work in some organizations.[17] Overall, however, ERG theory represents a more valid version of the need hierarchy.

Three Needs Theory

You've got one beanbag and there are five targets set up in front of you. Each one is progressively farther away and, hence, more difficult to hit. Target A is a cinch. It sits almost within arm's reach of you. If you hit it, you get $2. Target B is a bit farther out, but about eighty percent of the people who try can hit it. It pays $4. Target C pays $8, and about half the people who try can hit it. Very few people can hit Target D, but the payoff is $16 if you do. Finally, Target E pays $32, but it's almost impossible to achieve. Which target would you try for? If you selected C, you're very likely to be a high achiever. Why? Read on.

In Chapter 4, we introduced the need to achieve as a personality characteristic. It is also one of **three needs** proposed by David McClelland and others as being important in organizational settings for understanding motivation.[18] These three needs are achievement, power, and affiliation. They are identified as follows:

Three Needs Theory
Achievement, power, and affiliation are three important needs that help to understand motivation.

■ **Need for achievement**—the drive to excel, to achieve in relation to a set of standards, to strive to succeed

Power Need The desire to make others behave in a way that they would not otherwise have behaved.

Affiliation Need The desire for friendly and close interpersonal relationships.

- **Need for power**—the need to make others behave in a way that they would not have behaved otherwise
- **Need for affiliation**—the desire for friendly and close interpersonal relationships

As described previously, some people who have a compelling drive to succeed are striving for personal achievement rather than the rewards of success per se. They have a desire to do something better or more efficiently than it has been done before. This drive is the achievement need (*nAch*). From research into the achievement need, McClelland found that high achievers differentiate themselves from others by their desire to do things better.[19] They seek situations where they can attain personal responsibility for finding solutions to problems, where they can receive rapid feedback on their performance so they can tell easily whether they are improving or not, and where they can set moderately challenging goals. High achievers are not gamblers; they dislike succeeding by chance. They prefer the challenge of working at a problem and accepting the personal responsibility for success or failure rather than leaving the outcome to chance or the actions of others. Importantly, they avoid what they perceive to be very easy or very difficult tasks.

Again as noted in Chapter 4, high achievers perform best when they perceive their probability of success as being 0.5, that is, where they estimate that they have a 50–50 chance of success. They dislike gambling with high odds because they get no achievement satisfaction from happenstance success. Similarly, they dislike low odds (high probability of success) because then there is no challenge to their skills. They like to set goals that require stretching themselves a little. When there is an approximately equal chance of success or failure, there is the optimum opportunity to experience feelings of accomplishment and satisfaction from their efforts.

The need for power (*nPow*) is the desire to have impact, to be influential, and to control others. Individuals high in *nPow* enjoy being "in charge," strive for influence over others, prefer to be placed into competitive and status-

High achievers, like this salesperson at Schering-Plough, do well in sales positions because such jobs provide employees with freedom, personal responsibility for outcomes, immediate feedback on their performance, and the opportunity to take on moderate risks.
Rhoda Baer.

oriented situations, and tend to be more concerned with prestige and gaining influence over others than with effective performance.

The third need isolated by McClelland is affiliation (*nAff*). This need has received the least attention from researchers. Affiliation can be viewed as a Dale Carnegie-type of need—the desire to be liked and accepted by others. Individuals with a high affiliation motive strive for friendship, prefer cooperative situations rather than competitive ones, and desire relationships involving a high degree of mutual understanding.

Based on an extensive amount of research, some reasonably well-supported predictions can be made based on the relationship between achievement need and job performance. Although less research has been done on power and affiliation needs, there are consistent findings here, too.

First, as shown in Figure 7–5, individuals with a high need to achieve prefer job situations with personal responsibility, feedback, and an intermediate degree of risk. When these characteristics are prevalent, high achievers will be strongly motivated. The evidence consistently demonstrates, for instance, that high achievers are successful in entrepreneurial activities such as running their own businesses and managing a self-contained unit within a large organization.[20]

Second, a high need to achieve does not necessarily lead to being a good manager, especially in large organizations. People with a high achievement need are interested in how well they do personally and not in influencing others to do well. High-*nAch* sales people do not necessarily make good sales managers, and the good general manager in a large organization does not typically have a high need to achieve.[21]

Third, the needs for affiliation and power tend to be closely related to managerial success. The best managers are high in their need for power and low in their need for affiliation.[22] In fact, a high power motive may be a requirement for managerial effectiveness.[23] Of course, what is the cause and what is the effect is arguable. It has been suggested that a high power need may occur simply as a function of one's level in a hierarchical organization.[24] This latter argument proposes that the higher the level an individual rises to in the organization, the greater is the incumbent's power motive. As a result, powerful positions would be the stimulus to a high power motive.

Lastly, employees have been successfully trained to stimulate their achievement need. If the job calls for a high achiever, management can select a person with a high *nAch* or develop its own candidate through achievement training.[25]

FIGURE 7–5   Matching Achievers and Jobs

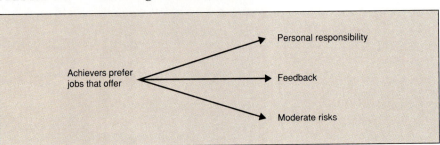

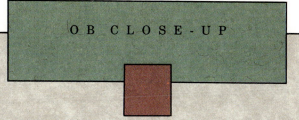

OB CLOSE-UP

Teaching People to Be Achievers

Successful achievement training is essentially a five step process conducted by professional trainers with groups of nine to twenty-five participants.[26]

The first step introduces the idea of achievement motivation. Participants are introduced to the idea that motives can be changed, and to results of research on achievement motivation.

The meaning of the achievement motive is taught in the second step. Participants learn how to measure the achievement motive by writing stories about pictures they're shown. As an example, the picture might show a male, in a suit, sitting at a desk in a relaxed position, staring out toward one of the walls in his office. Participants will write a story describing what they think is going on, what preceded this situation, and what will happen in the future. Participants will compare their stories to one written by a high achiever. The high achiever's story will contain references to accomplishments, winning, success, and the like. So, in our example, the high achiever might say that the person in the picture is the president of a large corporation who wants to get a major contract for his company. The bidding competition will be tough. But victory will enhance his company's position in the industry and probably result in a large bonus for him. He is, at the moment, feeling optimistic about getting the contract. He has just reviewed his company's proposal and he is confident that his production costs are lower than the competition, allowing him to be able to submit the lowest cost bid.

In the third step, participants learn how to *act* in a "high achievement" way. Specifically, they learn that achievers prefer situations where they have personal responsibility, feedback, and moderate risks. The trainer will use case studies and draw on the participants' own experiences to illustrate these concepts.

Next, the trainer provides feedback to the individual participants on their achievement-oriented behavior. This allows participants to compare their actions with achievement behavior.

Finally, the course concludes with each participant setting goals about how he or she will behave in an achievement-oriented fashion. These goals are written down, as are specific action plans for executing them, and a basis for evaluating progress toward attaining the goals is defined.

Cognitive Evaluation Theory

Cognitive Evaluation Theory Extrinsic rewards allocated for behavior that had been previously intrinsically rewarded tends to decrease the overall level of motivation.

In the late 1960s, one researcher proposed that the introduction of extrinsic rewards, such as pay, for work effort that had been previously intrinsically rewarding due to the pleasure associated with the content of the work itself, would tend to decrease the overall level of motivation.[27] This proposal—which has come to be called the **cognitive evaluation theory**—has been extensively researched, and a large number of studies have been supportive.[28] The importance of this theory cannot be overstated because, as we'll show, it has major implications for the way in which people are paid in organizations.

Historically, motivation theorists have generally assumed that intrinsic motivations such as achievement, responsibility, and competence were independent from extrinsic motivators like high pay, promotions, good supervisor relations, and pleasant working conditions. That is, the stimulation of one would not affect the other. But the cognitive evaluation theory suggests otherwise. It argues that when extrinsic rewards are used by organizations as payoffs for superior performance, the intrinsic rewards, which are derived from individuals doing what they like, are reduced. In other words, when extrinsic rewards are given to someone for performing an interesting task, it causes intrinsic interest in the task itself to decline.

Why would such an outcome occur? The popular explanation is that the individual experiences a loss of control over his or her own behavior so that the previous intrinsic motivation diminishes. Further, the elimination of extrinsic rewards can produce a shift—from an external to an internal explanation—in an individual's perception of causation of why he or she works on a task. If you're reading a novel a week because your English literature instructor requires you to, you can attribute your reading behavior to an external source. However, after the course is over, if you find yourself continuing to read a novel a week, your natural inclination is to say, "I must enjoy reading novels, because I'm still reading one a week!"

If the cognitive evaluation theory is valid, it should have major implications for managerial practices. It has been a truism among compensation specialists for years that if pay or other extrinsic rewards are to be effective motivators, they should be made contingent on an individual's performance. But, cognitive evaluation theorists would argue, this will only tend to decrease the internal satisfaction that the individual receives from doing the job. We have substituted an external stimulus for an internal stimulus. In fact, if cognitive evaluation theory is correct, it would make sense to make an individual's pay *non*contingent on performance in order to avoid decreasing intrinsic motivation.

We noted earlier that the cognitive evaluation theory has been supported in a number of studies. Yet it has also met with attacks, specifically on the methodology used in these studies[29] and in the interpretation of the findings.[30] But where does this theory stand today? Can we say that when organizations use extrinsic motivators like pay and promotions to stimulate workers' performance they do so at the expense of reducing intrinsic interest and motivation in the work being done? The answer is not a simple "Yes" or "No."

While further research is needed to clarify some of the current ambiguity, the evidence does lead us to conclude that the nonadditivity of extrinsic and intrinsic rewards is a real phenomenon.[31] But its impact on employee motivation at work, in contrast to motivation in general, may be considerably less than originally thought. First, many of the studies testing the theory were done with students, not paid organizational employees. The researchers would observe what happens to a student's behavior when a reward that had been allocated is stopped. This is interesting, but it does not represent the typical work situation. In the real world, when extrinsic rewards are stopped it usually means the individual is no longer part of the organization. Second, evidence indicates that very high intrinsic motivation levels are strongly resistant to the detrimental impacts of extrinsic rewards.[32] Even when a job is inherently interesting, there still exists a powerful norm for extrinsic payment.[33] At the other extreme, on dull tasks extrinsic rewards appear to increase intrinsic motivation.[34] Therefore, the theory may have limited applicability to work organizations because most low-level jobs are not inherently satisfying enough to foster high intrinsic interest and many managerial and professional positions offer intrinsic rewards. Cognitive evaluation theory may be relevant to that set of organizational jobs that falls in between—those that are neither extremely dull nor extremely interesting.

Task Characteristics Theories

"Every day was the same thing," Frank Greer began. "Put the right passenger seat into Jeeps as they came down the assembly line, pop in four bolts locking the seat frame to the car body, then tighten the bolts with my electric wrench. Thirty cars and 120 bolts an hour, eight hours a day. I didn't care that they were paying me $14 an hour, I was going crazy. I did it for almost a year and a half. Finally, I just said to my wife that this isn't going to be the way I'm going to spend the rest of my life. My brain was turning to Jello on that job. So I quit. Now I work in a print shop and I make less than $10 an hour. But let me tell you, the work I do is really interesting. It challenges me! I look forward every morning to going to work again."

Frank Greer is acknowledging two facts we all know: (1) Jobs are different and (2) some are more interesting and challenging than others. These facts have not gone unnoticed by OB researchers. They have responded by developing a number of **task characteristics theories** that seek to identify specific task characteristics of jobs, how these characteristics are combined to form different jobs, and the relationship of these task characteristics to employee motivation, satisfaction, and performance.

There are at least seven different task characteristics theories.[35] Fortunately, there is a significant amount of overlap between them.[36] For instance, Herzberg's motivation-hygiene theory and the research on the achievement need are essentially task characteristic theories. You'll remember that Herzberg argued that jobs that provided opportunities for achievement, recognition, responsibility, and the like would increase employee satisfaction. Similarly, McClelland demonstrated that high achievers performed best in jobs that offered personal responsibility, feedback, and moderate risks.

In this section, we'll review the two most important contributions among the task characteristic theories—requisite task attributes theory and the job characteristics model—and then show how the characteristics of a job might affect employee motivation.

REQUISITE TASK ATTRIBUTES THEORY The task characteristics approach began with the pioneering work of Turner and Lawrence in the mid-1960s.[37] They developed a research study to assess the effect of different kinds of jobs on employee satisfaction and absenteeism. They predicted that employees would prefer jobs that were complex and challenging; that is, such jobs would increase satisfaction and result in lower absence rates. They defined job complexity in terms of six task characteristics: (1) variety; (2) autonomy; (3) responsibility; (4) knowledge and skill; (5) required social interaction; and (6) optional social interaction. The higher a job scored on these characteristics, according to Turner and Lawrence, the more complex it was.

Their findings confirmed their absenteeism prediction. Employees in high-complexity tasks had better attendance records. But they found no general correlation between task complexity and satisfaction—until they broke their data down by the background of employees. When individual differences in the form of urban-vs.-rural background were taken into account, employees from urban settings were shown to be more satisfied with low-complexity jobs. Employees with rural backgrounds reported higher satisfaction in high-complexity jobs. Turner and Lawrence concluded that workers in larger communities had a variety of nonwork interests and thus were less involved and motivated by their work. In contrast, workers from smaller towns

Task Characteristic Theories Seek to identify specific task characteristics of jobs, how these characteristics are combined to form different jobs, and their relationship to employee motivation, satisfaction, and performance.

had fewer nonwork interests and were more receptive to the complex tasks of their jobs.

Turner and Lawrence's requisite task attributes theory was important for at least three reasons. First, they demonstrated that employees did respond differently to different types of jobs. Second, they provided a preliminary set of task attributes by which jobs could be assessed. And third, they focused attention on the need to consider the influence of individual differences on employees' reaction to jobs.

THE JOB CHARACTERISTICS MODEL   Turner and Lawrence's requisite task attributes theory laid the foundation for what is, today, the dominant framework for defining task characteristics and understanding their relationship to employee motivation. That is Hackman and Oldham's **job characteristics model** (JCM).[38]

According to the JCM, any job can be described in terms of five core job dimensions, defined as follows:

1. **Skill variety**—the degree to which the job requires a variety of different activities so the worker can use a number of different skills and talents
2. **Task identity**—the degree to which the job requires completion of a whole and identifiable piece of work
3. **Task significance**—the degree to which the job has a substantial impact on the lives or work of other people
4. **Autonomy**—the degree to which the job provides substantial freedom, independence, and discretion to the individual in scheduling the work and in determining the procedures to be used in carrying it out
5. **Feedback**—the degree to which carrying out the work activities required by the job results in the individual obtaining direct and clear information about the effectiveness of his or her performance.

Table 7–1 offers examples of job activities that rate high and low for each characteristic.

Figure 7–6 presents the model. Notice how the first three dimensions—skill variety, task identity, and task significance—combine to create meaning-

Job Characteristics Model Identifies five job characteristics and their relationship to personal and work outcomes.

Skill Variety The degree to which the job requires a variety of different activities.

Task Identity The degree to which the job requires completion of a whole and identifiable piece of work.

Task Significance The degree to which the job has a substantial impact on the lives or work of other people.

Autonomy The degree to which the job provides substantial freedom and discretion to the individual in scheduling the work and in determining the procedures to be used in carrying it out.

Feedback The degree to which carrying out the work activities required by a job results in the individual obtaining direct and clear information about the effectiveness of his or her performance.

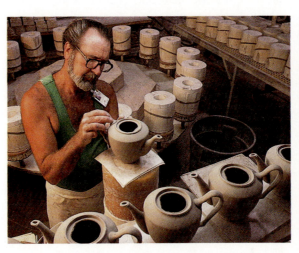

A Lenox craftsman applies finishing touches to fine china. An employee at Sanford, which makes Sharpie marking pens, caps pens on an assembly line. The former job scores higher in motivating potential than does the latter. Why?   Left, John S. Abbott; right, David Walberg.

TABLE 7-1   Examples of High and Low Job Characteristics

Skill Variety

High variety	The owner-operator of a garage who does electrical repair, rebuilds engines, does body work, and interacts with customers
Low variety	A body shop worker who sprays paint eight hours a day

Task Identity

High identity	A cabinetmaker who designs a piece of furniture, selects the wood, builds the object, and finishes it to perfection
Low identity	A worker in a furniture factory who operates a lathe solely to make table legs

Task Significance

High significance	Nursing the sick in a hospital intensive care unit
Low significance	Sweeping hospital floors

Autonomy

High autonomy	A telephone installer who schedules his or her own work for the day, makes visits without supervision, and decides on the most effective techniques for a particular installation
Low autonomy	A telephone operator who must handle calls as they come according to a routine, highly specified procedure

Feedback

High feedback	An electronics factory worker who assembles a radio and then tests it to determine if it operates properly
Low feedback	An electronics factory worker who assembles a radio and then routes it to a quality control inspector who tests it for proper operation and makes needed adjustments

Source: G. Johns, *Organizational Behavior: Understanding Life at Work,* 2nd ed. (Glenview, IL: Scott, Foresman, 1988), p. 198. With permission.

ful work. That is, if these three characteristics exist in a job, we can predict that the incumbent will view the job as being important, valuable, and worthwhile. Notice, too, that jobs that possess autonomy give the job incumbent a feeling of personal responsibility for the results and that, if a job provides feedback, the employee will know how effectively he or she is performing. From a motivational standpoint, the model says that internal rewards are obtained by an individual when he *learns* (knowledge of results) that he *personally* (experienced responsibility) has performed well on a task that he *cares* about (experienced meaningfulness).[39] The more that these three psychological states are present, the greater will be the employee's motivation, performance, and satisfaction, and the lower his or her absenteeism and likelihood of leaving the organization. As Figure 7–6 shows, the links between the job dimensions and the outcomes are moderated or adjusted by the strength of the individual's growth need, that is, by the employee's desire for self-esteem and self-actualization. This means that individuals with a high growth need are more likely to experience the psychological states when their jobs are enriched than are their counterparts with a low growth need. Moreover, they will respond more positively to the psychological states, when they are present, than will low-growth-need individuals.

Motivating Potential Score A predictive index suggesting the motivation potential in a job.

The core dimensions can be combined into a single predictive index, called the **motivating potential score** (MPS). Its computation is shown in Figure 7–7.

Jobs that are high on motivating potential must be high on at least one of the three factors that lead to experienced meaningfulness, and they must be high on both autonomy and feedback. If jobs score high on motivating potential, the model predicts that motivation, performance, and satisfaction

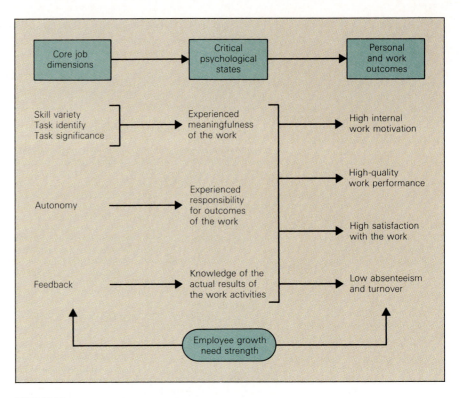

FIGURE 7–6   The Job Characteristics Model

Source: J. R. Hackman, "Work Design," in *Improving Life at Work,* eds. J. R. Hackman and J. L. Suttle (Glenview, IL: Scott, Foresman and Company, 1977), p. 129.

will be positively affected, while the likelihood of absence and turnover is lessened.

The job characteristics model has been well researched. Most of the evidence supports the general framework of the theory—that is, there is a multiple set of job characteristics and these characteristics impact behavioral outcomes.[40] But there is still considerable debate around the five specific core dimensions in the JCM, the multiplicative properties of the MPS, and whether other moderating variables may not be as good or better than growth-need strength.

FIGURE 7–7   Computing a Motivating Potential Score

$$\text{Motivating Potential Score (MPS)} = \left[\frac{\text{Skill variety} + \text{Task identity} + \text{Task significance}}{3} \right] \times \text{Autonomy} \times \text{Feedback}$$

There is some question whether task identity adds to the model's predictive ability,[41] and there is evidence suggesting that skill variety may be redundant with autonomy.[42] Further, a number of studies have found that by adding all the variables in the MPS, rather than adding some and multiplying by others, the MPS becomes a better predictor of work outcomes.[43] Finally, while the strength of an individual's growth needs has been found to be a meaningful moderating variable in many studies,[44] other variables—such as the presence or absence of social cues, perceived equity with comparison groups, and propensity to assimilate work experience[45]—have also been found to moderate the job characteristics–outcome relationship. Given the current state of research on moderating variables, one should be cautious in unequivocally accepting growth-need strength as originally included in the JCM.

Where does this leave us? Given the current state of evidence, we can make the following statements with relative confidence: (1) People who work on jobs with high core job dimensions are generally more motivated, satisfied, and productive than are those who do not; and (2) job dimensions operate through the psychological states in influencing personal and work outcome variables rather than influencing them directly.[46]

Goal-Setting Theory

Gene Broadwater, coach of the Hamilton High School cross-country team, gave his squad these last words before they approached the line for the league championship race: "Each one of you is physically ready. Now, get out there and do your best. No one can ever ask more of you than that."

You've heard the phrase a number of times yourself: "Just do your best. That's all anyone can ask for." But what does "do your best" mean? Do we ever know if we've achieved that vague goal? Would the cross-country runners have recorded faster times if Coach Broadwater had given each a specific goal to shoot for? Might you have done better in your high school English class if your parents had said, "You should strive for eighty-five percent or higher on all your work in English" rather than telling you to "do your best"? The research on **goal setting** addresses these issues, and the findings, as you will see, are impressive in terms of the impact specific and challenging goals have on performance.

In the late 1960s, Edwin Locke proposed that intentions to work toward a goal are a major source of work motivation.[47] That is, goals tell an employee what needs to be done and how much effort will need to be expended.[48] The evidence strongly supports the value of goals. More to the point, we can say that specific goals increase performance; that difficult goals, when accepted, result in higher performance than do easy goals; and that feedback leads to higher performance than does nonfeedback.[49]

Specific hard goals produce a higher level of output than does a generalized goal of "do your best." The specificity of the goal itself acts as an internal stimulus. For instance, when a trucker commits to making eighteen round-trip hauls between Baltimore and Washington, D.C., each week, this intention gives him a specific objective to reach for. We can say that, all things being equal, the trucker with a specific goal will outperform his counterpart operating with no goals or the generalized goal of "do your best."

If factors like ability and acceptance of the goals are held constant, we can also state that the more difficult the goal, the higher the level of performance. However, it's logical to assume that easier goals are more likely

Goal-setting Theory The theory that specific and difficult goals lead to higher performance.

to be accepted. But once an employee accepts a hard task, he or she will exert a high level of effort until it is achieved, lowered, or abandoned.

People will do better when they get feedback on how well they are progressing toward their goals, because feedback helps to identify discrepancies between what they have done and what they want to do; that is, feedback acts to guide behavior. But all feedback is not equally potent. Self-generated feedback—where the employee is able to monitor his or her own progress—has been shown to be a more powerful motivator than externally generated feedback.[50]

If employees have the opportunity to participate in the setting of their own goals, will they try harder? The evidence is mixed regarding the superiority of participative over assigned goals.[51] In some cases, participatively set goals elicit superior performance, while in other cases individuals performed best when assigned goals by their boss. But a major advantage of participation may be in increasing acceptance of the goal, itself, as a desirable one to work toward.[52] As we noted, resistance is greater when goals are difficult. If people participate in goal setting, they are more likely to accept even a difficult goal than if they are arbitrarily assigned it by their boss. The reason is that individuals are more committed to choices in which they have a part. Thus, although participative goals may have no superiority over assigned goals when acceptance is taken as a given, participation does increase the probability that more difficult goals will be agreed to and acted upon.

Our overall conclusion is that intentions—as articulated in terms of hard and specific goals—are a potent motivating force. They do lead to higher performance. However, there is no evidence that such goals are associated with increased job satisfaction.[53]

Reinforcement Theory

Reinforcement Theory
Behavior is a function of its consequences.

A counterpoint to goal-setting theory is **reinforcement theory.** The former is a cognitive approach, proposing that an individual's purposes direct his or her action. In reinforcement theory we have a behavioristic approach, which argues that reinforcement conditions behavior. The two are clearly at odds philosophically. Reinforcement theorists see behavior as being environmentally caused. You need not be concerned, they would argue, with internal cognitive events; what controls behavior are reinforcers—any consequence that, when immediately following a response, increases the probability that the behavior will be repeated.

Reinforcement theory ignores the inner state of the individual and concentrates solely on what happens to a person when he or she takes some action. Because it does not concern itself with what initiates behavior, it is not, strictly speaking, a theory of motivation. But it does provide a powerful means of analysis of what controls behavior, and it is for this reason that it is typically considered in discussions of motivation.[54]

We discussed the reinforcement process in detail in Chapter 4. We showed how using reinforcers to condition behavior gives us considerable insight into how people learn. Yet we cannot ignore the fact that reinforcement has a wide following as a motivational device. In its pure form, however, reinforcement theory ignores feelings, attitudes, expectations, and other cognitive variables that are known to impact behavior. In fact, some researchers look at the same experiments that reinforcement theorists use to support their position and interpret the findings in a cognitive framework.[55]

Reinforcement is undoubtedly an important influence on behavior, but few scholars are prepared to argue that it is the *only* influence. The behaviors you engage in at work and the amount of effort you allocate to each task *is* affected by the consequences that follow from your behavior. If you are consistently reprimanded for outproducing your colleagues, you will likely reduce your productivity. But your lower productivity may also be explained in terms of goals, inequity, or expectancies.

Equity Theory

Jane Pearson graduated last year from the State University with a degree in accounting. After interviews with a number of organizations on campus, she accepted a position with one of the nation's largest public accounting firms and was assigned to their Boston office. Jane was very pleased with the offer she received: challenging work with a prestigious firm, an excellent opportunity to gain important experience, and the highest salary any accounting major at State was offered last year—$2,600 a month. But Jane was the top student in her class; she was ambitious and articulate and fully expected to receive a commensurate salary.

Twelve months have passed since Jane joined her employer. The work has proved to be as challenging and satisfying as she had hoped. Her employer is extremely pleased with her performance; in fact, she recently received a $200-a-month raise. However, Jane's motivational level has dropped dramatically in the past few weeks. Why? Her employer has just hired a fresh college graduate out of State University, who lacks the one-year experience Jane has gained, for $2,850 a month—$50 more than Jane now makes! It would be an understatement to describe Jane in any other terms than livid. Jane is even talking about looking for another job.

Jane's situation illustrates the role that equity plays in motivation. Employees make comparisons of their job inputs and outcomes relative to those of others. We perceive what we get from a job situation (outcomes) in relation to what we put into it (inputs), and then we compare our outcome–input ratio with the outcome–input ratio of relevant others. This is shown in Table 7–2. If we perceive our ratio to be equal to the relevant others with whom we compare ourselves, a state of equity is said to exist. We perceive our situation as fair—that justice prevails. If the ratios are unequal, inequality exists; that is, we tend to view ourselves as underrewarded or overrewarded. J. Stacy Adams proposed that an equity process takes place in which people who view any inequity as aversive will attempt to correct it.[56]

TABLE 7–2   Equity Theory

Ratio Comparisons	Perception
$\dfrac{O}{I_A} < \dfrac{O}{I_B}$	Inequity due to being underrewarded
$\dfrac{O}{I_A} = \dfrac{O}{I_B}$	Equity
$\dfrac{O}{I_A} > \dfrac{O}{I_B}$	Inequity due to being overrewarded

where $\dfrac{O}{I_A}$ represents the employee and $\dfrac{O}{I_B}$ represents relevant others

Equity Theory Individuals compare their job inputs and outcomes with those of others and then respond so as to eliminate any inequities.

The referent that an employee selects adds to the complexity of **equity theory.** Evidence indicates that the referent chosen is an important variable in equity theory.[57] There are four referent comparisons that an employee can use:

1. *Self-inside*—An employee's experiences in a different position inside his or her current organization
2. *Self-outside*—An employee's experiences in a situation or position outside his or her current organization
3. *Other-inside*—Another individual or group of individuals inside the employee's organization
4. *Other-outside*—Another individual or group of individuals outside the employee's organization

So employees might compare themselves to friends, neighbors, co-workers, colleagues in other organizations, or past jobs they themselves have had. Which referent an employee chooses will be influenced by the information the employee holds about referents as well as the attractiveness of the referent. This has led to focusing on three moderating variables—the employee's salary level, amount of education, and length of tenure.[58] Employees with higher salaries and more education tend to be more cosmopolitan and have better information; thus, they're more likely to make comparisons with outsiders. Employees with short tenure in their current organization tend to have little information about others inside the organization, so they rely on their own personal experiences. On the other hand, employees with long tenure rely more heavily on co-workers for comparisons.

Based on equity theory, when employees perceive an inequity they can be predicted to make one of six choices:[59]

Most chief executives of public corporations are equity sensitive, especially since their compensation is widely publicized in business periodicals. In 1989, Martin S. Davis, CEO of Paramount Communicatons, earned $11,635,000—$4,095,000 in salary and bonus plus another $7,540,000 in long-term compensation. CEOs at other entertainment firms like Walt Disney and MCA undoubtedly compare their companies' performance to Paramount and then contrast their total pay and benefits package to Davis's. Gerd Ludwig/Woodfin Camp & Associates.

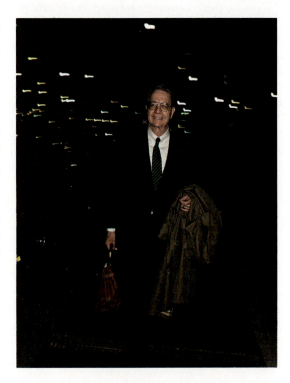

1. Change their inputs (for example, don't exert as much effort)
2. Change their outcomes (for example, individuals paid on a piece-rate basis can increase their pay by producing a higher quantity of units of lower quality)
3. Distort perceptions of self (for example, "I used to think I worked at a moderate pace but now I realize that I work a lot harder than everyone else.")
4. Distort perceptions of others (for example, "Mike's job isn't as desirable as I previously thought it was.")
5. Choose a different referent (for example, "I may not make as much as my brother-in-law, but I'm doing a lot better than my Dad did when he was my age.")
6. Leave the field (for example, quit the job)

Equity theory recognizes that individuals are concerned not only with the absolute amount of rewards they receive for their efforts, but also with the relationship of this amount to what others receive. They make judgments as to the relationship between their inputs and outcomes and the inputs and outcomes of others. Based on one's inputs, such as effort, experience, education, and competence, one compares outcomes such as salary levels, raises, recognition, and other factors. When people perceive an imbalance in their outcome–input ratio relative to others, tension is created. This tension provides the basis for motivation, as people strive for what they perceive as equity and fairness.

Specifically, the theory establishes four propositions relating to inequitable pay:

1. *Given payment by time, overrewarded employees will produce more than will equitably paid employees.* Hourly and salaried employees will generate high quantity or quality of production in order to increase the input side of the ratio and bring about equity.
2. *Given payment by quantity of production, overrewarded employees will produce fewer, but higher-quality, units than will equitably paid employees.* Individuals paid on a piece-rate basis will increase their effort to achieve equity, which can result in greater quality or quantity. However, increases in quantity will only increase inequity since every unit produced results in further overpayment. Therefore, effort is directed toward increasing quality rather than increasing quantity.
3. *Given payment by time, underrewarded employees will produce less or poorer quality of output.* Effort will be decreased, which will bring about lower productivity or poorer-quality output than equitably paid subjects.
4. *Given payment by quantity of production, underrewarded employees will produce a large number of low-quality units in comparison with equitably paid employees.* Employees on piece-rate pay plans can bring about equity because trading off quality of output for quantity will result in an increase in rewards with little or no increase in contributions.

These propositions have generally been supported, with a few minor qualifications.[60] First, inequities created by overpayment do not seem to have a very significant impact on behavior in most work situations. Apparently, people have a great deal more tolerance of overpayment inequities than of underpayment inequities, or are better able to rationalize them. Second, not all people are equity-sensitive. For example, there is a small part of the working population who actually prefer that their outcome–input ratio be less than the referent comparison. Predictions from equity theory are not likely to be very accurate with these "benevolent types."

In conclusion, equity theory demonstrates that, for most employees, motivation is influenced significantly by relative rewards as well as by absolute rewards. But some key issues are still unclear.[61] For instance, how do employees handle conflicting equity signals, such as when unions point to other employee groups who are substantially *better off,* while management argues how much things have *improved?* How do employees define inputs and outcomes? How do they combine and weigh their inputs and outcomes to arrive at totals? When and how do the factors change over time? Yet, regardless of these problems, equity theory continues to offer us some important insights into employee motivation.

Expectancy Theory

Currently, one of the most widely accepted explanations of motivation is Victor Vroom's **expectancy theory**.[62] Although it has its critics,[63] most of the research evidence is supportive of the theory.[64]

Essentially, the expectancy theory argues that the strength of a tendency to act in a certain way depends on the strength of an expectation that the act will be followed by a given outcome and on the attractiveness of that outcome to the individual. It includes three variables or relationships.[65]

1. *Attractiveness*—the importance that the individual places on the potential outcome or reward that can be achieved on the job. This considers the unsatisfied needs of the individual.
2. *Performance–reward linkage*—the degree to which the individual believes that performing at a particular level will lead to the attainment of a desired outcome.
3. *Effort–performance linkage*—the perceived probability by the individual that exerting a given amount of effort will lead to performance.

While this may sound pretty complex, it really is not that difficult to visualize. Whether one has the desire to produce at any given time depends on one's particular goals and one's perception of the relative worth of performance as a path to the attainment of these goals.

Figure 7–8 is a considerable simplification of expectancy theory, but it expresses its major contentions. The strength of a person's motivation to perform (effort) depends on how strongly he or she believes that he or she can achieve attempted tasks. If the person achieves this goal (performance), will he or she be adequately rewarded and, if rewarded by the organization, will the reward satisfy the person's individual goals? Let us consider the four steps inherent in the theory.

First, what perceived outcomes does the job offer the employee? Outcomes may be positive: pay, security, companionship, trust, fringe benefits, a chance to use talent or skills, congenial relationships. On the other hand,

Most Professional Athletes Seem Very Equity Sensitive

No early season in professional sports would be complete without some athletes "holding out" for more money. And are these athletes impoverished? Hardly! They are people making half-million or million-dollar-a-year salaries. Do they argue that they can't make ends meet on their current pay? Not very often! Their arguments are almost always couched in terms of equity.

Take the case of San Diego Padre baseball star Tony Gwynn. In 1987, the outfielder signed a two-year contract extension that locked him into the Padres until 1992. His pay? One million dollars a year! A lot of money at the time, but Gwynn was a lot of ballplayer. After only five full seasons in the big leagues, he was a five-time All-Star and four-time batting champion. But baseball salaries exploded in the next couple of years. The result was that, in 1990, Gwynn had become only the *seventh*-highest paid Padre player!

Was Gwynn upset? You bet he was! For example, in December 1989 the Padres signed another outfielder, Joe Carter. Acquired as a free agent, Carter signed a three-year, $9.2 million contract with the Padres. Gwynn's response? "Joe Carter can't hit for average the way I can. He's considered just an average outfielder. And he's never made the All-Star team. I mean, Joe is one of my dearest friends, but I don't think anyone in this game is $2 million better than I am. . . . Nowadays, utility players are making more than me, and that just doesn't seem right. . . . It's not fair, but they got me signed on the dotted line, and there's nothing I can do." At the same time, Gwynn's agent asked, "Where's the money for the guys who are loyal and dedicated to the organization? My God, who's a better organization man than Tony?"

Even though you and I might be euphoric over the opportunity to work six months a year for a couple of hundred thousand dollars a month—exclusive of earnings from endorsements and other promotional activities—professional athletes like Tony Gwynn are rarely concerned with the absolute dollars they receive. What they are doing is comparing themselves to other athletes who play similar positions and who have comparable or less impressive accomplishments. When they see a pay discrepancy, they seek equity. And when the management of these professional franchises fail to correct these inequities, they frequently find themselves with disgruntled and demotivated athletes.

anxiety, harsh supervision, threat of dismissal. Importantly, reality is not relevant here; the critical issue is what the individual employee *perceives* the outcome to be, regardless of whether or not his or her perceptions are accurate. employees may view the outcomes as negative: fatigue, boredom, frustration,

FIGURE 7–8   Simplified Expectancy Model

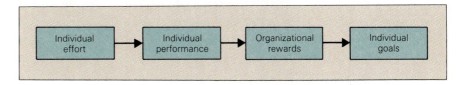

Second, how attractive do employees consider these outcomes? Are they valued positively, negatively, or neutrally? This obviously is an internal issue to the individual and considers his or her personal values, personality, and needs. The individual who finds a particular outcome attractive—that is, positively valued—would prefer attaining it to not attaining it. Others may find it negative and, therefore, prefer not attaining it to attaining it. Still others may be neutral.

Third, what kind of behavior must the employee produce in order to achieve these outcomes? The outcomes are not likely to have any effect on the individual employee's performance unless the employee knows, clearly and unambiguously, what he or she must do in order to achieve them. For example, what is "doing well" in terms of performance appraisal? What are the criteria the employee's performance will be judged on?

Fourth and last, how does the employee view his or her chances of doing what is asked? After the employee has considered his or her own competencies and ability to control those variables that will determine success, what probability does he or she place on successful attainment?[66]

The key to expectancy theory, therefore, is the understanding of an individual's goals and the linkage between effort and performance, between performance and rewards, and, finally, between the rewards and individual goal satisfaction. As a contingency model, expectancy theory recognizes that there is no universal principle for explaining everyone's motivations. Additionally, just because we understand what needs a person seeks to satisfy does not ensure that the individual himself perceives high performance as necessarily leading to the satisfaction of these needs.

Let us summarize some of the issues expectancy theory has brought forward. First, it emphasizes payoffs or rewards. As a result, we have to believe

Expectancy theory can be used to better understand student motivation. It would say that studying and preparation for a class (effort) is conditioned by its resulting in answering questions on exams correctly (performance), which will produce a high grade (reward), which will lead to the security, prestige, and other benefits that accrue from obtaining a desired job or getting into a good graduate school (individual goal). Among other things, for students to exert a high level of effort, they must believe that increased preparation is related to grades, that the tests fairly measure what they know, and they must value high grades.   Four By Five.

that the rewards the organization is offering align with what the employee wants. It is a theory based on self-interest, wherein each individual seeks to maximize his or her expected satisfaction: "Expectancy theory is a form of calculative, psychological *hedonism* in which the ultimate motive of every human act is asserted to be the maximization of pleasure and/or the minimization of pain."[67] Second, we have to be concerned with the attractiveness of rewards, which requires an understanding and knowledge of what value the individual puts on organizational payoffs. We want to reward the individual with those things he or she values positively. Third, expectancy theory emphasizes expected behaviors. Does the person know what is expected and how he or she will be appraised? Finally, the theory is concerned with expectations. What is realistic or rational is irrelevant. An individual's own expectations of performance, reward, and goal satisfaction outcomes will determine his or her level of effort, not the objective outcomes themselves.

Does the expectancy theory work? Attempts to validate the theory have been complicated by methodological, criterion, and measurement problems. As a result, many published studies that purport to support or negate the theory must be viewed with caution. Importantly, most studies have failed to replicate the methodology as it was originally proposed. For example, the theory proposes to explain different levels of effort within the same person under different circumstances, but almost all replication studies have looked at different people. By correcting for this flaw, support for the validity of the expectancy theory has been greatly improved.[68] Some critics suggest that the theory has only limited use, arguing that it tends to be more valid for predicting in situations where effort–performance and performance–reward linkages are clearly perceived by the individual.[69] Since few individuals perceive a high correlation between performance and rewards in their jobs, the theory tends to be idealistic. If organizations actually rewarded individuals for performance, rather than criteria such as seniority, effort, skill level, or job difficulty, then the theory's validity might be considerably greater. However, rather than invalidating expectancy theory, this criticism can be used in support of the theory and for explaining why a large segment of the work force exerts a minimal level of effort in carrying out their job responsibilities.

Don't Forget Ability and Opportunity

Robin and Chris both graduated from college a couple of years ago with their degrees in elementary education. They each took jobs as first-grade teachers, but in different school districts. Robin immediately confronted a number of obstacles on the job: a large class (forty-two students), a small and dingy classroom, and inadequate supplies. Chris' situation couldn't have been more different. He had only fifteen students in his class, plus a teaching aide for fifteen hours each week, a modern and well-lighted room, a well-stocked supply cabinet, the unlimited use of a personal computer for class planning, and a highly supportive principal. Not surprisingly, at the end of their first school year, Chris had been considerably more effective as a teacher than had Robin.

The preceding episode illustrates an obvious but often overlooked fact. Success on a job is facilitated or hindered by the existence or absence of support resources.

A popular, although arguably simplistic, way of thinking about employee performance is as a function of the interaction of ability and motivation; that

Different Strokes for Different Folks

What motivates me doesn't necessarily motivate you. Expectancy theory recognizes this by proposing that rewards be tailored to the individual. But can we generalize among subgroups of employees as to what they might place greater importance upon? A recent study of 1,000 employees asked them to rank order ten work-related factors.[70] Their answers were then tabulated by subgroups on the basis of sex, age, income level, job type, and organization level. The results are shown in Table 7–3.

While the results suggest that there is a great deal of similarity in preferences, especially between men and women, there are a few important differences. For instance, younger workers, those with low incomes, and those in lower, nonsupervisory positions are most concerned with money. Job security also is significantly less important to older workers and to those higher in the organization. If nothing else, these results challenge those who might simplistically assume that *everybody* considers factors such as good pay and promotion in the organization to be a high priority.

TABLE 7–3   What Workers Want, Ranked by Subgroups[1]

	Sex		Age				Income Level				Job Type				Organization Level		
	Men	Women	Under 30	31–40	41–50	Over 50	Under $12,000	$12,001–$18,000	$18,001–$25,000	Over $25,000	Blue-Collar Unskilled	Blue-Collar Skilled	White-Collar Unskilled	White-Collar Skilled	Lower Nonsupervisory	Middle Nonsupervisory	Higher Nonsupervisory
Interesting work	2	2	4	2	3	1	5	2	1	1	2	1	1	2	3	1	1
Full appreciation of work done	1	1	5	3	2	2	4	3	3	2	1	6	3	1	4	2	2
Feeling of being in on things	3	3	6	4	1	3	6	1	2	4	5	2	5	4	5	3	3
Job security	5	4	2	1	4	7	2	4	4	3	4	3	7	5	2	4	6
Good wages	4	5	1	5	5	8	1	5	6	8	3	4	6	6	1	6	8
Promotion and growth in organization	6	6	3	6	8	9	3	6	5	7	6	5	4	3	6	5	5
Good working conditions	7	7	7	7	7	4	8	7	7	6	9	7	2	7	7	7	4
Personal loyalty to employees	8	8	9	9	6	5	7	8	8	5	8	9	9	8	8	8	7
Tactful discipline	9	9	8	10	9	10	10	9	9	10	7	10	10	9	9	9	10
Sympathetic help with personal problems	10	10	10	8	10	6	9	10	10	9	10	8	8	10	10	10	9

[1]Ranked from 1 (highest) to 10 (lowest).

Source: Reprinted from *Business Horizons*, September–October 1987. Copyright 1987 by the Foundation for the School of Business at Indiana University. Used with permission. K. A. Kovach, "What Motivates Employees? Workers and Supervisors Give Different Answers," *Business Horizons*, September–October 1987, p. 61.

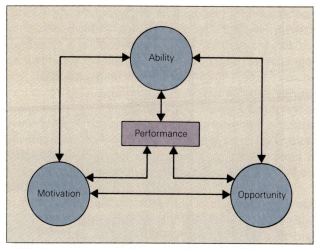

FIGURE 7–9   Performance Dimensions

Source: Adapted from M. Blumberg and C. D. Pringle, "The Missing Opportunity in Organizational Research: Some Implications for a Theory of Work Performance," *Academy of Management Review,* October 1982, p. 565.

Opportunity to Perform High levels of performance are partially a function of an absence of obstacles that constrain the employee.

is, performance = $f(A \times M)$. If either is inadequate, performance will be negatively affected. This helps to explain, for instance, the hardworking athlete or student with modest abilities who consistently outperforms his or her more gifted, but lazy, rival. So, as we noted in Chapter 4, an individual's intelligence and skills (subsumed under the label "ability") must be considered in addition to motivation if we are to be able to accurately explain and predict employee performance. But a piece of the puzzle is still missing. We need to add **opportunity to perform** to our equation—performance = $f(A \times M \times O)$.[71] Even though an individual may be willing and able, there may be obstacles that constrain performance. This is shown in Figure 7–9.

When you attempt to assess why an employee may not be performing to the level that you believe he or she is capable of, take a look at the work environment to see if it's supportive. Does the employee have adequate tools, equipment, materials, and supplies; does the employee have favorable working conditions, helpful co-workers, supportive rules and procedures to work under, adequate time to do a good job, and the like? If not, performance will suffer.

INTEGRATING CONTEMPORARY THEORIES OF MOTIVATION

We've looked at a lot of motivation theories in this chapter. The fact that a number of these theories have been supported only complicates the matter. How simple it would have been if, after presenting half-a-dozen theories, only one was found valid. So the challenge is now to tie these theories together to help you understand their interrelationship.

Figure 7–10 presents a model that integrates much of what we know about motivation. Its basic foundation is the simplified expectancy model shown in Figure 7–8. Let's work through Figure 7–10.

Motivation Theories Are Culture-Bound

Most current motivation theories were developed in the United States by Americans and about Americans.[72] Maybe the most blatant pro-American characteristics inherent in these theories is the strong emphasis on what we defined in Chapter 3 as individualism and masculinity. For instance, both goal-setting and expectancy theories emphasize goal accomplishment as well as rational and individual thought. Let's take a look at how this bias has affected a few of the motivation theories introduced in this chapter.

Maslow's need hierarchy argues that people start at the physiological level and then move progressively up the hierarchy in this order: physiological, safety, social, esteem, and self-actualization. This hierarchy, if it has any application at all, aligns with American culture. In countries like Japan, Greece, or Mexico, where uncertainty avoidance characteristics are strong, security needs would be on top of the need hierarchy. Countries that score high on femininity characteristics—Denmark, Sweden, Norway, the Netherlands, and Finland—would have social needs on top.[73] We would predict, for instance, that group work will motivate employees more when the country's culture scores high on the femininity criterion.

Another motivation concept that clearly has an American bias is the achievement need. The view that a high achievement need acts as an internal motivator presupposes two cultural characteristics—a willingness to accept a moderate degree of risk (which excludes countries with strong uncertainty avoidance characteristics) and a concern with performance (which applies almost singularly to countries with strong masculinity characteristics). This combination is found in Anglo-American countries like the United States, Canada, and Great Britain.[74] On the other hand, these characteristics are relatively absent in countries such as Chile and Portugal.

Goal-setting certainly is also culture-bound. It is well adapted to the United States because its key components align reasonably well with American culture. It assumes that subordinates will be reasonably independent (not too high a score on power distance), that managers and subordinates will seek challenging goals (low in uncertainty avoidance), and that performance is considered important by both (high in masculinity). Goal-setting's recommendations are not likely to increase motivation in countries such as Yugoslavia, Portugal, and Chile, where the opposite conditions exist.

REINFORCEMENT THEORY   This theory has an impressive record for predicting factors like quality and quantity of work, persistence of effort, absenteeism, tardiness, and accident rates. It does not offer much insight into employee satisfaction or the decision to quit.

EQUITY THEORY   Equity theory deals with all four dependent variables. However, it is strongest when predicting absence and turnover behaviors and weak when predicting differences in employee productivity.

EXPECTANCY THEORY   Our final theory focused on performance variables. It has proven to offer a relatively powerful explanation of employee productivity, absenteeism, and turnover. But expectancy theory assumes that employees have few constraints on their decision discretion. It makes many of

TABLE 7–4   **Power of Motivation Theories**[a]

			THEORIES			
VARIABLE	**Need**	**Task Characteristics**	**Goal-setting**	**\Reinforcement**	**Equity**	**Expectancy**
Productivity	3[b]	3[c]	5	3	3	4[d]
Absenteeism		3		4	4	4
Turnover		3			4	5
Satisfaction	2	4			2	

[a]Theories are rated on a scale of 1 to 5, 5 being highest.
[b]Applies to individuals with a high need to achieve.
[c]Applies to individuals with a high need for growth.
[d]Limited value in jobs where employees have little discretionary choice.
Source: Based on F. J. Landy and W. S. Becker, "Motivation Theory Reconsidered," in L. L. Cummings and B. M. Staw (eds.), *Research in Organizational Behavior*, Vol. 9 (Greenwich, CT: JAI Press, 1987), p. 33.

the same assumptions that the optimizing model makes about individual decision making (see Chapter 5). This acts to restrict its applicability.

For major decisions, like accepting or resigning from a job, expectancy theory works well, because people don't rush into decisions of this nature. They're more prone to take the time to carefully consider the costs and benefits of all the alternatives. But expectancy theory is *not* a very good explanation for more typical types of work behavior, especially for individuals in lower-level jobs, because such jobs come with considerable limitations imposed by work methods, supervisors, and company policies. We would conclude, therefore, that expectancy theory's power in explaining employee productivity increases where the jobs being performed are more complex and higher in the organization where discretion is greater.

SUMMARY   Table 7–4 attempts to summarize what we know about the power of the more well-known motivation theories to explain and predict our four dependent variables. While based on a wealth of research, it also includes some subjective judgments. However, it does provide a reasonable guide through the motivation theory maze.

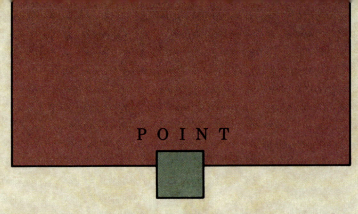

POINT

Money Motivates!

The importance of money as a motivator has been consistently downgraded by most behavioral scientists. They prefer to point out the value of challenging jobs, goals, participation in decision making, feedback, cohesive work groups, and other nonmonetary factors as stimulants to employee motivation. We will argue otherwise here—that money is *the* crucial incentive to work motivation. As a medium of exchange, it is the vehicle by which employees can purchase the numerous need-satisfying things they desire. Further, money also performs the function of a scorecard, by which employees assess the value that the organization places on their services and by which employees can compare their value to others.

Money's value as a medium of exchange is obvious. People may not work *only* for money, but take the money away and how many people would come to work? For the vast majority of the work force, a regular paycheck is absolutely necessary in order to meet their basic physiological and safety needs.

As equity theory suggests, money has symbolic value in addition to its exchange value. We use pay as the primary outcome against which we compare our inputs to determine if we are being treated equitably. That an organization pays one executive $80,000 a year and another $95,000 means more than the latter's merely earning $15,000 a year more. It is a message, from the organization to both employees, of how much it values the contribution of each.

In addition to equity theory, both reinforcement and expectancy theories attest to the value of money as a motivator. In the former, if pay is contingent on performance, it will encourage workers to high levels of effort. Consistent with expectancy theory, money will motivate to the extent that it is seen as being able to satisfy an individual's personal goals and is perceived as being dependent upon performance criteria.

The best case for money as a motivator is a review of studies done by Edwin Locke of the University of Maryland.* Locke looked at four methods of motivating employee performance: money, goal setting, participation in decision making, and redesigning jobs to give workers more challenge and responsibility. He found that the average improvement from money was thirty percent; goal setting increased performance sixteen percent; participation improved performance by less than one percent; and job redesign positively impacted performance by an average of seventeen percent. Moreover, every study Locke reviewed that used money as a method of motivation resulted in some improvement in employee performance. Such evidence demonstrates that money may not be the *only* motivator, but it is difficult to argue that it *doesn't* motivate!

*E. A. Locke et al., "The Relative Effectiveness of Four Methods of Motivating Employee Performance," in *Changes in Working Life*, eds. K. D. Duncan, M. M. Gruneberg, and D. Wallis (London: John Wiley, Ltd., 1980), pp. 363–83.

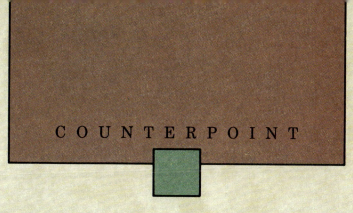

Money Doesn't Motivate Most Employees Today!

Money can motivate *some* people under *some* conditions. So the issue isn't really whether or not money *can* motivate. The answer to that is: It can! The more relevant question is: Does money motivate most employees in the work force today to higher performance? The answer to this question, we'll argue, is "No."

For money to motivate an individual's performance, certain conditions must be met. First, money must be important to the individual. Second, money must be perceived by the individual as being a direct reward for performance. Third, the marginal amount of money offered for the performance must be perceived by the individual as being significant. Finally, management must have the discretion to reward high performers with more money. Let's take a look at each of these conditions.

Money is not important to all employees. High achievers, for instance, are intrinsically motivated. Money should have little impact on these people. Similarly, money is relevant to those individuals with strong lower-order needs; but for most of the work force, their lower-order needs are substantially satisfied.

Money would motivate if employees perceived a strong linkage between performance and rewards in organizations. Unfortunately, pay increases are far more often determined by community pay standards, the national cost-of-living index, and the organization's current and future financial prospects than by each employee's level of performance.

For money to motivate, the marginal difference in pay increases between a high performer and an average performer must be significant. In practice, it rarely is. For instance, a high-performing employee who currently is earning $30,000 a year is given a $200 a month raise. After taxes, that amounts to about $35 a week. But this employee's $30,000-a-year co-worker, who is an average performer, is rarely passed over at raise time. Instead of getting an eight percent raise, he is likely to get half of that. The net difference in their weekly paychecks is probably less than $20. How much motivation is there in knowing that if you work really hard you're going to end up with $20 a week more than someone who is doing just enough to get by? For a large number of people, not much!

Our last point relates to the degree of discretion that managers have in being able to reward high performers. Where unions exist, that discretion is almost zero. Pay is determined through collective bargaining and is allocated by job title and seniority, not level of performance. In nonunionized environments, the organization's compensation policies will constrain managerial discretion. Each job typically has a pay grade. So a Systems Analyst III can earn between $3,525 and $4,140 a month. No matter how good a job that analyst does, her boss cannot pay her more than $4,140 a month. Similarly, no matter how poorly someone does in that job, he will earn at least $3,525 a month. In most organizations, managers have a very small area of discretion within which they can reward their higher-performing employees. So money might be theoretically capable of motivating employees to higher levels of performance, but most managers aren't given enough flexibility to do much about it.

1. Define motivation. Describe the motivation process.

2. What are the implications of Theories X and Y to motivation practices?

3. Compare and contrast Maslow's hierarchy of needs theory with (a) Alderfer's ERG theory, and (b) Herzberg's motivation-hygiene theory.

4. Describe the three needs isolated by McClelland. How are they related to worker behavior?

5. "The cognitive evaluation theory is contradictory to reinforcement and expectancy theories." Do you agree or disagree? Explain.

6. According to the job characteristics model, how does a job score high in motivating potential?

7. "Goal setting is part of both reinforcement and expectancy theories." Do you agree or disagree? Explain.

8. Do you think workaholics and high achievers are the same thing? Discuss.

9. Explain Figure 7–10 in your own words.

10. Can an individual be *too* motivated, so that his or her performance declines as a result of excessive effort? Discuss.

11. Explain the formula: Performance $= f(A \times M \times O)$ and give an example.

12. Identify three activities you *really enjoy* (for example, playing tennis, reading a novel, going shopping). Next, identify three activities you *really dislike* (for example, going to the dentist, cleaning the house, staying on a restricted calorie diet). Using the expectancy model, analyze each of your answers to assess why some activities stimulate your effort while others don't.

FOR FURTHER READING

Evans, M. G., "Organizational Behavior: The Central Role of Motivation," *Yearly Review of Management of the Journal of Management,* Summer 1986, pp. 203–22. Discusses individual behavior in terms of motivation theory, with emphasis on goals, feedback, attributions, and consequences of performance.

Greenberg, J., "Cultivating an Image of Justice: Looking Fair on the Job," *Academy of Management Executive,* May 1988, pp. 155–57. Fairness is an important element in equity theory. Research finds that fairness, as viewed by corporate management, is as much a matter of "appearing fair" as of actually "being fair."

Griffin, R. W., "Toward an Integrated Theory of Task Design," in L. L. Cummings and B. M. Staw (eds.), *Research in Organizational Behavior,* Vol. 9 (Greenwich, CT: JAI Press, 1987), pp. 79–120. Reviews the literature on task design and then presents a conceptual framework to integrate various approaches.

Kenton, S. B., "The Role of Communication in Managing Perceived Inequity," *Management Communication Quarterly,* May 1989, pp. 536–43. Offers suggestions for applications of effective communication as a tool to deter undesirable behavior resulting from the perception of inequity.

Miller, L. E. and J. E. Grush, "Improving Predictions in Expectancy Theory Research: Effects of Personality, Expectancies, and Norms," *Academy of Manage-*

ment Journal, March 1988, pp. 107–22. This article helps to establish the conditions under which expectancies determine behavior and demonstrates that social norms may determine behavior when those conditions aren't met.

STEERS, R. M., and L. W. PORTER, *Motivation and Work Behavior,* 4th ed. (New York: McGraw-Hill, 1987). Reprints some of the major articles in the study of work motivation.

Needs Test

Indicate how important each of the following is in the job you would like to get. Write the numbers 1, 2, 3, 4, or 5 on the line after each item.

1 = Not important
2 = Slightly important
3 = Moderately important
4 = Very important
5 = Extremely important

1. Cooperative relations with my co-workers. ____

2. Developing new skills and knowledge at work. ____

3. Good pay for my work. ____

4. Being accepted by others. ____

5. Opportunity for independent thought and action. ____

6. Frequent raises in pay. ____

7. Opportunity to develop close friendships at work. ____

8. A sense of self-esteem. ____

9. A complete fringe benefit program. ____

10. Openness and honesty with my co-workers. ____

11. Opportunities for personal growth and development. ____

12. A sense of security from bodily harm. ____

Turn to page 689 for scoring directions and key.

Source: Adapted with permission of The Free Press, a Division of Macmillan, Inc. from *Existence, Relatedness, and Growth: Human Needs in Organizational Settings*, by Clayton P. Alderfer. Copyright © 1972 by The Free Press.

Women, Motivation, and Top Management

Ellen Marram graduated from Harvard with an MBA in 1970, went to work for Lever Brothers, left for a position with Johnson & Johnson, and then joined RJR Nabisco. By 1987, Marram had been promoted four times and found herself in charge of more than 4,000 employees and eight major brand products as president of RJR Nabisco's grocery division. As a young graduate, she was sensitive to money matters, felt that she needed to be extremely innovative to survive in a man's world, and single-mindedly set out to make a career in product marketing, with its fast-track promise of new opportunities.

As head of a $1.2 billion-a-year miniconglomerate within RJR Nabisco—now part of KKR Enterprises—Ellen Marram is an obvious candidate for a CEO position in her industry, and being a woman can be an important advantage today. However, at age forty, Marram is not conscious of being unusual or of competing for new corporate laurels. She feels her success has nothing to do with gender, and her world revolves around her responsibilities as a line manager in a highly volatile industry. Money is no longer an object for Marram, whose estimated compensation package is more than a quarter of a million dollars a year, and she has no interest in the adornments of success. She does get excited about being creative, and is reputed to be a ferocious competitor within the industry.

In contrast, Roxanne Decyk, senior vice president of administration for Navistar Corporation, started as a corporate secretary in 1981. After four promotions in seven years, she now has a pivotal role in everything from strategic planning to labor relations. She is conscious of long-entrenched male cultures in major companies, and drove hard to achieve a top-officer's role before she was thirty-four years old. Instead of juggling the demands of home and office, like so many women executives in the past, Decyk's goals center on her career, although she has broad interests beyond the corporate walls. These include the fine arts; for example, she is a board member of the Chicago Ballet. She cautions aspiring women executives not to rely solely on their jobs for satisfaction, to be competitive and aggressive, but not to emulate male qualities.

Navistar promoted Roxanne Decyk to bring to the corporation a sense of participative management. This unusual move was based strongly on Decyk's ability to work closely with her peers and to get management and nonmanagement employees to join in team efforts. Top management defended her appointment by saying that women typically show more warmth and concern about human relationships, and this was certainly needed at Navistar.

Many women in executive positions leave their corporate jobs as their priorities shift or they become disenchanted with corporate life. In surveys over a ten-year period, *Fortune* magazine found that nearly a third of the women studied had resigned from their jobs, but not because of the oft-cited conflict between work and family. Instead, they departed because of a perception that there was no place to go (for men or women) in their organization or because they felt there were better things to do. Still, many women want to have families, and feel that in order to do so they must forgo a corporate career. For example, J. Diane Folzenlogen Stanley was among the top 100 corporate women in 1976. She was treasurer of Electronic Data Systems Corporation (EDS), and slated for a brilliant, high-profile career. But in 1977, she walked away from it all to start a family. Now she enjoys shooting marbles with Cub Scouts as much as she did being a financial wizard at EDS. She explains that her motives changed, and the corporate thrill lost its appeal.[76]

Questions

1. Contrast the motivation needs of the corporate women discussed here and explain each woman's motives in terms of Maslow's need hierarchy.

2. Examine each executive's profile in terms of McClelland's theory of achievement. How would you characterize each woman's career decisions?

3. As an exercise, choose a woman executive profiled in the press and discuss what you believe motivated her to succeed. How might her behavior reflect expectancy theory or reinforcement theory?

NOTES

[1]Based on "Why This 'Obsolete' Company is a 'Great Place to Work'," *International Management,* April 1986, pp. 46–51; and S. J. Modic, "Fine-Tuning a Classic," *Industry Week,* March 6, 1989, pp. 15–18.

[2]R. Katerberg and G. J. Blau, "An Examination of Level and Direction of Effort and Job Performance," *Academy of Management Journal,* June 1983, pp. 249–57.

[3]A. Maslow, *Motivation and Personality* (New York: Harper & Row, 1954).

[4]See for example, E. E. Lawler III and J. L. Suttle, "A Causal Correlation Test of the Need Hierarchy Concept," *Organizational Behavior and Human Performance,* April 1972, pp. 265–87; D. T. Hall and K. E. Nougaim, "An Examination of Maslow's Need Hierarchy in an Organizational Setting," *Organizational Behavior and Human Performance,* February 1968, pp. 12–35; and J. Rauschenberger, N. Schmitt, and J. E. Hunter, "A Test of the Need Hierarchy Concept by a Markov Model of Change in Need Strength," *Administrative Science Quarterly,* December 1980, pp. 654–70.

[5]A. K. Korman, J. H. Greenhaus, and I. J. Badin, "Personnel Attitudes and Motivation," in M. R. Rosenzweig and L. W. Porter (eds.), *Annual Review of Psychology* (Palo Alto, CA: Annual Reviews, 1977), p. 178.

[6]Ibid., p. 179.

[7]M. A. Wahba and L. G. Bridwell, "Maslow Reconsidered: A Review of Research on the Need Hierarchy Theory," *Organizational Behavior and Human Performance,* April 1976, pp. 212–40.

[8]D. McGregor, *The Human Side of Enterprise* (New York: McGraw-Hill, 1960). For an up-dated analysis of Theory X and Theory Y constructs, see R. J. Summers and S. F. Cronshaw, "A Study of McGregor's Theory X, Theory Y and the Influence of Theory X, Theory Y Assumptions on Causal Attributions for Instances of Worker Poor Performance," in S. L. McShane, ed., *Organizational Behavior,* ASAC 1988 Conference Proceedings, Vol. 9, Part 5. Halifax, Nova Scotia, 1988, pp. 115–23.

[9]F. Herzberg, B. Mausner, and B. Snyderman, *The Motivation to Work* (New York: John Wiley, 1959).

[10]R. J. House and L. A. Wigdor, "Herzberg's Dual-Factor Theory of Job Satisfaction and Motivations: A Review of the Evidence and Criticism," *Personnel Psychology,* Winter 1967, pp. 369–89; D. P. Schwab and L. L. Cummings, "Theories of Performance and Satisfaction: A Review," *Industrial Relations,* October 1970, pp. 403–30; and R. J. Caston and R. Braito, "A Specification Issue in Job Satisfaction Research," *Sociological Perspectives,* April 1985, pp. 175–97.

[11]C. N. Weaver, "What Workers Want from Their Jobs," *Personnel,* May–June 1976, p. 49.

[12]"What Motivates Managers," *INC.,* June 1989, p. 115.

[13]D. Guest, "What's New in Motivation," *Personnel Management,* May 1984, pp. 20–23.

[14]C. P. Alderfer, "An Empirical Test of a New Theory of Human Needs," *Organizational Behavior and Human Performance,* May 1969, pp. 142–75.

[15]M. Haire, E. E. Ghiselli, and L. W. Porter, "Cultural Patterns in the Role of the Manager," *Industrial Relations,* February 1963, pp. 95–117.

[16]C. P. Schneider and C. P. Alderfer, "Three Studies of Measures of Need Satisfaction in Organizations," *Administrative Science Quarterly,* December 1973, pp. 489–505.

[17]J. P. Wanous and A. Zwany, "A Cross-Sectional Test of Need Hierarchy Theory," *Organizational Behavior and Human Performance,* May 1977, pp. 78–97.

[18]D. C. McClelland, *The Achieving Society* (New York: Van Nostrand Reinhold, 1961); J. W. Atkinson and J. O. Raynor, *Motivation and Achievement* (Washington, D.C.: Winston, 1974); D. C. McClelland, *Power: The Inner Experience* (New York: Irvington, 1975); and M. J. Stahl, *Managerial and Technical Motivation: Assessing Needs for Achievement, Power, and Affiliation* (New York: Praeger, 1986).

[19]McClelland, *The Achieving Society.*

[20]D. C. McClelland and D. G. Winter, *Motivating Economic Achievement* (New York: Free Press, 1969).

[21]McClelland, *Power;* McClelland and D. H. Burnham, "Power Is the Great Motivator," *Harvard Business Review,* March–April 1976, pp. 100–10; and R. E. Boyatzis, "The Need for Close Relationships and the Manager's Job," in D. A. Kolb, I. M. Rubin, and J. M. McIntyre, *Organizational Psychology: Readings on Human Behavior in Organizations,* 4th ed. (Englewood Cliffs, NJ: Prentice Hall, 1984), pp. 81–86.

[22]Ibid.

[23]J. B. Miner, *Studies in Management Education* (New York: Springer, 1965).

[24]D. Kipnis, "The Powerholder," in J. T. Tedeschi (ed.), *Perspectives in Social Power* (Chicago: Aldine, 1974), pp. 82–123.

[25]D. Miron and D. C. McClelland, "The Impact of Achievement Motivation Training on Small Businesses," *California Management Review,* Summer 1979, pp. 13–28.

[26]D. McClelland, "Toward a Theory of Motive Acquisition," *American Psychologist,* May 1965, pp. 321–33; and J. B. Miner, *Theories of Organizational Behavior* (Hinsdale, IL: Dryden Press, 1980), pp. 67–69.

[27]R. de Charms, *Personal Causation: The Internal Affective Determinants of Behavior* (New York: Academic Press, 1968).

[28]E. L. Deci, *Intrinsic Motivation* (New York: Plenum, 1975); R. D. Pritchard, K. M. Campbell, and D. J. Campbell, "Effects of Extrinsic Financial Rewards on Intrinsic Motivation," *Journal of Applied Psychology,* February 1977, pp. 9–15; E. L. Deci, G. Betly, J. Kahle, L. Abrams, and J. Porac, "When Trying to Win: Competition and Intrinsic Motivation," *Personality and Social Psychology Bulletin,* March 1981, pp. 79–83; and P. C. Jordan, "Effects of an Extrinsic Reward on Intrinsic Motivation: A Field Experiment," *Academy of Management Journal,* June 1986, pp. 405–12.

[29]W. E. Scott, "The Effects of Extrinsic Rewards on 'Intrinsic Motivation': A Critique," *Organizational Behavior and Human Performance,* February 1976, pp. 117–19; B. J. Calder and B. M. Staw, "Interaction of Intrinsic and Extrinsic Motivation: Some Methodological Notes," *Journal of Personality and Social Psychology,* January 1975, pp. 76–80; and K. B. Boal and L. L. Cummings, "Cognitive Evaluation Theory: An Experimental Test of Processes and Outcomes," *Organizational Behavior and Human Performance,* December 1981, pp. 289–310.

[30]G. R. Salancik, "Interaction Effects of Performance and Money on Self-Perception of Intrinsic Motivation," *Organizational Behavior and Human Performance,* June 1975, pp. 339–51; and F. Luthans, M. Martinko, and T. Kess, "An Analysis of the Impact of Contingency Monetary Rewards on Intrinsic Motivation," *Proceedings of the Nineteenth Annual Midwest Academy of Management,* St. Louis, 1976, pp. 209–21.

[31]Miner, *Theories of Organizational Behavior,* p. 157.

[32]H. J. Arnold, "Effects of Performance Feedback and Extrinsic Reward upon High Intrinsic Motivation," *Organizational Behavior and Human Performance,* December 1976, pp. 275–88.

[33]B. M. Staw, "Motivation in Organizations: Toward Synthesis and Redirection," in B. M. Staw and G. R. Salancik (eds.), *New Directions in Organizational Behavior* (Chicago: St. Clair, 1977), p. 76.

[34]B. J. Calder and B. M. Staw, "Self-Perception of Intrinsic and Extrinsic Motivation," *Journal of Personality and Social Psychology,* April 1975, pp. 599–605.

[35]R. M. Steers and R. T. Mowday, "The Motivational Properties of Tasks," *Academy of Management Review,* October 1977, pp. 645–58.

[36]D. G. Gardner and L. L. Cummings, "Activation Theory and Job Design: Review and Reconceptualization," in B. M. Staw and L. L. Cummings (eds.), *Research in Organizational Behavior,* Vol. 10 (Greenwich, Conn.: JAI Press, 1988), p. 100.

[37]A. N. Turner and P. R. Lawrence, *Industrial Jobs and the Worker* (Boston: Harvard University Press, 1965).

[38]J. R. Hackman and G. R. Oldham, "Motivation Through the Design of Work: Test of a Theory," *Organizational Behavior and Human Performance,* August 1976, pp. 250–79.

[39]J. R. Hackman, "Work Design," in J. R. Hackman and J. L. Suttle (eds.), *Improving Life at Work* (Santa Monica, CA: Goodyear, 1977), p. 129.

[40]See "Job Characteristics Theory of Work Redesign," in J. B. Miner, *Theories of Organizational Behavior* (Hinsdale, IL: Dryden Press, 1980), pp. 231–66; B. T. Loher, R. A. Noe, N. L. Moeller, and M. P. Fitzgerald, "A Meta-Analysis of the Relation of Job Characteristics to Job Satisfaction," *Journal of Applied Psychology,* May 1985, pp. 280–89; W. H. Glick, G. D. Jenkins, Jr., and N. Gupta, "Method Versus Substance: How Strong Are Underlying Relationships Between Job Characteristics and Attitudinal Outcomes?," *Academy of Management Journal,* September 1986, pp. 441–64; Y. Fried and G. R. Ferris, "The Validity of the Job Characteristics Model: A Review and Meta-Analysis," *Personnel Psychology,* Summer 1987, pp. 287–322; and S. J. Zaccaro and E. F. Stone, "Incremental Validity of an Empirically Based Measure of Job Characteristics," *Journal of Applied Psychology,* May 1988, pp. 245–52.

[41]See R. B. Dunham, "Measurement and Dimensionality of Job Characteristics," *Journal of Applied Psychology,* August 1976, pp. 404–09; J. L. Pierce and R. B. Dunham, "Task Design: A Literature Review," *Academy of Management Review,* January 1976, pp. 83–97; and D. M. Rousseau, "Technological Differences in Job Characteristics, Employee Satisfaction, and Motivation: A Synthesis of Job Design Research and Sociotechnical Systems Theory," *Organizational Behavior and Human Performance,* October 1977, pp. 18–42.

[42]Ibid.; and Y. Fried and G. R. Ferris, "The Dimensionality of Job Characteristics: Some Neglected Issues," *Journal of Applied Psychology,* August 1986, pp. 419–26.

[43]See, for instance, Y. Fried and G. R. Ferris, "The Dimensionality of Job Characteristics;" and M. G. Evans and D. A. Ondrack, "The Motivational Potential of Jobs: Is a Multiplicative Model Really Necessary?," in S. L. McShane (ed.), *Organizational Behavior,* ASAC Conference Proceedings, Vol. 9, Part 5, Halifax, Nova Scotia, 1988, pp. 31–39.

[44]See, for instance, P. E. Spector, "Higher-Order Need Strength as a Moderator of the Job Scope–Employee Outcome Relationship: A Meta-Analysis," *Journal of Occupational Psychology,* June 1985, pp. 119–27; G. B. Graen, T. A. Scandura, and M. R. Graen, "A Field Experimental Test of the Moderating Effects of Growth Need Strength on Productivity," *Journal of Applied Psychology,* August 1986, pp. 484–91; and Y. Fried and G. R. Ferris, "The Validity of the Job Characteristics Model."

[45]C. A. O'Reilly and D. F. Caldwell, "Informational Influence as a Determinant of Perceived Task Characteristics and Job Satisfaction," *Journal of Applied Psychology,* April 1979,

MOTIVATION: FROM CONCEPTS TO APPLICATIONS

LEARNING OBJECTIVES

After studying this chapter, you should be able to:

1. *Identify the four ingredients common to MBO programs*
2. *Outline the typical five-step problem-solving model in OB Mod*
3. *Explain why managers might want to use participative decision making*
4. *Describe the link between performance-based compensation and expectancy theory*
5. *Explain how flexible benefits turn benefits into motivators*
6. *Summarize why two-tier pay systems are inconsistent with sound motivation theory*
7. *Describe how flextime schedules work*
8. *Explain how managers can enrich jobs*

Harbor Sweets has a uniquely flexible work environment. Production is organized into work stations, where groups of employees perform the same task. Workers are cross trained in several jobs, increasing the company's flexibility. Additionally, because the manufacturing of handmade candy is highly labor-intensive, few machines are used. So supervisors have greater flexibility in adjusting to the changing size of the daily workforce. If a crew is short handed, for example, fewer people can work there. Jeffery Titcomb.

*Set me anything to do as a task, and it is inconceivable
the desire I have to do something else.*

G. B. SHAW

B illie Phillips is thirty-nine years old and holds a master's degree
in counseling psychology.[1] She works twenty-five hours a week as the
personnel manager for Salem, Massachusetts-based Harbor Sweets Inc., a
manufacturer of handmade candy. They pay her only $15,000 a year and she
gets no health insurance, no pension plan, and no paid sick days. Pretty lousy
job? On the contrary! She loves working at Harbor Sweets. So much so that she
regularly brings work home with her, takes calls at home, and often works
overtime. What motivates Ms. Phillips and others at Harbor Sweets? It's
certainly not the money!

The founder and chief executive of Harbor Sweets, Ben Strohecker,
thinks he has the answers. Flexibility and autonomy. Says Billie Phillips, "I
feel satisfied because I also get something from this job that I can't have in
another job. I can leave when my kids need me."

Harbor Sweets employs 150 people, most working only part-time. Instead
of creating typical eight-hour shifts, the company has four-hour ones. This
allows employees to set any schedule that suits them, as long as it includes at
least twenty hours a week. Harbor Sweets pays only $5 an hour to start—in a
region where fast-food workers earn more—but employees are incredibly free
to determine their own work schedules. The company's stated policy, in fact, is
that if you want unpaid time off, take it!

In addition to flexible hours, there are other benefits to working at
Harbor Sweets. There are no time clocks. All employees are responsible for
quality control, and their individual decisions to junk product that doesn't
meet their standards are never questioned. Each month, employees even
receive a simplified version of the company's profit-and-loss statement so they
know how business is going. In the past, when times have been bad, employees
have responded with cost-cutting suggestions to improve company profitability.

The Harbor Sweets' work environment creates loyal employees. While
fast-food restaurants typically report annual turnover of 285 percent or more,
Harbor Sweets loses only about one-quarter of its people each year. Forty
percent have worked there for three or more years.

Ben Strohecker has drawn from concepts such as the motivation-hygiene
theory, expectancy theory, and the job characteristics model to create a
workplace where his employees are motivated, highly productive, and look
forward to coming to work.

In this chapter, we want to focus on how to apply motivation concepts. We want to link theories to practice. For it's one thing to be able to regurgitate motivation theories. It's often another to see how, as a manager, you could use them.

In the following pages, we'll review a number of techniques and programs that have gained varying degrees of acceptance in practice. For example, there will be discussions on popular programs such as management by objectives, two-tier pay systems, and flexible work hours. Specific attention will be given to showing how these programs build on one or more of the motivation theories we covered previously.

MANAGEMENT BY OBJECTIVES

Goal-setting theory has an impressive base of research support. But as a manager, how do you make goal setting operational? The best answer to that question is: Install a management by objectives (MBO) program.

What Is MBO?

Management by Objectives (MBO) A program that encompasses specific goals, participatively set, for an explicit time period, with feedback on goal progress.

Management by objectives emphasizes participatively set goals that are tangible, verifiable, and measurable. It's not a new idea. In fact, it was originally proposed by Peter Drucker more than thirty-five years ago as a means of using goals to motivate people rather than to control them.[2] Today, no introduction to basic management concepts would be complete without a discussion of MBO.

MBO's appeal undoubtedly lies in its emphasis on converting overall organizational objectives into specific objectives for organizational units and individual members. MBO operationalizes the concept of objectives by devising a process by which objectives cascade down through the organization. As depicted in Figure 8–1, the organization's overall objectives are translated into specific objectives for each succeeding level (that is, divisional, departmental, individual) in the organization. But because lower unit managers jointly participate in setting their own goals, MBO works from the "bottom up" as well as the "top down." The result is a hierarchy of objectives that link objectives at one level to those at the next level. And for the individual employee, MBO provides specific personal performance objectives. Each person, therefore, has an identified specific contribution to make to his or her unit's performance. If all the individuals achieve their goals, then their unit's goals will be attained and the organization's overall objectives become a reality.

There are four ingredients common to MBO programs. These are goal specificity, participative decision making, an explicit time period, and performance feedback.[3]

The objectives in MBO should be concise statements of expected accomplishments. It's not adequate, for example, to merely state a desire to cut costs, improve service, or increase quality. Such desires have to be converted into tangible objectives that can be measured and evaluated. To cut departmental costs *by seven percent,* to improve service by ensuring that all telephone orders are processed *within twenty-four hours of receipt,* or to increase quality by keeping returns to *less than one percent of sales* are examples of specific objectives.

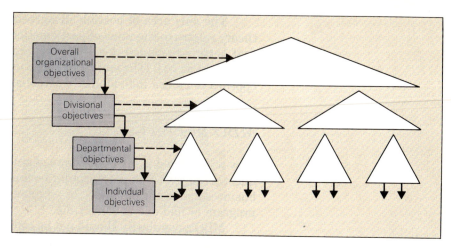

FIGURE 8–1   Cascading of Objectives

The objectives in MBO are not unilaterally set by the boss and then assigned to subordinates. MBO replaces imposed goals with participatively determined goals. The superior and subordinate jointly choose the goals and agree on how they will be measured.

Each objective has a specific time period in which it is to be completed. Typically the time period is three months, six months, or a year. So not only do managers and subordinates have specific objectives but stipulated time periods in which to accomplish them.

The final ingredient in an MBO program is feedback on performance. MBO seeks to give continuous feedback on progress toward goals. Ideally, this is accomplished by ongoing feedback to individuals so they can monitor and correct their own actions. This is supplemented by periodic managerial evaluations, when progress is reviewed. This applies at the top of the organization as well as at the bottom. The vice president of sales, for instance, has objectives for overall sales and for each of his or her major products. He or she will monitor ongoing sales reports to determine progress toward the sales division's objectives. Similarly, district sales managers have objectives, as does each salesperson in the field. Feedback in terms of sales and performance data is provided to let these people know how they are doing. Formal appraisal meetings also take place at which superiors and subordinates can review progress toward goals and further feedback can be provided.

Linking MBO and Goal-Setting Theory

Goal-setting theory demonstrates that hard goals result in a higher level of individual performance than do easy goals, that specific hard goals result in higher levels of performance than do no goals at all or the generalized goal of "do your best," and that feedback on one's performance leads to higher performance. Compare these findings with MBO.

MBO directly advocates specific goals and feedback. MBO implies, rather than explicitly states, that goals must be perceived as feasible. Consistent with goal setting, MBO would be most effective when the goals are difficult enough to require the person to do some stretching.

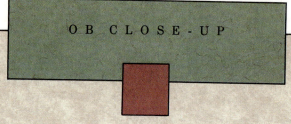

Hot Executive Benefits for the 1990s

What benefits are gaining in popularity? The following suggests some of the flexible benefits executives are likely to choose in the 1990s:[36]

Financial counseling. This includes everything from tax preparation to estate planning.

Company car. The purchase and upkeep of a car, especially a luxury one, is expensive. Why not let the company provide that Cadillac or Mercedes?

Flying first-class. As business becomes more global and long-distance trips the norm, wider seats, increased leg room, gourmet food, and other amenities of first class become more attractive.

High-tech communication devices. Car phones, portable brief case phones, laptop computers, and home fax machines can make the executive more efficient.

Child care. With both husband and wife working, quality child care becomes more attractive to many couples.

Elder care. Executives increasingly find themselves concerned with caring for elderly relatives.

Education benefits. Executives confronted with the high cost of tuition for their children at private schools and colleges are looking to their companies to pay all or part of the cost.

benefits are even becoming routinely available for companies with as few as fifty employees.[38] Clearly, flexible benefits is an idea whose time has come.

Now, let's look at the benefits and drawbacks. For employees, flexibility is attractive because they can tailor their benefits and levels of coverage to their own needs. The major drawback, from the employee's standpoint, is that the costs of individual benefits often go up so fewer total benefits can be purchased. For example, low-risk employees keep the cost of medical plans low for everyone. As they are allowed to drop out, the high-risk population occupies a larger segment and the cost of medical benefits go up. From the organization's standpoint, the good news is that flexible benefits often produce savings. Many organizations use the introduction of flexible benefits to raise deductibles and premiums. Moreover, once in place, costly increases in things like health insurance premiums often have to be substantially absorbed by the employee. The bad news for the organization is that these plans are more cumbersome for management to oversee and administering the programs is often expensive.

TWO-TIER PAY SYSTEMS

Kathy Schwab and Kathy Knoop are both flight attendants for American Airlines. Their job descriptions are essentially the same. Schwab, however, earns $1,200 a month, while Knoop averages around $3,300 a month.[39] True, Knoop is a fifteen-year veteran and Schwab is in her first year on the job. But should this justify a 175 percent premium for *experience* in the *same* job?

What's going on here? The answer is that American Airlines has negotiated a two-tier pay system with its flight attendants' union.

What Is a Two-Tier Pay System?

A **two-tier pay system** provides for new employees to be hired at significantly lower wage rates than those already employed in the same job. For instance, new machinists at Boeing start at $6.70 an hour while coworkers, hired before the two-tier contract, make a minimum of $11.38 an hour.[40]

There are two basic versions of the system. One establishes a temporary lower rate that catches up, in steps, to the higher level. Typically, contracts call for a three-to-ten year catch-up period. The other version keeps new employees permanently trailing the top-tier rate. American Airlines, as a case in point, negotiated a two-tier system for their pilots and flight attendants. Senior pilots, hired before the two-tier contract, can earn $127,900 a year. The lower tier, however, restricts new hires to only about half as much, regardless of how many years they fly.

Why would unions agree to a two-tier system? They would do so because it is an alternative to the pay cut that current employees would otherwise have to take. As a result of deregulation, nonunionized competitors, and low-cost foreign competition, many employers have had to find some way to significantly cut expenses. The two-tier pay system is such an alternative. It does drastically cut labor costs.

Linking Two-Tier Pay Systems and Equity Theory

A two-tier pay system may sound like a viable option for management, but it directly contradicts equity theory. In fact, based on equity theory predictions, you'd expect that to pay people such obviously different wages for doing essentially similar jobs would demotivate employees. Employees compare their input–outcome ratio against others. One of the most obvious "others" is co-workers. If you're doing the same job as someone else for significantly less money, yet feel your background and abilities are essentially similar, you're not likely to ignore this perceived discrepancy. The evidence suggests this to be the case.[41]

Two-tier pay systems build resentment among new hires, undermine employee loyalty, work against new employees exerting a high level of work effort, and increase the turnover rate among the newer hires.

Two-Tier Pay Systems in Practice

Two-tier systems were seen by many managers in the early 1980s as a quick and simple solution to high labor costs. But it didn't turn out to be the instant panacea that management had hoped for.[42] As noted earlier, it creates perceived inequities which, in turn, act to demotivate the newer, lower-paid employees. So two-tier pay systems are rapidly falling out of fashion. Their frequency has declined from a peak of eleven percent of union–management contracts in major industries in 1985, to nine percent in 1987, and six percent in 1989.[43]

ALTERNATIVE WORK SCHEDULES

Susan Ross is your classic "morning person." She rises each day at 5 A.M. sharp, full of energy. On the other hand, as she puts it, "I'm usually ready for bed right after the 7 P.M. news."

Susan's work schedule as a claims processor at Hartford Insurance is flexible. It allows her some degree of freedom as to when she comes to work and when she leaves. Her office opens at 6 A.M. and closes at 7 P.M. It's up to her how she schedules her eight-hour day within this thirteen-hour period. Because Susan is a morning person and also has a seven-year-old son who gets out of school at 3 P.M. every day, she opts to work from 6 A.M. to 3 P.M. "My work hours are perfect. I'm at the job when I'm mentally most alert, and I can be home to take care of Sean after he gets out of school."

What Are Alternative Work Schedules?

Most people work an eight-hour day, five days a week.[44] They start at a fixed time and leave at a fixed time. But a number of organizations have introduced alternative work schedule options, such as the compressed workweek, flextime, and job sharing, as a way to improve employee motivation and to better utilize human resources.

Compressed Workweek A four-day week, with employees working ten hours a day.

The most popular form of **compressed workweek** is four ten-hour days. The 4–40 program was conceived to allow workers more leisure time and shopping time, and to permit them to travel to and from work at nonrush-hour times. Supporters suggest that such a program can increase employee enthusiasm, morale, and commitment to the organization; increase productivity and reduce costs; reduce machine downtime in manufacturing; reduce overtime, turnover, and absenteeism; and make it easier for the organization to recruit employees.

Proponents argue that the compressed workweek may positively affect productivity in situations in which the work process requires significant start-up and shutdown periods.[45] When start-up and shutdown times are a major factor, productivity standards take these periods into consideration in determining the time required to generate a given output. Consequently, in such cases the compressed workweek will increase productivity even though worker performance is not affected, because the improved work scheduling reduces nonproductive time.

The evidence on 4–40 program performance is generally positive.[46] While some employees complain of fatigue near the end of the day, and about the difficulty of coordinating their jobs with their personal lives—the latter a problem especially for working mothers—most like the 4–40 program. In one study, for instance, when employees were asked whether they wanted to continue their 4–40 program, which had been in place for six months, or go back to a traditional five-day week, seventy-eight percent wanted to keep the shorter workweek.[47]

The compressed workweek doesn't increase employee discretion. Management still sets the work hours. Flextime, however, is a scheduling option that allows employees, within specific parameters, to decide when to go to work. Susan Ross' work schedule at Hartford Insurance is an example of flextime. But what specifically is flextime?

Flextime Employees work during a common core time period each

Flextime is short for flexible work hours. It allows employees some discretion over when they arrive and leave work. Employees have to work a

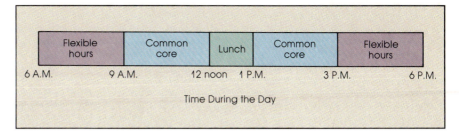

| Flexible hours | Common core | Lunch | Common core | Flexible hours |

6 A.M.　　　　　　9 A.M.　　　　　　12 noon　1 P.M.　　　　　3 P.M.　　　　　　6 P.M.

Time During the Day

FIGURE 8–4　　Example of a Flextime Schedule

day but have discretion in forming their total workday from a flexible set of hours outside the core.

specific number of hours a week, but they are free to vary the hours of work within certain limits. As shown in Figure 8–4, each day consists of a common core, usually six hours, with a flexibility band surrounding the core. For example, exclusive of a one-hour lunch break, the core may be 9:00 A.M. to 3:00 P.M., with the office actually opening at 6:00 A.M. and closing at 6:00 P.M. All employees are required to be at their jobs during the common core period, but they are allowed to accumulate their other two hours before and/or after the core time. Some flextime programs allow extra hours to be accumulated and turned into a free day off each month.

The benefits claimed for flextime are numerous. They include reduced absenteeism, increased productivity, reduced overtime expenses, a lessening in hostility toward management, reduced traffic congestion around work sites, elimination of tardiness, and increased autonomy and responsibility for employees that may increase employee job satisfaction.[48] But beyond the claims, what's flextime's record?

Most of the performance evidence stacks up favorably. Flextime tends to reduce absenteeism and frequently improves worker productivity,[49] probably

Jim Campbell is one of a growing number of Pacific Bell's 62,000 employees with customized work schedules. A single father of four sons, this account executive finds that Pac Bell's flextime program leaves him more time for his sons. He can drop them off at school and be in the office by 8 A.M. And if there's an emergency, "I can run my son over to the doctor and be back in the office without losing the whole day."

David Strick/Onyx.

for several reasons. Employees can schedule their work hours to align with personal demands, thus reducing tardiness and absences, and employees can adjust their work activities to those hours in which they are individually more productive.

Flextime's major drawback is that it's not applicable to every job. It works well with clerical tasks where an employee's interaction with people outside his or her department is limited. It is not a viable option for receptionists, sales personnel in retail stores, or similar jobs where comprehensive service demands that people be at their work stations at predetermined times.

Job Sharing The practice of having two or more people split a forty-hour-a-week job.

A recent work-scheduling innovation is **job sharing.** It allows two or more individuals to split a traditional forty-hour-a-week job. So, for example, one person might perform the job from 8 A.M. to noon, while another performs the same job from 1 P.M. to 5 P.M; or the two could work full, but alternate, days. From management's standpoint, job sharing allows the organization to draw upon the talents of more than one individual in a given job. It also opens up the opportunity to acquire skills—for instance, women with school-age children and retirees—that might not be available on a full-time basis. From the employee's viewpoint, job sharing increases flexibility. As such, it can increase motivation and satisfaction for those to whom a forty-hour a week job is just not practical.

Telecommuting Employees do their work at home on a computer that is linked to their office.

Linking Alternative Work Schedules and Motivation Theories

Not everyone prefers the traditional fixed eight-hour day. The larger blocks of leisure time created by the compressed workweek, for example, may be very appealing to the employee with a boat, a weekend house in the country, or a long daily commute. Employees with young children or other responsibilities that make high demands on their time find that scheduling alternatives like flextime and job sharing allow them more freedom to balance their work and personal commitments.[51]

In terms of motivation theories, alternative work schedules respond to the diverse needs of the work force. Flextime, for example, increases employee autonomy and responsibility. Therefore, it is consistent with the underlying concepts in motivation-hygiene theory.

Alternative Work Schedules in Practice

Alternatives to the traditional workweek have gained popularity over the past decade. The compressed workweek, as an example, grew 4.5 times as fast as did total employment between the mid-1970s and mid-1980s.[52] But the compressed workweek is still used by a small percentage of organizations. It's also interesting that it has been estimated that about twenty-eight percent of compressed workweek experiments end as failures.[53]

Flextime is more widely used and, where careful thought has been given to its applicability, is more successful. Thirty-one percent of American businesses now offer flexible time schedules. This is about twice as many as a decade ago.[54] Most of these, though, are small organizations, so the percentage of the total work force on flextime is probably about half that. Yet, based on current trends, you should expect to see more use of flextime in the coming years.

Job Enla
horizontal

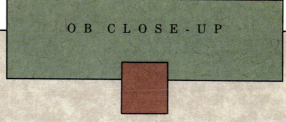

OB CLOSE-UP

Telecommuting: The Ultimate Flextime?

It might be close to the ideal job for many people. No commuting, flexible hours, freedom to dress as you please, and little or no interruptions from colleagues. It's called **telecommuting,** and refers to employees who do their work at home on a computer that is linked to their office.[50] Currently, over four million people work at home doing things like taking orders over the phone, filling out reports and other forms, and processing or analyzing information. Forecasters predict that ten to twenty million people could be telecommuting by the year 2000.

Whether the forecasts prove accurate depends on some questions for which we do not yet have answers. Will people balk at losing the regular social contact that a formal office provides? Would employees who do their work at home be at a political disadvantage? Might they be less likely to be considered for salary increases and promotions? Is being out of sight equivalent to being out of mind? Will nonwork-related distractions like children, neighbors, and the close proximity of the refrigerator significantly reduce productivity? Will nontelecommuters in the organization feel discriminated against? As we answer questions such as these, the future of telecommuting will become far more clear.

Job sharing is currently not widely practiced but should expand in future years. This prediction is based on the forecast near-term labor shortage and the growing number of retirees and women with children who want to work but can't commit to the demands of full-time employment.

Job Enrich
expansion

JOB REDESIGN

When you think about how mass-produced automobiles are made, what images come to mind? Do you think of cars moving along an assembly line, with workers bolting on fenders and hooking on doors? That may be the way most cars are mass-produced, but not at Volvo's new manufacturing plant in Uddevalla, Sweden.[55]

Uddevalla produces the midline Volvo 740 model using teams. Each team is made up of seven to ten workers. The teams work in one area and each assembles four cars per shift. Each team largely manages itself, handling scheduling, quality control, hiring, and other duties normally performed by supervisors. The teams, in fact, have no first-line supervisors. Each team appoints a spokesperson, who reports to one of six plant managers, who in turn reports to the president of the entire complex.

The major plus of the Uddevalla plant is that it overcomes the routine and boredom that workers experience on the conventional automobile assembly line where work cycles are only one or two minutes long. At Uddevalla, work team members are trained to handle all assembly jobs, so they work an average of three hours before having to repeat the same task.

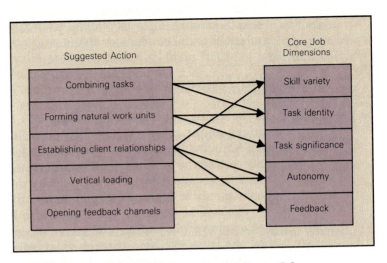

FIGURE 8–5   Guidelines for Enriching a Job
Source: From *Improving Life at Work* by J. R. Hackman and J. L. Suttle. Copyright ©
1977 by Scott, Foresman and Company. Reprinted by permission.

4. *Expand jobs vertically.* Vertical expansion gives employees responsibilities and control that was formerly reserved for management. It seeks to partially close the gap between the "doing" and the "controlling" aspects of the job, and it increases employee autonomy.

5. *Open feedback channels.* By increasing feedback, employees not only learn how well they are performing their jobs, but also whether their performance is improving, deteriorating, or remaining at a constant level. Ideally, this feedback about performance should be received directly as the employee does the job, rather than from management on an occasional basis.[57]

Citibank used the previous suggestions to design a job enrichment program for its back office personnel who processed all the firm's financial transactions.[58] These jobs had been split up so that each person performed a single, routine task over and over again. Employees had become dissatisfied with these mundane jobs, and this dissatisfaction showed in their work. Severe backlogs had developed, and error rates were unacceptably high. Citibank's management redesigned the work around customer types. Tasks were combined and individual employees were given complete processing and customer-service responsibility for a small group of customers in a defined product area. In the newly designed jobs, employees dealt directly with customers and handled entire transactions from the time they came into the bank until they left. As might be predicted, this enrichment program improved the quality of work as well as employee motivation and satisfaction.

Autonomous Work Teams

Autonomous Work Teams
Groups that are free to determine how the goals assigned to them are to be accomplished and how tasks are to be allocated.

Autonomous work teams represent job enrichment at the group level. As illustrated in the Volvo example at the beginning of this section on job redesign, work groups are given a high degree of self-determination in the

Teams like this at General Mills cereal plant in Lodi, California, schedule, operate, and maintain machinery so effectively that the factory runs with no managers present during the night shift. Since General Mills introduced autonomous work teams to this plant, productivity has risen up to 40 percent.

Doug Menuez/Reportage.

management of their day-to-day work. Typically this includes collective control over the pace of work, determination of work assignments, organization of breaks, and collective choice of inspection procedures. Fully autonomous work teams even select their own members and have the members evaluate each other's performance. As a result, supervisory positions take on decreased importance and may even be eliminated. Autonomous work teams draw from the job characteristics model. Self-managed work teams have three features: (1) employees with functionally interrelated tasks who collectively are responsible for end products; (2) individuals who have a variety of skills so they may undertake all or a large proportion of groups' tasks; and (3) feedback and evaluation in terms of the performance of whole groups.[59]

The first major experiment with these self-managed teams in the U.S. was in the early 1970s, by General Foods, at a new pet food plant it built in Kansas.[60] Today, a number of organizations have implemented the concept. For instance, General Motors is using teams in its joint venture with Toyota in California to make Chevrolet Novas and Toyota Corollas.[61] Factory workers are divided into small teams that define their own jobs and monitor the quality of their output. The groups even conduct their own daily quality audits, a chore that once was relegated to a separate group of inspectors. They also have "stop-line" cords that allow them to shut down the line if they encounter a problem. GM is now attempting to transfer what they have learned from their joint venture with Toyota to more than a third of their thirty-two car-and-truck assembly plants.

IMPLICATIONS FOR PERFORMANCE AND SATISFACTION

There are a number of techniques and programs for applying motivation theories. In this chapter, we reviewed eight of them: management by objectives, OB Mod, participative management, performance-based compensation, flexible benefits, two-tier pay systems, alternative work schedules, and job redesign. While it is always dangerous to synthesize a large number of complex ideas into a few simple guidelines, the following suggestions tap the essence of what we know about applying motivation theories toward improving employee performance and satisfaction.

RECOGNIZE INDIVIDUAL DIFFERENCES   Employees have different needs. Don't treat them all alike. Moreover, spend the time to understand what's important to each employee. This will allow you to individualize rewards, schedule work, and design jobs to align with individual needs.

USE GOALS AND FEEDBACK   Employees should have hard, specific goals, as well as feedback on how well they fare in pursuit of those goals.

ALLOW EMPLOYEES TO PARTICIPATE IN DECISIONS THAT AFFECT THEM   Employees can contribute to a number of decisions that affect them: setting work goals, choosing their own fringe benefit packages, selecting preferred work schedules, and the like. This can increase employee productivity, commitment to work goals, motivation, and job satisfaction.

LINK REWARDS TO PERFORMANCE   Rewards should be contingent on performance. Importantly, employees must perceive a clear linkage. Regardless of how closely rewards are actually correlated to performance criteria, if individuals perceive this correlation to be low, the result will be low performance, a decrease in job satisfaction, and an increase in turnover and absenteeism statistics.

CHECK THE SYSTEM FOR EQUITY   Rewards should also be perceived by employees as equating with the inputs they bring to the job. At a simplistic level, this should mean that experience, abilities, effort, and other obvious inputs should explain differences in performance and, hence, pay, job assignments and other obvious rewards.

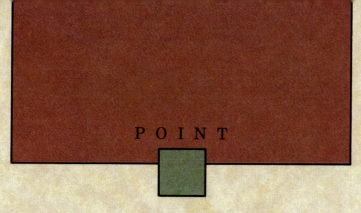

P O I N T

Organizations Should Provide Family Benefits to Employees

Progressive organizations are adapting their human resource policies to reflect the changing needs of their work force. They are grasping a basic fact of business in the era of the two-career household; that is, organizations don't hire an employee for forty or so hours a week, detached from his or her personal life. They buy the whole package. When firms hire employees, families and all of their home-life headaches are taken on as well.

As a result, an increasing number of organizations are doing the right thing. They are introducing innovative programs to increase employee productivity, motivation, and satisfaction, while cutting down on absenteeism and turnover. For example, one in ten American firms now provides some form of child-care assistance to employees. Here are some examples of what some organizations are doing to meet the personal needs of their employees:

- Group 243, an advertising firm in Ann Arbor, Michigan, with 110 employees, has set up an on-site day-care center at an annual cost of $100,000. The firm charges $100 a week per child, although actual costs are $175 a week. The company absorbs the difference.
- In Dade County, Florida, the American Bankers Insurance Group operates a kindergarten and first-grade class, using teachers, classroom, and supplies provided by the local school district.
- Stride Rite Corporation has an intergenerational center near its Cambridge, Massachusetts, headquarters to provide day care for up to sixty children and thirty elderly relatives of its employees.
- Haemonetics Corporation, of Braintree, Massachusetts, spends $40,000 a year to support a summer camp for its employees' children. Kids come to work with their parents and then get bused off for swimming lessons and hiking; they come back for lunch with mom or dad and finish up their afternoon activities by around 5 P.M. so they can return home with their parents.
- Arthur Andersen, the accounting and consulting firm, provides a family-care referral service. It researches and outlines options for employees at no charge.
- Capital Cities/ABC contributes up to $3,000 when one of its employees adopts a child.

Twenty years ago, few if any employers were offering these types of benefits to employees. But times have changed. A vice-president of Union Bank of California, whose wife is an engineer at a computer firm and whose two preschool sons attend his bank's day-care center, cogently captured the reason why companies are offering benefits like day-care: "My commitment has increased and I feel a new level of goodwill toward the bank because my employers have shown concern about my family. There is a direct connection between the existence of the day-care center and my job performance."

Based on "Home Is Where the Heart Is," *Time,* October 3, 1988, pp. 46–53; and "The Mommy and Daddy Track," *Forbes,* April 16, 1990, pp. 162–64.

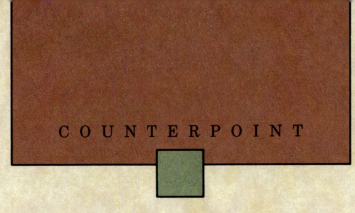

Let's Keep the Organization Out of the Employee's Personal Life

There is no argument that employers *are* expanding the breadth of benefits offered employees to better meet their increased commitments to their personal needs. The issue is whether or not organizations *should* be doing this. We'll argue that employers have no business providing day-care, elder-care, and similar family benefits for employees.

In the early part of this century, a number of logging and mining firms created company towns in places like Oregon, Montana, and West Virginia. The company owned the houses and rented them to workers. The company also owned and ran the stores, the schools, and everything else in town. Because of this, the company controlled the lives of their employees.

We don't look back on the days of the company town nostalgically. Management's intentions may have been good but we are a society that values freedom over paternalism. Today, company towns are viewed with suspicion. They are seen as potential opportunities to control and exploit employees. In a similar vein, when employers offer family benefits like day-care they are meddling in the personal lives of employees. They are gaining control over decisions that should properly be made by employees.

To illustrate, when companies provide day-care for the children of employees, the employer controls the content and the quality of the program. What skills does management have in designing or selecting a day-care program? Why shouldn't employees be completely free to choose the day-care center they want? If employers want to help employees with this expense, why not pay the employees more and let them make their own choices?

Regardless of how good their intentions are, management must be careful not to cross the line between an employee's work life and personal life. Whether an employee has preschool-age children or elderly dependent relatives should be irrelevant when the hiring decision is made. Similarly, it should be irrelevant once an employee has joined the organization. If employees need day-care or elder-care, let them personally take responsibility for providing it. It is not management's job or responsibility to be a substitute parent.

FOR DISCUSSION

1. Relate goal-setting theory with the MBO process. How are they similar? Different?

2. What factors in public sector organizations might work against an effective MBO program?

3. How might a college instructor use OB Mod to improve learning in the classroom?

4. Do you think participative management is likely to be more effective in certain types of organizations? With certain types of employees? Discuss.

5. Identify five different criteria by which organizations can compensate employees. Based on your knowledge and experience, do you think performance is the criterion most used in practice? Discuss.

6. What drawbacks, if any, do you see to implementing flexible benefits? (Consider this question from the perspectives of both the organization and the employee.)

7. If two-tier pay systems run counter to equity theory logic, why would intelligent managers seek to negotiate such programs? What other ways could management lower labor costs without the negative side-effects from two-tier systems?

8. Does flextime have an impact on any of the five core dimensions in the JCM? Discuss.

9. Would you want a full-time job telecommuting? How do you think most of your friends would feel about such a job? Do you think telecommuting has a future?

10. As a manager, what would you do to enrich an employee's job?

11. "Employees should have jobs that give them autonomy and diversity." Build an argument to support this statement. Then negate your argument.

12. Students often complain about doing group projects in a class. Why is that? Relate your answer to autonomous work teams. Would you want to be a member of one? Discuss.

FOR FURTHER READING

BOWERS, M. H., and R. D. RODERICK, "Two-Tier Pay Systems: The Good, the Bad, and the Debatable," *Personnel Administrator*, June 1987, pp. 101–12. Assesses the costs and benefits to management in implementing a two-tier pay system.

CAMPION, M. A., "Interdisciplinary Approaches to Job Design: A Constructive Replication With Extension," *Journal of Applied Psychology*, August 1988, pp. 467–81. Describes four approaches to job design and their corresponding outcomes: motivational approach with satisfaction outcomes, mechanistic approach with efficiency outcomes, biological approach with comfort outcomes, and perceptual/motor approach with reliability outcomes.

DALTON, D. R., and W. D. TODOR, "The Attenuating Effects of Internal Mobility on Employee Turnover: Multiple Field Assessments," *Journal of Management*, Winter 1987, pp. 705–11. Demonstrates that job rotation acts as a surrogate for employee turnover.

LEANA, C. R., E. A. LOCKE, and D. M. SCHWEIGER, "Fact and Fiction in Analyzing Research on Participative Decision Making: A Critique of Cotton, Vollrath,

Froggatt, Lengnick-Hall, and Jennings," *Academy of Management Review,* January 1990, pp. 137–46. Challenges previous analyses of participative decision-making studies.

McGuire, J. B., and J. R. Liro, "Absenteeism and Flexible Work Schedules," *Public Personnel Management,* Spring 1987, pp. 47–59. Argues for the advantage of a staggered fixed time schedule in which individual workers can vary their work schedule on a quarterly basis.

Miller, C. S., and M. H. Schuster, "Gainsharing Plans: A Comparative Analysis," *Organizational Dynamics,* Summer 1987, pp. 44–67. Compares six gain-sharing or productivity-sharing plans and offers suggestions for choosing the best one for an organization's needs.

Improving Your Understanding of How to Motivate Others

This exercise is designed to help increase awareness of how and why one motivates others and to help focus on the needs of those we are attempting to motivate.

1. Begin by breaking the class into groups of five to seven each. Then each student should individually read and respond to the following:
Situation 1: You are the owner and CEO of a moderate-size corporation. Your objective is to motivate all your subordinates to the highest level possible.
Task 1A: On a separate sheet of paper, list the factors you would use to motivate your employees. Avoid generalities—be as specific as possible.
Task 1B: Rank-order the factors you listed in 1A above.

2. Now complete the following in the same manner.
Situation 2: You are an employee of a moderate-size corporation. The company CEO has asked all employees to help in developing an effective motivational system. The CEO has asked for your response to Task 2A and 2B.
Task 2A: List the factors which would most effectively motivate you. Avoid generalities—be as specific as possible.
Task 2B: Rank-order the factors you listed in 2A above.

3. After completing both 1 and 2 above, each group should do the following:
   a. Share the list of motivational factors (1A) and ranking (1B) with other members of their group.
   b. Share the list of motivational factors (2A) and ranking (2B) with other members of their group.

4. Group members should discuss the following:
   a. Are each individual's (1A) and (2A) lists more similar or more dissimilar? What does this mean?
   b. Does everyone's (1A) and (2A) list in your group contain basically the same items? What does this mean?
   c. Are the 1B and 2B lists in your group more similar or more dissimilar? What does this mean?
   d. What have you learned about how and why you motivate others as you do and how can you apply these data?

5. Each group should appoint a spokesperson to present their answers to 4a-d above.

Adapted from B. E. Smith, "Why Don't They Respond: A Motivational Experience," *Organizational Behavior Teaching Review,* Vol. X, No. 2, 1985–86, pp. 98–100. With permission.

Springfield Remanufacturing Company: Motivating After International Harvestor

International Harvestor experienced financial difficulties throughout most of the 1970s and early 1980s. In February 1983, the Springfield, Missouri facility was sold to a small group of managers and was renamed the Springfield Remanufacturing Corporation (SRC). Since its purchase, the company has averaged almost 40 percent growth per year, has been featured on the cover of *INC.* magazine, and was the subject of a PBS special.

The person most responsible for the success of SRC is Jack Stack. He attributes his success to achieving a common focus among employees and achieving consensus about the way the organization should be run.

The common focus started with creating a common enemy for the employees to work toward overcoming. The common enemy is the financial statistics Stack and the employees at SRC use as their measure of success. Every Tuesday, Stack and upper management go over all corporate financial data, including information on cash flow, a weekly income statement, and summaries of sales and expense information. On Wednesday, these managers conduct similar meetings with their personnel so that everyone in the organization knows how money is being spent, what receipts are and what is needed to make a profit. Everyone from Stack to the janitor realizes their impact on corporate performance and are reminded of it weekly.

Bonuses are then paid to employees for beating predetermined corporate goals (the enemy). Employees as a group can receive up to 18 percent of their salaries each quarter for beating corporate goals for inventory control, profits, sales increases, and labor control.

Stack's philosophy is that "Everyone has to have an enemy. We keep our enemies outside of our operation. We focus the innate anger in people. If you can focus it outside your operation they (employees) won't turn on you (or themselves) internally."

QUESTIONS

1. Which theory of motivation is Stack using?

2. How was Stack able to motivate employees?

3. How do the weekly discussions of financial information contribute to performance?

4. How can goal setting be applied in other contexts, perhaps to your class schedule?

This case was contributed by R. Earl Thomas and Joe G. Thomas, Middle Tennessee State University. It is based on D. K. Denton and B. L. Wisdom, "Shared Vision," *Business Horizons.* July/August, 1989.

NOTES

[1]Based on M. E. Mangelsdorf, "Managing the New Work Force," *INC.*, January 1990, pp. 78–83.

[2]P. F. Drucker, *The Practice of Management* (New York: Harper & Row, 1954).

[3]See, for instance, S. J. Carroll and H. L. Tosi, *Management by Objectives: Applications and Research* (New York, Macmillan, 1973).

[4]See, for instance, F. Schuster and A. F. Kendall, "Management by Objectives, Where We Stand—A Survey of the *Fortune* 500," *Human Resource Management,* Spring 1974, pp. 8–11; F. Luthans, "Management by Objectives in the Public Sector: The Transference Problem," unpublished paper presented at the 35th Annual Academy of Management Conference, New Orleans, Louisiana, 1975; R. C. Ford, F. S. MacLaughlin, and J. Nixdorf, "Ten Questions about MBO," *California Management Review,* Winter 1980, p. 89; and C. H. Ford, "MBO: An Idea Whose Time Has Gone?," *Business Horizons,* December 1979, p. 49.

[5]C. H. Ford, "MBO: An Idea Whose Time Has Gone?"

[6]"At Emery Air Freight: Positive Reinforcement Boosts Performance," *Organizational Dynamics,* Winter 1973, pp. 41–50.

[7]F. Luthans and R. Kreitner, *Organizational Behavior Modification and Beyond: An Operant and Social Learning Approach* (Glenview, IL: Scott, Foresman, 1985).

[8]F. Luthans and R. Kreitner, "The Management of Behavioral Contingencies," *Personnel,* July–August 1974, pp. 7–16.

[9]F. Luthans and R. Kreitner, *Organizational Behavior Modification and Beyond,* Chapter 8.

[10]W. C. Hamner and E. P. Hamner, "Behavior Modification on the Bottom Line," *Organizational Dynamics,* Spring 1976, pp. 12–24; and "Productivity Gains from a Pat on the Back," *Business Week,* January 23, 1978, pp. 56–62.

[11]D. C. Anderson, C. R. Crowell, M. Doman, and G. S. Howard, "Performance Posting, Goal Setting, and Activity-Contingent Praise as Applied to a University Hockey Team," *Journal of Applied Psychology,* February 1988, pp. 87–95.

[12]See, for example, E. Locke, "The Myths of Behavior Mod in Organizations," *Academy of Management Review,* October 1977, pp. 543–53.

[13]B. Saporito, "The Revolt Against 'Working Smarter,'" *Fortune,* July 21, 1986, pp. 58–65; "Quality Circles: Rounding up Quality at USAA," *AIDE Magazine,* Fall 1983, p. 24; and L. Kuzela, "Boeing, Unions Plan New Plant," *Industry Week,* April 3, 1989, p. 27.

[14]J. L. Cotton, D. A. Vollrath, K. L. Froggatt, M. L. Lengnick-Hall, and K. R. Jennings, "Employee Participation: Diverse Forms and Different Outcomes," *Academy of Management Review,* January 1988, pp. 8–22.

[15]M. Sashkin, "Participative Management Is an Ethical Imperative," *Organizational Dynamics,* Spring 1984, pp. 5–22.

[16]R. Tannenbaum, I. R. Weschler, and F. Massarik, *Leadership and Organization: A Behavioral Science Approach* (New York: McGraw-Hill, 1961), pp. 88–100.

[17]E. Locke and D. Schweiger, "Participation in Decision Making: One More Look," in B. M. Staw (ed.), *Research in Organizational Behavior,* Vol. 1, Greenwich, CT: JAI Press, 1979; E. A. Locke, D. B. Feren, V. M. McCaleb, K. N. Shaw, and A. T. Denny, "The Relative Effectiveness of Four Methods of Motivating Employee Performance," in K. D. Duncan, M. M. Gruneberg, and D. Wallis (eds.), *Changes in Working Life* (London: Wiley, 1980), pp. 363–88; K. L. Miller and P. R. Monge, "Participation, Satisfaction, and Productivity: A Meta-Analytic Review," *Academy of Management Journal,* December 1986, pp. 727–53; J. A. Wagner III and R. Z. Gooding, "Effects of Societal Trends on Participation Research," *Administrative Science Quarterly,* June 1987, pp. 241–62; and J. A. Wagner III and R. Z. Gooding, "Shared Influence and Organizational Behavior: A Meta-Analysis of Situational Variables Expected to Moderate Participation-Outcome Relationships," *Academy of Management Journal,* September 1987, pp. 524–41.

[18]See, for example, G. W. Meyer and R. G. Stott, "Quality Circles: Panacea or Pandora's Box?," *Organizational Dynamics,* Spring 1985, pp. 34–50; M. L. Marks, P. H. Mirvis, E. J. Hackett, and J. F. Grady, Jr., "Employee Participation in a Quality Circle Program: Impact on Quality of Work Life, Productivity, and Absenteeism," *Journal of Applied Psychology,* February 1986, pp. 61–69; E. E. Lawler III and S. A. Mohrman, "Quality Circles: After the Honeymoon," *Organizational Dynamics,* Spring 1987, pp. 42–54; R. P. Steel and R. F. Lloyd, "Cognitive, Affective, and Behavioral Outcomes of Participation in Quality Circles: Conceptual and Empirical Findings," *Journal of Applied Behavioral Science,* Vol. 24, No. 1, 1988, pp. 1–17.

[19]"A Quality Concept Catches on Worldwide," *Industry Week,* April 16, 1979, p. 125.

[20]W. E. Halal and B. S. Brown, "Participative Management," p. 21.

[21]B. Saporito, "The Revolt Against 'Working Smarter,'" p. 59.

[22]W. E. Halal and B. S. Brown, "Participative Management," p. 20.

[23]Cited in *Harvard Business Review,* January–February 1985, p. 66.

[24]J. Main, "The Trouble with Managing Japanese-Style," *Fortune,* April 2, 1984, p. 51.

[25]Ibid., p. 50.

[26]A. Bennett, "Pay for Performance," *Wall Street Journal,* April 18, 1990, p. R7.

[27]"How A&P Fattens Profits by Sharing Them," *Business Week,* December 22, 1986, p. 44.

[28]Cited in "For Whom Were the Golden Eighties Most Golden?," *Business Week,* May 7, 1990, p. 60.

[29]M. Fein, "Work Measurement and Wage Incentives," *Industrial Engineering,* September 1973, pp. 49–51.

[30]See, for instance, N. J. Perry, "Here Comes Richer, Riskier Pay Plans," *Fortune,* December 19, 1988, pp. 50–58; and "Some Motivators Get Short Shrift," *Industry Week,* September 19, 1988, p. 5.

[31]"All Pulling Together, To Get the Carrot," *Wall Street Journal,* April 30, 1990, p. B1.

[32]Cited in "Pay for Performance," *Wall Street Journal,* February 20, 1990, p. 1.

[33]This box is based on J. S. Lublin, "The Continental Divide," *Wall Street Journal,* April 18, 1990, p. R28–30.

[34]See, for instance, "When You Want to Contain Costs and Let Employees Pick Their Benefits: Cafeteria Plans," *INC.,* December 1989, p. 142; and "More Benefits Bend With Workers' Needs," *Wall Street Journal,* January 9, 1990, p. B1.

[35]E. E. Lawler III, "Reward Systems," in *Improving Life at Work,* J. R. Hackman and J. L. Suttle (eds.), p. 182.

[36]See "Elder Care Comes of Age," *Industry Week,* January 2, 1989, pp. 54–55; and "Trendy Toys to Show You Arrived," *Business Month,* May 1990, p. 27.

[37]"Flexible Benefits Are Offered by More Firms, Spurred by Tax Reform Act," *Wall Street Journal,* September 15, 1987, p. 1.

[38]"When You Want to Contain Costs and Let Employees Pick Their Benefits."

[39]I. Ross, "Employers Win Big in the Move to Two-Tier Contracts," *Fortune,* April 29, 1985, p. 83.

[40]S. Flax, "Pay Cuts Before the Job Even Starts," *Fortune,* January 9, 1984, p. 75.

[41]R. A. White, "Employee Preferences for Nontaxable Compensation Offered in a Cafeteria Compensation Plan: An Empirical Study," *Accounting Review,* July 1983, pp. 539–61; M. Charlier and F. C. Brown III, "American Air Attendants Seek to Topple Two-Tier Pay," *Wall Street Journal,* March 25, 1987, p. 6; and J. E. Martin and M. M. Peterson, "Two-Tier Wage Structures: Implications for Equity Theory," *Academy of Management Journal,* June 1987, pp. 297–315.

[42]Ibid.

[43]R. Tomsho, "Employers and Unions Feeling Pressure to Eliminate Two-Tier Labor Contracts," *Wall Street Journal,* April 20, 1990, p. B1.

[44]S. J. Smith, "The Growing Diversity of Work Schedules," *Monthly Labor Review,* November 1986, pp. 7–13.

[45]E. J. Calvasina and W. R. Boxx, "Efficiency of Workers on the Four-Day Workweek," *Academy of Management Journal,* September 1975, pp. 604–10.

[46]See, for example, J. W. Seybolt and J. W. Waddoups, "The Impact of Alternative Work Schedules on Employee Attitudes: A Field Experiment," paper presented at the Western Academy of Management Meeting; Hollywood, CA, April 1987.

[47]J. C. Goodale and A. K. Aagaard, "Factors Relating to Varying Reactions to the 4-Day Work Week," *Journal of Applied Psychology,* February 1975, pp. 33–38.

[48]W. F. Glueck, "Changing Hours of Work: A Review and Analysis of the Research," *The Personnel Administrator,* March 1979, pp. 44–47.

[49]See, for example, D. A. Ralston and M. F. Flanagan, "The Effect of Flextime on Absenteeism and Turnover for Male and Female Employees," *Journal of Vocational Behavior,* April 1985, pp. 206–17; D. A. Ralston, W. P. Anthony, and D. J. Gustafson, "Employees May Love Flextime, but What Does It Do to the Organization's Productivity?," *Journal of Applied Psychology,* May 1985, pp. 272–79; J. B. McGuire and J. R. Liro, "Flexible Work Schedules, Work Attitudes, and Perceptions of Productivity," *Public Personnel Management,* Spring 1986, pp. 65–73; and P. Bernstein, "The Ultimate in Flextime: From Sweden, By Way of Volvo," *Personnel,* June 1988, pp. 70–74.

[50]See, for example, C. Ansberry, "When Employees Work at Home, Management Problems Often Arise," *Wall Street Journal,* April 20, 1987, p. 25; K. Christensen, "A Hard Day's Work in the Electronic Cottage," *Across the Board,* April 1987, pp. 17–22; C. A. Hamilton, "Telecommuting," *Personnel Journal,* April 1987, pp. 91–101; and D. C. Bacon, "Look Who's Working At Home," *Nation's Business,* October 1989, pp. 20–31.

[51]R. B. Dunham, J. L. Pierce, and M. B. Castaneda, "Alternative Work Schedules: Two Field Quasi-Experiments," *Personnel Psychology,* Summer 1987, pp. 215–42.

[52]S. J. Smith, "The Growing Diversity of Work Schedules," p. 9.

[53]S. D. Nollen, *New Work Schedules in Practice: Managing Time in a Changing Society* (New York: Van Nostrand Reinhold, 1982).

[54]E. G. Thomas, "Flextime Doubles in a Decade," *Management World,* April/May 1987, pp. 18–19; and "Flextime Pros and Cons," *Boardroom Reports,* March 1, 1989, p. 15.

[55]J. Kapstein, "Volvo's Radical New Plant: 'The Death of the Assembly Line'?," *Business Week,* August 28, 1989, pp. 92–93.

[56]B. G. Posner, "Role Changes," *INC.,* February 1990, pp. 95–98.

[57]J. R. Hackman, "Work Design," in J. R. Hackman and J. L. Suttle (eds.), *Improving Life at Work* (Santa Monica, CA: Goodyear, 1977), pp. 132–33.

[58]R. W. Walters, "The Citibank Project: Improving Productivity Through Work Design," in *How to Manage Change Effectively,* ed. D. L. Kirkpatrick (San Francisco: Jossey-Bass, 1985), pp. 195–208.

[59]T. D. Wall, N. J. Kemp, P. R. Jackson, and C. W. Clegg, "Outcomes of Autonomous Workgroups: A Long-Term Field Experiment," *Academy of Management Journal,* June 1986, pp. 280–304.

[60]See R. E. Walton, "From Hawthorne to Topeka to Kalmar," in *Man and Work in Society,* eds. E. L. Cass and F. G. Zimmer (New York: Van Nostrand Reinhold, 1975), pp. 118–21.

[61]"Why Image Counts: A Tale of Two Industries," *Business Week,* June 8, 1987, pp. 138–39; and "GM's Bootstrap Battle: The Factory-Floor View," *U.S. News & World Report,* September 21, 1987, pp. 52–53.

FOUNDATIONS OF GROUP BEHAVIOR

LEARNING OBJECTIVES

After studying this chapter, you should be able to:

1. *Differentiate between formal and informal groups*
2. *Explain why people join groups*
3. *List the five stages of group development*
4. *Identify the key factors in explaining group behavior*
5. *Describe how role requirements change in different situations*
6. *Describe how norms exert influence on an individual's behavior*
7. *Summarize the importance of the Hawthorne studies to the understanding of group behavior*
8. *List the benefits and disadvantages of cohesive groups*

Crew member teamwork aboard United's Flight 232 was instrumental in getting the crippled jet to the Sioux City, Iowa airfield. A stunning 185 of the 296 people on board survived this crash.   Kusel/Sipa Press.

One of the truly remarkable things about work groups is that they can make 2 + 2 = 5. Of course, they also have the capability of making 2 + 2 = 3.

S.P.R.

*I*n July 1989, the flight crew aboard United Airlines Flight 232 found the hours of teamwork training they had undergone paid off.[1] As soon as he heard the aircraft's tail engine explode, Capt. Dennis Fitch, a United DC-10 training pilot aboard as a passenger, sent word to the cockpit that he was available to help. Capt. Alfred Haynes, a 33-year United veteran, readily accepted. The airliner, with the hydraulics that allow pilots to control it crippled, was spiraling downward at about 2,400 feet a minute.

Scrunching down on his knees between the crew seats, Capt. Fitch experimented with the throttles. The two pilots found that they could keep the nose of the plane up if they advanced the two remaining engines to full throttle, and that they could steer, with great difficulty, by varying the thrust of each engine. Meanwhile, Capt. Haynes talked with air-traffic controllers about possible landing sites, and the flight engineer, D. J. Dvorak, sought advice by radio from United's San Francisco maintenance base and its Denver operations center.

Flight 232 crash-landed in Sioux City, Iowa. Safety experts say teamwork and resourcefulness in the cockpit were primarily what got the crippled jet to the airfield and allowed 185 of the 296 people on board to survive.

Every major airline and most small ones now train their crews in teamwork. They seek to create a coordinated, self-correcting team, so that if an individual makes a mistake the team which is working well together can correct it. A good team member communicates well, listens to others, and isn't afraid to question other team members if he or she thinks that something is wrong.

Ironically, teamwork doesn't come naturally to many pilots. They often enter commercial aviation after years in the military, flying fighter jets solo. If something happens, their natural response is to take control and do everything themselves.

This chapter introduces groups. Two facts make this chapter critical for your understanding of organizational behavior. First, the behavior of individuals in groups is something more than the sum total of each acting in his or her own way. In other words, when individuals are in groups, they act differently than they do when they are alone. Second, work groups are a vital part of every organization. Examples include production teams, committees, task forces, staff groups, investigative commissions, boards of directors, cockpit crews, surgical teams, quality circles, and repair crews. This chapter defines groups, reviews the various reasons why people join them, describes how groups develop, and then presents a comprehensive model that will help you to explain work group behavior.

DEFINING AND CLASSIFYING GROUPS

Group Two or more individuals, interacting and interdependent, who come together to achieve particular objectives.

Formal Group A designated work group defined by the organization's structure.

Informal Group A group that is neither formally structured nor organizationally determined; appears in response to the need for social contact.

Command Group A manager and his or her immediate subordinates.

Task Group Those working together to complete a job task.

Interest Group Those working together to attain a specific objective with which each is concerned.

Friendship Group Those brought together because they share one or more common characteristics.

A **group** is defined as two or more individuals, interacting and interdependent, who come together to achieve particular objectives. Groups can be either formal or informal. By **formal,** we mean defined by the organization's structure, with designated work assignments establishing tasks and work groups. In formal groups, the behaviors that one should engage in are stipulated by and directed toward organizational goals. The three members making up an airline flight crew are an example of a formal group. In contrast, **informal groups** are alliances that are neither formally structured nor organizationally determined. These groups are natural formations in the work environment, which appear in response to the need for social contact.

It is possible to subclassify groups further as command, task, interest, or friendship groups.[2] Command and task groups are dictated by the formal organization, whereas interest and friendship groups are informal alliances.

A **command group** is determined by the organization chart. It is composed of the subordinates who report directly to a given manager. An elementary school principal and her twelve teachers form a command group, as do the director of postal audits and his five inspectors.

Task groups, also organizationally determined, represent those working together to complete a job task. However, a task group's boundaries are not limited to its immediate hierarchical superior. It can cross command relationships. For instance, if a college student is accused of a campus crime, it may require communication and coordination among the Dean of Academic Affairs, the Dean of Students, the Registrar, the Director of Security, and the student's advisor. Such a formation would constitute a task group. It should be noted that all command groups are also task groups, but because task groups can cut across the organization, the reverse need not be true.

People who may or may not be aligned into common command or task groups may affiliate to attain a specific objective with which each is concerned. This is an **interest group.** Employees who band together to have their vacation schedule altered, to support a peer who has been fired, or to seek increased fringe benefits represent the formation of a united body to further their common interest.

Groups often develop because the individual members have one or more common characteristics. We call these formations **friendship groups.** Social allegiances, which frequently extend outside the work situation, can be based on similar age, support for "Big Red" Nebraska football, having attended the same college, or the holding of similar political views, to name just a few such characteristics.

Informal groups provide a very important service by satisfying their members' social needs. Because of interactions that result from the close proximity of workstations or task interactions, we find workers playing golf together, riding to and from work together, lunching together, and spending their breaks around the water cooler together. We must recognize that these types of interactions among individuals, even though informal, deeply affect their behavior and performance.

WHY DO PEOPLE JOIN GROUPS?

There is no single reason why individuals join groups. Since most people belong to a number of groups, it is obvious that different groups provide different benefits to their members. The most popular reasons for joining a group are related to our needs for security, status, self-esteem, affiliation, power, and goal achievement.

Security

"There's strength in numbers." By joining a group, we can reduce the insecurity of "standing alone"—we feel stronger, have fewer self-doubts, and are more resistant to threats. New employees are particularly vulnerable to a sense of isolation, and turn to the group for guidance and support. However, whether we are talking about new employees or those with years on the job, we can state that few individuals like to stand alone. We get reassurances from interacting with others and being part of a group. This often explains the appeal of unions—if management creates an environment in which employees feel insecure, they are likely to turn to unionization to reduce their feelings of insecurity.

Status

"I'm a member of our company's running team. Last month, at the National Corporate Relays, we won the national championship. Didn't you see our picture in the company newsletter?" These comments demonstrate the role that a group can play in giving prestige. Inclusion in a group viewed as important by others provides recognition and status for its members.

Self-Esteem

"Before I was asked to pledge Phi Omega Chi, I felt like a nobody. Being in a fraternity makes me feel much more important." This quote demonstrates that groups can provide people with feelings of self-worth. That is, in addition to conveying status to those outside the group, membership can also give increased feelings of worth to the group members themselves. Our self-esteem is bolstered, for example, when we are accepted by a highly valued group. Being assigned to a task force whose purpose is to review and make recommendations for the location of the company's new corporate headquarters can fulfill one's needs for competence and growth, as well as for status.

Affiliation

"I'm independently wealthy, but I wouldn't give up my job. Why? Because I really like the people I work with!" This quote, from a $45,000-a-year purchasing agent who inherited several million dollars' worth of real estate, verifies that groups can fulfill our social needs. People enjoy the regular interaction that comes with group membership. For many people, these on-the-job interactions are their primary source for fulfilling their needs for affiliation. For almost all people, work groups significantly contribute to fulfilling their needs for friendships and social relations.

Power

"I tried for two years to get the plant management to increase the number of restrooms for women on the production floor to the same number as the men have. It was like talking to a wall. But I got about fifteen other women who were production employees together and we jointly presented our demands to management. The construction crews were in here adding restrooms for us within ten days!"

This episode demonstrates that one of the appealing aspects of groups is that they represent power. What often cannot be achieved individually becomes possible through group action. Of course, this power may not be sought only to make demands on others. It may be desired merely as a countermeasure. In order to protect themselves from unreasonable demands by management, individuals may align with others.

Informal groups additionally provide opportunities for individuals to exercise power over others. For individuals who desire to influence others, groups can offer power without a formal position of authority in the organization. As a group leader, you may be able to make requests of group members and obtain compliance without any of the responsibilities that traditionally go with formal managerial positions. So, for people with a high power need, groups can be a vehicle for fulfillment.

Goal Achievement

"I'm part of a three-person team studying how we can cut our company's transportation costs. They've been going up at over thirty percent a year for several years now so the corporate controller assigned representatives from cost accounting, shipping, and marketing to study the problem and make recommendations."

This task group was created to achieve a goal that would be considerably more difficult if pursued by a single person. There are times when it takes more than one person to accomplish a particular task—there is a need to pool talents, knowledge, or power in order to get a job completed. In such instances, management will rely on the use of a formal group.

STAGES OF GROUP DEVELOPMENT

Group development is a dynamic process. Most groups are in a continual state of change. But just because groups probably never reach complete stability doesn't mean that there isn't some general pattern that describes how most groups evolve. There is strong evidence that groups pass through a standard sequence of five stages.[6] As shown in Figure 9–1, these five stages have been labeled *forming*, *storming*, *norming*, *performing*, and *adjourning*.

The first stage, **forming,** is characterized by a great deal of uncertainty about the group's purpose, structure, and leadership. Members are "testing the waters" to determine what types of behavior are acceptable. This stage is

Forming The first stage in group development, characterized by much uncertainty.

Management Is Learning the Value of Teamwork

After decades of hostility, managers at USX Corp. (formerly U. S. Steel) are teaming up with workers.[3] Why? Because they've learned that cooperation is the key to quality and high productivity. For example, at the company's Lorrain, Ohio plant, more than thirty teams made up of four hourly and salaried employees meet daily to solve quality control problems. The teams have devised improvements in the production system and significantly cut the plant's rejection rate.

But USX is not alone. Teamwork is spreading to automobile, food processing, electronics, paper, oil refining, and electrical products firms. The idea is also expanding into financial services and insurance. For instance, one large Wisconsin insurance company has reorganized its entire five-hundred-person staff into teams of twenty to thirty employees, who can perform all of the 167 tasks that were formerly split among functional departments.[4] The use of teams has increased productivity by twenty percent and reduced the time to process claims by as much as seventy-five percent.

The team concept seeks to reduce worker alienation in highly regimented work settings. When group members learn all the tasks performed by their team, they can rotate from job to job. The teams can also make their own operating decisions. Camaraderie and the opportunity to participate, in turn, builds loyalty and pride of workmanship. Work teams create the potential for improved quality and productivity, while making for more rewarding jobs for the team members.[5]

This team of ten at Milacron poses with a Vista machine they developed. The team was able to cut the standard development time from two years down to nine months.

Bob Kinmonth.

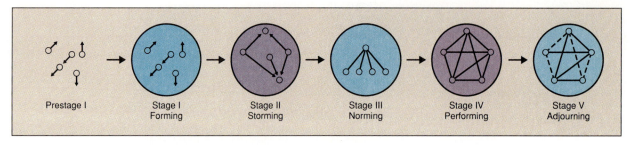

FIGURE 9–1   Stages of Group Development

complete when members have begun to think of themselves as part of a group.

The **storming** stage is one of intragroup conflict. Members accept the existence of the group, but there is resistance to the control that the group imposes on individuality. Further, there is conflict over who will control the group. When this stage is complete, there will be a relatively clear hierarchy of leadership within the group.

The third stage is one in which close relationships develop and the group demonstrates cohesiveness. There is now a strong sense of group identity and camaraderie. This **norming** stage is complete when the group structure solidifies and the group has assimilated a common set of expectations of what defines correct member behavior.

The fourth stage is **performing.** The structure at this point is fully functional and accepted. Group energy has moved from getting to know and understand each other to performing the task at hand.

For permanent work groups, performing is the last stage in their development. However, for temporary committees, task forces, teams, and similar groups that have a limited task to perform, there is an **adjourning** stage. In this stage, the group prepares for its disbandment. High task performance is no longer the group's top priority. Instead, attention is directed toward wrapping-up activities. Responses of group members vary in this stage. Some are upbeat, basking in the group's accomplishments. Others may be depressed over the loss of camaraderie and friendships gained during the work group's life.

Should one assume from the foregoing that a group becomes more effective as it progresses through the first four stages? While some argue that effectiveness of work units increases at advanced stages, it is not that simple.[7] While this assumption may be generally true, what makes a group effective is a complex issue. Under some conditions, high levels of conflict are conducive to high group performance. So we might expect to find situations where groups in Stage II outperform those in Stages III or IV. Similarly, groups do not always proceed clearly from one stage to the next. Sometimes, in fact, several stages go on simultaneously, as when groups are storming and performing at the same time. Groups even occasionally regress to previous stages. Therefore, one should not always assume that all groups precisely follow this developmental process or that Stage IV is always the most preferable. It is better to think of this model as a general framework. It reminds you that groups are dynamic entities and can help you better understand the problems and issues most likely to surface during a group's life.

Storming The second stage of group development, characterized by intragroup conflict.

Norming The third stage of group development, characterized by close relationships and cohesiveness.

Performing The fourth stage in group development, when the group is fully functional.

Adjourning The final stage in group development for temporary groups, characterized by concern with wrapping-up activities rather than task performance.

TOWARD EXPLAINING WORK GROUP BEHAVIOR

Why are some group efforts more successful than others? The answer to that question is complex, but it includes variables such as the ability of the group's members, the size of the group, the level of conflict, and the internal pressures on members to conform to the group's norms. Figure 9–2 presents the major components that determine group performance and satisfaction.[8] It can help you sort out the key variables and their interrelationships.

Work groups don't exist in isolation. They are part of a larger organization. A research team in Dow's Plastic Products division, for instance, must live within the rules and policies dictated from the division's headquarters and Dow's corporate offices. So every work group is influenced by external conditions imposed from outside it. The work group itself has a distinct set of resources determined by its membership. This includes things such as intelligence and motivation of members. It also has an internal structure that defines member roles and norms. These factors—group member resources and structure—determine interaction patterns and other processes within the group. Finally, the group process-performance/satisfaction relationship is moderated by the type of task that the group is working on. In the following pages, we'll elaborate on each of the basic boxes identified in Figure 9–2.

EXTERNAL CONDITIONS IMPOSED ON THE GROUP

To begin understanding the behavior of a work group, you need to view it as a subsystem embedded in a larger system.[9] That is, when we realize that groups are a subset of a larger organization system, we can extract part of the explanation of the group's behavior from an explanation of the organization to which it belongs.

FIGURE 9–2   Group Behavior Model

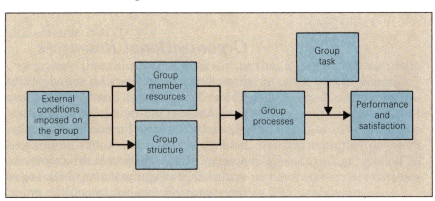

financial and career interests to accept a relocation, the conflict comes down to choosing between family and career role expectations.

The issue of ethics in business demonstrates a well-publicized area of role conflict among corporate executives. For example, one study found that fifty-seven percent of *Harvard Business Review* readers had experienced the dilemma of having to choose between what was profitable for their firms and what was ethical.[22]

All of us have faced and will continue to face role conflicts. The critical issue, from our standpoint, is how conflicts, imposed by divergent expectations within the organization, impact on behavior. Certainly they increase internal tension and frustration. There are a number of behavioral responses one may engage in. For example, one can give a formalized bureaucratic response. The conflict is then resolved by relying on the rules, regulations, and procedures that govern organizational activities. For example, a worker faced with the conflicting requirements imposed by the corporate controller's office and his own plant manager decides in favor of his immediate boss—the plant manager. Other behavioral responses may include withdrawal, stalling, negotiation or, as we found in our discussion of dissonance in Chapter 6, redefining the facts or the situation to make them appear congruent.

AN EXPERIMENT: ZIMBARDO'S SIMULATED PRISON One of the more illuminating role experiments was done by Stanford University psychologist Philip Zimbardo and his associates.[23] They created a "prison" in the basement of the Stanford psychology building; hired at $15 a day two dozen emotionally stable, physically healthy, law-abiding students who scored "normal average" on extensive personality tests; randomly assigned them the role of either "guard" or "prisoner"; and established some basic rules. The experimenters then stood back to see what would happen.

At the start of the planned two-week simulation, there were no measurable differences between those individuals assigned to be guards and those chosen to be prisoners. Additionally, the guards received no special training in how to be prison guards. They were told only to "maintain law and order" in the prison and not to take any nonsense from the prisoners: Physical violence was forbidden. To simulate further the realities of prison life, the prisoners were allowed visits from relatives and friends, but while the mock guards worked eight-hour shifts, the mock prisoners were kept in their cells around

Students at Stanford University play roles of "guard" and "prisoner" in a simulated prison experiment.   Philip G. Zimbardo, Stanford University.

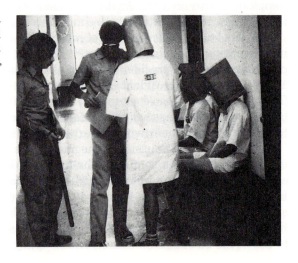

the clock and were allowed out only for meals, exercise, toilet privileges, head-count lineups, and work details.

It took the "prisoners" little time to accept the authority positions of the guards or the mock guards to adjust to their new authority roles. After the guards crushed a rebellion attempt on the second day, the prisoners became increasingly passive. Whatever the guards "dished out," the prisoners took. The prisoners actually began to believe and act as if they were, as the guards constantly reminded them, inferior and powerless. And every guard, at some time during the simulation, engaged in abusive, authoritative behavior. For example, one guard said, "I was surprised at myself . . . I made them call each other names and clean the toilets out with their bare hands. I practically considered the prisoners cattle, and I kept thinking: 'I have to watch out for them in case they try something.'" Another guard added, "I was tired of seeing the prisoners in their rags and smelling the strong odors of their bodies that filled the cells. I watched them tear at each other on orders given by us. They didn't see it as an experiment. It was real and they were fighting to keep their identity. But we were always there to show them who was boss."

The simulation actually proved *too* successful in demonstrating how quickly individuals learn new roles. The researchers had to stop the experiment after only six days because of the pathological reactions that the participants were demonstrating. And remember, these were individuals chosen precisely for their normalcy and emotional stability.

What should you conclude from this prison simulation? The participants in this prison simulation had, like the rest of us, learned stereotyped conceptions of guard and prisoner roles from the mass media and their own personal experiences in power and powerlessness relationships gained at home (parent–child), in school (teacher–student), and in other situations. This, then, allowed them easily and rapidly to assume roles that were very different from their inherent personalities. In this case, we saw that people with no prior personality pathology or training in their roles could execute extreme forms of behavior consistent with the roles they were playing.

Norms

Norms Acceptable standards of behavior within a group that are shared by the group's members.

Did you ever notice that golfers don't speak while their partners are putting on the green or that employees don't criticize their bosses in public? This is because of **"norms."**

All groups have established norms; that is, acceptable standards of behavior that are shared by the group's members. Norms tell members what they ought or ought not to do under certain circumstances. From an individual's standpoint, they tell what is expected of you in certain situations. When agreed to and accepted by the group, norms act as a means of influencing the behavior of group members with a minimum of external controls. Norms differ among groups, communities, and societies, but they all have them.

Formalized norms are written up in organizational manuals, setting out rules and procedures for employees to follow. By far, the majority of norms in organizations are informal. You do not need someone to tell you that throwing paper airplanes or engaging in prolonged gossip sessions at the water cooler are unacceptable behaviors when the "big boss from New York" is touring the office. Similarly, we all know that when we are in an employment interview discussing what we did not like about our previous job, there are certain things we should not talk about (difficulty in getting along with co-workers or our supervisor), while it is very appropriate to talk about other things (inadequate opportunities for advancement or unimportant and meaningless work). Evidence suggests that even high school students recognize that in such interviews certain answers are more socially desirable than others.[24]

Students quickly learn how to assimilate classroom norms. Depending upon the environment created by the instructor, the norms may support unequivocal acceptance of the material suggested by the instructor, or, at the other extreme, students may be expected to question and challenge the instructor on any point that is unclear. For example, in most classroom situations, the norms dictate that one not engage in loud, boisterous discussion that makes it impossible to hear the lecturer, or humiliate the instructor by pushing him or her "too far," even if one has obviously located a weakness in something the instructor has said. Should some in the classroom group behave in such a way as to violate these norms, we can expect pressure to be applied against the deviant members so as to bring their behavior into conformity with group standards.

THE HAWTHORNE STUDIES It is generally agreed among behavioral scientists that full-scale appreciation of the importance norms play in influencing worker behavior did not occur until the early 1930s. This enlightment grew out of a series of studies undertaken at Western Electric Company's Hawthorne Works in Chicago between 1924 and 1932.[25] Originally initiated by Western Electric officials and later overseen by Harvard professor Elton Mayo, the Hawthorne studies concluded that a worker's behavior and sentiments were closely related, that group influences were significant in affecting individual behavior, that group standards were highly effective in establishing individual worker output, and that money was less a factor in determining worker output than group standards, sentiments, and security. Let us briefly review the Hawthorne investigations and demonstrate the importance of these findings in explaining group behavior.

The Hawthorne researchers began by examining the relation between the physical environment and productivity. Illumination and other working conditions were selected to represent this physical environment. The researchers' initial findings contradicted their anticipated results.

They began the illumination experiments with various groups of workers. The researchers manipulated the intensity of illumination upward and downward, while at the same time noting changes in group output. Results varied, but one thing was clear: In no case was the increase or decrease in output in proportion to the increase or decrease in illumination. So the researchers introduced a control group: An experimental group was presented with varying intensity of illumination, while the controlled unit worked under a constant illumination intensity. Again, the results were bewildering to the Hawthorne researchers. As the light level was increased in the experimental unit, output rose for each group. But to the surprise of the researchers, as the light level was dropped in the experimental group, productivity continued to increase in both. In fact, a productivity decrease was observed in the experimental group only when the light intensity had been reduced to that of moonlight. The Hawthorne researchers concluded that illumination intensity was only a minor influence among the many influences that affected an employee's productivity, but they could not explain the behavior they had witnessed.

As a follow-up to the illumination experiments, the researchers began a second set of experiments in the relay assembly test room at Western Electric.

Western Electric employees participate in one of the famous group studies conducted at the company's Hawthorne Works plant. Courtesy Western Electric.

A small group of women was isolated from the main work group so that their behavior could be more carefully observed. They went about their job of assembling small telephone relays in a room laid out to resemble their normal department. The only significant difference was the placement in the room of a research assistant who acted as an observer, keeping records of output, rejects, working conditions, and a daily log sheet describing everything that happened. Observations covering a multiyear period found that this small group's output increased steadily. The number of personal absences and those due to sickness were approximately one-third of those recorded by women in the regular production department. What became evident was that this group's performance was significantly influenced by its status as a "special" group. The women in the test room thought that being in the experimental group was fun, that they were in sort of an elite group, and that management showed it was interested in them by engaging in such experimentation.

A third study in the bank wiring observation room was introduced to ascertain the effect of a sophisticated wage incentive plan. The assumption was that individual workers would maximize their productivity when they saw that it was directly related to economic rewards. The most important finding coming out of this study was that employees did not individually maximize their outputs. Rather, their output became controlled by a group norm that determined what was a proper day's work. Output was not only being restricted, but individual workers were giving erroneous reports. The total for a week would check with the total week's output, but the daily reports showed a steady, level output regardless of actual daily production. What was going on?

Interviews determined that the group was operating well below its capability and was leveling output in order to protect itself. Members were afraid that if they significantly increased their output, the unit incentive rate would be cut, the expected daily output would be increased, layoffs might occur, or slower workers would be reprimanded. So the group established its idea of a fair output—neither too much nor too little. They helped each other out to ensure that their reports were nearly level.

The norms that the group established included a number of "don'ts." *Don't* be a rate-buster, turning out too much work. *Don't* be a chiseler, turning out too little work. *Don't* be a squealer on any of your peers.

How did the group enforce these norms? Their methods were neither gentle nor subtle. They included sarcasm, name calling, ridicule, and even physical punches to the upper arm of members who violated the group's norms. Members would also ostracize individuals whose behavior was against the group's interest.

The Hawthorne studies made an important contribution to our understanding of group behavior—particularly the significant place that norms have in determining individual work behavior.

COMMON CLASSES OF NORMS   A work group's norms are like an individual's fingerprints—each is unique. Yet there are still some common classes of norms that appear in most work groups.[26]

Probably the most widespread norms deal with *performance-related processes*. Work groups typically provide their members with explicit cues on how hard they should work, how to get the job done, their level of output, appropriate communication channels, and the like. These norms are extremely powerful in affecting an individual employee's performance—they are capable of significantly modifying a performance prediction that was based solely on the employee's ability and level of personal motivation.

A second category of norms encompasses *appearance factors*. This includes things like appropriate dress, loyalty to the work group or organization, when to look busy, and when it's acceptable to goof off. Some organizations have formal dress codes. However, even in their absence, norms frequently develop to dictate the kind of clothing that should be worn to work. Presenting the appearance of loyalty is important in many work groups and organizations. For instance, in many organizations, especially among professional employees and those in the executive ranks, it is considered inappropriate to be openly looking for another job. This concern for demonstrating loyalty, incidentally, often explains why ambitious aspirants to top management positions in an organization willingly take work home at night, come in on weekends, and accept transfers to cities they would otherwise not prefer to live in.

Another class of norms concerns *informal social arrangements*. These norms come from informal work groups and primarily regulate social interactions within the group. With whom group members eat lunch, friendships on and off the job, social games, and the like are influenced by these norms. Many of the games and social patterns that Mayo and his associates found at the Hawthorne Works plant were dictated by informal social arrangement norms.

A final category of norms relates to *allocation of resources*. These norms can originate in the group or in the organization and cover things like pay, assignment of difficult jobs, and allocation of new tools and equipment. In some organizations, for example, new personal computers are distributed equally to all groups. So every department might get five, regardless of the number of people in the department or their need for the computers. In another organization, equipment is allocated to those groups who can make the best use of it. So some departments might get twenty computers and some none. These resource allocation norms can have a direct impact on employee satisfaction and an indirect effect on group performance.

THE "HOW" AND "WHY" OF NORMS   *How* do norms develop? *Why* are they enforced? A review of the research allows us to answer these questions.[27]

Norms typically develop gradually as group members learn what behaviors are necessary for the group to function effectively. Of course, critical events in the group might short-circuit the process and act quickly to solidify new norms. Most norms develop in one or more of the following four ways: (1)

Explicit statements made by a group member—often the group's supervisor or a powerful member. The group leader might, for instance, specifically say that no personal phone calls are allowed during working hours or that coffee breaks are to be kept to ten minutes. (2) *Critical events in the group's history.* These set important precedents. A bystander is injured while standing too close to a machine, and, from that point on, members of the work group regularly monitor each other to ensure that no one other than the operator gets within five feet of any machine. (3) *Primacy.* The first behavior pattern that emerges in a group frequently sets group expectations. Friendship groups of students often stake out seats near each other on the first day of class and become perturbed if an outsider takes "their" seats in a later class. (4) *Carry-over behaviors from past situations.* Group members bring expectations with them from other groups of which they have been members. This can explain why work groups typically prefer to add new members who are similar to current ones in background and experience. This is likely to increase the probability that the expectations they bring are consistent with those already held by the group.

But groups do not establish or enforce norms for every conceivable situation. The norms that the group will enforce tend to be those that are important to it. But what makes a norm important? (1) *If it facilitates the group's survival.* Groups don't like to fail, so they look to enforce those norms that increase their chances for success. This means that they will try to protect themselves from interference from other groups or individuals. (2) *If it increases the predictability of group members' behaviors.* Norms that increase predictability enable group members to anticipate each other's actions and to prepare appropriate responses. (3) *If it reduces embarrassing interpersonal problems for group members.* Norms are important if they ensure the satisfaction of their members and prevent as much interpersonal discomfort as possible. (4) *If it allows members to express the central values of the group and clarify what is distinctive about the group's identity.* Norms that encourage expression of the group's values and distinctive identity help to solidify and maintain the group.

Conformity Adjusting one's behavior to align with the norms of the group.

CONFORMITY As a member of a group, you desire acceptance by the group. Because of your desire for acceptance, you are susceptible to **conforming** to the group's norms. There is considerable evidence that groups can place strong pressures on individual members to change their attitudes and behaviors to conform to the group's standard.[28]

Do individuals conform to the pressures of all the groups they belong to? Obviously not, because people belong to many groups and their norms vary. In some cases, they may even have contradictory norms. So what do people do? They conform to the important groups to which they belong or hope to belong. The important groups have been referred to as *reference* groups and are characterized as ones where the person is aware of the others, the person defines himself or herself as a member, or would like to be a member, and the person feels that the group members are significant to him or her.[29] The implication, then, is that *all* groups do not impose equal conformity pressures on their members.

The impact that group pressures for conformity can have on an individual member's judgment and attitudes was demonstrated in the now classic studies by Solomon Asch.[30] Asch made up groups of seven or eight people, who sat in a classroom and were asked to compare two cards held by the experimenter. One card had one line, the other had three lines of varying length. As shown in

O B I N A
G L O B A L C O N T E X T

Social Loafing May Be a Culturally-Bound Phenomenon

Is the social-loafing phenomenon universal? Preliminary evidence suggests not.[36] Let's look at why the social loafing effect is probably consistent with a highly individualistic society like the United States and not collectivist societies like Japan or the People's Republic of China.

An individualistic culture is dominated by self-interest. Social loafing is likely to occur in such cultures because it will maximize an individual's personal gain. But social loafing shouldn't appear in collective societies since individuals in such cultures are motivated by in-group goals rather than self-interest. Work group members in countries like Japan will work to attain their group's collective goals regardless of the identifiability of their inputs. That is, they view their actions as a component essential to the group's goal attainment.

As noted, the preliminary evidence confirms this logic. A comparison of managerial trainees from the United States and the People's Republic of China found that the social-loafing effect surfaced among the Americans but not the Chinese. The Chinese didn't demonstrate any social loafing effect and, in fact, appeared to actually perform better in a group than working alone.

What this research suggests is that social loafing does not appear in all cultural settings. Predominantly studied by American researchers, it seems to be most applicable to such highly individualistic countries as the United States. As a result, the implications for OB of this effect on work groups need to be qualified to reflect cultural differences. In highly collectivistic societies, managers should feel comfortable in using groups even if individual efforts cannot be readily identified.

Composition

Most group activities require a variety of skills and knowledge. Given this requirement, it would be reasonable to conclude that heterogeneous groups—those composed of dissimilar individuals—would be more likely to have diverse abilities and information and should be more effective. Research studies substantiate this conclusion.[37]

When a group is heterogeneous in terms of personalities, opinions, abilities, skills, and perspectives, there is an increased probability that the group will possess the needed characteristics to complete its tasks effectively.[38] The group may be more conflict-laden and less expedient as diverse positions are introduced and assimilated, but the evidence generally supports the conclusion that heterogeneous groups perform more effectively than do those that are homogeneous.

A more specific offshoot of the composition issue has recently received a great deal of attention by group researchers. This is the degree to which members of a group share a common demographic attribute such as age, sex, race, educational level, or length of service in the organization, and the impact of these attributes on turnover. We'll call this variable **"group demography."**

Group Demography The degree to which members of a group share a common demographic

We discussed individual demographic factors in Chapter 4. Here we consider the same type of factors but in a group context—that is, it is not

attribute such as age, sex, race, educational level, or length of service in the organization, and the impact of these attributes on turnover.

Cohorts Individuals who, as part of a group, hold a common attribute.

whether a person is male or female, or has been employed with the organization a year rather than ten years. What now becomes our focus of attention is the individual's attribute in relationship to the others with whom he or she works. Let's work through the logic of group demography, review the evidence, and then consider the implications.

Groups and organizations are composed of **cohorts,** which we define as individuals who hold a common attribute. For instance, everyone in a group born in 1960 is of the same age. This means they also have shared common experiences. People born in 1960 have experienced the women's movement but not the Korean conflict. People born in 1945 shared the Vietnam War but not the Great Depression. Women in organizations today who were born prior to 1945 matured prior to the women's movement and have substantially different experiences from women born after 1960. Group demography, therefore, suggests that such attributes as age or the date that someone joins a specific work group or organization should help us to predict turnover. How would this occur? Essentially the logic would go like this: Turnover will be greater among those with dissimilar experiences because communication is more difficult; conflict and power struggles more likely, and more severe when they occur. The increased conflict makes group membership less attractive, so employees are more likely to quit. Similarly, the losers in a power struggle are more apt to leave voluntarily or be forced out.

Several studies have sought to test this thesis, and the evidence is quite encouraging.[39] For example, in departments or separate work groups where a large portion of members entered at the same time, there is considerably more turnover among those outside this cohort. Also, where there are large gaps between cohorts, turnover is higher. People who enter together or at approximately the same time are more likely to associate with one another, have a similar perspective of the group or organization, and thus are more likely to stay. On the other hand, discontinuities or bulges in the group's date-of-entry distribution is likely to result in a higher turnover rate within that group.

The implication of this line of inquiry is that the composition of a group may be an important predictor of turnover. Differences, per se, may not predict turnover. But large differences in similarity within a single group will lead to turnover. If everyone is moderately dissimilar from everyone else in a group, the feelings of being an outsider are reduced. So, it's the degree of dispersion

The research on group demography indicates that group members who are different from the majority—because of age, sex, race, educational level, or length of service in the organization—are more likely to quit. Danny Turner.

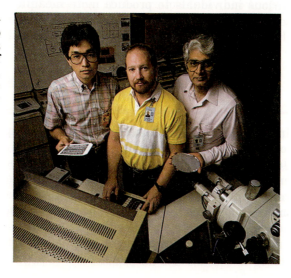

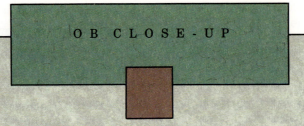

Groupware: Integrating Computer Networks and Work Groups

Computer programs are changing the way groups of people work together.[43] Software, or what more aptly is being called **groupware,** enables employees to collaborate across barriers of space and time to revolutionize the way people interact at work and, very importantly, to improve group productivity.

Current groupware has applications for face-to-face meetings, support between meetings, and support for electronic meetings. It includes such aids as presentation software and computer interconnection for group writing, project-management software and electronic calendaring, and personal-computer screen-sharing software and computer conferencing. Groupware can allow management to confer with subordinates, peers, superiors, suppliers, and customers via computer networks. Meetings can take place among employees thousands of miles apart, with computer software guiding the discussion and keeping the meeting on track.

Examples of sophisticated groupware that is currently available to facilitate groups of people working together include INTO and The Coordinator. INTO combines electronic mail, a group calendar, and other functions to keep everyone on a network organized. The Coordinator was developed on the assumption that business is essentially a set of action-oriented conversations such as requests, offers, counteroffers, and promises. The program lets a user compose a message on a personal computer, assign it to a conversation category, and transmit it via standard telephone lines to other users. The system then tracks every user's conversations, reminds each of his or her pending commitments, and keeps records of the status of group projects.

Groupware Computer software programs that allow employees to collaborate across barriers of space and time.

degree to which members are attracted to one another and share the group's goals. That is, the more that members are attracted to each other and the more that the group's goals align with their individual goals, the greater the group's cohesiveness. In the following pages, we'll review the factors that have been found to influence group cohesiveness and then look at the effect of cohesiveness on group productivity.[44]

Determinants of Cohesiveness

What factors determine whether group members will be attracted to one another? Cohesiveness can be affected by such factors as time spent together, the severity of initiation, group size, external threats, and previous successes.

TIME SPENT TOGETHER   If you rarely get an opportunity to see or interact with other people, you're unlikely to be attracted to them. The amount of time that people spend together, therefore, influences cohesiveness. As people spend more time together, they become more friendly. They naturally begin to talk, respond, gesture, and engage in other interactions. These interactions typically lead to the discovery of common interests and increased attraction.[45]

The opportunity for group members to spend time together is dependent on their physical proximity. We would expect more close relationships among members who are located close to one another rather than far apart. People who live on the same block, ride in the same car pool, or share a common office are more likely to become a cohesive group because the physical distance between them is minimal. For instance, among clerical workers in one organization it was found that the distance between their desks was the single most important determinant of the rate of interaction between any two of the clerks.[46]

SEVERITY OF INITIATION   The more difficult it is to get into a group, the more cohesive that group becomes. The hazing through which fraternities typically put their pledges is meant to screen out those who don't want to "pay the price" and to intensify the desire of those who do to become fraternity actives. But group initiation needn't be as blatant as hazing. The competition to be accepted to a good medical school results in first-year medical school classes that are highly cohesive. The common initiation rites—applications, test taking, interviews, and the long wait for a final decision—all contribute to creating this cohesiveness.

GROUP SIZE   If group cohesiveness tends to increase with the time members are able to spend together, it seems logical that cohesiveness should decrease as group size increases, since it becomes more difficult for a member to interact with all the members. This is generally what the research indicates.[47] As group size expands, interaction with all members becomes more difficult, as does the ability to maintain a common goal. Not surprisingly, too, as a single group's size increases, the likelihood of cliques forming also

The months or often years that an apprentice trade worker must put into developing his or her skills before being advanced to journeyman status results in union journeymen generally being a cohesive group. Lawrence Migdale/Stock, Boston.

IMPLICATIONS FOR PERFORMANCE AND SATISFACTION

We've covered a lot of territory in this chapter. Since we essentially organized our discussion around the group behavior model in Figure 9–2, let's use this model to draw our conclusions regarding performance and satisfaction.

Performance

Any predictions about a group's performance must begin by recognizing that work groups are part of a larger organization and that factors such as the organization's strategy, authority structure, selection procedures, and reward system can provide a favorable or unfavorable climate for the group to operate within. For example, if an organization is characterized by distrust between management and workers, it is more likely that work groups in that organization would develop norms to restrict effort and output than in an organization where trust is high. So don't look at any group in isolation. Rather, begin by assessing the degree of support external conditions provide the group. It is obviously a lot easier for any work group to be productive when the overall organization of which it is a part is growing, and it has both top management's support and abundant resources. Similarly, a group is more likely to be productive when its members have the requisite skills to do the group's tasks and the personality characteristics that facilitate working well together.

A number of structural factors show a relationship to performance. Among the more prominent are role perception, norms, the size of the group, and its demographic makeup.

There is a positive relationship between role perception and an employee's performance evaluation.[53] The degree of congruence that exists between an employee and his or her boss, in the perception of the employee's job, influences the degree to which that employee will be judged as an effective performer by the boss. To the extent that the employee's role perception fulfills the boss's role expectation, the employee will receive a higher performance evaluation.

Norms control group member behavior by establishing standards of right or wrong. If we know the norms of a given group, it can help us to explain the behaviors of its members. Where norms support high output, we can expect individual performance to be markedly higher than where group norms aim to restrict output. Similarly, acceptable standards of absence will be dictated by the group norms.

The impact of size on a group's performance depends upon the type of task in which the group is engaged. Larger groups are more effective in fact-finding activities. Smaller groups are more effective in action-taking tasks. Our knowledge of social loafing suggests that if management uses larger groups, efforts should be made to provide measures of individual performance within the group.

We found the group's demographic composition to be a key determinant of individual turnover. Specifically, the evidence indicates that group members who share a common age or date of entry into the work group are less prone to resign.

The primary contingency variable moderating the relationship between group processes and performance is the group's task. The more complex and interdependent the tasks, the more that inefficient processes will lead to reduced group performance.

Finally, we found that cohesiveness can play an important function in influencing a group's level of productivity. Whether or not it does depends on the group's performance-related norms.

Satisfaction

As with the role perception–performance relationship, high congruence between a boss and employee, as to the perception of the employee's job, shows a significant association with high employee satisfaction.[54] Similarly, role conflict is associated with job-induced tension and job dissatisfaction.[55]

The group size–satisfaction relationship is what one would intuitively expect: Larger groups are associated with lower satisfaction.[56] As size increases, opportunities for participation and social interaction decrease, as does the ability for members to identify with the group's accomplishments. At the same time, having more members also prompts dissension, conflict, and the formation of subgroups, which all act to make the group a less pleasant entity to be a part of.

Finally, we can make a set of predictions regarding both performance and satisfaction based on the impact of task as a moderating variable and research on the job characteristics model discussed in Chapter 7. A group can be expected to work especially hard on its tasks and members of that group are likely to be satisfied with their work when: (a) the group task requires members to use a variety of relatively high-level skills; (b) the group task is a whole and meaningful piece of work, with a visible outcome; (c) the outcomes of the group's work on the task have significant consequences for other people either inside or outside the organization; (d) the task provides group members with substantial autonomy for deciding about how they do the work; and (e) work on the task generates regular, trustworthy feedback about how well the group is performing.[57]

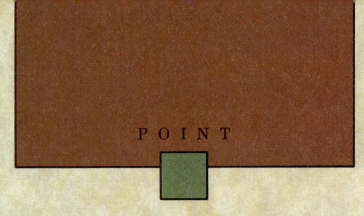

Designing Jobs Around Groups

It's time to take small groups seriously; that is, to use groups, rather than individuals, as the basic building blocks for an organization. I propose that we can design organizations from scratch around small groups rather than the way we have always done it—around individuals.

Why would management want to do such a thing? At least seven reasons can be identified. First, small groups seem to be good for people. They can satisfy important membership needs. They can provide a moderately wide range of activities for individual members. They can provide support in times of stress and crisis. They are settings in which people can learn not only cognitively but empirically to be reasonably trusting and helpful to one another. Second, groups seem to be good problem-finding tools. They seem to be useful in promoting innovation and creativity. Third, in a wide variety of decision situations, they make better decisions than individuals do. Fourth, they are great tools for implementation. They gain commitment from their members so that group decisions are likely to be willingly carried out. Fifth, they can control and discipline individual members in ways that are often extremely difficult through impersonal quasi-legal disciplinary systems. Sixth, as organizations grow large, small groups appear to be useful mechanisms for fending off many of the negative effects of large size. They help to prevent communication lines from growing too long, the hierarchy from growing too steep, and the individual from getting lost in the crowd. There is also a seventh, but altogether different, kind of argument for taking groups seriously. Groups are natural phenomena, and facts of organizational life. They can be created, but their spontaneous development cannot be prevented.

Operationally, how would an organization that was designed around groups function? One answer to this question is merely to take the things that organizations do with individuals and apply them to groups. The idea would be to raise the level from the atom to the molecule and *select* groups rather than individuals, *train* groups rather than individuals, *pay* groups rather than individuals, *promote* groups rather than individuals, *fire* groups rather than individuals, and so on down the list of activities that organizations have traditionally carried on in order to use human beings in their organizations.

In the past, the human group has been primarily used for patching and mending organizations that were built around the individual. The time is rapidly approaching, and it may already be here, for management to begin redesigning organizations around groups.

Adapted from H. J. Leavitt, "Suppose We Took Groups Seriously," in E. L. Cass and F. G. Zimmer (eds.), *Man and Work in Society* (New York: Van Nostrand Reinhold, 1975), pp. 67–77.

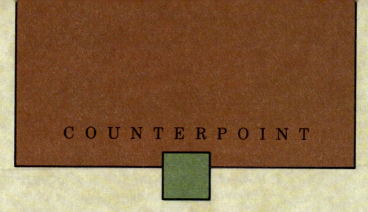

Jobs Should Be Designed Around Individuals

The argument that organizations can and should be designed around groups might hold in a socialistic society, but not in the United States. The following response directly relates to the United States and American workers, although it is probably generalizable to other economically advanced capitalistic countries. In fact, given the recent political changes in Eastern Europe and the increasing acceptance of profit-motivated businesses, the case for the individually oriented organization may be applicable throughout the world.

America was built on the ethic of the individual. This ethic has been pounded into us from birth. The result is that it is deeply embedded in the psyche of every American. We strongly value individual achievement. We praise competition. Even in team sports, we want to identify individuals for recognition. Sure, we enjoy group interaction. We like being part of a team, especially a winning team. But it is one thing to be a member of a work group while maintaining a strong individual identity and another to sublimate your identity to that of the group. The latter is inconsistent with the values of American life.

The American worker likes a clear link between his or her individual effort and a visible outcome. It is not happenstance that the United States, as a nation, has a considerably larger proportion of high achievers than exists in socialistic countries. America breeds achievers, and achievers seek personal responsibility. They would be frustrated in job situations where their contribution is commingled and homogenized with the contributions of others.

Americans want to be hired based on their individual talents. They want to be evaluated on their individual efforts. They also want to be rewarded with pay raises and promotions based on their individual performances. Americans believe in an authority and status hierarchy. They accept a system where there are bosses and subordinates. They are not likely to accept a group's decision on such issues as their job assignments and wage increases.

One of the more interesting illustrations of America's commitment to the individualistic ethic is research that has assessed the public's views on the American tax structure. We'd expect the rich to favor low tax rates on individuals with high incomes —$80,000 a year or more. But studies consistently find that Americans below the government's defined "poverty level" also strongly favor lower tax rates for high-income earners. A reasonable interpretation of these findings is that there is a very strong belief, held across the full range of economic levels, that anyone can make it in America. And when they make it, they don't want to be saddled with a heavy tax burden! Isn't this consistent with the stereotype of the individualistic American, motivated by his or her self-interest? Yes! Is this a worker who would be satisfied, and reach his or her full productive capacity, in a group-centered organization? Not likely!

*General Motors' executives are learning to listen to their employees. Turning around
a long tradition of top-down directives, GM's management has come to realize that
it empowers employees by encouraging upward communication.*
Courtesy General Motors.

*Every improvement in communication makes the bore
more terrible.*

F. M. COLBY

T he 1980s was a horrible decade for General Motors. It was aggressively attacked by Ford, Chrysler, and a host of Japanese competitors. It saw its United States market share drop from forty-six to thirty-five percent. Moreover, the company's incredibly burdensome organization structure and long-time tradition of top-down management only further hindered it in responding to its problems.

However, as the decade came to an end, GM's senior management seemed to have finally gotten the message.[1] It could no longer continue to manage its operations as it had in the past. A GM executive vice-president expressed this new found "religion" in a recent speech, when he said, "People, not fixed assets or technology, are what really make the difference in the bottom line."

Changing GM's autocratic, top-down management style isn't easy, but the effort at least is now underway. Managers, with the help of some in-house consultants, are learning to listen to, and trust, their employees. The humanization of General Motors involves persuading managers to accept ideas and challenges from their subordinates—a truly novel idea at GM—and convincing subordinates that management is sincerely open to their input. Top managers, middle managers, lower-level managers, and union employees all are participating in mini-retreats, workshops, and informal rap sessions to encourage discussion both within and between managerial levels.

One of the more positive outcomes from this improved communication has been the performance at the company's Buick City plant in Lake Orion, Michigan. The plant's management has actively sought ideas from rank-and-file workers. For instance, managers told the local union leaders that they needed more production and presented figures showing how the plant was using more labor-hours per car than virtually any other GM facility. The managers then asked the union officials to figure out what to do, and the union helped rearrange the work. The result was an increase in productivity of eight percent. Over a recent two-year period, the opening up of communication at the Buick City plant has helped to cut overall defects by ninety percent and assembly hours per car by forty-one percent.

The efforts going on at General Motors demonstrate the importance of good communication to any group's or organization's effectiveness. In fact, research indicates that poor communication is probably the most frequently cited source of interpersonal conflict.[2] Because individuals spend nearly seventy percent of their waking hours communicating—writing, reading, speaking, listening—it seems reasonable to conclude that one of the most inhibiting forces to successful group performance is a lack of effective communication.

No group can exist without **communication:** the transference of meaning among its members. It is only through transmitting meaning from one person to another that information and ideas can be conveyed. Communication, however, is more than merely imparting meaning. It must also be understood. In a group where one member speaks only German and the others do not know German, the individual speaking German will not be fully understood. Therefore, communication must include both the *transference and understanding of meaning.*

An idea, no matter how great, is useless until it is transmitted and understood by others. Perfect communication, if there were such a thing, would exist when a thought or idea was transmitted so that the mental picture perceived by the receiver was exactly the same as that envisioned by the sender. Although elementary in theory, perfect communication is never achieved in practice, for reasons we shall expand upon later.

Before making too many generalizations concerning communication and problems in communicating effectively, we need to review briefly the functions that communication performs and describe the communication process.

Communication The transference and understanding of meaning.

FUNCTIONS OF COMMUNICATION

Communication serves four major functions within a group or organization: control, motivation, emotional expression, and information.[3]

Communication acts to *control* member behavior in several ways. Organizations have authority hierarchies and formal guidelines that employees are required to follow. When employees, for instance, are required to first communicate any job-related grievance to their immediate boss, to follow their job description, or to comply with company policies, communication is performing a control function. But informal communication also controls behavior. The Hawthorne experiments, discussed in the previous chapter, showed how the group maintained control by communicating—sometimes very explicitly— the norms that were to be followed.

Communication fosters *motivation* by clarifying to employees what is to be done, how well they are doing, and what can be done to improve performance if it's subpar. We saw this operating in our review of goal-setting and reinforcement theories in Chapter 7. The formation of specific goals, feedback on progress toward the goals, and reinforcement of desired behavior all stimulate motivation and require communication.

For many employees, their work group is a primary source for social interaction. The communication that takes place within the group is a fundamental mechanism by which members show their frustrations and feelings of satisfaction. Communication, therefore, provides a release for the *emotional expression* of feelings and for fulfillment of social needs.

The final function that communication performs relates to its role in facilitating decision making. It provides the *information* that individuals and groups need to make decisions by transmitting the data to identify and evaluate alternative choices.

No one of these four functions should be seen as being more important than the others. For groups to perform effectively, they need to maintain some form of control over members, stimulate members to perform, provide a means for emotional expression, and make decision choices. You can assume that almost every communication interaction that takes place in a group or organization performs one or more of these four functions.

THE COMMUNICATION PROCESS

Communication Process The steps between a source and a receiver that result in the transference and understanding of meaning.

Communication can be thought of as a process or flow. Communication problems occur when there are deviations or blockages in that flow. In this section, we will describe the **process** in terms of a communication model and then consider how distortions can disrupt the process.

A Communication Model

Before communication can take place, a purpose, expressed as a message to be conveyed, is·needed. It passes between a source (the sender) and a receiver. The message is encoded (converted to symbolic form) and is passed by way of some medium (channel) to the receiver, who retranslates (decodes) the message initiated by the sender. The result is a transference of meaning from one person to another.[4]

Figure 10–1 depicts the communication process. This model is made up of seven parts: (1) the communication source, (2) encoding, (3) the message, (4) the channel, (5) decoding, (6) the receiver, and (7) feedback.

The source initiates a message by **encoding** a thought. Four conditions have been described that affect the encoded message: skill, attitudes, knowledge, and the social–cultural system.

Encoding Converting a communication message to symbolic form.

My success in communicating to you is dependent upon my writing skills; in the writing of textbooks, if the authors are without the requisite skills, their messages will not reach students in the form desired. One's total communicative success includes speaking, reading, listening, and reasoning skills as well. As we discussed in Chapter 6, our attitudes influence our behavior. We hold predisposed ideas on numerous topics, and our communications are affected by these attitudes. Further, we are restricted in our communicative activity by the extent of our knowledge on the particular topic. We cannot communicate what we do not know, and should our knowledge be too extensive, it is possible

FIGURE 10–1   The Communication Process Model

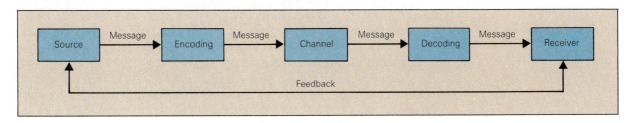

that our receiver will not understand our message. Clearly, the amount of knowledge the source holds about his or her subject will affect the message he or she seeks to transfer. And, finally, just as attitudes influence our behavior, so does our position in the social–cultural system in which we exist. Your beliefs and values, all part of your culture, act to influence you as a communicative source.

Message What is communicated.

The **message** is the actual physical product from the source encoding. "When we speak, the speech is the message. When we write, the writing is the message. When we paint, the picture is the message. When we gesture, the movements of our arms, the expressions on our face are the message."[5] Our message is affected by the code or group of symbols we use to transfer meaning, the content of the message itself, and the decisions that the source makes in selecting and arranging both codes and content.

Channel The medium through which a communication message travels.

The **channel** is the medium through which the message travels. It is selected by the source, who must determine which channel is formal and which one is informal. Formal channels are established by the organization and transmit messages that pertain to the job-related activities of members. They traditionally follow the authority network within the organization. Other forms of messages, such as personal or social, follow the informal channels in the organization.

Decoding Retranslating a sender's communication message.

The receiver is the object to whom the message is directed. But before the message can be received, the symbols in it must be translated into a form that can be understood by the receiver. This is the **decoding** of the message. Just as the encoder was limited by his or her skills, attitudes, knowledge, and social–cultural system, so is the receiver equally restricted. Just as the source must be skillful in writing or speaking, the receiver must be skillful in reading or listening, and both must be able to reason. One's level of knowledge, attitudes, and cultural background influences one's ability to receive, just as it does the ability to send.

Feedback Loop The final link in the communication process; puts the message back into the system as a check against misunderstandings.

The final link in the communication process is a **feedback loop.** "If a communication source decodes the message that he encodes, if the message is put back into his system, we have feedback."[6] Feedback is the check on how successful we have been in transferring our messages as originally intended. It determines whether understanding has been achieved.

Sources of Distortion

Unfortunately, most of the seven components in the process model have the potential to create distortion and, therefore, impinge upon the goal of communicating perfectly. These sources of distortion explain why the message that is decoded by the receiver is rarely the exact message that the sender intended.

If the encoding is done carelessly, the message decoded by the sender will have been distorted. The message itself can also cause distortion. The poor choice of symbols and confusion in the content of the message are frequent problem areas. Of course, the channel can distort a communication if a poor one is selected or if the noise level is high. The receiver represents the final potential source for distortion. His or her prejudices, knowledge, perceptual skills, attention span, and care in decoding are all factors that can result in interpreting the message somewhat differently than envisioned by the sender.

COMMUNICATION FUNDAMENTALS

A working knowledge of communication requires a basic understanding of some fundamental concepts. In this section, we'll review those concepts. Specifically, we'll look at the flow patterns of communication, compare formal and informal communication networks, describe the importance of nonverbal communication, and summarize the major barriers to effective communication.

Direction of Communication

Communication can flow vertically or laterally. The vertical dimension can be further divided into downward and upward directions.[7]

DOWNWARD   Communication that flows from one level of a group or organization to a lower level is a downward communication. This is the type of communication that managers at General Motors traditionally relied upon.

When we think of managers communicating with subordinates, the downward pattern is the one we usually think of. It is used by group leaders and managers to assign goals, provide job instructions, inform underlings of policies and procedures, point out problems that need attention, and offer feedback about performance. But downward communication doesn't have to be oral or face-to-face contact. When management sends letters to employees' homes to advise them of the organization's new sick leave policy, it is using downward communication.

UPWARD   Upward communication flows to a higher level in the group or organization. It is used to provide feedback to higher-ups, inform them of progress toward goals, and relay current problems. Upward communication keeps managers aware of how employees feel about their jobs, coworkers, and the organization in general. Managers also rely on upward communication for ideas on how things can be improved.

Some organizational examples of upward communication include performance reports prepared by lower management for review by middle and top

Lacy Edwards, chief executive of California-based software maker XA Systems Corp., recognized the problem of staying in touch with his employees as his firm grew. So he created annual "skip-level" interviews to facilitate upward communication. Once a year, employees have a one-on-one interview with their boss's boss. "It gives you a legitimate opportunity to explore without going around somebody," says Edwards, who interviews everyone who reports to his six vice-presidents.   Pat Kirk.

management, suggestion boxes, employee attitude surveys, grievance procedures, superior-subordinate discussions, and informal "gripe" sessions where employees have the opportunity to identify and discuss problems with their boss or representatives of higher management. General Motors' efforts to make their managers better listeners is essentially an attempt to emphasize the organization's upward communication channels.

LATERAL   When communication takes place among members of the same work group, among members of work groups at the same level, among managers at the same level, or among any horizontally equivalent personnel, we describe it as lateral communications.

Why would there be a need for horizontal communications if a group or organization's vertical communications are effective? The answer is that horizontal communications are often necessary to save time and facilitate coordination. In some cases, these lateral relationships are formally sanctioned. Often, they are informally created to short-circuit the vertical hierarchy and expedite action. So lateral communications can, from management's viewpoint, be good or bad. Since strict adherence to the formal vertical structure for all communications can impede the efficient and accurate transfer of information, lateral communications can be beneficial. In such cases, they occur with the knowledge and support of superiors. But they can create dysfunctional conflicts when the formal vertical channels are breached, when members go above or around their superiors to get things done, or when bosses find out that actions have been taken or decisions made without their knowledge.

Formal vs. Informal Networks

Communication networks define the channels by which information flows. These channels are one of two varieties—either formal or informal. **Formal networks** are typically vertical, follow the authority chain, and are limited to task-related communications. In contrast, the **informal network**—usually better known as the *grapevine*—is free to move in any direction, skip authority levels, and is as likely to satisfy group members' social needs as it is to facilitate task accomplishments.

FORMAL SMALL-GROUP NETWORKS   Figure 10–2 illustrates three common small-group networks. These are the chain, wheel, and all-channel. The chain rigidly follows the formal chain of command. The wheel relies on the leader to act as the central conduit for all the group's communication. The all-channel permits all group members to actively communicate with each other.

As Table 10–1 demonstrates, the effectiveness of each network depends on the dependent variable you are concerned about. For instance, the structure of the wheel facilitates the emergence of a leader, the all-channel network is best if you are concerned with having high member satisfaction, and the chain is best if accuracy is most important. So Table 10–1 leads us to the conclusion that no single network will be best for all occasions.

THE INFORMAL NETWORK   The previous discussion of networks emphasized formal communication patterns, but the formal system is not the only communication system in a group or between groups. Let us, therefore, turn

Communication Networks Channels by which information flows.

Formal Networks Task-related communications that follow the authority chain.

Informal Network The communication grapevine.

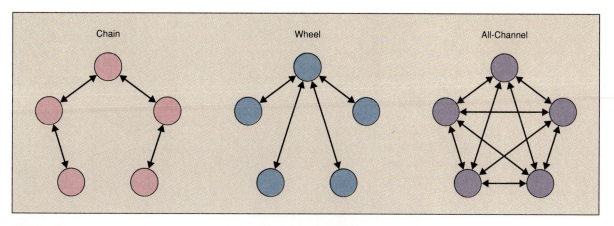

FIGURE 10–2   **Three Common Small-Group Networks**

our attention to the informal system, where information flows along the well-known grapevine and rumors can flourish.

The grapevine has three main characteristics.[8] First, it is not controlled by management. Second, it is perceived by most employees as being more believable and reliable than formal communiques issued by top management. Third, it is largely used to serve the self-interests of those people within it.

One of the most famous studies of the grapevine investigated the communication pattern among sixty-seven managerial personnel in a small manufacturing firm.[9] The basic approach used was to learn from each communication recipient how he first received a given piece of information and then trace it back to its source. It was found that, while the grapevine was an important source of information, only ten percent of the executives acted as liaison individuals; that is, passed the information on to more than one other person. For example, when one executive decided to resign to enter the insurance business, eighty-one percent of the executives knew about it, but only eleven percent transmitted this information on to others.

Two other conclusions from this study are also worth noting. Information on events of general interest tended to flow between the major functional groups (that is, production, sales) rather than within them. Also, no evidence surfaced to suggest that members of any one group consistently acted as liaisons; rather, different types of information passed through different liaison persons.

TABLE 10–1   **Small-Group Networks and Effectiveness Criteria**

Criteria	Networks		
	Chain	**Wheel**	**All-Channel**
Speed	Moderate	Fast	Fast
Accuracy	High	High	Moderate
Emergence of a leader	Moderate	High	None
Member satisfaction	Moderate	Low	High

Most American business firms have proven themselves more skilled at making scientific discoveries than at capitalizing on those discoveries. One exception is Hewlett-Packard. H-P CEO John Young (left) and director of Labs, Frank Carrubba, appreciate the value of gossip and other forms of informal communication at H-P to stimulate the transfer of the company's R & D discoveries into viable products.   Ed Kashi.

An attempt to replicate this study among employees in a small state government office also found that only ten percent act as liaison individuals.[10] This is interesting since the replication contained a wider spectrum of employees—including rank-and-file as well as managerial personnel. However, the flow of information in the government office took place within rather than between functional groups. It was proposed that this discrepancy might be due to comparing an executive-only sample against one which also included rank-and-file workers. Managers, for example, might feel greater pressure to stay informed and thus cultivate others outside their immediate functional group. Also, in contrast to the findings of the original study, the replication found that a consistent group of individuals acted as liaisons by transmitting information in the government office.

Is the information that flows along the grapevine accurate? The evidence indicates that about seventy-five percent of what is carried is accurate.[11] But what conditions foster an active grapevine? What gets the rumor mill rolling?

It is frequently assumed that rumors start because they make titillating gossip. Such is rarely the case. Rumors have at least four purposes: to structure and reduce anxiety; to make sense of limited or fragmented information; to serve as a vehicle to organize group members, and possibly outsiders, into coalitions; and to signal a sender's status ("I'm an insider and, with respect to this rumor, you're an outsider") or power ("I have the power to make you into an insider").[12] Research indicates that rumors emerge as a response to situations that are *important* to us, where there is *ambiguity,* and under conditions that arouse *anxiety.*[13] Work situations frequently contain these three elements, which explains why rumors flourish in organizations. The secrecy and competition that typically prevail in large organizations— around such issues as the appointment of new bosses, the relocation of offices, and the realignment of work assignments—create conditions that encourage and sustain rumors on the grapevine. A rumor will persist either until the wants and expectations creating the uncertainty underlying the rumor are fulfilled or until the anxiety is reduced.

What can we conclude from this discussion? Certainly the grapevine is an important part of any group or organization's communication network and well worth understanding. It identifies for managers those confusing issues that employees consider important and anxiety provoking. It acts, therefore, as both a filter and a feedback mechanism, picking up the issues that employees consider relevant. Maybe more important, again from a managerial perspective, it seems possible to analyze grapevine information and to predict its flow, given that only a small set of individuals (around ten percent) actively passes on information to more than one other person. By assessing which liaison individuals will consider a given piece of information to be relevant, we can improve our ability to explain and predict the pattern of the grapevine.

Can management entirely eliminate rumors? No! What management *can* do, however, is minimize the negative consequences of rumors by limiting their range and impact. Table 10–2 offers a few suggestions for minimizing those negative consequences.

Nonverbal Communications

Nonverbal Communication
Messages conveyed through body movements, the intonations or emphasis we give to words, facial expressions, and the physical distance between the sender and receiver.

Kinesics The study of body motions.

Anyone who has ever paid a visit to a singles bar or a nightclub is aware that communication need not be verbal in order to convey a message. A glance, a stare, a smile, a frown, a provocative body movement—they all convey meaning. This example illustrates that no discussion of communication would be complete without a discussion of **nonverbal communications.** This includes body movements, the intonations or emphasis we give to words, facial expressions, and the physical distance between the sender and receiver.

The academic study of body motions has been labeled **kinesics.** It refers to gestures, facial configurations, and other movements of the body. But it is a relatively new field, and it has been subject to far more conjecture and popularizing than the research findings support. Hence, while we acknowledge that body movement is an important segment of the study of communication and behavior, conclusions must be necessarily guarded. Recognizing this qualification, let us briefly consider the ways in which body motions convey meaning.

It has been argued that every *body movement* has a meaning and that no movement is accidental.[15] For example, through body language,

> We say, "Help me, I'm lonely. Take me, I'm available. Leave me alone, I'm depressed." And rarely do we send our messages consciously. We act out our state of being with nonverbal body language. We lift one eyebrow for disbelief. We rub our noses for puzzlement. We clasp our arms to isolate

TABLE 10–2   Suggestions for Reducing the Negative Consequences of Rumors

1. Announce timetables for making important decisions.
2. Explain decisions and behaviors that may appear inconsistent or secretive.
3. Emphasize the downside, as well as the upside, risks of current decisions and future plans.
4. Openly discuss worst case possibilities—it is almost never as anxiety provoking as the unspoken fantasy.

Source: Adapted from L. Hirschhorn, "Managing Rumors," in L. Hirschhorn (ed.), *Cutting Back* (San Francisco: Jossey-Bass, 1983), pp. 54–56. With permission.

Managers Can Make Office Gossip Work for Them

Managers often view office gossip with mixed feelings. On one hand they see it as harmful, potentially undermining formal communication channels, especially when it conveys erroneous information. On the other hand, managers want to have access to the gossip chain. It gives them early warnings of others' plans and problems that may be brewing.

The best managers are selective in using gossip.[14] They keep their ears open to grapevine information. They recognize that gossip is a natural phenomenon whenever people get together. It helps bind people together, lets the powerless blow off steam, and conveys concerns of employees. But effective managers aren't perceived as part of the gossip chain. For instance, they may have a loyal subordinate or colleague who discreetly shares grapevine information with them. Then they only pass along news that is likely to improve relationships in the organization while, at the same time, acting quickly to stamp out gossip that might be harmful to specific individuals or to their unit's overall performance.

ourselves or to protect ourselves. We shrug our shoulders for indifference, wink one eye for intimacy, tap our fingers for impatience, slap our forehead for forgetfulness.[16]

While we may disagree with the specific meaning of these movements, body language adds to and often complicates verbal communication. A body

As this photograph demonstrates, nonverbal messages can be a very powerful mode for conveying meaning.
Alen MacWeeney.

position or movement does not by itself have a precise or universal meaning, but when it is linked with spoken language, it gives fuller meaning to a sender's message.

If you read the verbatim minutes of a meeting, you could not grasp the impact of what was said in the same way you could if you had been there or saw the meeting on video. Why? There is no record of nonverbal communication. The emphasis given to words or phrases is missing. To illustrate how *intonations* can change the meaning of a message, consider the student in class who asks the instructor a question. The instructor replies, "What do you mean by that?" The student's reaction will be different depending on the tone of the instructor's response. A soft, smooth tone creates a different meaning from an intonation that is abrasive with strong emphasis placed on the last word.

The facial expression of the instructor will also convey meaning. A snarled face says something different from a smile. Facial expressions, along with intonations, can show arrogance, aggressiveness, fear, shyness, and other characteristics that would never be communicated if you read a transcript of what had been said.

The way individuals space themselves in terms of *physical distance* also has meaning. What is considered proper spacing is largely dependent on cultural norms. For example, what is "businesslike" distance in some European countries would be viewed as "intimate" in many parts of North America. If someone stands closer to you than is considered appropriate, it may indicate aggressiveness or sexual interest. If farther away than usual, it may mean disinterest or displeasure with what is being said.

It is important for the receiver to be alert to these nonverbal aspects of communication. You should look for nonverbal cues as well as listen to the literal meaning of a sender's words. You should particularly be aware of contradictions between the messages. The boss may say that she is free to talk to you about that raise you have been seeking, but you may see nonverbal signals that suggest that this is *not* the time to discuss the subject. Regardless of what is being said, an individual who frequently glances at her wristwatch is giving the message that she would prefer to terminate the conversation. We misinform others when we express one emotion verbally, such as trust, but nonverbally communicate a contradictory message that reads, "I don't have confidence in you." These contradictions often suggest that "actions speak louder (and more accurately) than words."

Barriers to Effective Communication

We conclude our discussion of communication fundamentals by reviewing several of the more prominent barriers to effective communication of which you should be aware.

Filtering A sender's manipulation of information so that it will be seen more favorably by the receiver.

FILTERING   **Filtering** refers to a sender manipulating information so that it will be seen more favorably by the receiver. For example, when a manager tells his boss what he feels his boss wants to hear, he is filtering information. Does this happen much in organizations? Sure! As information is passed up to senior executives, it has to be condensed and synthesized by underlings so those on top don't become overloaded with information. The personal interests and perceptions of what is important by those doing the synthesizing is going to result in filtering. As a former group vice-president of General Motors described it, the filtering of communications through levels at

GM made it impossible for senior managers to get objective information because "lower-level specialists . . . provided information in such a way that they would get the answer they wanted. I know. I used to be down below and do it."[17]

The major determinant of filtering is the number of levels in an organization's structure. The more vertical levels in the organization's hierarchy, the more opportunities there are for filtering.

SELECTIVE PERCEPTION   We have mentioned selective perception before in this book. It appears again because the receivers in the communication process selectively see and hear based on their needs, motivations, experience, background, and other personal characteristics. Receivers also project their interests and expectations into communications as they decode them. The employment interviewer who *expects* a female job applicant to put her family ahead of her career is likely to *see* that in female applicants, regardless of whether the applicants feel that way or not. As we said in Chapter 5, we don't see reality; rather, we interpret what we see and call it reality.

EMOTIONS   How the receiver feels at the time of receipt of a communication message will influence how he or she interprets it. The same message received when you're angry or distraught is likely to be interpreted differently when you're in a neutral disposition. Extreme emotions—such as jubilation or depression—are most likely to hinder effective communication. In such instances, we are most prone to disregard our rational and objective thinking processes and substitute emotional judgments.

LANGUAGE   Words mean different things to different people. "The meanings of words are *not* in the words; they are in us."[18] Age, education, and cultural background are three of the more obvious variables that influence the language a person uses and the definitions they give to words. The language of William F. Buckley, Jr., is clearly different from that of the typical high school-educated Burger King employee. The latter, in fact, would undoubtedly have trouble understanding much of Buckley's vocabulary (but then, so do a lot of people with graduate degrees!).

In an organization, employees usually come from diverse backgrounds. Additionally, the grouping of employees into departments creates specialists who develop their own jargon or technical language. In large organizations, members are also frequently widely dispersed geographically—even operating in different countries—and individuals in each locale will use terms and phrases that are unique to their area.

The existence of vertical levels can also cause language problems. For instance, differences in meaning with regard to words such as *incentives* and *quotas* have been found at different levels in management. Top managers often speak about the need for incentives and quotas, yet these terms imply manipulation and create resentment among many lower managers.

The point is that while you and I both speak a common language—English—our usage of that language is far from uniform. If we knew how each of us modified the language, communication difficulties would be minimized. The problem is that members in an organization usually don't know how others, with whom they interact, have modified the language. Senders tend to assume that the words and terms they use mean the same to the receiver as they do to them. This, of course, is often incorrect, thus creating communication difficulties.

Beware of the Communicaholic Manager!

The executive of twenty years ago relied heavily on telephones, memos, telegrams, and "just going out walking the halls" as his or her primary means of communicating with employees. Today's executive stays in touch by phone, but it is probably a portable or a car phone. In addition, today's executive also relies on high-tech communication devices like fax machines, computer networks, and voice mail systems to keep in close touch with "the troops."

New technologies have made it easier for people at work to communicate with one another, but they have turned many managers into communicaholics.[19] The idea of not having ready access to subordinates, peers, and superiors makes them extremely uncomfortable. These managers blur the traditional line separating work and nonwork time by seeking to be in constant touch with the office. You may know one or more of these managers. They're the ones with the $400-a-month car-phone bills, the fax machine at home, and the travel agent who has strict

instructions never to book them on a commercial flight that doesn't offer air-to-ground phone service.

We know the value of good communication. We know that it's an essential part of the manager's job. But a greater quantity of communication isn't always more *effective* communication. Managers may become prone to make decisions *too* quickly. The rapid access to data can preclude thoughtful deliberation. Communicaholic managers also tend to become obsessed with control. They closely monitor their employees' every action or decision and, in the process, frequently demotivate their employees. Still another problem created by the communicaholic manager is failure to build face-to-face relationships. The personal touch in managing is often lost. Finally, of course, is the reality that more information is not necessarily better information or even relevant information. More, faster, and easier communication opens up the possibility for managers to waste a lot of time on junky communications.

KEY COMMUNICATION SKILLS

Given the potential barriers that exist to retard effective communications, what can a person do to reduce those barriers?

Good communication skills take considerable effort to learn and years to perfect. But they *can* be learned. In this section, we'll briefly introduce two of the more critical skills related to effective communication—active listening and providing feedback—and demonstrate how you can begin to apply them immediately and develop your proficiency with them.[20]

Active Listening Skills

Too many people take their listening skills for granted. They confuse hearing with listening. What's the difference? Hearing is merely picking up sound vibrations. Listening is making sense out of what we hear. That is, listening requires paying attention, interpreting, and remembering sound stimuli.

Active Listening Listening with intensity, empathy, acceptance, and a willingness to take responsibility for completeness.

ACTIVE VERSUS PASSIVE LISTENING   Effective listening is active rather than passive. In passive listening, you're much like a tape recorder. You absorb the information given. If the speaker provides you with a clear message and makes his or her delivery interesting enough to keep your attention, you'll probably get most of what the speaker is trying to communicate. But **active listening** requires you to get inside the speaker so that you can understand the communication from his or her point of view. As you'll see, active listening is hard work. You have to concentrate and you have to want to fully understand what a speaker is saying. Students who use active listening techniques for an entire fifty-minute lecture are as tired as their instructor when that lecture is over because they have put as much energy into listening as the instructor put into speaking.

There are four essential requirements for active listening. You need to listen with (1) intensity, (2) empathy, (3) acceptance, and (4) a willingness to take responsibility for completeness.[21]

Our brain is capable of handling a speaking rate of about four times the speed of the average speaker. That leaves a lot of time for idle mind-wandering while listening. The active listener concentrates intensely on what the speaker is saying and tunes out the thousands of miscellaneous thoughts (about money, sex, vacations, parties, friends, getting the car fixed, and the like) that create distractions. What do active listeners do with their idle brain time? Summarize and integrate what has been said! They put each new bit of information into the context of what has preceded it.

Empathy requires you to put yourself in the speaker's shoes. You try to understand what the *speaker* wants to communicate rather than what *you* want to understand. Notice that empathy demands both knowledge of the speaker and flexibility on your part. You need to suspend your own thoughts and feelings and adjust what you see and feel to your speaker's world. In that way, you increase the likelihood that you will interpret the message being spoken in the way the speaker intended.

An active listener demonstrates acceptance. He or she listens objectively without judging content. This is no easy task. It is natural to be distracted by the content of what a speaker says, especially when we disagree with it. When we hear something we disagree with, we begin formulating our mental arguments to counter what is being said. Of course, in doing so, we miss the rest of the message. The challenge for the active listener is to absorb what is being said and to withhold judgment on content until the speaker is finished.

The final ingredient of active listening is taking responsibility for completeness. That is, the listener does whatever is necessary to get the full intended meaning from the speaker's communication. Two widely used active listening techniques to achieve this end are listening for feelings as well as for content and asking questions to ensure understanding.

DEVELOPING EFFECTIVE ACTIVE LISTENING SKILLS   Based on a review of the active listening literature, we can identify eight specific behaviors that effective listeners demonstrate.[22] (See Table 10–3.) As you review these behaviors, ask yourself the degree to which they describe your listening practices. If you're not currently using these techniques, there is no better time than today to begin developing them.

MAKE EYE CONTACT   How do you feel when somebody doesn't look at you when you're speaking? If you're like most people, you're likely to interpret this as aloofness or disinterest. It's ironic that while "you listen with your ears, people judge whether you are listening by looking at your eyes."[23]

TABLE 10–3   Behaviors Related to Effective Active Listening

- Make eye contact
- Exhibit affirmative head nods and appropriate facial expressions
- Avoid distracting actions or gestures
- Ask questions
- Paraphrase
- Avoid interrupting the speaker
- Don't overtalk
- Make smooth transitions between the roles of speaker and listener

EXHIBIT AFFIRMATIVE HEAD NODS AND APPROPRIATE FACIAL EXPRES-SIONS   The effective listener shows interest in what is being said. How? Through nonverbal signals. Affirmative head nods and appropriate facial expressions, when added to good eye contact, convey to the speaker that you're listening.

AVOID DISTRACTING ACTIONS OR GESTURES   The other side of showing interest is avoiding actions that suggest your mind is somewhere else. When listening, *don't* look at your watch, shuffle papers, play with your pencil, or engage in similar distractions. They make the speaker feel you're bored or uninterested. Maybe more importantly, they indicate that you *aren't* fully attentive and may be missing part of the message that the speaker wants to convey.

ASK QUESTIONS   The critical listener analyzes what he or she hears and asks questions. This behavior provides clarification, ensures understanding, and assures the speaker that you're listening.

Paraphrasing Restating what the speaker has said in one's own words.

PARAPHRASE   **Paraphrasing** means restating what the speaker has said *in your own words*. The effective listener uses phrases like: "What I hear you saying is . . ." or "Do you mean . . .?" Why rephrase what's already been said? Two reasons! First, it's an excellent control device to check on whether you're listening carefully. You can't paraphrase accurately if your mind is wandering or if you're thinking about what you're going to say next. Second, it's a control for accuracy. By rephrasing what the speaker has said in your own words and feeding it back to the speaker, you verify the accuracy of your understanding.

AVOID INTERRUPTING THE SPEAKER   Let the speaker complete his or her thought before you try to respond. Don't try to second-guess where the speaker's thoughts are going. When the speaker is finished, you'll know it!

DON'T OVERTALK   Most of us would rather speak our own ideas than listen to what someone else says. Too many of us listen only because it's the price we have to pay to get people to let us talk. While talking may be more fun and silence may be uncomfortable, you can't talk and listen at the same time. The good listener recognizes this fact and doesn't overtalk.

MAKE SMOOTH TRANSITIONS BETWEEN THE ROLES OF SPEAKER AND LISTENER   As a student sitting in a lecture hall, you find it relatively easy to get into an effective listening frame of mind. Why? Because communication is essentially one-way: The teacher talks and you listen. But the teacher–student dyad is atypical. In most work situations, you're continually shifting back and forth between the roles of speaker and listener. The effective listener, therefore, makes transitions smoothly from speaker to listener and back to speaker. From a listening perspective, this means concentrating on what a speaker has to say and practicing not thinking about what you're going to say as soon as you get your chance.

Feedback Skills

Ask a manager how much feedback he or she gives subordinates and you're likely to get a qualified answer. If the feedback is positive, it's likely to be given promptly and enthusiastically. Negative feedback, however, is often treated very differently. Managers, like most of us, don't particularly enjoy being the bearers of bad news. They fear offending or having to deal with defensiveness by the recipient. The result is that negative feedback is often avoided, delayed, or substantially distorted.[24] The purposes of this section are to show you the importance of providing both positive and negative feedback and to identify specific techniques to make your feedback more effective.

POSITIVE VERSUS NEGATIVE FEEDBACK   We said that managers treat positive and negative feedback differently. So, too, do recipients. You need to understand this fact and adjust your style accordingly.

Positive feedback is more readily and accurately perceived than negative feedback. Further, while positive feedback is almost always accepted, the negative variety often meets resistance.[25] Why? The logical answer seems to be that people want to hear good news and block out the bad. Positive feedback fits what most people wish to hear and already believe about themselves.

Does this mean that you should avoid giving negative feedback? No! What it means is that you need to be aware of potential resistance and learn to use negative feedback in situations where it is most likely to be accepted.[26] What are those situations? Research indicates that negative feedback is most likely to be accepted when it comes from a credible source or if it is objective in form. Subjective impressions carry weight only when they come from a person with

Kristina Hooper, Head of Apple Computer's multi-media laboratory, shows a group of students an interactive video system. The system communicates with a student and illustrates the importance of feedback in communication.   Ed Kashi.

high status and credibility.[27] This suggests that negative feedback that' is supported by hard data—numbers, specific examples, and the like—has a good chance of being accepted. Negative feedback that is subjective can be a meaningful tool for experienced managers, particularly those high in the organization who have earned the respect of their employees. From less experienced managers, those in the lower ranks of the organization, and those whose reputation has not yet been established, negative feedback is not likely to be well received.

DEVELOPING EFFECTIVE FEEDBACK SKILLS There are six specific suggestions we can make to help you be more effective in providing feedback (see Table 10–4).

FOCUS ON SPECIFIC BEHAVIORS Feedback should be specific rather than general.[28] Avoid statements like "You have a`bad attitude" or "I'm really impressed with the good job you did." They're vague, and while they provide information, they don't tell the recipient enough to correct the "bad attitude" or *on what basis* you concluded that a "good job" had been done.

Suppose you said something like "Bob, I'm concerned with your attitude toward your work. You were a half hour late to yesterday's staff meeting, and then told me you hadn't read the preliminary report we were discussing. Today you tell me you're taking off three hours early for a dental appointment"; or "Jan, I was really pleased with the job you did on the Phillips account. They increased their purchases from us by twenty-two percent last month and I got a call a few days ago from Dan Phillips complimenting me on how quickly you responded to those specification changes for the MJ-7 microchip." Both of these statements focus on specific behaviors. They tell the recipient *why* you are being critical or complimentary.

KEEP FEEDBACK IMPERSONAL Feedback, particularly the negative kind, should be descriptive rather than judgmental or evaluative.[29] No matter how upset you are, keep the feedback job-related and never criticize someone personally because of an inappropriate action. Telling people they're "stupid," "incompetent," or the like is almost always counterproductive. It provokes such an emotional reaction that the performance deviation itself is apt to be overlooked. When you're criticizing, remember that you're censuring a job-related behavior, not the person. You may be tempted to tell someone he or she is "rude and insensitive" (which may well be true); however, that's hardly impersonal. Better to say something like "You interrupted me three times, with questions that were not urgent, when you knew I was talking long distance to a customer in Scotland."

KEEP FEEDBACK GOAL-ORIENTED Feedback should not be given primarily to "dump" or "unload" on another.[30] If you have to say something negative,

TABLE 10–4 Behaviors Related to Providing Effective Feedback

- Focus on specific behaviors
- Keep feedback impersonal
- Keep feedback goal-oriented
- Make feedback well-timed
- Ensure understanding
- Direct negative feedback toward behavior that is controllable by the recipient

make sure it's directed toward the *recipient's* goals. Ask yourself whom the feedback is supposed to help. If the answer is essentially *you*—"I've got something I just want to get off my chest"—bite your tongue. Such feedback undermines your credibility and lessens the meaning and influence of future feedback.

MAKE FEEDBACK WELL-TIMED   Feedback is most meaningful to a recipient when there is a very short interval between his or her behavior and the receipt of feedback about that behavior.[31] To illustrate, a new employee who makes a mistake is more likely to respond to his manager's suggestions for improvement right after the mistake or at the end of that working day than during a performance-review session several months later. If you have to spend time recreating a situation and refreshing someone's memory of it, the feedback you're providing is likely to be ineffective.[32] Moreover, if you are particularly concerned with *changing* behavior, delays providing feedback on the undesirable actions lessen the likelihood that the feedback will be effective in bringing about the desired change.[33] Of course, making feedback prompt merely for promptness' sake can backfire if you have insufficient information, if you're angry, or if you're otherwise emotionally upset. In such instances, "well-timed" may mean "somewhat delayed."

ENSURE UNDERSTANDING   Is your feedback concise and complete enough so that the recipient clearly and fully understands your communication? Remember, every successful communication requires both transference and understanding of meaning. So if feedback is to be effective, you need to ensure that the recipient understands it.[34] Consistent with our discussion of listening techniques, you should have the recipient rephrase the content of your feedback to see whether it fully captures the meaning you intended.

DIRECT NEGATIVE FEEDBACK TOWARD BEHAVIOR THAT IS CONTROLLABLE BY THE RECIPIENT   There's little value in reminding a person of some shortcoming over which he or she has no control. Negative feedback, therefore, should be directed toward behavior the recipient can do something about.[35] So, for example, to criticize an employee who is late because he forgot to set his wake-up alarm is valid. To criticize him for being late when the subway he takes to work every day had a power failure, trapping him underground for half an hour, is pointless. There is nothing he could have done to correct what happened.

Additionally, when negative feedback is given concerning something that is controllable by the recipient, it may be a good idea to indicate specifically *what* can be done to improve the situation. This takes some of the sting out of the criticism and offers guidance to recipients who understand the problem but don't know how to resolve it.

GROUP DECISION MAKING

One of the more obvious applications of communication concepts is in the area of group decision making. We communicate information, and information is used in the making of decisions. Moreover, group decisions require transmitting of messages between members, and the effectiveness of this communica-

Four Rules for Improving Cross-Cultural Communication

Effective communication is difficult under the best of conditions. Cross-cultural factors clearly create the potential for increased communication problems.[36]

The encoding and decoding of messages into symbols is based on an individual's cultural background and, as a result, is not the same for each person. The greater the differences in backgrounds between sender and receiver, the greater the differences in meanings attached to particular words or behaviors. People from different cultures see, interpret, and evaluate things differently, and consequently act upon them differently.

When communicating with people from a different culture, what can you do to reduce misperceptions, misinterpretations, and misevaluations? Following these four rules can be helpful:

1. *Assume differences until similarity is proven.* Most of us assume that others are more similar to us than they actually are. But people from different countries often are very different from us. So you are far less likely to make an error if you assume others are different from you rather than assuming similarity until difference is proven.

2. *Emphasize description rather than interpretation or evaluation.* Interpreting or evaluating what someone has said or done, in contrast to description, is based more on the observer's culture and background than on the observed situation. As a result, delay judgment until you've had sufficient time to observe and interpret the situation from the differing perspectives of all the cultures involved.

3. *Practice empathy.* Before sending a message, put yourself in the recipient's shoes. What are his or her values, experiences, and frames of reference? What do you know about his or her education, upbringing, and background that can give you added insight? Try to see the other person as he or she really is.

4. *Treat your interpretations as a working hypothesis.* Once you've developed an explanation for a new situation or think you empathize with someone from a foreign culture, treat your interpretation as a hypothesis that needs further testing rather than as a certainty. Carefully assess the feedback provided by recipients to see if it confirms your hypothesis. For important decisions or communiques, you can also check with other foreign and home-country colleagues to make sure that your interpretations are on target.

tion process will have a significant impact on the quality of the group's decisions.

The belief—characterized by juries—that two heads are better than one has long been accepted as a basic component of our legal system. This belief has expanded to the point that, today, many decisions in organizations are made by groups or committees. There are permanent executive committees that meet on a regular basis, special task forces created to analyze unique problems, temporary project teams used to develop new products, and "quality circles" made up of representatives from management and labor who meet to

Are all groups equally vulnerable to groupthink? The evidence suggests not. Researchers have focused in on three moderating variables—the group's cohesiveness, its leader's behavior, and its insulation from outsiders—but the findings have not been consistent.[43] At this point, the most valid conclusions we can make would be: (1) highly cohesive groups have more discussion and bring out more information but it's unclear whether such groups discourage dissent, (2) groups with impartial leaders who encourage member input generate and discuss more alternative solutions, (3) leaders should avoid expressing a preferred solution early in the group's discussion because this tends to limit critical analysis and significantly increases the likelihood that the group will adopt this solution as the final choice, and (4) insulation of the group leads to fewer alternatives being generated and evaluated.

GROUPSHIFT   In comparing group decisions with the individual decisions of members within the group, evidence suggests that there are differences.[44] In some cases, the group decisions are more conservative than the individual decisions. More often, the shift is toward greater risk.[45]

What appears to happen in groups is that the discussion leads to a significant shift in the positions of members toward a more extreme position in the direction toward which they were already leaning before the discussion. So conservative types become more cautious and the more aggressive types take on more risk. The group discussion tends to *exaggerate* the initial position of the group.

The groupshift can be viewed as actually a special case of groupthink. The decision of the group reflects the dominant decision-making norm that develops during the group's discussion. Whether the shift in the group's decision is toward greater caution or more risk depends on the dominant prediscussion norm.

The greater occurrence of the shift toward risk has generated several explanations for the phenomena.[46] It's been argued, for instance, that the discussion creates familiarization among the members. As they become more comfortable with each other, they also become more bold and daring. Another argument is that our society values risk, that we admire individuals who are willing to take risks, and that group discussion motivates members to show that they are at least as willing as their peers to take risks. The most plausible explanation of the shift toward risk, however, seems to be that the group diffuses responsibility. Group decisions free any single member from accountability for the group's final choice. Greater risk can be taken because even if the decision fails, no one member can be held wholly responsible.

So how should you use the findings on groupshift? You should recognize that group decisions exaggerate the initial position of the individual members, that the shift has been shown more often to be toward greater risk, and that whether a group will shift toward greater risk or caution is a function of the members' prediscussion inclinations.

Group Decision Making Techniques

The most common form of group decision making takes place in face-to-face **interacting groups.** But as our discussion of groupthink demonstrated, interacting groups often censor themselves and pressure individual members toward conformity of opinion. Brainstorming, nominal group, and Delphi techniques have been proposed as ways to reduce many of the problems inherent in the traditional interacting group. We'll discuss each in this section.

Interacting Groups Typical groups, where members interact with each other face to face.

Brainstorming An idea-generation process that specifically encourages any and all alternatives, while withholding any criticism of those alternatives.

BRAINSTORMING　　**Brainstorming** is meant to overcome pressures for conformity in the interacting group that retard the development of creative alternatives.[47] It does this by utilizing an idea-generation process that specifically encourages any and all alternatives while withholding any criticism of those alternatives.

In a typical brainstorming session, a half-dozen to a dozen people sit around a table. The group leader states the problem in a clear manner so that it is understood by all participants. Members then "free wheel" as many alternatives as they can in a given length of time. No criticism is allowed, and all the alternatives are recorded for later discussion and analysis. That one idea stimulates others and that judgment of even the most bizarre suggestions are withheld until later encourages group members to "think the unusual."

Brainstorming, however, is merely a process for generating ideas. The next two techniques go further by offering techniques for actually arriving at a preferred solution.[48]

NOMINAL GROUP TECHNIQUE　　The **nominal group technique** restricts discussion or interpersonal communication during the decision making process; hence, the term *nominal*. Group members are all physically present, as in a traditional committee meeting, but members operate independently. Specifically, a problem is presented and then the following steps take place:

Nominal Group Technique A group decision method in which individual members meet face to face to pool their judgments in a systematic but independent fashion.

1. Members meet as a group but, before any discussion takes place, each member independently writes down his or her ideas on the problem.
2. This silent period is followed by each member presenting one idea to the group. Each member takes his or her turn, going around the table, presenting a single idea until all ideas have been presented and recorded (typically on a flip chart or chalkboard). No discussion takes place until all ideas have been recorded.
3. The group now discusses the ideas for clarity and evaluates them.
4. Each group member silently and independently rank orders the ideas. The final decision is determined by the idea with the highest aggregate ranking.

The chief advantage of the nominal group technique is that it permits the group to meet formally but does not restrict independent thinking as does the interacting group.

Delphi Technique A group decision method in which individual members, acting separately, pool their judgment in a systematic and independent fashion.

DELPHI TECHNIQUE　　A more complex and time-consuming alternative is the **Delphi technique.** It is similar to the nominal group technique except that it does not require the physical presence of the group's members. In fact, the Delphi technique never allows the group members to meet face to face. The following steps characterize the Delphi techniques:

1. The problem is identified and members are asked to provide potential solutions through a series of carefully designed questionnaires.
2. Each member anonymously and independently completes the first questionnaire.
3. Results of the first questionnaire are compiled at a central location, transcribed, and reproduced.
4. Each member receives a copy of the results.

5. After viewing the results, members are again asked for their solutions. The results typically trigger new solutions or cause changes in the original position.

6. Steps 4 and 5 are repeated as often as necessary until consensus is reached.

Like the nominal group technique, the Delphi technique insulates group members from the undue influence of others. Because it does not require the physical presence of the participants, the Delphi technique can be used for decision making among geographically scattered groups. For instance, Sony could use the technique to query its managers in Tokyo, Brussels, Paris, London, New York, Toronto, Rio de Janeiro, and Melbourne as to the best worldwide price for one of the company's products. The cost of bringing the executives together at a central location is avoided. Of course, the Delphi technique has its drawbacks. Because the method is extremely time consuming, it is frequently not applicable where a speedy decision is necessary. Additionally, the method may not develop the rich array of alternatives that the interacting or nominal group technique does. The ideas that might surface from the heat of face-to-face interaction may never arise.

SUMMARY: EVALUATING EFFECTIVENESS   How do these various techniques stack up against the traditional interacting group? As we find so often, each technique has its own unique set of strengths and weaknesses. The choice of one technique over the others depends on the criteria you seek to emphasize. For instance, as Table 10–6 indicates, the interacting group is good for building group cohesiveness, brainstorming keeps social pressures to a minimum, and the Delphi technique minimizes interpersonal conflict. The "best" technique is defined by the criteria you use to evaluate the group.

IMPLICATIONS FOR PERFORMANCE
AND SATISFACTION

A careful review of this chapter finds a common theme regarding the relationship between communication and employee satisfaction: The less the uncertainty, the greater the satisfaction. Distortions, ambiguities, and incongruities all increase uncertainty and, hence, have a negative impact on satisfaction.[49]

The less distortion that occurs in communication, the more that goals, feedback, and other management messages to employees will be received as they were intended.[50] This, in turn, should reduce ambiguities and clarify the group's task. Extensive use of vertical, lateral, and informal channels will increase communication flow, reduce uncertainty, and improve group performance and satisfaction. We should also expect incongruities between verbal and nonverbal communiqués to increase uncertainty and reduce satisfaction.

Findings in the chapter further suggest that the goal of perfect communication is unattainable. Yet, there is evidence that demonstrates a positive relationship between effective communication (which includes factors such as perceived trust, perceived accuracy, desire for interaction, top management receptiveness, and upward information requirements) and worker productivity.[51] Choosing the correct channel, clarifying jargon, and utilizing feedback may, therefore, make for more effective communication, but candidness

TABLE 10–6   Evaluating Group Effectiveness

Effectiveness Criteria	Type of Group			
	Interacting	Brainstorming	Nominal	Delphi
Number of ideas	Low	Moderate	High	High
Quality of ideas	Low	Moderate	High	High
Social pressure	High	Low	Moderate	Low
Time/money costs	Moderate	Low	Low	High
Task orientation	Low	High	High	High
Potential for interpersonal conflict	High	Low	Moderate	Low
Feelings of accomplishment	High to low	High	High	Moderate
Commitment to solution	High	Not applicable	Moderate	Low
Builds group cohesiveness	High	High	Moderate	Low

Source: Reprinted by permission of the publisher from "Group Decision Making: What Strategies Should You Use?" J. K. Murnighan, *Management Review,* February 1981, p. 61. © AMACOM, a division of American Management Association, New York. All rights reserved.

requires the admission that the human factor generates distortions that can never be fully eliminated. The communication process represents an exchange of messages, but the outcome is meanings that may or may not approximate those that the sender intended. Whatever the sender's expectations, the decoded message in the mind of the receiver represents his or her reality. And it is this "reality" that will determine performance, along with the individual's level of motivation and his or her degree of satisfaction. The issue of motivation is critical, so we should briefly review how communication is central in determining an individual's degree of motivation.

You will remember from expectancy theory that the degree of effort an individual exerts depends on his or her perception of the effort–performance, performance–reward, and reward–goal satisfaction linkages. If individuals are not given the data necessary to make the perceived probability of these linkages high, motivation will be less than it could be. If rewards are not made clear, if the criteria for determining and measuring performance are ambiguous, or if individuals are not relatively certain that their effort will lead to satisfactory performance, then effort will be reduced. So communication plays a significant role in determining the level of motivation.

A final implication from the communication literature relates to predicting turnover. The use of realistic job previews acts as a communication device for clarifying role expectations. Employees who have been exposed to a realistic job preview have more accurate information about that job. Comparisons of turnover rates between organizations that use the realistic job preview versus either no preview or only presentation of positive job information show that those *not* using the realistic preview have, on average, almost twenty-nine percent higher turnover.[52] This makes a strong case for management conveying honest and accurate information about a job to applicants during the recruiting and selection process.

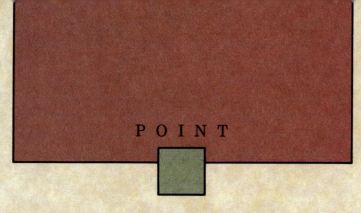

The Case for Improved Understanding

The major barrier to mutual interpersonal communication is our very natural tendency to judge, to evaluate, and to approve (or disapprove) the statements of the other person or the other group. Let me illustrate this view with a couple of simple examples. Suppose that someone, commenting on this discussion, says, "I didn't like what that man said." What will you respond? Almost invariably your reply will be either approval or disapproval of the attitude expressed. Either you respond, "I didn't either; I thought it was terrible," or else you tend to reply, "Oh, I thought it was really good." In other words, the primary reaction is to evaluate it from *your* point of view, your own frame of reference.

Or take another example. Suppose that I say with some feeling. "I think the Republicans are showing a lot of good sound sense these days." What is the response that arises in your mind? The overwhelming likelihood is that it will be evaluative. In other words, you will find yourself agreeing, or disagreeing, or making some judgment about me such as "He must be a conservative" or "He seems solid in his thinking."

Although the tendency to make evaluations is common in almost all interchange of language, it is greatly heightened in those situations where feelings and emotions are deeply involved. So the stronger our feelings, the more likely it is that there will be no mutual element in the communication. There will be just two ideas, two feelings, two judgments, missing each other in psychological space.

I am sure you recognize this from your own experience. When you have not been emotionally involved yourself and have listened to a heated discussion, you often go away thinking, "Well, actually they weren't talking about the same thing." And they were not. Each was making a judgment, an evaluation, from his or her own frame of reference. There was really nothing that could be called communication in any genuine sense. This tendency to react to any emotionally meaningful statement by forming an evaluation of it from our own point of view is, I repeat, the major barrier to interpersonal communication.

The solution to this evaluative tendency is to see the expressed idea and attitudes from the other person's point of view, to sense how it feels to him, or her, to achieve his or her frame of reference in regard to the thing about which he or she is talking. When each of the different parties comes to *understand* the other from the *other's* point of view rather than *judge* that point of view, the insincerities, the lies, and the "false fronts" drop away with astonishing speed.

Adapted from C. R. Rogers, in C. R. Rogers and F. J. Roethlisberger, "Barriers and Gateways to Communication," *Harvard Business Review,* August 1952, pp. 46–50.

The Case for Ambiguous Communication

The major barrier to communication is the naive assumption that individuals actually want to *improve* communication. Most of us seem to overlook a very basic fact: It is often in the sender's and/or receiver's best interest purposely to keep communication ambiguous.

"Lack of communication" seems to have replaced original sin as the explanation for the ills of the world. We're continually hearing that problems would go away if we could "just communicate better." Some of the basic assumptions underlying this view need to be looked at carefully.

One assumption is the way in which poor communication resembles original sin: Both tend to get tangled up with control of the situation. If one defines communication as mutual understanding, this does not imply control for either party and certainly not for both. However, equating good communication with control appears in the assumption that better communication will necessarily reduce strife and conflict. Each individual's definition of better communication, like his or her definition of virtuous conduct, becomes that of having the other party accept his or her views, which would reduce conflict at that party's expense. A better understanding of the situation might serve only to underline the differences rather than to resolve them. Indeed, many of the techniques thought of as poor communication were apparently developed with the aim of bypassing or avoiding confrontation.

Another assumption that grows from this view is that when a conflict has existed for a long time and shows every sign of continuing, lack of communication must be one of the basic problems. Usually if the situation is examined more carefully, plenty of communication will be found; the problem is again one of equating communication with agreement.

Still a third assumption, somewhat related but less squarely based on the equation of communication with controls, is that it is always in the interest of at least one of the parties to an interaction and often of both to attain maximum clarity as measured by some more or less objective standard. Aside from the difficulty of setting up this standard —whose standard? and doesn't this give *him* or *her* control of the situation?—there are some sequences, and perhaps many of them, in which it is to the interests of both parties to leave the situation as fuzzy and undefined as possible. This is notably true in culturally or personally sensitive and taboo areas involving prejudices, preconceptions, and so on, but it can also be true when the area is merely a new one that could be seriously distorted by using old definitions and old solutions.

Too often we forget that keeping organizational communications fuzzy cuts down on questions, permits faster decision making, minimizes objections, reduces opposition, makes it easier to deny one's earlier statements, preserves freedom to change one's mind, helps to preserve mystique and hide insecurities, allows one to say several things at the same time, permits one to say "no" diplomatically, and helps to avoid confrontation and anxiety.

If you want to see the fine art of ambiguous communication up close, all you have to do is watch a television interview with a politician who is running for office. The interviewer attempts to get specific information, while the politician tries to retain multiple possible interpretations. Such ambiguous communications allow the politician to approach his or her ideal image of being "all things to all people."

Based on C. O. Kursh, "The Benefits of Poor Communication," *The Psychoanalytic Review,* Summer-Fall 1971, pp. 189–208; and E. M. Eisenberg and M. G. Witten, "Reconsidering Openness in Organizational Communication," *Academy of Management Review,* July 1987, pp. 418–26.

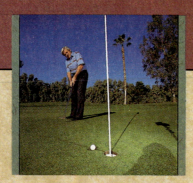

CHAPTER ELEVEN

LEADERSHIP

LEARNING OBJECTIVES

After studying this chapter, you should be able to:

1. *Describe the nature of leadership*
2. *Summarize the conclusions of trait theories*
3. *Identify the limitations of behavioral theories*
4. *Describe Fiedler's contingency model*
5. *Summarize the path–goal theory*
6. *State the situational leadership theory*
7. *Explain leader–member exchange theory*
8. *Describe the leader–participation model*
9. *Explain why no one leadership style is ideal in all situations*
10. *Define the qualities that characterize charismatic leaders*

A Fiedler Update: Cognitive Resource Theory

Recently, Fred Fiedler and Joe Garcia reconceptualized the former's original theory[25] to deal with "some serious oversights that need to be redressed."[26] Specifically, they are concerned with trying to explain the *process* by which a leader obtains effective group performance. They call this reconceptualization *cognitive resource theory*.

They begin by making two assumptions. First, intelligent and competent leaders make more effective plans, decisions, and action strategies than less intelligent and competent leaders. Second, leaders communicate their plans, decisions, and strategies through directive behavior. They then show how stress and cognitive resources such as experience, tenure, and intelligence act as important influences on leadership effectiveness.

The essence of the new theory can be culled down to three predictions: (1) directive behavior results in good performance only if linked with high intelligence in a supportive, nonstressful leadership environment; (2) in highly stressful situations, there is a positive relationship between job experience and performance; and (3) the intellectual abilities of leaders correlate with group performance in situations which the leader perceives as nonstressful.

Fiedler and Garcia admit that the data supporting cognitive resource theory is far from overwhelming. More research is certainly needed. Yet, given the impact of Fiedler's original contingency model of leadership on organizational behavior, the new theory's link to this earlier model, and the new theory's introduction of the leader's cognitive abilities as important influences on leadership effectiveness, cognitive resource theory should not be dismissed out of hand.

- *Selling* (high task-high relationship). The leader provides both directive behavior and supportive behavior.
- *Participating* (low task-high relationship). The leader and follower share in decision making, with the main role of the leader being facilitating and communicating.
- *Delegating* (low task-low relationship). The leader provides little direction or support.

The final component in Hersey and Blanchard's theory is defining four stages of maturity:

- *M1*. People are both unable and unwilling to take responsibility to do something. They are neither competent nor confident.
- *M2*. People are unable but willing to do the necessary job tasks. They are motivated but currently lack the appropriate skills.
- *M3*. People are able but unwilling to do what the leader wants.
- *M4*. People are both able and willing to do what is asked of them.

Figure 11–5 integrates the various components into the situational leadership model. As followers reach high levels of maturity, the leader

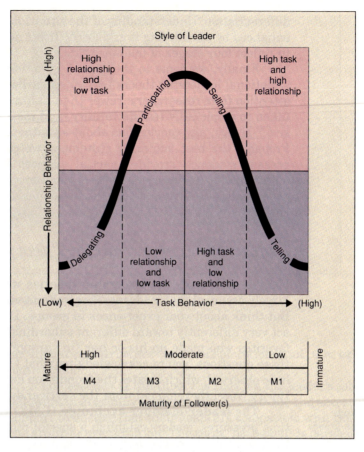

FIGURE 11–5   Situational Leadership Model

Source: Adapted from P. Hersey and K. Blanchard, *Management of Organizational Behavior: Utilizing Human Resources,* 4th ed. © 1982, p. 152. Reprinted by permission of Prentice-Hall Inc., Englewood Cliffs, N.J.

responds by not only continuing to decrease control over activities, but also by continuing to decrease relationship behavior as well. At stage M1, followers need clear and specific directions. At stage M2, both high-task and high-relationship behavior is needed. The high-task behavior compensates for the followers' lack of ability, and the high-relationship behavior tries to get the followers psychologically to "buy into" the leader's desires. M3 creates motivational problems that are best solved by a supportive, nondirective, participative style. Finally, at stage M4, the leader doesn't have to do much because followers are both willing and able to take responsibility.

The astute reader might have noticed the high similarity between Hersey and Blanchard's four leadership styles and the four extreme "corners" in the Managerial Grid. The telling style equates to the 9,1 leader; selling equals 9,9; participating is equivalent to 1,9; and delegating is the same as the 1,1 leader. Is situational leadership, then, merely the Managerial Grid with one major difference—the replacement of the 9,9 ("one style for all occasions") contention with the recommendation that the "right" style should align with the maturity of the followers? Hersey and Blanchard say "No!"[29] They argue that the grid emphasizes *concern* for production and people, which are attitudinal dimensions. Situational leadership, in contrast, emphasizes task and relationship *behavior.* In spite of Hersey and Blanchard's claim, this is a pretty minute

All This Talk About Leadership . . . But What About Followership?

When someone was once asked what it took to be a great leader, he responded: Great followers! While the response may have seemed sarcastic, it has some truth. We have long known that many managers can't lead a horse to water. But many subordinates can't follow a parade.

Only recently have we begun to recognize that in addition to having leaders that can lead, successful organizations need followers who can follow.[63] In fact, it's probably fair to say that all organizations have far more followers than leaders, so ineffective followers may be more of a handicap to an organization than ineffective leaders.

What qualities do effective followers have? One writer focuses on four:[64]

1. *They manage themselves well.* They are able to think for themselves. They can work independently and without close supervision.

2. *They are committed to a purpose outside themselves.* Effective followers are committed to something—a cause, a product, a work group, an organization, an idea—in addition to the care of their own lives. Most people like working with colleagues who are emotionally, as well as physically, committed to their work.

3. *They build their competence and focus their efforts for maximum impact.* Effective followers master skills that will be useful to their organizations, and they hold higher performance standards than their job or work group requires.

4. *They are courageous, honest, and credible.* Effective followers establish themselves as independent, critical thinkers whose knowledge and judgment can be trusted. They hold high ethical standards, give credit where credit is due, and aren't afraid to own up to their mistakes.

Predictive ability increased as a result of the recognition that inclusion of situational factors was critical. Recent efforts have moved beyond mere recognition toward specific attempts to isolate these situational variables. We can expect further progress to be made with leadership models, but in the last decade we have taken several large steps—large enough that we now can make moderately effective predictions as to who can best lead a group and explain under what conditions a given approach (such as task oriented or people oriented) is likely to lead to high performance and satisfaction.

In addition, the study of leadership has expanded to include implicit theories, especially the transformational or charismatic view of leadership. As we learn more about the personal characteristics that followers attribute to charismatic leaders and the conditions that facilitate its emergence, we should be increasingly able to predict situations when followers will exhibit extraordinary commitment and loyalty to their leaders and to their leaders' goals.

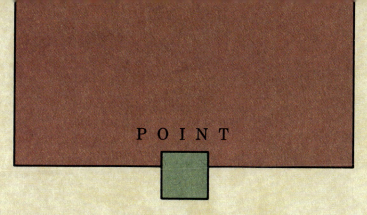

Leaders Make a Real Difference!

There can be little question that the success of an organization, or any group within an organization, depends largely on the quality of its leadership. Whether in business, government, education, medicine, or religion, the quality of an organization's leadership determines the quality of the organization itself. Successful leaders anticipate change, vigorously exploit opportunities, motivate their followers to higher levels of productivity, correct poor performance, and lead the organization toward its objectives.

The importance relegated to the leadership function is well known. Rarely does a week go by that we don't hear or read about some leadership concern: "President Fails to Provide the Leadership America Needs!" "Montana Leads 49ers to Super Bowl Victory!" "The Democratic Party Searches for New Leadership!" "Sculley Leads Apple Turnaround!" A review of the leadership literature led two academics to conclude that the research shows "a consistent effect for leadership explaining twenty to forty-five percent of the variance on relevant organizational outcomes."*

Why is leadership so important to an organization's success? The answer lies in the need for coordination and control. Organizations exist to achieve objectives that are either impossible or extremely inefficient to achieve if done by individuals acting alone. The organization itself is a coordination and control mechanism. Rules, policies, job descriptions, and authority hierarchies are illustrations of devices created to facilitate coordination and control. But leadership, too, contributes toward integrating various job activities, coordinating communication between organizational subunits, monitoring activities, and controlling deviations from standard. No amount of rules and regulations can replace the experienced leader who can make rapid and decisive decisions.

The importance of leadership is not lost on those who staff organizations. Corporations, government agencies, school systems, and institutions of all shapes and sizes cumulatively spend billions of dollars every year to recruit, select, evaluate, and train individuals for leadership positions. The best evidence, however, of the importance organizations place on leadership roles is exhibited in salary schedules. Leaders are routinely paid ten, twenty, or more times the salary of those in nonleadership positions. The head of General Motors earns more than $1 million annually. The highest skilled auto worker, in contrast, earns under $50,000 a year. The president of this auto worker's union makes better than $100,000 a year. Police officers typically make around $25,000 to $35,000 a year. Their boss probably earns twenty-five percent more, and his or her boss another twenty-five percent. The pattern is well established. The more responsibility a leader has, as evidenced by his or her level in the organization, the more he or she earns. Would organizations voluntarily pay their leaders so much more than their nonleaders if they didn't strongly believe that leaders make a real difference?

*D. V. Day and R. G. Lord, "Executive Leadership and Organizational Performance: Suggestions for a New Theory and Methodology," *Journal of Management,* Fall 1988, pp. 453–64.

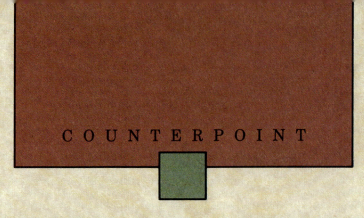

Leaders Don't Make a Difference!

Given the resources that have been spent on studying, selecting, and training leaders, you'd expect there to be clear evidence supporting the positive impact of leadership on a group or organization's performance. That evidence has failed to surface!

Analyses of leadership have frequently presumed that leadership style or leader behavior was an independent variable that could be selected or trained at will to conform to what research would find to be optimal. Even theorists who took a more contingent view of appropriate leadership behavior generally assumed that with proper training, appropriate behavior could be produced. Fiedler, noting how hard it is to change behavior, suggested changing the situational characteristics rather than the person, but this was an unusual suggestion in the context of prevailing literature that suggested that leadership style was something to be strategically selected according to the variables of the particular leadership theory.

But the leader is embedded in a social system, which constrains behavior. The leader has a role set, in which members have expectations for appropriate behavior and persons make efforts to modify the leader's behavior. Pressures to conform to the expectations of peers, subordinates, and superiors are all relevant in determining actual behavior.

Leaders, even in high-level positions, have unilateral control over fewer resources and fewer policies than might be expected. Investment decisions may require approval of others, while hiring and promotion decisions may be accomplished by committees. Leader behavior is constrained both by the demands of others in the role set and by organizationally prescribed limitations on the sphere of activity and influence.

Many factors that may affect organizational performance are outside a leader's control, even if he or she were to have complete discretion over major areas of organizational decision. For example, consider the executive in a home construction firm.

Costs are largely determined by operation of commodities and labor markets, and demand is largely affected by interest rates, availability of mortgage money, and economic conditions that are affected by governmental policies over which the executive has little control. School superintendents have little control over birth rates and community economic development, both of which profoundly affect school system budgets. While the leader may react to contingencies as they arise, or may be a better or worse forecaster, in accounting for variation in organizational outcomes, he or she may account for relatively little compared to external factors.

The leader's success or failure may also be partly due to circumstances unique to the organization but still outside his or her control. Leader positions in organizations vary in terms of the strength and position of the organization. The choice of a new executive does not fundamentally alter a market and financial position that has developed over years and affects the leader's ability to make strategic changes and the likelihood that the organization will do well or poorly. Organizations have relatively enduring strengths and weaknesses. The choice of a particular leader for a particular position has limited impact on these capabilities.

There is a basic myth associated with leadership. We believe in attribution—when something happens, we believe something has *caused* it. Leaders play that role in organizations. They take the credit for successes and the blame for failures. A more realistic conclusion would probably be that except in times of rapid growth, change, or crisis, leaders don't make much of a difference in an organization's performance.

Much of this argument is based on J. Pfeffer, "The Ambiguity of Leadership," *Academy of Management Review,* January 1977, pp. 104–11. See also A. B. Thomas, "Does Leadership Make a Difference to Organizational Performance?, *Administrative Science Quarterly,* September 1988, pp. 388–400, for a recent review of this issue.

FOR DISCUSSION

1. Trace the development of leadership research.
2. Discuss the strengths and weaknesses in the trait approach to leadership.
3. "Behavioral theories of leadership are static." Do you agree or disagree? Discuss.
4. What is the Managerial Grid? Contrast its approach to leadership with the Ohio State and Michigan groups.
5. Develop an example where you operationalize the Fiedler model.
6. Contrast the situational leadership theory with the Managerial Grid.
7. How do Hersey and Blanchard define *maturity?* Is this contingency variable included in any other contingency theory of leadership?
8. Develop an example where you operationalize path-goal theory.
9. Reconcile Hersey and Blanchard's situational leadership theory, path-goal theory, and substitutes for leadership.
10. Describe the leader-participation model. What are its contingency variables?
11. When might leaders be irrelevant?
12. What kind of activities could a college student pursue that might lead to the perception that he or she was a charismatic leader? In doing those activities, what might the student do to further enhance this perception of being charismatic?

FOR FURTHER READING

BASS, B. M., *Bass and Stogdill's Handbook of Leadership,* 3rd ed. New York: Free Press, 1990. This 1,200 page treatise is probably the most comprehensive resource available on leadership theories and models.

CONGER, J. A. and R. N. KANUNGO, *Charismatic Leadership.* San Francisco: Jossey-Bass, 1988. Brings together articles from experts in a variety of fields; providing one of the most comprehensive and diverse looks at charismatic leadership.

FIELD, R. H. G., "The Self-Fulfilling Prophecy Leader: Achieving the Metharme Effect," *Journal of Management Studies,* March 1989, pp. 151–75. Presents a model of leadership based on developing high member expectations.

KOTTER, J. P., "How Leaders Grow Leaders," *Across the Board,* March 1988, pp. 38–42. Describes the activities in which successful firms engage to attract, develop, retain, and motivate leadership talent.

YUKL, G., "Managerial Leadership: A Review of Theory and Research," *Journal of Management,* June 1989, pp. 251–89. An excellent review of all major theories and the current state of leadership research.

ZALEZNIK, A., "The Leadership Gap," *Academy of Management Executive,* February 1990, pp. 7–22. A critical assessment of a mystique that places a premium on the team over the individual as practiced in business and taught in business schools.

Compute Your LPC Score

Think of the person with whom you work least well. He or she may be someone you work with now, or may be someone you knew in the past. He or she does not have to be the person you like least well, but should be the person with whom you now have or have had the most difficulty in getting a job done. Describe this person as he or she appears to you by placing an "x" at that point which you believe best describes that person. Do this for each pair of adjectives.

	8	7	6	5	4	3	2	1	
Pleasant	8	7	6	5	4	3	2	1	Unpleasant
Friendly	8	7	6	5	4	3	2	1	Unfriendly
Rejecting	1	2	3	4	5	6	7	8	Accepting
Helpful	8	7	6	5	4	3	2	1	Frustrating
Unenthusiastic	1	2	3	4	5	6	7	8	Enthusiastic
Tense	1	2	3	4	5	6	7	8	Relaxed
Distant	1	2	3	4	5	6	7	8	Close
Cold	1	2	3	4	5	6	7	8	Warm
Cooperative	8	7	6	5	4	3	2	1	Uncooperative
Supportive	8	7	6	5	4	3	2	1	Hostile
Boring	1	2	3	4	5	6	7	8	Interesting
Quarrelsome	1	2	3	4	5	6	7	8	Harmonious
Self-assured	8	7	6	5	4	3	2	1	Hesitant
Efficient	8	7	6	5	4	3	2	1	Inefficient
Gloomy	1	2	3	4	5	6	7	8	Cheerful
Open	8	7	6	5	4	3	2	1	Guarded

Source: From *Leadership and Effective Management* by F. E. Fiedler and M. M. Chemers. Copyright © 1974 by Scott, Foresman & Co. Reprinted by permission.

Turn to page 689 for scoring directions and key.

Oliver North—A Leader or the Led?

Oliver North, the Marine Lieutenant Colonel, made national news and became a hero during the Iran Contra Hearings before Congress. North was perceived by many as a freedom fighting, anti-communist soldier. In his answers to most questions, North projected himself as the patriotic soldier doing what he believed was in the best interest of the U.S., even if his actions violated the law. North testified that even though he knew that selling arms to Iran was illegal, the need to avoid the spread of communism to countries neighboring the United States was so critical that circumventing laws was necessary.

Throughout his testimony, North stressed that he was guided by the need to use extraordinary means to help the United States win its war against communism in Central America. North's belief in what he was doing was so strong that he was able to convince subordinates, including his secretary, Fawn Hall, to knowingly violate laws. The most highly publicized of these violations was Hall's alteration of documents to hamper the Congressional investigation. Public sentiment was sufficiently strong that there was discussion in some circles of North being a candidate for President or Vice-President.

In his subsequent trial for his actions, North presented himself as a "scapegoat" and "fall guy," contending that he was simply following orders and being blamed for decisions made by others. He further argued that he was simply following the orders and examples set by former President Reagan and current President Bush. Government released documents showed that both Presidents Reagan and Bush were directly involved in getting other governments to provide aid and support to the contras in return for U.S. aid to their countries. North testified that he never anticipated his actions as a member of the National Security Council could be illegal and that he was simply being a loyal subordinate and not questioning instructions given him by his superiors.

QUESTIONS

1. What characteristics of a charismatic leader are displayed by North?

2. What characteristics of an effective follower does North display?

3. How are charismatic leaders able to establish credibility and support from followers?

4. Do followers have an obligation to evaluate the actions of the leader and to take responsibility for their own behavior?

This case is contributed by Dr. Joe G. Thomas, Middle Tennessee State University. It is based on facts presented in Jill Abramson, "North Trial, No Dreary Anticlimax, Has Offered Odd Turnings, Altered Egos and a Showstopper," *The Wall Street Journal*, April 19, 1989, p. A20.

NOTES

[1]Based on L. Armstrong, "The American Drivers Steering Japan Through the States," *Business Week,* March 12, 1990, p. 98.

[2]A. Zaleznik, "Excerpts from 'Managers and Leaders: Are They Different?'" *Harvard Business Review,* May–June 1986, p. 54.

[3]V. H. Vroom, "The Search for a Theory of Leadership," in J. W. McGuire (ed.), *Contemporary Management: Issues and Viewpoints* (Englewood Cliffs, NJ: Prentice Hall, 1974), p. 396.

[4]J. G. Geier, "A Trait Approach to the Study of Leadership in Small Groups," *Journal of Communication,* December 1967, pp. 316–23.

[5]R. M. Stogdill, *Handbook of Leadership: A Survey of Theory and Research* (New York: Free Press, 1974).

[6]Ibid.

[7]See, for instance, D. A. Kenny and S. J. Zaccaro, "An Estimate of Variance Due to Traits in Leadership," *Journal of Applied Psychology,* November 1983, pp. 678–85.

[8]R. M. Stogdill and A. E. Coons (eds.), *Leader Behavior: Its Description and Measurement,* Research Monograph No. 88 (Columbus: Ohio State University, Bureau of Business Research, 1951). For an updated review of the Ohio State research, see S. Kerr, C. A. Schriesheim, C. J. Murphy, and R. M. Stogdill, "Toward a Contingency Theory of Leadership Based upon the Consideration and Initiating Structure Literature," *Organizational Behavior and Human Performance,* August 1974, pp. 62–82; and B. M. Fisher, "Consideration and Initiating Structure and Their Relationships with Leader Effectiveness: A Meta-Analysis," F. Hoy (ed.), *Proceedings of the 48th Academy of Management Conference,* Anaheim, Calif., 1988, pp. 201–05.

[9]R. Kahn and D. Katz, "Leadership Practices in Relation to Productivity and Morale," D. Cartwright and A. Zander (eds.), *Group Dynamics: Research and Theory,* 2nd ed. (Elmsford, NY: Row, Paterson, 1960).

[10]R. R. Blake and J. S. Mouton, *The Managerial Grid* (Houston: Gulf, 1964).

[11]See, for example, R. R. Blake and J. S. Mouton, "A Comparative Analysis of Situationalism and 9,9 Management by Principle," *Organizational Dynamics,* Spring 1982, pp. 20–43.

[12]See, for example, L. L. Larson, J. G. Hunt, and R. N. Osborn, "The Great Hi-Hi Leader Behavior Myth: A Lesson from Occam's Razor," *Academy of Management Journal,* December 1976, pp. 628–41; and P. C. Nystrom, "Managers and the Hi-Hi Leader Myth," *Academy of Management Journal,* June 1978, pp. 325–31.

[13]See, for example, the three styles—autocratic, participative, and laissez-faire—proposed by K. Lewin and R. Lippitt, "An Experimental Approach to the Study of Autocracy and Democracy: A Preliminary Note," *Sociometry,* no. 1 (1938), pp. 292–380; or the 3-D theory proposed by W. J. Reddin, *Managerial Effectiveness* (New York: McGraw-Hill, 1970).

[14]J. P. Howell, P. W. Dorfman, and S. Kerr, "Moderating Variables in Leadership Research," *Academy of Management Review,* January 1986, pp. 88–102.

[15]R. Tannenbaum and W. H. Schmidt, "How to Choose a Leadership Pattern," *Harvard Business Review,* March–April 1958, pp. 95–101.

[16]A. C. Filley, R. J. House, and S. Kerr, *Managerial Process and Organizational Behavior,* 2nd ed. (Glenview, IL: Scott, Foresman, 1976), p. 223.

[17]W. C. Hamner and D. W. Organ, *Organizational Behavior: An Applied Psychological Approach* (Dallas: Business Publications, 1978), pp. 396–97.

[18]F. E. Fiedler, *A Theory of Leadership Effectiveness* (New York: McGraw-Hill, 1967).

[19]S. Shiflett, "Is There a Problem with the LPC Score in LEADER MATCH?," *Personnel Psychology,* Winter 1981, pp. 765–69.

[20]F. E. Fiedler, M. M. Chemers, and L. Mahar, *Improving Leadership Effectiveness: The Leader Match Concept* (New York: John Wiley, 1977).

[21]L. H. Peters, D. D. Hartke, and J. T. Pohlmann, "Fiedler's Contingency Theory of Leadership: An Application of the Meta-Analysis Procedures of Schmidt and Hunter," *Psychological Bulletin,* March 1985, pp. 274–85.

[22]Ibid.

[23]See, for instance, R. W. Rice, "Psychometric Properties of the Esteem for the Least Preferred Coworker (LPC) Scale," *Academy of Management Review,* January 1978, pp. 106–18; C. A. Schriesheim, B. D. Bannister, and W. H. Money, "Psychometric Properties of the LPC Scale: An Extension of Rice's Review," *Academy of Management Review,* April 1979, pp. 287–90; and J. K. Kennedy, J. M. Houston, M. A. Korgaard, and D. D. Gallo, "Construct Space of the Least Preferred Co-Worker (LPC) Scale," *Educational & Psychological Measurement,* Fall 1987, pp. 807–14.

[24]See E. H. Schein, *Organizational Psychology,* 3rd ed. (Englewood Cliffs, NJ: Prentice Hall, 1980), pp. 116–17; and B. Kabanoff, "A Critique of Leader Match and Its Implications for Leadership Research," *Personnel Psychology,* Winter 1981, pp. 749–64.

[25]F. E. Fiedler and J. E. Garcia, *New Approaches to Effective Leadership: Cognitive Resources and Organizational Performance* (New York: John Wiley & Sons, 1987).

[26]*Ibid.,* p. 6.

[27]P. Hersey and K. H. Blanchard, "So You Want to Know Your Leadership Style?" *Training and Development Journal,* February 1974, pp. 1–15; and P. Hersey and K. H. Blanchard,

Management of Organizational Behavior: Utilizing Human Resources, 4th ed. (Englewood Cliffs, NJ: Prentice Hall, 1982), pp. 150–61.

[28]Hersey and Blanchard, *Management of Organizational Behavior,* p. 171.

[29]P. Hersey and K. H. Blanchard, "Grid Principles and Situationalism: Both! A Response to Blake and Mouton," *Group and Organization Studies,* June 1982, pp. 207–10.

[30]R. K. Hambleton and R. Gumpert, "The Validity of Hersey and Blanchard's Theory of Leader Effectiveness," *Group & Organizational Studies,* June 1982, pp. 225–42; C. L. Graeff, "The Situational Leadership Theory: A Critical View," *Academy of Management Review,* April 1983, pp. 285–91; W. Blank, J. R. Weitzel, and S. G. Green, "Situational Leadership Theory: A Test of Underlying Assumptions," paper presented at the National Academy of Management Conference, Chicago, August 1986; R. P. Vecchio, "Situational Leadership Theory: An Examination of a Prescriptive Theory," *Journal of Applied Psychology,* August 1987, pp. 444–51; and J. R. Goodson, G. W. McGee, and J. F. Cashman, "Situational Leadership Theory: A Test of Leadership Prescriptions," *Group & Organization Studies,* December 1989, pp. 446–61.

[31]R. P. Vecchio, "Situational Leadership Theory."

[32]F. Dansereau, J. Cashman, and G. Graen, "Instrumentality Theory and Equity Theory as Complementary Approaches in Predicting the Relationship of Leadership and Turnover Among Managers," *Organizational Behavior and Human Performance,* October 1973, pp. 184–200; and G. Graen, M. Novak, and P. Sommerkamp, "The Effects of Leader-Member Exchange and Job Design on Productivity and Satisfaction: Testing a Dual Attachment Model," *Organizational Behavior and Human Performance,* August 1982, pp. 109–31.

[33]G. Graen and J. Cashman, "A Role-Making Model of Leadership in Formal Organizations: A Development Approach," in J. G. Hunt and L. L. Larson (eds.), *Leadership Frontiers* (Kent, OH: Kent State University Press, 1975), pp. 143–65; and R. Liden and G. Graen, "Generalizability of the Vertical Dyad Linkage Model of Leadership," *Academy of Management Journal,* September 1980, pp. 451–65.

[34]D. Duchon, S. G. Green, and T. D. Taber, "Vertical Dyad Linkage: A Longitudinal Assessment of Antecedents, Measures, and Consequences," *Journal of Applied Psychology,* February 1986, pp. 56–60.

[35]See, for example, G. Graen, M. Novak, and P. Sommerkamp, "The Effects of Leader-Member Exchange;" T. Scandura and G. Graen, "Moderating Effects of Initial Leader-Member Exchange Status on the Effects of a Leadership Intervention," *Journal of Applied Psychology,* August 1984, pp. 428–36; and R. P. Vecchio and B. C. Gobdel, "The Vertical Dyad Linkage Model of Leadership: Problems and Prospects," *Organizational Behavior and Human Performance,* August 1984, pp. 5–20.

[36]A. Jago, "Leadership: Perspectives in Theory and Research," *Management Science,* March 1982, pp. 331.

[37]R. J. House, "A Path-Goal Theory of Leader Effectiveness," *Administrative Science Quarterly,* September 1971, pp. 321–38; R. J. House and T. R. Mitchell, "Path-Goal Theory of Leadership," *Journal of Contemporary Business,* Autumn 1974, p. 86; and R. J. House, "Retrospective Comment," in L. E. Boone and D. D. Bowen, *The Great Writings in Management and Organizational Behavior,* 2nd ed. (New York: Random House, 1987), pp. 354–64.

[38]See J. Indik, "Path-Goal Theory of Leadership: A Meta-Analysis," paper presented at the National Academy of Management Conference, Chicago, August 1986; and R. T. Keller, "A Test of the Path-Goal Theory of Leadership With Need for Clarity as a Moderator in Research and Development Organizations," *Journal of Applied Psychology,* April 1989, pp. 208–12.

[39]V. H. Vroom and P. W. Yetton, *Leadership and Decision-Making* (Pittsburgh: University of Pittsburgh Press, 1973).

[40]From V. H. Vroom, "A New Look at Managerial Decision Making," *Organizational Dynamics,* Spring 1973, pp. 66–80. With permission.

[41]See, for example, R. H. G. Field, "A Test of the Vroom-Yetton Normative Model of Leadership," *Journal of Applied Psychology,* October 1982, pp. 523–32; C. R. Leana, "Power Relinquishment Versus Power Sharing: Theoretical Clarification and Empirical Comparison of Delegation and Participation," *Journal of Applied Psychology,* May 1987, pp. 228–33; and J. T. Ettling and A. G. Jago, "Participation Under Conditions of Conflict: More on the Validity of the Vroom-Yetton Model," *Journal of Management Studies,* January 1988, pp. 73–83.

[42]V. H. Vroom and A. G. Jago, *The New Leadership: Managing Participation in Organizations* (Englewood Cliffs, N.J.: Prentice Hall, 1988). See especially Chapter 8.

[43]S. Kerr and J. M. Jermier, "Substitutes for Leadership: Their Meaning and Measurement," *Organizational Behavior and Human Performance,* December 1978, pp. 375–403; J. P. Howell and P. W. Dorfman, "Substitutes for Leadership: Test of a Construct," *Academy of Management Journal,* December 1981, pp. 714–28; P. W. Howard and W. F. Joyce, "Substitutes for Leadership: A Statistical Refinement," paper presented at the 42nd Annual Academy of Management Conference, New York, August 1982; J. P. Howell, P. W. Dorfman, and S. Kerr, "Leadership and Substitutes for Leadership," *Journal of Applied Behavioral Science,* Vol. 22, No. 1, 1986, pp. 29–46; and N. J. Pitner, "Leadership Substitutes: Their Factorial Validity in Educational Organizations," *Educational & Psychological Measurement,* Summer 1988, pp. 307–15.

[44]B. Karmel, "Leadership: A Challenge to Traditional Research Methods and Assumptions," *Academy of Management Review,* July 1978, pp. 477–79.

[45]Schein, *Organizational Psychology,* p. 132.

[46]Margerison and Glube, "Leadership Decision-Making."

[47]K. Blanchard and S. Johnson, *The One Minute Manager* (New York: William Morrow, 1982).

[48]See, for instance, J. C. McElroy, "A Typology of Attribution Leadership Research," *Academy of Management Review,* July 1982, pp. 413–17; and J. R. Meindl and S. B. Ehrlich, "The Romance of Leadership and the Evaluation of Organizational Performance," *Academy of Management Journal,* March 1987, pp. 91–109.

[49]R. G. Lord, C. L. DeVader, and G. M. Alliger, "A Meta-Analysis of the Relation Between Personality Traits and Leadership Perceptions: An Application of Validity Generalization Procedures," *Journal of Applied Psychology,* August 1986, pp. 402–10.

[50]G. N. Powell and D. A. Butterfield, "The 'High-High' Leader Rides Again!," *Group and Organization Studies,* December 1984, pp. 437–50.

[51]B. M. Staw and J. Ross, "Commitment in an Experimenting Society: A Study of the Attribution of Leadership from Administrative Scenarios," *Journal of Applied Psychology,* June 1980, pp. 249–60.

[52]J. A. Conger and R. N. Kanungo, "Behavioral Dimensions of Charismatic Leadership," in J. A. Conger, R. N. Kanungo and Associates, *Charismatic Leadership* (San Francisco: Jossey-Bass, 1988), p. 79.

[53]J. M. Burns, *Leadership* (New York: Harper & Row, 1978); and B. M. Bass, *Leadership and Performance Beyond Expectations* (New York: Free Press, 1985).

[54]B. M. Bass, *Leadership and Performance Beyond Expectations.*

[55]R. J. House, "A 1976 Theory of Charismatic Leadership," in J. G. Hunt and L. L. Larson (eds.), *Leadership: The Cutting Edge* (Carbondale: Southern Illinois University Press, 1977), pp. 189–207.

[56]W. Bennis, "The 4 Competencies of Leadership," *Training and Development Journal,* August 1984, pp. 15–19.

[57]J. A. Conger and R. N. Kanungo, "Behavioral Dimensions of Charismatic Leadership," pp. 78–97.

[58]R. J. House, J. Woycke, and E. M. Fodor, "Charismatic and Noncharismatic Leaders: Differences in Behavior and Effectiveness," in J. A. Conger and R. N. Kanungo, *Charismatic Leadership,* pp. 103–04.

[59]J. A. Conger and R. N. Kanungo, "Training Charismatic Leadership: A Risky and Critical Task," in J. A. Conger and R. N. Kanungo, *Charismatic Leadership,* pp. 309–23.

[60]J. M. Howell and P. J. Frost, "A Laboratory Study of Charismatic Leadership," *Organizational Behavior and Human Decision Processes,"* April 1989, pp. 243–69.

[61]R. J. House, "A 1976 Theory of Charismatic Leadership."

[62]D. Machan, "The Charisma Merchants," *Forbes,* January 23, 1989, pp. 100–01.

[63]R. E. Kelley, "In Praise of Followers," *Harvard Business Review,* November–December 1988, pp. 142–48.

[64]*Ibid.*

POWER AND POLITICS

LEARNING OBJECTIVES

After studying this chapter, you should be able to:

1. Define the four bases of power

2. Define the four sources of power

3. List seven power tactics and their contingencies

4. Explain how power is achieved

5. Clarify what creates dependency in power relationships

6. Describe the importance of a political perspective

7. List those individual and organizational factors that stimulate political behavior

8. Identify seven techniques for managing the impression one makes on others

In the film industry, there are three levels of influence: some, a lot, and Spielberg. Unquestionably the most powerful movie maker in Hollywood, Steven Spielberg has studio heads fighting each other to secure his services, and he is able to pick the projects he wants and demand and get free rein on his films.   Mark Sennet/Onyx.

*You can get much farther with a kind word and a gun
than you can with a kind word alone.*

A. CAPONE

The song lyric goes: "You don't pull on Superman's cape, you don't spit in the wind, you don't pull the mask off the old Lone Ranger, and you don't mess around with Jim."* In the movie industry, that last line could be rewritten to ". . . and you don't mess around with Steven." The Steven we're talking about here is Spielberg.[1]

Steven Spielberg is unquestionably the most powerful film maker in Hollywood. That power comes from his string of megahits. He has produced or directed five of the ten top-grossing movies in Hollywood's history—*E. T. The Extraterrestrial, Jaws, Raiders of the Lost Ark, Back to the Future,* and *Indiana Jones and the Temple of Doom*. In all, his twenty-five films have sold more than two billion dollars worth of tickets worldwide. As the president of Columbia Pictures put it, "Who's going to argue with his track record?"

Spielberg's power in his industry is truly awesome. He can pick the projects he wants—and can choose from among any of the seven major studios to make them. Says the chairman of Warner Communications Inc.: "I'd take anything the man does."

While Spielberg, because he is an independent producer, is free to shop his projects around, Universal Pictures tried to get on his good side in 1984 by spending six million dollars to build a sprawling complex for his Amblin Entertainment operations on the Universal lot. However, between 1982 and 1989 Spielberg made only one film at Universal. Sources say that was because he didn't like Universal's two former presidents. Universal's current president, Thomas Pollock, knows the importance of keeping Spielberg happy: "One of the most important things I can do in this job is make sure that Steven wants to work with us."

Power has been described as the last dirty word. It is easier for most of us to talk about money or even sex than it is to talk about power. People who have it deny it, people who want it try not to appear to be seeking it, and those who are good at getting it are secretive about how they got it.[2]

Fifteen years ago, we knew little about power. That's no longer true. In recent years we've gained considerable insights into the topic.[3] We can now make some fairly accurate predictions, for example, about what one should do if one wants to have power in a group or organization. In this chapter, we'll demonstrate that the acquisition and distribution of power is a natural process in any group or organization. Power determines the goals to be sought and how

*By Jim Croce, copyright 1974, 1985 DenJac Music Co. Used by permission. All rights reserved.

resources will be distributed. These, in turn, have important implications for member performance and satisfaction.

A DEFINITION OF POWER

Power A capacity that A has to influence the behavior of B so that B does things he or she would not otherwise do.

Dependency B's relationship to A when A possesses something that B requires.

Power refers to a capacity that A has to influence the behavior of B, so that B does something he or she would not otherwise do. This definition implies (1) a *potential* that need not be actualized to be effective, (2) a *dependence* relationship, and (3) the assumption that B has some *discretion* over his or her own behavior. Let's look at each of these points more closely.

Power may exist but not be used. It is, therefore, a capacity or potential. One can have power but not impose it.

Probably the most important aspect of power is that it is a function of **dependence.** The greater B's dependence on A, the greater is A's power in the relationship. Dependence, in turn, is based on alternatives that B perceives and the importance that B places on the alternative(s) that A controls. A person can have power over you only if he or she controls something you desire. If you want a college degree and have to pass a certain course to get it, and your current instructor is the only faculty member in the college who teaches that course, he or she has power over you. Your alternatives are highly limited and you place a high degree of importance on obtaining a passing grade. Similarly, if you're attending college on funds totally provided by your parents, you probably recognize the power that they hold over you. You are dependent on them for financial support. But once you're out of school, have a job, and are making a solid income, your parents' power is reduced significantly. Who among us, though, has not known or heard of the rich relative who is able to control a large number of family members merely through the implicit or explicit threat of "writing them out of the will"?

For A to get B to do something he or she otherwise would not do means that B must have the discretion to make choices. At the extreme, if B's job behavior is so programmed that he is allowed no room to make choices, he obviously is constrained in his ability to do something other than what he is doing. For instance, job descriptions, group norms, and organizational rules and regulations, as well as community laws and standards, constrain people's choices. As a nurse, you may be dependent on your supervisor for continued employment. But, in spite of this dependence, you're unlikely to comply with her request to perform heart surgery on a patient or steal several thousand dollars from petty cash. Your job description and laws against stealing constrain your ability to make these choices.

CONTRASTING LEADERSHIP AND POWER

A careful comparison of our description of power with our description of leadership in the previous chapter should bring the recognition that the two concepts are closely intertwined. Leaders use power as a means of attaining group goals. Leaders achieve goals, and power is a means of facilitating their achievement.

What differences are there between the two terms? One difference relates to goal compatibility. Power does not require goal compatibility, merely dependence. Leadership, on the other hand, requires some congruence between the goals of the leader and the led. A second difference relates to the direction of influence. Leadership focuses on the downward influence on one's subordinates. It minimizes the importance of lateral and upward influence patterns. Power does not. Still another difference deals with research emphasis. Leadership research, for the most part, emphasizes style. It seeks answers to such questions as: How supportive should a leader be? How much decision making should be shared with subordinates? In contrast, the research on power has tended to encompass a broader area and focus on tactics for gaining compliance. It has gone beyond the individual as exerciser because power can be used by groups as well as by individuals to control other individuals or groups.

BASES AND SOURCES OF POWER

Referent Power Influence held by A based on B's admiration and desire to model himself or herself after A.

Where does power come from? What is it that gives an individual or group influence over others? The early answer to these questions was a five-category classification scheme identified by French and Raven.[4] They proposed that there were five bases or sources of power that they termed coercive, reward, expert, legitimate, and referent power. Coercive power depends on fear; reward power derives from the ability to distribute anything of value (typically money, favorable performance appraisals, interesting work assignments, friendly colleagues, and preferred work shifts or sales territories); expert power refers to influence that derives from special skills or knowledge; legitimate power is based on the formal rights one receives as a result of holding an authoritative position or role in an organization; and **referent power** develops out of others' admiration for one and their desire to model their behavior and attitudes after that person. While French and Raven's classification scheme provided an extensive repertoire of possible bases of power, their categories created ambiguity because they confused bases of power with sources of power.[5] The result was much overlapping. We can improve our understanding of the power concept by separating bases and sources so as to develop clearer and more independent categories.

Bases of Power What powerholders control that allow them to manipulate the behavior of others.

Bases of power refers to what the powerholder has that gives him or her power. Assuming that you're the powerholder, your bases are what you control that enables you to manipulate the behavior of others. There are four power bases—coercive power, reward power, persuasive power, and knowledge power.[6] We'll expand on each in a moment.

Sources of Power How powerholders come to control the bases of power.

How are **sources of power** different from bases of power? The answer is that sources tell us where the power holder gets his or her power bases. That is, sources refer to how you come to control the bases of power. There are four sources—the position you hold, your personal characteristics, your expertise, and the opportunity you have to receive and obstruct information.[7] Each of these will also be discussed in a moment.

Let us now consider the four bases of power.

Bases of Power

Coercive Power Power that is based on fear.

COERCIVE POWER   The **coercive** base depends on fear. One reacts to this power out of fear of the negative ramifications that might result if one fails to comply. It rests on the application, or the threat of application, of physical sanctions such as infliction of pain, deformity, or death; the generation of frustration through restriction of movement; or the controlling through force of basic physiological or safety needs.

In the 1930s, when John Dillinger went into a bank, held a gun to the teller's head, and asked for the money, he was incredibly successful at getting compliance with his request. His power base? Coercive. A loaded gun gives its holder power because others are fearful that they will lose something that they hold dear—their lives.

> Of all the bases of power available to man, the power to hurt others is possibly most often used, most often condemned, and most difficult to control . . . the state relies on its military and legal resources to intimidate nations, or even its own citizens. Businesses rely upon the control of economic resources. Schools and universities rely upon their right to deny students formal education, while the church threatens individuals with loss of grace. At the personal level, individuals exercise coercive power through a reliance upon physical strength, verbal facility, or the ability to grant or withhold emotional support from others. These bases provide the individual with the means to physically harm, bully, humiliate, or deny love to others.[8]

At the organization level, A has coercive power over B if A can dismiss, suspend, or demote B, assuming that B values his or her job. Similarly, if A can assign B work activities that B finds unpleasant or treat B in a manner that B finds embarrassing, A possesses coercive power over B.

REWARD POWER   The opposite of coercive power is the power to reward. People comply with the wishes of another because it will result in positive benefits; therefore, one who can distribute rewards that others view as valuable will have power over them. Our definition of rewards is here limited to only material rewards. This would include salaries and wages, commissions, fringe benefits, and the like.

Persuasive Power The ability to allocate and manipulate symbolic rewards.

PERSUASIVE POWER   **Persuasive power** rests on the allocation and manipulation of symbolic rewards. If you can decide who is hired, manipulate the mass media, control the allocation of status symbols, or influence a group's norms, you have persuasive power. For instance, when a teacher uses the class climate to control a deviant student, or when a union steward arouses the members to use their informal power to bring a deviant member into line, you are observing the use of persuasive power.

Knowledge Power The ability to control unique and valuable information.

KNOWLEDGE POWER   **Knowledge,** or access to information, is the final base of power. We can say that when an individual in a group or organization controls unique information, and when that information is needed to make a decision, that individual has knowledge-based power.

To summarize, the bases of power refer to what the powerholder controls that enables him or her to manipulate the behavior of others. The coercive base of power is the control of punishment, the reward base is the control of material rewards, the persuasive base is the control of symbolic rewards, and the knowledge base is the control of information. Table 12–1 offers some common symbols that would suggest that a manager has developed strong power bases.

TABLE 12–1   Common Symbols of a Manager's Power

To what extent a manager can
• Intercede favorably on behalf of someone in trouble with the organization
• Get a desirable placement for a talented subordinate
• Get approval for expenditures beyond the budget
• Get above-average salary increases for subordinates
• Get items on the agenda at policy meetings
• Get fast access to top decision makers
• Get regular, frequent access to top decision makers
• Get early information about decisions and policy shifts

Sources of Power

POSITION POWER   In formal groups and organizations, probably the most frequent access to one or more of the power bases is one's structural position. A teacher's position includes significant control over symbols, a secretary frequently is privy to important information, and the head coach of an NFL team has substantial coercive resources at his disposal. All of these bases of

FIGURE 12–1
Source: Drawing by Leo Cullum; © 1986 The New Yorker Magazine, Inc.

"I was just going to say 'Well, I don't make the rules.' But, of course, I do make the rules."

power are achieved as a result of the formal position each holds within their structural hierarchy.

PERSONAL POWER   Personality traits were discussed in Chapter 4 and again in the previous chapter on leadership. They reappear within the topic of power when we acknowledge the fact that one's **personal** characteristics can be a source of power. If you are articulate, domineering, physically imposing, or possessing of that mystical quality called "charisma," you hold personal characteristics that may be used to get others to do what you want.

EXPERT POWER   Expertise is a means by which the powerholder comes to control specialized information (rather than the control itself, which we have discussed as the knowledge base of power). Those who have expertise in terms of specialized information can use it to manipulate others. Expertise is one of the most powerful sources of influence, especially in a technologically-oriented society. As jobs become more specialized, we become increasingly dependent on "experts" to achieve goals. So, while it is generally acknowledged that physicians have expertise and hence **expert power**—when your doctor talks, you listen—you should also recognize that computer specialists, tax accountants, solar engineers, industrial psychologists, and other specialists are able to wield power as a result of their expertise.

OPPORTUNITY POWER   Finally, being in the right place at the right time can give one the **opportunity** to exert power.[9] One need not hold a formal position in a group or organization to have access to information that is important to others or to be able to exert coercive influence. An example of how one can use an opportunity to create a power base is the story of the former United States President Lyndon Johnson when he was a student at Southwestern Texas State Teachers College. He had a job as special assistant to the college president's personal secretary.

> As special assistant, Johnson's assigned job was simply to carry messages from the president to the department heads and occasionally to other faculty members. Johnson saw that the rather limited function of messenger had possibilities for expansion; for example, encouraging recipients of the messages to transmit their own communications through him. He occupied a desk in the president's outer office, where he took it upon himself to announce the arrival of visitors. These added services evolved from a helpful convenience into an aspect of the normal process of presidential business. The messenger had become an appointments secretary, and, in time, faculty members came to think of Johnson as a funnel to the president. Using a technique which was later to serve him in achieving mastery over the Congress, Johnson turned a rather insubstantial service into a process through which power was exercised.[10]

Johnson eventually broadened his informal duties to include handling the president's political correspondence, preparing his reports for state agencies, and even regularly accompanying him on his trips to the state capital—the president eventually relying on his young apprentice for political counsel. Certainly this represents an example of someone using an opportunity to redefine his job and to give himself power.

Personal Power Influence attributed to one's personal characteristics.

Expert Power Influence based on special skills or knowledge.

Opportunity Power Influence obtained as a result of being in the right place at the right time.

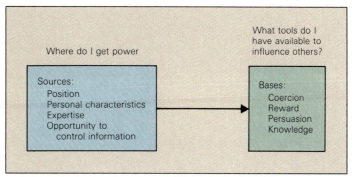

FIGURE 12–2   Sources and Bases of Power

Summary

The foundation to understanding power begins by identifying where power comes from (sources) and, given that one has the means to exert influence, what it is that one manipulates (bases). Figure 12–2 visually depicts the relationship between sources and bases. Sources are the means. Individuals can use their position in the structure, rely on personal characteristics, develop expertise, or take advantage of opportunities to control information. Control of one or more of these sources allows the powerholder to manipulate the behavior of others via coercion, reward, persuasion, or knowledge bases. To reiterate, sources are *where* you get power. Bases are *what* you manipulate. Those who seek power must develop a source of power. Then, and only then, can they acquire a power base.

DEPENDENCY: THE KEY TO POWER

Earlier in this chapter it was said that probably the most important aspect of power is that it is a function of dependence. In this section, we'll show how an understanding of dependency is central to furthering your understanding of power itself.

The General Dependency Postulate

Let's begin with a general postulate: *The greater B's dependency on A, the greater the power A has over B.* When you possess anything that others require but that you alone control, you make them dependent upon you and, therefore, you gain power over them.[12] Dependency, then, is inversely proportional to the alternative sources of supply. If something is plentiful, possession of it will not increase your power. If everyone is intelligent, intelligence gives no special advantage. Similarly, among the superrich, money is no longer power. But, as the old saying goes, "In the land of the blind, the one-eyed man is king!" If you can create a monopoly by controlling information, prestige, or anything that others crave, they become dependent on you. Conversely, the more that you can expand your options, the less power you place in the hands of others. This explains, for example, why most organizations develop multiple suppliers rather than give their business to only one. It also explains why so many of us

Predictions About People with a High Need for Power

David McClelland and his associates have conducted nearly one hundred studies on the power motive.[11] These studies provide convincing evidence that there is, in fact, something called *a need for power* (see Chapter 7), and that it allows for meaningful predictions of behavior. The following represent some of the more interesting findings related to individuals high in the need for power:

- They show partiality toward ingratiating followers.

- They inhibit group discussion when they are group leaders, resulting in the group considering fewer alternatives and having lower quality of decisions.

- They pursue occupations such as teaching, psychology, journalism, and business, that allow them to exert significant influence over others.

- High-power males report that they have more arguments, play competitive sports more, have less stable interpersonal relations, experience more emotional problems, and are more impulsively aggressive than low-power males.

---

aspire to financial independence. Financial independence reduces the power that others can have over us.

Joyce Fields provides an example of the role that dependency plays in a work group or organization.[13] In 1975, she took a job with the Times Mirror Company in its Los Angeles headquarters. Fields moved quickly up the organization ladder, eventually becoming treasurer of the company. Among her many accomplishments at Times Mirror has been setting up a full-scale commercial-paper borrowing program from scratch and negotiating one billion dollars of new debt to finance the company's media purchases. In 1988, Fields' husband was offered a promotion to chief financial officer at Paramount Communications in New York City. The job was too good to pass up, so the couple decided to pack up and move to Manhattan. However, Times Mirror didn't want to lose Fields to a New York company. So, in a tribute to her importance, top management at Times Mirror moved the company's entire treasury operations across the country to New York.

What Creates Dependency?

Dependency is increased when the resource you control is *important, scarce,* and *nonsubstitutable*.[14]

IMPORTANCE   If nobody wants what you've got, it's not going to create dependency. To create dependency, therefore, the thing(s) you control must be perceived as being important. It's been found, for instance, that organizations actively seek to avoid uncertainty.[15] We should, therefore, expect that those individuals or groups who can absorb an organization's uncertainty will be perceived as controlling an important resource. For instance, a study of industrial organizations found that the marketing departments in these firms were consistently rated as the most powerful.[16] It was concluded by the researcher that the most critical uncertainty facing these firms was selling their products. This might suggest that during a labor strike, the organization's negotiating representatives have increased power, or that engineers, as a group, would be more powerful at Apple Computer than at Procter & Gamble. These inferences appear to be generally valid. Labor negotiators do become more powerful within the personnel area and the organization as a whole during periods of labor strife. An organization such as Apple Computer, which is heavily technologically oriented, is highly dependent on its engineers to maintain its products' technical advantages and quality. And, at Apple, engineers are clearly the most powerful group. At Procter & Gamble, marketing is the name of the game, and marketers are the most powerful occupational group. These examples support not only the view that the ability to reduce uncertainty increases a group's importance and, hence, its power but also that what's important is situational. It varies between organizations and undoubtedly also varies over time within any given organization.

SCARCITY   As noted previously, if something is plentiful, possession of it will not increase your power. A resource needs to be perceived as scarce to create dependency.

This can help to explain how low-ranking members in an organization who have important knowledge not available to high-ranking members gain power over the high-ranking members. Possession of a scarce resource—in this case, important knowledge—makes the high-ranking member dependent on the low-ranking member. This also helps to make sense out of behaviors of low-ranking members that, otherwise, might seem illogical, such as destroy-

In the early 1980s, the power of basketball superstar Magic Johnson in the Laker Organization was strong enough to bring down his coach, Paul Westhead. Frustrated with Westhead's system, Johnson told the press he wanted to be traded. The reality was that Magic Johnson was a more important and scarce commodity to the Lakers than Westhead. So, in spite of the coach's outstanding win-loss record and leading the Lakers to a recent NBA championship, Westhead was fired. Magic stayed and the Lakers dominated the NBA during the 1980s.

Ken Levine/Allsport.

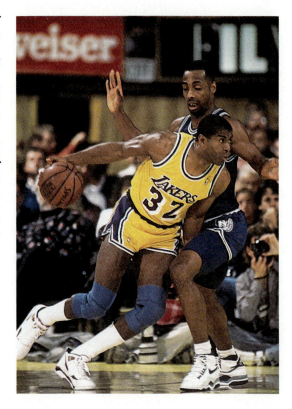

Elementary school teachers are suddenly a hot property. Enrollments are up and school districts are competing for a limited number of new teachers. As a result, the power of recent elementary education majors to select the kinds of jobs they want, with the resources they need, and in the geographic locations they prefer is much higher than 15 years ago—when there was a large oversupply of elementary education majors.   Laima Druskis.

ing the procedure manuals that describe how a job is done, refusing to train people in their jobs or even to show others exactly what they do, creating specialized language and terminology that inhibits others from understanding their jobs, or operating in secrecy so an activity will appear more complex and difficult than it really is.

The scarcity–dependency relationship can further be seen in the power of occupational categories. Individuals in occupations in which the supply of personnel is low relative to demand can negotiate compensation and benefit packages far more attractive than can those in occupations where there is an abundance of candidates. College administrators have no problem today finding English instructors. The market for accounting teachers, in contrast, is extremely tight, with the demand high and the supply limited. The result is that the bargaining power of accounting faculty allows them to negotiate higher salaries, lighter teaching loads, and other benefits.

NONSUBSTITUTABILITY   The more that a resource has no viable substitutes, the more power that control over that resource provides. This is illustrated in a concept we'll call the **"elasticity of power."**

Elasticity of Power The relative responsiveness of power to change in available alternatives.

In economics, considerable attention is focused on the elasticity of demand, which is defined as the relative responsiveness of quantity demanded to change in price. This concept can be modified to explain the strength of power.

Elasticity of power is defined as the relative responsiveness of power to change in available alternatives. One's ability to influence others is viewed as being dependent on how these others perceive their alternatives.

As shown in Figure 12–3, assume that there are two individuals. Mr. A's power elasticity curve is relatively inelastic. This would describe, for example, an employee who believed that he had a large number of employment opportunities outside his current organization. Fear of being fired would have only a moderate impact on Mr. A, for he perceives that he has a number of other alternatives. Mr. A's boss finds that threatening A with termination has only a minimal impact on influencing his behavior. A reduction in alternatives (from X to $X-1$) only increases the power of A's boss slightly (A' to A''). However, Mr. B's curve is relatively elastic. He sees few other job opportunities. His age, education, present salary, or lack of contacts may severely limit his ability to find a job somewhere else. As a result, Mr. B is dependent on his

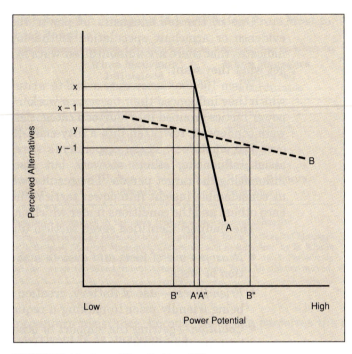

FIGURE 12–3   Elasticity of Power

present organization and boss. If B loses his job (Y to $Y-1$), he may face prolonged unemployment, and it shows itself in the increased power of B's boss. As long as B perceives his options as limited and B's boss holds the power to terminate his employment, B's boss will hold considerable power over him. In such a situation, it is obviously important for B to get his boss to believe that his options are considerably greater than they really are. If this is not achieved, B places his fate in the hands of his boss and makes him captive to almost any demands the boss devises.

Higher education provides an excellent example of how this elasticity concept operates. In universities where there are strong pressures for the faculty to publish, we can say that a department head's power over a faculty member is inversely related to that member's publication record. The more recognition the faculty member receives through publication, the more mobile he or she is. That is, since other universities want faculty who are highly published and visible, there is an increased demand for his or her services. Although the concept of tenure can act to alter this relationship by restricting the department head's alternatives, those faculty members with little or no publications have the least mobility and are subject to the greatest influence from their superiors.

POWER TACTICS

Power Tactics Identifies how individuals manipulate the power bases.

This section is a logical extension of our previous discussions. We've reviewed *where* power comes from and *what* it is that powerholders manipulate. Now, we go the final step—to **power tactics.** Tactics tell us *how* to manipulate the bases. The following discussion will show you how employees translate their power bases into specific actions.

individuals. Studies of college teachers and sales personnel found coercion the least preferred power base.[51] A study of insurance company employees also drew the same conclusion.[52]

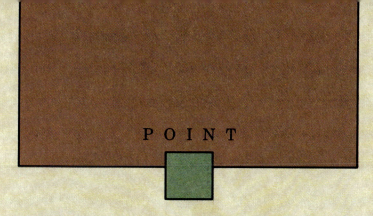

It's a Political Jungle Out There!

Politics in organizations is simply a fact of life. Those who fail to acknowledge political behavior ignore the reality that organizations are political systems.

It would be nice if all organizations or formal groups within organizations could be described in such terms as supportive, harmonious, objective, trusting, collaborative, or cooperative. A nonpolitical perspective can lead one to believe that employees will always behave in ways consistent with the interests of the organization. In contrast, a political view can explain much of what may seem to be irrational behavior in organizations. It can help to explain, for instance, why employees withhold information, restrict output, attempt to "build empires," publicize their successes, hide their failures, distort performance figures to make themselves look better, and engage in similar activities that appear to be at odds with the organization's desire for effectiveness and efficiency.

For those who want tangible evidence that "it's a political jungle out there" in the real world, let's look at two studies. The first analyzed what it takes to get promoted fast in organizations. The second addressed the performance appraisal process.

Luthans and his associates* studied more than 450 managers. They found that these managers engaged in four managerial activities: traditional management (decision making, planning, and con-

trolling); communication (exchanging routine information and processing paperwork); human resource management (motivating, disciplining, managing conflict, staffing, and training), and networking (socializing, politicking, and interacting with outsiders). Those managers who got promoted fastest spent forty-eight percent of their time networking. The average managers spent most of their efforts on traditional management and communication activities and only nineteen percent of their time networking. We suggest that this provides strong evidence of the importance that social and political skills play in getting ahead in organizations.

Longenecker and his associates† held in-depth interviews with sixty upper-level executives to find out what went into performance ratings. What they found was that executives frankly admitted to deliberately manipulating formal appraisals for political purposes. Accuracy was *not* a primary concern of these executives. Rather, they manipulated the appraisal results in an intentional and systematic manner to get the outcomes they wanted.

*F. Luthans, R. M. Hodgetts, and S. A. Rosenkrantz, *Real Managers* (Cambridge, Mass.: Ballinger, 1988).
†C. O. Longenecker, D. A. Gioia, and H. P. Sims, Jr., "Behind the Mask: The Politics of Employee Appraisal," *Academy of Management Executive*, August 1987, pp. 183–94.

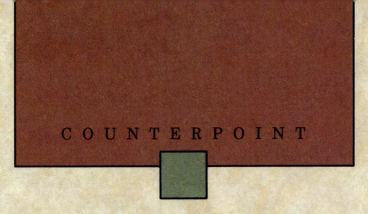

The Myth of the Corporate Political Jungle

Organizational behavior currently appears to be undergoing a period of fascination with workplace politics. Proponents argue that politics is inevitable in organizations—that power struggles, alliance formations, strategic maneuverings, and cut-throat actions are as endemic to organizational life as are planning, organizing, leading, and controlling.

While political behavior certainly occurs, it is not inevitable in organizations. This myth is based on the erroneous assumption that there is a universal power motive, and it is perpetuated because its acceptance works in the best interest of management.

Organizational members are not necessarily driven by a power motive. On the contrary, highly variable data gathered from personality inventories indicate that the power motive may be subordinate to such other motives as affiliation or achievement or may be absent altogether. So why the belief in the universality of the power motive? It is consistent with the philosophical belief that human beings are primarily motivated to achieve their own good. The innateness of self-interest is difficult to refute, for it can be located in any personal goal, even the goal of advancing the interests of others. However, self-interest does not necessarily require the maximization of power, but rather may be satisfied by nothing more ambitious than survival. The competitive na-ture of some organizations requires individuals to *appear* to seek power maximization but that is only a survival measure. Under less competitive conditions, self-interest may be satisfied without engaging in defensive measures that appear to be power-related. So the lessening of competitive pressures can make political behavior unnecessary.

There is no doubt that the political jungle myth provides important benefits to those managers who are already in power. A few examples will illustrate this point. By arguing the need for political skills to achieve managerial positions, and given that managers are already incumbents, they demonstrate that they already have proven that they possess the political skills to acquire and retain resources for the organization. The existence of workplace politics also lessens the need for managers to be concerned with objectivity, fairness, and performance criteria when they allocate rewards. If organizations are political systems—and others accept them as such —managers have a greater latitude of discretion to legitimately reward their friends and punish their enemies.

Much of this argument is based on J. I. Klein, "The Myth of the Corporate Political Jungle: Politicization as a Political Strategy," *Journal of Management Studies,* January 1988, pp. 1–11.

FOR DISCUSSION

1. What is power? How is it different from leadership?

2. Contrast French and Raven's power classification to the bases and sources presented in this chapter.

3. What is the difference between a source of power and a base of power?

4. Contrast power tactics with power bases and sources. What are some of the key contingency variables that determine which tactic a powerholder is likely to use?

5. "Knowledge power and expert power are the same thing." Do you agree or disagree? Discuss.

6. What is a coalition? When is it likely to develop?

7. Based on the information presented in this chapter, what would you do as a new college graduate entering a new job to maximize your power and accelerate your career progress?

8. How are power and politics related?

9. "More powerful managers are good for an organization. It is the powerless, not the powerful, who are the ineffective managers." Do you agree or disagree with this statement? Discuss.

10. Define political behavior. Differentiate between legitimate and illegitimate political actions.

11. "Politicking in organizations is bad." Do you agree or disagree with this statement? Discuss.

12. What factors contribute to political activity?

FOR FURTHER READING

BAUM, H. S., "Organizational Politics Against Organizational Culture: A Psychoanalytic Perspective," *Human Resource Management,* Summer 1989, pp. 191–206. Organizational politics arouses anxiety that induces workers to withdraw emotionally. Argues that politics makes it psychologically difficult for workers to feel loyal to an organization.

EISENHARDT, K. M., and L. J. BOURGEOIS III, "Politics of Strategic Decision Making in High-Velocity Environments: Toward a Midrange Theory," *Academy of Management Journal,* December 1988, pp. 737–70. Research study found that politics arises from power centralization. Autocratic CEOs engage in politics and generate political behavior among subordinates.

HINKIN, T. R., and C. A. SCHRIESHEIM, "Power and Influence: The View from Below," *Personnel,* May 1988, pp. 47–50. The way employees view their supervisor's use of power and influence affects their level of satisfaction and commitment to the organization.

KUMAN, P., and R. GHADIALLY, "Organizational Politics and Its Effects on Members of Organizations," *Human Relations,* April 1989, pp. 305–14. Finds that political behaviors have significant negative consequences for interpersonal relationships and performance in organizations.

RAGINS, B. R., and E. SUNDSTROM, "Gender and Power in Organizations: A Longitudinal Perspective," *Psychological Bulletin,* January 1989, pp. 51–88. Presents a model of power in organizations and uses it to organize a comprehensive review of empirical research and related theory concerning differences between the genders in power. Research reveals a consistent difference favoring men in accessibility to resources for power.

STEWART, T. A., "New Ways to Exercise Power," *Fortune,* November 6, 1989, pp. 52–64. Provides a practical perspective on power in organizations today. Argues that power is changing within organizations, but that power ultimately derives from performance.

Power Orientation Test

Instructions: For each statement, circle the number that most closely resembles your attitude.

Statement	Disagree		Neutral	Agree	
	A Lot	A Little		A Little	A Lot
1. The best way to handle people is to tell them what they want to hear.	1	2	3	4	5
2. When you ask someone to do something for you, it is best to give the real reason for wanting it rather than giving reasons that might carry more weight.	1	2	3	4	5
3. Anyone who completely trusts anyone else is asking for trouble.	1	2	3	4	5
4. It is hard to get ahead without cutting corners here and there.	1	2	3	4	5
5. It is safest to assume that all people have a vicious streak, and it will come out when they are given a chance.	1	2	3	4	5
6. One should take action only when it is morally right.	1	2	3	4	5
7. Most people are basically good and kind.	1	2	3	4	5
8. There is no excuse for lying to someone else.	1	2	3	4	5
9. Most people more easily forget the death of their father than the loss of their property.	1	2	3	4	5
10. Generally speaking, people won't work hard unless they're forced to do so.	1	2	3	4	5

Source: R. Christie and F. L. Geis, *Studies in Machiavellianism.* © Academic Press 1970. Reprinted by permission.

Turn to page 689 for scoring directions and key.

The Shake-up at the Business School

The business school at this urban, midwest university had experienced very rapid growth. In a period of four or five years, the number of faculty members increased from approximately fifteen to thirty-five. Most of these new members were young, having recently finished their own graduate studies.

The dominant power coalition within the business school was made up of the dean, Jack Halpert, and his department heads. All the department heads had been at the university for many years and ruled with considerable strength. Although the dean had come from another university and had been in his position only a few years, he was in his late fifties and had been hand-picked by the department chairmen because he was seen as someone who would not "shake up the ship." What the dominant coalition had overlooked, however, was that there were now more young faculty than "old-timers" and that the university's top administrators believed that the future of the business school resided with the new faculty.

The young faculty had quickly become frustrated by the power of Halpert and his department heads. Their ideas carried little weight in the school and all the key committees were run by the dominant power coalition. Rather than look for jobs somewhere else, the young faculty decided to stage a palace revolt. They felt they had the numbers and the support of the top administration to overthrow the dominant coalition.

Several of the young faculty went to the university's vice president and outlined a long list of problems facing the business school. They also presented evidence to support their position that the dean was not effectively dealing with these problems. A few visits with the vice president, followed by her own evaluation of the situation, resulted in Dean Halpert being asked to resign. An acting dean was appointed from among the department chairs.

Interestingly, few of the dominant coalition saw that a revolt was brewing. The fact that one of the chairs was made acting dean reassured the

dominant coalition that they were still in control. The department chairs fully expected the next dean to maintain the status quo.

At a faculty meeting several months after Halpert's resignation, one of the items on the agenda was nominations to the search committee for selecting a new dean. When that item came up, the young faculty members were ready. Within less than a minute, they had succeeded in nominating and seconding five of their own to the five committee positions. The nominations were closed. Suddenly it became obvious to everyone at the meeting that the young faculty had stacked the deck.

The search committee wanted the power coalition changed, and only those candidates that supported such a change were recommended as finalists to the vice president. When the new dean was appointed, the young faculty members took control. All the chair positions were changed. The old-timers were replaced by members of the young faculty coalition. The business school was subsequently reorganized, and the interests of the young faculty were paramount in this structural change. These changes, it was argued, were necessary to improve the effectiveness of the business school. Whether they did is problematic. But there is no question that they furthered the interests of the young faculty by legitimizing their power. The young faculty totally revamped the goals and structure of the business school in their interests.

QUESTIONS

1. What, if anything, could Dean Halpert and his department heads have done to maintain their power?

2. Why did the young faculty need a coalition to exert power?

3. What was the source of the younger faculty's power?

4. How does this case illustrate the politics in defining organizational effectiveness?

[1]Based on R. Grover, "Fear Not, Hollywood: Golden Boy is Still Golden," *Business Week,* May 29, 1989, pp. 64–65.

[2]R. M. Kanter, "Power Failure in Management Circuits," *Harvard Business Review,* July–August 1979, p. 65.

[3]See, for example, D. Kipnis, *The Powerholders* (Chicago: University of Chicago Press, 1976); S. B. Bacharach and E. J. Lawler, *Power and Politics in Organizations* (San Francisco: Jossey-Bass, 1980); J. Pfeffer, *Power in Organizations* (Marshfield, MA: Pitman, 1981); H. Mintzberg, *Power In and Around Organizations* (Englewood Cliffs, NJ: Prentice Hall, 1983); and R. J. House, "Power and Personality in Complex Organizations," in B. M. Staw and L. L. Cummings (eds.), *Research in Organizational Behavior,* Vol. 10 (Greenwich, Conn.: JAI Press, 1988), pp. 305–57.

[4]J. R. P. French, Jr., and B. Raven, "The Bases of Social Power," in D. Cartwright (ed.), *Studies in Social Power* (Ann Arbor: University of Michigan, Institute for Social Research, 1959), pp. 150–67. For an update on French and Raven's work, see D. E. Frost and A. J. Stahelski, "The Systematic Measurement of French and Raven's Bases of Social Power in Workgroups," *Journal of Applied Social Psychology,* April 1988, pp. 375–89; and T. R. Hinkin and C. A. Schriesheim, "Development and Application of New Scales to Measure the French and Raven (1959) Bases of Social Power," *Journal of Applied Psychology,* August 1989, pp. 561–67.

[5]Bacharach and Lawler, *Power and Politics,* pp. 34–36.

[6]Adapted from Ibid., and A. Etzioni, *Comparative Analysis of Complex Organizations* (New York: Free Press, 1961).

[7]Bacharach and Lawler, *Power and Politics,* pp. 34–36.

[8]Kipnis, *Powerholders,* pp. 77–78.

[9]D. J. Brass, "Being in the Right Place: A Structural Analysis of Individual Influence in an Organization," *Administrative Science Quarterly,* December 1984, pp. 518–39; and R. Lachman, "Power from What? A Reexamination of Its Relationships with Structural Conditions," *Administrative Science Quarterly,* June 1989, pp. 231–51.

[10]D. Kearns, "Lyndon Johnson and the American Dream," *The Atlantic Monthly,* May 1976, p. 41.

[11]D. C. McClelland, *Human Motivation* (Glenview, Il: Scott, Foresman, 1985). For a condensed version of this research, see R. J. House, "Power and Personality in Complex Organizations," pp. 319–24.

[12]R. E. Emerson, "Power-Dependence Relations," *American Sociological Review,* Vol. 27 (1962), pp. 31–41.

[13]Cited in *Business Month,* April 1989, p. 41.

[14]Mintzberg, *Power In and Around Organizations,* p. 24.

[15]R. M. Cyert and J. G. March, *A Behavioral Theory of the Firm* (Englewood Cliffs, NJ: Prentice Hall, 1963).

[16]C. Perrow, "Departmental Power and Perspective in Industrial Firms," in M. N. Zald (ed.), *Power in Organizations* (Nashville, TN: Vanderbilt University Press, 1970).

[17]See, for example, D. Kipnis, S. M. Schmidt, C. Swaffin-Smith, and I. Wilkinson, "Patterns of Managerial Influence: Shotgun Managers, Tacticians, and Bystanders," *Organizational Dynamics,* Winter 1984, pp. 58–67; T. Case, L. Dosier, G. Murkison, and B. Keys, "How Managers Influence Superiors: A Study of Upward Influence Tactics," *Leadership and Organization Development Journal,* Vol. 9, No. 4, 1988, pp. 25–31; and D. Kipnis and S. M. Schmidt, "Upward-Influence Styles: Relationship With Performance Evaluations, Salary, and Stress," *Administrative Science Quarterly,* December 1988, pp. 528–42.

[18]This section is adapted from Kipnis, Schmidt, Swaffin-Smith, and Wilkinson, "Patterns of Managerial Influence."

[19]P. P. Poole, "Coalitions: The Web of Power," in D. J. Vredenburgh and R. S. Schuler (eds.), *Effective Management: Research and Application,* Proceedings of the 20th Annual Eastern Academy of Management, Pittsburgh, May 1983, pp. 79–82.

[20]See Pfeffer, *Power in Organizations,* pp. 155–57.

[21]N. J. Adler, *International Dimensions of Organizational Behavior* (Boston: Kent Publishing, 1986), p. 40.

[22]S. A. Culbert and J. J. McDonough, *The Invisible War: Pursuing Self-interest at Work* (New York: John Wiley, 1980), p. 6.

[23]Mintzberg, *Power In and Around Organizations,* p. 26.

[24]D. J. Vredenburgh and J. G. Maurer, "A Process Framework of Organizational Politics," *Human Relations,* January 1984, pp. 47–66.

[25]D. Farrell and J. C. Petersen, "Patterns of Political Behavior in Organizations," *Academy of Management Review,* July 1982, p. 405.

[26]Ibid., pp. 406–07; and A. Drory, "Politics in Organization and Its Perception Within the Organization," *Organization Studies,* Vol. 9, No. 2, 1988, pp. 165–79.

[27]Based on T. C. Krell, M. E. Mendenhall, and J. Sendry, "Doing Research in the Conceptual Morass of Organizational Politics." Paper presented at the Western Academy of Management Conference, Hollywood, CA, April 1987.

²⁸See, for example, B. T. Mayes and R. W. Allen, "Toward a Definition of Organizational Politics," *Academy of Management Review,* October 1977, pp. 672–78; D. J. Moberg, "Factors Which Determine the Perception and Use of Organizational Politics," paper presented at the 38th Annual Academy of Management Conference, San Francisco, 1978; L. W. Porter, R. W. Allen, and H. L. Angle, "The Politics of Upward Influence in Organizations," in L. L. Cummings and B. M. Staw (eds.), *Research in Organizational Behavior,* Vol. 3 (Greenwich, CT: JAI Press, 1981), pp. 121–22; and G. Biberman, "Personality and Characteristic Work Attitudes of Persons With High, Moderate, and Low Political Tendencies," *Psychological Reports,* October 1985, pp. 1303–10.

²⁹See, for example, J. E. Haas and T. E. Drabek, *Complex Organizations: A Sociological Perspective* (New York: Macmillan, 1973); R. T. Mowday, "The Exercise of Upward Influence in Organizations," *Administrative Science Quarterly,* March 1978, pp. 137–56; and D. L. Madison, R. W. Allen, L. W. Porter, P. A. Renwick, and B. T. Mayes, "Organizational Politics: An Exploration of Manager's Perceptions," *Human Relations,* February 1980, pp. 79–100.

³⁰Farrell and Petersen, "Patterns of Political Behavior," p. 408.

³¹S. C. Goh and A. R. Doucet, "Antecedent Situational Conditions of Organizational Politics: An Empirical Investigation," paper presented at the Annual Administrative Sciences Association of Canada Conference, Whistler, B. C.; May 1986; and C. Hardy, "The Contribution of Political Science to Organizational Behavior," in J. W. Lorsch (ed.), *Handbook of Organizational Behavior* (Englewood Cliffs, NJ: Prentice Hall, 1987), p. 103.

³²See, for example, Madison et al., "Organizational Politics"; Porter et al., "The Politics of Upward Influence in Organizations," pp. 113–20; Vredenburgh and Maurer, "A Process Framework of Organizational Politics"; Farrell and Petersen, "Patterns of Political Behavior," p. 409; and P. M. Fandt and G. R. Ferris, "The Management of Information and Impressions: When Employees Behave Opportunistically," *Organizational Behavior and Human Decision Processes,* February 1990, pp. 140–58.

³³M. R. Leary and R. M. Kowalski, "Impression Management: A Literature Review and Two-Component Model," *Psychological Bulletin,* January 1990, pp. 34–47.

³⁴*Ibid.,* p. 34.

³⁵See, for instance, B. R. Schlenker, *Impression Management: The Self-Concept, Social Identity, and Interpersonal Relations* (Monterey, Calif.: Brooks/Cole, 1980); J. Tedeschi and V. Melburg, "Impression Management and Influence in the Organization," in S. Bacharach and E. Lawler (eds.), *Research in the Sociology of Organizations,* Vol. 3 (Greenwich, Conn.: JAI Press, 1984), pp. 31–58; W. L. Gardner and M. J. Martinko, "Impression Management in Organizations," *Journal of Management,* June 1988, pp. 321–38; and D. C. Gilmore and G. R. Ferris, "The Effects of Applicant Impression Management Tactics on Interviewer Judgments," *Journal of Management,* December 1989, pp. 557–64.

³⁶Based on B. R. Schlenker, *Impression Management;* and W. L. Gardner and M. J. Martinko, "Impression Management in Organizations," p. 332.

³⁷M. R. Leary and R. M. Kowalski, "Impression Management," p. 40.

³⁸W. L. Gardner and M. J. Martinko, "Impression Management in Organizations," p. 333.

³⁹R. A. Baron, "Impression Management by Applicants During Employment Interviews: The 'Too Much of a Good Thing' Effect," in R. W. Eder and G. R. Ferris (eds.), *The Employment Interview: Theory, Research, and Practice* (Newbury Park, Calif.: Sage Publishers, 1989), pp. 204–15.

⁴⁰G. R. Ferris, G. S. Russ, and P. M. Fandt, "Politics in Organizations," in R. A. Giacalone and P. Rosenfeld (eds.), *Impression Management in the Organization* (Hillsdale, New Jersey: Erlbaum, 1990).

⁴¹R. A. Baron, "Impression Management by Applicants During Employment Interviews;" and D. C. Gilmore and G. R. Ferris, "The Effects of Applicant Impression Management Tactics on the Interviewer Judgments."

⁴²D. C. Gilmore and G. R. Ferris, "The Effects of Applicant Impression Management Tactics on Interviewer Judgments."

⁴³See, for example, M. A. Rahim, "Relationships of Leader Power to Compliance and Satisfaction with Supervision: Evidence from a National Sample of Managers," *Journal of Management,* December 1989, pp. 545–56.

⁴⁴J. G. Bachman, D. G. Bowers, and P. M. Marcus, "Bases of Supervisory Power: A Comparative Study in Five Organizational Settings," in A. S. Tannenbaum (ed.), *Control in Organizations* (New York: McGraw-Hill, 1968), p. 236.

⁴⁵K. Student, "Supervisory Influence and Work-Group Performance," *Journal of Applied Psychology,* June 1968, pp. 188–94.

⁴⁶J. Ivancevich, "An Analysis of Control, Bases of Control, and Satisfaction in an Organizational Setting," *Academy of Management Journal,* December 1970, pp. 427–36.

⁴⁷J. G. Bachman, "Faculty Satisfaction and the Dean's Influence: An Organizational Study of Twelve Liberal Arts Colleges," *Journal of Applied Psychology,* February 1968, pp. 55–61; and J. G. Bachman, C. G. Smith, and J. A. Slesinger, "Control, Performance and Satisfaction: An Analysis of Structure and Individual Effort," *Journal of Personality and Social Psychology,* August 1966, pp. 127–36.

⁴⁸Bachman, Bowers, and Marcus, "Bases of Supervisory Power."

⁴⁹P. Busch, "The Sales Managers' Bases of Social Power and Influence Upon the Sales

Force," *Journal of Marketing,* Fall 1980, pp. 91–101; and M. A. Rahim, "Relationships of Leader Power to Compliance and Satisfaction."

[50]P. Busch, "The Sales Managers' Bases of Social Power."

[51]See note 47.

[52]Ivancevich, "Analysis of Control."

CONFLICT AND INTERGROUP BEHAVIOR

LEARNING OBJECTIVES

After studying this chapter, you should be able to:

1. *Differentiate between the traditional, human relations, and interactionist views of conflict*
2. *Outline the conflict process*
3. *Differentiate between functional and dysfunctional conflict*
4. *Summarize the sources of conflict*
5. *Describe the five methods for reducing conflict*
6. *List the benefits and disadvantages of conflict*
7. *Explain the factors that affect intergroup relations*
8. *Identify methods for managing intergroup relations*

Andrew Kay, founder of Kaypro, at work at his home. He has seen most of his centimillion dollar fortune vanish with the bankruptcy of his Kaypro Corp.
Chad Slattery.

*Part of my job as a coach is to keep the five guys who
hate me away from the five guys who are undecided.*

C. STENGEL

T he rise and fall of Kaypro Corp. is a story about how nepotism
and conflict undermined one of the early "bright lights" of the personal
computer industry.[1]

Kaypro's founder, Andrew Kay, was a brilliant graduate of MIT. When
personal computers appeared in the late 1970s, he became fascinated by them
and decided to build his own. The Kaypro 2, launched in the early 1980s,
became an instant hit. The little machine was inexpensive and reliable. Sales
zoomed from $5 million to $120 million between 1982 and 1984.

To manage his San Diego-based company, Kay, now 71, turned to his own
family. His son David was appointed vice-president for marketing, although
his qualifications for this job were minimal. Another son, Allan, became
vice-president for administration. Kay's wife, Mary, was Kaypro's secretary;
his brother ran the firm's print shop. Even his father, now 94, got into the act;
he looked after maintenance.

Family squabbles, especially between David and his father, soon surfaced. Andrew Kay had been an authoritarian father when his sons were
growing up and he found it hard to let David make decisions. David,
meanwhile, felt as if he constantly had to rein in his father's overoptimism. For
instance, at one point in 1984 the company had enough parts in inventory to
build six months worth of computers. Most computer companies rarely keep
more than half that on hand. Yet Andrew Kay kept on buying more parts.
David, tired of arguing with his dad, took action. He physically moved his desk
down to the loading dock and sent truck drivers away before they could unload
their shipments.

The squabbling between father and son increased. It distracted the
company from moving into new products. The company failed to recognize the
need to introduce a computer that was compatible with IBM's popular PC and,
by the time it had a competitive clone, it was too late. Yet the conflicts
continued. David was named president in 1985, but his father remained very
much in charge. It got to the point that it seemed as if every decision turned
into a fight between the two men. And so it continued until David left the
company at the end of 1988.

Kaypro went into bankruptcy in the Spring of 1990. Looking back,
Andrew says, "I used to talk to David a lot when he was young. But when we
worked together, he didn't talk to me. To him, my questions seemed like
threats. We weren't getting along at all." Not surprisingly, David sees things
differently. "I had no control over what was happening," he says.

The interactionist view of conflict supports disagreements and open questioning of others as is taking place in this group when it aids the group's performance.   Andy Freeberg.

Given the interactionist view—and it is the one we shall take in this chapter—it becomes evident that to say conflict is all good or bad is inappropriate and naive. Whether a conflict is good or bad depends on the type of conflict. Specifically, it's necessary to differentiate between functional and dysfunctional conflicts.

FUNCTIONAL VERSUS DYSFUNCTIONAL CONFLICT

Functional Conflict Conflict that supports the goals of the group and improves its performance.

Dysfunctional Conflict Conflict that hinders group performance.

The interactionist view does not propose that *all* conflicts are good. Rather, some conflicts support the goals of the group and improve its performance; these are **functional,** constructive forms of conflict. Additionally, there are conflicts that hinder group performance; these are **dysfunctional** or destructive forms.

Of course, it is one thing to argue that conflict can be valuable for the group, but how does one tell if a conflict is functional or dysfunctional?

The demarcation between functional and dysfunctional is neither clear nor precise. No one level of conflict can be adopted as acceptable or unacceptable under all conditions. The type and level of conflict that creates healthy and positive involvement toward one group's goals may, in another group or in the same group at another time, be highly dysfunctional.

The important criterion is group performance. Since groups exist to attain a goal or goals, it is the impact that the conflict has on the group, rather than on any singular individual, that defines functionality. The impact of conflict on the individual and on the group is rarely mutually exclusive, so the ways that individuals perceive a conflict may have an important influence on its effect on the group. However, this need not be the case, and when it is not, our orientation will be to the group. For us to appraise the impact of conflict on group behavior—to consider its functional and dysfunctional effects—we shall consider whether the individual group members perceive the conflict as being good or bad to be irrelevant. A group member may perceive an action as dysfunctional, in that the outcome is personally dissatisfying to him or her. However, for our analysis, it would be functional if it furthers the objectives of the group.

THE CONFLICT PARADOX

Conflict Paradox Conflict contributes to a group's performance but most groups and organizations try to eliminate it.

If some conflict has been proven to be beneficial to a group's performance, why do most of us continue to look at conflict as undesirable? The answer to this **conflict paradox** is that we live in a society that has been built upon the traditional view. Tolerance of conflict is counter to most cultures in developed nations. In North America, the home, school, and church are generally the most influential institutions during the early years, when our attitudes are forming. These institutions, for the most part, have historically reinforced anticonflict values and emphasized the importance of getting along with others.

The home has historically reinforced the authority pattern through the parent figure. Parents knew what was right and children complied. Conflict between children or between parents and children has generally been actively discouraged. The traditional school systems in developed countries reflected the structure of the home. Teachers had *the* answers and were not to be challenged. Disagreements at all levels were viewed negatively. Examinations reinforced this view: Students attempted to get their answers to agree with those the teacher had determined were right. The last major influencing institution, the church, also has supported anticonflict values. The religious perspective emphasizes peace, harmony, and tranquility. Church doctrines, for the most part, advocate acceptance rather than argument. This is best exemplified by the teachings of the Roman Catholic Church. According to its beliefs, when the pope speaks officially (*ex cathedra*) on religious matters, he is infallible. Such dogma has discouraged questioning the teachings of the Church.

Should we be surprised, then, that the traditional view of conflict continues to receive wide support in spite of the evidence to the contrary?

Let us now proceed to move beyond definitions and philosophy, to describe and analyze the evolutionary process leading to conflict outcomes.

THE CONFLICT PROCESS

The conflict process can be seen as comprising four stages: potential opposition, cognition and personalization, behavior, and outcomes. The process is diagrammed in Figure 13–1.

Stage I: Potential Opposition

The first step in the conflict process is the presence of conditions that create opportunities for conflict to arise. They *need not* lead directly to conflict, but can only lead to conflict when one or more of the parties are affected by, and aware of, the conflict.

As we noted in our definition of conflict, perception is required. Therefore, one or more of the parties must be aware of the existence of the antecedent conditions. However, because a conflict is **perceived** does not mean that it is personalized. In other words, "A may be aware that B and A are in serious disagreement . . . but it may not make A tense or anxious, and it may have no effect whatsoever on A's affection towards B."[7] It is at the **felt** level, when individuals become emotionally involved, that parties experience anxiety, tenseness, frustration, or hostility.

Stage III: Behavior

We are in the third stage of the conflict process when a member engages in action that frustrates the attainment of another's goals or prevents the furthering of the other's interests. This action must be intended; that is, there must be a knowing effort to frustrate another. At this juncture, the conflict is out in the open.

Overt conflict covers a full range of behaviors—from subtle, indirect, and highly controlled forms of interference to direct, aggressive, violent, and uncontrolled struggle. At the low range, this overt behavior is illustrated by the student who raises his or her hand in class and questions a point the instructor has made. At the high range, strikes, riots, and wars come to mind.

Stage III is also where most conflict-handling behaviors are initiated. Once the conflict is overt, the parties will develop a method for dealing with the conflict. This does not exclude conflict-handling behaviors from being initiated in Stage II, but in most cases, these techniques for reducing the frustration are used when the conflict has become observable rather than as preventive measures.

Figure 13–2 represents one author's effort at identifying the primary conflict-handling orientations. Using two dimensions—*cooperativeness* (the degree to which one party attempts to satisfy the other party's concerns) and *assertiveness* (the degree to which one party attempts to satisfy his or her own

Perceived Conflict Awareness by one or more parties of the existence of conditions that create opportunities for conflict to arise.

Felt Conflict Emotional involvement in a conflict creating anxiety, tenseness, frustration, or hostility.

Overt conflict recently surfaced between United Parcel Service and its Teamster employees. Although UPS' 140,000 Teamsters earn 30 percent more than at nonunion Federal Express, these workers complained about UPS' rigorous, minutely timed work schedules. After a long period of intense negotiation, an agreement was reached and the Teamsters' record of never calling a national strike against UPS was kept intact.
Michael L. Abramson.

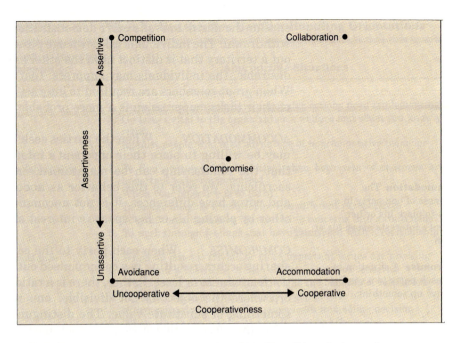

FIGURE 13–2   Dimensions of Conflict-Handling Orientations

Source: K. Thomas, "Conflict and Conflict Management," in M. D. Dunnette (ed.), *Handbook of Industrial and Organizational Psychology*, p. 900. Copyright © 1976 Rand McNally. Reprinted by permission of John Wiley & Sons, Inc.

concerns)—five conflict-handling orientations can be identified: *competition* (assertive and uncooperative), *collaboration* (assertive and cooperative), *avoidance* (unassertive and uncooperative), *accommodation* (unassertive and cooperative), and *compromise* (midrange on both assertiveness and cooperativeness).[8]

COMPETITION   When one person seeks to achieve his or her goals or further his or her interests, regardless of the impact on the parties to the conflict, he or she **competes** and dominates. These win–lose struggles, in formal groups or in an organization, frequently utilize the formal authority of a mutual superior as the dominant force, and the conflicting individuals both will use their own power bases in order to resolve a victory in their favor.

COLLABORATION   When the parties to conflict each desire to satisfy fully the concern of all parties, we have cooperation and the search for a mutually beneficial outcome. In **collaboration,** the behavior of the parties is aimed at solving the problem, at clarifying the differences rather than accommodating various points of view. The participants consider the full range of alternatives, the similarities and differences in viewpoint become more clearly focused, and the causes or differences become outwardly evident. Because the solution sought is advantageous to all parties, collaboration is often thought of as a win–win approach to resolving conflicts. It is, for example, a frequent tool of marriage counselors. Behavioral scientists, who value openness, trust, authenticity, and spontaneity in relationships, are also strong advocates of a collaborative approach to resolving conflicts.

AVOIDANCE   A person may recognize that a conflict exists but react by withdrawing or by suppressing the conflict. We call this **avoidance.** Indiffer-

Competition Rule-regulated efforts to obtain a goal without regard for the impact on others.

Collaboration A situation where the parties to a conflict each desire to satisfy fully the concern of all parties.

Avoidance Withdrawing from or suppressing conflict.

Approaches to Resolving Conflicts Vary Across Cultures

Americans have a reputation for being open, direct, and competitive. This characteristic is consistent with a society marked by relatively low uncertainty avoidance and high masculinity rankings.

As we discovered in Chapter 3, people in countries low in uncertainty avoidance feel secure and relatively free from threats of uncertainty. Their organizations, therefore, tend to be more open and flexible. Countries high in masculinity emphasize assertiveness. The cultural climate of low uncertainty avoidance and high masculinity tends to shape a society that is open, direct, and competitive. It would also tend to create individuals who favor such conflict-handling behaviors as competition and collaboration.

The above suggests that uncertainty avoidance and masculinity–femininity rankings would be fairly good predictors of which conflict styles are preferred in different countries. It suggests, for instance, that when one is in a Scandinavian country—which tend to rate high on femininity—avoidance or accommodation behaviors should be emphasized. The same recommendation would apply in Japan, Greece, or other countries that rate high on uncertainty avoidance, because the extensive use of formal rules and employment guarantees tend to minimize conflicts and encourage cooperation.

Research studies in diverse settings confirm the functionality of conflict. Consider the following findings:

The comparison of six major decisions made during the administration of four different United States presidents found that conflict reduced the chance that groupthink would overpower policy decisions. The comparisons demonstrated that conformity among presidential advisors was related to poor decisions, while an atmosphere of constructive conflict and critical thinking surrounded the well-developed decisions.[11]

The bankruptcy of the Penn Central Railroad has been generally attributed to mismanagement and a failure of the company's board of directors to question actions taken by management. The board was composed of outside directors who met monthly to oversee the railroad's operations. Few questioned decisions made by the operating management, though there was evidence that several board members were uncomfortable with many decisions made by them. Apathy and a desire to *avoid* conflict allowed poor decisions to stand unquestioned.[12] This, however, should not be surprising, since a review of the relationship between bureaucracy and innovation has found that conflict encourages innovative solutions.[13] The corollary of this finding also appears true: Lack of conflict results in a passive environment with reinforcement of the status quo.

Not only do better and more innovative decisions result from situations where there is some conflict, but there is evidence indicating that conflict can be positively related to productivity. It was demonstrated that, among established groups, performance tended to improve more when there was conflict among members than when there was fairly close agreement. The investiga-

How to Create Functional Conflict

How can an organization encourage functional conflict?[20] For most organizations, it's a tough job. As one consultant put it, "A high proportion of people who get to the top are conflict avoiders. They don't like hearing negatives, they don't like saying or thinking negative things. They frequently make it up the ladder in part because they don't irritate people on the way up." Another suggests that at least seven out of ten people in American business hush up when their opinions are at odds with those of their superiors, allowing bosses to make mistakes even when they know better.

Such anticonflict cultures may have been tolerable in the past, but not in today's fiercely competitive global economy. Those organizations that don't encourage and support dissent may not survive the 1990s. Let's look at some of the approaches firms are taking to encourage their people to challenge the system and develop fresh ideas.

Hewlett-Packard rewards dissenters by recognizing go-against-the-grain types, or people who stay with the ideas they believe in even when those ideas are rejected by management. Herman Miller Inc., an office-furniture manufacturer, has a formal system in which employees evaluate and criticize their bosses. IBM also has a formal system that encourages dissension. Employees can question their boss with impunity. If the disagreement can't be resolved, the system provides a third party for counsel.

Royal Dutch-Shell Group, General Electric, and Anheuser-Busch build devil's advocates into the decision process. For instance, when the policy committee at Anheuser-Busch considers a major move, such as getting into or out of a business, or making a major capital expenditure, it often assigns teams to make the case for each side of the question. This process frequently results in decisions and alternatives that previously hadn't been considered.

One common ingredient in organizations that successfully create functional conflict is that they reward dissent and punish conflict-avoiders. The president of Innovis Interactive Technologies, for instance, fired a top executive who refused to dissent. His explanation: "He was the ultimate yes-man. In this organization I can't afford to pay someone to hear my own opinion." But the real challenge for managers is when they hear news that they don't want to hear. The news may make their blood boil or their hopes collapse, but they can't show it. They have to learn to take the bad news without flinching. No tirades, no tight-lipped sarcasm, no eyes rolling upward, no gritting of teeth. Rather, managers should ask calm, even-tempered questions: "Can you tell me more about what happened?" "What do you think we ought to do?" A sincere "Thank you for bringing this to my attention" is likely to reduce the likelihood that they will be cut off from similar communications in the future.

tors observed that when groups analyzed decisions that had been made by the individual members of that group, the average improvement among the high-conflict groups was seventy-three percent greater than was that of those groups characterized by low-conflict conditions.[14] Others have found similar results: Groups composed of members with different interests tend to produce higher-quality solutions to a variety of problems than do homogeneous groups.[15]

Similarly, studies of professionals—systems analysts and research and

General Motors and the Price of Eliminating Conflict

H. Ross Perot is an outspoken superpatriot and a self-made billionaire. In 1984, he sold Electronic Data Systems, the Dallas-based computer services company he founded in the early 1960s, to General Motors for $2.5 billion and immediately became GM's largest stockholder and a member of the board.

GM's decision to buy EDS was motivated by the desire to improve its internal coordination. EDS had the people and experience to coordinate GM's massive information systems and to help GM achieve its goal of becoming a world leader in factory automation. GM's chairman, Roger Smith, also looked forward to having Perot's fiery spirit to reinvigorate GM's bureaucracy for the big battle with the Japanese.

Unfortunately, the marriage was not a happy one. Perot saw problems at GM and felt compelled to speak out.[22] He was particularly frustrated about how slow GM was in responding to the actions of competitors, as evidenced by these types of comments: "The first EDSer to see a snake kills it. At GM, the first thing you do is go hire a consultant on snakes. Then you get a committee on snakes, and then you discuss it for a couple of years." Or, "It takes this company [GM] four years to get a car from the drawing board to a showroom. Good Heavens, we won World War II in less time!" Or, "At GM the stress is not on getting results—on winning—but on bureaucracy, on conforming to the GM system. You get to the top of General Motors not by doing something, but by not making a mistake."

Roger Smith had wanted Perot to act as an irritant inside GM—to shake things up. And that he did. Perot loudly and enthusiastically questioned many of GM's longstanding management practices. He went down to the factory floor to talk to workers about new ideas. He even anonymously shopped for cars at GM dealerships to assess customer service. But in December 1986, Smith had apparently had enough of Perot's criticism of GM practices. To silence Perot and get his resignation from GM's board, Smith agreed to pay Perot roughly double the market price—a whopping $750 million—for his stake in GM. GM had decided that it was worth the money to eliminate the conflict, whether it was functional or otherwise.

development scientists—support the constructive value of conflict. An investigation of twenty-two teams of systems analysts found that the more incompatible groups were likely to be more productive.[16] Research and development scientists have been found to be most productive where there is a certain amount of intellectual conflict.[17]

Conflict can even be constructive on sports teams and in unions. Studies of sports teams indicate that moderate levels of group conflict contribute to team effectiveness and provide an additional stimulus for high achievement.[18] An examination of local unions found that conflict between members of the local was positively related to the union's power and to member loyalty and participation in union affairs.[19] These findings might suggest that conflict within a group indicates strength rather than, as in the traditional view, weakness.

DYSFUNCTIONAL OUTCOMES   The destructive consequences of conflict upon a group or organization's performance are generally well known. A reasonable summary might state: Uncontrolled opposition breeds discontent, which acts to dissolve common ties, and eventually leads to the destruction of the group. And, of course, there is a substantial body of literature to document how conflict—the dysfunctional varieties—can reduce group effectiveness.[21] Among the more undesirable consequences are a retarding of communication, reductions in group cohesiveness, and subordination of group goals to the primacy of infighting between members. At the extreme, conflict can bring group functioning to a halt and potentially threaten the group's survival.

This discussion has again returned us to the issue of what is functional and what is dysfunctional. Research on conflict has yet to identify those situations where conflict is more likely to be constructive than destructive. However, the difference between functional and dysfunctional conflict is important enough for us to go beyond the substantive evidence and propose at least two hypotheses. The first is that extreme levels of conflict—exemplified by overt struggle or violence—are rarely, if ever, functional. Functional conflict is probably most often characterized by low to moderate levels of subtle and controlled opposition. Second, the type of group activity should be another factor determining functionality. We hypothesize that the more creative or unprogrammed the decision-making tasks of the group, the greater the probability that internal conflict is constructive. Groups that are required to tackle problems requiring new and novel approaches—as in research, advertising, and other professional activities—will benefit more from conflict than groups performing highly programmed activities—for instance, those of work teams on an automobile assembly line.

INTERGROUP RELATIONS

For the most part, the concepts from Chapter 9 on have dealt with *intra*group activities. For instance, the previous material in this chapter emphasized interpersonal and intragroup conflict. But we need to understand relationships between groups as well as within groups. In this section, we'll focus on *inter*group relationships. These are the coordinated bridges that link two distinct organizational groups.[23] As we'll show, the efficiency and quality of these relationships can have a significant bearing on one or both of the groups' performances and their members' satisfaction.

Factors Affecting Intergroup Relations

Successful intergroup performance is a function of a number of factors. The umbrella concept that overrides these factors is *coordination*. Each of the following can affect efforts at coordination.

INTERDEPENDENCE   The first overriding question we need to ask is: Do the groups really need coordination? The answer to this question lies in determining the degree of interdependence that exists between the groups. That is, do the groups depend on each other and, if so, how much? The three

The work of designers at Chadick & Kimball, a Washington, D.C. design firm that specializes in developing corporate identity programs, requires reciprocal interdependence with the firm's marketing staff. Design and marketing people are required to exchange information in order to meet client needs.
T. Michael Keza.

most frequently identified types of interdependence are pooled, sequential, and reciprocal.[24] Each requires an increasing degree of group interaction (see Figure 13–3).

When two groups function with relative independence but their combined output contributes to the organization's overall goals, **pooled interdependence** exists. At a firm such as Apple Computer, for instance, this would describe the relationship between the Product Development department and the Shipping department. Both are necessary if Apple is to develop new products and get those products into consumers' hands, but each is essentially separate and distinct from the other. All other things being equal, coordination requirements between groups linked by pooled interdependence are less than with sequential or reciprocal interdependence.

The Purchasing and Parts Assembly departments at Apple are **sequen-**

Pooled Interdependence
Where two groups function with relative independence but their combined output contributes to the organization's overall goals.

FIGURE 13–3   Types of Interdependence

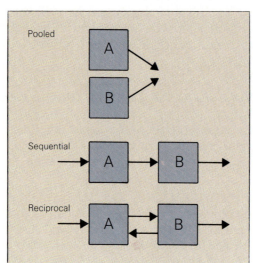

Sequential Interdependence
One group depends on another for its input but the dependency is only one way.

Reciprocal Interdependence
Where groups exchange inputs and outputs.

tially interdependent. One group—Parts Assembly—depends on another—Purchasing—for its inputs, but the dependency is only one way. Purchasing is not directly dependent on Parts Assembly for its inputs. In sequential interdependence, if the group that provides the input doesn't perform its job properly, the group that is dependent on the first will be significantly affected. In our Apple example, if Purchasing fails to order an important component that goes into the assembly process, then the Parts Assembly department may have to slow down or temporarily close its assembly operations.

The most complex form of interdependence is **reciprocal.** In these instances, groups exchange inputs and outputs. For example, Sales and Product Development groups at Apple are reciprocally interdependent. Sales people, in contact with customers, acquire information about their future needs. Sales then relays this back to Product Development so they can create new computer products. The long-term implications are that if Product Development doesn't come up with new products that potential customers find desirable, Sales personnel are not going to get orders. So there is high interdependence—Product Development needs Sales for information on customer needs so it can create successful new products, and Sales depends on the Product Development group to create products that it can successfully sell. This high degree of dependency translates into greater interaction and increased coordination demands.

TASK UNCERTAINTY The next coordination question is: What type of tasks are the groups involved in? For simplicity's sake, we can think of a group's tasks as ranging from highly routine to highly nonroutine.[25] (See Figure 13–4.)

Highly routine tasks have little variation. Problems that group members face tend to contain few exceptions and are easy to analyze. Such group activities lend themselves to standardized operating procedures. For example, manufacturing tasks in a tire factory are made up of highly routine tasks. At the other extreme are nonroutine tasks. These are activities that are unstructured, with many exceptions and problems that are hard to analyze. Many of the tasks undertaken by marketing research and product development groups are of this variety. Of course, a lot of group tasks fall somewhere in the middle or combine both routine and nonroutine tasks.

Task Uncertainty The greater the uncertainty in a task, the more custom the response. Conversely, low uncertainty encompasses routine tasks with standardized activities.

The key to **task uncertainty** is that nonroutine tasks require considerably more processing of information. Tasks with low uncertainty tend to be standardized. Further, groups that do such tasks do not have to interact much with other groups. In contrast, groups that undertake tasks that are high in uncertainty face problems that require custom responses. This, in turn, leads to a need for more and better information. We would expect the people in the

FIGURE 13–4   Task Continuum

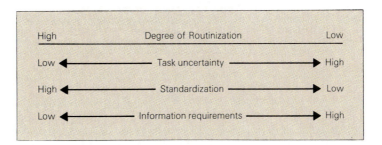

marketing research department at Goodyear Tire & Rubber to interact much more with other departments and constituencies—marketing, sales, product design, tire dealers, advertising agencies, and the like—than would people in Goodyear's manufacturing group.

TIME AND GOAL ORIENTATION   How different are the groups in terms of their members' background and thinking? This is the third question relevant to the degree of coordination necessary between groups. Research demonstrates that a work group's perceptions of what is important may differ on the basis of the time frame that governs their work and their goal orientation.[26] This can make it difficult for groups with different perceptions to work together.

Why might work groups have different time and goal orientations? Top management divides work up by putting common tasks into common functional groups and assigning these groups specific goals. Then, people are hired with the appropriate background and skills to complete the tasks and help the group achieve its goals. This differentiation of tasks and hiring of specialists makes it easier to coordinate intragroup activities. But it makes it increasingly difficult to coordinate interaction between groups.

To illustrate how orientations differ between work groups, manufacturing personnel have a short-term time focus. They worry about today's production schedule and this week's productivity. In contrast, people in research and development focus on the long run. They're concerned about developing new products that may not be produced for several years. Similarly, work groups often have different goal orientations. Sales, as a case in point, wants to sell anything and everything. Their goals center on sales volume, and increasing revenue and market share. Their customers' ability to pay for the sales they make are not their concern. But people in the credit department want to ensure that sales are made only to credit-worthy customers. These

FIGURE 13–5

differences in goals often make it difficult for sales and credit to communicate. It also makes it harder to coordinate their interactions.

Methods for Managing Intergroup Relations

What coordination methods are available for managing intergroup relations? There are a number of options; the seven most frequently used are identified in Figure 13–6. These seven are listed on a continuum, in order of increasing cost.[27] They also are cumulative in the sense that succeeding methods higher on the continuum add to, rather than are substituted for, lower methods.

RULES AND PROCEDURES   The most simple and least costly method for managing intergroup relations is to establish, in advance, a set of formalized rules and procedures that will specify how group members are to interact with each other. In large organizations, for example, standard operating procedures are likely to specify that when additional permanent staff are needed in any department, a "request for new staff" form is to be filed with the personnel department. Upon receipt of this form, the personnel department begins a standardized process to fill the request. Notice that such rules and procedures minimize the need for interaction and information flow between the departments or work groups. The major drawback to this method is that it works well only when intergroup activities can be anticipated ahead of time and when they recur often enough to justify establishing rules and procedures for handling them.

HIERARCHY   If rules and procedures are inadequate, the use of the organization's hierarchy becomes the primary method for managing intergroup relations. What this means is that coordination is achieved by referring problems to a common superior higher in the organization. In a college, if the chairpersons for the English and Speech Communication departments can't

FIGURE 13–6   Methods for Managing Intergroup Relations

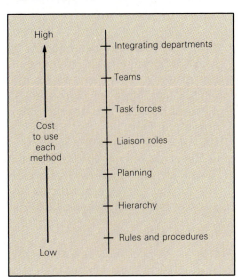

This production line at Westinghouse illustrates the application of rules and procedures to facilitate intergroup relations. Standard operating procedures define how group members are to interact with each other.

Insight magazine/Brig Cabe.

agree on where the new courses in debate will be taught, they can take the issue to the college dean for a resolution. The major limitation to this method is that it increases demands on the common superior's time. If all differences were resolved by this means, the organization's chief executive would be overwhelmed with resolving intergroup problems, leaving little time for other matters.

PLANNING   The next step up the continuum is the use of planning to facilitate coordination. If each work group has specific goals for which it is responsible, then each knows what it is supposed to do. Intergroup tasks that create problems are resolved in terms of the goals and contributions of each group. In a state motor vehicle office, the various work groups—testing and examinations, driving permits, vehicle registration, cashiering, and the like— each has a set of goals that define its area of responsibility and acts to reduce intergroup conflicts. Planning tends to break down as a coordination device where work groups don't have clearly defined goals or where the volume of contacts between groups is high.

LIAISON ROLES   Liaison roles refers to individuals with specialized roles designed to facilitate communication between two interdependent work units. In one organization where accountants and engineers had a long history of conflict, management hired an engineer with an MBA degree and several years of experience in public accounting. This person could speak the language of both groups and understood their problems. As a result of this new liaison role, conflicts that had previously made it difficult for the accounting and engineering departments to coordinate their activities were significantly reduced. The major drawback to this coordination device is that there are limits to any liaison person's ability to handle information flow between interacting groups, especially where the groups are large and interactions are frequent.

TASK FORCES   A task force is a temporary group made up of representatives from a number of departments. It exists only long enough to solve the problem it was created to handle. After a solution is reached, task force participants return to their normal duties.

Task forces are an excellent device for coordinating activities when the number of interacting groups is more than two or three. For example, when Audi began receiving numerous complaints about its cars accelerating when the transmission was put in reverse, even when drivers swore that their feet were firmly on the brakes, the company created a task force to assess the problem and develop a solution. Representatives from design, production, legal, and engineering departments were brought together. After a solution was determined, the task force was disbanded.

TEAMS   As tasks become more complex, additional problems arise during the act of execution. Previous coordination devices are no longer adequate. If the delays in decisions become long, lines of communication become extended, and top managers are forced to spend more time on day-to-day operations, the next response is to use permanent teams. They are typically formed around frequently occurring problems—with team members maintaining a responsibility to both their primary functional department and to the team. When the team has accomplished its task, each member returns full time to his or her functional assignment.

This form of coordination device is popular in aerospace firms. There are functional departments based on common functions. Teams are formed around the major problem areas or projects on which the firm is working. So, for instance, manufacturing operations might have a wing team located in one place in the plant (see Figure 13–7), with members coming from the various functional areas.

INTEGRATING DEPARTMENTS   When intergroup relations become too complex to be coordinated through plans, task forces, teams, and the like, organizations may create integrating departments. These are permanent

FIGURE 13–7   Example of a Team Intergroup-Coordination Device
Source: J. R. Galbraith, *Organization Design* (Reading, MA: Addison-Wesley, 1977), p. 117.

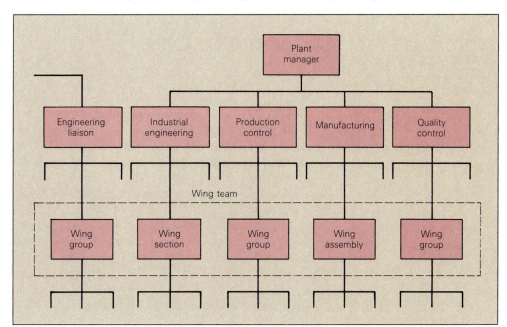

departments with members formally assigned to the task of integration between two or more groups. While they're permanent and expensive to maintain, they tend to be used when an organization has a number of groups with conflicting goals, nonroutine problems, and intergroup decisions that have a significant impact on the organization's total operations. They are also excellent devices to manage intergroup conflicts for organizations facing long-term retrenchments. When organizations are forced to shrink in size—as has recently occurred in industries such as steel, mining, and oil exploration—conflicts over how cuts are to be distributed and how the smaller resource pie is to be allocated become major and ongoing dilemmas. The use of integrating departments in such cases can be an effective means for managing these intergroup relations.

SUMMARY   It may help to put this discussion in perspective by considering methods for managing intergroup relations in terms of effectiveness.

Researchers state that the effectiveness of intergroup relations can be evaluated in terms of efficiency and quality.[28] Efficiency considers the costs to the organization of transforming an intergroup conflict into actions agreed to by the groups. Quality refers to the degree to which the outcome results in a well-defined and enduring exchange agreement. Using these definitions, the seven methods introduced in this section were presented, in order, from most efficient to least efficient. That is, ignoring outcomes for a moment, rules and procedures are less costly to implement than hierarchy, hierarchy is less costly than planning, and so forth. But, of course, keeping costs down is only one consideration. The other element of effectiveness is quality, or how well the coordination device works in facilitating interaction and reducing dysfunctional conflicts. As we've shown, the least costly alternative may not be adequate. So managers have a number of options at their disposal for managing intergroup relations. But since they tend to be cumulative, with costs rising as you move up the continuum in Figure 13–6, the most effective coordination device will be the one lowest on the continuum that facilitates an enduring integrative exchange.

IMPLICATIONS FOR PERFORMANCE AND SATISFACTION

Many people assume that conflict is related to lower group and organizational performance. This chapter has demonstrated that this assumption is frequently fallacious. Conflict can be either constructive or destructive to the functioning of a group or unit. As shown in Figure 13–8, levels of conflict can be either too high or too low. Either extreme hinders performance. An optimal level is where there is enough conflict to prevent stagnation, stimulate creativity, allow tensions to be released, and initiate the seeds for change; yet not so much as to be disruptive or deter coordination of activities.

Inadequate or excessive levels of conflict can hinder the effectiveness of a group or an organization, resulting in reduced satisfaction of group members, increased absence and turnover rates, and, eventually, lower productivity. On the other hand, when conflict is at an optimal level, complacency and apathy should be minimized, motivation should be enhanced through the creation of a challenging and questioning environment with a vitality that makes work

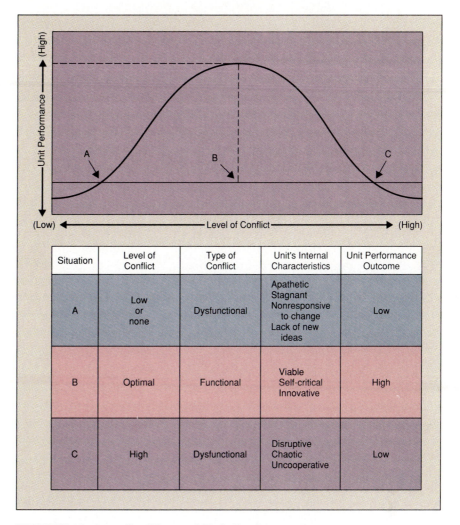

Situation	Level of Conflict	Type of Conflict	Unit's Internal Characteristics	Unit Performance Outcome
A	Low or none	Dysfunctional	Apathetic Stagnant Nonresponsive to change Lack of new ideas	Low
B	Optimal	Functional	Viable Self-critical Innovative	High
C	High	Dysfunctional	Disruptive Chaotic Uncooperative	Low

FIGURE 13–8   Conflict and Unit Performance

interesting, and there should be the needed turnover to rid the organization of misfits and poor performers.

Intergroup conflicts can also affect an organization's performance. Emphasis at this level, however, has tended to focus on dysfunctional conflicts and methods for managing them. Where organizational performance depends on effective group relations and where there is high interdependence between groups, management needs to insure that the proper integrative device is put in place. However, consistent with the interactionist perspective on conflict, there is no reason to believe that *all* intergroup conflicts are dysfunctional. Some minimal levels of conflict can facilitate critical thinking among group members, make a group more responsive to the need for change, and provide similar benefits that can enhance group and organizational performance.

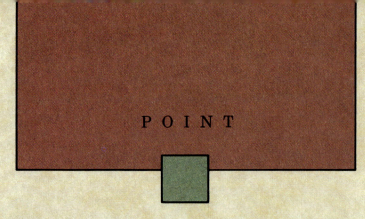

Conflict Is Good for an Organization

We've made considerable progress in the last twenty years toward overcoming the negative stereotype given to conflict. Most behavioral scientists and an increasing number of practitioners now accept that the goal of effective management is not to eliminate conflict. Rather, it is to create the right intensity of conflict so as to reap its functional benefits.

Since conflict can be good for an organization, it is only logical to acknowledge that there may be times when managers will purposely want to increase its intensity. Let's briefly review how stimulating conflict can provide benefits to the organization.

Conflict is a means by which to bring about radical change. It is an effective device by which management can drastically change the existing power structure, current interaction patterns, and entrenched attitudes.

Conflict facilitates group cohesiveness. While conflict increases hostility between groups, external threats tend to cause a group to pull together as a unit. Intergroup conflicts raise the extent to which members identify with their own group and increase feelings of solidarity, while, at the same time, internal differences and irritations dissolve.

Conflict improves group and organizational effectiveness. The stimulation of conflict initiates the search for new means and goals and clears the way for innovation. The successful solution of a conflict leads to greater effectiveness, to more trust and openness, to greater attraction of members for each other, and to depersonalization of future conflicts. In fact, it has been found that as the number of minor disagreements increases, the number of major clashes decreases.

Conflict brings about a slightly higher, more constructive level of tension. This enhances the chances of solving the conflicts in a way satisfactory to all parties concerned. When the level of tension is very low, the parties are not sufficiently motivated to do something about a conflict.

These points are clearly not comprehensive. As noted in the chapter, conflict provides a number of benefits to an organization. However, groups or organizations devoid of conflict are likely to suffer from apathy, stagnation, groupthink, and other debilitating diseases.

The points presented here were influenced by E. Van de Vliert, "Escalative Intervention in Small-Group Conflicts," *Journal of Applied Behavioral Science,* Vol. 21, No. 1, 1985, pp. 19–36.

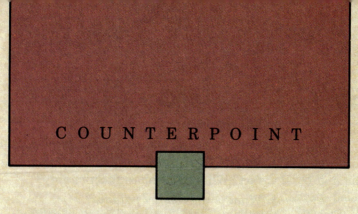

All Conflicts Are Dysfunctional!

It may be true that conflict is an inherent part of any group or organization. It may not be possible to eliminate it completely. However, just because conflicts exist is no reason to deify them. *All* conflicts are dysfunctional, and it is one of management's major responsibilities to keep conflict intensity as low as humanly possible. A few points will support my case.

The negative consequences from conflict can be devastating. The list of negatives associated with conflict are awesome. The most obvious include increased turnover, decreased employee satisfaction, inefficiencies between work units, sabotage, labor grievances and strikes, and physical aggression.

Effective managers build teamwork. A good manager builds a coordinated team. Conflict works against such an objective. A successful work group is like a successful sports team; each member knows his or her role and supports his or her teammates. When a team works well, the whole becomes greater than the sum of the parts. Management creates teamwork by minimizing internal conflicts and facilitating internal coordination.

Competition is good for an organization, but not conflict. Competition and conflict should not be confused with each other. *Conflict* is behavior directed against another party, whereas *competition* is behavior aimed at obtaining a goal without interference from another party. Competition is healthy; it is the source of organizational vitality. Conflict, on the other hand, is destructive.

Managers who accept and stimulate conflict don't survive in organizations. The whole argument on the value of conflict may be moot as long as senior executives in organizations view conflict from the traditional view. In the traditional view, *any* conflict will be seen as bad. Since the evaluation of a manager's performance is made by higher-level executives, those managers who do not succeed in eliminating conflicts are likely to be appraised negatively. This, in turn, will reduce opportunities for advancement. Any manager who aspires to move up in such an environment will be wise to follow the traditional view and eliminate any outward signs of conflict. Failure to follow this advice might result in the premature departure of the manager.

FOUNDATIONS OF ORGANIZATION STRUCTURE

LEARNING OBJECTIVES

After studying this chapter, you should be able to:

1. *Define organization structure*
2. *Identify the advantages and disadvantages to division of labor*
3. *Explain the reason for maintaining unity of command*
4. *Differentiate line from staff authority*
5. *Define the span of control*
6. *List the ways an organization can departmentalize*
7. *Explain why structure may be a perceptual phenomenon*

Michele Chen works in an informal, loosely structured organization where she operates under minimum controls. Her brother, Tony, however, works in a highly formalized and impersonal organization where there are tight controls over employee behavior. Both photos courtesy of Hewlett-Packard.

One man's red tape is another man's system.

D. WALDO

ichele and Tony Chen are twins. Both grew up in Seattle, attended the University of Washington, and graduated with degrees in computer science in 1989. Upon graduation, Michele joined a San Francisco consulting firm as a systems specialist. Tony went to work for a Boston firm that writes computer software programs. At a recent family Thanksgiving dinner, the two spent some time comparing their job impressions.

"Did I ever make a mistake," began Tony. "I had four job offers and I took the one I did because it was a well-known company, provided me the opportunity to specialize in writing expert systems programs, and the promotion potential looked good because there were a number of levels of management. Well, there are many opportunities to move up here, but there's also a lot of competition. Of course, I've never been afraid of competition. It's just that jobs are so specialized and top management so removed from the daily routine that no one seems to notice what I do. I'm just a cog in this wheel. I'm a number—employee number HO 297, to be exact—and except for my boss and a few people in adjoining cubicles, no one even knows my name. It couldn't be more impersonal. You wouldn't believe the umpteen-zillion rules and regulations we have to follow. The company's policy manual has over 500 pages! I spent my first four weekends with the firm in my office reading that manual. The actual work I do is really interesting and I've learned a lot of technical aspects about programming. But I hate this feeling of alienation I have. This company, day by day, is stripping me of my identity. I've begun making a few calls to some of our old college friends to let them know I'm back in the job market and to let me know if they hear of anything interesting. But maybe it's me. Maybe all companies are like this. What's your firm like?"

"It's nothing like yours," was Michele's reply. "Managers are purposely given a large number of people to supervise. This cuts down on the number of managers and minimizes the number of levels from the top of the company to the bottom. The place is really very informal. No policy manuals, no job descriptions, no complex chain of command. If I have a question or problem, I can take it up with anyone. We're all treated as equals. I think our firm is about the same size as yours—between 400 and 500 people—but we operate very loosely. The office layouts don't even include walls, which encourages us to communicate regularly with people at different ranks and in different areas. I'm on a first-name basis with everyone, including the president. They ask for my ideas on projects. And my ideas are always listened to and often implemented. We're all supposed to be professionals, and we're treated as such."

Tony and Michele work in organizations with very different structures. And as their comments suggest, these structures have a bearing on each twin's attitudes and behavior. In this chapter, we'll lay the foundation for an understanding of organization structure. We'll define the key dimensions that make up structure, describe the basic structural components, and consider how they affect organizational behavior.

WHAT IS STRUCTURE?

Organizations create structure to facilitate the coordination of activities and to control the actions of their members. Structure, itself, is made up of three components. The first has to do with the degree to which activities within the organization are broken up or differentiated. We call this *complexity*. Second is the degree to which rules and procedures are utilized. This component is referred to as *formalization*. The third component of structure is *centralization,* which considers where decision-making authority lies. Combined, these three components make up an organization's structure.[1] Some organizations, such as General Electric or the United States Department of Defense, are rigidly structured. They have lots of differentiated units, a great number of vertical levels between top management and the workers at the bottom, numerous rules and regulations that members are required to follow, and elaborate decision-making networks. At the other extreme are organizations that are loosely structured—few differentiated units, only a couple of levels of management hierarchy, little in terms of formalized regulations to restrict employees, and a simple system for making decisions. Of course, in between these two extremes lie a number of structural combinations. But while organizations differ in the ways they are structured, our primary interest is what impact these structural differences have on employee attitudes and behavior. First, however, let's briefly elaborate on the three components we have identified to ensure we have a common understanding of what is meant when we use the term **organization structure.**

Organization Structure The degree of complexity, formalization, and centralization in the organization.

Complexity

Complexity encompasses three forms of differentiation: horizontal, vertical, and spatial. **Horizontal differentiation** considers the degree of horizontal separation between units. The larger the number of different occupations within an organization that require specialized knowledge and skills, the more horizontally complex that organization is, because diverse orientations make it more difficult for organizational members to communicate and more difficult for management to coordinate their activities. When organizations have coordination problems because the cost accountants can't understand the priorities of the industrial engineers or because marketing and credit personnel have conflicting goals, the source of the problems is horizontal differentiation.

   Vertical differentiation refers to the depth of the organizational hierarchy. The more levels that exist between top management and the operatives, the more complex the organization is. This is because there is a greater potential for communication distortion, it's more difficult to coordinate the decisions of managerial personnel, and it's harder for top management to oversee closely the actions of operatives where there are more vertical levels.

Complexity The degree of vertical, horizontal, and spatial differentiation in an organization.

Horizontal Differentiation The degree of differentiation between units based on the orientation of members, the nature of the tasks they perform, and their education and training.

Vertical Differentiation The number of hierarchical levels in the organization.

For example, it's a lot more likely that information having to go through eight or ten levels of management hierarchy will become distorted or misinterpreted than if that information had to move through only two or three levels.

Spatial differentiation encompasses the degree to which the location of an organization's physical facilities and personnel are geographically dispersed. As spatial differentiation increases so does complexity, because communication, coordination, and control become more difficult. Coordinating Sheraton's hundreds of hotels, located around the world, is a far more complex undertaking than coordinating the dozen New York City hotels that make up the Helmsley chain.

Spatial Differentiation The degree to which the location of an organization's offices, plants, and personnel are geographically dispersed.

Formalization

The second component of structure is **formalization.** This term refers to the degree to which jobs within the organization are standardized. If a job is highly formalized, then the job incumbent has a minimum amount of discretion over what is to be done, when it is to be done, and how he or she should do it. Employees can be expected always to handle the same input in exactly the same way, resulting in a consistent and uniform output. There are explicit job descriptions, lots of organizational rules, and clearly defined procedures covering work processes in organizations where there is high formalization. Where formalization is low, job behaviors are relatively nonprogrammed and employees have a great deal of freedom to exercise discretion in their work. Since an individual's discretion on the job is inversely related to the amount of behavior that is preprogrammed by the organization, the greater the standardization, the less input the employee has into how his or her work is to be done. Standardization not only eliminates the possibility of employees engaging in alternative behaviors, but it even removes the need for employees to consider alternatives.

Formalization The degree to which jobs within the organization are standardized.

The degree of formalization can vary widely between organizations and within organizations. Certain jobs, for instance, are well known to have little formalization. College book travelers—the representatives of publishers who call on professors to inform them of their company's new publications—have a great deal of freedom in their jobs. They have no standard sales "spiel," and the extent of rules and procedures governing their behavior may be little more than the requirement that they submit a weekly sales report and some suggestions on what to emphasize for the various new titles. At the other extreme, there are clerical and editorial positions in the same publishing houses where employees are required to "clock in" at their workstations by 8:00 A.M. or be docked a half-hour of pay and, once at that workstation, to follow a set of precise procedures dictated by management.

Centralization

In some organizations, top managers make all the decisions. Lower-level managers merely carry out top management's directives. At the other extreme, there are organizations where decision making is pushed down to those managers who are closest to the action. The former case is called **centralization;** the latter is decentralization.

Centralization The degree to which decision making is concentrated at a single point in the organization.

The term centralization refers to the degree to which decision making is concentrated at a single point in the organization. The concept includes only formal authority, that is, the rights inherent in one's position. Typically, it is said that if top management makes the organization's key decisions with little or no input from lower-level personnel, then the organization is centralized. In contrast, the more that lower-level personnel provide input or are actually given the discretion to make decisions, the more decentralized the organization.

An organization characterized by centralization is an inherently different structural animal from one that is decentralized. In a decentralized organization, action can be taken more quickly to solve problems, more people provide input into decisions, and employees are less likely to feel alienated from those who make the decisions that affect their work lives.

BASIC ORGANIZATIONAL CONCEPTS

Both management practitioners and theorists have been concerned with developing organizational principles since before the turn of the century. For instance, Adam Smith wrote on the advantages of division of labor in his celebrated *The Wealth of Nations* in the late eighteenth century.[2] During the first half of this century, a group of management practitioners and academics postulated a set of principles to guide managers in making structural decisions.[3] This group has come to be known as the *classical theorists* and their recommendations as the *classical principles*.

A number of decades have passed since most of these principles were originally proposed. Given the passing of that much time and all the changes that have taken place in our society, you might think these principles would be pretty worthless today. Surprisingly, they're not! For the most part, they still provide valuable insight into understanding the structure of organizations. Of course, we've also gained a great deal of knowledge over the years as to the limitations of these principles. In this section, we'll discuss the five basic classical principles. We'll also present an updated analysis of how each has had to be modified to reflect the increasing complexity and changing nature of today's organizational activities.

Division of Labor

Division of Labor
Specialization; breaking jobs down into simple and repetitive tasks.

THE CLASSICAL VIEW   **Division of labor** means that, rather than an entire job being done by one individual, it is broken down into a number of steps, each step being completed by a separate individual. In essence, individuals specialize in doing part of an activity rather than the entire activity. Assembly-line production, in which each worker does the same standardized task over and over again, is an example of division of labor.

The classical theorists were strong proponents of division of labor. They saw it as a way to significantly increase the economic efficiencies of organizations.

Division of labor makes efficient use of the diversity of skills that workers hold. In most organizations, some tasks require highly developed skills; others can be performed by the untrained. If all workers were engaged in each step of, say, an organization's manufacturing process, all must have the skills necessary to perform both the most demanding and the least demanding jobs. The result would be that, except when performing the most skilled or highly

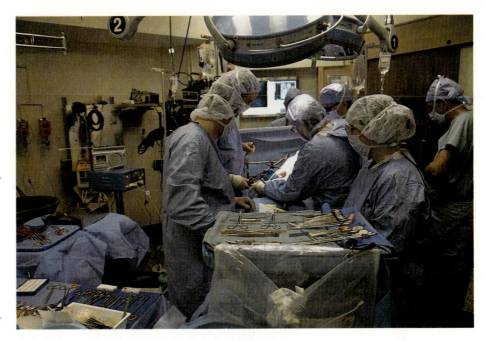

We see the results of division of labor in medical organizations. In this operating room, doctors, nurses, and other medical professionals each perform a precise and repetitive set of tasks. Much of the progress in modern medicine can be traced to increased expertise made possible by high degrees of specialization.   Richard Pasley / Stock, Boston.

sophisticated tasks, employees would be working below their skill levels. And since skilled workers are paid more than unskilled workers and their wages tend to reflect their highest level of skill, it represents an inefficient usage of organizational resources to pay highly skilled workers to do easy tasks.

A number of other efficiencies are achieved through division of labor. One's skills at performing a task successfully increase through repetition. Less time is spent in changing tasks, in putting away one's tools and equipment from a prior step in the work process, and in getting ready for another. Equally important, training for specialization is more efficient from the organization's perspective. It is easier and less costly to find and train workers to do specific and repetitive tasks. This is especially true of highly sophisticated and complex operations. For example, could Lear produce one Lear jet a year if one person had to build the entire plane alone? Finally, division of labor increases efficiency and productivity by encouraging the creation of special inventions and machinery.

THE CONTEMPORARY VIEW   The classical theorists viewed division of labor as an unending source of increased productivity. At the turn of the century and earlier, this generalization was undoubtedly accurate. Because specialization was not widely practiced, its introduction almost always generated higher productivity. But a good thing can be carried too far. There is a point when the human diseconomies from division of labor—which surface as boredom, fatigue, stress, low productivity, poor quality, increased absenteeism, and high turnover—exceed the economic advantages. (See Figure 14–1.)

By the 1960s, it became clear that that point had been reached in a number of jobs. In such cases, productivity could be increased by enlarging, rather than narrowing, the scope of job activities. If you'll remember back to Chapters 7 and 8, where we discussed motivation, we dealt with job characteristics and design. We demonstrated that when employees are given a variety of activities to do, allowed to do a whole and complete piece of work, and put together into teams, they often achieved higher productivity and satisfaction.

Responsibility An obligation to perform.

When we delegate authority, the classicists argued, we must allocate commensurate **responsibility.** That is, when one is given *rights,* one also assumes a corresponding *obligation* to perform. To allocate authority without responsibility creates opportunities for abuse, and no one should be held responsible for what he or she has no authority over.

Classical theorists recognized the importance of equating authority and responsibility. Additionally, they stated that responsibility cannot be delegated. They supported this contention by noting that the delegator was held responsible for the actions of his or her delegates. But how is it possible to have equal authority and responsibility, if responsibility cannot be delegated?

The classicists' answer was to recognize two forms of responsibility: *operating* responsibility and *ultimate* responsibility. Managers pass on operating responsibility, which in turn may be passed on further. But there is an aspect of responsibility—its ultimate component—that must be retained. A manager is ultimately responsible for the actions of his or her subordinates to whom the operating responsibility has been passed. Therefore, managers should delegate operating responsibility equal to the delegated authority; however, ultimate responsibility can never be delegated.

Line Authority Authority to direct the work of a subordinate.

Chain of Command The superior–subordinate authority chain that extends from the top of the organization to the lowest echelon.

The classical theorists also distinguished between two forms of authority relations: line authority and staff authority. **Line authority** is the authority that entitles a manager to direct the work of a subordinate. It is the superior–subordinate authority relationship that extends from the top of the organization to the lowest echelon, following what is called the **chain of command.** As a link in the chain of command, a manager with line authority has the right to direct the work of subordinates and to make certain decisions without consulting others. Of course, in the chain of command, every manager is also subject to the direction of his or her superior.

Sometimes the term *line* is used to differentiate *line* managers from *staff* managers. In this context, line emphasizes those managers whose organizational function contributes directly to the achievement of the organizational objectives. In a manufacturing firm, line managers are typically in the production function, whereas executives in personnel or accounting are considered staff managers. But whether a manager's function is classified as

EDS Corp. provides supportive computer and information services to organizations. In the typical manufacturing firm, management information specialists are in a staff function. However, at EDS, such specialists are line. Courtesy of EDS Corporation, Dallas, Texas.

line or staff depends on the organization's objectives. At a firm like Kelly Services, which is a temporary personnel placement organization, personnel interviewers have a line function. Similarly, at the accounting firm of Price Waterhouse, accounting is a line function.

The definitions given above are not contradictory but, rather, represent two ways of looking at the term *line*. Every manager has line authority over his or her subordinates, but not every manager is in a line function or position. This latter determination depends on whether or not the function directly contributes to the organization's objectives.

As organizations get larger and more complex, line managers find that they do not have the time, expertise, or resources to get their jobs done effectively. In response, they create **staff authority** functions to support, assist, advise, and in general reduce some of the informational burdens they have. The hospital administrator can't effectively handle all the purchasing of supplies that the hospital needs, so she creates a purchasing department. The purchasing department is a staff department. Of course, the head of the purchasing department has line authority over her subordinate purchasing agents. The hospital administrator may also find that she is overburdened and needs an assistant. In creating the position of assistant-to-the-hospital administrator, she has created a staff position.

Figure 14–3 illustrates line and staff authority.

THE CONTEMPORARY VIEW The classical theorists were enamored with authority. They naively assumed that the rights inherent in one's formal position in an organization were the sole source of influence. They believed that managers were all-powerful.

Staff Authority Positions that support, assist, and advise line managers.

FIGURE 14–3   Line and Staff Authority

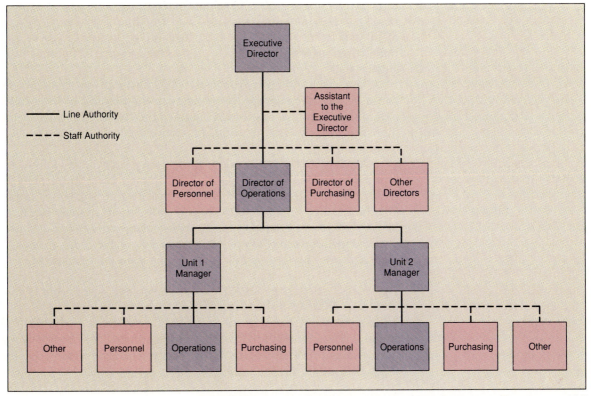

This may have been true fifty or more years ago. Organizations were simpler. Staff was less important. Managers were only minimally dependent on technical specialists. Under such conditions, influence is the same as authority; and the higher a manager's position in the organization, the more influence he or she had. But, as we described in Chapter 12, those conditions no longer hold. Researchers and practitioners of management now recognize that you don't have to be a manager to have power, nor is power perfectly correlated to one's level in the organization. Authority is an important concept in organizations, but an exclusive focus on it produces a narrow and unrealistic view of influence in organizations. Today we recognize that authority is but one element in the larger concept of power.

Moreover, as we have mentioned many times previously, organizations today have increasingly turned to participation, teams, and other devices to downplay authoritative, superior–subordinate relationships. Managers are increasingly viewing their jobs as liberating and enabling their employees rather than supervising them. As one former chief executive of a large office furniture manufacturer put it: "Take a 33-year-old man who assembles chairs. He's been doing it several years. He has a wife and two children. He knows what to do when the children have earaches, and how to get them through school. He probably serves on a volunteer board. And when he comes to work we give him a supervisor. He doesn't need one."[4]

Span of Control

THE CLASSICAL VIEW   How many subordinates can a manager efficiently and effectively direct? This question of **span of control** received a great deal of attention from the classicists. While there is no consensus on a specific number, the classical theorists favored small spans—typically no more than six—in order to maintain close control.[5] Several, however, did acknowledge level in the organization as a contingency variable. They argued that as a manager rises in an organization, he or she has to deal with a greater number of ill-structured problems, so top executives need a smaller span than do middle managers, and middle managers require a span smaller than do supervisors.

Span of Control The number of subordinates a manager can efficiently and effectively direct.

The span of control concept was important to the classical theorists because, to a large degree, it determines the number of levels and managers an organization has. All things being equal, the wider or larger the span, the more efficient the organization. An example can illustrate the validity of this statement.

Assume that we have two organizations, both of which have approximately 4,100 operative-level employees. As Figure 14–4 illustrates, if one has a uniform span of four and the other a span of eight, the wider span would have two fewer levels and approximately 800 fewer managers. If the average manager made $40,000 a year, the wider span would save $32 million a year in management salaries! Obviously, wider spans are more *efficient* in terms of cost. However, at some point wider spans reduce *effectiveness*.

THE CONTEMPORARY VIEW   Management guru Tom Peters recently predicted that Wal-Mart would pass Sears, Roebuck as the number one retailer in the United States: "Sears doesn't have a chance!," he said. "A twelve-layer company can't compete with a three-layer company."[6] Peters may have exaggerated the point a bit, but it clearly reflects the fact that the

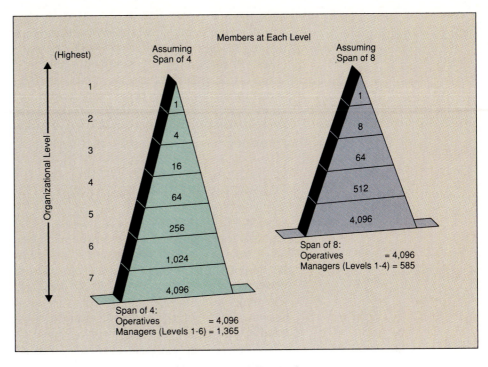

Members at Each Level

(Highest)	Assuming Span of 4	Assuming Span of 8

Organizational Level

1 — 1 — 1
2 — 4 — 8
3 — 16 — 64
4 — 64 — 512
5 — 256 — 4,096
6 — 1,024
7 — 4,096

Span of 8:
Operatives = 4,096
Managers (Levels 1-4) = 585

Span of 4:
Operatives = 4,096
Managers (Levels 1-6) = 1,365

FIGURE 14–4   Contrasting Spans of Control

pendulum has swung in recent years toward creating flat structures with wide spans of control.

More and more organizations today are increasing their spans of control. For example, the span for managers at companies such as General Electric and Reynolds Metals has expanded to ten or twelve subordinates—twice the number of ten years ago.[7] The span of control is increasingly being determined by looking at contingency variables. For instance, it's obvious that the more

James Emshoff is president of Citicorp's Diners Club unit. To better service customers, he has slashed layers of management between himself and first-line supervisors to four from eight. Mr. Emshoff's span of control has also doubled from four to eight. In addition to cutting costs, the credit-card company's biggest customers can now receive customized products and services, and there's speedier handling of customer complaints.   Courtesy of Citicorp Diners Club.

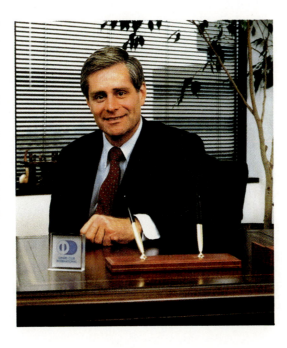

training and experience subordinates have, the less direct supervision they need. This is fully consistent with the research findings on the path-goal theory of leadership presented in Chapter 11. So managers who have well-trained and experienced employees can function with a wider span. Other contingency variables that will determine the appropriate span include similarity of subordinate tasks, the complexity of those tasks, the physical proximity of subordinates, the degree to which standardized procedures are in place, and the preferred style of the manager.[8]

Departmentalization

THE CLASSICAL VIEW   The classical theorists argued that activities in an organization should be specialized and grouped into departments. Division of labor creates specialists who need coordination. This coordination is facilitated by putting specialists together in departments under the direction of a manager. Creation of these departments is typically based on the work functions being performed, the product or service being offered, the target customer or client, the geographic territory being covered, or the process being used to turn inputs into outputs. No single method of departmentalization was advocated by the classical theorists. The method or methods used should reflect the grouping that would best contribute to the attainment of the organization's objectives and the goals of individual units.

Functional Departmentalization Grouping activities by function performed.

One of the most popular ways to group activities is by functions performed—**functional departmentalization.** A manufacturing manager might organize his or her plant by separating engineering, accounting, manufacturing, personnel, and purchasing specialists into common departments. (See Figure 14–5). Of course, departmentalization by function can be used in all types of organizations. Only the functions change to reflect the organization's objectives and activities. A hospital might have departments devoted to research, patient care, accounting, and so forth. A professional football franchise might have departments entitled Player Personnel, Ticket Sales, and Travel and Accommodations. The major advantage to this type of grouping is obtaining efficiencies from putting like specialists together. Functional departmentalization seeks to achieve economies of scale by placing people with common skills and orientations into common units.

Product Departmentalization Grouping activities by product line.

Figure 14–6 illustrates the **product departmentalization** method used at Sun Petroleum Products. Each major product area in the corporation is placed under the authority of a vice president who is a specialist in, and responsible for, everything having to do with his or her product line. Notice, for example, in contrast to functional departmentalization, that manufacturing and other major activities have been divided up to give the product managers (vice presidents, in this case) considerable autonomy and control. The major advantage to this type of grouping is increased accountability for product performance.

If an organization's activities are service- rather than product-related, each service would be autonomously grouped. For instance, an accounting firm would have departments for tax, management consulting, auditing, and the like. Each would offer a common array of services under the direction of a product or service manager.

The particular type of customer the organization seeks to reach can also be used to group employees. The sales activities in an office supply firm, for instance, can be broken down into three departments to service retail,

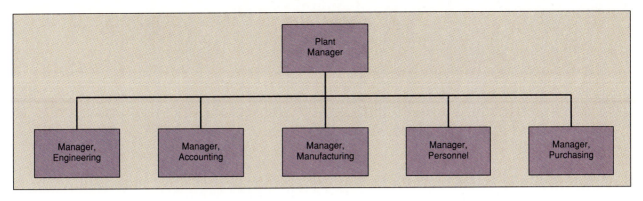

FIGURE 14–5   **Departmentalization by Function**

Customer Departmentalization Grouping activities on the basis of common customers.

Geographic Departmentalization Grouping activities on the basis of territory.

wholesale, and government customers. (See Figure 14–7.) A large law office can segment its staff on the basis of whether they service corporate or individual clients. The assumption underlying **customer departmentalization** is that customers in each department have a common set of problems and needs that can best be met by having specialists for each.

Another way to departmentalize is on the basis of geography or territory **—geographic departmentalization.** The sales function may have western, southern, midwestern, and eastern regions. (See Figure 14–8.) A large school district may have six high schools to provide for each of the major geographical territories within the district. If an organization's customers are scattered over a large geographic area, then this form of departmentalization can be valuable.

FIGURE 14–6   **Departmentalization by Product**

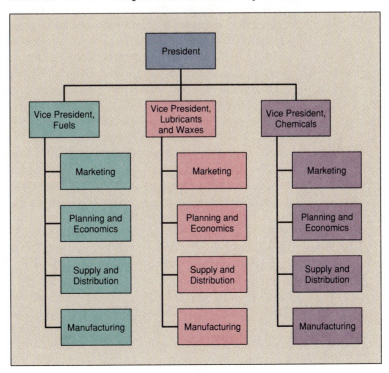

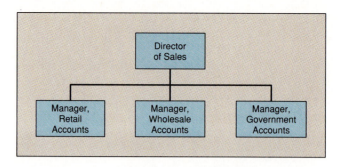

FIGURE 14–7   Departmentalization by Customer

Figure 14–9 depicts the various production departments in an aluminum plant. Each department specializes in one specific phase in the production of aluminum tubing. The metal is cast in huge furnaces; sent to the press department, where it is extruded into aluminum pipe; transferred to the tube mill, where it is stretched into various sizes and shapes of tubing; moved to finishing, where it is cut and cleaned; and finally arrives in the inspect, pack, and ship department. Since each process requires different skills, this method offers a basis for the homogeneous categorizing of activities.

Process Departmentalization
Grouping activities on the basis of product or customer flow.

Process departmentalization can be used for processing customers as well as products. If you have ever been to a state motor vehicle office to get a driver's license, you probably went through several departments before receiving your license. In one state, applicants must go through three steps, each handled by a separate department: (1) validation, by motor vehicles division; (2) processing, by the licensing department; and (3) payment collection, by the treasury department.

THE CONTEMPORARY VIEW   Most large organizations continue to use most or all of the departmental groupings suggested by the classical theorists. A major electronics firm, for instance, organizes each of its divisions along functional lines and its manufacturing units around processes; departmentalizes sales around four geographic regions; and divides each sales region into three customer groupings. But two recent trends need to be mentioned. First, customer departmentalization has become increasingly emphasized. Second, rigid departmentalization is being complemented by the use of teams that cross over traditional departmental lines.

Today's competitive environment has refocused management's attention on its customers. In order to better monitor the needs of customers and to be

FIGURE 14–8   Departmentalization by Geography

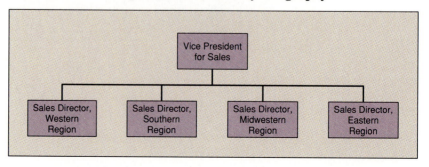

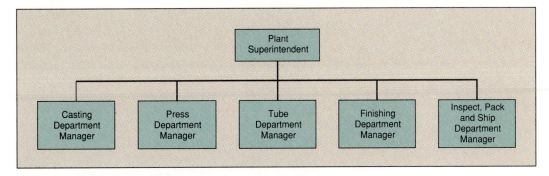

FIGURE 14–9   Departmentalization by Process

able to respond to changes in those needs, many organizations have given greater emphasis to customer departmentalization. Xerox, for example, has eliminated its corporate marketing staff and placed marketing specialists out in the field.[9] This allows the company to better understand who their customers are and to respond faster to their requirements.

As discussed in a number of previous places in this book, you see a great deal more use of teams today as a device for accomplishing organizational objectives. As tasks have become more complex and more diverse skills are needed to accomplish them, management has introduced the use of teams and task forces. For example, when Ford decided to create an entirely new car concept it went to a temporary task force that crossed the company's traditional departmental lines. Team Taurus brought together people from design, manufacturing, sales, marketing, public relations, legal, and other departments to create the most successful new-car introduction in American history.

STRUCTURAL VARIABLES AND ORGANIZATIONAL BEHAVIOR

We opened this chapter by implying that an organization's structure can have profound effects on its members. In this section we want to directly assess just what those effects might be.[10] Let's look again at each of the five basic organizational concepts we've just reviewed, but this time consider their implications on organizational behavior.

Division of Labor

Generalizing across the population, the evidence indicates that division of labor contributes to higher employee productivity but at the price of reduced job satisfaction. However, this generalization ignores individual differences and the type of job tasks people do.

As we noted previously, division of labor is not an unending source of higher productivity. Problems start to surface, and productivity begins to suffer, when the human diseconomies of doing repetitive and narrow tasks overtake the economies of specialization. As the workforce has become more highly educated and desirous of jobs that are intrinsically rewarding, the point where productivity begins to decline seems to be reached more quickly than in decades past.

While more people today are undoubtedly turned off by overly-specialized jobs than were their parents or grandparents, it would be naive to ignore the reality that there is still a segment of the workforce that prefers the routine and repetitiveness of highly specialized jobs. Some individuals want work that makes minimal intellectual demands and provides the security of routine. For these people, high division of labor is a source of job satisfaction. The empirical question, of course, is whether this represents two percent of the workforce or fifty-two percent. Given that there is some self-selection operating in the choice of careers, we might conclude that negative behavioral outcomes from high division of labor are most likely to surface in professional jobs occupied by individuals with high needs for personal growth and diversity.

Unity of Command

There is little evidence to indicate that any significant segment of the work force actually *prefers* jobs where they must live under the rule of multiple bosses. It's hard—sometimes impossible—to serve two masters. The exception is when those bosses coordinate their actions so as not to place unrealistic or conflicting demands upon their mutual subordinates.

From the worker's perspective, organizations that closely apply the unity of command concept reduce ambiguity and hence lessen employee stress. But not without a price! The clarity and predictability that the unity of command concept provides also tends to contribute toward making organizations hierarchically-obsessed. Everything has to "go through channels." Communication becomes highly formalized. The result is that employees can become frustrated from a feeling of being "boxed in."

Combine strict adherence to the unity of command with high division of labor and you have the probable explanation for some of your worst personal experiences in dealing with large corporations or government agencies. For example, have you ever been frustrated when trying to return merchandise to a big department store or in seeking clarification on a tax matter with the Internal Revenue Service? Well, the frustration works both ways. Organizations that divide jobs up into narrow tasks and require employees to closely follow the unity of command create an impersonal climate for their employees. Just as this can frustrate you as a customer or client, it can also frustrate those people who have to work in such places.

Authority and Responsibility

Authority provides employees with clarity and minimizes ambiguity because people know whose directives they are expected to follow.

While the classical theorists may have viewed authority as the glue that held organizations together, an overreliance by managers on their formal authority is likely to cause problems in organizations today. The "might makes right" thesis was effective, for the most part, when people in organizations had minimal levels of education and supervisors could do their subordinates' jobs as well or better than the subordinates could. Nowadays, as jobs have become more technical and specialized, those "in authority" often don't know exactly what their people do or how they do it. As a result, they are more dependent on their employees. An overreliance on formal authority, in such situations, is likely to alienate employees.

Close supervision at the Army's SDI battle-management center in Alabama is possible with a small span of control while the printers at Banta Corporation in Wisconsin work with less supervision. Some employees may find the close supervision at the SDI battle-management center frustrating or dehumanizing but those new to a job or with minimal experience are likely to find that small spans of control mean their bosses are readily available when they need them.   Left, courtesy of U.S. Army Strategic Defense Command, Huntsville, Ala.; right, © James Schnepf.

Competence and respect are not necessarily perfectly correlated with authority. When managers rely on authority rather than on knowledge, persuasive skills, or other bases of power, they can lose credibility among their followers. Managers who hide behind their formal rights are likely to have less productive and less satisfied employees than those who develop additional sources of power.

Span of Control

A review of the research indicates that it is probably safe to say there is no evidence to support a relationship between span of control and employee performance. While it is intuitively attractive to argue that large spans might lead to higher employee performance because they provide more distant supervision and more opportunity for personal initiative, the research fails to support this notion. At this point it is impossible to state that any particular span of control is best for producing high performance or high satisfaction among subordinates. The reason is probably individual differences. That is, some people like to be left alone, while others prefer the security of a boss who is quickly available at all times. Consistent with several of the contingency theories of leadership, we would expect factors such as employees' experiences and abilities and the degree of structure in their tasks to explain when wide or narrow spans of control are likely to contribute to their performance and job satisfaction. However, there is some evidence indicating that a *manager's* job satisfaction increases as the number of subordinates he or she supervises increases.

Departmentalization

Organizations departmentalize in order to increase efficiency and effectiveness. But what effect does it have on the people in the organization?

From an employee's perspective, putting together people who share similar interests, skills, concerns for a product, or the like facilitates intradepartmental communication. For instance, in functional departmentalization, marketing people get to work closely with other marketing people and design engineers get to do the same. In product departmentalization, all the members of a department can put their individual efforts into developing, making, and selling a common product and can experience the common feeling of accomplishment when the product succeeds.

As with all the other structural variables we've discussed, there is a downside to departmentalization. It develops a narrow perspective among its department members. In some cases, especially in the functional and process varieties, jobs can become repetitive and boring. Additionally, rigid departmentalization tends to create barriers to effective interdepartmental communication and to cross-fertilization of ideas. These barriers, then, can contribute to reducing employee productivity and satisfaction.

ARE ORGANIZATIONAL STRUCTURES REAL OR IN PEOPLE'S MINDS?

Complexity, formalization, and centralization are objective structural components that can be measured by organizational researchers. Every organization can be evaluated as to the degree to which it is high or low in all three. But employees don't objectively measure these components. They observe things around them in an unscientific fashion and then form their own implicit models of what the organization's structure is like. How many different people did they have to interview with before they were offered their jobs? How many people work in their departments and buildings? How visible is the organization's policy manual, if one exists? Is everyone given a copy? If not, is one readily available? Is it referred to frequently? How is the organization and its top management described in newspapers and periodicals? Answers to questions such as these, when combined with an employee's past experiences and comments made by peers, leads members to form an overall subjective image of what their organization's structure is like. This image, though, may in no way resemble the organization's actual objective structural characteristics.

The importance of implicit models of organization structure should not be overlooked. As we noted in Chapter 5, people respond to their perceptions rather than to objective reality. The research, for instance, on the relationship between many structural variables and subsequent levels of performance or job satisfaction are inconsistent. Some of this is explained as being attributable to individual differences. Some employees, for instance, prefer narrowly defined and routine jobs; others abhor such characteristics. Additionally, however, a contributing cause to these inconsistent findings may be diverse perceptions of the objective characteristics. Researchers have focused on actual levels of the various structural components, but these may be irrelevant if people interpret similar components differently. The bottom line, therefore, is to understand how employees interpret their organization's structure. That should prove a more meaningful predictor of their behavior than the objective characteristics themselves.

IMPLICATIONS FOR PERFORMANCE AND SATISFACTION

This chapter defined organization structure, presented the classical cornerstones of organizing, and updated the discussion by reviewing contemporary

National Differences and Organization Structure

The willingness to accept unquestioningly a superior's authority or the determination of what is the right size for a manager's span of control must take into consideration the cultural values of the society in which an organization operates. Let's see how these two structural variables might need to be modified in different countries.

To what degree are people in a given country likely to unquestioningly accept the authority of their bosses? To what degree will managers in that country delegate authority? The concept of power distance can help us answer these questions. In high power-distance cultures, people accept wide differences in power. As a result, they should also readily accept directives from a boss, even if they strongly disagree with those orders. So formal authority is likely to be a potent influencing device in such places as Mexico or the Phillipines. In contrast, in low power-distance countries such as Austria or Denmark, authoritative directives are likely to be rejected by employees. We might also speculate that in low power-distance cultures people are more willing to ac-

cept or even seek delegated authority. In high power-distance countries, employees expect to be told what to do rather than actually to make decisions themselves.

In our updated discussion on span of control we noted the emphasis on contingency variables to help managers identify the most effective group size. To that list of contingency variables should be added *national culture*. For example, feminine cultures emphasize human relationships. This is consistent with confidence in subordinates and wide spans of control. So we could expect resistance to the imposition of narrow spans in Scandinavian countries like Sweden or Norway. Additionally, research on human nature discussed in Chapter 3 indicates cultures vary on whether they view people as good or evil. Clearly, in those countries where the evil perspective dominates, tight spans of control should be more readily accepted by employees. In fact, these employees may expect tight controls and be *less* productive and satisfied when not closely supervised.

theories and practices. We introduced these concepts because there is clear evidence that an organization's internal structure contributes to explaining and predicting behavior. That is, in addition to individual and group factors, the structural relationships in which people work have an important bearing on employee attitudes and behavior.

What is the basis for the argument that structure has an impact on both attitudes and behavior? To the degree that an organizations' structure reduces ambiguity for employees and clarifies such concerns as "What am I supposed to do?" "How am I supposed to do it?" "Who do I report to?" and "Who do I go to if I have a problem?" it shapes their attitudes and facilitates and motivates them to higher levels of performance.

Of course, structure also constrains employees to the extent that it limits and controls what they do.[11] For example, organizations structured around high levels of formalization and division of labor, strict adherence to the unity of command, limited delegation of authority, and narrow spans of control give employees little autonomy. Controls in such organizations are tight and behavior will tend to vary within a narrow range. In contrast, organizations that are structured around limited division of labor, low formalization, wide spans of control, and the like provide employees greater freedom and, thus, will be characterized by greater behavioral diversity. As we pointed out previously, the effect of these structural variables on employee performance and satisfaction will be substantially a function of an employee's preferences and how he or she cognitively interprets the actual structure.

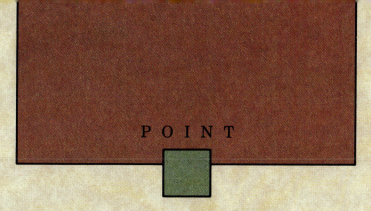

Tomorrow's Organizations Will Be Like Large Symphony Orchestras

Tomorrow's organizations are going to be flatter, less hierarchical, and more decentralized. In structural terminology, they're going to be less complex, less formalized, and more decentralized. What are they going to look like? Not like a pyramid, which has been the traditional metaphor for organization structure. No! Tomorrow's organizations will resemble a large symphony orchestra.

Why is the pyramid doomed? There are at least four reasons:

1. RAPID AND UNEXPECTED CHANGE The pyramid's strength is its capacity to manage efficiently the routine and predictable events that an organization confronts. The pyramid, with its nicely defined chain of command, its rules, and its rigidities, is ill adapted to the rapid changes that all organizations now face.

2. INCREASING DIVERSITY Today's organizational activities require people with very diverse and highly specialized levels of competence. The narrow departmental boxes of the pyramid are inappropriate for handling diversity.

3. CHANGE IN MANAGERIAL BEHAVIOR Managers no longer rule by dictum. Managerial philosophy has changed. Managers increasingly project humanistic–democratic values. Moreover, they increasingly rely on collaboration and reason rather than coercion and threats to lead their people.

4. ADOPTION OF COMPUTER TECHNOLOGY Computers are changing the way things are done within organizations. Information-based technology demands a higher degree of flexibility.

The first three points are rather straightforward, but we should elaborate on our fourth point.

Knowledge-based organizations are composed largely of specialists who direct and discipline their own performances through organized feedback from colleagues, customers, and headquarters. This requires a structure that looks a lot like that of a symphony orchestra. Instead of doing things sequentially—research, development, manufacturing, and marketing—they'll be done by *synchrony*. Clear, simple, common objectives will allow the chief executive directly to "conduct" hundreds of employees or musicians. The CEO will be able to have a wide span of control because each employee will be a specialist who knows his or her part. Similarly, rules and regulations will be minimal because employees will be skilled professionals who had their standards of performance and expectations "indoctrinated" into them during their professional training. Like conductors, managers won't have to explain much. They'll merely need to provide the musical score or plan, and then give subtle overall direction.

This argument is largely based on P. F. Drucker, "The Coming of the New Organization," *Harvard Business Review,* January–February 1988, pp. 45–53.

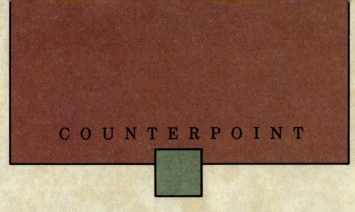

The Future Still Belongs to the Pyramid!

There is no doubt that organizations are changing. But are these changes leaving the pyramid-shaped structure behind? Nothing could be further from the truth! The pyramid is alive, well, and flourishing. We'll make our position by emphasizing four points.

1. THE FUTURE LIES WITH LARGE ORGANIZA-TIONS   Large size demands the efficiency that division of labor, high formalization, and other pyramid-creating devices use to maintain control. While many "experts" have predicted the demise of large organizations, the globalization of markets has turned the tide back in favor of large size. Global competition in major industries will require resources and managerial skills not available to small organizations. The pendulum, in the 1990s, is swinging back toward large organizations that will be able to compete aggressively in markets throughout the world.

2. EMPLOYEES LIKE PYRAMIDS   Employees like the predictability and security that pyramid-shaped organizations offer. They minimize ambiguity. Employees know what to do, who to report to, and the like.

3. MANAGERS LIKE PYRAMIDS   Managers, too, like pyramids, because they provide tight controls. Humanistic–democratic values sound good, and many managers prefer to use collaboration and reason, but when the pressure is on and managers must perform, they often fall back on coercion and threats.

4. THE "INFORMATION–TECHNOLOGY" THEME HAS BEEN OVERSOLD IN NORTH AMERICA   Some 82 million jobs in the United States do not require a four-year college education. Moreover, American business has been moving toward de-skilling jobs—that is, downgrading skills—in order to cut wages and increase productivity. A recent study found that less than ten percent of employers are creating jobs that call for workers with broad-based skills and the ability to adapt to fast-changing technology and markets. The symphony orchestra metaphor might be appropriate for managing groups of Ph.D. research scientists, but the de-skilling of jobs such as machine operator, retail clerk, assembler, and health service worker is more compatible with the tight control provided by the pyramid-shaped organization.

These facts argue for a very different scenario than that predicted in the previous argument. Tomorrow's organizations won't look like symphony orchestras. A few might, but they're likely to be quite small in size. The organization of tomorrow will look like the organization of yesterday—it will be a tightly-controlled structure shaped like a pyramid.

Facts on de-skilling mentioned here are from J. Hoerr, "Business Shares the Blame for Workers' Low Skills," *Business Week*, June 25, 1990, p. 71.

FOR DISCUSSION

1. Describe a highly *complex* organization.
2. What characteristics would describe an organization that is high in formalization?
3. Why isn't division of labor an unending source of increased productivity?
4. Why is the unity of command concept important?
5. All things being equal, which is more efficient, a wide or narrow span of control?
6. Why did the classical theorists argue that authority should equal responsibility?
7. Can the manager of a staff department have line authority? Explain.
8. In what ways can management departmentalize?
9. "Employees prefer to work in flat, decentralized organizations." Do you agree or disagree? Discuss.
10. Do you think most employees prefer high formalization? Support your position.
11. Which form of departmentalization has become increasingly popular in recent years? Why?
12. What is the importance of the statement: "Employees form implicit models of organization structure."

FOR FURTHER READING

CARTER, N. M., and T. L. KEON, "The Rise and Fall of the Division of Labor, the Past 25 Years," *Organization Studies,* Vol. 7, No. 1, 1986, pp. 57–74. Reviews empirical research published during the past 25 years on the division of labor.

DE CHAMBEAU, F. A., "Keeping the Corporate Tall Ships Afloat," *Across the Board,* March 1987, pp. 54–56. Argues that many of the ills of the traditional pyramid-shaped organization can be traced to diffusion of power, ambiguity of purpose, and leadership that is not of one mind.

ORTON, J. D., and K. E. WEICK, "Loosely Coupled Systems: A Reconceptualization," *Academy of Management Review,* April 1990, pp. 203–23. Loosely-coupled organizations have low levels of interdependence. This article reviews the literature on this concept.

PERROW, C., *Complex Organizations: A Critical Essay,* 3rd ed. New York: Random House, 1986. Provides a developmental overview of the major schools of organization thought and a close examination of recent approaches.

PETERS, T., *Thriving on Chaos.* New York: Alfred Knopf, 1988. Argues that organizations of tomorrow will thrive on chaos and appear to be similar to focused anarchy.

ROBBINS, S. P., *Organization Theory: Structure, Design, and Applications,* 3rd ed. Englewood Cliffs, N.J.: Prentice Hall, 1990. Provides a comprehensive overview of the organization theory literature and its practical applications.

Authority Figures

Purpose: To learn about one's experiences with, and feelings about, authority.

Time required: Approximately 75 minutes.

Instructions:

1. Your instructor will separate class members into groups based on their *birth* order. Groups are formed consisting of "Only children," "Eldest," "Middle," and "Youngest," according to placement in families. Larger groups will be broken into smaller ones, with four or five members, to allow for freer conversation.

2. Each group member should talk about how he or she "typically *reacts* to the authority of others." Focus should be on specific situations that offer general information about how individuals deal with authority figures (for example, bosses, teachers, parents, or coaches). The group has 25 minutes to develop a written list of how the *group* generally deals with others' authority. Be sure to separate tendencies that group members share and those they do not.

3. Repeat step 2 above, except this time discuss how group members "typically are *as* authority figures." Again make a list of shared characteristics.

4. Each group will share its general conclusions with the entire class.

5. Class discussion will focus on questions such as:
   a. What patterned differences surface between the groups?
   b. What may account for these differences?
   c. What hypotheses might explain the connection between how individuals react to the authority of others and how they are as authority figures?

This exercise is adapted from W. A. Kahn, "An Exercise of Authority," *Organizational Behavior Teaching Review,* Vol. XIV, Issue 2, 1989–90, pp. 28–42.

People Express: A Successful Failure?

People Express was founded in the early 1980s as an alternative to full-price, full-service airlines such as American, United, and TWA. It started small. For instance, in 1981, it had three planes and only 200 employees. But its founder, Don Burr, had a vision that the public would respond positively to what he had to offer. What was that? Low costs, no frills, and enthusiastic employees.

By 1984, People Express had become the fastest growing airline ever. It had 45 planes and thousands of employees. And it was scaring the pants off the competition. It was charging $149 on its New York–London route. The competition was charging $395. Normal fares from New York to Houston were $320. People charged $69. It also avoided going head-to-head against major carriers by flying less heavily traveled routes out of New York—to places like Buffalo and West Palm Beach. But not only was People Express cheap, it was very profitable. The main reason was that it was the low-cost operator. Its operating costs were 5.3 cents per passenger mile compared to 11 cents for other airlines.

How did People Express get such low costs? There were a number of reasons. The company was nonunion. Employees accepted considerably less pay than the competition. In return they participated in a generous stock option plan based on performance that greatly enhanced each employee's earnings. Moreover, all employees were required to buy stock in the company at the time they were hired. So every employee was also an owner. People Express additionally had a minimal amount of overhead. They operated out of an abandoned terminal at Newark Airport. There were no secretaries or plush offices. And everyone rotated among jobs, even executives. Managers, for instance, might work the reservation desk, unload baggage, or help serve passengers coffee. A flight attendant, when not flying, might check in passengers or teach in a company training program. At People Express, there were no direct supervisors. Rather, people worked in teams. They took turns being team leaders and everyone got to manage others some of the time. To further keep costs down, customers had to pay for optional services that the other airlines provided for free. At People Express, it cost $3 to check each bag and customers had to pay for in-flight meals.

By the mid-1980s, Don Burr was running an airline that had a highly dedicated staff and over $100 million cash in the bank. But the seeds were being sowed for failure. In 1985, Burr began a major growth program. He bought additional planes, doubled his routes to include major cities like Chicago and Dallas, added first-class seating, and bought out Frontier Airlines. In so doing, the company lost its identity. As its costs went up, the competition cut prices to match People Express' low fares. People Express didn't have the financial resources to successfully compete in a rate war. When it raised its prices, customers began turning to the company's more established competitors. People Express essentially died in 1986 when it merged with Texas Air Corporation, which operated Continental, Eastern, and New York Air.

QUESTIONS

1. Describe People Express' organization structure.
2. In what ways did this company's organization structure contribute to its success? To its failure?
3. Would you have liked working at People Express? Explain.

Source: Based on "How People Does It," *Time,* February 21, 1983, p. 53; and J.R. Norman, "People Is Plunging But Burr Is Staying Cool," *Business Week,* July 7, 1986, pp. 31-32.

NOTES

¹S. P. Robbins, *Organization Theory: Structure, Design, and Applications,* 3rd ed. (Englewood Cliffs, NJ: Prentice Hall, 1990), Chapter 4.

²A. Smith, *An Inquiry into the Nature and Causes of the Wealth of Nations* (New York: Modern Library 1937). Originally published in 1776.

³See, for example, H. Fayol, *Administration Industrielle et Generale* (Paris: Dunod, 1916); M. Weber, *The Theory of Social and Economic Organizations,* ed., T. Parsons, trans. A. M. Henderson and T. Parsons (New York: Free Press, 1947); and R. C. Davis, *The Fundamentals of Top Management* (New York: Harper & Row, 1951).

⁴"Max DePree: It's Not What You Preach But How You Behave," *Fortune,* March 26, 1990, p. 36.

⁵L. Urwick, *The Elements of Administration* (New York: Harper & Row, 1944), pp. 52–53.

⁶Quoted in J. Braham, "Money Talks," *Industry Week,* April 17, 1989, p. 23.

⁷J. S. McClenahen, "Managing More People in the '90s," *Industry Week,* March 20, 1989, p. 30.

⁸D. Van Fleet, "Span of Management Research and Issues," *Academy of Management Journal,* September 1983, pp. 546–52.

⁹J. H. Sheridan, "Sizing Up Corporate Staffs," *Industry Week,* November 21, 1988, p. 47.

¹⁰A number of the conclusions presented in this section are drawn from L. W. Porter and E. E. Lawler III, "Properties of Organization Structure in Relation to Job Attitudes and Job Behavior," *Psychological Bulletin,* July 1965, pp. 23–51; L. R. James and A. P. Jones, "Organization Structure: A Review of Structural Dimensions and Their Conceptual Relationships with Individual Attitudes and Behavior," *Organizational Behavior and Human Performance,* June 1976, pp. 74–113; D. R. Dalton, W. D. Todor, M. J. Spendolini, G. J. Fielding, and L. W. Porter, "Organization Structure and Performance: A Critical Review," *Academy of Management Review,* January 1980, pp. 49–64; and W. Snizek and J. H. Bullard, "Perception of Bureaucracy and Changing Job Satisfaction: A Longitudinal Analysis," *Organizational Behavior and Human Performance,* October 1983, pp. 275–87.

¹¹D. A. Nadler, J. R. Hackman, and E. E. Lawler III, *Managing Organizational Behavior* (Boston: Little, Brown, 1979), pp. 182–84.

ORGANIZATION DESIGN

LEARNING OBJECTIVES

After studying this chapter, you should be able to:

1. *Differentiate between mechanistic and organic structures*
2. *List the factors that favor different organization structures*
3. *Identify the five basic parts to any organization*
4. *Describe Mintzberg's five design configurations*
5. *Explain the behavioral implications of each design configuration*
6. *Summarize the strengths and weaknesses of the matrix structure*
7. *Explain why there is a growth bias in organizations*
8. *Describe how organizational decline affects employees*

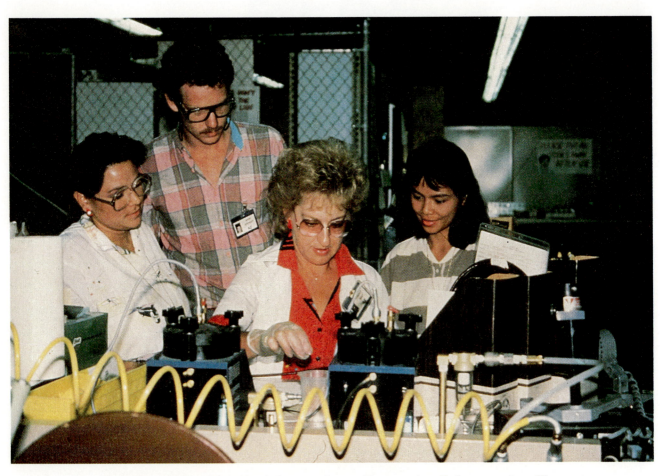

W. L. Gore & Associates doesn't have employees. Everyone is called an associate. The company goes to great lengths to minimize formal structural mechanisms and to maximize flexibility.   Courtesy of W. L. Gore & Associates Inc.

The problem with a bureaucracy is that it can't respond rapidly to change. Its motto is: "Ready, aim, aim, aim, aim . . . " It just can't pull the trigger!

ANONYMOUS

W. L. Gore & Associates is a company with sales in excess of $200 million a year. The firm is best known for producing the highly successful Gore-Tex fabric. Impervious to sunlight, heat, cold, or water, the fiber is used in high-quality tents, sleeping bags, gloves, ski clothes, boots, and other outdoor products. But the most fascinating fact about this company is that it employs 3,000 people but has *no formal hierarchy or structure*.[1] There are no job titles, no bosses, no chains of command. Everyone is an "associate," with equal authority. To keep this hierarchy-free organization running smoothly, work groups are limited to two hundred people. The result is a bunch of small plants. The company claims that this unusual form of organization generates double the productivity of an average manufacturing work force and triple the creativity.

Contrast W. L. Gore & Associates with the typical firm that employs 3,000 people. As described in the previous chapter, its workers probably perform specialized activities in departments. Departments will have supervisors who report to middle managers who, in turn, report to top-level managers! And this pyramid-shaped hierarchy is justified as necessary to achieve efficiency, to establish clear lines of responsibility, and to maintain control. Yet, as the Gore company illustrates, there is more than one way to structure a successful organization. Moreover, the different structural designs that organizations use do not emerge at random. They are chosen by management for certain reasons. In this chapter we'll build on concepts introduced in Chapter 14. More specifically, we'll review the factors that influence management's choice of an organization design, present a framework for categorizing design options, and consider the effect of various organization designs on the employees in those organizations.

MECHANISTIC VS. ORGANIC STRUCTURES

Before we begin reviewing the factors that influence management's choice of an organization design, we need to introduce a simple designation device for generalizing about organization structures.

There are many ways that management can mix and match the three structural components of complexity, formalization, and centralization. However, an organization's overall structure generally falls into one of two designs.[2] One is the **mechanistic structure,** which is characterized by high complexity (especially a great deal of horizontal differentiation), high formalization, a limited information network (mostly downward communication), and

Mechanistic Structure A structure characterized by high complexity, high formalization, and centralization.

Organic Structure A structure characterized by low complexity, low formalization, and decentralization.

little participation by low-level members in decision making. The mechanistic structure is synonymous with the rigid pyramid-shaped organization. At the other extreme is the **organic structure.** It is low in complexity and formalization, it possesses a comprehensive information network (utilizing lateral and upward communication as well as downward), and it involves high participation in decision making. W. L. Gore & Associates has many of the characteristics associated with the organic structure.

As Figure 15–1 depicts, mechanistic structures are rigid, relying on authority and a well-defined hierarchy to facilitate coordination. The organic structure, on the other hand, is flexible and adaptive. Coordination is achieved through constant communication and adjustment.

In the next section, you'll find that we regularly refer back to these two generic structural designs.

WHY DO STRUCTURES DIFFER?

Why are some organizations structured along more mechanistic lines while others follow organic characteristics? What are the forces that influence the form that is chosen? In the following pages, we'll present the major forces that have been identified as causes or determinants of an organization's structure.

Strategy

An organization's structure is a means to help management achieve its objectives. Since objectives are derived from the organization's overall strate-

FIGURE 15–1   Mechanistic vs. Organic Structures

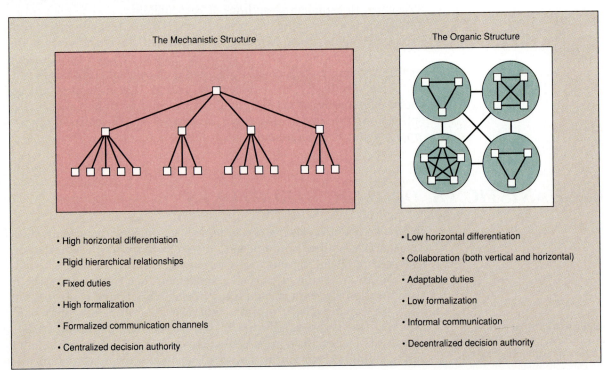

The Mechanistic Structure

The Organic Structure

• High horizontal differentiation

• Rigid hierarchical relationships

• Fixed duties

• High formalization

• Formalized communication channels

• Centralized decision authority

• Low horizontal differentiation

• Collaboration (both vertical and horizontal)

• Adaptable duties

• Low formalization

• Informal communication

• Decentralized decision authority

gy, it is only logical that strategy and structure should be closely linked. More specifically, structure should follow strategy. If management makes a significant change in its organization's strategy, the structure will need to be modified to accommodate and support this change.

CHANDLER'S STRATEGY–STRUCTURE THESIS The classic research supporting this strategy–structure relationship was a study of close to one hundred large United States companies conducted by Alfred Chandler and published in the early 1960s.[3] Tracing the development of these organizations over a period of fifty years, and compiling extensive case histories of companies such as DuPont, General Motors, Standard Oil of New Jersey, and Sears, Roebuck, Chandler concluded that changes in corporate strategy precede and lead to changes in an organization's structure. Chandler found that organizations usually begin with a single product or line. They do only one thing, like manufacturing, sales, or warehousing. The simplicity of the strategy requires only a simple, or loose, form of structure to execute it. Decisions can be centralized in the hands of a single senior manager, while complexity and formalization will be low.

As organizations grow, their strategies become more ambitious and elaborated. From the single product line, companies often expand their activities within their industry. This vertical integration strategy makes for increased interdependence between organizational units and creates the need for a more complex coordination device. This is achieved by redesigning the structure to form specialized units based on functions performed.

Finally, if growth proceeds further into product diversification, structure needs to be adjusted again to gain efficiency. A product diversification strategy demands a structural form that allows for the efficient allocation of resources, accountability for performance, and coordination between units. This can be achieved best by creating many independent divisions, each responsible for a specified product line.

In summary, Chandler's thesis argued that as strategies move from single product through vertical integration to product diversification, management will need to develop more elaborate structures to maintain effectiveness. That is, they will begin with an organic structure and, over time, move to a more mechanistic structure.

CONTEMPORARY RESEARCH ON THE STRATEGY–STRUCTURE THESIS More recent research confirms the strategy–structure thesis, but the notion of strategy has been rethought from Chandler's original framework.[4] Most strategy frameworks now focus on three strategy dimensions—innovation, cost-minimization, and imitation—and the structural design that works best with each.

Innovation Strategy A strategy that emphasizes the introduction of major new products or services.

To what degree does an organization introduce major new products or services? An **innovation strategy** does not mean a strategy merely for simple or cosmetic changes from previous offerings but rather one for meaningful and unique innovations. Obviously, not all firms pursue innovation. This strategy may appropriately characterize 3M Co., but it certainly is not a strategy pursued by Reader's Digest.

Cost-Minimization Strategy A strategy that emphasizes tight cost controls, avoidance of unnecessary innovation or marketing expenses, and price cutting.

An organization that is pursuing a **cost-minimization strategy** tightly controls costs, refrains from incurring unnecessary innovation or marketing expenses, and cuts prices in selling a basic product. This would describe the strategy pursued by Wal-Mart or the sellers of generic grocery products.

Organizations following an **imitation strategy** try to capitalize on the

3M Co. is a classic example of an organization that pursues an innovative strategy. It has a stated goal of generating a minimum of 30 percent of its sales from products introduced within any prior five year period. One of those new products is this filter for metalworking shops, shown by its developer, Tony Flannery.   Steve Woit.

Imitation Strategy A strategy that seeks to move into new products or new markets only after their viability has been already proven.

best of both of the previous strategies. They seek to minimize risk and maximize opportunity for profit. Their strategy is to move into new products or new markets only after viability has been proven by innovators. They take the successful ideas of innovators and copy them. Manufacturers of mass-marketed fashion goods that are rip-offs of designer styles follow the imitation strategy. This label also probably characterizes such well-known firms as IBM and Caterpillar. They essentially follow their smaller and more innovative competitors with superior products, but only after their competitors have demonstrated that the market is there.

Table 15–1 describes the structural option that best matches each strategy. Innovators need the flexibility of the organic structure, while cost-minimizers seek the efficiency and stability of the mechanistic structure. Imitators combine the two structures. They use a mechanistic structure in order to maintain tight controls and low costs in their current activities while at the same time they create organic subunits in which to pursue new undertakings.

Organization Size

Organization Size The number of people employed in an organization.

A quick glance at the organizations we deal with regularly in our lives would lead most of us to conclude that **size** would have some bearing on an organization's structure. The more than 800,000 employees of the United States Postal Service, for example, do not neatly fit into one building, or into several departments supervised by a couple of managers. It's pretty hard to envision 800,000 people being organized in any manner other than one that contains a great deal of horizontal, vertical, and spatial differentiation, uses a large number of procedures and regulations to ensure uniform practices, and follows a high degree of decentralized decision making. On the other hand, a local messenger service that employs ten people and generates less than $300,000 a year in service fees is not likely to need decentralized decision making or formalized procedures and regulations.

TABLE 15-1   Contemporary Strategy–Structure Thesis

Strategy	Structural Option
Innovation	Organic. A loose structure; low division of labor, low formalization, decentralized
Cost minimization	Mechanistic. Tight control; extensive division of labor, high formalization, high centralization
Imitation	Mechanistic and organic. Mix of loose with tight properties. Tight controls over current activities and looser controls for new undertakings

A little more thought suggests that the same conclusion—size influences structure—can be arrived at through a more sophisticated reasoning process. As an organization hires more operative employees, it will attempt to take advantage of the economic benefits of specialization. The result will be increased horizontal differentiation. Grouping like functions together will facilitate intragroup efficiencies, but will cause intergroup relations to suffer as each performs its different activities. Management, therefore, will need to increase vertical differentiation to coordinate the horizontally differentiated units. This expansion in size is also likely to result in spatial differentiation. All of this increase in complexity will reduce top management's ability to directly supervise the activities within the organization. The control achieved through direct surveillance, therefore, will be replaced by the implementation of formal rules and regulations. This increase in formalization may also be accompanied by still greater vertical differentiation as management creates new units to coordinate the expanding and diverse activities of organizational members. Finally, with top management further removed from the operating level, it becomes difficult for senior executives to make rapid and informative decisions. The solution is to substitute decentralized decision making for centralization. Following this reasoning, we see changes in size leading to major structural changes.

But does it actually happen this way? Does structure change directly as a result in a change in the total number of employees? A review of the evidence indicates that size has a significant influence on some but certainly not all elements of structure.

Size appears to have a decreasing rate of impact on complexity.[5] That is, increases in organization size are accompanied by initially rapid and subsequently more gradual increases in differentiation. The biggest effect, however, is on vertical differentiation.[6] As organizations increase their number of employees, more levels are added, but at a decreasing rate.

The evidence linking size and formalization is quite strong.[7] There is a logical connection between the two. Management seeks to control the behavior of its employees. This can be achieved by direct surveillance or by the use of formalized regulations. While not perfect substitutes for each other, as one increases the need for the other should decrease. Because surveillance costs should increase very rapidly as an organization expands in size, it seems reasonable to expect that it would be less expensive for management to substitute formalization for direct surveillance as size increases.

There is also a strong inverse relationship between size and centralization.[8] In small organizations, it's possible for management to exercise control by keeping decisions centralized. As size increases, management is physically unable to maintain control in this manner and, therefore, is forced to decentralize.

called complex. This is essentially the current environment in the computer software business. Every day there is another "new kid on the block" with whom established software firms have to deal.

Figure 15–4 summarizes our definition of the environment along its three dimensions. The arrows in this figure are meant to indicate movement toward higher uncertainty. So organizations that operate in environments characterized as scarce, dynamic, and complex face the greatest degree of uncertainty. Why? Because they have little room for error, high unpredictability, and a diverse set of elements in the environment to constantly monitor.

Given this three-dimensional definition of environment, we can offer some general conclusions. There is evidence that relates the degrees of environmental uncertainty to different structural arrangements. Specifically, the more scarce, dynamic, and complex the environment, the more organic a structure should be. The more abundant, stable, and simple the environment, the more the mechanistic structure will be preferred.

Power-Control

Power-control An organization's structure is the result of a power struggle by internal constituencies who are seeking to further their interests.

An increasingly popular and insightful approach to the question of what causes structure is to look to a political explanation. Strategy, size, technology, and environment—even when combined—can at best explain only fifty to sixty percent of the variability in structure.[22] There is a growing body of evidence that suggests that power and control can explain a good portion of the residual variance. More specifically, the **power-control** explanation states that an organization's structure is the result of a power struggle by internal constituencies who are seeking to further their interests.[23] Like all decisions in an organization, the structural decision is not fully rational. Managers do not necessarily choose those alternatives that will maximize the organization's interest. They choose criteria and weight them so that the "best choice" will meet the minimal demands of the organization, and also satisfy or enhance the interests of the decision maker. Strategy, size, technology, and environmental uncertainty act as constraints by establishing parameters and defining how much discretion is available. Almost always, within the parameters, there is a great deal of room for the decision maker to maneuver. The power-control position, therefore, argues that those in power will choose a

FIGURE 15–4   Three-Dimensional Model of the Environment

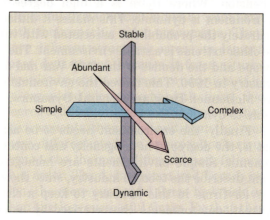

National Culture Is Part of the Environment

Strategy, size, technology, and environment have been shown to be major factors influencing the structural design an organization has. Environment, of course, would include differences across national cultures.

In a country with a high power distance rating, people prefer that decisions be centralized. Similarly, uncertainty avoidance characteristics relate to formalization. That is, high uncertainty avoidance relates to high formalization. Based on these relationships, we should expect to find certain patterns. The French and Italians tend to create rigid mechanistic structures, high in both centralization and formalization. In India, preference is given to centralization and low formalization. Germans prefer formalization with decentralization.[21]

The above suggests that multinational organizations face a real challenge. They have to balance the dual objectives of adjusting the structure of their units to the unique characteristics of each country in which they operate while, at the same time, developing uniform practices to facilitate interunit coordination. This may explain why many multinationals have had trouble in countries that differ significantly from their home country. In management's effort to achieve common standards of coordination and control, it has imposed standardized structures on its units. When those structures fit poorly with a country's culture, it results in lower organizational performance.

structure that will maintain or enhance their control. Consistent with this perspective, we should expect structures to change very slowly, if at all. Significant changes would occur only as a result of a political struggle in which new power relations evolve. But this rarely occurs. Transitions in the executive suite are usually peaceful. They are evolutionary rather than revolutionary. However, major shake-ups in top management occasionally do occur. Not surprisingly, they are typically followed by major structural changes.

Predictions based on the power-control viewpoint differ from those based on the four previous approaches in that those approaches were basically contingency models: Structures change to reflect changes in strategy, size, technology, or environmental uncertainty. The power-control approach, however, is essentially noncontingent. It assumes little change within the organization's power coalition. Hence, it would propose that structures are relatively stable over time. More important, power-control advocates would predict that after taking into consideration strategy, size, technology, and environmental factors, those in power would choose a structure that would best serve their personal interests. What type of structure would that be? Obviously one that would be low in complexity, high in formalization, and centralized. These structural dimensions will most likely maximize control in the hands of senior management. A structure with these properties becomes the single "one best way" to organize. Of course, *best* in this context refers to "maintenance of control" rather than enhancement of organizational performance.

Is the power-control position an accurate description? The evidence suggests that it explains a great deal of why organizations are structured the

IBM's size and market power permit it to operate effectively with a relatively mechanistic structure, even though its industry is essentially characterized by a dynamic and uncertain environment.   Courtesy of IBM.

way they are.[24] The dominant structural forms in organizations today are essentially mechanistic. Organic structures have received a great deal of attention by academicians, but the vast majority of real organizations, especially those of moderate and large size, are mechanistic.

Applying the Contingency Factors

Under what conditions would each of the contingency factors we've introduced —strategy, organization size, technology, and environment—be the dominant determinant of an organization's structure? More specifically, when should we expect to find mechanistic structures and when should organic structures be most prevalent?

STRATEGY   The strategy-determines-structure thesis argues that managers change their organization's structure to align with changes in strategy. Organizations that seek innovation demand a flexible structure. Organizations that attempt to be low-cost operators must maximize efficiency, and the mechanistic structure helps achieve that. Those organizations that pursue an imitation strategy need structures that contain elements of both the mechanistic and the organic forms.

Studies generally support that strategy influences structure at the top levels of business firms.[25] But strategy undoubtedly has less impact on the structure of sub-units within the overall organization. Additionally, it is not clear how the strategy–structure relationship operates in service businesses or among not-for-profit organizations such as hospitals, educational institutions, and government agencies.

ORGANIZATION SIZE   The larger an organization's size, in terms of the number of members it employs, the more likely it is to use the mechanistic structure. The creation of extensive rules and regulations only makes sense when there is a large number of people to be coordinated. Similarly, given the fact that a manager's ability to supervise a set of subordinates directly has some outside limit, as more people are hired to do the work, more managers will be needed to oversee these people. This creates increased complexity.

We should not, however, expect the size–structure relationship to be linear over a wide range. This is because once an organization becomes relatively large—with 1,500 to 2,000 employees or more—it will tend to have already acquired most of the properties of a mechanistic structure. So the addition of 500 employees to an organization that has only 100 employees is likely to lead to significantly increased levels of complexity and formalization. Yet adding 500 employees to an organization that already employs 10,000 is likely to have little or no impact on that organization's structure.

TECHNOLOGY   The evidence demonstrates that routine technologies are associated with mechanistic structures, whereas organic structures are best for dealing with the uncertainties inherent with nonroutine technologies. But we shouldn't expect technology to affect all parts of the organization equally.

The closer a department or unit within the organization is to the operating core, the more it will be affected by technology and, hence, the more technology will act to define structure. The primary activities of the organization take place at the operating core. State motor vehicle divisions, for example, process driver's license applications, distribute vehicle license plates, and monitor the ownership of vehicles within their state. Those departments within the motor vehicle division that are at the operating core—giving out driver's tests, collecting fees for plates, and so on—will be significantly affected by technology. But as units become removed from this core, technology will play a less important role. The structure of the executive offices at the motor vehicle division, for instance, are not likely to be affected much by technology. So, to continue with the motor vehicle example, the use of routine technology at the operating core should result in the units at the core being high in both complexity and formalization. As units within the division move farther away from activities at the operating core, technology will become less of a constraint on structural choices.

ENVIRONMENT   Will a dynamic and uncertain environment always lead to an organic structure? Not necessarily. Whether environment is a major determinant of an organization's structure depends on the degree of dependence of the organization on its environment.

IBM operates in a highly dynamic environment—the result of a continual stream of new competitors introducing products to compete against theirs. But IBM's size, reputation for quality and service, and marketing expertise act as potent forces to lessen the impact of this uncertain environment on IBM's performance. IBM's ability to lessen its dependence on its environment results in a structure that is much more mechanistic in design than would be expected given the uncertain environment within which it exists. In contrast, firms like Apple Computer and Digital Equipment Corporation have been far less successful in managing their dependence on their environment. Environment, therefore, is a much stronger influence on Apple and DEC's structure than at IBM.

MINTZBERG'S FIVE DESIGN CONFIGURATIONS

Now it's time to move from the general to the specific. While up to this point we've used the terms *mechanistic* and *organic* to classify organizations, these labels are too generic and abstract to be of much practical value. They really don't capture much of the details in actual organization designs. In this

Computers and Organization Design

When organizations introduce sophisticated, computer-based management information systems, they are changing technology. For instance, a computer-based MIS lessens the need to depend on direct supervision and staff reports as control mechanisms. A senior executive can monitor what's going on on the operating floor or in the accounts payable department by simply pushing a few keys on his or her desktop terminal. And such changes in technology have a very real effect on the organization's structure.[26] The most obvious result: Organizations become flatter and more organic.

Computer-based information systems allow managers to handle more subordinates because computer control substitutes for personal supervision. As a result, managers can effectively oversee more people and the organization will require fewer managers and, hence, there will be fewer levels in the hierarchy. The need for staff support is also reduced with a computer-based information system. Managers can tap information directly which makes large staff support groups redundant. Both forces—wider spans of supervision and reduced staff—lead to flatter organizations.

One of the more interesting phenomena created by sophisticated information systems is that they have allowed management to make organizations more organic without any loss in control.[27] Management can lessen formalization and become more decentralized—thus making their organizations more organic—without giving up control. Why? An MIS substitutes computer control for rules and decision discretion. Computer technology rapidly apprises top managers of the consequences of any decision and allows them to take corrective action if the decision is not to their liking. Thus there's the appearance of decentralization without any commensurate loss of control.

---

section, we'll present Henry Mintzberg's work, which develops a richer classification scheme that allows us to discuss organization designs and their impact on employee behavior.

Common Elements in Organizations

Mintzberg proposes that there are five basic parts to any organization.[28] They are shown in Figure 15–5 and defined as follows:

Operating Core Employees who perform the basic work related to the production of products and services.

Strategic Apex Top-level managers.

Middle Line Managers who connect the operating core to the strategic apex.

1. **The operating core.** Employees who perform the basic work related to the production of products and services.
2. **The strategic apex.** Top-level managers, who are charged with the overall responsibility for the organization.
3. **The middle line.** Managers who connect the operating core to the strategic apex.
4. **The technostructure.** Analysts, who have the responsibility for effecting certain forms of standardization in the organization.

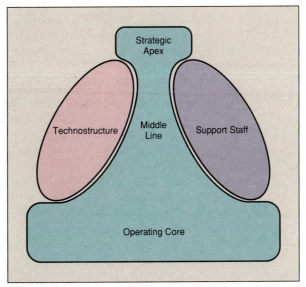

FIGURE 15–5   Five Basic Elements of an Organization

Source: H. Mintzberg, *Structure in Fives: Designing Effective Organizations,* © 1983, p. 11. Reprinted by permission of Prentice Hall, Englewood Cliffs, NJ.

Technostructure Analysts in the organization.

Support Staff People in an organization who fill the staff units.

5. **The support staff.** People who fill the staff units, who provide indirect support services for the organization.

Any one of these five parts can dominate an organization. Moreover, depending on which part is in control, a given structural configuration is likely to be used. So, according to Mintzberg, there are five distinct design configurations, and each one is associated with the domination by one of the five basic parts. If control lies with the operating core, decisions are decentralized. This creates the *professional bureaucracy.* When the strategic apex is dominant, control is centralized and the organization is a *simple structure.* If middle management is in control, you'll find groups of essentially autonomous units operating in a *divisional structure.* Where the analysts in the technostructure are dominant, control will be through standardization, and the resultant structure will be a *machine bureaucracy.* Finally, in those situations where the support staff rules, control will be via mutual adjustment and the *adhocracy* arises.

Let's look at these five designs, present each one's strengths and weaknesses, and consider what effect each might have on its members.

The Simple Structure

What do a small retail store, an electronics firm run by a hard driving entrepreneur, a new Planned Parenthood office, and an airline in the midst of a companywide pilot's strike have in common? They probably all utilize the simple structure.

The simple structure is said to be characterized most by what it is not rather than what it is. The simple structure is not elaborated.[29] It is low in complexity, has little formalization, and has authority centralized in a single

Simple Structure A structure characterized by low complexity, low formalization, and authority centralized in a single person.

person. As shown in Figure 15–6, the **simple structure** is depicted best as a flat organization, with an organic operating core and almost everyone reporting to a one-person strategic apex where the decision-making power is centralized.

STRENGTHS AND WEAKNESSES   The strength of the simple structure lies in its simplicity. It's fast and flexible and requires little cost to maintain. There are no layers of cumbersome structure. Accountability is clear. There is a minimum amount of goal ambiguity because members are able to identify readily with the organization's mission, and it is fairly easy to see how one's actions contribute to the organization's goals.

The simple structure's predominant weakness is its limited applicability. When confronted with increased size, this structure generally proves inadequate. Additionally, the simple structure concentrates power in one person. Rarely does the structure provide countervailing forces to balance the chief executive's power. Therefore, the simple structure can easily succumb to the abuse of authority by the person in power. This concentration of power, of course, can work against the organization's effectiveness and survival. The simple structure, in fact, has been described as the "riskiest of structures hinging on the health and whims of one individual."[30] One heart attack can literally destroy the organization's decision-making center.

BEHAVIORAL IMPLICATIONS   Many people enjoy working in a small, intimate organization under a strong leader. It's easy for employees to feel involved in a simple structure. Because they tend to be small, these organizations also provide high task identity. Employees can readily relate to the organization's goals and see how their work contributes to those goals. Simple structures can be especially exciting for employees when an organization is new and entrepreneurial. Apple Computer and Microsoft, for instance, began as simple structures. Reports by those who were part of these organizations' early years indicate they experienced a kind of psychological "rush" by being part of something new and innovative.

How individuals respond to the simple structure largely depends on their relationship to the central authority figure. Since one boss "calls the shots," the interpersonal relations between the boss and employees becomes critical in determining employee satisfaction. At its worst, the simple structure becomes highly restrictive and paternalistic. "Big brother" is constantly

FIGURE 15–6   The Simple Structure
Source: H. Mintzberg, *Structure in Fives: Designing Effective Organizations,* © 1983, p. 159. Reprinted by permission of Prentice Hall, Englewood Cliffs, NJ.

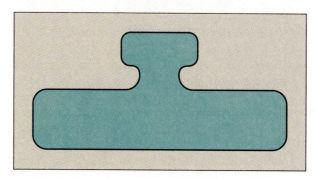

Government agencies, like this Internal Revenue Service office, are typically machine bureaucracies. They rate high in complexity, have numerous rules and procedures that employees must follow, and concentrate decision authority in high-ranking officials.   Andrew Popper / Picture Group.

watching over you and all important decisions will be made, or at least approved, by the person in power.

The Machine Bureaucracy

Standardization! That's the key concept that underlies all machine bureaucracies. Take a look at the bank where you keep your checking account; the department store where you buy your clothes; or the government offices that collect your taxes, enforce health regulations, or provide local fire protection. They all rely on standardized work processes for coordination and control.

Machine Bureaucracy A structure that rates high in complexity, formalization, and centralization.

The **machine bureaucracy** has highly routine operating tasks, very formalized rules and regulations, tasks that are grouped into functional departments, centralized authority, decision making that follows the chain of command, and an elaborate administrative structure with a sharp distinction between line and staff activities. It is Mintzberg's operationalizing of what we've been calling the mechanistic structure.

Figure 15–7 depicts the machine bureaucracy. Rules and regulations permeate the entire structure. While not explicitly evident from Figure 15–7, the key part of this design is the technostructure. That's because this is where the staff analysts who do the standardizing—time-and-motion engineers, job-description designers, planners, budgeters, accountants, auditors, systems-and-procedures analysts—are housed.

STRENGTHS AND WEAKNESSES   The primary strength of the machine bureaucracy lies in its ability to perform standardized activities in a highly efficient manner. Putting like specialties together results in economies of scale, minimization of duplication of personnel and equipment, and comfortable and satisfied employees who have the opportunity to talk "the same language" among their peers. Further, machine bureaucracies can get by nicely with less talented—and, hence less costly—middle- and lower-level managers. The pervasiveness of rules and regulations substitute for managerial discretion. Standardized operations, coupled with high formalization, allow decision making to be centralized. There is little need, therefore, for

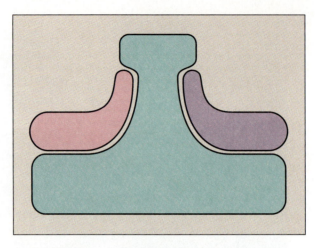

FIGURE 15–7   The Machine Bureaucracy

Source: H. Mintzberg, *Structure in Fives: Designing Effective Organizations,* © 1983, p. 170. Reprinted by permission of Prentice Hall, Englewood Cliffs, NJ.

innovative and experienced decision makers below the level of senior executives.

One of the major weaknesses of the machine bureaucracy is illustrated in the following dialogue between four executives in one company: "Ya know, nothing happens in this place until we *produce* something," said the production executive. "Wrong," commented the research-and-development manager, "nothing happens until we *design* something!" "What are you talking about?" asked the marketing executive. "Nothing happens here until we *sell* something!" Finally, the exasperated accounting manager responded, "It doesn't matter what you produce, design or sell. No one knows what happens until we *tally up the results!*"

This conversation points up the fact that specialization creates subunit conflicts. Functional unit goals can override the overall goals of the organization.

The other major weakness of the machine bureaucracy is something we've all experienced at one time or another when having to deal with people who work in these organizations: obsessive concern with following the rules. When cases arise that don't precisely fit the rules, there is no room for modification. The machine bureaucracy is efficient only as long as employees confront problems that they have previously encountered and for which programmed decision rules have already been established.

BEHAVIORAL IMPLICATIONS   The machine bureaucracy is obsessed with control. But, in contrast to the simple structure where control is exercised through direct supervision, the machine bureaucracy achieves its control over people through rules and regulations. Consistent with our discussion of power-control, we should expect that top management will like this design.

Whether or not employees like the machine bureaucracy and perform well under its restrictions depends on their bureaucratic orientation. (See Exercise 15 at the end of this chapter.) For people who enjoy routine work, this structure provides security and regularity. High division of labor, high formalization, narrow spans of control, and limited decision discretion make jobs seem menial. For the most part, jobs in this structure will score low on skill variety, task identity, task significance, and autonomy. So employee alienation often surfaces in response to unchallenging job tasks and management's obsession with ensuring that everyone follow the rules, with a feeling that they are treated as machines rather than human beings with individual needs and concerns.

The Professional Bureaucracy

The last quarter of a century has seen the birth of a new structural animal. It has been created to allow organizations to hire highly trained specialists for the operating core, while still achieving the efficiencies from standardization. The configuration is called the **professional bureaucracy,** and it combines standardization with *decentralization*.

Professional Bureaucracy A structure that rates high in complexity and formalization, and low in centralization.

The jobs that people do today increasingly require a high level of specialized expertise. An undergraduate college degree is required for more and more jobs. So, too, are graduate degrees. The knowledge explosion has created a whole class of organizations that require professionals to produce their goods and services. Obvious examples include hospitals, school districts, universities, museums, libraries, engineering design firms, social service agencies, and public accounting firms. This has created the need for an organizational design that substitutes *individuals* who are specialized for *work* that is specialized. By hiring professionals, who through years of schooling and training have mastered specific skills, the organization can free them up to perform their activities relatively autonomously.

Figure 15–8 illustrates the configuration for professional bureaucracies. The power in this design rests with the operating core because they have the critical skills that the organization needs, and they have the autonomy— provided through decentralization—to apply their expertise. The only other part of the professional bureaucracy that is fully elaborated is the support staff, but their activities are focused on serving the operating core.[31]

The New York City Public Library, like most libraries, is a professional bureaucracy. Decision making is decentralized to free up professional librarians so they can perform their activities relatively autonomously.
Naoki Okamoto / Black Star.

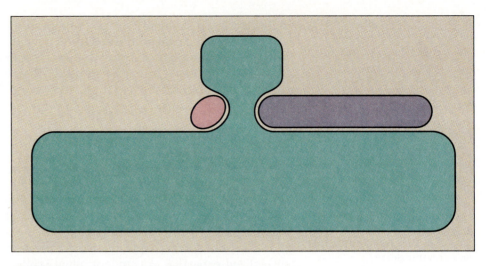

FIGURE 15–8   The Professional Bureaucracy

Source: H. Mintzberg, *Structure in Fives: Designing Effective Organizations,* © 1983, p. 194. Reprinted by permission of Prentice Hall, Englewood Cliffs, NJ.

STRENGTHS AND WEAKNESSES   The strength of the professional bureaucracy is that it can perform specialized tasks—ones that require the skills of highly trained professionals—with the same relative efficiency as the machine bureaucracy can. Why then, you may ask, didn't management just choose the latter? It's not because management wouldn't *prefer* the machine form! In power-control terms, the professional bureaucracy requires top management to give up a considerable degree of control. But what's their alternative? The professionals need the autonomy to do their jobs effectively.

The weaknesses of the professional bureaucracy are the same as for the machine form. First, there is the tendency for subunit conflicts to develop. The various professional functions seek to pursue their own narrow objectives, often sublimating the interests of other functions and the organization as a whole. Second, the specialists in the professional bureaucracy, like their counterparts in the machine form, are compulsive in their determination to follow the rules. Only the rules in professional bureaucracies are the making of the professionals themselves. Standards of professional conduct and codes for ethical practices have been socialized into the employees during their training. So, for example, while lawyers or nurses have autonomy on their jobs, their professional standards of how their work is to be done can be a hindrance to an organization's effectiveness when the standards are rigid and unable to adjust to unique or changing conditions.

BEHAVIORAL IMPLICATIONS   This design provides employees with the best of both worlds: the benefits of being attached to a large organization, yet the freedom to serve clients as they see fit, constrained only by the standards of their profession. The professional bureaucracy, then, allows people with professional skills, high levels of education, and strong needs for autonomy to survive—even thrive—in a large organization.

In contrast to the machine bureaucracy, this design empowers its employees and creates enriched jobs. For professionals who are competent and conscientious, this structure should produce high job performance.

The Divisional Structure

Divisional Structure A set of autonomous units coordinated by a central headquarters.

General Motors, Hershey Foods, Du Pont, Burlington Industries, and Xerox are examples of organizations that use the divisional structure.

As Figure 15–9 illustrates, the power in the divisional structure lies with middle management. The reason is that the **divisional structure** is actually a set of autonomous units, each typically a machine bureaucracy unto itself, coordinated by a central headquarters. Since the divisions are autonomous, it allows middle management—the division managers—a great deal of control.[32]

STRENGTHS AND WEAKNESSES One of the problems associated with the machine bureaucracy is that the goals of the functional units tend to override the organization's overall goals. One of the strengths of the divisional structure is that it seeks to remedy this problem by placing full responsibility for a product or service in the hands of the divisional manager. So one of the advantages to the divisional structure is that it provides more accountability and focus on outcomes than does the machine bureaucracy alone.

Another strength of the divisional structure is that it frees up the headquarters staff from being concerned with the day-to-day operating details so they can pay attention to the long term. Big-picture, strategic decision making is done at headquarters. At General Motors, for instance, senior executives in Detroit can wrestle with the world's future transportation needs while the division managers can go about the business of producing Chevrolets and Buicks as efficiently as possible.

It should be obvious that the autonomy and self-containment characteristics of the divisional form make it an excellent vehicle for training and developing general managers. This is a distinct advantage over the machine bureaucracy and its emphasis on specialization. That is, the divisional structure gives managers a broad range of experience with the autonomous units.

It's evident that the real strengths of the divisional form come from its creation of self-contained "businesses within a business." The divisions have

FIGURE 15–9   The Divisional Structure

Source: H. Mintzberg, *Structure in Fives: Designing Effective Organizations,* © 1983, p. 225. Reprinted by permission of Prentice Hall, Englewood Cliffs, NJ.

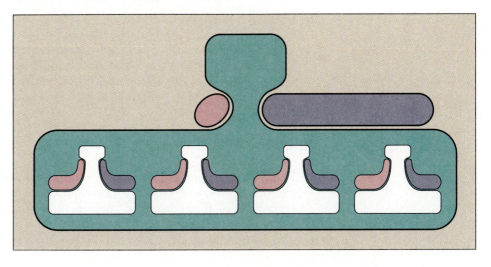

the responsiveness, the accountability, and the benefits of specialization and are able to process information as if they were organizations unto themselves. Yet they also have the benefits of large size that allow economies of scale in planning, acquisition of capital, and spreading of risk. Returning to our example of General Motors, when its Saturn Corporation needs $500 million to build a new plant, GM is able to borrow that money at a rate several percentage points below what Saturn could negotiate if it were not part of General Motors. Similarly, that division can be provided with legal expertise that could never be available "in house" if Saturn were a separate corporation independent of GM.

Let us turn now to the weaknesses of the divisional structure, of which there are no shortage. First is the duplication of activities and resources. Each division, for instance, may have a marketing research department. In the absence of autonomous divisions, all the organization's marketing research might be centralized and done for a fraction of the cost that divisionalization requires. So the divisional form's duplication of functions increases the organization's costs and reduces efficiency.

Another disadvantage is the propensity of the divisional form to stimulate conflict. There is little incentive with this structural design to encourage cooperation among divisions. Further conflicts are created as divisions and headquarters argue about where to locate support services. The more the divisions succeed in having these services decentralized to their level, the less dependent they are on headquarters and, hence, the less power headquarter's personnel can wield over them.

The autonomy of the divisions, to the degree that it is more theory than practice, can breed resentment in the division managers. While the structure gives general autonomy to the divisions, the autonomy is exercised within constraints. The division manager is being held fully accountable for results in his or her unit, but because he or she must operate within the uniform policies imposed from headquarters, the manager is likely to be resentful and argue that his or her authority is less than the responsibility.

Finally, the divisional form creates coordination problems. Personnel are frequently unable to transfer between divisions, especially when the divisions operate in highly diverse product or service markets. Du Pont employees in the Remington Arms Division, for instance, have little transferability to the Textile Fibers or Petro-Chemicals divisions. This reduces the flexibility of headquarters' executives to allocate and coordinate personnel.

BEHAVIORAL IMPLICATIONS In giant corporations, where you're most likely to find this design, the divisional structure concentrates enormous amounts of power in very few hands. In this sense, it is not unlike the machine bureaucracy. In fact, the behavioral implications of the divisional structure are the same as those of the machine bureaucracy since the former is nothing more than a grouping of machine bureaucracies under a common umbrella.

The Adhocracy

When Steven Spielberg or George Lucas goes about making a film, he brings together a diverse group of professionals. This team—composed of producers, scriptwriters, film editors, set designers, and hundreds of other specialists— exists for the singular purpose of making a single movie. They may be called back by Spielberg or Lucas when they begin another film, but that is irrelevant when the current project begins. These professionals frequently find themselves with overlapping activities because no formal rules or regulations are provided to guide them. While there is a production schedule, it often must be modified to take into consideration unforeseen contingencies. The film's production team may be together for a few months, or, in some unusual cases, for several years. But the organization is temporary. In contrast to bureaucracies or divisional structures, the filmmaking organizations have no entrenched hierarchy, no permanent departments, no formalized rules, and no standardized procedures for dealing with routine problems. Welcome to our last design configuration: the **adhocracy.** It's characterized by high horizontal differentiation, low vertical differentiation, low formalization, decentralization, and great flexibility and responsiveness. As such, it is synonymous with the organic structure.

Horizontal differentiation is great because adhocracies are staffed predominantly by professionals with a high level of expertise. Vertical differentiation is low because the many levels of administration would restrict the organization's ability to adapt. Also, the need for supervision is minimal because professionals have internalized the behaviors that management wants.

There are few rules and regulations in adhocracies. Those that exist tend to be loose and unwritten. The reason is that flexibility demands an absence of formalization. Rules and regulations are effective only where standardization of behavior is sought. In this context, it may be valuable to compare the professional bureaucracy with adhocracy. Both employ professionals. The key difference is that the professional bureaucracy, when faced with a problem, immediately classifies it into some standardized program so that the professionals can treat it in a uniform manner. In an adhocracy, a novel solution is needed so that standardization and formalization are inappropriate.

Decision making in adhocracies is decentralized. This is necessary for speed and flexibility and because senior management cannot be expected to possess the expertise necessary to make all decisions. So the adhocracy depends on decentralized teams of professionals for decision making.

The adhocracy is a very different design from those we've encountered earlier. This can be seen in Figure 15–10. Because the adhocracy has little standardization or formalization, the technostructure is almost nonexistent. Because middle managers, the support staff, and operatives are typically all professionals, the traditional distinctions between supervisor and employee and line and staff become blurred. The result is a central pool of expert talent that can be drawn from to innovate, solve unique problems, and perform flexible activities. Power flows to anyone in the adhocracy with expertise, regardless of his or her position.[33]

Adhocracies are best conceptualized as groups of teams. Specialists are grouped together into flexible teams that have few rules, regulations, or standardized routines. Coordination between team members is through mutual adjustment. As conditions change, so do the activities of the members. But adhocracies don't have to be devoid of horizontally differentiated departments. Frequently, departments are used for clarity, but then department members are deployed into small teams, which cut across functional units, to do their tasks.

STRENGTHS AND WEAKNESSES   The history of adhocracy can be traced to the development of task forces during World War II, when the military created ad hoc teams that were disbanded after completion of their missions.

Adhocracy A structure characterized as low in complexity, formalization, and centralization.

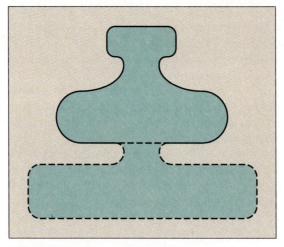

FIGURE 15–10   The Adhocracy

Source: H. Mintzberg, *Structure in Fives: Designing Effective Organizations,* © 1983, p. 262. Reprinted by permission of Prentice Hall, Englewood Cliffs, NJ.

There was no rigid time span for their existence—teams could last a day, a month, or a year. Roles performed in the teams were interchangeable, and, depending upon the nature and complexity of the mission, the group could be divided into subunits, each responsible for different facets of the job to be performed. The advantages of these ad hoc teams included their ability to respond rapidly to change and innovation and to facilitate the coordination of diverse specialists. More than forty-five years have passed since World War II, but the advantage of ad hoc teams, or what we call adhocracy, continues today. When it is important that the organization be adaptable and creative, when individual specialists from diverse disciplines are required to collaborate to achieve a common goal, and when tasks are technical, nonprogrammed, and too complex for any one person to handle, the adhocracy represents a viable alternative.

On the negative side, conflict is a natural part of adhocracy. There are no clear boss–subordinate relationships. Ambiguities exist over authority and responsibilities. Activities cannot be compartmentalized. In short, adhocracy lacks the advantages of standardized work.

In contrast to bureaucracy, adhocracy is clearly an inefficient configuration. It is also a vulnerable design. As one author noted, "Many of them either die early or else shift to bureaucratic configurations to escape the uncertainty."[34] So why, you might ask, would it ever be used? Because its inefficiencies, in certain circumstances, are more than offset by the need for flexibility and innovation.

BEHAVIORAL IMPLICATIONS   The adhocracy is the antithesis of the machine bureaucracy. Nothing is standardized. There are no rules or procedures. It's exhilarating for members because every day brings new and unexpected challenges. But with this exhilaration comes ambiguity and confusion.

Adhocracy can create social stress and psychological tension for its members. It is not easy to quickly set up and dismantle work relationships on a continuing basis. Some employees find it difficult to cope with rapid change, living in temporary work systems, and having to share responsibilities with other team members.

Adhocracy also creates highly competitive and, at times, ruthless work climates. Because there are no well-defined ground rules, politics can often run rampant. This can add further to employee stress and reduce job satisfaction.

THE MATRIX STRUCTURE

Matrix Structure A structure that creates dual lines of authority; combines functional and product departmentalization.

One of the more recent organizational design innovations is the **matrix structure.** You'll find it being used in advertising agencies, aerospace firms, research and development laboratories, construction companies, hospitals, government agencies, universities, management consulting firms, and entertainment companies.[35] Essentially, the matrix combines two forms of departmentalization—functional and product.

Combining Functions and Products

Referring back to our discussion in the previous chapter, the strength of functional departmentalization lies in putting like specialists together, which minimizes the number necessary, while it allows the pooling and sharing of specialized resources across products. Its major disadvantage is the difficulty of coordinating the tasks of diverse functional specialists so that their activities are completed on time and within budget. Product departmentalization, on the other hand, has exactly the opposite benefits and disadvantages. It facilitates coordination among specialties to achieve on-time completion and meet budget targets. Further, it provides clear responsibility for all activities related to a product, but with duplication of activities and costs. The matrix attempts to gain the strengths of each, while avoiding their weaknesses.

The most obvious structural characteristic of the matrix is that it breaks the unity of command concept. Employees in the matrix have two bosses—their functional department managers and their product managers. Therefore, the matrix has a dual chain of command.

Figure 15–11 shows the matrix form as used in a college of business administration. The academic departments of accounting, economics, marketing, and so forth are functional units. Additionally, specific programs (that is, products) are overlaid on the functions. In this way, members in a matrix structure have a dual assignment—to their functional department, and to their product groups. For instance, a professor of accounting teaching an undergraduate course reports to the director of undergraduate programs as well as to the chairperson of the accounting department.

Strengths and Weaknesses

The strength of the matrix lies in its ability to facilitate coordination when the organization has a multiplicity of complex and interdependent activities. As an organization gets larger, its information-processing capacity can become overloaded. In a bureaucracy, complexity results in increased formalization. The direct and frequent contact between different specialties in the matrix can make for better communication and more flexibility. Information permeates the organization and more quickly reaches those people who need to take

Programs / Academic Departments	Undergraduate	Master's	Ph. D.	Research	Executive Programs	Community-Service Programs
Accounting						
Administrative Studies						
Economics						
Finance						
Marketing						
Organizational Behavior						
Quantitative Methods						

FIGURE 15–11   Matrix Structure for a College of Business Administration

account of it. Further, the matrix reduces bureaupathologies. The dual lines of authority reduce tendencies of departmental members to become so busy protecting their little worlds that the organization's overall goals become secondary.

There are other advantages to the matrix. It facilitates the efficient allocation of specialists. When individuals with highly specialized skills are lodged in one functional department or product group, their talents are monopolized and underutilized. The matrix achieves the advantages of economies of scale by providing the organization with both the best resources and an effective way of ensuring their efficient deployment. Further advantages of the matrix are that it creates (1) increased ability to respond rapidly to changes in the environment, (2) an effective means for balancing the customer's or client's requirements for product performance with the organization's need for economic efficiency and development of technical capability for the future, and (3) increased motivation by providing an environment more in line with the democratic norms preferred by scientific and professional employees.[36]

The major disadvantages of the matrix lie in the confusion it creates, its propensity to foster power struggles, and the stress it places on individuals.[37] When you dispense with the unity of command concept, ambiguity is significantly increased and ambiguity often leads to conflict. For example, it's frequently unclear who reports to whom, and it is not unusual for product managers to fight over getting the best specialists assigned to their products. Confusion and ambiguity also create the seeds of power struggles. Bureaucracy reduces the potential for power grabs by defining the rules of the game. When those rules are "up for grabs," power struggles between functional and product managers result. For individuals who desire security and absence from ambiguity, this work climate can produce stress. Reporting to more than one boss introduces role conflict, and unclear expectations introduce role ambiguity. The comfort of bureaucracy's predictability is absent, replaced by insecurity and stress.

ORGANIZATIONS IN MOTION: GROWTH VS. DECLINE

To this point, we've treated organizations as static entities. In reality, of course, they're not. Organizations are fluid—in a constant state of change. Some are growing and expanding. Others are shrinking. In recent years, we've seen a definite trend toward the latter in North America. Terms such as *retrenchment, downsizing,* and *lean and mean* have become increasingly used to describe the direction in which management has been taking organizations in the late 1980s and early 1990s.

In this section, we'll briefly discuss the historical growth bias in organizations, what has precipitated the recent emphasis on making organizations smaller, and the differing effects that decline and growth have on employees in organizations.

The Growth Bias

There has been an historical bias, especially in the United States, toward growth. It reflects an inherent optimism about the future that permeates American values. Let's look at a few ways in which this bias has infiltrated managerial thinking.

BIGGER IS BETTER   One of the strong forces for growth has been the "bigger is better" notion in America. Although under attack in recent years, this view still has its advocates. For instance, many Americans still covet large incomes and large homes. This bias, when applied to organizations, was often couched in economic terms. Growth was desirable because with increases in size came economies of scale. Bigger, in fact, was frequently more efficient.

GROWTH INCREASES THE LIKELIHOOD OF SURVIVAL   Large organizations are not permitted to go out of existence the way small organizations are. In 1980, for instance, the United States government came to the rescue of Chrysler Corporation by guaranteeing $1.5 billion in loans. Chrysler's large size alone assured it of strong constituencies who would fight for its survival. Wherever Chrysler had assembly plants, suppliers, bankers it owed money to, and dealers—which included just about every state in the Union—the company had supporters fighting for government assistance. Your community drugstore or laundromat, should it face financial difficulties, certainly would not attract that kind of support.

In addition to providing a large constituency, growth facilitates survival by providing more resources with which the organization can buffer itself against uncertainty. Larger organizations can make errors and live to talk about them. Similarly, more resources provide a buffer in times of setbacks. Growing organizations have slack resources that can be cut more easily than those of small or stable organizations.

GROWTH BECOMES SYNONYMOUS WITH EFFECTIVENESS   Growth is often used by managers to imply success. Business executives flaunt that "sales are up significantly." Hospital administrators produce charts showing that they are handling more patients than ever. College deans brag about having record enrollments. If those in the environment on whom the organization depends for continued support—suppliers, customers, lenders, and the like—also equate growth with effectiveness, managers will obviously be predisposed to the values of growth.

GROWTH IS POWER   Growth is almost always consistent with the self-interest of the top management in the organization. It increases prestige, power, and job security for this group. It should certainly be of more than passing interest to know that growth is linked to executive compensation. Size, in fact, is a better predictor of executive salaries than is profit margin.[38]

Growth also provides an organization more power relative to other organizations and groups in its environment. Larger organizations have more influence with suppliers, unions, large customers, government, and the like.

Pressures Toward Retrenchment

The twenty-five year period immediately following World War II was generally a time of growth and prosperity for organizations in the United States. The last two decades, however, have witnessed a sharp change in direction. In fact, it is the unusual *Fortune* 500 company that has *not* cut back the size of its operations in recent years. What has brought this about?

The initial impetus came from the dramatic increase in energy costs in the early 1970s. Oil and gas were no longer available in unlimited supplies at low costs. This jolted many industries and forced cutbacks.

The globalization of markets shocked many companies that had gotten fat by competing within protected borders. General Motors, as a case in point, found that Honda, Toyota, and a host of other foreign competitors could build higher quality and more innovative products at extremely competitive prices. GM saw its United States market-share drop by more than twenty-five percent, requiring the closing of inefficient plants and the layoff of tens of thousands of employees. The same also occurred in such other industries as steel, rubber, textiles, and consumer electronics.

Three other forces in the 1980s ganged up to further increase the pressures on management to shrink their organizations—reduction of inflation, aggressive corporate raiders, and expanded merger and acquisition activities. The stabilizing of inflation made it harder for companies to pass on higher costs to consumers, so management had to prune excessive costs. Corporate raiders aggressively sought out firms that were overstaffed and inefficient, then cut costs in order to improve profitability. Mergers and acquisitions (including leveraged buyouts) typically result in significant cutbacks to eliminate waste and redundant operations.

Effect on Employees

Growth creates opportunities to work on new projects, more promotion possibilities, and higher salary increases. It's not surprising that Apple Computer's management had no problem finding and keeping highly talented computer engineers in its early years. These employees, in the early 1980s, worked sixty or more hours a week, yet expressed very high levels of job satisfaction. Employee turnover was negligible. The reason, of course, was that Apple's rapid growth created exciting opportunities and enough excess resources to enable them to reward high performers generously.

Organizational retrenchment, unfortunately, creates a very different work climate. Let's look at what retrenchment does to organizations and their employees.[39]

CONFLICT   Growth creates slack that acts as a grease to smooth over conflict-creating forces. Management uses this slack as a currency for buying off potentially conflicting interest groups within the organization. Conflicts can be resolved readily by expanding everyone's resources. However, in retrenchment, conflict over resources increases because there is less slack to divvy up.

POLITICKING   Less slack also translates into more politicking. Many organized and vocal groups will emerge, each actively pursuing its own self-interest. Politically naive managers will find their jobs difficult, if not impossible, as they are unable to adjust to the changing decision-making criteria. Remember, in retrenchment, the pie of resources shrinks. If one department can successfully resist a cut, typically the result will be that other departments have to cut deeper. Weak units not only will take a disproportional part of the cut but may be most vulnerable to elimination. In a "fight-for-life" situation, the standard rules are disregarded. Critical data for decisions are twisted and interpreted by various coalitions so as to further their groups' interests. Such a climate encourages "no holds barred" politicking.

WORK FORCE COMPOSITION   Retrenchment requires personnel cuts. The most popular criterion for determining who gets laid off is seniority; that is, the most recent hires are the first to go. Laying off personnel on the basis of seniority, however, tends to reshape the composition of the organization's work force.

Since newer employees tend to be younger, seniority-based layoffs typically create an older work force. When organizations operating in mature industries are required to make substantial cuts, the average age of employees may increase ten years or more.

One of the most disheartening results of seniority-based layoffs is that it undermines much of the progress made in the past twenty-five years toward opening up job opportunities for women and minorities. Members of these groups tend to be among the most recently hired and therefore are the first to be let go. The organization's labor force will become more homogeneous as a result of retrenchment, looking more white and male.

VOLUNTARY TURNOVER   The other side of employee departures are voluntary quits. This becomes a major potential problem in retrenchment because the organization will want to retain its most valuable employees. Yet some of the first people to voluntarily leave a shrinking organization are the most mobile individuals, such as skilled technicians, professionals, and talented managerial personnel. These, of course, are the individuals who the organization can least afford to lose.

MOTIVATION   Employee motivation is different when an organization is contracting than when it is enjoying growth. On the growth side, motivation can be provided by promotional opportunities and the excitement of being associated with a dynamic organization. During decline, there are layoffs, reassignments of duties that frequently require absorbing the tasks that were previously done by others, and similar stress-inducing changes. It's usually hard for employees to stay motivated when there is high uncertainty as to whether they will still have a job next month or next year. Retrenchment, in other words, directly attacks an employee's basic lower-order needs.

IMPLICATIONS FOR PERFORMANCE AND SATISFACTION

Figure 15–12 visually depicts what we have discussed in this chapter. Strategy, size, technology, environment, and power-control determine the type of structure an organization will have. Complexity, formalization, and centralization represent the structural components that can be mixed and matched to form various structural designs. For simplicity's sake, we can classify structural designs as mechanistic or organic. The former rates high on complexity, formalization, and centralization; the latter rates low on the same three components. Mintzberg's machine and professional bureaucracies plus his divisional form fall into the mechanistic category. His simple structure and adhocracy are examples of organic forms. Common structural components, however, do not necessarily have a uniform impact on every employee's level of performance and satisfaction. The impact of objective structural characteristics on members of the organization is moderated by the employees' individual preferences and their subjective interpretation of the objective characteristics. Let us now offer some general thoughts.

For a large proportion of the population, high structure—that is, high complexity, high formalization, and centralization—leads to reduced job satisfaction. High vertical differentiation tends to alienate lower-level employees because vertical communication becomes more difficult and one can feel like "low man on the totem pole." On the other hand, upper management undoubtedly finds that the rewards that go with *their* positions enhance job satisfaction.

Specialization would also tend to be inversely related to satisfaction, especially where jobs have been divided into extremely minute tasks. This conclusion would have to be moderated to reflect individual differences among employees. While most prefer variety in their work, not *all* do.

For individuals who value autonomy and self-actualization, large size, when accompanied by high centralization, results in lower satisfaction. As we have noted, there are fewer opportunities to participate in decision making, less proximity and identification with organizational goals, and less feeling that individual effort is linked to an identifiable outcome. In other words, the larger the organization, the more difficult it is for the individual to see the impact of his or her contribution to the final goods or service produced.

Organic structures increase cohesiveness among unit members and more closely align their authority with the responsibility for completion of a particular assignment. For certain types of activities, these structures are undoubtedly superior from management's standpoint. For instance, if tasks are nonroutine and there exists a great deal of environmental uncertainty, the organization can be more responsive when structured along organic rather than mechanistic lines. But these more responsive structures provide both advantages and disadvantages to employees. They rarely have restrictive job descriptions or excessive rules and regulations, and they do not require workers to obey commands that are issued by distant executives. But they usually have overlapping layers of responsibility and play havoc with individuals who need the security of doing standardized tasks. To maximize

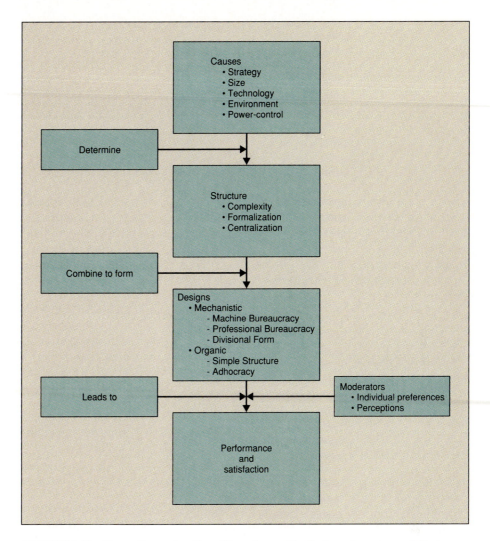

FIGURE 15–12   Organization Structure: Its Determinants and Outcomes

employee performance and satisfaction, individual differences should be taken into account. Individuals with a high degree of bureaucratic orientation tend to place a heavy reliance on higher authority, prefer formalized and specific rules, and prefer formal relationships with others on the job. These people are better suited to mechanistic structures. Those individuals with a low degree of bureaucratic orientation would be better suited to organic structures.

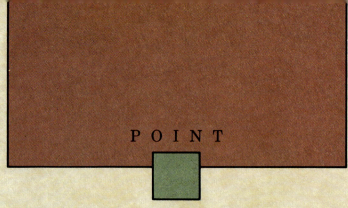

Management Can Control Its Environment

The external environment has received a great deal of attention in the organization literature because it is one (if not *the*) of the most important contingency factors that managers must take into consideration when making organization design decisions. The flaw in this analysis is that it ignores the fact that the environment can be controlled by management, and, for that reason, is relatively unimportant in influencing the structural decision.

Almost all large and powerful organizations, and many small ones as well, clearly have the means to shape major elements of their environment. In so doing, they reduce environmental uncertainty and minimize the impact of the environment on the organization. The following provides a quick overview of some of the techniques managers use to reduce environmental uncertainty.

DOMAIN CHOICE The most comprehensive action management can take when faced with an unfavorable environment is to change to a domain with less environmental uncertainty. Management could consider, for instance, staking out a niche that has fewer or less powerful competitors; barriers that keep other competitors out as a result of high entry costs, economies of scale, or regulatory approval; little regulation; numerous suppliers; no unions; less powerful public-pressure groups, and the like.

RECRUITMENT The practice of selective hiring to reduce environmental uncertainty is widespread. For example, corporations hire executives from competing firms to acquire information about their competitors' future plans.

ENVIRONMENTAL SCANNING This entails scrutinizing the environment to identify actions by competitors, government, unions, and the like, that might impinge on the organization's operations. To the extent that this scanning can lead to accurate forecasts of environmental fluctuations, it can reduce uncertainty.

BUFFERING Organizations can protect their organization's operations by ensuring supplies or absorption of outputs. When organizations stockpile materials, use multiple suppliers, engage in preventive maintenance, or create finished-goods inventories, they are buffering their operations from environmental uncertainties.

GEOGRAPHIC DISPERSION Environmental uncertainty sometimes varies with location. To lessen location-induced uncertainty, organizations can move to a different community or lessen risk by operating in multiple locations.

CONTRACTING Contracting protects the organization from changes in quantity or price on either the input or output side. For instance, management may agree to a long-term fixed contract to purchase materials and supplies or to sell a certain part of the organization's output.

COOPTING Organizations can absorb those individuals or organizations in the environment that threaten their stability. This is most frequently accomplished in business firms through selective appointments to the organization's board of directors.

COALESCING Mergers, joint ventures, and cooperative (though illegal) agreements to fix prices or split markets are examples of how organizations can combine with one or more other organizations for joint action. Many mergers, for instance, reduce environmental uncertainty by lessening interorganizational competition and dependency.

LOBBYING Using influence—for example, through trade associations and political action committees—to achieve favorable outcomes is a widespread practice used by organizations to control their environments.

This argument is based on S. Robbins, *Organization Theory: Structure, Design, and Applications,* 3rd ed. (Englewood Cliffs, NJ: Prentice Hall, 1990), pp. 362–77.

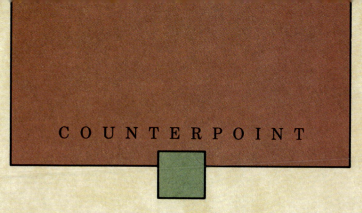

The Environment Controls Management

Organizations are not merely *influenced* by their environment, they are *totally captive* to it. Management is impotent in determining an organization's success or failure. The environment selects certain types of organizations to survive and others to perish based on the fit between their structural characteristics and the characteristics of their environment.

Look at any population of organizations—for example, fast-food restaurants, chemical firms, general hospitals, or private colleges—and you will find variations in organizational forms; that is, there will be diversity in organization structures. But some of these variations are better suited to their environments than others. They may, for example, have lower costs, superior service, higher quality, or more convenient locations. Those that are well suited survive, while others either fail or change to match their environmental requirements. As long as the carrying capacity of an environment is limited, there will be a competitive arena where some organizations will succeed and others will fail. For instance, there are only so many hospitals that a given community's size can absorb. Regardless of how good management is, survival of the fittest argues that the strongest and most adaptable organizations will survive over time.

Management, at least in the short or interme-diate term, has little impact on an organization's survival. Managers are merely observers. If there is a shift in the environmental niche that an organization occupies, there is little that management can do. Survival is determined solely by how well the environment supports the organization. Success, therefore, is a result of luck or chance. Organizations that survive are merely in the right place at the right time, and positioning has nothing to do with managerial choice.

For a vivid illustration of this argument, consider the fate of afternoon daily newspapers. In most major cities they have gone the way of the horse and buggy. Their failure had little to do with the quality of their management or any actions that their management did or didn't take. Rather, the environment changed—the evening news on television could provide the same information in a more timely manner; and fewer people, in general, are reading newspapers. Those newspapers that have survived in metropolitan areas have tended to be the large morning papers. For the management of afternoon dailies, their problem was merely being in the wrong place at the wrong time.

This argument is based on D. Ulrich, "The Population Perspective: Review, Critique, and Relevance," *Human Relations,* March 1987, pp. 137–52.

FOR DISCUSSION

1. Explain Chandler's strategy–structure thesis.

2. What type of structure works best with an innovation strategy? A cost-minimization strategy? An imitation strategy?

3. Summarize the size–structure relationship.

4. Define and give an example of what is meant by the term *technology*.

5. Summarize the technology–structure relationship.

6. Summarize the environment–structure relationship.

7. Describe the power-control thesis.

8. How do coordination and control change in each of Mintzberg's five configurations?

9. Contrast the machine and professional bureaucracy.

10. Does management ever blend designs; for example, combining the machine bureaucracy with adhocracy? Discuss.

11. What is a matrix structure? When would management use it?

12. Why is organizational retrenchment currently so widespread?

FOR FURTHER READING

BOSCHKEN, H. L., "Strategy and Structure: Reconceiving the Relationship," *Journal of Management,* March 1990, pp. 135–50. Presents a framework that looks at subunit strategies and microstructures within an overall organization.

BURKHART, M. E. and D. J. BRASS, "Changing Patterns or Patterns of Change: The Effects of a Change in Technology on Social Network Structure and Power," *Administrative Science Quarterly,* March 1990, pp. 104–27. Reviews the effects of a change in technology on organizational structure and power in a longitudinal study of the introduction and diffusion of a computerized information system.

CAMERON, K. S., R. I. SUTTON, and D. A. WHETTON, *Readings in Organizational Decline.* Cambridge, Mass.: Ballinger Publishing, 1988. A book of readings that includes the key articles written in the past decade on organizational retrenchment.

COURTRIGHT, J. A., G. T. FAIRHURST, and L. E. ROGERS, "Interaction Patterns in Organic and Mechanistic Systems," *Academy of Management Journal,* December 1989, pp. 773–802. Provides empirical support for hypotheses suggesting that communicative forms are consultative in organic systems and command-like in mechanistic systems.

HENKOFF, R., "Cost Cutting: How to Do It Right," *Fortune,* April 9, 1990, pp. 40–49. Argues that downsizing should focus on eliminating work rather than reducing employees.

ROBEY, D., *Designing Organizations,* 3rd ed. Homewood, Ill.: Richard D. Irwin, 1991. A comprehensive source on organization design theory and practice.

Bureaucratic Orientation Test

Instructions. For each statement, check the response (either mostly agree or mostly disagree) that best represents your feelings.

	MOSTLY AGREE	MOSTLY DISAGREE
1. I value stability in my job.	_____	_____
2. I like a predictable organization.	_____	_____
3. The best job for me would be one in which the future is uncertain.	_____	_____
4. The U.S. Army would be a nice place to work.	_____	_____
5. Rules, policies, and procedures tend to frustrate me.	_____	_____
6. I would enjoy working for a company that employed 85,000 people worldwide.	_____	_____
7. Being self-employed would involve more risk than I'm willing to take.	_____	_____
8. Before accepting a job, I would like to see an exact job description.	_____	_____
9. I would prefer a job as a freelance house painter to one as a clerk for the Department of Motor Vehicles.	_____	_____
10. Seniority should be as important as performance in determining pay increases and promotion.	_____	_____
11. It would give me a feeling of pride to work for the largest and most successful company in its field.	_____	_____
12. Given a choice, I would prefer to make $40,000 per year as a vice-president in a small company to $45,000 as a staff specialist in a large company.	_____	_____
13. I would regard wearing an employee badge with a number on it as a degrading experience.	_____	_____
14. Parking spaces in a company lot should be assigned on the basis of job level.	_____	_____
15. If an accountant works for a large organization, he or she cannot be a true professional.	_____	_____
16. Before accepting a job (given a choice), I would want to make sure that the company had a very fine program of employee benefits.	_____	_____
17. A company will probably not be successful unless it establishes a clear set of rules and procedures.	_____	_____
18. Regular working hours and vacations are more important to me than finding thrills on the job.	_____	_____
19. You should respect people according to their rank.	_____	_____
20. Rules are meant to be broken.	_____	_____

Turn to page 690 for scoring directions and key.

Source: A. J. DuBrin, *Human Relations: A Job Oriented Approach* © 1978, pp. 687–88. Reprinted with permission of Reston Publishing Co., a Prentice-Hall Co., 11480 Sunset Hills Road, Reston, Va. 22090.

Ben & Jerry's Homemade Inc.

In the summer of 1978, Ben Cohen and Jerry Greenfield opened an ice cream parlor in a renovated Burlington, Vermont, gas station. Their goal was to make and sell super-premium ice cream and have fun doing it. During the next ten years, Ben & Jerry's Homemade Inc. grew into a $45-million-a-year company with 150 employees. Along the way, however, Ben Cohen has become afraid that the company has lost, or at least is losing, its unique character—with its emphasis on fun, charity, and goodwill toward fellow workers. Ben has begun to wonder whether his firm can be true to its founders' vision of a company that is genuinely sensitive to the needs of its employees and the community while, at the same time, pursuing rapid internal growth.

Ben & Jerry's began as more than just a "profit-making venture." It authentically wanted to act as a force for social change. Ben and Jerry were going to show other people that you could run a business differently from the way most businesses were run. For example, managers would wear jeans and T-shirts, and no executive would be allowed to earn more than five times what the lowest paid employee made. They would hire the handicapped. They would provide free therapy sessions to any employee. They'd stop production so every employee could participate in monthly staff meetings, and they would rely on all employees to participate in company decision making.

By 1988, Ben Cohen wasn't sure whether growth was compatible with his company's original mission. All he had to do was look around his new plant and offices in his headquarters in Waterbury, Vermont, and see the changes that had taken place. They had a chief operating officer with an M.B.A.! There were cost controls, departments, and memos. Product introductions now took much more effort than they used to and required numerous approvals. Some company managers were wearing ties. While production still stopped for the monthly staff meet-ings, they were no longer vehicles for two-way communication but, rather, one-way affairs with management telling employees what was happening. Employees also talked about the stress of meeting production goals.

Ben was also lamenting the fact that growth had brought malaise. What was once a small group of employees who were like family was becoming an impersonal, and maybe even an inefficient, organization. Employees were no longer privy to every decision management made. Departments were duplicating work. Communications broke down. Employees, for example, found out about the company's new Springfield, Vermont, plant from newspaper accounts. Even the company's most visible egalitarian symbol—the five-to-one salary ratio—was under attack. The highest possible salary in 1988 was $84,240. Consistent with Ben & Jerry's original philosophy, if managers wanted more money, they would first have to raise the lowest salaries. But the director of sales is now complaining that he's making only 60 to 70 percent of what he'd make elsewhere and the chief operating officer says that this policy is making recruiting difficult.

QUESTIONS

1. "This case demonstrates that organizations control people as much or more than people control organizations." Do you agree or disagree with this statement? Discuss.

2. What type of structure did Ben & Jerry's have in its early years? Today? What factors brought about this change?

3. Can a $45-million-a-year company have an organic structure? Explain.

Source: Based on E. Larson, "Forever Young," *INC.*, July 1988, pp. 50-62.

NOTES

[1]S. W. Angrist, "Classless Capitalists," *Forbes,* May 9, 1983, pp. 122–24.

[2]See T. Burns and G. M. Stalker, *The Management of Innovation* (London: Tavistock, 1961); and J. A. Courtright, G. T. Fairhurst, and L. E. Rogers, "Interaction Patterns in Organic and Mechanistic Systems," *Academy of Management Journal,* December 1989, pp. 773–802.

[3]A. D. Chandler, Jr., *Strategy and Structure: Chapters in the History of the Industrial Enterprise* (Cambridge, MA: MIT Press, 1962).

[4]See R. E. Miles and C. C. Snow, *Organizational Strategy, Structure, and Process* (New York: McGraw–Hill, 1978); and D. Miller, "The Structural and Environmental Correlates of Business Strategy,: *Strategic Management Journal,* January–February 1987, pp. 55–76.

[5]P. M. Blau, "A Formal Theory of Differentiation in Organizations," *American Sociological Review,* April 1970, pp. 201–18.

[6]D. S. Mileti, D. F. Gillespie, and J. E. Haas, "Size and Structure in Complex Organizations," *Social Forces,* September 1977, pp. 208–17.

[7]W. A. Rushing, "Organizational Size, Rules, and Surveillance," in J. A. Litterer (ed.), *Organizations: Structure and Behavior,* 3rd ed. (New York: John Wiley, 1980), pp. 396–405; and Y. Samuel and B. F. Mannheim, "A Multidimensional Approach Toward a Typology of Bureaucracy," *Administrative Science Quarterly,* June 1970, pp. 216–28.

[8]See, for example, P. M. Blau and R. A. Schoenherr, *The Structure of Organizations* (New York: Basic Books, 1971); and J. Child and R. Mansfield, "Technology, Size, and Organization Structure," *Sociology,* September 1972, pp. 369–93.

[9]J. Woodward, *Industrial Organization: Theory and Practice* (London: Oxford University Press, 1965).

[10]C. Perrow, "A Framework for the Comparative Analysis of Organizations," *American Sociological Review,* April 1967, pp. 194–208.

[11]J. D. Thompson, *Organizations in Action* (New York: McGraw-Hill, 1967).

[12]*Ibid.,* p. 17.

[13]J. Hage and M. Aiken, "Routine Technology, Social Structure, and Organizational Goals," *Administrative Science Quarterly,* September 1969, pp. 366–77.

[14]D. Gerwin, "Relationships Between Structure and Technology at the Organizational and Job Levels," *Journal of Management Studies,* February 1979, pp. 70–79.

[15]A. Van De Ven, A. Delbecq, and R. Koenig, Jr., "Determinants of Coordination Modes Within Organizations," *American Sociological Review,* April 1976, pp. 322–38.

[16]J. Hage and M. Aiken, "Relationship of Centralization to Other Structural Properties," *Administrative Science Quarterly,* June 1967, pp. 72–92.

[17]J. Pfeffer and G. R. Salancik, *The External Control of Organizations: A Resource Dependence Perspective* (New York: Harper & Row, 1978), p. 29.

[18]F. E. Emery and E. Trist, "The Causal Texture of Organizational Environments," *Human Relations,* February 1965, pp. 21–32.

[19]P. Lawrence and J. W. Lorsch, *Organization and Environment: Managing Differentiation and Integration* (Boston: Harvard Business School, Division of Research, 1967).

[20]G. G. Dess and D. W. Beard, "Dimensions of Organizational Task Environments," *Administrative Science Quarterly,* March 1984, pp. 52–73.

[21]G. Hofstede, "Motivation, Leadership, and Organization: Do American Theories Apply Abroad?" *Organizational Dynamics,* Summer 1980, p. 60.

[22]J. Child, "Organization Structure, Environment and Performance: The Role of Strategic Choice," *Sociology,* January 1972, pp. 1–22; and D. S. Pugh, "The Management of Organization Structures: Does Context Determine Form?" *Organizational Dynamics,* Spring 1973, pp. 19–34.

[23]Pfeffer, *Organizational Design.*

[24]Ibid.

[25]For a review of this research, see S. P. Robbins, *Organization Theory: Structure, Design, and Applications,* 3rd ed. (Englewood Cliffs, N.J.: Prentice Hall, 1990), pp. 123–24.

[26]See S. Zuboff, *In the Age of the Smart Machine: The Future of Work and Power* (New York: Basic Books, 1988); and J. Chalykoff and T. A. Kochan, "Computer-Aided Monitoring: Its Influence on Employee Job Satisfaction and Turnover," *Personnel Psychology,* Winter 1989, pp. 807–29.

[27]S. P. Robbins, *Organization Theory,* p. 107.

[28]H. Mintzberg, *Structure in Fives: Designing Effective Organizations* (Englewood Cliffs, NJ: Prentice Hall, 1983).

[29]*Ibid.,* p. 157.

[30]H. Mintzberg, *The Structuring of Organizations* (Englewood Cliffs, NJ: Prentice Hall, 1979), p. 312.

[31]H. Mintzberg, *Structure in Fives,* p. 194.

[32]*Ibid.,* p. 217.

[33]*Ibid.,* p. 261.

[34]D. Miller and P. H. Friesen, *Organizations: A Quantum View* (Englewood Cliffs, N.J.: Prentice Hall, 1984), p. 85.

[35]S. M. Davis and P. R. Lawrence, "The Matrix Diamond," *Wharton Magazine,* Winter 1978, pp. 19–27.

[36]K. Knight, "Matrix Organization: A Review," *Journal of Management Studies,* May 1976, pp. 111–30.

[37]*Ibid.,* and S. M. Davis and P. R. Lawrence, "Problems of Matrix Organizations," *Harvard Business Review,* May–June 1978, pp. 131–42.

[38]J. Pfeffer and G. R. Salancik, *The External Control of Organizations.*

[39]This section is based on S. P. Robbins, *Organization Theory: Structure, Design, and Applications,* pp. 481–85.

HUMAN RESOURCE POLICIES AND PRACTICES

LEARNING OBJECTIVES

After studying this chapter, you should be able to:

1. *Define the purposes of job analysis*
2. *Explain when to use interviews in selection*
3. *List the advantages of performance simulation tests over written tests*
4. *Define three skill categories*
5. *Summarize the four stages in a career*
6. *Describe five specific career anchors*
7. *Outline the best procedure for making an individual career choice*
8. *Explain the purposes of performance evaluation*
9. *Identify the advantages to using behaviors rather than traits in evaluating performance*
10. *Describe the potential problems in performance evaluation and actions that can correct these problems*
11. *Outline the various types of rewards*
12. *Clarify how the existence of a union affects employee behavior*

In his 15-year career at DuPont, Don Pippins has had several promotions. But at the age of 38, he is already having to face the possibility that his career at DuPont is plateauing.   Geoffrey Biddle.

I failed to get this job I wanted because I answered one of the questions on the application wrong. The question asked "Do you advocate the overthrow of the United States government by revolution or violence?" I chose violence!

D. CAVETT

Today's "up-and-comers" are different from earlier generations. First, they're as likely to be a "she" as a "he." Second, they're probably part of a two-career couple, attempting to balance two sets of goals and aspirations. And third, the large cohort of baby-boomers now in their 30s or early 40s plus the trend toward downsizing in many large corporations has significantly increased the competition among these up-and-comers for a reduced number of promotion slots. Don Pippins' career pattern and frustrations are typical among this group.[1]

After earning an engineering degree at Georgia Tech, Don joined DuPont in 1976 as a $16,000-a-year shift supervisor in a company plant in Richmond, Virginia. Although he had to rotate hours every four or five days and rarely had time to spend with his wife, he considered it to be "paying his dues." It was part of the price for moving up in the company. In 1981, Don was promoted to a job as a marketing representative in carpet fibers, working out of DuPont's headquarters in Wilmington, Delaware. This job, however, required extensive traveling. It was hard on him and his family but, again, Don considered it part of paying his dues. In his fifth year in Wilmington, he got a one-year staff assignment in public relations. This increased his visibility in the company and resulted in a promotion to a business strategist position on a new fibers venture. This is where he is today, earning more than $50,000 a year, putting in long hours, and wondering if he'll ever get his hoped-for next promotion to marketing manager.

At the age of 38, Don Pippins is recognizing that his career may be already plateauing. He's been a very loyal DuPont employee, but he has a lot of competition for promotion slots. He also worries that DuPont's commitment to promoting more women and minorities could affect him. Even though Don feels he's been loyal and paid his dues, he is beginning to recognize that he faces a future that will require lowered expectations. Either that or he'll have to leave DuPont and the security of a DuPont career. But that's a dilemma increasingly facing today's ambitious professional.

Don Pippins' frustrations provide one small illustration of how an organization's human resource policies and practices—in this case, DuPont's career development policies—can affect an employee's attitudes and behavior. In this chapter, we'll discuss a number of human resource concerns that add important pieces to our puzzle as we attempt to explain and predict employee behavior. Specifically, we'll look at selection practices, training and career development programs, performance evaluation, reward systems, and union–management relations.

SELECTION PRACTICES

The objective of effective selection is to match individual characteristics (ability, experience, and so on) with the requirements of the job.[2] When management fails to get a proper match, both employee performance and satisfaction suffer. In this search to achieve the right individual–job fit, where does management begin? The answer is to assess the demands and requirements of the job. The process of assessing the activities within a job is called job analysis.

Job Analysis

Job Analysis Developing a detailed description of the tasks involved in a job, determining the relationship of a given job to other jobs, and ascertaining the knowledge, skills, and abilities necessary for an employee to perform the job.

Job Description A written statement of what a jobholder does, how it is done, and why it is done.

Job Specification States the minimum acceptable qualifications that an employee must possess to perform a given job successfully.

Job analysis involves developing a detailed description of the tasks involved in a job, determining the relationship of a given job to other jobs, and ascertaining the knowledge, skills, and abilities necessary for an employee to successfully perform the job.[3]

How is this information attained? Table 16–1 describes the more popular job analysis methods.

Information gathered by using one or more of the job analysis methods results in the organization being able to create a **job description** and **job specification.** The former is a written statement of what a jobholder does, how it is done, and why it is done. It should accurately portray job content, environment, and conditions of employment. The job specification states the minimum acceptable qualifications that an employee must possess to perform a given job successfully. It identifies the knowledge, skills, and abilities needed to do the job effectively. So job descriptions identify characteristics of the job, while job specifications identify characteristics of the successful job incumbent.

The job description and specification are important documents for guiding the selection process. The job description can be used to describe the

TABLE 16–1   Popular Job Analysis Methods

1. **Observation Method.** An analyst watches employees directly or reviews films of workers on the job.
2. **Individual Interview Method.** Selected job incumbents are extensively interviewed, and the results of a number of these interviews are combined into a single job analysis.
3. **Group Interview Method.** Same as individual except that a number of job incumbents are interviewed simultaneously.
4. **Structured Questionnaire Method.** Workers check or rate the items they perform in their jobs from a long list of possible task items.
5. **Technical Conference Method.** Specific characteristics of a job are obtained from "experts," who typically are supervisors with extensive knowledge of the job.
6. **Diary Method.** Job incumbents record their daily activities in a diary.

job to potential candidates. The job specification keeps the attention of those doing the selection on the list of qualifications necessary for an incumbent to perform a job and assists in determining whether or not candidates are qualified.

Selection Devices

What do application forms, interviews, employment tests, background checks, and personal letters of recommendation have in common? Each is a device for obtaining information about a job applicant that can help the organization determine whether the applicant's skills, knowledge, and abilities are appropriate for the job in question. In this section, we review the more important of these selection devices—interviews, written tests, and performance simulation tests.

INTERVIEWS   Do you know anyone who has gotten a job without at least one interview? You may have an acquaintance who got a part-time or summer job through a close friend or relative without having to go through an interview, but such instances are rare. There is little doubt that the interview is the most widely used selection device that organizations rely upon to differentiate candidates. It plays a part in over ninety percent of selection decisions.[4]

With a bit less certainty, we can also say that the interview seems to carry a great deal of weight. That is, not only is it widely used, but its results tend to carry a disproportionate amount of influence in the selection decision. The candidate who performs poorly in the employment interview is likely to be cut from the applicant pool, regardless of his or her experience, test scores, or letters of recommendation. Conversely, "all too often, the person most polished in job-seeking techniques, particularly those used in the interview process, is the one hired, even though he or she may not be the best candidate for the position."[5]

These findings are important because, to many people's surprise, the typical loosely-structured interview is a poor selection device for most jobs.[6] Why? Because the data gathered from such interviews are often biased and unrelated to future job performance. Research indicates that prior knowledge about an applicant biases the interviewer's evaluation, that interviewers tend to favor applicants who share their attitudes, that the order in which applicants are interviewed influences evaluations, that negative information is given unduly high weight, and that an applicant's ability to do well in an interview is irrelevant in most jobs.[7] On this last point: What relevance do "good interviewing skills" have for successful performance as a bricklayer, drillpress operator, data-entry operator, or laboratory technician? The answer is: "Little or none!" These jobs don't require this skill. Yet employers typically use the interview as a selection device for such jobs.

The evidence suggests that interviews are good for assessing an applicant's intelligence, level of motivation, and interpersonal skills. Where these qualities are related to job performance, the interview should be a valuable tool. For example, these qualities have demonstrated relevance for performance in upper managerial positions. So the use of the interview in selecting senior executives makes sense. But its use in identifying "good performers" for most lower-level jobs appears questionable.

One factor that can improve the validity of any interview is structuring the content.[8] Unstructured interviews—those without a predetermined set of questions—have too much variability to be effective decision guides. The most valid interviews use a consistent structure and ask applicants questions that require answers giving detailed accounts of actual behaviors they have displayed on the job.

WRITTEN TESTS   Typical written tests include tests of intelligence, aptitude, ability, and interest. Long popular as selection devices, there has been a marked decline in their use since the late 1960s. The reason is that such tests have frequently been characterized as discriminating, and many organizations have not, or cannot, validate such tests as being job related.

Tests in intellectual ability, spatial and mechanical ability, perceptual accuracy, and motor ability have shown to be moderately valid predictors for many semiskilled and unskilled operative jobs in industrial organizations.[9] Intelligence tests are reasonably good predictors for supervisory positions.[10] But the burden is on management to demonstrate that any test used is job related. Since the characteristics that many of these tests tap are considerably removed from the actual performance of the job itself, getting high validity coefficients has often been difficult. The result has been a decreased use of traditional written tests and increased interest in performance simulation tests.

PERFORMANCE SIMULATION TESTS   What better way is there to find out if an applicant can do a job successfully than by having him or her do it? The logic of this question has resulted in increased usage of performance simulation tests. Undoubtedly the enthusiasm for these tests lies in the fact that they are based on job analysis data and, therefore, should more easily meet the requirement of job relatedness than do written tests. Performance simulation tests are made up of actual job behaviors rather than surrogates, as are written tests.

Super Valu, a giant Minneapolis-based food wholesaler, sends hundreds of managers and prospective managers to a one-day assessment center that includes two and a half hours of exercises to measure reasoning, analysis, and problem-solving skills; an hour-and-a-half long "in-basket" exercise—memos that call for immediate action—to flush out decision-making habits, priorities, values, and thoughtfulness; and an interview with a psychologist who sizes up the style and substance of each answer. Super Valu estimates the cost of this test at $950 per candidate.   Courtesy Personnel Decisions, Inc.

Work Sampling Creating a miniature replica of a job to evaluate the performance abilities of job candidates.

The two best known performance simulation tests are work sampling and assessment centers. The former is suited to routine jobs, whereas the latter is relevant for the selection of managerial personnel.

Work sampling is an effort to create a miniature replica of a job. Applicants demonstrate that they possess the necessary talents by actually doing the tasks. By carefully devising work samples based on job analysis data, the knowledge, skills, and abilities needed for each job are determined. Then each work sample element is matched with a corresponding job performance element. For instance, a work sample for a job where the employee has to use computer spreadsheet software would require the applicant to actually solve a problem using a spreadsheet.

The results from work sample experiments are impressive. Studies almost consistently demonstrate that work samples yield validities superior to written aptitude and personality tests.[11]

A more elaborate set of performance simulation tests, specifically designed to evaluate a candidate's managerial potential, is administered in **assessment centers.** In assessment centers, line executives, supervisors, and/or trained psychologists evaluate candidates as they go through two to four days of exercises that simulate real problems that they would confront on the job. Based on a list of descriptive dimensions that the actual job incumbent has to meet, activities might include interviews, inbasket problem-solving exercises, group discussions, and business decision games.

Assessment Centers A set of performance simulation tests designed to evaluate a candidate's managerial potential.

The evidence on the effectiveness of assessment centers is extremely impressive. They have consistently demonstrated results that predict later job performance in managerial positions.[12] Although they are not cheap—AT&T, which has assessed more than 200,000 employees, computes its assessment costs at $800 to $1,500 per employee—the selection of an ineffective manager is unquestionably far more costly.

TRAINING AND DEVELOPMENT PROGRAMS

Competent employees will not remain competent forever. Their skills can deteriorate; technology may make their skills obsolete; the organization may move into new areas, changing the type of jobs that exist and the skills necessary to do them. This reality has not been overlooked by management. It has been estimated, for instance, that United States business firms spend an astounding thirty billion dollars a year on formal courses and training programs to build workers' skills.[14] Of course, managers themselves can and do benefit from skill development efforts. A national survey found that, in a typical year, approximately ten million managers receive an average of about thirty-five hours of skill training.[15]

In this section we'll look at the type of skills that training can improve; then we will review skill training methods, as well as the career development programs that can prepare employees for a future that's different from today.

Skill Categories

We can dissect skills into three categories: technical, interpersonal, and problem solving. Most training activities seek to modify one or more of these skills.

A Challenge for the '90s: Managing Diversity

The make-up of the workforce has undergone, and is continuing to undergo, dramatic changes.[13] The 1950s version of an employee—a white male, with a wife and 2.3 children, who was the sole family breadwinner—is history. The only generalization we can accurately make about the workforce of the 1990s is that you *can't generalize about it!*

The employees of the 1990s come from a wide range of racial and ethnic groups; have diverse sexual preferences; and differ on demographics such as marital status, dependents, and age. Rather than being married white males, they will be female, single males and females with preschool children, physically impaired, black, Asian, Hispanic, gay, lesbian, teens, or octogenarians. A Digital Equipment Corp. plant in Boston provides a partial preview of the future. The factory's 350 employees include men and women from forty-four countries, who speak nineteen languages. When plant management issues written announcements, they are printed in English, Chinese, French, Spanish, Portuguese, Vietnamese, and Haitian Creole.

To grasp the changes that are taking place, consider the following statistics. Over the next decade, women will account for fifty-one percent of United States employment growth, Hispanics fifteen percent, blacks thirteen percent, and Asians and other minorities will represent six percent. By the year 2000, the white, non-Hispanic male will have become the true minority, comprising only thirty-nine percent of the total workforce.

The management of successful organizations will learn how to manage diversity. The reason is that we're entering a period where organizations will face serious labor shortages. Those organizations that fail to attract, train, and promote people who are different will find themselves with a shrinking workforce.

How are organizations managing diversity? They're providing extensive training to make employees more tolerant of language and cultural differences. They're providing programs to increase awareness and to reject racial and sexual prejudices, and to be more accommodating to the physically and mentally impaired. They're offering workshops where employees experience unorthodox styles and different values, and learn that the differences also bring fresh ideas and perspectives that can help business. And they're also expanding childcare and eldercare benefits.

TECHNICAL Most training is directed at upgrading and improving an employee's technical skills. This applies as much to white-collar as to blue-collar jobs. Jobs change as a result of new technologies and improved methods. Postal sorters have had to undergo technical training in order to learn to operate automatic sorting machines. Many auto repair personnel have had to undergo extensive training to fix and maintain recent models with front-wheel-drive trains, electronic ignitions, fuel injection, and other innovations. Not many clerical personnel during the past decade have been unaffected by the computer. Literally millions of such employees have had to be trained to operate and interface with a computer terminal.

INTERPERSONAL Almost all employees belong to a work unit. To some degree, their work performance depends on their ability to effectively interact with their co-workers and their boss. Some employees have excellent interpersonal skills, but others require training to improve theirs. This includes learning how to be a better listener, how to communicate ideas more clearly, and how to reduce conflict.

One employee who had had a history of being difficult to work with found that a three-hour group session in which she and co-workers openly discussed how each perceived the others significantly changed the way she interacted with her peers. Her coworkers were unanimous in describing her as arrogant. They all interpreted her requests as sounding like orders. Once she was made aware of this tendency, she began to make conscious efforts to change the tone and content of her requests, and these changes had very positive results in her relationships with her colleagues.

PROBLEM SOLVING   Managers, as well as many employees who perform nonroutine tasks, have to solve problems on their job. When people require these skills, but are deficient, they can participate in problem-solving training. This would include activities to sharpen their logic, reasoning, and skills at defining problems, assessing causation, developing alternatives, analyzing alternatives, and selecting solutions.

Training Methods

Most training takes place on the job. This can be attributed to the simplicity of such methods and their usually lower cost. However, on-the-job training can disrupt the workplace and result in an increase in errors as learning proceeds. Also, some skill training is too complex to learn on the job. In such cases, it should take place outside the work setting.[16]

ON-THE-JOB TRAINING   Popular on-the-job training methods include job rotation and understudy assignments. *Job rotation* involves lateral transfers that enable employees to work at different jobs. Employees get to learn a wide

These auto body students are participating in an off-the-job training program at a center near Dayton, Ohio. In this exercise, they are learning customer service by simulating a day on the job.   John S. Abbott.

variety of jobs and gain increased insight into the interdependency between jobs and a wider perspective on organizational activities. New employees frequently learn their jobs by understudying a seasoned veteran. In the trades, this is usually called an *apprenticeship*. In white-collar jobs, it is called a *coaching,* or *mentor,* relationship. In each, the understudy works under the observation of an experienced worker, who acts as a model whom the understudy attempts to emulate.

Both job rotation and understudy assignments apply to the learning of technical skills. Interpersonal and problem-solving skills are acquired more effectively by training that takes place off the job.

OFF-THE-JOB TRAINING　　There are a number of off-the-job training methods that managers may want to make available to employees. The more popular are classroom lectures, films, and simulation exercises. *Classroom lectures* are well suited for conveying specific information. They can be used effectively for developing technical and problem-solving skills. *Films* can also be used to explicitly demonstrate technical skills that are not easily presented by other methods. Interpersonal and problem-solving skills may be best learned through *simulation exercises* such as case analyses, experiential exercises, role playing, and group interaction sessions. However, complex computer models, such as those used by airlines in the training of pilots, are another kind of simulation exercise, which in this case is used to teach technical skills. So, too, is *vestibule training,* in which employees learn their jobs on the same equipment they will be using, only the training is conducted away from the actual work floor.

Career Development

Career development is a means by which an organization can sustain or increase its employees' current productivity, while, at the same time, prepare them for a changing world. Effective career development programs can reduce employee turnover and increase productivity.[17] For example, a formal career counseling program in a bank saved $1.95 million in one year, an estimate based on a sixty-five percent reduction in turnover, a twenty-five percent increase in productivity, and a seventy-five percent increase in promotability.[18]

To help you personalize the value of career development, consider the fact that the average corporation loses fifty percent of its college recruits within five years.[19] Apparently, employees' goals, satisfaction, and needs have been incongruent with their company's operating styles and policies, which led to dissatisfaction and eventually the decision to leave. Research tells us that the implementation of career development programs by companies can help to lessen this high turnover rate.

Career A sequence of positions occupied by a person during the course of a lifetime.

Career Stages The four steps most people go through in their careers: exploration, establishment, midcareer, and late career.

CAREER STAGES　　A **career** is a "sequence of positions occupied by a person during the course of a lifetime."[20] This definition does not imply advancement or success or failure. Any work, paid or unpaid, pursued over an extended period of time, can constitute a career. In addition to formal job work, it may include schoolwork, homemaking, or volunteer work.[21]

Careers can be more easily understood if we think of them as proceeding through **stages.**[22] Most of us have or will go through four stages: exploration, establishment, midcareer, and late career.

Exploration begins prior to even entering the work force on a paid basis and ends for most of us in our mid-twenties as we make the transition from school to our primary work interest. It's a time of self-exploration and an assessment of alternatives. The *establishment* stage includes being accepted by our peers, learning the job, and gaining tangible evidence of successes or failures in the "real world." Most people don't face their first severe career dilemmas until they reach the *midcareer* stage, a stage that is typically reached between the ages of thirty-five and fifty. This is a time where one may continue to improve one's performance, level off, or begin to deteriorate. At this stage, the first dilemma is accepting the fact that you're no longer seen as a "learner." Mistakes carry greater penalties. At this point in a career, you are expected to have moved beyond apprenticeship to journeyman status. For those who continue to grow through the midcareer stage, the *late career* usually is a pleasant time when you are allowed the luxury to relax a bit and enjoy playing the part of the elder statesman. For those who have stagnated or deteriorated during the previous stage, the late career brings the reality that they will not have an everlasting impact or change the world as they once thought. It is a time when individuals recognize that they have decreased work mobility and may be locked into their current jobs. They begin to look forward to retirement and the opportunities of doing something different.

If employees are to remain productive, career development and training programs need to be available that can support an employee's task and emotional needs at each stage. Table 16–2 identifies the more important of these needs.

TABLE 16–2   Training Needs within Career Stages

Stage	Task Needs	Emotional Needs
Exploration	1. Varied job activities 2. Self-exploration	1. Make preliminary job choices 2. Settling down
Establishment	1. Job challenge 2. Develop competence in a specialty area 3. Develop creativity and innovation 4. Rotate into new area after three to five years	1. Deal with rivalry and competition; face failures 2. Deal with work/family conflicts 3. Support 4. Autonomy
Midcareer	1. Technical updating 2. Develop skills in training and coaching others (younger employees) 3. Rotation into new job requiring new skills 4. Develop broader view of work and own role in organization	1. Express feelings about midlife 2. Reorganize thinking about self in relation to work, family, community 3. Reduce self-indulgence and competitiveness
Late career	1. Plan for retirement 2. Shift from power role to one of consultation and guidance 3. Identify and develop successors 4. Begin activities outside the organization	1. Support and counseling to see one's work as a platform for others 2. Develop sense of identity in extraorganizational activities

Source: Adapted from D. T. Hall and M. Morgan, "Career Development and Planning," in K. Perlman, F. L. Schmidt, and W. C. Hamner, *Contemporary Problems in Personnel* (3rd ed.). Copyright © 1983 by John Wiley & Sons. Reprinted by permission of John Wiley & Sons.

Career Anchors Distinct patterns of self-perceived talents and abilities, motives and needs, and attitudes and values that guide and stabilize a person's career after several years of real-world experience and feedback.

CAREER ANCHORS   In addition to stages, another concept that can help to understand people in their jobs is that of career anchors.[23]

Just as boats put down anchors to keep them from drifting too far, people put down anchors to stabilize their career decisions and keep them within constraints. **Career anchors,** then, are distinct patterns of self-perceived talents and abilities, motives and needs, and attitudes and values that guide and stabilize a person's career after several years of real-world experience and feedback.

As people reach their late 20s and early 30s, they have to begin making decisions about which jobs to pursue and how to balance personal and work life. To avoid erratic or random decisions, they develop these career anchors. If they sense that a job or job situation will not be consistent with their talents, needs, and values, their anchor pulls them back into situations that are more congruent with their self-image.

Research has identified five specific patterns:

TECHNICAL/FUNCTIONAL COMPETENCE   This anchor focuses on the actual content of a person's work. Someone with an accounting degree and a C.P.A. certificate might find jobs outside of accounting as a challenge to her feelings of competence yet inconsistent with her basic occupational self-concept.

MANAGERIAL COMPETENCE   This anchor emphasizes holding and exercising managerial responsibility. These people seek situations where they can be analytical, utilize their interpersonal skills, and exercise power.

SECURITY   For some people, a key factor in career decision making is work stability. A new position with great opportunities and challenges, but that provides little job security, would be incongruent with this type of people's needs. They prefer job and organizational stability, employment contracts, good employment benefits, attractive pension plans, and the like.

AUTONOMY   The overriding factor for some people in career decisions is to maintain their independence and freedom. They seek to minimize organizational constraints. These people, not surprisingly, prefer small, organic type of organizations in which to work.

CREATIVITY   The last group of people is driven by an overarching desire to create something that is entirely of their own making. For creativity-anchored people, starting a new business, working in a research laboratory, being a major player on a new project's team, or similar activities are important in their assessment of their self-worth.

The career-anchor perspective has both selection and motivational implications. For example, it can help to explain why dramatic changes in career focus are so difficult for people to make. They require great effort and are not likely to occur very frequently. The perspective also helps to explain why individuals may have very different reactions to similar jobs. Any understanding of how job characteristics will affect an individual has to take into consideration the dynamics between the job's task attributes and the career anchors of the person in that job.

EFFECTIVE CAREER DEVELOPMENT PRACTICES   What kind of practices would characterize an organization that understood the value of career development? The following summarizes a few of the more effective practices.

There is an increasing body of evidence indicating that employees who receive especially *challenging job assignments* early in their careers do better on later jobs.[24] More specifically, the degree of stimulation and challenge in a person's initial job assignment tends to be significantly related to later career success and retention in the organization.[25] Apparently, initial challenges, particularly if they are successfully met, stimulate a person to perform well in subsequent years.

To provide information to all employees about job openings, job opportunities should be posted. *Job postings* list key job specification data—abilities, experience, and seniority requirements to qualify for vacancies—and are typically communicated through bulletin board displays or organizational publications.

One of the most logical parts of career development is *career counseling*. An effective program will cover the following issues with employees:

1. The employee's career goals, aspirations, and expectations for five years or longer

2. Opportunities available within the organization and the degree to which the employee's aspirations are realistic and match the opportunities available

3. Identification of what the employee would have to do in the way of further self-development to qualify for new opportunities

4. Identification of the actual next steps in the form of plans for new development activities or new job assignments that would prepare the employee for further career growth[26]

Organizations can offer group *workshops* to facilitate career development. By bringing together groups of employees with their supervisors and managers, problems and misperceptions can be identified and, it is hoped, resolved. These workshops can be general, or they can be designed to deal with problems common to certain groups of employees—new members, minorities, older workers, and so forth.

Periodic job changes can prevent obsolescence and stimulate career growth.[27] The changes can be lateral transfers, vertical promotions, or temporary assignments. The important element in periodic job changes is that they give the employee a variety of experiences that offer diversity and new challenges.

A PERSONAL FOOTNOTE: INDIVIDUAL CAREER DEVELOPMENT   Career development is a two-way street. While students of organizational behavior are concerned with the issue in the interests of improving organizational performance, individuals should be concerned about it for their own self-interest. This personal footnote from your author presents a framework for helping you make your occupational and career choices.

Most young people go at the problem of choosing an occupation backwards. They start by identifying a market or job opportunity and then attempt to assess whether they like it or not. I can't count the number of students I've had who tell me, for instance, that they're majoring in accounting because of the job opportunities in that area. When I ask them if they like accounting work, a number tell me "Not really, but the starting salaries are great!" My experience leads me to conclude that the market-driven job choice often leads to frustration and establishment-stage career changes for people.

You should begin by assessing your basic strengths. Figure out what you do best. What skill or skills do you excel at? Writing, speaking, concentrating,

Lynn Wilson is someone who has taken responsibility for her career development. When she was turned down in the late 1960s for a job in a commercial design firm in Miami, she decided to start her own commercial interior design firm. Today, Lynn Wilson Associates has annual revenues of over $250 million and offices in Tokyo, London, and Paris as well as New York, Los Angeles, and Coral Gables, Florida. Courtesy Lynn Wilson Associates.

interacting with people, organizing things, logical reasoning? (See Table 16–3.) Everyone has something that he or she does better than other things. What's yours? The idea here is to play off your strengths.

Next, determine what it is you like to do. Forget, for a moment, what you're good at and think about what "turns you on." Do you like to talk to people? Be left alone? Participate in sports? Read? Explain things to others? Research subjects? Do something risky?

Now, you should merge what you do *best* with what you *like* to do. If you're a good writer but like to be left alone, maybe your life's work should be as a novelist or researcher. If your strength is writing but you like to interact with people, maybe you should consider journalism. Think about linking jobs with your strengths and preferences. Strong interpersonal skills are needed in management, sales, and a host of other jobs. If you're good at organizing things, management may be right for you—or a career as a library cataloger. If you like sports, coaching is a possibility. If you like to explain things, you'd probably find a great deal of satisfaction in teaching. Keep in mind that the *Dictionary of Occupational Titles,* published by the U.S. federal government, lists over 30,000 job titles!

Once you've got a set of jobs that you think you'd like and also do well at, ask yourself: Where do I want to work? In a large organization? A small firm? For myself? In a major urban center or a rural community?

The final step in a personal career assessment is to evaluate market conditions. Where are the opportunities? It does little good to identify the perfect job if it doesn't exist or if the probability of your getting it is extremely remote. For example, regardless of your predilections, you should think hard nowadays before deciding on a career in the United States military. Not that

TABLE 16–3   Where Does Your Strength Lie?

Analytical skills: Comparing, evaluating, and understanding complex problems or situations

Interpersonal communication skills: Speaking with clarity, clarifying misunderstandings, and listening effectively

Making presentations: Presenting ideas to groups of people with a clear and logical presentation

Writing skills: Writing with clarity and conciseness

Manipulating data and numbers: Processing information and numbers skillfully; handling budgets and statistical reports

Entrepreneurial skills and innovation: Recognizing and seizing opportunities for new ideas or products, creating new services or processes or products

Leading and managing others: Inspiring others, assessing others' abilities, delegating effectively, motivating others to achieve a set of goals

Learning skills: Grasping new information quickly, using common sense to deal with new situations, using feedback effectively

Team membership skills: Working well on committees, incorporating a variety of perspectives toward a common goal

Conflict resolution skills: Dealing with differences, confronting others effectively

Developing, helping, teaching, training others: Encouraging, guiding, and evaluating others; explaining and/or demonstrating new ideas or skills, creating an environment for learning and growth

Source: Adapted from D. Marcic Hai, *Organizational Behavior: Experiences and Cases* (St. Paul, Minn.: West Publishing, 1986), pp. 251–52.

the military can't be challenging and rewarding. It's just that in the 1990s and maybe well into the twenty-first century—with the demise of the Cold War and the reduction in United States military operations worldwide—factors don't favor the military as an occupation. So don't ignore the market. It's a critical variable in your choice of an occupation. However, consider it only as a constraint that you impose after you've considered your strengths and preferences.

One last point: No matter how thorough your career plans, there can be no guarantees. Market demand and your personal preferences change. Just as you might have wanted to be a fire fighter or flight attendant at six but not today, your current choice may not be appealing twenty years from now.

PERFORMANCE EVALUATION

Would you study differently or exert a different level of effort in a college course graded on a pass-fail basis than one where letter grades from A to F are used? When I ask that question of students, I usually get an affirmative answer. Students typically tell me that they study harder when letter grades are at stake. Additionally, they tell me that when they take a course on a pass-fail basis, they tend to do just enough to ensure a passing grade.

This finding illustrates how performance evaluation systems influence behavior. Major determinants of your in-class behavior and out-of-class studying effort in college are the criteria and techniques your instructor uses to evaluate your performance. Of course, what applies in the college context also applies to employees at work. In this section, we'll show how the choice of a performance evaluation system and the way it's administered can be an important force influencing employee behavior.

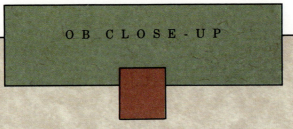

Job Security Is Still Elusive in the United States

The promise of "employment security," not long ago a bright hope for curing America's competitive problems, has faded.[28]

For more than a century, United States employers responded to declining sales and profit margins by laying off people. This tradition came under fire in the early 1980s, as United States management attempted to implement "lifetime job security" as practiced in Japan. The notion was not altruistically motivated. Rather, United States management thought that job security would lead to a workforce that would be committed to quality and productivity.

There are a handful of companies with more than 1,000 employees that have introduced no-layoff policies and stuck with them. These include Delta Airlines, Digital Equipment, Federal Express, IBM, and Xerox. These firms tend to avoid layoffs by first hiring temporary workers to meet unexpected increases in demand or requiring permanent employees to work overtime. If business falls, the temps are fired, and overtime or even regular hours are cut. Work performed by outside contractors are also brought back in-house. If all else fails, surplus production workers are reassigned to sales and maintenance jobs, new product task forces, or training programs.

The trend, however, has been toward reverting to old ways of handling overstaffing. Companies like Bank of America, Chase Manhattan, Eastman Kodak, and Hewlett-Packard have bowed to competitive pressures and dropped their no-layoff policies. In fact, although only about 0.25 percent of all manufacturing concerns in the United States are Japanese-owned, more of them currently operate with no-layoff policies than all the United States-owned companies.

Purposes of Performance Evaluation

Performance evaluation serves a number of purposes in organizations (see Table 16–4 for survey results on primary uses of evaluations).[29] Management uses evaluations for general *personnel decisions*. Evaluations provide input into such important decisions as promotions, transfers, and terminations. Evaluations *identify training and development needs*. They pinpoint employee skills and competencies that are currently inadequate but for which programs can be developed to remedy. Performance evaluations can be used as a *criterion against which selection and development programs are validated*. Newly hired employees who perform poorly can be identified through performance evaluation. Similarly, the effectiveness of training and development programs can be determined by assessing how well those employees who have participated do on their performance evaluation. Evaluations also fulfill the purpose of *providing feedback to employees* on how the organization views their performance. Further, performance evaluations are used as the *basis for reward allocations*. Decisions as to who gets merit pay increases and other rewards are frequently determined by performance evaluations.

Each of these functions of performance evaluation is important. Yet their importance to us depends on the perspective we're taking. Several are clearly relevant to personnel management decisions. But our interest is in organiza-

TABLE 16–4   Primary Uses of Performance Evaluations

Use	Percent[a]
Compensation	85.6
Performance feedback	65.1
Training	64.3
Promotion	45.3
Personnel planning	43.1
Retention/discharge	30.3
Research	17.2

[a]Based on responses from 600 organizations.
Source: Based on "Performance Appraisal: Current Practices and Techniques," *Personnel,* May–June 1984, p. 57.

tional behavior. As a result, we shall be emphasizing performance evaluation in its role as a mechanism for providing feedback and as a determinant of reward allocations.

Performance Evaluation and Motivation

In Chapter 7, considerable attention was given to the expectancy model of motivation. We argued that this model currently offers one of the best explanations of what conditions the amount of effort an individual will exert on his or her job. A vital component of this model is performance, specifically the effort–performance and performance–reward linkages. Do people see effort leading to performance and performance to the rewards that they value? Clearly, they have to know what is expected of them. They need to know how their performance will be measured. Further, they must feel confident that if they exert an effort within their capabilities, it will result in a satisfactory performance as defined by the criteria by which they are being measured. Finally, they must feel confident that if they perform as they are being asked, they will achieve the rewards they value.

In brief, if the objectives that employees are expected to achieve are unclear, if the criteria for measuring those objectives are vague, and if the employees lack confidence that their efforts will lead to a satisfactory appraisal of their performance or believe that there will be an unsatisfactory payoff by the organization when their performance objectives are achieved, we can expect individuals to work considerably below their potential.

What Do We Evaluate?

The criteria or criterion that management chooses to evaluate, when appraising employee performance, will have a major influence on what employees do. Two examples illustrate this:

In a public employment agency, which served workers seeking employment and employers seeking workers, employment interviewers were appraised by the number of interviews they conducted. Consistent with the thesis that the evaluating criteria influence behavior, interviewers emphasized the *number* of interviews conducted rather than the *placements* of clients in jobs.[30]

A management consultant specializing in police research noticed that, in one community, officers would come on duty for their shift, proceed to get into their police cars, drive to the highway that cut through the town, and speed back and forth along this highway for their entire shift. Clearly this fast cruising had little to do with good police work, but this behavior made considerably more sense once the consultant learned that the community's City Council used mileage on police vehicles as an evaluative measure of police effectiveness.[31]

These examples demonstrate the importance of criteria in performance evaluation. This, of course, begs the question: What should management evaluate? The three most popular sets of criteria are individual task outcomes, behaviors, and traits.

INDIVIDUAL TASK OUTCOMES If ends count, rather than means, then management should evaluate an employee's task outcomes. Using task outcomes, a plant manager could be judged on criteria such as quantity produced, scrap generated, and cost per unit of production. Similarly, a salesperson could be assessed on overall sales volume in his or her territory, dollar increase in sales, and number of new accounts established.

BEHAVIORS In many cases, it's difficult to identify specific outcomes that can be directly attributable to an employee's actions. This is particularly true of personnel in staff positions and individuals whose work assignments are intrinsically part of a group effort. In the latter case, the group's performance may be readily evaluated, but the contribution of each group member may be difficult or impossible to identify clearly. In such instances, it is not unusual for management to evaluate the employee's behavior. Using the previous examples, behaviors of a plant manager that could be used for performance evaluation purposes might include promptness in submitting his or her monthly reports or the leadership style that the manager exhibits. Pertinent salesperson behaviors could be average number of contact calls made per day or sick days used per year.

TRAITS The weakest set of criteria, yet one that is still widely used by organizations, is individual traits. We say they are weaker than either task outcomes or behaviors because they are farthest removed from the actual performance of the job itself. Traits such as having "a good attitude," showing "confidence," being "intelligent" or "friendly," "looking busy," or possessing "a wealth of experience" may or may not be highly correlated with positive task outcomes, but only the naive would ignore the reality that such traits are frequently used in organizations as criteria for assessing an employee's level of performance.

Methods of Performance Evaluation

The previous section explained *what* we evaluate. Now we ask: *How* do we evaluate an employee's performance? That is, what are the specific techniques for evaluation? The following reviews the major performance evaluation methods.

WRITTEN ESSAYS   Probably the simplest method of evaluation is to write a narrative describing an employee's strengths, weaknesses, past performance, potential, and suggestions for improvement. The written essay requires no complex forms or extensive training to complete. But the results often reflect the ability of the writer. A good or bad appraisal may be determined as much by the evaluator's writing skill as by the employee's actual level of performance.

Critical Incidents Evaluating those behaviors that are key in making the difference between executing a job effectively or ineffectively.

CRITICAL INCIDENTS   **Critical incidents** focus the evaluator's attention on those behaviors that are key in making the difference between executing a job effectively or ineffectively. That is, the appraiser writes down anecdotes that describe what the employee did that was especially effective or ineffective. The key here is that only specific behaviors, and not vaguely defined personality traits, are cited. A list of critical incidents provides a rich set of examples from which the employee can be shown those behaviors that are desirable and those that call for improvement.

Graphic Rating Scales An evaluation method where the evaluator rates performance factors on an incremental scale.

GRAPHIC RATING SCALES   One of the oldest and most popular methods of evaluation is the use of **graphic rating scales.** In this method, a set of performance factors, such as quantity and quality of work, depth of knowledge, cooperation, loyalty, attendance, honesty, and initiative, are listed. The evaluator then goes down the list and rates each on incremental scales. The scales typically specify five points, so a factor like *job knowledge* might be rated 1 ("poorly informed about work duties") to 5 ("has complete mastery of all phases of the job").

Why are graphic ratings scales so popular? Though they don't provide the depth of information that essays or critical incidents do, they are less time-consuming to develop and administer. They also allow for quantitative analysis and comparison.

Behaviorally Anchored Rating Scales An evaluation method where actual job related behaviors are rated along a continuum.

BEHAVIORALLY ANCHORED RATING SCALES   Behaviorally anchored rating scales have received a great deal of attention in recent years.[32] These scales combine major elements from the critical incident and graphic rating scale approaches: The appraiser rates the employees based on items along a continuum, but the points are examples of actual behavior on the given job rather than general description or traits.

Behaviorally anchored rating scales specify definite, observable, and measurable job behavior. Examples of job-related behavior and performance dimensions are found by asking participants to give specific illustrations of effective and ineffective behavior regarding each performance dimension. These behavioral examples are then translated into a set of performance dimensions, each dimension having varying levels of performance. The results of this process are behavioral descriptions, such as anticipates, plans, executes, solves immediate problems, carries out orders, and handles emergency situations.

Group Order Ranking An evaluation method that places employees into particular classifications such as quartiles.

MULTIPERSON COMPARISONS   Multiperson comparisons evaluate one individual's performance against one or more others. It is a relative rather than an absolute measuring device. The three most popular comparisons are group order ranking, individual ranking, and paired comparisons.

The **group order ranking** requires the evaluator to place employees into a particular classification, such as top one-fifth or second one-fifth. This method is often used in recommending students to graduate schools. Evaluators are asked to rank the student in the top five percent, the next five percent, the next fifteen percent, and so forth. But when used by managers to appraise employees, managers deal with all their subordinates. Therefore, if a rater has twenty subordinates, only four can be in the top fifth and, of course, four must also be relegated to the bottom fifth.

Individual Ranking An evaluation method that rank-orders employees from best to worst.

The **individual ranking** approach rank orders employees from best to worst. If the manager is required to appraise thirty subordinates, this approach assumes that the difference between the first and second employee is the same as that between the twenty-first and twenty-second. Even though some of the employees may be closely grouped, this approach allows for no ties. The result is a clean ordering of employees, from the highest performer down to the lowest.

Paired Comparison An evaluation method that compares each employee with every other employee and assigns a summary ranking based on the number of superior scores that the employee achieves.

The **paired comparison** approach compares each employee with every other employee and rates each as either the superior or the weaker member of the pair. After all paired comparisons are made, each employee is assigned a summary ranking based on the number of superior scores he or she achieved. This approach ensures that each employee is compared against every other, but it can obviously become unwieldly when many employees are being compared.

Multiperson comparisons can be combined with one of the other methods to blend the best from both absolute and relative standards. For example, a college might use the graphic rating scale and the individual ranking method to provide more accurate information about its students' performance. The student's relative rank in the class could be noted next to an absolute grade of A, B, C, D, or F. A prospective employer or graduate school could then look at two students who each got a "B" in their different financial accounting courses and draw considerably different conclusions about each where next to one grade it says "ranked fourth out of twenty-six," while the other says "ranked seventeenth out of thirty." Obviously, the latter instructor gives out a lot more high grades!

Potential Problems

While organizations may seek to make the performance evaluation process free from personal biases, prejudices, or idiosyncracies, a number of potential problems can creep into the process. To the degree that the following factors are prevalent, an employee's evaluation is likely to be distorted.

SINGLE CRITERION   The typical employee's job is made up of a number of tasks. An airline flight attendant's job, for example, includes welcoming passengers, seeing to their comfort, serving meals, and offering safety advice. If performance on this job were assessed by a single criterion measure—say the time it took to provide food and beverages to a hundred passengers—the result would be limited evaluation of that job. More important, flight attendants whose performance evaluation included assessment on only this single criterion would be motivated to ignore those other tasks in their job. Similarly, if a football quarterback were appraised only on his percentage of completed passes, he would be likely to throw short passes and only in situations where he felt assured that they will be caught. Our point is that where employees are evaluated on a single job criterion, and where successful performance on that job requires good performance on a number of criteria, employees will emphasize the single criterion to the exclusion of other job-relevant factors.

Leniency Error The tendency to evaluate a set of employees too high (positive) or too low (negative).

LENIENCY ERROR   Every evaluator has his or her own value system that acts as a standard against which appraisals are made. Relative to the true or actual performance an individual exhibits, some evaluators mark high and others low. The former is referred to as positive **leniency error,** and the latter as negative leniency error. When evaluators are positively lenient in their appraisal, an individual's performance becomes overstated, that is, rated higher than it actually should be. Similarly, a negative leniency error understates performance, giving the individual a lower appraisal.

If all individuals in an organization were appraised by the same person, there would be no problem. Although there would be an error factor, it would be applied equally to everyone. The difficulty arises when we have different raters with different leniency errors making judgments. For example, assume that Jones and Smith are performing the same job for different supervisors, but they have absolutely identical job performance. If Jones' supervisor tends to err toward positive leniency, while Smith's supervisor errs toward negative leniency, we might be confronted with two dramatically different evaluations.

HALO ERROR   The halo effect or error, as we noted in Chapter 5, is the tendency for an evaluator to let the assessment of an individual on one trait influence his or her evaluation of that person on other traits. For example, if an employee tends to be dependable, we might become biased toward that individual to the extent that we will rate him or her high on many desirable attributes.

People who design teaching appraisal forms for college students to fill out to evaluate the effectiveness of their instructor each semester must confront the halo effect. Students tend to rate a faculty member as outstanding on all criteria when they are particularly appreciative of a few things he or she does in the classroom. Similarly, a few bad habits—like showing up late for lectures, for example, or being slow in returning papers, or assigning an extremely demanding reading requirement—might result in students' evaluating the instructor as "lousy" across the board.

Similarity Error Giving special consideration when rating others to those qualities that the evaluator perceives in himself or herself.

SIMILARITY ERROR   When evaluators rate other people giving special consideration to those qualities that they perceive in themselves, they are making a **similarity error.** For example, the evaluator who perceives himself as aggressive may evaluate others by looking for aggressiveness. Those who demonstrate this characteristic tend to benefit, while others are penalized.

Again, this error would tend to wash out if the same evaluator appraised all the people in the organization. However, interrater reliability obviously suffers when various evaluators are utilizing their own similarity criteria.

LOW DIFFERENTIATION   It is possible that, regardless of whom the appraiser evaluates and what traits are used, the pattern of evaluation remains the same. It is possible that the evaluator's ability to appraise objectively and accurately has been impeded by social differentiation, that is, the evaluator's style of rating behavior.

It has been suggested that evaluators may be classified as (1) high differentiators, who use all or most of the scale, or (2) low differentiators, who use a limited range of the scale.[34]

Low differentiators tend to ignore or suppress differences, perceiving the universe as being more uniform than it really is. High differentiators, on the other hand, tend to utilize all available information to the utmost extent and thus are better able to perceptually define anomalies and contradictions than are low differentiators.[35]

Does Physical Attractiveness Affect Performance Evaluations?

A research study examined whether a person's physical attractiveness affected his or her performance evaluation.[33] The results are interesting, although a bit disturbing.

Thirty-four graduate business students received a set of four relatively equivalent performance review forms that presented information varying according to the job, sex, and appearance of the employee being evaluated. The students were asked to evaluate present performance, predict future success, and indicate the appropriateness of various personnel actions.

The results showed that attractiveness was advantageous for women in nonmanagerial positions and disadvantageous for women in managerial ones. But appearance had no effect whatsoever on evaluations of men. Apparently, the student evaluators believed that attractiveness enhanced the perceived femininity of females but did not enhance the perceived masculinity of the males. Moreover, the students may be assuming that femininity is inconsistent with managerial effectiveness. We described these findings as disturbing because they illustrate the possibility that sexual stereotypes may cloud an appraiser's judgment and result in biased evaluations.

This finding tells us that evaluations made by low differentiators need to be carefully inspected and that the people working for a low differentiator have a high probability of being appraised as being significantly more homogeneous than they really are.

FORCING INFORMATION TO MATCH NONPERFORMANCE CRITERIA While rarely advocated, it is not an infrequent practice to find the formal evaluation taking place *following* the decision as to how the individual has been performing. This may sound illogical, but it merely recognizes that subjective, yet formal, decisions are often arrived at prior to the gathering of objective information to support that decision. For example, if the evaluator believes that the evaluation should not be based on performance, but rather seniority, he or she may be unknowingly adjusting each "performance" evaluation so as to bring it into line with the employee's seniority rank. In this and other similar cases, the evaluator is increasing or decreasing performance appraisals to align with the nonperformance criteria actually being utilized.

Overcoming the Problems

That organizations can encounter problems with performance evaluations should not lead managers to give up on the process. Some things can be done to overcome most of the problems we have identified.[36]

USE MULTIPLE CRITERIA Since successful performance on most jobs requires doing a number of things well, all those "things" should be identified and evaluated. The more complex the job, the more criteria that will need to be identified and evaluated. But everything need not be assessed. The critical activities that lead to high or low performance are the ones that need to be evaluated.

DEEMPHASIZE TRAITS   Many traits often considered to be related to good performance may, in fact, have little or no performance relationship. For example, traits like loyalty, initiative, courage, reliability, and self-expression are intuitively appealing as desirable characteristics in employees. But the relevant question is: Are individuals who are evaluated as high on those traits higher performers than those who rate low? We can't answer this question. We know that there are employees who rate high on these characteristics and are poor performers. We can find others who are excellent performers but do not score well on traits such as these. Our conclusion is that traits like loyalty and initiative may be prized by managers, but there is no evidence to support that certain traits will be adequate synonyms for performance in a large cross section of jobs.

Another weakness in traits is the judgment itself. What is "loyalty"? When is an employee "reliable"? What you consider "loyalty," I may not. So traits suffer from weak interrater agreement.

USE MULTIPLE EVALUATORS   As the number of evaluators increases, the probability of attaining more accurate information increases. If rater error tends to follow a normal curve, an increase in the number of appraisers will tend to find the majority congregating about the middle. You see this approach being used in athletic competitions in such sports as diving and gymnastics. A multiple set of evaluators judges a performance, the highest and lowest scores are dropped, and the final performance evaluation is made up from the cumulative scores of those remaining. The logic of multiple evaluators applies to organizations as well.

If an employee has had ten supervisors, nine having rated her excellent and one poor, we can discount the value of the one poor evaluation. Therefore, by moving employees about within the organization so as to gain a number of evaluations, we increase the probability of achieving more valid and reliable evaluations.

The United States Army has made good use of this technique. For individuals who have been evaluated by ten or fifteen officers during their first five or six years in the service, there is less chance that one or two "slanted" evaluations will seriously influence decisions made on the basis of these performance appraisals.

EVALUATE SELECTIVELY   It has been suggested that appraisers should evaluate in only those areas in which they have some expertise.[37] If raters make evaluations on *only* those dimensions on which they are in a good position to rate, we increase the interrater agreement and make the evaluation a more valid process. This approach also recognizes that different organizational levels often have different orientations toward ratees and observe them in different settings. In general, therefore, we would recommend that appraisers should be as close as possible, in terms of organizational level, to the individual being evaluated. Conversely, the more levels that separate the evaluator and evaluatee, the less opportunity the evaluator has to observe the individual's behavior and, not surprisingly, the greater the possibility for inaccuracies.

club is not available to all middle- and upper-level executives, but only to those who have shown particular performance ratings, then it is a motivating reward. Similarly, if company-owned automobiles and aircraft are made available to certain employees based on their performance rather than their "entitlement," we should view these indirect compensations as motivating rewards for those who might deem these forms of compensation as attractive.

As with direct compensation, indirect compensation may be viewed in an individual, group, or organizational context. However, if rewards are to be linked closely with performance, we should expect individual rewards to be emphasized. On the other hand, if a certain group of managers within the organization has made a significant contribution to the effective performance of the organization, a blanket reward such as a membership in a social club might be appropriate. Again, it is important to note that since rewards achieve the greatest return when they are specifically designed to meet the needs of each individual, and since group and organizational rewards tend to deal in homogeneity—that is, they tend to treat all people alike—these types of rewards must, by definition, be somewhat less effective than individual rewards. The only exceptions to that statement are those instances where there is a high need for cohesiveness and group congeniality. In such instances, individuals may find group rewards more personally satisfying than individual rewards.

The classification of nonfinancial rewards tends to be a smorgasbord of desirable "things" that are potentially at the disposal of the organization. The creation of nonfinancial rewards is limited only by managers' ingenuity and ability to assess "payoffs" that individuals with the organization find desirable and that are within the managers' discretion.

The old saying "One man's food is another man's poison" certainly applies to rewards. What one employee views as highly desirable, another finds superfluous. Therefore *any* reward may not get the desired result; however, where selection has been done assiduously, the benefits to the organization by way of higher worker performance should be impressive.

Some workers are very status conscious. A paneled office, a carpeted

An increasingly popular status symbol today is the cellular telephone. This manager, working at a site overlooking London's St. Paul Cathedral, uses his phone to keep in touch with headquarters.   Barry Lewis— Network/Contact.

floor, a large walnut desk, or a private bathroom may be just the office furnishing that stimulates an employee toward top performance. Status-oriented employees may also value an impressive job title, their own business cards, their own secretary, or a well-located parking space with their name clearly painted underneath the "Reserved" sign.

Some employees value having their lunch at, say, 1 P.M. to 2 P.M. If lunch is normally from 11 A.M. to 12 noon, the benefit of being able to take their lunch at another, more desirable time can be viewed as a reward. Having a chance to work with congenial colleagues or achieving a desired work assignment or an assignment where the worker can operate without close supervision are all rewards that are within the discretion of management and, when carefully aligned to individual needs, can provide stimulus for improved performance.

THE UNION–MANAGEMENT INTERFACE

Labor Unions An organization, made up of employees, that acts collectively to protect and promote employee interests.

Labor unions are a vehicle by which employees act collectively to protect and promote their interests. Currently, in the United States, approximately sixteen percent of the work force belongs to and is represented by a union. For this segment of the labor force, wage levels and conditions of employment are explicitly articulated in a contract that is negotiated, through collective bargaining, between representatives of the union and the organization's management. But the impact of unions on employees is broader than their sixteen percent representation figure might imply. This is because nonunionized employees benefit from the gains that unions make. There is a spillover effect so that the wages, benefits, and working conditions provided nonunionized employees tend to mirror—with some time lag—those negotiated for union members.

Labor unions influence a number of organizational activities.[43] Recruitment sources, hiring criteria, work schedules, job design, redress procedures, safety rules, and eligibility for training programs are examples of activities that are influenced by unions. The most obvious and pervasive area of influence, of course, is wage rates and working conditions. Where unions exist, performance evaluation systems tend to be less complex because they play a relatively small part in reward decisions. Wage rates, when determined through collective bargaining, emphasize seniority and downplay performance differences.

Figure 16–2 shows what impact a union has on an employee's performance and job satisfaction. The union contract affects motivation through determination of wage rates, seniority rules, layoff procedures, promotion criteria, and security provisions. Unions can influence the competence with which employees perform their jobs by offering special training programs to their members, by requiring apprenticeships, and by allowing members to gain leadership experience through union organizational activities. The actual level of employee performance will be further influenced by collective bargaining restrictions placed on the amount of work produced, the speed with which work can be done, overtime allowances per worker, or the kind of tasks a given employee is allowed to perform.

Are union members more satisfied with their jobs than their nonunion counterparts? The answer to this question is more complicated than a simple "Yes" or "No." The evidence consistently demonstrates that unions have only

Training and Development Programs

Training programs can affect work behavior in two ways. The most obvious is by directly improving the skills necessary for the employee to successfully complete his or her job. An increase in ability improves the employee's potential to perform at a higher level. Of course, whether that potential becomes realized is largely an issue of motivation.

A second benefit from training is that it increases an employee's self-efficacy. **Self-efficacy** is a person's expectation that he or she can successfully execute the behaviors required to produce an outcome.[45] For employees, those behaviors are work tasks and the outcome is effective job performance. Employees with high self-efficacy have strong expectations about their abilities to perform successfully in new situations. They're confident and expect to be successful. Training, then, is a means to positively affect self-efficacy. In so doing, employees may be more willing to undertake job tasks and exert a high level of effort. Or in expectancy terms (see Chapter 7), individuals are more likely to perceive their effort as leading to performance.

We also discussed career development programs in this chapter. Organizations that provide formal career development activities and match them to needs that employees experience at various stages in their careers reduce the likelihood that productivity will decrease as a result of obsolescence or that job frustrations will create reduced satisfaction.[46]

In today's job environment—with cutbacks, increasingly wider spans of control, and reduced promotion opportunities—employees will increasingly confront the reality of career plateauing. Out of frustration, employees may look for other jobs. Organizations that have well-designed career programs will have employees with more realistic expectations and career tracking systems that will lessen the chance that good employees will leave because of inadequate opportunities.

Performance Evaluation

A major goal of performance evaluation is to assess accurately an individual's performance contribution as a basis for making reward allocation decisions. If the performance evaluation process emphasizes the wrong criteria or inaccurately appraises actual job performance, employees will be over- or underrewarded. As equity theory demonstrated in Chapter 7, this can lead to negative consequences such as reduced effort, increases in absenteeism, or search for alternative job opportunities.

Reward Systems

If employees perceive that their efforts will be accurately appraised, and if they further perceive that the rewards they value are closely linked to their evaluations, the organization will have optimized the motivational properties from its evaluation and reward procedures and policies. More specifically, based on the contents of this chapter and our discussion of motivation in Chapters 7 and 8, we can conclude that rewards are likely to lead to high employee performance and satisfaction when they are (1) perceived as being equitable by the employee, (2) tied to performance, and (3) tailored to the

Self-Efficacy A person's expectation that he or she can successfully execute behaviors required to produce an outcome.

needs of the individual. These conditions should foster a minimum of dissatisfaction among employees, reduce withdrawal patterns, and increase organizational commitment. If these conditions do not exist, the probability of
withdrawal behavior increases, and the prevalence of marginal or barely
adequate performance increases. If workers perceive that their efforts are not
recognized or rewarded, and if they view their alternatives as limited, they
may continue working, but perform at a level considerably below their
capability.

Employee benefits like flexible workhours, paternity leaves, and day care
centers may be most relevant for the impact they have on reducing absenteeism and improving job satisfaction. These rewards reduce barriers that many
employees—particularly those with significant responsibilities outside the
job—find get in the way of being at work on time or even making it to work at
all. To the degree that these benefits lessen an employee's worries over outside
responsibilities, they may increase satisfaction with the job and the organization.

Union–Management Interface

The existence of a union in an organization adds another variable in our
search to explain and predict employee behavior. The union has been found to
be an important contributor to employees' perceptions, attitudes, and behavior.

The power of the union surfaces in the collective bargaining agreement
that it negotiates with the organization's management. Much of what an
employee can and cannot do on the job is formally stipulated in this
agreement. In addition, the informal norms that union cohesiveness fosters
can encourage or discourage high productivity, organizational commitment,
and morale.

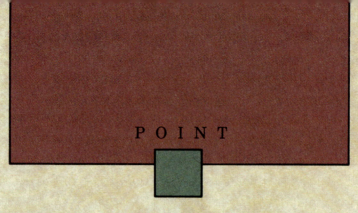

College Students Shouldn't Be Asked to Grade Their Teachers

The evaluation of teacher performance by students is now a fixture of campus life. The results have become an important factor in faculty promotion and retention decisions. In practice, this translates into faculty members with higher student evaluation scores receiving more favorable consideration.

Treating student evaluations as though they were a straightforward measure of good teaching invites abuse. Most important, it fails to recognize the applicability of the "journeyman principle" to college faculty members. This principle acknowledges that those who wish to be practitioners of a skilled trade or profession must undergo rigorous training. Those who complete the training are known as journeymen and are assumed competent to perform satisfactorily the range of tasks ordinarily required. They are not required to prove competence, since journeymen status itself attests to such competence. It is the judgment of incompetence that is made on the basis of special evidence.

Use of this principle would result in a radically different approach to the evaluation of good teaching: It would no longer be important to obtain a fine measurement of the teaching performance of every faculty member. Small distinctions among the ranks of the competent would cease to be important, because they are insignificant with respect to the work. For example, any journeyman plumber can fix your sink, any competent pediatrician can diagnose a child's ear infection, and any competent mathematician can teach calculus. Following the journeyman principle, attention would be focused on identifying those at the extremes. It is important to detect the incompetent—those who cannot be trusted to perform the ordinary tasks properly. It is equally important to detect the exceptional—those who can handle the extraordinary tasks.

Do college faculty members fit the definition of journeyman? There are several reasons to suggest they do. Members of a college faculty have usually successfully completed some amount of graduate training, which may be taken to certify a certain high level of intellectual competence and mastery of subject matter. The ability to present material in a clear and organized fashion is generally a prerequisite for successfully completing a graduate degree. There is, additionally, the process of self-selection: Those who dislike teaching, or feel inarticulate or uncomfortable addressing groups, tend to avoid choosing teaching as a profession.

We may fairly conclude that college faculty members are intelligent, know their subject matter, express themselves reasonably well, and care about teaching. They are a highly selected sample who are, with a few exceptions, clustered at the upper end of the competence continuum. The current idea that it is important to evaluate the teaching performance of every faculty member so as to obtain proof of competence seems to derive from the contrary notion that college teachers are uniformly distributed over the whole continuum of competence.

Adapted from M. J. Rodin, "By a Faculty Member's Yardstick, Student Evaluations Don't Measure Up," *Chronicle of Higher Education,* May 3, 1982, p. 63.

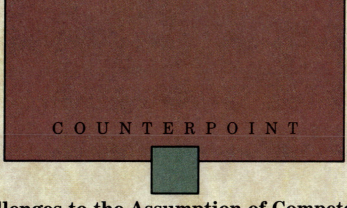

COUNTERPOINT

Challenges to the Assumption of Competence

The journeyman principle is thought-provoking, but it is vulnerable on at least four points: (1) Teaching students is not like fixing a leaking sink; (2) most college teachers' apprenticeships don't emphasize teaching skills; (3) competence, even if demonstrated at one point in time, need not hold constant for an indefinite time period; and (4) the overt evidence that there is a good deal of bad teaching out there can't be ignored.

Teaching is not a routine task in the way sink repair may be considered routine. Every student is different. A standardized approach isn't likely to succeed in meeting the various learning styles and needs of students.

The successful completion of a graduate degree program is no assurance that a teacher can teach. Graduate study emphasizes research. Most graduate students are not required to teach in order to obtain their degree, and those who do so are evaluated infrequently, if at all. Sure, subject matter competence is needed to complete a graduate degree, but knowledge of a subject is no assurance that one can teach that material.

Even if we assumed that all faculty members were competent teachers at the time they were hired, why should we believe that competence will remain a constant over a teaching career? In many fields, subject matter is rapidly made obsolete and displaced. The knowledge held by the teacher of information processing in 1971 would be totally inadequate in 1991. And teaching ability can change over time. Changes in college administrative policy, salary levels, and colleagues can alter the teacher's motivation. The faculty member's interests may also change over his or her career. Thirty years or more of tenure-protected job security (a luxury not offered those in the plumbing profession) can further act to deter a faculty member's motivation to keep up in his or her field or put in the extra effort to make classroom lectures interesting.

Finally, you can't ignore the reality that college teachers *aren't* "clustered at the upper end of the competence continuum." College teachers, like most populations on most competence scales, tend to be distributed along a bell-shaped curve. Some are excellent and some are poor, with most centered around the median. Without student evaluation information, faculty members are deprived of the kind of feedback that is necessary to assess their strengths and weaknesses and work toward reducing those weaknesses.

College faculty, in spite of superior academic qualifications, are not beyond evaluation. To follow the journeyman analogy would suggest, for instance, that a bridge should never be inspected since both the contractor who built it and the architects and engineers who designed it have met the journeyman requirement. The journeyman principle assumes that all teachers are competent when they enter the profession and that that competence is maintained throughout one's teaching career. These assumptions just are not valid.

Ideas expressed here were influenced by "Letters to the Editor," *Chronicle of Higher Education*, June 2, 1982, p. 25.

1. What is job analysis? How is it related to those the organization hires?

2. If you were a dean of a college of business, how would you determine which job candidates would be effective teachers?

3. Describe several *on-the-job* training methods and several *off-the-job* methods.

4. What would an effective career development program look like?

5. What effect do career anchors have on employee behavior?

6. If you were a dean of a college of business, how would you evaluate the performance of your faculty members?

7. What relationship, if any, is there between job analysis and performance evaluation?

8. Why do organizations evaluate employees?

9. What are the advantages and disadvantages of the following performance evaluation methods: (1) written essays, (b) graphic rating scales, and (c) behaviorally anchored rating scales?

10. How can an organization's performance evaluation system affect employee behavior?

11. Some organizations have a personnel policy that pay information be kept secret. Not only is pay information not given out by management but employees are also discouraged from talking about their pay with co-workers. How do you think this practice affects employee behavior?

12. What impact do unions have on an organization's reward system?

FOR FURTHER READING

DESHPANDE, S. P., and J. FIORITO, "Specific and General Beliefs in Union Voting Models," *Academy of Management Journal,* December 1989, pp. 883–97. Survey data revealed that roughly three-fourths of nonunion employees view unions as effective in improving wages and working conditions, yet only about one-third would vote for unionization of their workplace. This article explains why.

FELDMAN, D. C., "Careers in Organizations: Recent Trends and Future Directions," *Journal of Management,* June 1989, pp. 135–56. Explores some of the important trends in the study of careers in organizations during the 1980s.

GUION, R. M., and W. M. GIBSON, "Personnel Selection and Placement," in M. R. Rosenzweig and L. W. Porter (eds.), *Annual Review of Psychology,* Vol. 39. Palo Alto, Calif.: Annual Reviews Inc., 1988, pp. 349–74. Presents an extensive review of the recent literature on selection procedures and predictors.

KERR, J. L., and E. F. JACKOFSKY, "Aligning Managers With Strategies: Management Development Versus Selection," *Strategic Management Journal,* Summer 1989, pp. 157–70. Recent research has stressed the importance of matching managerial talent with organizational strategy. Most have argued for the use of selection to "fit" the manager to the strategy. This article proposes the use of management development as an alternate means of achieving manager–strategy alignment.

LATHAM, G. P., "Human Resource Training and Development," in M. R. Rosenzweig and L. W. Porter (eds.), *Annual Review of Psychology,* Vol. 39. Palo Alto, Calif.: Annual Reviews Inc., 1988, pp. 545–82. Reviews recent findings related to identifying training needs, training of raters, evaluating training programs, training in other cultures, leadership training, and maximizing trainee learning.

NEVELS, P., "Why Employees Are Being Asked to Rate Their Supervisors," *Supervisory Management,* December 1989, pp. 5–11. Traditional top-down evaluations are being supplemented by new bottom-up evaluations. This article reviews why this is being done and the potential problems it might create.

Career Assessment Test

Complete the following questionnaire by circling the answer that best describes your feelings about each statement. For each item, circle your response according to the following:

SA = Strongly Agree, A = Agree, D = Disagree, SD = Strongly Disagree.

1. I would leave my company rather than be promoted out of my area of expertise.	SA	A	D	SD
2. Becoming highly specialized and highly competent in some specific functional or technical area is important to me.	SA	A	D	SD
3. A career that is free from organization restriction is important to me.	SA	A	D	SD
4. I have always sought a career in which I could be of service to others.	SA	A	D	SD
5. A career that provides a maximum variety of types of assignments and work projects is important to me.	SA	A	D	SD
6. To rise to a position in general management is important to me.	SA	A	D	SD
7. I like to be identified with a particular organization and the prestige that accompanies that organization.	SA	A	D	SD
8. Remaining in my present geographical location rather than moving because of a promotion is important to me.	SA	A	D	SD
9. The use of my skills in building a new business enterprise is important to me.	SA	A	D	SD
10. I would like to reach a level of responsibility in an organization where my decisions really make a difference.	SA	A	D	SD
11. I see myself more as a generalist as opposed to being committed to one specific area of expertise.	SA	A	D	SD
12. An endless variety of challenges in my career is important to me.	SA	A	D	SD
13. Being identified with a powerful or prestigious employer is important to me.	SA	A	D	SD
14. The excitement of participating in many areas of work has been the underlying motivation behind my career.	SA	A	D	SD
15. The process of supervising, influencing, leading, and controlling people at all levels is important to me.	SA	A	D	SD
16. I am willing to sacrifice some of my autonomy to stabilize my total life situation.	SA	A	D	SD
17. An organization that will provide security through guaranteed work, benefits, a good retirement, and so forth, is important to me.	SA	A	D	SD
18. During my career I will be mainly concerned with my own sense of freedom and autonomy.	SA	A	D	SD
19. I will be motivated throughout my career by the number of products that I have been directly involved in creating.	SA	A	D	SD
20. I want others to identify me by my organization and job.	SA	A	D	SD

21. Being able to use my skills and talents in the service of an important cause is important to me.   SA   A   D   SD

22. To be recognized by my title and status is important to me.   SA   A   D   SD

23. A career that permits a maximum of freedom and autonomy to choose my own work, hours, and so forth, is important to me.   SA   A   D   SD

24. A career that gives me a great deal of flexibility is important to me.   SA   A   D   SD

25. To be in a position in general management is important to me.   SA   A   D   SD

26. It is important for me to be identified by my occupation.   SA   A   D   SD

27. I will accept a management position only if it is in my area of expertise.   SA   A   D   SD

28. It is important for me to remain in my present geographical location rather than move because of a promotion or new job assignment.   SA   A   D   SD

29. I would like to accumulate a personal fortune to prove to myself and others that I am competent.   SA   A   D   SD

30. I want to achieve a position that gives me the opportunity to combine analytical competence with supervision of people.   SA   A   D   SD

31. I have been motivated throughout my career by using my talents in a variety of different areas of work.   SA   A   D   SD

32. An endless variety of challenges is what I really want from my career.   SA   A   D   SD

33. An organization that will give me long-run stability is important to me.   SA   A   D   SD

34. To be able to create or build something that is entirely my own product or idea is important to me.   SA   A   D   SD

35. Remaining in my specialized area, as opposed to being promoted out of my area of expertise, is important to me.   SA   A   D   SD

36. I do not want to be constrained by either an organization or the business world.   SA   A   D   SD

37. Seeing others change because of my efforts is important to me.   SA   A   D   SD

38. My main concern in life is to be competent in my area of expertise.   SA   A   D   SD

39. The chance to pursue my own life-style and not be constrained by the rules of an organization is important to me.   SA   A   D   SD

40. I find most organizations to be restrictive and intrusive.   SA   A   D   SD

41. Remaining in my area of expertise, rather than being promoted into general management, is important to me.   SA   A   D   SD

42. I want a career that allows me to meet my basic needs through helping others.   SA   A   D   SD

43. The use of my interpersonal and helping skills in the service of others is important to me.   SA   A   D   SD

44. I like to see others change because of my efforts.   SA   A   D   SD

Turn to page 691 for scoring direction and key.

Adapted, by permission of the publisher, from "Reexamining the Career Anchor Model", by T. J. Delong, *PERSONNEL*, May–June 1982, pp. 56–57. © 1982 AMACOM, a division of American Management Associations, New York. All rights reserved.

Dan Moore's Dilemma

"Where are we going to find people?," Dan Moore asked his Wellesley restaurant manager, Anne Priebe. Anne just shrugged her shoulders. The problem was as frustrating for her as it was for Dan.

Dan Moore owns three Burger King franchises in an upscale area of the Boston suburbs. In contrast to many fast-food operators, Dan has no complaints about business. He has improved comparable monthly sales every single month since he bought the franchises in 1987. His major problem is finding and keeping responsible, hard-working, and conscientious employees.

"I'm at my wits end," Dan related to this case writer. "I just don't know what to do. Each of my places needs a base of at least 25 employees. But our *average* turnover rate is 170 percent a year! Can you believe that?

"One cause of this problem is the decline in the pool of 18 to 21 year olds. This group historically provided the primary labor supply for businesses like mine. But this group has shrunken drastically. Additionally, I'm facing increased competition for these potential employees from other service firms. We're all fighting for low-skilled, minimum-wage people. I know of a McDonalds in nearby Newton

that's paying $6.50 an hour to start. I'm paying close to a dollar over minimum wage with little success. This is a highly labor-intensive business and I can't afford to pay $6 or more an hour. And, to be frank, I'm not sure I can get people at even $6 an hour.

"My best source of labor is inner-city kids. They're anxious to work and job opportunities are limited in the central city. But these kids live at least ten miles away and they don't have cars. Public transportation by bus is available but it means probably two or three transfers and an hour bus commute each way. The kids just aren't willing to go through such a hassle to come out here. And I can't blame them."

QUESTIONS

1. What sources or other ideas can you offer Dan to help him find and attract possible job applicants?

2. What selection devices are most appropriate for the jobs he is trying to fill?

3. What suggestions would you offer Dan to help him reduce his turnover rate?

NOTES

[1]"The Middleman," *U.S. News & World Report,* January 16, 1989, pp. 45–46.

[2]See C. T. Dortch, "Job–Person Match," *Personnel Journal,* June 1989, pp. 49–57.

[3]See, for example, J. V. Ghorpade, *Job Analysis: A Handbook for the Human Resource Director* (Englewood Cliffs, NJ: Prentice Hall, 1988).

[4]G. Johns, *Organizational Behavior: Understanding Life at Work,* 2nd ed. (Glenview, IL: Scott, Foresman, 1988), p. 19.

[5]T. J. Hanson and J. C. Balestreri-Spero, "An Alternative to Interviews," *Personnel Journal,* June 1985, p. 114.

[6]See R. D. Arvey and J. E. Campion, "The Employment Interview: A Summary and Review of Recent Research," *Personnel Psychology,* Summer 1982, pp. 281–322; and M. M. Harris, "Reconsidering the Employment Interview: A Review of Recent Literature and Suggestions for Future Research," *Personnel Psychology,* Winter 1989, pp. 691–726.

[7]See, for example, A. P. Phillips and R. L. Dipboye, "Correlational Tests of Predictions From a Process Model of the Interview," *Journal of Applied Psychology,* February 1989, pp. 41–52.

[8]See, for example, M. M. Harris, "Reconsidering the Employment Interview;" and J. Solomon, "The New Job Interview: Show Thyself," *Wall Street Journal,* December 4, 1989, p. B1.

[9]E. E. Ghiselli, "The Validity of Aptitude Tests in Personnel Selection," *Personnel Psychology,* Winter 1973, p. 475.

[10]G. Grimsley and H. F. Jarrett, "The Relation of Managerial Achievement to Test Measures Obtained in the Employment Situation: Methodology and Results," *Personnel Psychology,* Spring 1973, pp. 31–48; and A. K. Korman, "The Prediction of Managerial Performance: A Review," *Personnel Psychology,* Summer 1968, pp. 295–322.

[11]J. J. Asher and J. A. Sciarrino, "Realistic Work Sample Tests: A Review," *Personnel Psychology,* Winter 1974, pp. 519–33; and I. T. Robertson and R. S. Kandola, "Work Sample Tests: Validity, Adverse Impact and Applicant Reaction," *Journal of Occupational Psychology,* 1982, pp. 171–82.

[12]See, for example, B. B. Gaugher, D. B. Rosenthal, G. C. Thornton III, and C. Bentson, "Meta-Analysis of Assessment Center Validity," *Journal of Applied Psychology,* August 1987, pp. 493–511; G. M. McEvoy and R. W. Beatty, "Assessment Centers and Subordinate Appraisals of Managers: A Seven-Year Examination of Predictive Validity," *Personnel Psychology,* Spring 1989, pp. 37–52; and M. J. Papa, "A Comparison of Two Methods of Managerial Selection," *Management Communication Quarterly,* November 1989, pp. 191–218.

[13]Based on W. A. Henry III, "Beyond the Melting Pot," *Time,* April 9, 1990, pp. 28–31; and J. Dreyfuss, "Get Ready for the New Work Force," *Fortune,* April 23, 1990, pp. 165–81.

[14]"Corporate Training Has Itself Become Big Business," *Wall Street Journal,* August 5, 1986, p. 1.

[15]C. Lee, "Where the Training Dollars Go," *Training,* Vol. 24, No. 10, 1987, pp. 51–65.

[16]For an extended discussion of on-the-job and off-the-job training methods, see D. DeCenzo and S. P. Robbins, *Personnel/Human Resource Management,* 3rd ed. (Englewood Cliffs, NJ: Prentice Hall, 1988), pp. 248–51, 255–61.

[17]R. Wowk, D. Williams, and G. Halstead, "Do Formal Career Development Programs Really Increase Employee Participation?," *Training and Development Journal,* September 1983, pp. 82–83.

[18]M. Moravec, "A Cost-Effective Career Planning Program Requires a Strategy," *Personnel Administrator,* January 1982, pp. 28–32.

[19]From a study conducted by the Sterling Institute and reported in J. Keller and C. Piotrowski, "Career Development Programs in *Fortune* 500 Firms," *Psychological Reports,* December 1987, p. 921.

[20]D. E. Super and D. T. Hall, "Career Development Exploration and Planning," in M. R. Rosenzweig and L. W. Porter (eds.), *Annual Review of Psychology,* Vol. 29 (Palo Alto: Annual Reviews, 1978), p. 334.

[21]D. T. Hall, *Careers in Organizations* (Santa Monica, CA: Goodyear, 1976), pp. 3–4.

[22]See, for example, D. E. Super, *The Psychology of Careers* (New York: Harper & Row, 1957); and E. H. Schein, "The Individual, the Organization, and the Career: A Conceptual Scheme," *Journal of Applied Behavioral Science,* August 1971, pp. 401–26.

[23]E. H. Schein, "How Career Anchors Hold Executives to Their Career Paths," *Personnel,* May 1975, pp. 11–24; and E. H. Schein, *Career Dynamics: Matching Individual and Organizational Needs* (Reading, MA: Addison-Wesley, 1978).

[24]D. E. Berlew and D. T. Hall, "The Socialization of Managers: Effects of Expectations on Performance," *Administrative Science Quarterly,* September 1966, pp. 207–23; and D. W. Bray, R. J. Campbell, and D. L. Grant, *Formulative Years in Business: A Long-Term AT&T Study of Managerial Lives* (New York: John Wiley, 1974).

[25]See Super and Hall, "Career Development: Exploration and Planning," p. 362.

[26]J. Van Maanen and E. H. Schein, "Career Development," in J. R. Hackman and J. L. Suttle (eds.), *Improving Life at Work* (Santa Monica: CA: Goodyear, 1977), p. 87.

[27]H. G. Kaufman, *Obsolescence and Professional Career Development* (New York: AMACOM, 1974).

[28]Based on J. Hoerr, "A Japanese Import That's Not Selling," *Business Week,* February 26, 1990, pp. 86–87.

[29]See J. N. Cleveland, K. R. Murphy, and R. E. Williams, "Multiple Uses of Performance Appraisal: Prevalence and Correlates," *Journal of Applied Psychology,* February 1989, pp. 130–35.

[30]P. M. Blau, *The Dynamics of Bureaucracy,* rev. ed. (Chicago: University of Chicago Press, 1963).

[31]"The Cop-Out Cops," *National Observer,* August 3, 1974.

[32]For two diverse conclusions on behaviorally-anchored rating scales, see A. Tziner, "Effects of Rating Format on Goal-Setting Dimensions: A Field Experiment," *Journal of Applied Psychology,* May 1988, pp. 323–26; and L. R. Gomez-Mejia, "Evaluating Employee Performance: Does the Appraisal Instrument Make a Difference?," *Journal of Occupational Behavior Management,* Vol. 9, No. 2, 1988, pp. 155–72.

[33]M. E. Heilman and M. H. Stopeck, "Being Attractive, Advantage or Disadvantage? Performance-Based Evaluations and Recommended Personnel Actions as a Function of Appearance, Sex, and Job Type," *Organizational Behavior and Human Decision Processes,* April 1985, pp. 202–15.

[34]A. Pizam, "Social Differentiation—A New Psychological Barrier to Performance Appraisal," *Public Personnel Management,* July–August 1975, pp. 244–47.

[35]Ibid., pp. 245–46.

[36]See, for example, W. M. Fox, "Improving Performance Appraisal Systems," *National Productivity Review,* Winter 1987–88, pp. 20–27.

[37]W. C. Borman, "The Rating of Individuals in Organizations: An Alternate Approach," *Organizational Behavior and Human Performance,* August 1974, pp. 105–24.

[38]Ibid.

[39]G. P. Latham, K. N. Wexley, and E. D. Pursell, "Training Managers to Minimize Rating Errors in the Observation of Behavior," *Journal of Applied Psychology,* October 1975, pp. 550–55.

[40]H. J. Bernardin, "The Effects of Rater Training on Leniency and Halo Errors in Student Rating of Instructors," *Journal of Applied Psychology,* June 1978, pp. 301–08.

[41]Ibid.; and J. M. Ivancevich, "Longitudinal Study of the Effects of Rater Training on Psychometric Error in Ratings, *Journal of Applied Psychology,* October 1979, pp. 502–08.

[42]This section is based on W. Lobdell, "Who's Right for an Overseas Position?" *World Trade,* April/May 1990, pp. 20–26.

[43]This material was adapted from T. H. Hammer, "Relationship Between Local Union Characteristics and Worker Behavior and Attitudes," *Academy of Management Journal,* December 1978, pp. 560–77.

[44]See, for example, C. J. Berger, C. A. Olson, and J. W. Boudreau, "Effects of Unions on Job Satisfaction: The Role of Work-Related Values and Perceived Rewards," *Organizational Behavior and Human Performance,* December 1983, pp. 289–324.

[45]A. Bandura, "Self-Efficacy: Towards a Unifying Theory of Behavioral Change," *Psychological Review,* March 1977, pp. 191–215.

[46]M. K. Mount, "Managerial Career Stage and Facets of Job Satisfaction," *Journal of Vocational Behavior,* June 1984, pp. 340–54; and C. S. Granrose and J. D. Portwood, "Matching Individual Career Plans and Organizational Career Management," *Academy of Management Journal,* December 1987, pp. 699–720.

ORGANIZATIONAL CULTURE

LEARNING OBJECTIVES

After studying this chapter, you should be able to:

1. *Describe* institutionalization *and its relationship to organizational culture*
2. *Define the common characteristics making up organizational culture*
3. *Contrast strong and weak cultures*
4. *Identify the functional and dysfunctional effects of organizational culture on people*
5. *Explain the factors determining an organization's culture*
6. *List the factors that maintain an organization's culture*
7. *Clarify how culture is transmitted to employees*
8. *Outline the various socialization alternatives available to management*

McDonald's founder, Ray Kroc, died in 1984. But his philosophy is preserved on tape at company headquarters and continues to guide McDonald's current management.
Kevin Horan.

In any organization, there are the ropes to skip and the ropes to know.

R. RITTI AND G. FUNKHOUSER

With the possible exception of the Disney Co., McDonald's is the definitive example of a powerful and successful organizational culture.[1] If you walk into any one of the more than 10,000 McDonald's restaurants—whether it's in Moscow, Idaho or Moscow in the Soviet Union—you'll see a familiar layout, an essentially common menu, and one of the most efficient organizations in the world. It's not by chance that a McDonald's meal tastes pretty much the same everywhere.

No small part of McDonald's success is due to its strong culture. Every McDonald's employee knows the company's basic operating principles. Quality, service, cleanliness. Don't compromise. Use the best ingredients.

Where did McDonald's culture come from? Its founder, Ray Kroc. Though he died in 1984, his presence is as great today as it was during his lifetime. His office at corporate headquarters in Oak Brook, Illinois, is preserved as a museum, his reading glasses untouched in their leather case on the desk. In a headquarters exhibit called "Talk to Ray," a visitor can phone up Ray on a video screen and with a keyboard ask him questions. More than an hour-and-a-half of videotape has been accumulated from talk shows and other sources that allow visitors and employees to hear Kroc espouse his philosophy of what McDonald's is about.

Today's executives at McDonald's cite Mr. Kroc so often that he still seems to be in charge. His photo smiles down on every desk. When executives are faced with tough decisions, they typically ask themselves, "What would Ray do?" And because these executives have been so fully indoctrinated in Kroc's philosophy, they usually arrive at answers consistent with decisions made when Kroc headed the company. This explains, to a large degree, why McDonald's has become a symbol of stability and consistency.

A strong culture like that at McDonald's provides employees with a clear understanding of "the way things are done around here." In this chapter, we'll show that every organization has a culture and, depending on its strength, can have a significant influence in shaping the attitudes and behaviors of its members.

INSTITUTIONALIZATION: A FORERUNNER OF CULTURE

The idea of viewing organizations as cultures—where there is a system of shared meaning among members—is a relatively recent phenomenon. Fifteen years ago, organizations were, for the most part, simply thought of as rational means by which to coordinate and control a group of people. They had vertical levels, departments, authority relationships, and so forth. But organizations are more. They have personalities too, just like individuals. They can be rigid or flexible, unfriendly or supportive, innovative or conservative. General Electric offices and people *are* different from the offices and people at General Mills. Harvard and MIT are in the same business—education—and separated only by the width of the Charles River, but each has a unique feeling and character beyond its structural characteristics. Organizational theorists, in recent years, have begun to acknowledge this by recognizing the important role that culture plays in the lives of organization members. Interestingly, though, the origin of culture as an independent variable affecting an employee's attitudes and behavior can be traced back forty years ago to the notion of **institutionalization.**[2]

Institutionalization When an organization takes on a life of its own, apart from any of its members, and acquires immortality.

When an organization becomes institutionalized, it takes on a life of its own, apart from any of its members. The Internal Revenue Service, Chrysler Corporation, and Timex Corporation are examples of organizations that exist, and have existed, beyond the life of any one member. Additionally, when an organization becomes institutionalized, it becomes valued for itself, not merely for the goods or services it produces. It acquires immortality. If its original goals are no longer relevant, it doesn't go out of business. Rather, it redefines itself. When the demand for Timex's watches declined, the company merely redirected itself into the consumer electronics business—making, in addition to watches, clocks, computers, and health care products such as digital thermometers and blood pressure testing devices. Time took on an existence that went beyond its original mission to manufacture low-cost mechanical watches.

Institutionalization operates to produce common understandings among members about what is appropriate and, fundamentally, meaningful behavior.[3] So when an organization takes on institutional permanence, acceptable modes of behavior become largely self-evident to its members. As we'll see, this is essentially the same thing that organizational culture does. So an understanding of what makes up an organization's culture, and how it is created, sustained, and learned will enhance our ability to explain and predict the behavior of people at work.

WHAT IS ORGANIZATIONAL CULTURE?

Organizational culture is one of those topics about which many people will say, "Oh, yeah, I know what you mean," but one that is quite difficult to define in any specific form. In this section, we'll propose a specific definition and review several peripheral issues that revolve around this definition.

A Definition

Organizational Culture A common perception held by the organization's members; a system of shared meaning.

There seems to be wide agreement that **organizational culture** refers to a system of shared meaning held by members that distinguishes the organization from other organizations.[4] This system of shared meaning is, on closer analysis, a set of key characteristics that the organization values. There appear to be ten characteristics that, when mixed and matched, tap the essence of an organization's culture.[5]

As part of Toshiba's efforts to indoctrinate new employees in its organization's culture, recruits are even required to learn the company song.   R. Wallis/ SIPA-PRESS.

1. *Individual initiative:* the degree of responsibility, freedom, and independence that individuals have
2. *Risk tolerance:* the degree to which employees are encouraged to be aggressive, innovative, and risk-seeking
3. *Direction:* the degree to which the organization creates clear objectives and performance expectations
4. *Integration:* the degree to which units within the organization are encouraged to operate in a coordinated manner
5. *Management support:* the degree to which managers provide clear communication, assistance, and support to their subordinates
6. *Control:* the number of rules and regulations, and the amount of direct supervision that is used to oversee and control employee behavior
7. *Identity:* the degree to which members identify with the organization as a whole rather than with their particular work group or field of professional expertise
8. *Reward system:* the degree to which reward allocations (that is, salary increases, promotions) are based on employee performance criteria in contrast to seniority, favoritism, and so on
9. *Conflict tolerance:* the degree to which employees are encouraged to air conflicts and criticisms openly
10. *Communication patterns:* the degree to which organizational communications are restricted to the formal hierarchy of authority

Each of these characteristics exists on a continuum from low to high. By appraising the organization on these ten characteristics, then, a composite picture of the organization's culture is formed. This picture becomes the basis for feelings of shared understanding that members have about the organiza-

Les Wexner, founder of The Limited, seeds to create a culture that encourages risk taking. Buyers, for example, are graded not only on their successes, but also on their failures. Too many hits means buyers aren't taking enough chances. Lynn Johnson/Black Star.

tion, how things are done in it, and the way members are supposed to behave. Table 17–1 demonstrates how these characteristics can be mixed to create highly diverse organizations.

Culture Is a Descriptive Term

Organizational culture is concerned with how employees perceive the ten characteristics, not whether they like them or not. That is, it is a descriptive term. This is important because it differentiates this concept from that of job satisfaction.

Research on organizational culture has sought to measure how employees see their organization: Are there clear objectives and performance expectations? Does the organization reward innovation? Does it stifle conflict?

In contrast, job satisfaction seeks to measure affective responses to the work environment. It is concerned with how employees feel about the organization's expectations, reward practices, methods for handling conflict, and the like. Although the two terms undoubtedly have characteristics that overlap, keep in mind that the term organizational culture is descriptive, while job satisfaction is evaluative.

Do Organizations Have Uniform Cultures?

Organizational culture represents a common perception held by the organization's members. This was made explicit when we defined culture as a system of *shared* meaning. We should expect, therefore, that individuals with different backgrounds or at different levels in the organization will tend to describe the organization's culture in similar terms.

Acknowledgment that organizational culture has common properties does not mean, however, that there cannot be subcultures within any given

TABLE 17–1   Two Highly Diverse Organizational Cultures

Organization A	Organization B
This organization is a manufacturing firm. There are extensive rules and regulations that employees are required to follow. Every employee has specific objectives to achieve in his or her job. Managers supervise employees closely to ensure there are no deviations. People are allowed little discretion on their jobs. Employees are instructed to bring any unusual problem to their superior, who will then determine the solution. All employees are required to communicate through formal channels. Because management has no confidence in the honesty or integrity of its employees, it imposes tight controls. Managers and employees alike tend to be hired by the organization early in their careers, rotated into and out of various departments on a regular basis, and are generalists rather than specialists. Effort, loyalty, cooperation, and avoidance of errors are highly valued and rewarded.	This organization is also a manufacturing firm. Here, however, there are few rules and regulations. Employees are seen as hardworking and trustworthy, thus supervision is loose. Employees are encouraged to solve problems themselves, but to feel free to consult with their supervisors when they need assistance. Top management downplays authority differences. Employees are also encouraged to develop their unique specialized skills. Interpersonal and interdepartmental differences are seen as natural occurrences. Managers are evaluated not only on their department's performance but on how well their department coordinates its activities with other departments in the organization. Promotions and other valuable rewards go to employees who make the greatest contribution to the organization, even when those employees have strange ideas, unusual personal mannerisms, or unconventional work habits.

culture. Most large organizations have a dominant culture and numerous sets of subcultures.[6]

Dominant Culture Expresses the core values that are shared by a majority of the organization's members.

Subcultures Minicultures within an organization, typically defined by department designations and geographical separation.

Core Values The primary or dominant values that are accepted throughout the organization.

A **dominant culture** expresses the core values that are shared by a majority of the organization's members. When we talk about an *organization's* culture, we are referring to its dominant culture. It is this macro view of culture that gives an organization its distinct personality. **Subcultures** tend to develop in large organizations to reflect common problems, situations, or experiences that members face. These subcultures are likely to be defined by department designations and geographical separation. The purchasing department, for example, can have a subculture that is uniquely shared by members of that department. It will include the **core values** of the dominant culture plus additional values unique to members of the purchasing department. Similarly, an office or unit of the organization that is physically separated from the organization's main operations may take on a different personality. Again, the core values are essentially retained but modified to reflect the separated unit's distinct situation.

If organizations had no dominant culture and were composed only of numerous subcultures, the value of organizational culture as an independent variable would be significantly lessened, because there would be no uniform interpretation of what represented appropriate or inappropriate behavior. It is the "shared meaning" aspect of culture that makes it such a potent device for guiding and shaping behavior. But we cannot ignore the reality that many organizations also have subcultures that can influence the behavior of members.

Strong vs. Weak Cultures

It has become increasingly popular to differentiate between strong and weak cultures.[7] The argument here is that strong cultures have a greater impact on employee behavior and are more directly related to reduced turnover.

A **strong culture** is characterized by the organization's core values being both intensely held and widely shared.[8] The more members who accept the core values and the greater their commitment to those values, the stronger the culture is. Consistent with this definition, a strong culture will obviously have a greater influence on the behavior of its members. Religious organizations, cults, and Japanese companies are examples of organizations that have very strong cultures.[9] When a James Jones can entice nine hundred members of his Guyana cult to commit mass suicide, we see a behavioral influence considerably greater than that typically attributed to leadership. The culture of Jonestown had a degree of sharedness and intensity that allowed for extremely high behavioral control. Of course, the same strong cultural influence that can lead to the tragedy of a Jonestown can be directed positively to create immensely successful organizations like IBM, Mary Kay Cosmetics, and Sony.

A specific result of a strong culture should be lower employee turnover. A strong culture demonstrates high agreement among members about what the organization stands for. Such unanimity of purpose builds cohesiveness, loyalty, and organizational commitment. These, in turn, lessen the propensity for employees to leave the organization.[10]

CULTURE VS. FORMALIZATION A strong organizational culture increases behavioral consistency. In this sense, we should recognize that a strong culture can act as a substitute for formalization.

In Chapter 14, we discussed how formalization's rules and regulations act to regulate employee behavior. High formalization in an organization creates predictability, orderliness, and consistency. Our point is that a strong culture achieves the same end without the need for written documentation. Therefore, we should view formalization and culture as two different roads to a common destination. The stronger an organization's culture, the less management need be concerned with developing formal rules and regulations to guide employee behavior. Those guides will have been internalized in employees when they accept the organization's culture.

WHAT DOES CULTURE DO?

We've alluded to organizational culture's impact on behavior. We've also explicitly argued that a strong culture should be associated with reduced turnover. In this section, we will more carefully review the functions that culture performs and assess whether culture can be a liability for an organization.

Culture's Functions

Culture performs a number of functions within an organization. First, it has a boundary-defining role; that is, it creates distinctions between one organization and others. Second, it conveys a sense of identity for organization members. Third, culture facilitates the generation of commitment to something larger than one's individual self-interest. Fourth, it enhances social system stability. Culture is the social glue that helps hold the organization

There Are No "Right" Cultures!

A few years back, largely due to the tremendous commercial success and general acceptance of Tom Peters and Robert Waterman's book *In Search of Excellence*[11] (the book sold more than 5 million copies), many practicing managers thought that successful organizations had a set of common cultural characteristics. Peters and Waterman argued that well-managed or "excellent" companies like IBM, DuPont, 3M, McDonald's, and Procter & Gamble had common characteristics such as a bias for action, autonomy and entrepreneurship, and increased productivity through employee involvement.[12] Moreover, to quote Peters and Waterman, "without exception, the dominance and coherence of culture proved to be an essential quality of the excellent companies."[13]

While the idea that there might be a set of "right" cultural characteristics that differentiate successful from unsuccessful organizations is intuitively appealing, the evidence does not stack up that way.[14] What defines excellence in an organization is far from clear. Additionally, what was excellent yesterday is not necessarily excellent today. For instance, Peters and Waterman included firms such as Caterpillar Tractor, Schlumberger, and Wang Labs in their set of forty-three excellent firms, but each has had serious declines in financial performance since the publication of their book. Maybe most damning is the reality that there are undoubtedly hundreds, maybe thousands, of organizations that equal or exceed the performance of Peters and Waterman's excellent companies but have few, if any, of the "right" cultural characteristics.

To construe culture as a set of specific shared values implies that there are "right" cultures and "wrong" ones. Such a perspective misrepresents the concept of organizational culture and misdirects attention from *understanding what is* toward *prescribing what should be*. At this time, it is clearly presumptuous to state that we know the cultural characteristics prevalent in "excellent" organizations.

together by providing appropriate standards for what employees should say and do. Finally, culture serves as a sense-making and control mechanism that guides and shapes the attitudes and behavior of employees. It is this last function that is of particular interest to us. As the following quote makes clear, culture defines the rules of the game:

> Culture by definition is elusive, intangible, implicit, and taken for granted. But every organization develops a core set of assumptions, understandings, and implicit rules that govern day-to-day behavior in the workplace. . . . Until newcomers learn the rules, they are not accepted as full-fledged members of the organization. Transgressions of the rules on the part of high-level executives or front-line employees result in universal disapproval and powerful penalties. Conformity to the rules becomes the primary basis for reward and upward mobility.[15]

As we'll show later in this chapter, who is made job offers to join the organization, who is appraised as a high performer, and who gets the promotions are strongly influenced by the individual–organization "fit"—that is, whether the applicant or employee's attitudes and behavior are compatible with the culture. It is not a coincidence that employees at Disneyland and Disney World appear to be almost universally attractive, clean, and wholesome-looking, with bright smiles. That's the image Disney seeks. The company selects employees who will maintain that image. And once on the job, both the informal norms and formal rules and regulations ensure that Disney employees will act in a relatively uniform and predictable way.

Culture as a Liability

We are treating culture in a nonjudgmental manner. We haven't said that it's good or bad, only that it exists. Many of its functions, as outlined, are valuable for both the organization and the employee. Culture enhances organizational commitment and increases the consistency of employee behavior. These are clearly benefits to an organization. From an employee's standpoint, culture is valuable because it reduces ambiguity. It tells employees how things are done and what's important. But we shouldn't ignore the potentially dysfunctional aspects of culture, especially a strong one, on an organization's effectiveness.

Culture is a liability where the shared values are not in agreement with those that will further the organization's effectiveness. This is most likely to occur when the organization's environment is dynamic. When the environment is undergoing rapid change, the organization's entrenched culture may no longer be appropriate. So consistency of behavior is an asset to an organization when it faces a stable environment. It may, however, burden the organization and make it difficult to respond to changes in the environment. This helps to explain the challenges AT&T has had adapting to a deregulated environment.[17] Its strong service and technology-oriented culture, which originated in the nineteenth century, was amazingly effective as long as the company remained in the telephone business and held a monopoly there. But after deregulation, AT&T chose to compete in the telecommunications and computer industries against the likes of IBM, Xerox, and the Japanese. AT&T has had a difficult time adjusting to its new environment, largely due to the fact that it has had to try to create a new, more market-driven culture and that its pre-deregulation culture was so strong.

CREATING AND SUSTAINING CULTURE

An organization's culture doesn't pop out of thin air. Once established, it rarely fades away. What forces influence the creation of a culture? What reinforces and sustains these forces once they are in place? We'll answer both of these questions in this section.

How a Culture Begins

An organization's current customs, traditions, and general way of doing things are largely due to what it has done before and the degree of success it has had with those endeavors. This leads us to the ultimate source of an organization's culture: its founders.

The founders of an organization traditionally have a major impact in establishing the early culture. They have a vision or mission of what the

Which Organizational Culture Fits You?

Research conducted by Jeffrey Sonnenfeld of Emory University found four cultural "types" in today's organizations. Sonnenfeld labeled them *academy, club, baseball team,* and *fortress.*[16]

ACADEMY   An academy is the place for steady climbers who want to thoroughly master each new job they hold. These companies like to recruit young college graduates and then carefully steer them through a myriad of specialized jobs within a particular function. IBM is a classic academy. So, too, are Coca-Cola, Procter & Gamble, and General Motors.

CLUB   Clubs place a high value on "fitting in," on loyalty, and on commitment. Seniority is the key at clubs. Age and experience count. In contrast to an academy, clubs groom managers as generalists. Examples of clubs include United Parcel Service, Delta Airlines, the Bell operating companies, government agencies, and the military.

BASEBALL TEAM   These organizations are entrepreneurially-oriented havens for risk takers and innovators. Baseball teams seek out talent of all ages and experiences, then reward them for what they produce. Because they offer big dollars and great freedom to their star performers, job hopping among these organizations is common-

place. Organizations that fit the baseball team description include accounting, law, and consulting firms; advertising agencies; software developers; and bioresearch concerns.

FORTRESS   While baseball teams value inventiveness, fortresses are preoccupied with survival. Many are academies, clubs, or baseball teams seeking to reverse sagging fortunes. Fortresses offer little promise of job security, yet they can be exciting for those who like the challenge of a turnaround. Fortress organizations include large retailers, hotels, forest products companies, and oil and natural gas exploration firms.

Sonnenfeld found that many organizations can't be neatly categorized into one of the above four categories. Some have a blend of cultures; others are in transition. General Electric, for example, has distinctly different cultures within different units. Apple Computer started out as a baseball team but is maturing into an academy.

Sonnenfeld found that each of the four cultural types tends to attract certain personalities and the personality–organizational culture match affects how far and how easily a person will move up the management ranks. For instance, a risk taker will thrive at a baseball-team company but fall flat on his or her face at an academy.

organization should be. They are unconstrained by previous customs or ideologies. The small size that typically characterizes any new organization further facilitates the founders' imposing their vision on all organizational members. Because the founders have the original idea, they also typically have biases on how to get the idea fulfilled. The organization's culture results from the interaction between (1) the founders' biases and assumptions, and (2) what the original members who the founders initially employ learn subsequently from their own experiences.[18]

Henry Ford at the Ford Motor Company, Thomas Watson at IBM, J.

A Los Angeles law firm, Loeb & Loeb, uses its summer internship program to identify individuals who might make good full-time employees. In photo, summer interns salute their recruiter, Annette Roe, foreground. Alan D. Levenson/Loeb and Loeb.

Edgar Hoover at the FBI, Thomas Jefferson at the University of Virginia, Walt Disney at the Disney Co., Sam Walton at Wal-Mart, David Packard at Hewlett-Packard, and Steven Jobs and Stephen Wozniak at Apple Computer are just a few obvious examples of individuals who have had immeasurable impact in shaping their organization's culture. For instance, Watson's views on research and development, product innovation, employee dress attire, and compensation policies are still evident at IBM, though he died in 1956. The Disney Co. continues to focus on Walt Disney's original vision of a company that created fantasy entertainment. Wal-Mart's commitment to frugality, simplicity, and value come directly from Sam Walton's persona. The formality found today at the University of Virginia is due, in large part, to the original culture created by its founder, Thomas Jefferson. Apple's informal and creative culture was established by Steve Jobs.

Keeping a Culture Alive

Once a culture is in place, there are practices within the organization that act to maintain it by giving employees a set of similar experiences. For example, many of the human resource practices discussed in the previous chapter reinforce the organization's culture. The selection process, performance evaluation criteria, reward practices, training and career development activities, and promotion procedures ensure that those hired fit in with the culture, reward those who support it, and penalize (and even expel) those who challenge it. Three forces play a particularly important part in sustaining a culture—selection practices, the actions of top management, and socialization methods. Let's take a closer look at each.

SELECTION   The explicit goal of the selection process is to identify and hire individuals who have the knowledge, skills, and abilities to perform the jobs within the organization successfully. But, typically, more than one candidate will be identified who meets any given job's requirements. When that point is reached, it would be naive to ignore that the final decision as to who is hired will be significantly influenced by the decision maker's judgment of how well the candidates will fit into the organization. This attempt to ensure a proper match, whether purposely or inadvertently, results in the hiring of people who have common values (ones essentially consistent with those of the organization) or at least a good portion of those values.[19] Additionally, the selection process provides information to applicants about the organization. Candidates learn about the organization, and, if they perceive a conflict between their values and those of the organization, they can self-select themselves out of the applicant pool. Selection, therefore, becomes a two-way street, allowing either employer or applicant to abrogate a marriage if there appears to be a mismatch. In this way, the selection process sustains an organization's culture by selecting out those individuals who might attack or undermine its core values.

Applicants for entry-level positions in brand management at Procter & Gamble experience an exhaustive application and screening process. Their interviewers are part of an elite cadre who have been selected and trained extensively via lectures, video tapes, films, practice interviews, and role plays to identify applicants who will successfully fit in at P&G. Applicants are interviewed in depth for such qualities as their ability to "turn out high volumes of excellent work," "identify and understand problems," and "reach thoroughly substantiated and well reasoned conclusions that lead to action." P&G values rationality and seeks applicants who think that way. College applicants receive two interviews and a general knowledge test on campus, before being flown back to Cincinnati for three more one-on-one interviews and a group interview at lunch. Each encounter seeks corroborating evidence of the traits that the firm believes correlate highly with "what counts" for success at P&G.[20] Applicants for positions at Compaq Computer are carefully chosen for their ability to fit into the company's teamwork-oriented culture. As one executive put it, "We can find lots of people who are competent . . . The No. 1 issue is whether they fit into the way we do business."[21] At Compaq, that means job candidates who are easy to get along with and who feel comfortable with the company's consensus management style. To increase the likelihood that loners and those with big egos get screened out, it's not unusual for a new hire to be interviewed by fifteen people who represent all departments of the company and a variety of seniority levels.[22]

TOP MANAGEMENT   The actions of top management also have a major impact on the organization's culture.[23] Through what they say and how they behave, senior executives establish norms that filter down through the organization as to whether risk taking is desirable; how much freedom managers should give their subordinates; what is appropriate dress; what actions will pay off in terms of pay raises, promotions, and other rewards; and the like.

For example, look at Xerox Corp.[24] Its chief executive from 1961 to 1968 was Joseph C. Wilson. An aggressive, entrepreneurial type, he oversaw Xerox's staggering growth on the basis of its 914 copier, one of the most successful products in American history. Under Wilson, Xerox had an entrepreneurial environment, with an informal, high-camaraderie, innovative, bold, risk-taking culture. Wilson's replacement as CEO was C. Peter McColough, a Harvard MBA with a formal management style. He instituted bureaucratic controls and a major change in Xerox's culture. When McColough stepped down in 1982, Xerox had become stodgy and formal, with lots of politics and turf battles and layers of watchdog managers. His replacement was David T. Kearns. He believed the culture he inherited hindered Xerox's ability to compete. To increase the company's competitiveness, Kearns trimmed Xerox down by cutting 15,000 jobs, delegated decision making downward, and refocused the organization's culture around a simple theme: boosting the quality of Xerox products and services. By his actions and those of his senior managerial cadre, Kearns conveyed to everyone at Xerox that the company values and rewards quality, innovative thinking, efficiency, and staying on top of the competition.

SOCIALIZATION   No matter how good a job the organization does in recruiting and selection, new employees are not fully indoctrinated in the organization's culture. Maybe most important, because they are least familiar with the organization's culture, new employees are potentially most likely to disturb the beliefs and customs that are in place. The organization will, therefore, want to help new employees adapt to its culture. This adaptation process is called **socialization.**[25]

Socialization The process that adapts employees to the organization's culture.

All Marines must go through boot camp, where they "prove" their commitment. Of course, at the same time, the Marine trainers are indoctrinating new recruits in the "Marine way." The success of any cult depends on effective socialization. New Moonies undergo a "brainwashing" ritual that substitutes group loyalty and commitment for family. New Morgan Guaranty bank employees go through a one year training program that tests their intellect, and endurance, and that requires teamwork as an essential factor for survival. The reason is that Morgan Guaranty wants to mold new members into the firm's collegial style.

As we discuss socialization, keep in mind that the most critical socialization stage is at the time of entry into the organization. This is when the organization seeks to mold the outsider into an employee "in good standing." Those employees who fail to learn the essential or pivotal role behaviors risk being labeled "nonconformists" or "rebels," which often leads to expulsion. But the organization will be socializing every employee, though maybe not as explicitly, throughout his or her entire career in the organization. This further contributes to sustaining the culture.

Socialization can be conceptualized as a process made up of three stages: prearrival, encounter, and metamorphosis.[26] The first stage encompasses all the learning that occurs before a new member joins the organization. In the second stage, the new employee sees what the organization is really like and confronts the likelihood that expectations and reality may diverge. In the third stage, the relatively long-lasting changes take place. The new employee masters the skills required for his or her job, successfully performs his or her new roles, and makes the adjustments to his or her work group's values and norms.[27] This three-stage process impacts on the new employee's work productivity, commitment to the organization's objectives, and eventual decision to stay with the organization. Figure 17–1 depicts this process.

Prearrival Stage The period of learning in the socialization process that occurs before a new employee joins the organization.

The **prearrival stage** explicitly recognizes that each individual arrives with a set of values, attitudes, and expectations. These cover both the work to be done and the organization. For instance, in many jobs, particularly professional work, new members will have undergone a considerable degree of prior socialization in training and in school. One major purpose of a business school, for example, is to socialize business students to the attitudes and behaviors that business firms want. If business executives believe that successful employees value the profit ethic, are loyal, will work hard, desire to achieve, and willingly accept directions from their superiors, they can hire individuals out of business schools who have been premolded in this pattern. But prearrival socialization goes beyond the specific job. The selection process is used in most organizations to inform prospective employees about the organization as a whole. In addition, as noted previously, the selection process also acts to ensure the inclusion of the "right type"—those who will fit in. "Indeed, the ability of the individual to present the appropriate face during the selection process determines his ability to move into the organization in the first place. Thus, success depends on the degree to which the aspiring member

FIGURE 17–1   A Socialization Model

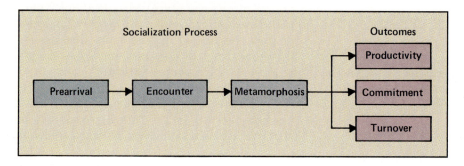

Encounter Stage The stage in the socialization process in which a new employee sees what the organization is really like and confronts the likelihood that expectations and reality may diverge.

Metamorphosis Stage The stage in the socialization process in which a new employee adjusts to his or her work group's values and norms.

has correctly anticipated the expectations and desires of those in the organization in charge of selection."[28]

Upon entry into the organization, the new member enters the **encounter stage.** Here the individual confronts the possible dichotomy between her expectations—about her job, her co-workers, her boss, and the organization in general—and reality. If expectations prove to have been more or less accurate, the encounter stage merely provides for a reaffirmation of the perceptions gained earlier. However, this is often not the case. Where expectations and reality differ, the new employee must undergo socialization that will detach her from her previous assumptions and replace them with another set that the organization deems desirable. At the extreme, a new member may become totally disillusioned with the actualities of her job and resign. Proper selection should significantly reduce the probability of the latter occurrence.

Finally, the new member must work out any problems discovered during the encounter stage. This may mean going through changes—hence, we call this the **metamorphosis stage.** The choices presented in Table 17–2 are alternatives designed to bring about the desired metamorphosis. But what is a desirable metamorphosis? We can say that metamorphosis and the entry socialization process is complete when the new member has become comfortable with the organization and his or her job. She has internalized the norms of the organization and her work group, and understands and accepts these norms. The new member feels accepted by her peers as a trusted and valued individual, is self-confident that she has the competence to complete the job successfully, and understands the system—not only her own tasks, but the rules, procedures, and informally accepted practices as well. Finally, she knows how she will be evaluated, that is, what criteria will be used to measure and appraise her work. She knows what is expected, and what constitutes a job "well done." As Figure 17–1 shows, successful metamorphosis should have a positive impact on the new employee's productivity and her commitment to the organization, and reduce her propensity to leave the organization.

Summary: How Cultures Form

Figure 17–2 summarizes how an organization's culture is established and sustained. The original culture is derived from the founder's philosophy. This, in turn, strongly influences the criteria used in hiring. The actions of the current top management set the general climate of what is acceptable behavior and what is not. How employees are to be socialized will depend on both the degree of success achieved in matching new employee's values to those of the organization's in the selection process and on top management's preference for socialization methods.

FIGURE 17–2   How Organization Cultures Form

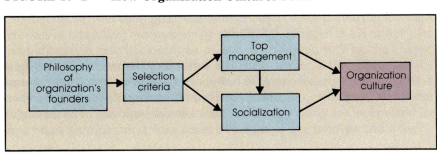

One of the best-known corporate rituals is Mary Kay Cosmetics' annual award meeting.[33] Looking like a cross between a circus and a Miss America pageant, the meeting takes place over a couple of days in a large auditorium, on a stage in front of a large, cheering audience, with all the participants dressed in glamorous evening clothes. Saleswomen are rewarded with an array of flashy gifts—gold and diamond pins, fur stoles, pink Cadillacs—based on success in achieving sales quota. This "show" acts as a motivator by publicly recognizing outstanding sales performance. In addition, the ritual aspect reinforces Mary Kay's personal determination and optimism, which enabled her to overcome personal hardships, found her own company, and achieve material success. It conveys to her salespeople that reaching their sales quota is important and that through hard work and encouragement they too can achieve success.

Material Symbols

Tandem Computers' headquarters in Cupertino, California, doesn't look like your typical head office operation. It has jogging trails, a basketball court, space for dance and yoga classes, and a large swimming pool—all for its employees' enjoyment. Every Friday afternoon at 4:30, employees partake in the weekly beer bust, courtesy of the company. This informal corporate headquarters conveys to employees that Tandem values openness and equality.

Some corporations provide their top executives with chauffeur-driven limousines and, when they travel by air, unlimited use of the corporate jet. Others may not get to ride in limousines or private jets but they might still get a car and air transportation paid for by the company. Only, the car is a Chevrolet (with no driver) and the jet seat is in the economy section of a commercial airliner.

The layout of corporate headquarters, the types of automobiles top executives are given, and the presence or absence of corporate aircraft are a few examples of material symbols. Others include the size and layout of offices, the elegance of furnishings, executive perks, and dress attire. These material symbols convey to employees who is important, the degree of egalitarianism desired by top management, and the kinds of behavior (for example, risk-taking, conservative, authoritarian, participative, individualistic, social) that are appropriate.

Language

Many organizations and units within organizations use language as a way to identify members of a culture or subculture. By learning this language, members attest to their acceptance of the culture and, in so doing, help to preserve it.

The following are examples of terminology used by employees at Dialog, a California-based data redistributor: *accession number* (a number assigned each individual record in a database); *KWIC* (a set of key-words-in-context); and *relational operator* (searching a database for names or key terms in some order). Librarians are a rich source of terminology foreign to people outside their profession. They sprinkle their conversations liberally with acronyms like *ARL* (Association for Research Libraries), *OCLC* (a center in Ohio that

Organizational Culture vs. National Culture

This chapter has taken the anthropologist's concept of societal cultures and applied it at the organizational level. Our main thesis has been that members of an organization develop common perceptions that, in turn, affect their attitudes and behavior. The strength of that affect, however, depends on the strength of the organization's culture.

Throughout this book we've argued that national differences—that is, national cultures—must be taken into account if accurate predictions are to be made about organizational behavior in different countries.

In this box, we want to address an integrated question: Does national culture override an organization's culture? Is an IBM facility in Germany, for example, more likely to reflect German ethnicity or IBM's corporate culture?

The research indicates that national culture has a greater impact on employees than does their organization's culture.[34] German employees at an IBM facility in Munich, therefore, will be influenced more by German culture than by IBM's culture. This means that as influencial as organizational culture is to understanding the behavior of people at work, national culture is even more so.

The above conclusion has to be qualified to reflect the self-selection that goes on at the hiring stage. IBM, for example, may be less concerned with hiring the "typical Italian" for its Italian operations than in hiring an Italian who fits within the IBM way of doing things.[35] Italians who have a high need for autonomy are more likely to go to Olivetti than IBM. Why? Because Olivetti's organizational culture is informal and nonstructured. It allows employees considerably more freedom than IBM.[36] In fact, Olivetti seeks to hire individuals who are impatient, risk-taking, and innovative—qualities in job candidates that IBM's Italian operations would purposely seek to exclude in new hires.

does cooperative cataloging), and *OPAC* (for on-line patron accessing catalog).

Organizations, over time, often develop unique terms to describe equipment, offices, key personnel, suppliers, customers, or products that relate to its business. New employees are frequently overwhelmed with acronyms and jargon that, after six months on the job, have become fully part of their language. But once assimilated, this terminology acts as a common denominator that unites members of a given culture or subculture.

ORGANIZATIONAL CULTURE IN ACTION

We now turn our attention to three specific organizations and their cultures—the Walt Disney Co., MCI, and BankAmerica Corp. They are of interest for different reasons. Disney is fascinating because of its culture's strength; MCI because it is so untraditional; and BankAmerica as an illustration of what happens when diverse cultures merge.

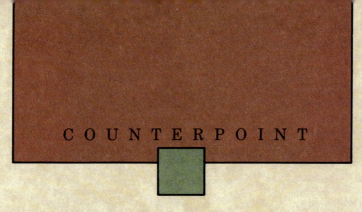

COUNTERPOINT

How to Change an Organization's Culture

Changing an organization's culture is extremely difficult, but cultures *can* be changed. For example, Lee Iacocca came to Chrysler Corp. in 1978, when the company appeared to be only weeks away from bankruptcy. It took him about five years but, in what is now a well-worn story, he took Chrysler's conservative, inward-looking, and engineering-oriented culture and changed it into an action-oriented, market-responsive culture.

The evidence suggests that cultural change is most likely to take place when most or all of the following conditions exist:

A dramatic crisis. This is the shock that undermines the status quo and calls into question the relevance of the current culture. Examples of these crises might be a surprising financial setback, the loss of a major customer, or a dramatic technological breakthrough by a competitor.

Turnover in leadership. New top leadership, which can provide an alternative set of key values, may be perceived as more capable of responding to the crisis. This would definitely be the organization's chief executive but also might need to include all senior management positions.

Young and small organization. The younger the organization is, the less entrenched its culture will be. Similarly, it's easier for management to communicate its new values when the organization is small.

Weak culture. The more widely held a culture is and the higher the agreement among members on its values, the more difficult it will be to change. Conversely, weak cultures are more amenable to change than strong ones.

If conditions support cultural change, you should consider the following suggestions:

1. Have top management people become positive role models, setting the tone through their behavior.
2. Create new stories, symbols, and rituals to replace those currently in vogue.
3. Select, promote, and support employees who espouse the new values that are sought.
4. Redesign socialization processes to align with the new values.
5. Change the reward system to encourage acceptance of a new set of values.
6. Replace unwritten norms with formal rules and regulations that are tightly enforced.
7. Shake up current subcultures through extensive use of job rotation.
8. Work to get peer group consensus through utilization of employee participation and creation of a climate with a high level of trust.

Implementing most or all of these suggestions will not result in an immediate or dramatic shift in the organization's culture. Cultural change is a lengthy process—measured in years rather than months. But if the question is, "*Can* culture be changed?" the answer is "Yes!"

592   THE ORGANIZATION SYSTEM

1. Contrast individual personality and organizational culture. How are they similar? How are they different?

2. What is the relationship between institutionalization, formalization, and organizational culture?

3. What's the difference between job satisfaction and organizational culture?

4. Can an employee survive in an organization if he or she rejects its core values? Explain.

5. What forces might contribute toward making a culture strong or weak?

6. How is an organization's culture maintained?

7. Is socialization brainwashing? Explain.

8. What benefits can socialization provide for the organization? For the new employee?

9. If management sought a culture characterized as innovative and autonomous, what might its socialization program look like?

10. If management sought a culture characterized as formalized and conflict-free, what might its socialization program look like?

11. Can you identify a set of characteristics that describe your college's culture? Compare them with several of your peers. How closely do they agree?

12. "We should be opposed to the manipulation of individuals for organizational purposes but a degree of social uniformity enables organizations to work better." Do you agree or disagree with this statement? Discuss.

■ *FOR FURTHER READING*

BUONO, A. F., and J. L. BOWDITCH, *The Human Side of Mergers and Acquisitions.* San Francisco: Jossey-Bass, 1989. Describes strategies that managers can use to handle the collisions between people, culture, and organizations that occur when mergers and acquisitions take place.

HIRSCHHORN, L., and T. N. GILMORE, "The Psychodynamics of a Cultural Change: Learning from a Factory," *Human Resource Management,* Summer 1989, pp. 211–33. A case study that explores the psychodynamics of a cultural change in a large electronics factory.

HOFSTEDE, G., B. NEUIJEN, D. D. OHAYV, and G. SANDERS, "Measuring Organizational Cultures: A Qualitative and Quantitative Study Across Twenty Cases," *Administrative Science Quarterly,* June 1990, pp. 286–316. Based on a study of organizational cultures in twenty units from ten different organizations in Denmark and the Netherlands, researchers found that organizational culture could be described on six independent dimensions.

KELLER, M., *Rude Awakening: The Rise, Fall, and Struggle for Recovery of General Motors.* New York: William Morrow, 1989. A description of GM's organization, culture, and products; plus an explanation of what went wrong in the 1970s and 1980s.

MEEK, V. L., "Organizational Culture: Origins and Weaknesses," *Organization Studies,* Vol. 9, No. 4, 1988, pp. 453–74. Reviews and critiques several theories of organizational culture.

SHOCKLEY-ZALABAK, P., and D. D. MORLEY, "Adhering to Organizational Culture," *Group & Organization Studies,* December 1989, pp. 483–500. Considers the interrelatedness of communication and organizational culture.

Rate Your Classroom Culture

Listed here are eight statements. Score each statement by indicating the degree to which you agree with it. If you strongly agree, give it a 5. If you strongly disagree, give it a 1.

1. My classmates are friendly and supportive. ____
2. My teacher is friendly and supportive. ____
3. I expect my final grade will accurately reflect the effort I make. ____
4. My teacher clearly expresses his or her expectations to the class. ____
5. My teacher encourages me to question and challenge him or her as well as other students. ____
6. I think the grading system used by my teacher is based on clear standards of performance. ____
7. My teacher makes me want to learn. ____
8. My teacher would give everyone in the class an A if we all earned it. ____

Turn to page 692 for scoring directions and key.

Nordstrom: Where Service Is a Serious Business

Nordstrom employees are fond of this story: When this specialty retail chain was in its infancy, a customer came in and wanted to return a set of automobile tires. The sales clerk was a bit uncertain how to handle the problem. As the customer and sales clerk spoke, Mr. Nordstrom walked by and overheard the conversation. He immediately interceded, asking the customer how much he paid for the tires. Mr. Nordstrom then instructed the clerk to take the tires back and provide a full cash refund. After the customer had received his refund and left, the perplexed clerk looked at the boss. "But, Mr. Nordstrom, we don't sell tires!" "I know," replied the boss, "but we do whatever we need to do to make the customer happy. I mean it when I say we have a no-questions-asked return policy." Nordstrom then picked up the telephone and called a friend in the auto parts business to see how much he could get for the tires.*

Without sacrificing style, variety, or value, Nordstrom distinguishes itself from its competition by its service. Cheerful Nordstrom employees are readily available to help customers and they will go to incredible lengths to make a sale. It is not unusual, for example, for a sales person to call a Nordstrom store hundreds of miles away to see if they have the item a customer wants. If they do, they have it shipped. Upon its arrival, the sales person may personally deliver the item to the customer's home.

In contrast to many retailers, every Nordstrom executive started on the selling floor. Nordstrom rewards its salespeople with a salary, commission, and profit sharing package that is among the highest in its industry. College graduates start at $20,000 a year, and store managers can earn in excess of $100,000. The firm's rapid growth has meant rapid promotions for those who produce. The company, which began in Seattle, now has more than fifty stores on the West Coast, recently opened its first stores on the East Coast, and is currently planning stores in Chicago and Minneapolis. Specialty retailers in these areas, many of whom have cut services to improve their profit margins, shiver at the thought of competing against Nordstrom. They know Nordstrom has a service culture that works. It also makes plenty of money. The company has the highest sales per square foot of any department store—more than one hundred percent above the industry average. And profit growth ranks in retailing's top tier.

QUESTIONS

1. Compare Nordstrom's culture with the culture at a large department store you're familiar with. How do they compare?

2. What is the impact of the Nordstrom culture on its employees?

3. If the Nordstrom culture has proven so successful, why don't competitors copy it?

*This case is partially based on T. Peters, "The Store Where the Action Is," *U.S. News & World Report,* May 12, 1986; and "Why Rivals Are Quaking as Nordstrom Heads East," *Business Week,* June 15, 1987, pp. 99–100. For an update on this case, see "Nordstrom's Push East Will Test Its Renown for the Best in Service," *Wall Street Journal,* August 1, 1989, p. 1; and "Will 'The Nordstrom Way' Travel Well?" *Business Week*, September 3, 1990, pp. 82-83.

NOTES

[1]R. Johnson, "McDonald's Combines a Dead Man's Advice With Lively Strategy," *Wall Street Journal,* December 18, 1987, p. 1; and P. Moser, "The McDonald's Mystique," *Fortune,* July 4, 1988, pp. 112–16.

[2]P. Selznick, "Foundations of the Theory of Organizations," *American Sociological Review,* February 1948, pp. 25–35.

[3]L. G. Zucker, "Organizations as Institutions," in S. B. Bacharach (ed.), *Research in the Sociology of Organizations* (Greenwich, CT: JAI Press, 1983), pp. 1–47; and A. J. Richardson, "The Production of Institutional Behaviour: A Constructive Comment on the Use of Institutionalization Theory in Organizational Analysis," *Canadian Journal of Administrative Sciences,* December 1986, pp. 304–16.

[4]See, for example, H. S. Becker, "Culture: A Sociological View," *Yale Review,* Summer 1982, pp. 513–27; and E. H. Schein, *Organizational Culture and Leadership* (San Francisco: Jossey-Bass, 1985), p. 168.

[5]Based on G. G. Gordon and W. M. Cummins, *Managing Management Climate* (Lexington, MA: Lexington Books, 1979); and C. A. Betts and S. M. Halfhill, "Organization Culture: Theory, Definitions, and Dimensions," presented at the National American Institute of Decision Sciences' Conference, Las Vegas, November 1985. See also S. R. Glaser, S. Zamanou, and K. Hacker, "Measuring and Interpreting Organizational Culture," *Management Communication Quarterly,* November 1987, pp. 173–98.

[6]See, for example, K. L. Gregory, "Native-View Paradigms: Multiple Cultures and Culture Conflicts in Organizations," *Administrative Science Quarterly,* September 1983, pp. 359–76.

[7]See, for example, T. E. Deal and A. A. Kennedy, *Corporate Cultures* (Reading, MA: Addison-Wesley, 1982); and T. J. Peters and R. H. Waterman, Jr., *In Search of Excellence* (New York: Harper & Row, 1982). For a counter argument, see G. S. Saffold, III, "Culture Traits, Strength, and Organizational Performance: Moving Beyond 'Strong' Culture," *Academy of Management Review,* October 1988, pp. 546–58.

[8]Y. Wiener, "Forms of Value Systems: A Focus on Organizational Effectiveness and Cultural Change and Maintenance," *Academy of Management Review,* October 1988, p. 536.

[9]C. A. O'Reilly III, "Corporations, Cults and Organizational Culture: Lessons from Silicon Valley Firms," paper presented at the 42nd Annual Meeting of the Academy of Management, Dallas, 1983.

[10]R. T. Mowday, L. W. Porter, and R. M. Steers, *Employee-Organization Linkages: The Psychology of Commitment, Absenteeism, and Turnover* (New York: Academic Press, 1982).

[11]T. J. Peters and R. H. Waterman, *In Search of Excellence.*

[12]Ibid.

[13]Ibid., p. 75.

[14]See, for instance, "Who's Excellent Now?," *Business Week,* November 5, 1984, pp. 76–78; K. E. Aupperle, W. Acar, and D. E. Booth, "An Empirical Critique of *In Search of Excellence:* How Excellent Are the Excellent Companies?," *Journal of Management,* Winter 1986, pp. 499–512; and M. A. Hitt and R. D. Ireland, "Peters and Waterman Revisited: The Unended Quest for Excellence," *Academy of Management Executive,* May 1987, pp. 91–98.

[15]T. E. Deal and A. A. Kennedy, "Culture: A New Look Through Old Lenses," *Journal of Applied Behavioral Science,* November 1983, p. 501.

[16]C. Hymowitz, "Which Corporate Culture Fits You?," *Wall Street Journal,* July 17, 1989, p. B1.

[17]M. Langley, "AT&T Has Call for a New Corporate Culture," *The Wall Street Journal,* February 28, 1984, p. 24; S. P. Feldman, "Culture and Conformity: An Essay on Individual Adaptation in Centralized Bureaucracy," *Human Relations,* April 1985, pp. 341–56; and J. J. Keller, "Bob Allen is Turning AT&T Into a Live Wire," *Business Week,* November 6, 1989, pp. 140–52.

[18]E. H. Schein, "The Role of the Founder in Creating Organizational Culture," *Organizational Dynamics,* Summer 1983, pp. 13–28.

[19]G. Salaman, "The Sociology of Assessment: The Regular Commissions Board Assessment Procedure," in *People and Organizations: Media Booklet II* (Milton Keynes, England: Open University Press, 1974).

[20]R. Pascale, "The Paradox of 'Corporate Culture': Reconciling Ourselves to Socialization," *California Management Review,* Winter 1985, pp. 26–27.

[21]"Who's Afraid of IBM?" *Business Week,* June 29, 1987, p. 72.

[22]Ibid.

[23]D. C. Hambrick and P. A. Mason, "Upper Echelons: The Organization as a Reflection of Its Top Managers," *Academy of Management Review,* April 1984, pp. 193–206.

[24]"Culture Shock at Xerox," *Business Week,* June 22, 1987, pp. 1, 6–10; and T. Vogel, "At Xerox, They're Shouting 'Once More Into the Breach'," *Business Week,* July 23, 1990, pp. 62–63.

[25]See, for instance, J. E. Hebden, "Adopting an Organization's Culture: The Socialization of Graduate Trainees," *Organizational Dynamics,* Summer 1986, pp. 54–72; and G. R. Jones, "Socialization Tactics, Self-Efficacy, and Newcomers' Adjustments to Organizations," *Academy of Management Journal,* June 1986, pp. 262–79.

[26]J. Van Maanen and E. H. Schein, "Career Development," in J. R. Hackman and J. L. Suttle (eds.), *Improving Life at Work* (Santa Monica, CA: Goodyear, 1977), pp. 58–62.

[27]D. C. Feldman, "The Multiple Socialization of Organization Members," *Academy of Management Review,* April 1981, p. 310.

[28]Van Maanen and Schein, "Career Development," p. 59.

[29]W. Rodgers, *Think* (New York: Stein & Day, 1969), pp. 153–54.

[30]J. Martin, M. S. Feldman, M. J. Hatch, and S. B. Sitkin, "The Uniqueness Paradox in Organizational Stories," *Administrative Science Quarterly,* September 1983, pp. 438–53.

[31]A. M. Pettigrew, "On Studying Organizational Cultures," *Administrative Science Quarterly,* December 1979, p. 576.

[32]Ibid.

[33]Cited in J. M. Beyer and H. M. Trice, "How an Organization's Rites Reveal Its Culture," *Organizational Dynamics,* Spring 1987, p. 15.

[34]See N. J. Adler, *International Dimensions of Organizational Behavior* (Boston: Kent Publishing, 1986), pp. 46–48.

[35]S. C. Schneider, "National vs. Corporate Culture: Implications for Human Resource Management," *Human Resource Management,* Summer 1988, p. 239.

[36]Ibid.

[37]This section is based on C. Knowlton, "How Disney Keeps the Magic Going," *Fortune,* December 4, 1989, pp. 111–32; C. M. Solomon, "How Does Disney Do It?," *Personnel Journal,* December 1989, pp. 50–57; and J. Van Maanen and G. Kunda, "'Real Feelings': Emotional Expression and Organizational Culture," in L. L. Cummings and B. M. Staw (eds.), *Research in Organizational Behavior,* Vol. 11 (Greenwich, Conn.: JAI Press, 1989), pp. 58–70.

[38]E. L. Andrews, "Out of Chaos," *Business Month,* December 1989, p. 33.

[39]See D. Hellriegel and J. W. Slocum, Jr., "Organizational Climate: Measures, Research, and Contingencies," *Academy of Management Journal,* June 1974, pp. 225–80; and B. M. Meglino, E. C. Ravlin, and C. L. Adkins, "Work Values Approach to Corporate Culture: A Field Test of the Value Congruence Process and Its Relationship to Individual Outcomes," *Journal of Applied Psychology,* June 1989, pp. 424–32.

[41]J. W. Lorsch and J. J. Morse, *Organizations and Their Members* (New York: Harper & Row, 1974).

[42]N. Nicholson and G. Johns, "The Absence Culture and the Psychological Contract— Who's in Control of Absence?" *Academy of Management Review,* July 1985, pp. 397–407.

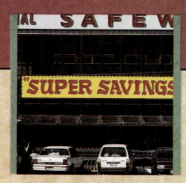

WORK STRESS

LEARNING OBJECTIVES

After studying this chapter, you should be able to:

1. *Define stress*
2. *Describe potential sources of stress*
3. *Explain individual difference variables that moderate the stress–outcome relationship*
4. *Identify stress consequences*
5. *Outline individual stress management strategies*
6. *List organizational stress management strategies*

Safeway Stores reduced its number of employees by 63,000. The restructuring has been stressful for both employees let go and those who remain. Susan May Tell/Picture Group.

Ulcers? I give 'em, I don't get 'em.

ANONYMOUS *CEO*

Safeway Stores, Inc. used to be a nice place to work. Its longtime motto—Safeway Offers Security—reflected this fact. In 1986, when the California-based company was taken private in a leveraged buyout, it had 2,000 supermarkets in twenty-nine states and in England, Australia, Canada, and Mexico. But immediately following the buyout, Safeway management introduced massive cost cuts. Three hundred staffers in its Oakland corporate headquarters were fired. A few months later, the Dallas division was shut down and nearly 9,000 more employees were dismissed—employees who had been with the company an average of seventeen years. By 1990, 63,000 managers and workers had been cut loose from Safeway through store sales or layoffs. The "new" Safeway's corporate statement reflects these changes. Displayed on a plaque in the lobby at corporate headquarters, it reads in part: "Targeted Returns on Current Investment."[1]

The majority of the former employees were reemployed by their new store owners, but at significantly lower pay. Many thousands have gone unemployed for several years. Those who have survived with the company find increased workloads and intense pressure to increase productivity.

The Safeway story is one of mixed results. It has proven a financial blessing for former shareholders, current investors, and top management. On the other hand, it has been a disaster for both its former and current employees. For example, James White, a Safeway trucker for nearly thirty years in Dallas, took his life a year after being fired. His widow said that he never could get over being let go from Safeway. Two other former employees tried to kill themselves. Hundreds of laid-off workers suffer from severe depression and have sought counseling.

For those who remain employed at Safeway, the work load and stress levels are high. Morale, not surprisingly, is at rock bottom. Truck drivers, for example, complain of having to pull sixteen-hour shifts. Store employees complain that clipboard-toting managers patrol the floors, closely monitoring performance and filing a blizzard of disciplinary reports. The company's new store quotas also create anxiety among everyone from managers to checkout clerks. A rash of store managers has even stepped down to become checkers, complaining of pressures to meet quotas.

What has happened at Safeway may be an extreme, but it dramatizes the stresses that some people are experiencing at work. In this chapter, we'll consider what causes stress, how it affects people differently, and ways in which individuals and organizations can manage stress.

The topic of stress and its relationship to worker behavior has only recently become a topic of interest to organizational researchers. Until the mid-1970s, research on stress was essentially confined to its effect on health and was conducted by individuals in the medical profession. Why the recent concern with stress as an OB topic? First, stress appears to be linked to employee performance and satisfaction, so the topic is a relevant independent variable. Second, there is an implicit obligation of management to improve the quality of organizational life for employees. Because stress has been directly linked to coronary heart disease, a reduction in stress can increase both the general health and the longevity of an organization's work force. Of course, this too can have performance implications.

One point of clarification is necessary before we proceed. The point is that the topic of stress has individual and group-level relevance as well as organization system implications. As we will show, an individual's stress level can be increased by such varied factors as his or her personality, role conflicts, or job's design. So work stress, while presented in this book's section on the organization system, is a multilevel concept.

WHAT IS STRESS?

Stress A dynamic condition in which an individual is confronted with an opportunity, constraint, or demand related to what he or she desires and for which the outcome is perceived to be both uncertain and important.

Stress is a dynamic condition in which an individual is confronted with an opportunity, constraint, or demand related to what he or she desires and for which the outcome is perceived to be both uncertain and important.[2] This is a complicated definition. Let's look at its components more closely.

Stress is not necessarily bad in and of itself. While stress is typically discussed in a negative context, it also has positive value. It is an opportunity when it offers potential gain. Consider, for example, the superior performance that an athlete or stage performer gives in "clutch" situations. Such individuals often use stress positively to rise to the occasion and perform at or near their maximum.

Constraints Forces that prevent individuals from doing what they desire.

Demands The loss of something desired.

More typically, stress is associated with **constraints** and **demands.** The former prevent you from doing what you desire. The latter refers to the loss of something desired. So when you take a test at school or you undergo your annual performance review at work, you feel stress because you confront opportunities, constraints, and demands. A good performance review may lead to a promotion, greater responsibilities, and a higher salary. But a poor review may prevent you from getting the promotion. An extremely poor review might even result in your being fired.

Two conditions are necessary for potential stress to become actual stress.[3] There must be uncertainty over the outcome and the outcome must be important. Regardless of the conditions, it is only when there is doubt or uncertainty regarding whether the opportunity will be seized, the constraint removed, or the loss avoided that there is stress. That is, stress is highest for those individuals who perceive that they are uncertain as to whether they will win or lose and lowest for those individuals who think that winning or losing is a certainty. But importance is also critical. If winning or losing is an unimportant outcome, there is no stress. If keeping your job or earning a promotion doesn't hold any importance to you, you have no reason to feel stress over having to undergo a performance review.

IS WORK STRESS WIDESPREAD?

Whether work stress is actually a widespread problem depends on your definition of "widespread." There are no reliable statistics on stress intensity at work or the percentage of the work population suffering serious stress symptoms. However, we can approach the question from several other directions.

First, a lot of people in general seem to suffer from stress symptoms. For instance, the American Academy of Family Physicians estimates that two-thirds of office visits to its members are attributable to stress-related symptoms.[4]

Second, stress-related health problems cost business and society a ton of money. The cost to business of stress-related problems and mental illness has been estimated as high as $150 billion a year, including health insurance and disability claims plus lost productivity.[5] In 1988, stress accounted for about fourteen percent of all occupational-disease worker-compensation claims.[6] And these claims on average draw medical and benefits payments totaling $15,000, or twice as much as those for workers with physical injuries.[7]

Third, some stress seems to come with every job. Can you name three or four jobs that are completely stress-free? It's not as easy as it seems. Most of us can identify jobs that are high in stress—air traffic controllers, police officers, fire fighters, emergency room physicians. But low-stress or, better yet, no-stress jobs are harder to identify.

Fourth, the dramatic changes that have taken place in the economy—mergers and acquisitions, increased global competition, new technological innovations, and the like—have resulted in large layoffs in many organizations and the restructuring of jobs. Few jobs are totally secure anymore. When co-workers or friends are losing their jobs and you fear for your own, stress levels are naturally going to increase.

An example of the dramatic changes that have recently taken place in the economy is the collapse of the investment banking business. The biggest player, Drexel Burnham Lambert, closed shop in the spring of 1990 and put thousands of young investment bankers on the street. Lee Celano/SIPA-PRESS.

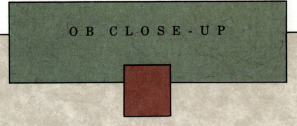

Rating Occupations by Stress

Recent research divides occupations into four categories: active jobs, low-strain jobs, passive jobs, and high-strain jobs.[8]

Active jobs have heavy pressure to perform but allow leeway for problem solving. The hours tend to be long, but are partly at the worker's discretion. Doctors, engineers, farmers, executives, and other professionals, for example, hold active jobs.

Low-strain jobs put low demands on people and give them a high degree of decision-making latitude. Tenured professors, carpenters, repair people, and successful artists, among others, hold low-strain jobs.

Passive jobs combine low demands on skills and mental processes with little leeway for learning or decision making. These jobs offer almost no latitude for innovation. Examples include the jobs held by billing clerks, night watchmen, janitors, dispatchers, and keypunchers.

High-strain jobs have heavy pressure to perform and little leeway in decision making. These jobs tend to have long hours, require following rigid procedures, and allow little latitude for taking breaks or time off for personal needs. Assembly-line workers, waiters and waitresses, nurse's aides, and telephone operators are good examples of people who hold high-strain jobs.

There is strong evidence indicating that people in high-strain jobs have the highest rates for many diseases. In fact, the risk of illness for such people is two to four times what it is for others, independent of all other risk factors.

Fifth, restructuring is not only undermining employee security, it is also putting pressure on employees—especially managers—to work longer hours. Twelve-hour days and six-day weeks have become the norm for many up-and-coming managers. A recent survey of CEOs found that they expect their middle managers to average forty-nine hours a week and their high-level executives to put in fifty-four hours. The CEOs themselves devote more than sixty hours a week to their jobs.[9]

Returning to our question—Is work stress widespread?—the answer would seem to be "yes." We're not saying that this stress level is necessarily high or even that it is seriously hindering most people in their work. A national survey of managers found that sixty-five percent believed that their jobs were more stressful than the average job.[10] But as Table 18–1 illustrates, the stressors that created above-average stress were factors such as interruptions, role conflicts, and workload demands. And the ratings on these factors indicate that they were nowhere near the "always stressful" point (4 on a scale of 1 to 4).

UNDERSTANDING STRESS AND ITS CONSEQUENCES

What causes stress? What are its consequences for individual employees? Why is it that the same set of conditions that creates stress for one person seems to

TABLE 18–1   The Impact of Workplace Stressors on Managerial Respondents (n = 315)

Stressor	Average Rating of All Respondents*
Interruptions	2.8
Role conflict (conflicting demands on time by others)	2.7
Work load	2.6
Managing time on the job	2.4
Organizational politics	2.3
Finding time for outside activities	2.3
Responsibility for subordinates	2.3
Firing someone	2.3
Reprimanding or disciplining	2.3
Balancing personal life with worklife	2.2
Dealing with upper management	2.1
Reviewing performance	2.0
Role ambiguity (uncertainty of what others expect)	2.0
Pay/compensation	1.8
Interviewing and hiring	1.8
Overtime	1.7
Working with budgets	1.7
Working with computers	1.5
Travel	1.4

*On a scale of 1 to 4, where 1 means never or rarely stressful and 4 means always stressful.
Source: Reprinted from *Management World,* June–August 1987, with permission from AMS, Trevose, PA 19047. Copyright (1987) AMS.

have little or no effect on another person? Figure 18–1 provides a model that can help to answer questions such as these.[11]

The model identifies three sets of factors—environmental, organizational, and individual—that act as *potential* sources of stress. Whether they become *actual* stress depends on individual differences such as job experience and personality. When stress is experienced by an individual, its symptoms can surface as physiological, psychological, and behavioral outcomes.

In the remainder of this chapter, we'll consider this model in more detail by reviewing the potential sources of stress, key individual difference variables, and stress consequences. Then we'll focus on stress management strategies that individuals themselves and organizations can utilize to help people cope with dysfunctional stress levels.

POTENTIAL SOURCES OF STRESS

As the model in Figure 18–1 shows, there are three categories of potential stressors: environmental, organizational, and individual. Let's take a look at each.[12]

Environmental Factors

Just as environmental uncertainty influences the design of an organization's structure, it also influences stress levels among employees in that organization.

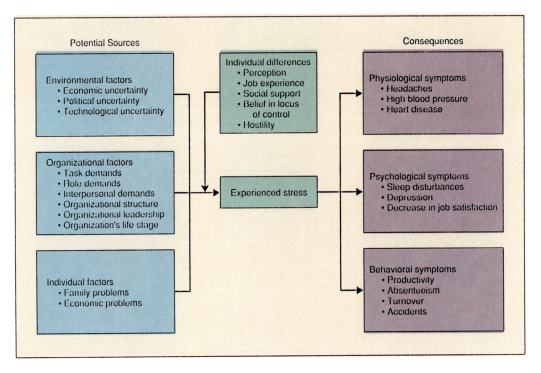

FIGURE 18–1   A Model of Stress

Changes in the business cycle create *economic uncertainties*. When the economy is contracting, people become increasingly anxious about their security. It was not a chance occurrence that suicide rates skyrocketed during the Great Depression of the 1930s. Minor recessions, too, increase stress levels. Downward swings in the economy are often accompanied by permanent reductions in force, temporary layoffs, reduced pay, shorter work weeks, and the like.

Political uncertainties don't tend to create stress among North Americans as they do for employees in countries like Nicaragua or Iraq. The obvious reason is that the United States and Canada have stable political systems where change is typically implemented in an orderly manner. Yet political threats and changes, even in countries like the United States and Canada, can be stress-inducing. The collapse of Canada's Meech Lake Accord in 1990, which sought to recognize Quebec's French-speaking majority and give unique status to the province, has significantly increased the likelihood that Quebec will seek some type of official separation from the rest of Canada. Such political uncertainty increases stress among many Quebequers, particularly those with little or no skills in the French language.

New innovations can make an employee's skills and experience obsolete in a very short period of time. *Technological uncertainty,* therefore, is a third type of environmental factor that can cause stress. Computers, robotics, automation, and other forms of technological innovations are a threat to many people and cause them stress.

Organizational Factors

There are no shortages of factors within the organization that can cause stress: Pressures to avoid errors or complete tasks in a limited time period,

Political uncertainties are far less in the United States than in the Middle East, but such uncertainties can still be stress-inducing for individuals.   Left, Susan Biddle/The White House; right, © Merlet/Rea/Saba.

work overload, a demanding and insensitive boss, and unpleasant co-workers are a few examples. (See Table 18–2.) We've categorized these factors around task, role, and interpersonal demands; organization structure; organizational leadership; and the organization's life stage.[13]

Task demands are factors related to a person's job. They include the design of the individual's job (autonomy, task variety, degree of automation), working conditions, and the physical work layout. Assembly lines can put pressure on people when their speed is perceived as excessive. The more interdependence between a person's tasks and the tasks of others, the more potential stress there is. Autonomy, on the other hand, tends to lessen stress. Jobs where temperatures, noise, or other working conditions are dangerous or undesirable can increase anxiety. So, too, can working in an overcrowded room or in a visible location where interruptions are constant.

Role demands relate to pressures placed on a person as a function of the particular role he or she plays in the organization. Role conflicts create expectations that may be hard to reconcile or satisfy. Role overload is experienced when the employee is expected to do more than time permits. Role

TABLE 18–2   Primary Causes of Stress at Work

What factors cause the most stress on the job? A *Wall Street Journal* survey reported:

Factor	Percentage Response*
Not doing the kind of work I want to	34
Coping with current job	30
Working too hard	28
Colleagues at work	21
A difficult boss	18

*Percentages exceed 100 as a result of some multiple responses.
Source: "Worries at Work," *Wall Street Journal*, April 7, 1988, p. 27. Reprinted by permission of *Wall Street Journal*, © 1988 Dow Jones & Company, Inc. All rights reserved worldwide.

So much mail; so little time. The pressure is high for many of these postal workers who have about one second to read an address and punch in the first three digits of the ZIP code, which is then translated into a bar code symbol for sorting mail by carrier route.   Jodi Buren/Time Magazine.

ambiguity is created when role expectations are not clearly understood and the employee is not sure what he or she is to do.

Interpersonal demands are pressures created by other employees. Lack of social support from colleagues and poor interpersonal relationships can cause considerable stress, especially among employees with a high social need.

Organization structure defines the level of differentiation in the organization, the degree of rules and regulations, and where decisions are made. Excessive rules and lack of participation in decisions that affect an employee are examples of structural variables that might be potential sources of stress.

Organizational leadership represents the managerial style of the organization's senior executives. Some chief executive officers create a culture characterized by tension, fear, and anxiety. They establish unrealistic pressures to perform in the short run, impose excessively tight controls, and routinely fire employees who don't "measure up." For instance, when Harold Geneen was chairman and CEO at ITT, division executives had to formally present their annual business plan to Geneen and his senior staff group. Each division executive would then be interrogated about every number in every graph, exhibit, and analysis in the plan. The exercise was known to put fear in the hearts of all the division executives and to occasionally bring tears to some of their eyes.

Organizations go through a cycle. They're established, they grow, become mature, and eventually decline. An *organization's life stage*—that is, where it is in this four-stage cycle—creates different problems and pressures for employees. The establishment and decline stages are particularly stressful. The former is characterized by a great deal of excitement and uncertainty, while the latter typically requires cutbacks, layoffs, and a different set of uncertainties. Stress tends to be least in maturity where uncertainties are at their lowest ebb.

Individual Factors

The typical individual only works about forty hours a week. The experiences and problems that people encounter in those other 128 nonwork hours each week can spill over to the job. Our final category, then, encompasses factors that comprise the employee's personal life. Primarily, this focuses on family and personal economic problems.

National surveys consistently show that people hold *family* and personal relationships dear. Marital difficulties, the breaking off of a relationship, and discipline troubles with children are examples of relationship problems that create stress for employees and that aren't left at the front door when they arrive at work.

Economic problems created by individuals overextending their financial resources is another set of personal troubles that can create stress for employees and distract their attention from their work. Regardless of income level—people who make $50,000 a year seem to have as much trouble handling their finances as those who earn $15,000—some people are poor money managers or have wants that always seem to exceed their earning capacity.

Table 18–3 lists more than forty life events that, according to research, create stress for individuals.[14] The mean value given to each life event represents its relative weight or importance. Higher numbers create greater stress and require more adaptive or coping behavior. Notice, for example, how four out of the first five are problems related to family and relationships. Notice, too, that life change events typically characterized as positive— marriage, outstanding personal achievements, vacations, Christmas—are stress-creating.

Most of the research using the scale in Table 18–3 has been to establish relationships between individual scores and later health problems. The logic underlying the scale is that the accumulation of life change events lowers the body's resistance and enhances the probability of illness, injuries, and related health problems. Researchers have found that individuals who report life change scores totalling less than 150 points in the previous year are generally in good health a year later. If the total score is above 150 but less than 300, individuals have about a fifty percent chance of developing a serious illness in the following year. For those in the high-risk category—300 points or above—the chance of developing a serious illness rises to seventy percent.[15]

Stressors Are Additive

As the life change events scale illustrates, stress is an additive phenomenon—a fact that tends to be overlooked when stressors are reviewed individually.[16] Stress builds up. Each new and persistent stressor adds to an individual's stress level. A single stressor, in and of itself, may seem relatively unimportant, but if it is added to an already high level of stress, it can be "the straw that breaks the camel's back." If we want to appraise the total amount of stress an individual is under, we have to sum up his or her opportunity stresses, constraint stresses, and demand stresses.

TABLE 18–3   Life Change Events and Their Rating

Rank	Life Event	Mean Value
1.	Death of spouse	100
2.	Divorce	73
3.	Marital separation from mate	65
4.	Detention in jail or other institution	63
5.	Death of a close family member	63
6.	Major personal injury or illness	53
7.	Marriage	50
8.	Being fired at work	47
9.	Marital reconciliation with mate	45
10.	Retirement from work	45
11.	Major change in the health or behavior of a family member	44
12.	Pregnancy	40
13.	Sexual difficulties	39
14.	Gaining a new family member (through birth, adoption, relative moving in, etc.)	39
15.	Major business readjustment (merger, reorganization, bankruptcy, etc.)	39
16.	Major change in financial state (a lot worse off or a lot better off than usual)	38
17.	Death of a close friend	37
18.	Changing to a different line of work	36
19.	Major change in the number of arguments with spouse (either a lot more or a lot less than usual regarding child-rearing, personal habits, etc.)	35
20.	Taking out a mortgage or loan for a major purchase (for a home, business, etc.)	31
21.	Foreclosure on a mortgage or loan	30
22.	Major change in responsibilities at work (promotion, demotion, lateral transfer)	29
23.	Son or daughter leaving home (marriage, attending college, etc.)	29
24.	Trouble with in-laws	29
25.	Outstanding personal achievement	28
26.	Spouse beginning or ceasing work outside the home	26
27.	Beginning or ceasing formal schooling	26
28.	Major change in living conditions (building a new home, remodeling, deterioration of home or neighborhood, etc.)	25
29.	Revision of personal habits (dress, manners, associations, etc.)	24
30.	Trouble with the boss	23
31.	Major change in working hours or conditions	20
32.	Change in residence	20
33.	Changing to a new school	20
34.	Major change in usual type and/or amount of recreation	19
35.	Major change in church activities (a lot more or a lot less than usual)	19
36.	Major change in social activities (clubs, dancing, movies, visiting, etc.)	18
37.	Taking out a mortgage or loan for a lesser purchase (for a car, TV, freezer, etc.)	17
38.	Major change in sleeping habits (a lot more or a lot less sleep, or change in part of day when asleep)	16
39.	Major change in number of family get-togethers (a lot more or a lot less than usual, etc.)	15
40.	Major change in eating habits (a lot more or a lot less food intake, or very different meal hours or surroundings)	15
41.	Vacation	13
42.	Christmas	12
43.	Minor violations of the law (traffic tickets, jaywalking, disturbing the peace, etc.)	11

Source: Adapted from T. H. Holmes and R. H. Rahe, "The Social Readjustment Scale," *Journal of Psychosomatic Research*, 11 (1967), p. 216. With permission from Pergamon Press, Ltd.

INDIVIDUAL DIFFERENCES

Not *everyone* who scores over 300 points on the life change events scale has a serious illness. On the other hand, some individuals who have incredibly stable and secure lives go to pieces when the smallest problem arises. Some people thrive on stressful situations, while others are totally overwhelmed by them. What is it that differentiates people in terms of their ability to deal with stress? What individual difference variables moderate the relationship between *potential* stressors and *experienced* stress? At least five variables—perception, job experience, social support, belief in locus of control, and hostility—have been found to be relevant moderators.

Perception

In Chapter 5, we demonstrated that employees react in response to their perception of reality rather than to reality itself. Perception, therefore, will moderate the relationship between a potential stress condition and an employee's reaction to it. One person's fear that he'll lose his job because his company is laying off personnel may be perceived by another as an opportunity to get a large severance allowance and start his own business. Similarly, what one employee perceives as an efficient and challenging work environment may be viewed as threatening and demanding by others. So the stress potential in environmental, organizational, and individual factors doesn't lie in their objective condition. Rather, it lies in an employee's interpretation of those factors.

Job Experience

Experience is said to be a great teacher. It can also be a great stress-reducer. Think back to your first date or your first few days in college. For most of us, the uncertainty and newness of these situations created stress. But as we gained experience, that stress disappeared or at least significantly decreased. The same phenomenon seems to apply to work situations. That is, experience on the job tends to be negatively related to work stress. Two explanations have been offered.[17] First is the idea of selective withdrawal. Voluntary turnover is more probable among people who experience more stress. Therefore, people who remain with the organization longer are those with more stress-resistant traits; or who are at least more resistant to the stress characteristics of their organization. Second, people eventually develop coping mechanisms to deal with stress. Because this takes time, senior members of the organization are more likely to be fully adapted and should experience less stress.

Social Support

There is increasing evidence that social support—that is, collegial relationships with co-workers or supervisors—can buffer the impact of stress.[18] The logic underlying this moderating variable is that social support acts as a palliative, mitigating the negative effects of even high-strain jobs.

For individuals whose work associates are unhelpful or even actively hostile, social support may be found outside the job. Involvement with family, friends, and community can provide the support—especially for those with a high social need—that is missing at work and that can make job stressors more tolerable.

Belief in Locus of Control

Locus of control was introduced in Chapter 4 as a personality attribute. Those with an internal locus of control believe they control their own destiny. Those with an external locus believe their lives are controlled by outside forces. Evidence indicates that internals perceive their jobs to be less stressful than do externals.[19]

When internals and externals confront a similar stressful situation, the internals are likely to believe that they can have a significant effect on the results. They, therefore, act to take control of events. Externals are more likely to be passive and defensive. Rather than do something to reduce the stress, they acquiesce. So externals, who are more likely to feel helpless in stressful situations, are also more likely to experience stress.

Hostility

Type A Behavior Aggressive involvement in a chronic, incessant struggle to achieve more and more in less and less time and, if necessary, against the opposing efforts of other things or other people.

For much of the 1970s and 1980s, a great deal of attention was directed at what became known as **Type A behavior**.[20] In fact, throughout the 1980s it was undoubtedly the most frequently used moderating variable related to stress.

Type A behavior is characterized by feeling a chronic sense of time urgency and by an *excessive* competitive drive. A Type A individual is "*aggressively* involved in a *chronic, incessant* struggle to achieve more and more in less and less time, and if required to do so, against the opposing efforts of other things or other persons."[21] In the North American culture, such characteristics tend to be highly prized and positively correlated with ambition and the successful acquisition of material goods. Type As

1. are always moving, walking, and eating rapidly,
2. feel impatient with the rate at which most events take place,
3. strive to think or do two or more things simultaneously,
4. cannot cope with leisure time, and
5. are obsessed with numbers; success is measured in terms of how much of everything they acquire.

Type B Behavior Rarely harried by the desire to obtain a wildly increasing number of things or to participate in an endlessly growing series of events in an ever decreasing amount of time.

The opposite of Type A is **Type B behavior.** Type Bs are "rarely harried by the desire to obtain a wildly increasing number of things or participate in an endless growing series of events in an ever decreasing amount of time."[22] Type Bs

1. never suffer from a sense of time urgency, with its accompanying impatience,
2. feel no need to display or discuss their achievements or accomplishments unless such exposure is demanded by the situation,
3. play for fun and relaxation, rather than to exhibit their superiority at any cost, and

4. can relax without guilt.

Until quite recently, researchers believed that Type As were more likely to experience stress on and off the job. More specifically, Type As were widely believed to be at higher risk for heart disease. A closer analysis of the evidence, however, has produced new conclusions.[23] By looking at various components of Type A behavior, it's been found that only the hostility and anger associated with Type A behavior actually is related to heart disease. The chronically angry, suspicious, and mistrustful person is the one at risk.

So just because a person is a workaholic, rushes around a lot, and is impatient or competitive does not mean that he or she is unduly susceptible to heart disease or the other negative effects of stress. Rather, it's the quickness to anger, the persistent hostile outlook, and the cynical mistrust of others that are harmful.

STRESS CONSEQUENCES

Stress shows itself in a number of ways. For instance, an individual who is experiencing a high level of stress may develop high blood pressure, ulcers, irritability, difficulty in making routine decisions, loss of appetite, accident proneness, and the like. These can be subsumed under three general categories: physiological, psychological, and behavioral symptoms.[24]

Physiological Symptoms

Physiological Symptoms
Changes in an individual's health as a result of stress.

Most of the early concern with stress was directed at **physiological symptoms.** This was predominately due to the fact that the topic was researched by specialists in the health and medical sciences. This research led to the

Fire department emergency medical personnel frequently experience all three types of stress symptoms—physiological, psychological, and behavioral—as a result of the stress from their jobs.   Jon A. Rembold/Insight Magazine.

conclusion that stress could create changes in metabolism, increase heart and breathing rates, increase blood pressure, bring on headaches, and induce heart attacks.

The link between stress and particular physiological symptoms is not clear. There are few, if any, consistent relationships.[25] This is attributed to the complexity of the symptoms and the difficulty of objectively measuring them. But of greater relevance is the fact that physiological symptoms have the least direct relevance to students of OB. Our concern is with behaviors and attitudes. Therefore, the two other symptoms of stress are more important to us.

Psychological Symptoms

Psychological Symptoms
Changes in an individual's attitudes and disposition due to stress.

Stress can cause dissatisfaction. Job-related stress can cause job-related dissatisfaction. Job dissatisfaction, in fact, is "the simplest and most obvious psychological effect" of stress.[26] But stress shows itself in other **psychological** states—for instance, tension, anxiety, irritability, boredom, and procrastination.

The evidence indicates that when people are placed in jobs that make multiple and conflicting demands or in which there is a lack of clarity as to the incumbent's duties, authority, and responsibilities, both stress and dissatisfaction are increased.[27] Similarly, the less control people have over the pace of their work, the greater the stress and dissatisfaction. While more research is needed to clarify the relationship, the evidence suggests that jobs that provide a low level of variety, significance, autonomy, feedback, and identity to incumbents create stress and reduce satisfaction and involvement in the job.[28]

Behavioral Symptoms

Behavioral Symptoms
Changes in an individual's behavior—including productivity, absence, and turnover—as a result of stress.

Behaviorally related stress symptoms include changes in productivity, absence, and turnover, as well as changes in eating habits, increased smoking or consumption of alcohol, rapid speech, fidgeting, and sleep disorders.

There has been a significant amount of research investigating the stress–performance relationship. The most thoroughly documented pattern in the stress–performance literature is the inverted-U relationship.[29] This is shown in Figure 18–2.

The logic underlying the inverted U is that low to moderate levels of stress stimulate the body and increase its ability to react. Individuals then often perform their tasks better, more intensely, or more rapidly. But too much stress places unattainable demands or constraints on a person, which results in lower performance. This inverted-U pattern may also describe the reaction to stress over time, as well as to changes in stress intensity. That is, even moderate levels of stress can have a negative influence on performance over the long term as the continued intensity of the stress wears down the individual and saps his or her energy resources. An athlete may be able to use the positive effects of stress to obtain a higher performance during every Saturday's game in the fall season, or a sales executive may be able to psych herself up for her presentation at the annual national meeting. But moderate levels of stress experienced continually over long periods of time—as typified by the emergency room staff in a large urban hospital—can result in lower performance. This may explain why emergency room staffs at such hospitals

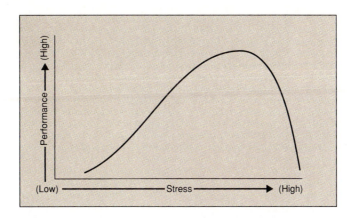

FIGURE 18–2   Relationship Between Stress and Job Performance

are frequently rotated and why it is unusual to find individuals who have spent the bulk of their career in such an environment. In effect, to do so would expose the individual to the risk of "career burnout."

Considerable attention has also been focused on how the Type A–Type B dichotomy affects job performance. Research findings, unfortunately, are inconclusive.[30] For instance, some indicate that Type As emphasize quantity of output while Type Bs focus on quality. Other studies, however, fail to replicate these findings. The most confident statement we can make is that Type As outperform Type Bs in those jobs calling for persistence or endurance. This is because Type As set higher performance goals and are not easily derailed by setbacks.

STRESS MANAGEMENT STRATEGIES

From the organization's standpoint, management may not be concerned when employees experience low-to-moderate levels of stress. The reason, as we showed earlier, is that such levels of stress can be functional and lead to higher employee performance. But high levels of stress, or even low levels sustained over long periods of time, can lead to reduced employee performance and, thus, require action by management.

While a limited amount of stress may benefit an employee's performance, don't expect employees to see it that way. From the individual's standpoint, even low levels of stress are likely to be perceived as undesirable. It's not unlikely, therefore, for employees and management to have different notions of what constitutes an acceptable level of stress on the job. What management may consider as "a positive stimulus that keeps the adrenalin running" is very likely to be seen as "excessive pressure" by the employee. Keep this in mind as we discuss individual and organizational approaches toward managing stress.[35]

Individual Approaches

An employee can take personal responsibility for reducing his or her stress level. Individual strategies that have proven effective include implementing

Job Burnout: The Malady of Our Age?

Many people have undoubtedly suffered from job burnout for decades but it didn't become a primary concern of health specialists and behavioral scientists until the 1980s. Now, some are calling it "the malady of our age."[31]

What *is* job burnout? Burnout is defined as a three-dimensional concept characterized by (1) depersonalization or a negative shift in responses to others; (2) a decreased sense of personal accomplishment; and (3) physical, mental, and emotional exhaustion.[32] It is this last characteristic that most of us associate with burnout—sufferers appear to have become worn out from their jobs. They are low in energy, fatigued, feel helpless and trapped, and exhibit negative attitudes about themselves, work, and life in general.

Is job burnout synonymous with stress? No, but it's closely related. Work-related stressors can culminate in burnout, but do not always do so. What conditions, then, lead to job burnout? First, there is the existence of such organizational or individual stressors as role ambiguity, performance pressures, work overload, or interpersonal conflicts. Second, the burnout candidate tends to hold unrealistic expectations or ambitions. These combine to create stress, fatigue, frustration, and feelings of helplessness and guilt.[33] When burnout sets in, the person finds that he or she has difficulty coping with the demands of the job. The eventual result is reduced organizational commitment and job satisfaction, increased absenteeism, and impairment of interpersonal relationships with work colleagues, friends, and family.

Who is vulnerable to job burnout? Maybe somewhat surprisingly, it tends to attack the best, the brightest, and the most highly motivated—those who had once been among the most idealistic and enthusiastic.[34] It seems particularly to strike middle managers and helping professionals such as nurses, physicians, social workers, lawyers, schoolteachers, and police officers.

The combination of stress and acceptance of the fact that many job problems have no clear-cut solutions may explain why some professionals drop out of the careers that they've spent years in and for which they underwent extensive training. The decision by many nurses and secondary school teachers, for instance, to switch to other careers after only ten or fifteen years in these professions is probably at least in part a response to job burnout. Some of the strategies for managing stress that we discuss in the next section can also help reduce the causes and symptoms of burnout.

time management techniques, increasing physical exercise, relaxation training, and expanding the social support network.

TIME MANAGEMENT   Many people manage their time poorly. The things they have to accomplish in any given day or week are not necessarily beyond completion if they manage their time properly. The well-organized employee, like the well-organized student, can often accomplish twice as much as the person who is poorly organized. So an understanding and utilization of basic time management principles can help individuals better cope with job demands. A few of the more well-known time management principles include: (1) making daily lists of activities to be accomplished; (2) prioritizing activities by importance and urgency; (3) scheduling activities according to the priorities set; and (4) knowing your daily cycle and handling the most demanding parts of your job during the high part of your cycle when you are most alert and productive.[36]

PHYSICAL EXERCISE   Noncompetitive physical exercise such as aerobics, race walking, jogging, swimming, and riding a bicycle have long been recommended by physicians as a way to deal with excessive stress levels. These forms of exercise increase heart capacity, lower at-rest heart rate, provide a mental diversion from work pressures, and offer a means to "let off steam."

RELAXATION TRAINING   Individuals can teach themselves to relax through techniques such as meditation, hypnosis, and biofeedback. The objective is to reach a state of **deep relaxation,** where one feels physically relaxed, somewhat detached from the immediate environment, and detached from body sensations.[37] Fifteen or twenty minutes a day of deep relaxation releases tension and provides a person with a pronounced sense of peacefulness. Importantly, significant changes in heart rate, blood pressure, and other physiological factors result from achieving the deep relaxation condition.

SOCIAL SUPPORT   As we noted earlier in this chapter, having friends, family, or work colleagues to talk to provides an outlet when stress levels become excessive. Expanding your social support network, therefore, can be a means for tension reduction. It provides you with someone to hear your problems and a more objective perspective on the situation. Research also demonstrates that social support moderates the stress–burnout relationship.[38] That is, high support reduces the likelihood that heavy work stress will result in job burnout.

Deep Relaxation A state of physical relaxation, where the individual is somewhat detached from both the immediate environment and body sensations.

Organizational Approaches

Several of the factors that cause stress—particularly task and role demands, and organization structure—are controlled by management. As such, they can be modified or changed. Strategies that management might want to consider include improved personnel selection and job placement, use of realistic goal setting, redesigning of jobs, use of participative decision making, improved organizational communication, and establishment of corporate wellness programs.

SELECTION AND PLACEMENT   While certain jobs are more stressful than others, we learned earlier in this chapter that individuals can differ in their response to stress situations. We know, for example, that individuals with little experience or an external locus of control, tend to be more stress-prone. Selection and placement decisions should take these facts into consideration. Obviously, while management shouldn't restrict hiring to only experienced individuals with an internal locus, such individuals may adapt better to high stress jobs and perform those jobs more effectively.

GOAL SETTING   We discussed goal setting in Chapter 7. Based on an extensive amount of research, we concluded that individuals perform better when they have specific and challenging goals and receive feedback on how well they are progressing toward these goals. The use of goals can reduce stress as well as provide motivation. Specific goals that are perceived as attainable clarify performance expectations. Additionally, goal feedback reduces uncertainties as to actual job performance. The result is less employee frustration, role ambiguity, and stress.

JOB REDESIGN   Redesigning jobs to give employees more responsibility, more meaningful work, more autonomy, and increased feedback can reduce stress, because these factors give the employee greater control over work activities and lessen dependence on others. But as we noted in our discussion of job design in Chapter 8, not all employees want enriched jobs. The right job redesign, then, for employees with a low need for growth might be less responsibility and increased division of labor. If individuals prefer structure and routine, reducing skill variety should also reduce uncertainties and stress levels.

PARTICIPATIVE DECISION MAKING   Role stress is detrimental to a large extent because employees feel uncertain about goals, expectations, how they'll be evaluated, and the like. By giving these employees a voice in those decisions that directly affect their job performances, management can increase employee control and reduce this role stress. So managers should consider increasing employee participation in decision making.[39]

ORGANIZATIONAL COMMUNICATION   Increasing formal communication with employees reduces uncertainty by lessening role ambiguity and role conflict. Given the importance that perceptions play in moderating the stress–response relationship, management can also use effective communications as a means to shape employee perceptions. Remember that what

FIGURE 18–3
Source: © 1990 by Sidney Harris, *The Wall Street Journal,* March 30, 1990.

"Since we began our corporate
stress-reduction seminars, production is
down – and no one seems to care."

Wellness Programs
Organizationally supported programs that focus on the employee's total physical and mental condition.

employees categorize as demands, threats, or opportunities are merely an interpretation, and that interpretation can be affected by the symbols and actions communicated by management.

WELLNESS PROGRAMS   Our final suggestion is to offer organizationally-supported **wellness programs.** These programs focus on the employee's total physical and mental condition.[40] For example, they typically provide workshops to help people quit smoking, control alcohol use, lose weight, eat better, and develop a regular exercise program. The assumption underlying most wellness programs is that employees need to take personal responsibility for their physical and mental health. The organization is merely a vehicle to facilitate this end.

Organizations, of course, aren't altruistic. They expect a payoff from their investment in wellness programs. And most of those firms that have introduced wellness programs have found the benefits to exceed the costs. For instance, Pillsbury calculates that every one dollar spent on its wellness program produces a $3.63 savings in health-related costs.[41] Johnson & Johnson computes the cost of its program at $200 per employee, yet claims that it saves $378 per employee by lowering absenteeism and slowing the rise in the company's health-care expenses.[42]

IMPLICATIONS FOR PERFORMANCE AND SATISFACTION

A number of factors (environmental, organizational, and individual), moderated by individual differences, cause employees to feel stressed. The more frequently these factors occur and the more intensely stressful they are for the employee, the greater the stress that he or she experiences. How intensely stressful the work situation is for a particular employee depends in part on his

Quaker Oats has installed a fitness center at its headquarters to encourage employees to stay healthy. To further encourage employees, the company offers financial incentives for employees who stay well.   David Walberg.

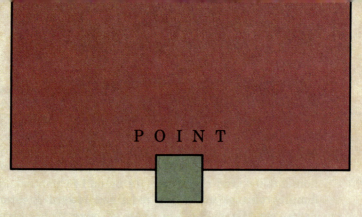

Employee Stress Isn't a Management Problem!

The recent attention given employee stress by behavioral scientists has been blown totally out of proportion. There is undoubtedly a small proportion of the working population that suffers from stress. These people have ongoing headaches, ulcers, high blood pressure, and the like. They may even turn to alcohol and drugs as an outlet to deal with their stress. But if there is a problem, it's a medical one. It is *not* a management problem. In support of this position, I'll argue that (1) stress is not that important because human beings are highly adaptive; (2) most stress that employees experience is of the positive type; and (3) even if the first two points weren't relevant, a good portion of what causes excessive work stress tends to be uncontrollable by management anyway.

Those who seem to be so concerned about employee stress forget that people are more adaptable than we traditionally give them credit for. They are amazingly resilient. Most successfully adjust to illnesses, misfortune, and other changes in their lives. All through their school years, they adapted to the demands that dozens of teachers put on them. They survived the trials of puberty, dating, beginning and ending relationships, and leaving home—to name a few of the more potentially stressful times we have all gone through. By the time individuals enter the work force, they have experienced many difficult situations and, for the most part, they have adjusted to each. There is no reason to believe that this ability to adapt to changing or uncomfortable conditions breaks down once people begin their working careers.

Stress, like conflict, has a positive as well as a negative side. But that positive side tends to be overshadowed by concern with the negative. A life without stress is a life without challenge, stimulation, or change. As Table 18–3 so clearly illustrates, many positive and exciting life events—marriage, the birth of a child, inheriting a large sum of money, buying a new home, a job promotion, vacations—create stress. Does that mean that these positive events should be avoided? The answer is obviously no. Unfortunately, when most people talk about stress and the need to reduce it, they tend to overlook its positive side.

Finally, there is the reality that many sources of employee stress are outside the control of management. Management can't control environmental factors. Most individual factors, too, are outside management's influence. Even if stresses created by such individual factors as family and economic problems can be influenced by managerial actions, there remains the ethical question: Does management have the right to interfere in an employee's personal life? Undoubtedly a good portion of any employee's total stress level is created by factors that are uncontrollable by management—marital problems; divorce; children who get into trouble; poor personal financial management; uncertainty over the economy; societal norms to achieve and acquire material symbols of success; pressures of living in a fast-paced, urban world, and the like. The actions of management didn't create these stressors. Most are just part of modern living. More importantly, there is little that employers can do to lessen these stressors without extending their influence beyond the organization and into the employee's personal life. That's something that most of us would agree is outside the province of the employer–employee relationship.

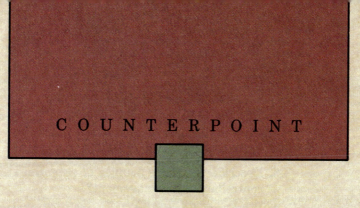

Stress Creates Real Costs to Organizations

Those who think management should ignore the problem of employee stress need to take a look at what stress is costing organizations.*

The total cost of work-related accidents in the United States is approximately $32 billion per year. It is estimated that at least three-quarters of all industrial accidents are caused by the inability of employees to cope with emotional distress.

Stress-related absenteeism, organizational medical expenses, and lost productivity are estimated to cost between $50 billion and $75 billion per year or an average of about $750 per worker. Stress-related headaches are the leading cause of lost work time in United States industry.

Coronary heart disease is a leading killer of Americans. Over one million Americans suffer heart attacks each year, and half of them are fatal. One out of every five average, healthy male Americans will suffer a heart attack before he reaches the age of sixty-five. Heart disease causes an annual loss of more than 135 million workdays. The premature loss of valued employees means the loss of experienced personnel and the additional cost of replacing these people. These facts are important because there now exists a wealth of research that links stress to heart disease.

More than sixty percent of long-term disability is related to psychological or psychosomatic problems often brought on or made worse by stress. State workers' compensation boards are increasingly awarding compensation for physical- and mental-stress claims. A single claim for permanent total disability can cost in excess of $250,000. Since each employer's workers' compensation costs are based on claims against that employer, any increase in awards is an added cost of doing business.

Two facts about stress cannot be ignored. First, people get sick from stress at work. Second, the costs associated with stress are significant to every employer. They include lost time, increased accidents, higher insurance premiums and health care costs, and lower productivity. The only natural conclusion one can draw is that managers cannot ignore the stress issue and must actively seek to do something about it. It is in management's self-interest to take an active stance because, if for no other reason, it provides a basis for defending the organization against claims that its jobs and working conditions are stress-creating and the primary cause for compensable emotional problems.

*These figures come from K. Albrecht, *Stress and the Manager* (Englewood Cliffs, NJ: Prentice Hall, 1979), pp. 33–34; "Stress: Can We Cope?," *Time*, June 6, 1983, pp. 48–54; J. W. Jones, "A Cost Evaluation for Stress Management," *EAP Digest*, November–December 1984, p. 34; "Stress Claims Are Making Business Jumpy," *Business Week*, October 14, 1985, pp. 152–54; and M. J. McCarthy, "Stressed Employees Look for Relief in Workers' Compensation Claims," *Wall Street Journal*, April 7, 1988, p. 27.

The "Stress for Success" Dilemma

Amy Redding was sitting in her office reviewing a speech she would be making the next day when Scott Oletta appeared at her doorway. Amy is head of research for a major securities and brokerage firm. Scott is an industry analyst who works for Amy. He is one of Amy's most valued analysts.

"Amy," Scott began, "I need to talk to you. You know I've been in this job for nearly four years. You hired me right out of graduate school. I thought the job would be challenging and it's been everything I had hoped for. I spend long hours here—I regularly put in twelve-hour days and have worked every Saturday for the past three months. But I'm not complaining. I love it. It's really challenging. But I've got no personal life. I was joking the other day with Nick in the mail room about not knowing what a love life is. The trouble is it's not a joke! Every time I meet someone and a relationship begins to develop, she gives me an ultimatum: 'It's either me or your work.' Women expect me to be free in the evenings and on weekends. And that just won't fly in this job. It consumes me.

"I weighed 170 pounds when I got out of school. This morning I weighed in at 205! I never smoked more than a pack a week in college. Did you know I'm up to three packs a day now? But what's got me really concerned is my drinking. For the past six months or so, I've had trouble sleeping. To help relax before bed, I began making myself a martini. Well, it worked, except I've been increasing the quantity lately. This morning, when I woke up, I looked at the vermouth bottle. It had been unopened until last night. It was half-empty. I figured out I had at least eight drinks last night! Amy, I'm scared. This job is my life, but the pressure to produce my industry reports and come up with continual recommendations at the rate we're expected to is getting to me.

"I called my sister down in Florida this morning and I ended up talking to her for an hour-and-a-half. She thinks I'm on a self-destructing course. She wants me to quit and come live with her for awhile. I'm afraid I'd go crazy without a job to consume me. You know I don't have any other interests. And I have to keep busy or I go crazy. There's so much I want to accomplish, career-wise, and I get frustrated that there are only twenty-four hours in the day.

"Amy, I don't know what to do. I think the best thing to do is quit this rat race and see if I can find a job with less pressure. I've written up my letter of resignation." Handing it to Amy, Scott said, "I'm not sure this is the answer, but I don't know what is."

QUESTIONS

1. What are the major stressors in Scott's life at the present time?

2. What stress symptoms is Scott displaying?

3. If you were Amy, how would you handle this situation?

NOTES

[1]S. C. Faludi, "Safeway LBO Yields Vast Profits But Exacts a Heavy Human Toll," *Wall Street Journal,* May 16, 1990, p. 1.

[2]Adapted from R. S. Schuler, "Definition and Conceptualization of Stress in Organizations," *Organizational Behavior and Human Performance,* April 1980, p. 189.

[3]Ibid., p. 191.

[4]C. Wallis, "Stress: Can We Cope?" *Time,* June 6, 1983.

[5]Cited in "Stress: The Test Americans Are Failing," *Business Week,* April 18, 1988, p. 74.

[6]M. J. McCarthy, "Stressed Employees Look for Relief in Workers' Compensation Claims," *Wall Street Journal,* April 7, 1988, p. 27.

[7]*Ibid.*

[8]R. Karasek and T. Theorell, *Healthy Work* (New York: Basic Books, 1990).

[9]S. Solo, "Stop Whining and Get Back to Work," *Fortune,* March 12, 1990, pp. 49–50.

[10]M. A. Tipgos, "The Things That Stress Us," *Management World,* June–August 1987, pp. 17–18.

[11]This model is based on D. F. Parker and T. A. DeCotiis, "Organizational Determinants of Job Stress," *Organizational Behavior and Human Performance,* October 1983, p. 166; S. Parasuraman and J. A. Alutto, "Sources and Outcomes of Stress in Organizational Settings: Toward the Development of a Structural Model," *Academy of Management Journal,* June 1984, p. 333; and C. L. Cooper, "The Stress of Work: An Overview," *Aviation, Space, and Environmental Medicine,* July 1985, p. 628.

[12]This section is adapted from C. Cooper and R. Payne, *Stress at Work;* and S. Parasuraman and J. A. Alutto, "Sources and Outcomes of Stress in Organizational Settings," pp. 330–50.

[13]See, for example, D. R. Frew and N. S. Bruning, "Perceived Organizational Characteristics and Personality Measures as Predictors of Stress/Strain in the Work Place," *Journal of Management,* Winter 1987, pp. 633–46.

[14]T. H. Holmes and R. H. Rahe, "The Social Readjustment Rating Scale," *Journal of Psychosomatic Research,* August 1967, pp. 213–18.

[15]Ibid.

[16]H. Selye, *The Stress of Life,* rev. ed. (New York: McGraw-Hill, 1956).

[17]S. J. Motowidlo, J. S. Packard, and M. R. Manning, "Occupational Stress: Its Causes and Consequences for Job Performance," *Journal of Applied Psychology,* November 1987, pp. 619–20.

[18]See, for instance, J. J. House, *Work Stress and Social Support* (Reading, Mass.: Addison Wesley, 1981); S. Jayaratne, D. Himle, and W. A. Chess, "Dealing with Work Stress and Strain: Is the Perception of Support More Important Than Its Use?," *The Journal of Applied Behavioral Science,* Vol. 24, No. 2, 1988, pp. 191–202; and R. C. Cummings, "Job Stress and the Buffering Effect of Supervisory Support," *Group & Organization Studies,* March 1990, pp. 92–104.

[19]See, for instance, G. R. Gemmill and W. J. Heisler, "Fatalism as a Factor in Managerial Job Satisfaction, Job Strain, and Mobility," *Personnel Psychology,* Summer 1972, pp. 241–50; and C. R. Anderson, D. Hellriegel, and J. W. Slocum, Jr., "Managerial Response to Environmentally Induced Stress," *Academy of Management Journal,* June 1977, pp. 260–72.

[20]M. Friedman and R. H. Rosenman, *Type A Behavior and Your Heart* (New York: Alfred A. Knopf, 1974).

[21]*Ibid.,* pg. 84.

[22]*Ibid.,* pp. 84–85.

[23]R. Williams, *The Trusting Heart: Great News About Type A Behavior* (New York: Times Books, 1989).

[24]Schuler, "Definition and Conceptualization of Stress," pp. 200–205.

[25]See T. A. Beehr and J. E. Newman, "Job Stress, Employee Health, and Organizational Effectiveness: A Facet Analysis, Model, and Literature Review," *Personnel Psychology,* Winter 1978, pp. 665–99; and B. D. Steffy and J. W. Jones, "Workplace Stress and Indicators of Coronary-Disease Risk," *Academy of Management Journal,* September 1988, pp. 686–98.

[26]Ibid., p. 687.

[27]C. L. Cooper and J. Marshall, "Occupational Sources of Stress: A Review of the Literature Relating to Coronary Heart Disease and Mental Ill Health," *Journal of Occupational Psychology,* Vol. 49, No. 1 (1976), pp. 11–28.

[28]J. R. Hackman and G. R. Oldham, "Development of the Job Diagnostic Survey," *Journal of Applied Psychology,* April 1975, pp. 159–70.

[29]See, for instance, J. E. McGrath, "Stress and Behavior in Organizations," in M. D. Dunnette (ed.), *Handbook of Industrial and Organizational Psychology* (Chicago: Rand McNally, 1976); J. M. Ivancevich and M. T. Matteson, *Stress and Work* (Glenview, IL: Scott, Foresman, 1981); and R. D. Allen, M. A. Hitt, and C. R. Greer, "Occupational Stress and Perceived Organizational Effectiveness in Formal Groups: An Examination of Stress Level and Stress Type," *Personnel Psychology,* Summer 1982, pp. 359–70.

[30]See, for instance, K. A. Matthews, "Psychological Perspectives on the Type A Behavior Pattern," *Psychological Bulletin,* March 1982, pp. 293–323; M. Jamal, "Type A Behavior and Job Performance: Some Suggestive Findings," *Journal of Human Stress,* Summer 1985, pp. 60–68;

and C. Lee, P. C. Earley, and L. A. Hanson, "Are Type As Better Performers?," *Journal of Organizational Behavior,* July 1988, pp. 263–69.

[31]S. J. Modic, "Surviving Burnout: The Malady of Our Age," *Industry Week,* February 20, 1989, pp. 29–34.

[32]See S. E. Jackson, R. L. Schwab, and R. S. Schuler, "Toward an Understanding of the Burnout Phenomenon," *Journal of Applied Psychology,* November 1986, pp. 630–40.

[33]D. P. Rogers, "Helping Employees Cope With Burnout," *Business,* October–December 1984, pp. 3–7.

[34]S. J. Modic, "Surviving Burnout," p. 29.

[35]The following discussion has been strongly influenced by J. E. Newman and T. A. Beehr, "Personal and Organizational Strategies for Handling Job Stress," *Personnel Psychology,* Spring 1979, pp. 1–38; A. P. Brief, R. S. Schuler, and M. Van Sell, *Managing Job Stress;* R. L. Rose and J. F. Veiga, "Assessing the Sustained Effects of a Stress Management Intervention on Anxiety and Locus of Control," *Academy of Management Journal,* March 1984, pp. 190–98; E. R. Kemery, A. G. Bedeian, K. W. Mossholder, and J. Touliatos, "Outcomes of Role Stress: A Multisample Constructive Replication," *Academy of Management Journal,* June 1985, pp. 363–75; N. S. Bruning and D. R. Frew, "Effects of Exercise, Relaxation, and Management Skills Training on Physiological Stress Indicators: A Field Experiment," *Journal of Applied Psychology,* November 1987, pp. 515–21; J. M. Ivancevich and M. T. Matteson, "Organizational Level Stress Management Interventions: A Review and Recommendations," *Journal of Organizational Behavior Management,* Fall–Winter 1986, pp. 229–48; and M. T. Matteson and J. M. Ivancevich, "Individual Stress Management Interventions: Evaluation of Techniques," *Journal of Management Psychology,* January 1987, pp. 24–30.

[36]See, for example, M. E. Haynes, *Practical Time Management: How to Make the Most of Your Most Perishable Resource* (Tulsa, OK: PennWell Books, 1985).

[37]H. Benson, *The Relaxation Response* (New York: William Morrow, 1975).

[38]D. Etzion, "Moderating Effects of Social Support on the Stress-Burnout Relationship," *Journal of Applied Psychology,* November 1984, pp. 615–22; and S. E. Jackson, R. L. Schwab, and R. S. Schuler, "Toward an Understanding of the Burnout Phenomenon."

[39]S. E. Jackson, "Participation in Decision Making as a Strategy for Reducing Job-Related Strain," *Journal of Applied Psychology,* February 1983, pp. 3–19.

[40]See, for instance, R. A. Wolfe, D. O. Ulrich, and D. F. Parker, "Employee Health Management Programs: Review, Critique, and Research Agenda," *Journal of Management,* Winter 1987, pp. 603–15; and "When You're Looking for a Long-Term Strategy: Wellness Programs," *INC.,* December 1989, pp. 151–53.

[41]Cited in H. Rothman, "Wellness Works for Small Firms," *Nation's Business,* December 1989, p. 42.

[42]N. Templin, "Johnson & Johnson 'Wellness' Program for Workers Shows Healthy Bottom Line," *Wall Street Journal,* May 21, 1990, p. B1.

[43]J. M. Horowitz, "A Puzzling Toll at the Top," *Time,* August 3, 1987, p. 46.

[44]Ibid.

[45]T. D. Jick and L. F. Mitz, "Sex Differences in Work Stress," *Academy of Management Review,* July 1985, pp. 408–20; and R. D. Hackett, "A Multiple Case Study of Employee Absenteeism," paper presented at the 1986 ASAC Conference, Whistler, British Columbia.

[46]See, for example, E. R. Kemery, A. G. Bedeian, K. W. Mossholder, and J. Touliatos, "Outcomes of Role Stress."

FOUNDATIONS OF ORGANIZATIONAL CHANGE

LEARNING OBJECTIVES

After studying this chapter, you should be able to:

1. *Describe forces that act as stimulants to change*
2. *Define planned change*
3. *Summarize sources of individual resistance to change*
4. *Explain sources of organizational resistance to change*
5. *List techniques for overcoming resistance to change*
6. *Summarize Lewin's three-step change model*
7. *Describe action research*
8. *Define organizational development*

Herbert Rogers is chief operating officer at General Dynamics—America's second largest weapons manufacturer. In light of cutbacks in U.S. defense spending, he has to oversee the company's transition to a leaner and more aggressive firm.   Max Aquilera-Hellweg.

Most people hate any change that doesn't jingle in their pockets.

ANONYMOUS

You think you've got things rough. How would you like to run a company with sales of $10 billion a year, $8.5 billion of which comes from one customer who may no longer need your product? That's the unfortunate dilemma facing Herbert Rogers, chief operating officer at General Dynamics, and his management team.[1]

There's an old joke in the defense industry that business is almost always good except for those occasional instances when "peace breaks out." Well, that joke is not so funny anymore for major defense contractors like General Dynamics. Peace has "broken out." The Berlin Wall has fallen, countries such as Hungary and Poland have installed democratic governments, and the once-menacing Soviet Union has become more concerned with feeding its people than building weapons. The Cold War, in other words, is over.

This is bad news indeed for General Dynamics, America's second largest weapons manufacturer. By the end of the 1980s, for example, its F-16 Fighting Falcon was the primary Air Force fighter; its Standard Missile was one of the Navy's basic missiles; its shoulder-fired Stinger was a mainstay in the Army's weapons chest; and its Trident Submarine and M1A1 Abrams battle tank were well-loved by the military. While in 1990 General Dynamics had a backlog of sales that would carry it for a couple of years, the intermediate and long-term was another story. The Secretary of Defense was recommending substantial cuts in the military budget and Congress was talking about slashing it even deeper.

Rogers' worst-case scenerio predicts a fall in General Dynamics' sales of fifty percent by the end of 1995. Major changes will have to be implemented throughout the company. Layoffs of between 10,000 and 20,000 people are possible. The company will almost certainly restructure some of its nine major divisions to increase their efficiency, while shutting down some major operations completely.

General Dynamics' management is pinning most of its hopes on its ability to grab a larger share of the shrinking defense budget. They essentially have decided to stay with what they know and not move into nonweapon manufacturing. As one knowledgeable observer remarked, "The characteristics that are the key to success in their industry—high tech, high quality, small production runs, little marketing capability—may not be easily translatable to other fields."[2]

In the defense industry of the 1990s, every player will have to adjust to a leaner diet and some will probably starve. As one of the biggest and strongest players, General Dynamics won't starve. But it will be forced to undergo changes that will substantially change the company.

This chapter introduces organizational change. We'll present major changes taking place that require action by management. We'll also consider why people and organizations resist changes and how this resistance can be overcome. Finally, we'll review various processes for managing organizational change.

FORCES FOR CHANGE

More and more organizations today face a dynamic and changing environment that, in turn, requires these organizations to adapt. In this section we'll look at six specific forces that are acting as stimulants for change—the changing nature of the work force, technology, economic shocks, changing social trends, the "new" world politics, and the changing nature of competition.

Nature of the Work Force

In a number of places in this book we've discussed the changing nature of the work force. This is as good a time as any to summarize these changes.

We pointed out the different work values expressed by different generations. Workers over fifty value loyalty to their employer. Workers in their mid-thirties to late forties are loyal to themselves. The late baby-boomers' generation or pragmatists value loyalty to their careers.

A recent cover story in *Time* magazine tried to characterize the latest entrants to the work force—the "twentysomething" generation.[3] These young people seem to be different again from earlier cohorts. They value flexibility, job satisfaction, and family relations. In contrast to the workaholic characteristics of the pragmatists, members of the twentysomething generation want nights and weekends to be work-free—they want to spend that time on relationships with friends, relatives, and children. One of the more interesting observations about these new labor-force entrants is their preference for short-term tasks with observable results. This was a generation raised on the importance of grades, class rank, and SAT scores. They want a quantification of their achievements. Unlike the pragmatists, who were driven from within, today's younger people seek external reinforcement.

We described the 1990s as a decade where organizations will have to learn to manage diversity. The work force is changing, with a rapid increase in the percentage of women and minorities. Human resource policies and practices will have to change in order to attract and keep this more diverse work force.

The increase in the participation rate of women in the work force also means more dual-career couples. Organizations are having to modify transfer and promotion policies, as well as make child-care and elder-care available, in order to respond to the needs of two-career couples.

It's easy to focus on the increasing educational levels of the work force. Yet there is a dark side that has important implications for organizations. A significant portion of new work force entrants do not have marketable skills. Many are high school dropouts. But a good number, and this is probably the most alarming, have high school and college degrees but can't adequately perform the basic reading, writing, and computational skills that organizations require. This is forcing organizations to introduce training programs to upgrade skills and, in some cases, deskill jobs so that they can be adequately performed by employees.

Technology

Changes in technology change the nature of work. The adoption of new technologies such as computers, telecommunication systems, robotics, and flexible manufacturing operations have a profound impact on the organizations that adopt them.

For instance, IBM has built a system of modular work stations at a plant in Austin, Texas, that uses flexible manufacturing concepts to build personal computers.[4] From receiving dock to exit dock, computers are assembled, tested, packed, and shipped without a human being so much as turning a screw. The entire operation is handled by thirteen robots. Moreover, the entire manufacturing system was built with flexibility in mind. The plant is designed to be able to build *any* electronic product that is no bigger than two feet by two feet by fourteen inches. So IBM's management can build printers, other types of computers, or even toasters in this plant.

Computers and sophisticated information systems, while only the tip of the technology iceberg, are having an enormous impact on organizations. They are stimulating widespread changes in the required skill levels of employees, the daily activities of managers, and the organization's ability to respond to the changing needs of customers. For instance, as many routine tasks are being automated, people are being freed up to take on more varied and challenging tasks. Of course, employee skills are also becoming obsolete more quickly, so organizations are having to increase their investment in employee training and education. The substitution of computer control for direct supervision is resulting in wider spans of control for managers and flatter organizations. Sophisticated information technology is also making organizations more responsive. Companies such as Motorola, General Electric, and AT&T can now develop, make, and distribute their products in a fraction of the time it took them a decade ago. And, as organizations have had to become more adaptable, so too have their employees. As we noted in our discussion of groups and organization design, many jobs are being reshaped. Individuals doing narrow, specialized, and routine jobs are being replaced by work teams whose members can perform multiple tasks and actively participate in team decisions.

Economic Shocks

We live in an "age of discontinuity." In the 1950s and 1960s, the past was a pretty good prologue to the future. Tomorrow was essentially an extended trend-line from yesterday. That is no longer true. Beginning in the early 1970s, with the overnight quadrupling of world oil prices, economic shocks have continued to impose changes on organizations. In an indirect way, the changes we'll mention have affected all organizations. However, economic shocks typically hit some industries and firms much harder than others.

In the last twenty years, we can pinpoint at least five major economic shocks experienced in the United States, beginning with the explosion in oil prices.

When OPEC raised the price of oil from under $3.00 to nearly $12.00 a barrel, automobile, recreational vehicle, and building-insulation manufacturers, for example, felt an immediate effect. General Motors and Winnebago, for instance, saw the demand for their "gas guzzling" vehicles collapse. Toyota, Honda, and other manufacturers of small, fuel-efficient cars, on the other hand, experienced a sales bonanza. Firms such as Johns-Mansville, which manufactured building insulation, found that, in spite of running multiple shifts, they were unable to meet the increased market demand for their product.

In the mid-1970s, the United States and Canada underwent a two-year-or-so period of accelerated inflation and interest rates never before experienced in this century. Inflation reached an annual peak of over thirteen percent, and interest rates exceeded sixteen percent. Potential home buyers found it difficult to qualify for loans and many homebuilders went bankrupt. Almost all well-managed companies changed their bill-paying and inventory policies. It made good sense, for instance, to use suppliers' money and delay paying bills for as long as possible. It also made good sense to reduce inventories to absolute minimum levels to reduce the high carrying costs. In terms of organizational behavior, employees' expectations for wage increases rose sharply. Many firms found it impossible even to provide merit increases because cost-of-living adjustments were consuming all of the pool of money they had set aside for wage increases. Morale in many organizations fell during this period and turnover increased.

The stock market crash of October 1987 is another example of an economic shock. While this had an impact upon the financing plans and market value of almost all publicly-held businesses, the crash proved devastating to the financial services industry. Large layoffs on Wall Street immediately followed. Several of the major brokerage firms were forced to restructure or merge in order to survive.

Another shock to the financial services industry hit in late 1989 with the collapse of the so-called junk-bond market. This almost single-handedly ended the corporate takeover and leveraged buyout frenzy of the 1980s. It also significantly reduced the assets of many insurance companies and pension funds.

One of the latest shocks to the economy has been the massive defaults of savings and loans. This, in turn, has depressed real estate prices and resulted in large losses for real estate developers and others closely connected with the real estate industry.

During the 1990s, we can forecast with almost one-hundred-percent certainty that there will be one or more economic shocks of similar magnitude to those of the past two decades. The only problem is that it is impossible to predict what those shocks will be and where they will come from. That is the irony of change in the age of discontinuity: We know almost for sure that tomorrow won't be like today but we don't know how it will be different.

Social Trends

Take a look at social trends during the 1970s and 1980s. They will suggest changes for the 1990s that organizations will need to adjust for. Consider, as examples, shifts in the value placed on higher education, views on marriage, and shopping preferences.

In the early 1960s, less than twenty-five percent of all United States high school graduates enrolled in college. By 1978, it was forty-nine percent. In

1988, the figure had reached fifty-nine percent. The higher-education industry now provides a mass-market product. The makeup of the typical student body has also changed a great deal in the past decade or two. Women have gone from a small minority to the majority, part-time students now outnumber full-timers, and an increasing proportion of students are over thirty years of age. Those colleges and universities that fail to respond to these changes in the student population may not be around at the end of the decade.

There has been a clear trend in marriages and divorce during the past two decades. Young people are delaying marriage, and half of all marriages are ending in divorce. One obvious result of this social trend is an increasing number of single households and demand for housing by singles.

Another social trend of interest, particularly to those organizations in the retail industry, has been the shift in consumer preferences for specialty stores. Large chains such as Sears, which try to be all things to all people, have suffered at the hands of discount and niche stores. Wal-Mart, K-mart, Circuit City, Toys R Us, Waldenbooks, Victoria's Secret, and Blockbuster Video are examples of firms that have responded positively to this trend. Many of the big retailers of yesterday—W. T. Grant, F. W. Woolworth, Montgomery Ward, Sears—are either dead or in extremely poor health.

World Politics

In Chapter 3 we argued strongly for the importance of seeing OB in a global context. We reinforced this argument with boxes in each of the following chapters. While business schools have been preaching a global perspective for nearly a decade, no one—not even the strongest proponents of globalization—could have imagined how world politics would change in 1989 and 1990.

A quick glance through recent headlines reveals a very different world from just a few years ago. The fall of the Berlin Wall. The release from jail of Nelson Mandela by the South African government. Free elections in Nicaragua and the ousting from power of the Sandinistas. Elections in Poland and

Coca Cola is a firm that adapts rapidly to change. When the Berlin Wall came down, Coca Cola employees could be found giving away thousands of cans of soft drinks to thirsty East Berliners.   Courtesy The Coca Cola Company.

the creation of a Solidarity-led government. Declarations of sovereignty by Soviet Union republics, including Russia, Moldavia, Estonia, Latvia, and Lithuania. A war inside Colombia—pitting 200,000 members of the government armed forces and police against the Medellín drug cartel—with the drug dealers winning more of the battles than the government. Iraq's invasion of Kuwait. And maybe the biggest surprise of all—the reunification of Germany.

What do the new world politics mean to students of management and organizational behavior? It's too soon to predict the full impact of these changes, yet some predictions seem relatively safe.

One certainty is that companies that have survived on defense contracts will be undergoing changes. General Dynamics, as described at the beginning of this chapter, is readying itself for reduced military spending. In the summer of 1990, the United States's largest defense contractor, McDonnell-Douglas, announced intentions to cut 17,000 jobs before that year ended. Employees in the various United States armed services and intelligence agencies should also be preparing themselves for new assignments as these organizations rethink their role in the post-Cold War world.

Managers of most firms and a good portion of their employees will need to become attuned to cultural differences. They will increasingly be interacting with people in other countries and working alongside people raised in different cultures. So don't be surprised to find yourself working for a boss who was raised in a different land. It also may not be a bad idea to brush up or begin developing your foreign language skills—especially in Japanese and German.

Ownership of companies and property by people and organizations from other countries is likely to continue worldwide. As long as currencies fluctuate and some economies outperform others, assets will flow across borders. In the 1980s, Japanese money flowed into the United States. In the 1990s, it may

Is this supermarket in Hong Kong? No! It's in suburban Los Angeles. This picture illustrates the changing makeup of many American communities and the need for managers to become attuned to cultural differences. Lynn Johnson/Black Star.

well be United States, Canadian, and Japanese funds that flow into Eastern Europe. Where investment goes will fluctuate at different times, but in a true global economy resources will constantly seek out their best return, wherever in the world that might be. What this means, of course, is the realization that some businesses in some countries will fail because their products or services can be more efficiently produced in another country. Along these lines, it is no longer preposterous to conceive of a General Motors Corp., headquartered in Detroit, that builds every one of its automobiles in plants outside the United States.

Competition

The last area we want to discuss is the changes that derive from increased competition. The global economy means that competitors are as likely to come from Japan, Mexico, or Germany as from the other side of town. But heightened competition also means that established organizations need to defend themselves against both traditional competitors who develop new products and services and small, entrepreneurial firms with innovative offerings.

Successful organizations will be the ones that can change in response to the competition. They'll be fast on their feet, capable of developing new products rapidly, and getting them to market quickly. They'll rely on short production runs, short product cycles, and an ongoing stream of new products. In other words, they'll be flexible. They will require an equally flexible and responsive work force which can adapt to rapidly and even radically changing conditions.

MANAGING PLANNED CHANGE

A group of employees who work in a small retail women's clothing store confronted the owner: "The air pollution in this store from cigarette smoking has gotten awful," said their spokeswoman. "We won't continue to work here if you allow smoking in the store. We want you to post no smoking signs on the entrance doors and not allow any employee to smoke on the floor. If people have to smoke, they can go into the mall." The owner listened thoughtfully to the group's ultimatum and agreed to their request. The next day the owner posted the no smoking signs and advised all of her employees of the new rule.

A major automobile manufacturer spent several billion dollars to install state-of-the-art robotics. One area that would receive the new equipment was quality control. Sophisticated computer-controlled equipment would be put in place to significantly improve the company's ability to find and correct defects. Since the new equipment would dramatically change the jobs of the people working in the quality control area, and since management anticipated considerable employee resistance to the new equipment, executives were developing a program to help people become familiar with the equipment and to deal with any anxieties they might be feeling.

Change Making things different.

Both of the previous scenarios are examples of **change.** That is, both were concerned with making things different. However, only the second scenario described a planned change. In this section, we want to clarify what

Are These Really Such Dynamic Times?

The picture we've drawn is one of accelerated change. Since the early 1970s, we've lived in an age of discontinuity. The implication is that today's world is more dynamic and turbulent than at any previous time. Moreover, we've implied that the current generation of employees must deal with a working world that is more chaotic than that faced by any prior generation.

While no one argues that these changes aren't real, maybe the uniqueness of these conditions has been overdramatized. Maybe the magnitude of changes that employees have experienced in recent years is actually less than that faced by their grandparents or great grandparents.

Just this notion has been proposed by Nobel laureate Herbert Simon.[5] He argues that the years of real change took place between the Civil War and World War I. During that time the world went from a rural, agricultural, horse-powered society to an urban, industrialized place with railroads, telegraphs, steamships, electric lights, automobiles, and airplanes. Dramatic technological breakthroughs were coming from all directions. Simon argues that nothing in the past seventy years, with the possible exception of the atomic bomb, has so changed the basic terms of human existence as did those technologies. So, Simon argues, in relative terms today's employees may be facing a far less dynamic workplace than were their counterparts of three generations ago.

Is Simon right? Probably! Does that mean that we're guilty of overkill for describing so dramatically the forces for change? No! The magnitude of change may have been greater a century ago, but not the speed of that change. It is the speed with which organizations are confronting change, and to which managers and employees have to respond, that makes organizational change such an important topic today in organizational behavior.

Planned Change Change activities that are intentional and goal-oriented.

we mean by planned change, describe its goals, and consider who is responsible for bringing about **planned change** in an organization.

Many changes in organizations are like the one that occurred in the retail clothing store—they just happen. Some organizations treat all change as an accidental occurrence. However, we're concerned with change activities that are proactive and purposeful. In this chapter, we'll address change as an intentional, goal-oriented activity.

What are the goals of planned change? Essentially there are two. First, it seeks to improve the ability of the organization to adapt to changes in its environment. Second, it seeks to change employee behavior.

If an organization is to survive, it must respond to changes in its environment. When competitors introduce new products or services, government agencies enact new laws, important sources of supply go out of business, or similar environmental changes take place, the organization needs to adapt. As you'll see in our next chapter, efforts to introduce work teams, decentralized decision making, and new organizational cultures are examples of planned change activities directed at responding to changes in the environment.

Since an organization's success or failure is essentially due to the things

Eastman Kodak's top executives have recently introduced massive changes at this conglomerate. Several noncritical businesses have been sold and 4,500 jobs have been cut. Major efforts to move into the electronic photography business may make the company's ubiquitous yellow box a relic. Bob Mahoney.

that employees do or fail to do, planned change also is concerned with changing the behavior of individuals and groups within the organization. Again, in the next chapter, we'll review a number of techniques that organizations can use to get people to behave differently in the tasks they perform and in their interaction with others.

Change Agents Persons who act as catalysts, and assume the responsibility for managing change activities.

Who in organizations is responsible for managing change activities? The answer is **change agents.** These change agents can be managers or nonmanagers, employees of the organization or outside consultants. For major change efforts, internal management often will hire the services of outside consultants to provide advice and assistance. Because they are from the outside, these individuals can offer an objective perspective often unavailable to insiders. However, outside consultants are disadvantaged because they usually have an inadequate understanding of the organization's history, culture, operating procedures, and personnel. Outside consultants also may be prone to initiating more drastic changes—which can be a benefit or a disadvantage—because they do not have to live with the repercussions after the change is implemented. In contrast, internal staff specialists or managers, when acting as change agents, may be more thoughtful (and possibly cautious) because they must live with the consequences of their actions.

RESISTANCE TO CHANGE

One of the most well-documented findings from studies of individual and organizational behavior is that organizations and their members resist change. In a sense, this is positive. It provides a degree of stability and predictability to behavior. If there wasn't some resistance, organizational behavior would take on characteristics of chaotic randomness. Resistance to change can also be a source of functional conflict. For example, resistance to a reorganization plan or a change in a product line can stimulate a healthy debate over the merits of the idea and result in a better decision. But there is a definite downside to resistance to change. It hinders adaptation and progress.

Resistance to change doesn't necessarily surface in standardized ways. Resistance can be overt, implicit, immediate, or deferred. It is easiest for management to deal with resistance when it is overt and immediate. For instance, a change is proposed and employees quickly respond by voicing complaints, engaging in a work slowdown, threatening to go on strike, or the like. The greater challenge is managing resistance that is implicit or deferred. Implicit resistance efforts are more subtle—loss of loyalty to the organization, loss of motivation to work, increased errors or mistakes, increased absenteeism due to "sickness"—and hence more difficult to recognize. Similarly, deferred actions cloud the link between the source of the resistance and the reaction to it. A change may produce what appears to be only a minimal reaction at the time it is initiated but surfaces weeks, months, or even years later. Or a single change, in and of itself, has little impact. But it becomes the straw that breaks the camel's back. Reactions to change can build up and then explode in some response that seems totally out of proportion to the change action it follows. The resistance, of course, has merely been deferred and stockpiled. What surfaces is a response to an accumulation of previous changes.

Let's look at the sources of resistance. For analytical purposes, we've categorized them by individual and organizational sources. In the real world, the sources often overlap.

Individual Resistance

Individual sources of resistance to change reside in basic human characteristics such as perceptions, personalities, and needs. The following summarizes five reasons why individuals may resist change. (See Figure 19–1.)

HABIT   Every time you go out to eat do you try a different restaurant? Probably not. If you're like most people, you find a couple of places you like and return to them on a somewhat regular basis.

As human beings, we're creatures of habit. Life is complex enough; we don't need to consider the full range of options for the hundreds of decisions we have to make every day. To cope with this complexity, we all rely on habits or programmed responses. But when confronted with change, this tendency to respond in our accustomed ways becomes a source of resistance. So when your department is moved to a new office building across town, it means you're likely to have to change many habits: waking up ten minutes earlier, taking a new set of streets to work, finding a new parking place, adjusting to the new office layout, developing a new lunchtime routine, and so on.

SECURITY   People with a high need for security are likely to resist change because it threatens their feeling of safety. When General Dynamics announces personnel cutbacks or Ford introduces new robotic equipment, many employees at these firms may fear that their jobs are in jeopardy.

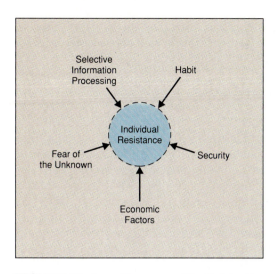

FIGURE 19–1   Sources of Individual Resistance to Change

ECONOMIC FACTORS   Another source of individual resistance is concern that changes will lower one's income. Changes in job tasks or established work routines also can arouse economic fears if people are concerned that they won't be able to perform the new tasks or routines to their previous standards, especially when pay is closely tied to productivity.

FEAR OF THE UNKNOWN   Changes substitute ambiguity and uncertainty for the known. Regardless of how much you may dislike attending college, at least you know what is expected of you. But when you leave college and venture out into the world of full-time employment, regardless of how much you want to get out of college, you have to trade the known for the unknown.

Employees in organizations hold the same dislike for uncertainty. If, for

Much of the resistance expressed by Greyhound bus drivers in the spring of 1990 was fear that they would get fewer hours of driving time and would have to take a cut in their hourly wage rate.   Bruce De Lis/ Gamma-Liaison.

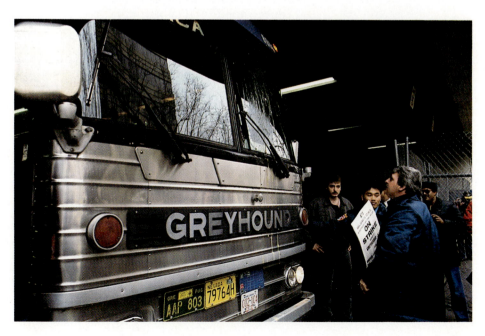

example, the introduction of word processors means that departmental secretaries will have to learn to operate these new pieces of equipment, some of the secretaries may fear that they will be unable to do so. They may, therefore, develop a negative attitude toward working with word processors or behave dysfunctionally if required to use them.

SELECTIVE INFORMATION PROCESSING   As we learned in Chapter 5, individuals shape their world through their perceptions. Once they have created this world, it resists change. So individuals are guilty of selectively processing information in order to keep their perceptions intact. They hear what they want to hear. They ignore information that challenges the world that they've created. To return to the secretaries who are faced with the introduction of word processors, they may ignore the arguments that their bosses make in explaining why the new equipment has been purchased or the potential benefits that the change will provide them.

Organizational Resistance

Organizations, by their very nature, are conservative.[6] They actively resist change. You don't have to look far to see evidence of this phenomenon. Government agencies want to continue doing what they have been doing for years, whether the need for their service changes or remains the same. Organized religions are deeply entrenched in their history. Attempts to change church doctrine requires great persistence and patience. Educational institutions, which exist to open minds and challenge established doctrine, are themselves extremely resistant to change. Most school systems are using essentially the same teaching technologies today as they were fifty years ago. The majority of business firms, too, appear highly resistant to change.

Six major sources of organizational resistance have been identified.[7] They are shown in Figure 19–2.

STRUCTURAL INERTIA   Organizations have built-in mechanisms to produce stability. For example, the selection process systematically selects

FIGURE 19–2   Sources of Organizational Resistance to Change

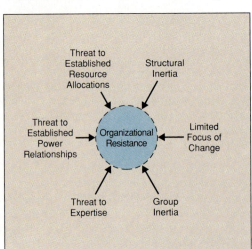

certain people in and certain people out. Training and other socialization techniques reinforce specific role requirements and skills. Formalization provides job descriptions, rules, and procedures for employees to follow.

The people who are hired into an organization are chosen for fit; they are then shaped and directed to behave in certain ways. When an organization is confronted with change, this structural inertia acts as a counterbalance to sustain stability.

LIMITED FOCUS OF CHANGE   Organizations are made up of a number of interdependent subsystems. You can't change one without effecting the others. For example, if management changes the technological processes without simultaneously modifying the organization's structure to match, the change in technology is not likely to be accepted. So limited changes in subsystems tend to get nullified by the larger system.

GROUP INERTIA   Even if individuals want to change their behavior, group norms may act as a constraint. An individual union member, for instance, may be willing to accept changes in his job suggested by management. But if union norms dictate resisting any unilateral change made by management, he's likely to resist.

THREAT TO EXPERTISE   Changes in organizational patterns may threaten the expertise of specialized groups. The introduction of decentralized personal computers, which allow managers to gain access to information directly from a company's mainframe, is an example of a change that was strongly resisted by many information systems departments in the early 1980s. Why? Because decentralized, end-user computing was a threat to the specialized skills held by those in the centralized information systems departments.

THREAT TO ESTABLISHED POWER RELATIONSHIPS   Any redistribution of decision-making authority can threaten long established power relationships within the organization. Introduction of participative decision making or autonomous work teams are examples of changes that are often seen as threats to the power of supervisors and middle managers.

THREAT TO ESTABLISHED RESOURCE ALLOCATIONS   Those groups in the organization that control sizable resources often see change as a threat. They tend to be content with the way things are. Will the change, for instance, mean a reduction in their budgets or a cut in their staff size? Those that most benefit from the current allocation of resources are often threatened by changes that may affect future allocations.

Overcoming Resistance to Change

Six tactics have been suggested for use by change agents in dealing with resistance to change.[8] Let's review them briefly.

EDUCATION AND COMMUNICATION   Resistance can be reduced through communicating with employees to help them see the logic of a change. This tactic basically assumes that the source of resistance lies in misinformation or poor communication: If employees receive the full facts and get any misunderstandings cleared up, resistance will subside. This can be achieved through one-on-one discussions, memos, group presentations, or reports. Does it work? It does, provided that the source of resistance is inadequate communication and that management–employee relations are characterized by mutual trust and credibility. If these conditions do not exist, the change is unlikely to succeed.

PARTICIPATION   It's difficult for individuals to resist a change decision in which they participated. Prior to making a change, those opposed can be brought into the decision process. Assuming that the participants have the expertise to make a meaningful contribution, their involvement can reduce resistance, obtain commitment, and increase the quality of the change decision. However, against these advantages are the negatives: potential for a poor solution and great time consumption.

FACILITATION AND SUPPORT   Change agents can offer a range of supportive efforts to reduce resistance. When employee fear and anxiety are high, employee counseling and therapy, new skills training, or a short paid leave of absence may facilitate adjustment. The drawback of this tactic is that, as with the others, it is time consuming. Additionally, it is expensive, and its implementation offers no assurance of success.

NEGOTIATION   Another way for the change agent to deal with potential resistance to change is to exchange something of value for a lessening of the resistance. For instance, if the resistance is centered in a few powerful individuals, a specific reward package can be negotiated that will meet their individual needs. Negotiation, as a tactic, may be necessary when resistance comes from a powerful source. Yet one cannot ignore its potentially high costs. Additionally, there is the risk that, once a change agent negotiates to avoid resistance, he or she is open to the possibility of being blackmailed by other individuals in positions of power.

MANIPULATION AND COOPTATION   Manipulation refers to covert influence attempts. Twisting and distorting facts to make them appear more attractive, withholding undesirable information, or creating false rumors to get employees to accept a change are all examples of manipulation. If corporate management threatens to close down a particular manufacturing plant if that plant's employees fail to accept an across-the-board pay cut, and if the threat is actually untrue, management is using manipulation. Cooptation, on the other hand, is a form of both manipulation and participation. It seeks to "buy off" the leaders of a resistance group by giving them a key role in the change decision. The leaders' advice is sought, not to seek a better decision, but to get their endorsement. Both manipulation and cooptation are relatively inexpensive and easy ways to gain the support of adversaries, but the tactics can backfire if the targets become aware that they are being tricked or used. Once discovered, the change agent's credibility may drop to zero.

COERCION   Last on the list of tactics is coercion; that is, the application of direct threats or force upon the resisters. If the corporate management mentioned in the previous discussion were really determined to close the manufacturing plant if employees did not acquiesce to a pay cut, then coercion would be the label attached to their change tactic. Other examples of coercion include threats of transfer, loss of promotions, negative performance evalua-

Harwood Manufacturing: A Classic Study in Participative Change

One of the most famous studies on organizational change took place in the late 1940s at a plant of the Harwood Manufacturing Co., where pajamas were made.[9]

The plant employed about 500 people and had a long history of disruptions every time changes were made in the way work was conducted. Although the changes were typically minor—for instance, pajama folders who formerly folded tops with prefolded pants would be required to fold the pants as well—the employees resisted. They would complain and some would openly refuse to make the changes. Production decreased, and grievances, absenteeism, and job turnover would increase.

The usual way that Harwood's management made changes was autocratically. Management made the decision, then would call a group meeting where they would announce the changes to employees and explain why they were necessary. The changes would then be implemented. But, as we said, employees continued to resist these changes in their jobs. So Harwood's executives brought in a consultant as an outside change agent to help with the problem. As an experiment, the consultant arranged for the next change to be conducted in three groups using three different methods. In the first group, the change was initiated in the usual manner—autocratically. This was the control group. The second involved employee participation through elected representatives. These representatives, with management, worked out the details of the change; then tried the new methods and trained others in the new procedures. In the third group, there was full participation. All employees shared in the designing of new methods with management.

The consultant gathered data over a forty-day period and what he found strongly supported the value of participation. In the control group, resistance occurred as before. Seventeen percent of the employees quit their jobs during the forty-day period, and grievances and absenteeism increased. However, in the representative and full participation groups, there were no quits, only one grievance, and no absenteeism. Moreover, participation was positively related to productivity. In the control group, output actually dropped from an average of sixty units per hour to forty-eight units during the experimental period. The participation-by-representation group generated sixty-eight units per hour and the total participation group averaged seventy-three units per hour.

tions, or a poor letter of recommendation. The advantages and drawbacks of coercion are approximately the same as those mentioned for manipulation and cooptation.

APPROACHES FOR MANAGING ORGANIZATIONAL CHANGE

We conclude our review of basic organizational change concepts by looking at several popular approaches to managing change. Specifically, we'll discuss Lewin's classic three-step model of the change process, present the action-

An International Look at Organizational Change

A number of the issues addressed in this chapter are culture-bound. To illustrate, let's briefly look at four questions: (1) Do people believe change is possible? (2) If it is possible, how long will it take to bring it about? (3) Is resistance to change greater in some cultures than in others? (4) Does culture influence how change efforts will be implemented?

Do people believe change is possible? Remember that cultures vary in terms of beliefs about their ability to control their environment. In cultures where people believe that they can dominate their environment, individuals will take a proactive view toward change. This would describe the United States and Canada. In other countries, such as Iran and Saudi Arabia, people see themselves as subjugated to their environment and thus will tend to take a passive approach toward change.

If change is possible, how long will it take to bring it about? A culture's time orientation can help us answer this question. Societies that focus on the long-term, such as Japan, will demon-

strate considerable patience while waiting for positive outcomes from change efforts. In societies with a short-term focus, such as the United States and Canada, people expect quick improvements and will seek change programs that promise fast results.

Is resistance to change greater in some cultures than in others? Resistance to change will be influenced by a society's reliance on tradition. Italians, as an example, focus on the past, while Americans emphasize the present. Italians, therefore, should generally be more resistant to change efforts than their American counterparts.

Does culture influence how change efforts will be implemented? Power distance can help with this issue. In high power-distance cultures, such as the Philippines or Venezuela, change efforts will tend to be autocratically implemented by top management. In contrast, low power-distance cultures value democratic methods. We'd predict, therefore, a greater use of participation in countries such as Denmark and Israel.

research model, and briefly introduce organizational development as a systematic framework for bringing about organizational change.

Lewin's Three-Step Model

Unfreezing Change efforts to overcome the pressures of both individual resistance and group conformity.

Refreezing Stabilizing a change intervention by balancing driving and restraining forces.

Kurt Lewin argued that successful change in organizations should follow three steps: **unfreezing** the status quo, *movement* to a new state, and **refreezing** the new change to make it permanent.[10] (See Figure 19–3.) The value of this model can be seen in the following example when the management of a large oil company decided to reorganize its marketing function in the western United States.

The oil company had three divisional offices in the west, located in Seattle, San Francisco, and Los Angeles. The decision was made to consolidate the divisions into a single regional office to be located in San Francisco. The reorganization meant transferring over 150 employees, eliminating some

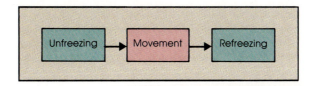

FIGURE 19–3   Lewin's 3-Step Change Model

duplicate managerial positions, and instituting a new hierarchy of command. As you might guess, a move of this magnitude was difficult to keep secret. The rumor of its occurrence preceded the announcement by several months. The decision itself was made unilaterally. It came from the executive offices in New York. Those people affected had no say whatsoever in the choice. For those in Seattle or Los Angeles, who may have disliked the decision and its consequences—the problems inherent in transferring to another city, pulling youngsters out of school, making new friends, having new co-workers, undergoing the reassignment of responsibilities—their only recourse was to quit. In actuality, less than ten percent did.

Driving Forces Forces that direct behavior away from the status quo.

Restraining Forces Forces that hinder movement from the status quo.

The status quo can be considered to be an equilibrium state. To move from this equilibrium—to overcome the pressures of both individual resistance and group conformity—unfreezing is necessary. It can be achieved in one of three ways. (See Figure 19–4.) The **driving forces,** which direct behavior away from the status quo, can be increased. The **restraining forces,** which hinder movement from the existing equilibrium, can be decreased. A third alternative is to *combine the first two approaches.*

The oil company's management could expect employee resistance to the consolidation. To deal with that resistance, management could use positive

FIGURE 19–4   Unfreezing the Status Quo

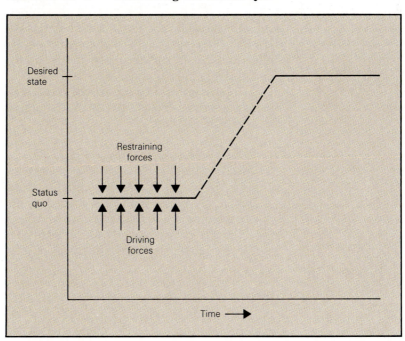

incentives to encourage employees to accept the change. For instance, increases in pay can be offered to those who accept the transfer. Very liberal moving expenses can be paid by the company. Management might offer low-cost mortgage funds to allow employees to buy new homes in San Francisco. Of course, management might also consider unfreezing acceptance of the status quo by removing restraining forces. Employees could be counseled individually. Each employee's concerns and apprehensions could be heard and specifically clarified. Assuming that most of the fears are unjustified, the counselor could assure the employees that there was nothing to fear and then demonstrate, through tangible evidence, that restraining forces are unwarranted. If resistance is extremely high, management may have to resort to both reducing resistance and increasing the attractiveness of the alternative if the unfreezing is to be successful.

Once the consolidation change has been implemented, if it is to be successful, the new situation needs to be refrozen so that it can be sustained over time. Unless this last step is taken, there is a very high chance that the change will be short-lived and that employees will attempt to revert to the previous equilibrium state. The objective of refreezing, then, is to stabilize the new situation by balancing the driving and restraining forces.

How could the oil company's management refreeze their consolidation change? By systematically replacing temporary forces with permanent ones. For instance, they might impose a permanent upward adjustment of salaries or permanently remove time clocks to reinforce a climate of trust and confidence in employees. The formal rules and regulations governing behavior of those affected by the change should also be revised to reinforce the new situation. Over time, of course, the work group's own norms will evolve to sustain the new equilibrium. But until that point is reached, management will have to rely on more formal mechanisms.

Action Research

Action Research A change process based on systematic collection of data and then selection of a change action based on what the analyzed data indicates.

Action research refers to a change process based on systematic collection of data and then selection of a change action based on what the analyzed data indicates.[11] Its importance lies in providing a scientific methodology for managing planned change.

The process of action research consists of five steps: diagnosis, analysis, feedback, action, and evaluation. You'll note that these steps closely parallel the scientific method.

DIAGNOSIS   The change agent, often an outside consultant in action research, begins by gathering information about problems, concerns, and needed changes from members of the organization. This diagnosis is analogous to the physician's search to find what specifically ails a patient. In action research, the change agent asks questions, interviews employees, reviews records, and listens to the concerns of employees.

ANALYSIS   The information gathered during the diagnostic stage is then analyzed. What problems do people key in on? What patterns do these problems seem to take? The change agent synthesizes this information into primary concerns, problem areas, and possible actions.

FEEDBACK   Action research includes extensive involvement of the change targets. That is, the people who will be involved in any change program must be actively involved in determining what the problem is and participating in creating the solution. So the third step is sharing with employees what has been found from steps one and two. The employees, with the help of the change agent, develop action plans for bringing about any needed change.

ACTION   Now the "action" part of action research is set in motion. The employees and the change agent carry out the specific actions to correct the problems that have been identified.

EVALUATION   Finally, consistent with the scientific underpinnings of action research, the change agent evaluates the effectiveness of the action plans. Using the initial data gathered as points of reference, any subsequent changes can be compared and evaluated.

Action research provides at least two specific benefits for an organization. First, it's problem-focused. The change agent objectively looks for problems and the type of problem determines the type of change action. While this may seem intuitively obvious, a lot of change activities aren't done this way. Rather, they're solution-centered. The change agent has a favorite solution—for example, implementing flextime or a management-by-objectives program—and then seeks out problems that his or her solution fits. Second, because action research so heavily involves employees in the process, resistance to change is reduced. In fact, once employees have actively participated in the feedback stage, the change process typically takes on a momentum of its own. The employees and groups that have been involved become an internal source of sustained pressure to bring about the change.

Organizational Development

No discussion of approaches to managing organizational change would be complete without inclusion of organizational development (OD). We'll provide only the briefest of introductions here because the next chapter is completely devoted to the topic.

Organizational Development
A collection of techniques that attempt to effect systematic planned change.

Organizational development refers to systematic, planned change. It's not an easily definable single concept. Rather, OD is a term used to encompass a collection of change techniques or interventions, from organization-wide changes in structure and systems to psychotherapeutic counseling sessions with groups and individuals, undertaken in response to changes in the external environment, that seek to improve organizational effectiveness and employee well-being.[12]

As we'll elaborate upon in the next chapter, OD is built on humanistic-democratic values. In addition, OD characteristics that distinguish it from more traditional change approaches include: (1) an emphasis on the work team as the key unit for learning more effective modes of organizational behavior; (2) an emphasis on participation and collaborative management; (3) an emphasis on changing the organization's culture; (4) the use of behavioral scientists as change agents; and (5) a view of the change effort as an ongoing process.[13]

IMPLICATIONS FOR PERFORMANCE
AND SATISFACTION

The need for change has been implied throughout this text. "A casual reflection on change should indicate that it encompasses almost all our concepts in the organizational behavior literature. Think about leadership, motivation, organizational environment, and roles. It is impossible to think about these and other concepts without inquiring about change."[14]

Changes occur outside organizations that require internal adaptation. Deregulation in the airline industry, for instance, dramatically changed the rules of the game for established players like Delta, TWA, and Continental; and single-handedly created a group of new players, including America West and Southwest Airlines. Cable networks, VCRs, and nationally syndicated programming is rapidly producing new competitors for the three traditional television networks, ABC, CBS, and NBC. If organizations fail to implement changes to adapt to their environments, their future survival can be at stake. Similarly, such internal forces as changes in the makeup of an organization's work force or the introduction of new equipment requires the implementation of planned change. Employees must adapt to these changes or their performances will suffer.

If environments were perfectly static, if employees' skills and abilities were always up-to-date and could never deteriorate, and if tomorrow were always exactly the same as today, organizational change would have little or no relevance to employee performance and satisfaction. But the real world is dynamic and turbulent, requiring organizations and their members to undergo change if they are to perform at competitive levels.

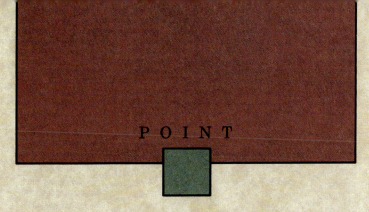

Change Is an Episodic Activity

The study of planned organizational change has, with very few exceptions, viewed it as an episodic activity. That is, it starts at some point, proceeds through a series of steps, and culminates in some outcome that those involved hope is an improvement over the starting point. When change is seen as an episodic activity, it has a beginning, a middle, and an end.

Both Lewin's three-step model and action research follow this perspective. In the former, change is seen as a break in the organization's equilibrium. The status quo has been disturbed, and change is necessary to establish a new equilibrium state. The objective of refreezing is to stabilize the new situation by balancing the driving and restraining forces. Action research begins with a diagnostic assessment, where problems are identified. These problems are then analyzed, shared with those who are effected, solutions developed, and action plans initiated. The process is brought to closure by an evaluation of the action plan's effectiveness. Even though supporters of action research recognize that the cycle may need to go through numerous iterations, the process is still seen as a cycle with a beginning and an end.

Some experts have argued that organizational change should be thought of as balancing a system made up of five interacting variables within the organization—people, tasks, technology, structure, and strategy. A change in any one variable has repercussions on one or more of the others. Again, this perspective is episodic in that it treats organizational change as essentially an effort to sustain an equilibrium. A change in one variable begins a chain of events which, if properly managed, requires adjustments in the other variables to achieve a new state of equilibrium.

Another way to conceptualize the episodic way of looking at change is to think of managing change as analogous to captaining a ship. The organization is like a large ship traveling across the calm Mediterranean Sea to a specific port. The ship's captain has made this exact trip hundreds of times before with the same crew. Every once in a while, however, a storm will appear, and the crew has to respond. The captain will make the appropriate adjustments —that is, implement changes—and, having maneuvered through the storm, will return to calm waters. Managing an organization should therefore be seen as a journey with a beginning and an end, and implementing change as a response to a break in the status quo and needed only in occasional situations.

Change Is an Ongoing Activity

The episodic approach may be the dominant paradigm for handling planned organizational change, but it has become obsolete. It applies to a world of certainty and predictability. The episodic approach was developed in the 1950s and 1960s, and it reflects the environment of those times. It treats change as the occasional disturbance in an otherwise peaceful world. However, it has little resemblance to the 1990s and an environment of constant and chaotic change.

If you want to understand what it's like to manage change in today's organizations, think of it as equivalent to permanent white-water rafting.* The organization is not a large ship, but more akin to a forty-foot raft. Rather than sailing a calm sea, this raft must traverse a raging river made up of an uninterrupted flow of permanent white-water rapids. To make things worse, the raft is manned by ten people who have never worked together, none of them has traveled the river before, much of the trip is in the dark, the river is dotted by unexpected turns and obstacles, the exact destination of the raft is not clear, and at irregular intervals the raft needs to pull to shore, where some new crew members are added and others leave. Change is a natural state and managing change is a continual process. That is, managers never get the luxury of escaping the white-water rapids.

To get a feeling for what managers are facing,

think of what it would be like to attend a college that had the following structure: Courses vary in length. When you sign up for a course, however, you don't know how long it will last. It might go for two weeks or thirty weeks. Furthermore, the instructor can end a course any time he or she wants, with no prior warning. If that wasn't frustrating enough, the length of the class changes each time it meets—sometimes it lasts twenty minutes, while other times it runs for three hours—and determination of when the next class meeting will take place is set by the instructor during the previous class. And one more thing: the exams are all unannounced, so you have to be ready for a test at any time.

A growing number of managers are coming to accept that their jobs are much like what a student would face in such a college. The stability and predictability of the episodic perspective doesn't exist. Nor are disruptions in the status quo only occasional, temporary, and followed by a return to an equilibrium state. Managers today face constant change, bordering on chaos. They are being forced to play a game they've never played before, governed by rules that are created as the game progresses.

*This perspective is based on P.B. Vaill, *Managing as a Performing Art: New Ideas for a World of Chaotic Change* (San Francisco: Jossey-Bass, 1989).

FOR DISCUSSION

1. How might changes in the makeup of an organization's workforce require implementation of organizational change programs?

2. What is meant by the phrase "we live in an age of discontinuity"?

3. "Managing today is easier than at the turn of the century because the years of real change took place between the Civil War and World War I." Do you agree or disagree? Discuss.

4. Are all managers change agents? Discuss.

5. "Resistance to change is an irrational response." Do you agree or disagree? Discuss.

6. Why do individuals resist change?

7. Why do organizations resist change?

8. How does Lewin's three-step model of change deal with resistance to change?

9. Describe the action research process.

10. What characteristics distinguish organizational development?

11. Discuss the link between learning theories discussed in Chapter 4 and the issue of organizational change.

12. Give some examples of motivation and leadership approaches that might be considered change programs.

FOR FURTHER READING

BEER, M., and A. E. WALTON, "Organization Change and Development," in M. R. Rosenzweig and L. W. Porter (eds.), *Annual Review of Psychology,* Vol. 38, pp. 339–67. Palo Alto, CA.: Annual Reviews, 1987. Updates the organizational change literature with discussions of trends in general management and human resource management.

DUNPHY, D. C., and D. A. STACE, "Transformational and Coercive Strategies for Planned Organizational Change: Beyond the O.D. Model," *Organization Studies,* Vol. 9, No. 3, 1988, pp. 317–34. Presents a contingency model of change based on incremental and transformational theories of change and participative versus coercive methods.

FRENCH, W. L., and C. H. BELL, JR., *Organization Development: Behavioral Science Interventions for Organization Improvement,* 4th ed. Englewood Cliffs, N.J.: Prentice Hall, 1990. A popular introductory text that reviews organizational change theories and practices.

HAMILTON, E. E., "The Facilitation of Organizational Change: An Empirical Study of Factors Predicting Change Agents' Effectiveness," *Journal of Applied Behavioral Science,* Vol. 24, No. 1, 1988, pp. 37–59. Study found that the personality characteristics and individual tendencies of effective change consultants differed significantly from those of less effective consultants.

ISABELLA, L. A., "Evolving Interpretations as a Change Unfolds: How Managers Construe Key Organizational Events," *Academy of Management Journal,* March 1990, pp. 7–41. Develops a model of how managers construe organizational events as a change unfolds. The model suggests that interpretations of key events unfold in four stages: anticipation, confirmation, culmination, and aftermath, linked to the process of change.

WOODMAN, R. W., and W. A. PASMORE, eds. *Research in Organizational Change and Development,* Vol. 2. Greenwich, Conn.: JAI Press, 1988. An annual volume of theories, models, ideas, and empirical data on organizational change.

Managing-in-a-Turbulent-World Tolerance Test

Instructions: Listed below are some statements a thirty-seven-year-old manager made about his job at a large, successful corporation. If your job had these characteristics, how would you react to them? After each statement are five letters, A to E. Circle the letter that best describes how you think you would react according to the following scale:

A   *I would enjoy this very much: it's completely acceptable.*
B   *This would be enjoyable and acceptable most of the time.*
C   *I'd have no reaction to this feature one way or another, or it would be about equally enjoyable and unpleasant.*
D   *This feature would be somewhat unpleasant for me.*
E   *This feature would be very unpleasant for me.*

1. I regularly spend 30 to 40 percent of my time in meetings.
    A B C D E

2. A year and a half ago, my job did not exist, and I have been essentially inventing it as I go along.   A B C D E

3. The responsibilities I either assume or am assigned consistently exceed the authority I have for discharging them.   A B C D E

4. At any given moment in my job, I have on the average about a dozen phone calls to be returned.   A B C D E

5. There seems to be very little relation in my job between the quality of my performance and my actual pay and fringe benefits.
    A B C D E

6. About two weeks a year of formal management training is needed in my job just to stay current.   A B C D E

7. Because we have very effective equal employment opportunity (EEO) in my company and because it is thoroughly multinational, my job consistently brings me into close working contact at a professional level with people of many races, ethnic groups, and nationalities and of both sexes.   A B C D E

8. There is no objective way to measure my effectiveness.   A B C D E

9. I report to three different bosses for different aspects of my job, and each has an equal say in my performance appraisal.   A B C D E

10. On average, about a third of my time is spent dealing with unexpected emergencies that force all scheduled work to be postponed.
    A B C D E

11. When I have to have a meeting of the people who report to me, it takes my secretary most of a day to find a time when we are all available, and even then, I have yet to have a meeting where everyone is present for the entire meeting.   A B C D E

12. The college degree I earned in preparation for this type of work is now obsolete, and I probably should go back for another degree.
    A B C D E

13. My job requires that I absorb 100–200 pages per week of technical materials.   A B C D E

14. I am out of town overnight at least one night per week.   A B C D E

15. My department is so interdependent with several other departments in the company that all distinctions about which departments are responsible for which tasks are quite arbitrary.   A B C D E

16. I will probably get a promotion in about a year to a job in another division that has most of these same characteristics.   A B C D E

17. During the period of my employment here, either the entire company or the division I worked in has been reorganized every year or so.   A B C D E

18. While there are several possible promotions I can see ahead of me, I have no real career path in an objective sense.   A B C D E

19. While there are several possible promotions I can see ahead of me, I think I have no realistic chance of getting to the top levels of the company.   A B C D E

20. While I have many ideas about how to make things work better, I have no direct influence on either the business policies or the personnel policies that govern my division.   A B C D E

21. My company has recently put in an "assessment center" where I and all other managers will be required to go through an extensive battery of psychological tests to assess our potential.   A B C D E

22. My company is a defendant in an antitrust suit, and if the case comes to trial, I will probably have to testify about some decisions that were made a few years ago.   A B C D E

23. Advanced computer and other electronic office technology is continually being introduced into my division, necessitating constant learning on my part.   A B C D E

24. The computer terminal and screen I have in my office can be monitored in my bosses' offices without my knowledge.   A B C D E

Turn to page 692 for scoring directions and key.

Source: From P. B. Vaill, *Managing as a Performing Art: New Ideas for a World of Chaotic Change* (San Francisco: Jossey-Bass, 1989), pp. 8–9. Reproduced with permission of publisher. All rights reserved.

Brusque or Efficient?

The people at WBFL had never seen anyone like Stan Moorhead before. WBFL is a television network affiliate in Buffalo, New York. Stan was the new station manager. He came to Buffalo after three years as manager of a smaller station in Memphis. In only two months, Stan has introduced a whole new management approach to WBFL. Maybe his most radical ideas relate to internal communications at the station. The following are a few examples (with selected quotes supplied by Stan):

"This place is memo crazy. In the first week I was here, I received over a dozen memos from staff members and the *shortest* was six pages long!" In response, Stan instituted a new rule: Any memo sent to him was not to exceed one page in length. Anything longer won't be read. "If these people can't make their point in 200 or 300 words, then they're not sure what they want to say."

"I told the people who report to me that they are well-paid professionals and I'm not their nursemaid. If they have a problem, fine, come to me and we'll discuss it. But here's the new catch: Don't come to me with a problem unless you've thoroughly thought it out and have a recommended solution to offer. It's not my job to make the decisions for my staff. I'm an advisor, not a dictator." Most of Stan's staff find this new procedure tough to follow. As the News Director noted, "I've been here for six years. When I had a problem in the past, I went to the station manager and he'd tell me how to handle it. This new policy makes my job twice as difficult. Now I have to review alternatives, select a solution, and be prepared to defend that solution to Stan. My job

was a whole lot easier before Stan got here."

Maybe the most radical action Stan has taken was to remove all the chairs from his office, except for his own. "I learned this trick when I was in Memphis. People would come into my office, sit down, and what should have been a five-minute meeting turned into a thirty-minute B.S.-session. Once people sit down and get comfortable, they think they have a right to talk on forever. Well, my time is valuable and so is theirs! So I took out all the chairs. My door is open and I'm available when needed. But when anyone comes into my office, they stand up. Sure it's a little strange. It makes people feel ill at ease. But it sure cuts out the idle chit-chat. People say what they have to say and leave. And, of course, if I really want to pursue a conversation at length, we can move next door to my conference room where there are plenty of chairs."

QUESTIONS

1. Have Stan's new management methods improved communication or created additional barriers? Explain.

2. Stan is convinced his ideas make WBFL more efficient but many of his employees have resisted the changes. Does this suggest that employees resist ideas that make an organization more efficient? Does it suggest that Stan's changes may not really be increasing efficiency? Discuss.

3. What impact do you think Stan's new ideas have on decision making at WBFL?

NOTES

[1]M. Kelly, "Sticking to Its Guns," *Business Month,* June 1990, pp. 58–61.

[2]*Ibid.,* p. 60.

[3]D. M. Gross and S. Scott, "Proceeding With Caution," *Time,* July 16, 1990, pp. 56–62.

[4]B. Saporito, "IBMs No-Hands Assembly Line," *Fortune,* September 15, 1986, pp. 105–09.

[5]H. A. Simon, *The New Science of Management Decision,* rev. ed. (Englewood Cliffs, N.J.: Prentice Hall, 1977), pp. 100–01.

[6]R. H. Hall, *Organizations: Structures, Processes, and Outcomes,* 4th ed. (Englewood Cliffs, N.J.: Prentice Hall, 1987), p. 29.

[7]D. Katz and R. L. Kahn, *The Social Psychology of Organizations,* 2nd ed. (New York: John Wiley & Sons, 1978), pp. 714–15.

[8]J. P. Kotter and L. A. Schlesinger, "Choosing Strategies for Change," *Harvard Business Review,* March–April 1979, pp. 106–14.

[9]L. Coch and J. R. P. French, Jr., "Overcoming Resistance to Change," *Human Relations,* Vol. 1, No. 4 (1948), pp. 512–32.

[10]K. Lewin, *Field Theory in Social Science* (New York: Harper & Row, 1951).

[11]See, for example, A. B. Shani and W. A. Pasmore, "Organization Inquiry: Towards a New Model of the Action Research Process," in D. D. Warrick (ed.), *Contemporary Organization Development: Current Thinking and Applications* (Glenview, Ill.: Scott, Foresman, 1985), pp. 438–48.

[12]M. Beer and A. E. Walton, "Organization Change and Development," in M. R. Rosenzweig and L. W. Porter (eds.), *Annual Review of Psychology,* Vol. 38 (Palo Alto, CA.: Annual Reviews, Inc., 1987), pp. 339–40.

[13]Based on W. L. French and C. H. Bell, Jr., *Organization Development: Behavioral Science Interventions for Organization Improvement, 4th ed.* (Englewood Cliffs, N.J.: Prentice Hall, 1990), p. 17.

[14]P. S. Goodman and L. B. Kurke, "Studies of Change in Organizations: A Status Report," in P. S. Goodman (ed.), *Change in Organizations* (San Francisco: Jossey-Bass, 1982), pp. 1–2.

ORGANIZATIONAL DEVELOPMENT

LEARNING OBJECTIVES

After studying this chapter, you should be able to:

1. *Outline OD values*
2. *Explain the political implications in a change intervention*
3. *Describe how OD interventions can reduce employee freedom and privacy*
4. *Summarize structural interventions*
5. *Describe task-technology interventions*
6. *Explain five specific people-focused interventions*
7. *List persuasive techniques for changing attitudes*

Mark Felver, a bagger and machine operator at Weaver Popcorn, helped purchase $134,000 worth of conveyor equipment. "I got gray hair," says Felver over the decision, "and I'm only 27." Like all Weaver employees, Felver has been actively involved in a change process that now involves company employees in decision making. Andy Goodwin.

The pace of change in the Nineties will make the Eighties look like a picnic—a walk in the park.

J. F. WELCH, JR.

H ow tough is it to produce good popcorn? It's not exactly rocket science. But to Mike Weaver, head of Weaver Popcorn Co., it's become a religion.[1]

When Weaver joined his family's firm right out of business school in 1972, the company was doing less than $6 million a year in revenue. Today it does about $70 million and is one of the world's largest processors of popcorn. A major turning point in the company's history was in November 1985. The company had just sent off one of its biggest shipments—280,000 pounds of popcorn—to a customer in Japan. The customer called to inform Weaver that, after inspecting the order, they were rejecting it because there was too much foreign material among the kernels. Shocked and ashamed, Mike Weaver and his executive team began to reassess their firm's approach to quality. What they quickly realized was that Weaver Popcorn had to change the way it did things. Its standards were no longer good enough.

Improving product quality proved a lot harder than Mike Weaver had originally thought it would. His first reaction was to spend over a million dollars to buy state-of-the-art, high-speed optical scanners that could identify foreign particles such as weed seeds and dirt clods. No one in his industry had them. This expenditure only made Weaver's management more aware of their quality problems. First, the new machines didn't *solve* the quality problem. They only made it easier to identify. Second, it became clear that nothing had a greater impact on the quality of the corn than the people in the plant. If quality was to significantly improve, Weaver Popcorn was going to have to make changes in the way people did their jobs. Mike Weaver continuously reminded people that the company couldn't rest on its past successes. "The only real job security for any of us is being the very best at what we do."

Since that Japanese order was rejected in 1985, Mike Weaver has been on a mission to change the way his people look at quality. How did he do it? By totally remaking his organization and getting employees involved in as many areas of the company as possible. For instance, employees who complained that they couldn't adequately inspect incoming popcorn supplies for contamination were allowed to buy tools that could do the job. Then they were given the authority to reject shipments that didn't meet company specifications. A bagger and machine operator helped purchase $134,000 worth of conveyor equipment. A truck dispatcher was invited to speak before a large customer group. The head of the company's consumer services department went to Sweden to help a customer.

In addition, Weaver Popcorn has implemented team management. Major policy decisions now are made by team leaders selected from different areas within the company. When three of the five plant supervisors quit—because they couldn't adjust to the changes—none were replaced. When the manager of the company's trucking subsidiary resigned, he was replaced by a team of four employees.

Weaver Popcorn is a very different company today than it was only half-a-dozen years ago. It is now a more efficient and aggressive competitor, produces a significantly higher-quality product, and has introduced processes that will allow it to continue to improve its quality.

Weaver Popcorn illustrates what many organizations have come to learn: Change or die! In this chapter, we want to discuss organizational development and various OD techniques for bringing about effective change.

OD VALUES AND OUTCOMES

We described organizational development in the previous chapter as a collection of change techniques or interventions built on humanistic-democratic values. Let's elaborate on this latter point because it helps to clarify the philosophy underlying the OD movement.

The OD paradigm values human and organizational growth, collaborative and participative processes, and a spirit of inquiry.[2] The change agent may be directive in OD; however, there is a strong emphasis on collaboration. Concepts such as power, authority, control, conflict, and coercion are held in relatively low esteem among OD change agents. The following briefly identifies the underlying values in most OD efforts:

1. *Respect for people.* Individuals are perceived as being responsible, conscientious, and caring. They should be treated with dignity and respect.
2. *Trust and support.* The effective and healthy organization is characterized by trust, authenticity, openness, and a supportive climate.
3. *Power equalization.* Effective organizations deemphasize hierarchical authority and control.
4. *Confrontation.* Problems shouldn't be swept under the rug. They should be openly confronted.
5. *Participation.* The more that people who will be affected by a change are involved in the decisions surrounding that change, the more they will be committed to implementing those decisions.

Table 20–1 summarizes the positive outcomes that advocates argue can result from successful OD interventions.

IMPLEMENTATION ISSUES IN OD

Why do some well-conceived and worthwhile change interventions fail? Can change intervention programs impinge on individual rights? These questions

TABLE 20–1   Ten Positive Results from OD

1. Improved organizational effectiveness (increased productivity and morale; more effective goal setting, planning, and organizing; clearer goals and responsibilities; better utilization of human resources; and bottom-line improvements)
2. Better management from top to bottom
3. Greater commitment and involvement from organizational members in making the organization successful
4. Improved teamwork within and between groups
5. A better understanding of an organization and its strengths and weaknesses
6. Improvement in communications, problem solving, and conflict resolution skills, resulting in increased effectiveness and less wasted time from communications breakdowns, game playing, and win–lose confrontations
7. Efforts to develop a work climate that encourages creativity and openness, provides opportunities for personal growth and development, and rewards responsible and healthy behavior
8. A significant decrease in dysfunctional behavior
9. Increased personal and organizational awareness that improves the organization's ability to adapt to a continuously changing environment and to continue to grow, learn, and stay competitive
10. The ability to attract and keep healthy and productive people

Source: *MODMAN: Managing Organization Change and Development* by D. D. (Don) Warrick, p. 10. Copyright © Science Research Associates, Inc., 1984. Reprinted by permission of the publisher.

relate to three current issues in OD. First, OD values don't fit into all organizational cultures. Second, many OD endeavors fail because the change agent doesn't understand the politics of change. And third, OD has ethical implications. Specifically, efforts to humanize organizations can create a dilemma between the goals of freedom and equality.

Differences in Organizational Cultures

OD values are not compatible with every organization's culture. OD embraces the values of collaboration, confrontation, authenticity, trust, support, and openness. These, however, are at odds with cultures that are characterized as risk aversive, low in integration, low in management support, high in control, and intolerant of conflict.

OD is clearly more compatible with organic structures and Theory Y assumptions (see Chapters 15 and 7, respectively) about human nature than with mechanistic designs and Theory X assumptions. Of course, a large proportion of organizations in North America are bureaucratically structured, with extensive formalization and centralized decision power. These organizations might benefit most from having OD programs yet, paradoxically, they are also the type of organizations that are also most likely to resist OD values and make interventions difficult, if not impossible. Our point is that OD success is, to a large degree, dependent on the mesh between OD's values and those of the organization. Efforts to impose OD values in an alien culture are very likely to result in failure.

The Politics of Change

In Chapter 12, we described organizations as political systems with individuals and groups vying for power. Political dynamics, however, escalate during times of change,[3] because any significant change has the potential to disrupt the current balance of power among groups. Uncertainty and ambiguity surface. The result is that individuals and groups in the organization can be expected to use what power they have to protect their vested interests and ensure that any change maintains or improves their current position.

The reality of organizational politics means that effective change agents should approach any change intervention by assessing how it might threaten the current power distribution. This perspective, incidentally, often disturbs many OD advocates. They would prefer to view organizations as cooperative systems, devoid of power struggles, self-serving coalitions, strategic maneuvering, and the like. But to ignore politics and the impact that change interventions can have on the balance of power within an organization is naive at best and, at worst, may predestine the change effort to failure.

Can a change agent do anything beyond recognizing the potential for resistance and being on the lookout for actions that seem to block the change? Yes.[4] First, the change agent can develop his or her power sources and bases. The possession of expertise, information, contacts, the ability to allocate rewards, and similar skills and resources can help convince others to go along with the change effort. Next, the change agent should assess the situation and key players. Who will be affected by the change? How powerful are they? Who has a positive, negative, or neutral stake in the change? How determined might those threatened by the change be in using their power to undermine the change effort? Remember, change cannot succeed unless there is a critical mass of support.[5]

After this assessment is complete, the change agent can select the proper power strategies. Table 20–2 describes a number of possible strategies for implementing change. In many cases, the change agent will want to use several of these strategies. But which one he or she chooses should reflect the political dynamics of the situation.

The Ethics of Control

We previously noted that OD interventions typically are based on humanistic-democratic values. They rely heavily on processes such as participation, collaboration, and confrontation. OD interventions are viewed as effective to the degree to which they increase openness, trust, risk-taking, autonomy, and respect for people, and equalize power within the organization. The assumption by OD proponents is that these outcomes are desirable and lead to more effective organizational performance. Some writers have correctly noted, however, that when OD change agents use humanistic processes to achieve democratic outcomes, they are imposing their values on organizational participants.[6] For example, if employees in a given department have had trouble working with each other over a fairly long period of time, an OD change agent might recommend that the department members get together in an informal session and openly discuss their perceptions of each other, the sources of their disagreements, and similar issues. But not everyone feels comfortable participating in a process that requires them to be open about their feelings and attitudes. For such individuals, OD interventions that demand openness reduce their privacy and freedom. Even if participation is voluntary, the decision not to participate might carry negative connotations, result in lower performance appraisals, and have adverse career effects. Moreover, what if an employee does participate, is authentically open, reveals to the group some

TABLE 20–2   Strategies for Implementing Change

- *Present a nonthreatening image.* When attempting to introduce innovative programs, it may be effective to be perceived as being conservative and essentially nonthreatening to existing organizational activities.
- *Present arguments in terms of the client's interests.* Don't distort information, but cast arguments for change proposals in terms of the benefits that will accrue to the client.
- *Diffuse opposition and bring out conflict.* Rather than stifle opposition, diffuse it through an open discussion of ideas. Conflicts that develop can be dealt with by engaging the opposition in legitimate discussion, answering objections, and allaying fears and facts. Open discussion can also spotlight any die-hard resistors, reducing opportunities for them to covertly thwart the change effort.
- *Align with powerful others.* In addition to gaining top management's approval, it can be beneficial to build alliances with operating or line managers who are directly affected by the change.
- *Bargain and make trade-offs.* Change is an on-going activity. Resistors may reduce their resistance if they are assured that other changes, which they favor, will be forthcoming.
- *Begin as an experiment.* Resistance may be lessened by introducing the change as an experiment. When something is viewed as temporary, it is less threatening. Having the change made permanent is easier once it is already in place.
- *Begin small.* Start small and slowly expand the change project. If an "all-or-nothing" stance has a reasonable chance of failing, it may be more effective to "get your foot in the door" and then expand the project slowly.

Source: Based on V. E. Schein, "Organizational Realities: The Politics of Change," *Training and Development Journal,* February 1985, pp. 39–40.

very personal fears and concerns, and then someone in the group uses this information vindictively against that employee at some later date? Haven't the employee's privacy and freedom been compromised?

Even voluntary participation in an OD intervention implies control by the change agent over participants. Of course, you might say that managers attempt to control employees all the time and that doesn't seem to generate concerns about ethics. Why should OD interventions? The answer is twofold. First, employees understand that they give up some freedom when they accept employment. There is a trade-off—they give up forty hours a week for fifty or so weeks a year and, in turn, they receive a paycheck and an assortment of valuable benefits. Second, OD interventions control people by seeking to make them more open, trusting, authentic, and the like. How can you rail against outcomes such as these? The answer is, you can't. You're not likely to impress your bosses by arguing that mutual avoidance, closed communication, and distrusting relationships are O.K. because "they protect my privacy." So employees are under pressure to participate. They must surrender some of their freedoms and privacy or be labeled as "uncooperative." Consider some typical OD interventions: (1) Employees are asked to complete questionnaires and participate in interviews to determine their satisfaction with their job, their immediate supervisor, and the organization itself. The focus is on identifying problems that management may not be aware of so they can be corrected. (2) A manager and his or her subordinates are asked to look at the former's leadership style. The manager describes his or her style, then subordinates provide feedback. The change focus is on getting the manager to understand the dysfunctions of autocratic leadership and the superiority of participative management. (3) Group members with a history of interpersonal problems are asked to reveal personal frustrations, and insecurities, and explain why they have difficulty working with each other. The change focus is on understanding others, improving communication, reducing conflicts, and improving work group performance. Employees can't easily decline participation in such apparently "worthwhile" change efforts.

Is something ethical if it promotes the greatest good for the greatest number? If so, OD interventions that reduce some employee rights might be considered ethical. But one can argue that management is unethical if it interferes with even one employee's freedoms. Does management have the right to even implicitly coerce employees to participate in an OD program "for the good of the organization?" This is not easy to answer. At the extreme, management could avoid all OD activities associated with the loss of employee freedom. But this might make planned change impossible. Why? Because changes don't occur unless there is some unfreezing of the status quo. And participation, confrontation, and similar OD processes contain risks for participants. These risks, in turn, stimulate the forces of change. If OD interventions minimize individual risk, the climate may be so bland as to have no effect on the change process. So the challenge for management in using OD interventions is to find the proper balance—where employees' rights and well-being are weighed against improvements in the organization's effectiveness.

OD INTERVENTIONS

What are some of the OD techniques and interventions for bringing about change? In this section, we'll review the more popular intervention techniques. We have categorized them under structural, task-technology, and people-focused interventions.

Structural Interventions

Structural OD interventions emphasize making organizations more organic and egalitarian. We can see this emphasis in OD programs that include major structural reorganization, introduction of new rewards systems, and efforts to change organizational cultures.

STRUCTURAL REORGANIZATION   Formal structures are not chiseled in stone. The structural configuration that was right for a firm in 1980 can put it at a competitive disadvantage in 1990. So structural reorganization may be necessary. Recent trends indicate that structures are becoming flatter, more decentralized, and more organic. Notice that these trends are all consistent with OD values.

OD change agents favor flatter organizations for at least three reasons. First, it provides economic benefits. By widening spans of control and cutting the number of vertical levels, the organization reduces administrative overhead costs because there are fewer managers. Second, fewer vertical levels improve communication. Third, wider spans of control typically result in employees having greater autonomy since managers can't directly oversee their subordinates as closely.

Decentralized decision making is a popular intervention favored by OD change agents. Pushing authority downward creates power equalization. It allows people closest and most knowledgeable about an issue to make decisions regarding that issue. Decentralization also gives lower-level employees greater control over their work.

OD Across National Boundaries

We know that effective motivational practices, leadership styles, and organization designs differ across national boundaries. Why, then, shouldn't OD interventions? The answer, as several recent studies demonstrate, is that they should.[7]

It has been argued that OD's values match well with countries who score low on power distance, low on uncertainty avoidance, low on masculinity, and moderate on individualism.[8] Countries with this profile value equality, confrontation, willingness to take risks, open expression of feelings, and collaboration rather than competition. It seems logical that the greater the match between OD's values and a country's cultural dimensions, the greater the potential for acceptance and success of OD interventions.

A review of the research comparing countries on their cultural dimensions allows us to make several predictions. First, OD interventions that emphasize openness, equality and the like are most likely to be accepted in countries such as Denmark, Norway, and Sweden, where the match between OD values and cultural dimensions is very high. Second, these forms of OD interventions are not likely to succeed in countries such as Colombia, Mexico, Italy, and Japan, where the match is low. Third, and somewhat surprising given that a large proportion of OD enthusiasts come from American behavioral scientists, the United States' cultural dimensions don't align

particularly well with those of general OD values. This may explain why OD has had some problems of acceptance and success in the United States, especially the more radical interventions that strive to democratize American bureaucracies. It can also provide insights into why Great Britain, where security, stability, and class structure are deeply-rooted values, has difficulty accepting OD interventions that focus on risk-taking and equality; or why interventions that seek to increase employee assertiveness would be inappropriate in Japan because success would only produce organizational deviants.

The following five steps have been recommended to increase the likelihood that any OD intervention is in harmony with the country where it is being considered for introduction.[9]

1. Evaluate the ranking of the dimensions of culture in the given situation.
2. Make a judgment as to which values are the most deeply held and unlikely to change.
3. Evaluate interventions in terms of their harmony with the culture identified in Step 1.
4. Choose the intervention that would clash least with the most rigidly held values.
5. Incorporate process modifications in the proposed intervention to fit with the given cultural situation.

One increasingly popular way to facilitate decentralized decision making has been through the introduction of computers. Sophisticated computerized information systems change access patterns to information. Many are currently being designed to allow lower-level managers and operative employees to gain direct access to the information they need to make operating decisions.

The trend in OD structural interventions has been toward making organizations more organic. Relating back to Chapter 15, OD change agents are trying to make organizations less bureaucratic so they can respond more quickly to changes in the environment. Where bureaucratic structures are necessary to maintain competitive efficiency, OD change agents have often favored adding organic subunits to gain flexibility. IBM, for instance, developed its personal computer in a small organic unit located in Florida, far from the company's headquarters in New York. Once the PC was designed by the Florida group, responsibility for the product was subsumed by the company's large and efficient production and marketing bureaucracies.

Major structural reorganizations are typically quite disruptive and threatening to those people affected. As a result, OD change agents favor employees actively participating in the reorganization process.

NEW REWARD SYSTEMS   OD change agents enthusiastically endorse operant conditioning's notion that behavior is a function of its consequences. (See Chapter 4.) This focuses attention on the organization's reward system.

Generally speaking, organizations did a poor job in the postwar era in linking rewards to employee performance. Production workers increasingly were paid by the hour rather than by output. Clerical and managerial personnel received a monthly salary that often had little direct relationship to productivity.

As discussed in Chapter 8, organizations have only recently moved to enact "pay-for-performance" programs. OD change agents have been actively involved in helping to develop and implement these programs. While individual-based bonus plans are most popular, OD change agents typically favor plans that emphasize group and organizational performance. For instance, a significant portion of an employee's compensation might be calculated on the productivity of his or her work team, or comprised of year-end bonuses based on the overall profitability of the company. The reason such programs are favored by OD specialists is that they are more likely than individual-based plans to facilitate teamwork and cooperation.

CHANGING ORGANIZATIONAL CULTURE   The challenges involved in changing an organization's culture was addressed in the Point–Counterpoint section in Chapter 17. As discussed, there is considerable debate about whether organizational cultures can be changed. Even among those who argue that change is possible, it is clear that it's a long-term process.

Regardless of the difficulty, many major corporations—for example, AT&T, Xerox, Scott Paper, and Ford Motor Co.—have undertaken the task. Interestingly, consistent with OD values, the changes have been almost exclusively toward introducing new cultural values that support less management control, increased tolerance for risk and conflict, and opening up communication channels. Many large and historically successful organizations have learned the hard way that cultures can become obsolete and create serious impediments for responding to a changing environment. Like Weaver Popcorn, presented in this chapter's opening, the emphasis has moved toward making organizational cultures more flexible, more responsive, and more focused on customer needs, service, and quality.

For those organizations taking on the task, what are they doing? They're reorganizing; replacing and reassigning people in key positions; changing their reward systems; creating new stories, symbols, and rituals; and modifying their selection and socialization processes to hire and support individuals who will espouse the new values.

Task-Technology Interventions

Task-technology interventions emphasize changing the actual jobs that people do and/or the technological processes and tools they use to perform these jobs.

Included in this category are job redesign, sociotechnical systems, and quality-of-worklife programs.

JOB REDESIGN   We discussed job redesign in Chapter 8. Examples of redesign interventions include job rotation, enlargement, enrichment, and autonomous work teams.

Job redesign is similar to structural reorganization except instead of focusing the change effort at the level of the organization, the focus is at the job level. As a result, in contrast to organization redesign, job redesign is more widely practiced and can be implemented by lower-level supervisors as well as by senior-level managers.

OD change agents have actively promoted the redesign of jobs along the lines suggested by the job characteristics model. That is, they have sought to take jobs and increase their skill variety, task identity and significance, autonomy, and feedback.

Successful job redesign interventions that follow the job characteristics model share several common qualities.[10] The organizations have cultures that support employee autonomy and participation, they have low formalization that allows flexibility in redesigning tasks, and they either are nonunionized or have the support of the union.

SOCIOTECHNICAL SYSTEMS   The accomplishment of any task requires a technology and a social system.[11] The technology consists of the tools, techniques, procedures, skills, knowledge, and devices used by employees to do their jobs. The social system comprises the people who work in the organization and their interrelationships. Proponents of a **sociotechnical systems** approach to change argue that any successful work design must jointly

Sociotechnical Systems Work design must jointly optimize both the social and the technological demands in the job.

The AccuTrac, which is used by roofers to fasten insulation, is changing their job. The machine allows a worker to singularly do what previously took two people.   James Schnepf.

optimize the social and the technological demands of the job.

When originally introduced in the 1950s, the sociotechnical systems perspective was one of the first to recognize that the needs of both the organization *and* the individual employee had to be considered in the design of work. Technology constrains the social system by shaping the behaviors required to operate it. However, if job designers ignore the personalities and attitudes of workers, their interaction patterns, their relationships with their supervisors, and the like, then the best designed technical system will fail to achieve its full potential.

For change agents who want to use sociotechnical systems as a guide in redesigning jobs, what should they do? Probably the best place to begin is to conceptualize work design as organizing *groups* of workers rather than *individuals* alone. Then the various technologies that are within the feasible set for achieving the group's objectives can be evaluated to find the proper match. Table 20–3 outlines some specific tenets derived from the sociotechnical systems philosophy.

Quality of Worklife (QWL) A process by which an organization responds to employee needs by developing mechanisms to allow them to share fully in making decisions that design their lives at work.

QUALITY OF WORKLIFE The term **quality of worklife (QWL)** describes a process by which an organization responds to employee needs by developing mechanisms to allow them to share fully in making the decisions that design their lives at work.[12] It may help to think of QWL as an umbrella concept that encompasses literally dozens of specific interventions that have a common goal of humanizing the workplace.

While QWL encompasses a large number of interventions, one author has divided them into eight specific categories:[13]

1. Adequate and fair compensation.
2. A safe and healthy environment.
3. Jobs that develop human capacities.
4. A chance for personal growth and security.
5. A social environment that provides personal identity, freedom from prejudice, a sense of community, and upward mobility.
6. Rights of personal privacy, dissent, and due process.
7. A work role that minimizes infringement on personal leisure and family needs.
8. Socially responsible organizational actions.

TABLE 20–3

Some Basic Tenets from Sociotechnical Systems
1. The work system becomes the basic unit rather than the single jobs into which it is decomposable.
2. Correspondingly, the work group rather than the individual jobholder becomes central.
3. Internal regulation of the system by the group rather than the external regulation of individuals by supervisors now becomes possible.
4. The individual becomes viewed as complementary to the machine rather than an extension of it.
5. Variety is increased for both the individual and the organization, rather than variety decreasing, as is common in machine bureaucracies.

Adapted from E. L. Trist, "The Sociotechnical Perspective," in A. H. Van de Ven and W. F. Joyce, eds., *Perspectives On Organization Design and Behavior* (New York: John Wiley & Sons, 1981), pp. 22–23. With permission.

Johnsonville Foods' personal development lifelong learning program enabled Michelle Stock to learn sign language so she could communicate with another worker. The company's CEO has found that company-sponsored personal-growth projects increase employee commitment. Kevin Horan.

Any comprehensive list of QWL programs would encompass job redesign, participative management, flextime, and quality circles, as well as programs that offer employees the opportunity to purchase equity in their firms, or programs that provide protection against arbitrary action by their supervisors.

People-Focused Interventions

The vast majority of OD intervention efforts have been directed at changing the attitudes and behaviors of organization members through the processes of communication, decision making, and problem solving. While this group of interventions could include corporate training programs and management development, OD has emphasized five specific people-focused interventions: sensitivity training, survey feedback, process consultation, team building, and intergroup development.

Sensitivity Training Training groups that seek to change behavior through unstructured group interaction.

SENSITIVITY TRAINING   It can go by a variety of names—laboratory training, **sensitivity training,** encounter groups, or T-groups (training groups)—but all refer to a method of changing behavior through unstructured group interaction. Members are brought together in a free and open environment in which participants discuss themselves and their interactive processes, loosely directed by a professional behavioral scientist. The group is process oriented, which means that individuals learn through observing and participating rather than being told. The professional creates the opportunity for participants to express their ideas, beliefs, and attitudes. He or she does not accept—in fact, overtly rejects—any leadership role.

FIGURE 20–1
Source: Reprinted by permission of United Feature Syndicate, Inc.

The objectives of the T-groups are to provide the subjects with increased awareness of their own behavior and how others perceive them, greater sensitivity to the behavior of others, and increased understanding of group processes. Specific results sought include increased ability to empathize with others, improved listening skills, greater openness, increased tolerance of individual differences, and improved conflict resolution skills.

If individuals lack awareness of how others perceive them, then the successful T-group can effect more realistic self-perceptions, greater group cohesiveness, and a reduction in dysfunctional interpersonal conflicts. Further, it will ideally result in a better integration between the individual and the organization.

SURVEY FEEDBACK   One tool for assessing attitudes held by organizational members, identifying discrepancies among member perceptions, and solving these differences is the **survey feedback** approach.

Everyone in an organization can participate in survey feedback, but of key importance is the organizational family—the manager of any given unit and those employees who report directly to him or her. A questionnaire is usually completed by all members in the organization or unit. Organization members may be asked to suggest questions or may be interviewed to determine what issues are relevant. The questionnaire typically asks members for their perceptions and attitudes on a broad range of topics, including decision making practices; communication effectiveness; coordination between units; and satisfaction with the organization, job, peers, and their immediate supervisor.

The data from this questionnaire are tabulated with data pertaining to an individual's specific "family" and to the entire organization and distributed to employees. These data then become the springboard for identifying problems and clarifying issues that may be creating difficulties for people. In some cases, the manager may be counseled by an external change agent about the meaning of the responses to the questionnaire and may even be given suggested guidelines for leading the organizational family in group discussion of the results. Particular attention is given to the importance of encouraging discussion and ensuring that discussions focus on issues and ideas and not on attacking individuals.

Finally, group discussion in the survey feedback approach should result in members identifying possible implications of the questionnaire's findings.

Survey Feedback The use of questionnaires to identify discrepancies among member perceptions; discussion follows and remedies are suggested.

Are people listening? Are new ideas being generated? Can decision making, interpersonal relations, or job assignments be improved? Answers to questions like these, it is hoped, will result in the group agreeing upon commitments to various actions that will remedy the problems that are identified.

Process Consultation
Consultant gives a client insight into what is going on around him or her, within him or her, and between him or her and other people; identifies processes that need improvement.

PROCESS CONSULTATION   No organization operates perfectly. Managers often sense that their unit's performance can be improved, but they are unable to identify what can be improved and how it can be improved. The purpose of **process consultation** is for an outside consultant to assist a client, usually a manager, "to perceive, understand, and act upon process events" with which he or she must deal.[14] These might include work flow, informal relationships among unit members, and formal communication channels.

Process consultation (PC) is similar to sensitivity training in its assumption that organizational effectiveness can be improved by dealing with interpersonal problems, and in its emphasis on involvement. But PC is more task directed than sensitivity training.

Consultants in PC are there to "give the client 'insight' into what is going on around him, within him, and between him and other people."[15] They do not solve the organization's problems. Rather, the consultant is a guide or coach who advises on the process to help the client solve his or her own problems.

The consultant works with the client in *jointly* diagnosing what processes need improvement. The emphasis is on "jointly," because the client develops a skill at analyzing processes within his or her unit that can be continually called on long after the consultant is gone. Additionally, by having the client actively participate in both the diagnosis and the development of alternatives, there will be greater understanding of the process and the remedy and less resistance to the action plan chosen.

Importantly, the process consultant need not be an expert in solving the particular problem that is identified. The consultant's expertise lies in diagnosis and developing a helping relationship. If the specific problem uncovered requires technical knowledge outside the client and consultant's expertise, the consultant helps the client to locate such an expert and then instructs the client in how to get the most out of this expert resource.

Team Building High interaction among group members to increase trust and openness.

TEAM BUILDING   Organizations are made up of people working together to achieve some common end. Since people are frequently required to work in groups, considerable attention has been focused in OD on **team building**.[16]

Team building can be applied within groups or at the intergroup level where activities are interdependent. For our discussion, we shall emphasize the intragroup level and leave intergroup development to the next section. As a result, our interest concerns applications to organizational families (command groups), as well as communities, project teams, and task groups.

Not all group activity has interdependence of functions. To illustrate, consider a football team and a track team:

> Although members on both teams are concerned with the team's total output they function differently. The football team's output depends synergistically on how well each player does his particular job in concert with his teammates. The quarterback's performance depends on the performance of his linemen and receivers, and ends on how well the quarterback throws the ball, and so on. On the other hand, a track team's performance is determined largely by the mere addition of the performances of the individual members.[17]

Chrysler Corp. has used team building to reduce historical conflicts with unionized employees. This group of employees from Chrysler's Newark assembly plant in Delaware implemented the first modern operating agreement negotiated between Chrysler and the United Auto Workers. It allows more flexibility and communication in the workplace and helps labor and management function as a team.   Courtesy Chrysler Corporation.

Team building is applicable to the case of interdependence, such as in football. The objective is to improve coordinative efforts of team members which will result in increasing the group's performance.

The activities considered in team building typically include goal setting, development of interpersonal relations among team members, role analysis to clarify each member's role and responsibilities, and team process analysis. Of course, team building may emphasize or exclude certain activities depending on the purpose of the development effort and the specific problems with which the team is confronted. Basically, however, team building attempts to use high interaction among group members to increase trust and openness.

It may be beneficial to begin by having members attempt to define the goals and priorities of the group. This will bring to the surface different perceptions of what the group's purpose may be. Following this, members can evaluate the group's performance—how effective are they in structuring priorities and achieving their goals? This should identify potential problem areas. This self-critique discussion of means and ends can be done with members of the total group present or, where large size impinges on a free interchange of views, may initially take place in smaller groups followed up by the sharing of their findings with the total group.

Team building can also address itself to clarifying each member's role in the group. Each role can be identified and clarified. Previous ambiguities can be brought to the surface. For some individuals, it may offer one of the few opportunities they have had to think through thoroughly what their job is all about and what specific tasks they are expected to carry out if the group is to optimize its effectiveness.

Still another team building activity can be similar to that performed by the process consultant, that is, to analyze key processes that go on within the team to identify the way work is performed and how these processes might be improved to make the team more effective.

INTERGROUP DEVELOPMENT   A major area of concern in OD is the dysfunctional conflict that exists between groups. As a result, this has been a subject to which change efforts have been directed.

Intergroup Development OD efforts to improve interaction between groups.

Intergroup development seeks to change the attitudes, stereotypes, and perceptions that groups have of each other. For example, in one company the engineers saw the accounting department as composed of shy and conservative types, and the personnel department as having a bunch of "smiley types who sit around and plan company picnics." Such stereotypes can have an obvious negative impact on the coordinative efforts between the departments.

Although there are several approaches for improving intergroup relations,[18] a popular method emphasizes problem solving.[19] In this method, each group meets independently to develop lists of its perception of themselves, the other group, and how they believe the other group perceives them. The groups then share their lists, after which similarities and differences are discussed. Differences are clearly articulated, and the groups look for the causes of the disparities.

Are the groups' goals at odds? Were perceptions distorted? On what basis were stereotypes formulated? Have some differences been caused by misunderstandings of intentions? Have words and concepts been defined differently by each group? Answers to questions like these clarify the exact nature of the conflict. Once the causes of the difficulty have been identified, the groups can move to the integration phase—working to develop solutions that will improve relations between the groups.

Subgroups, with members from each of the conflicting groups, can now be created for further diagnosis and to begin to formulate possible alternative actions that will improve relations.

IMPLICATIONS FOR PERFORMANCE AND SATISFACTION

In this chapter we've discussed structural, task-technology, and people-focused interventions for bringing about change. But do these OD interventions work?

A lot of the evaluative studies of OD interventions lack rigor, relying heavily on case studies and anecdotal data for support. Some researchers have gone so far as to claim that any positive results of OD interventions are due more to the weak or loose methodologies used for evaluation than to the effectiveness of the interventions, and that the more rigorous the research, the more likely the results are to show negative findings.[21] On the other hand, there is evidence that the quality of OD research designs have improved and that methodological weaknesses are more likely to be found in earlier studies.[22] Nevertheless, we should acknowledge that research in this area is far from flawless. However, given this caveat, what *can* we say about OD in its relation to behavior and attitudes?

One meta-analysis of 126 studies looked at the effect of task-technology and people-focused interventions on satisfaction. The authors concluded that: (1) people-focused interventions had a larger effect on attitudes than did task-technology interventions; (2) using two or more interventions is superior to using only one; and (3) the outcomes that result from OD interventions are in most instances situationally specific, so care should be taken in making generalizations.[23]

Changing Attitudes Through Persuasive Messages

You hear through the grapevine that one of your employees thinks you're insensitive to the needs of racial minorities. You know that not to be the case. Is there anything you can do to change this employee's attitude?

In Chapter 6, we introduced the concept of cognitive dissonance and evidence demonstrating that people dislike inconsistency. Based on that research, we know that one way for employees to reduce dissonance is to change their attitudes to bring them into line with other attitudes or behavior. So if you can arouse dissonance with your employee—possibly through making her aware of specific actions you've taken that clearly demonstrate your concern for racial minorities—you might be able to change her attitude about you.

Another technique for inducing attitude change involves the use of persuasive messages. That is, we can induce others to change their attitudes by consciously manipulating what we say to them. The following summarizes the research on persuasive skills.[20] It emphasizes oral persuasion but can be easily adapted for written communications.

1. *Establish your credibility*. Nothing undermines persuasive efforts more than lack of credibility. People don't want to listen to a person they don't trust or believe. Credibility is developed through demonstrating competence, objectivity, and high ethical standards.

2. *Use a positive, tactful tone*. Assume the person you're trying to persuade is intelligent and mature. Don't talk down to that person. Be respectful, direct, sincere, and tactful.

3. *Make your presentation clear*. Before you can

convincingly articulate your view to someone else, you need to be clear about what it is you want to say. Once your objective is clear, you should present your argument one idea at a time. Don't jump from issue to issue, and avoid unrelated topics. Focus on your end objective, and then present your ideas in a straight path that will lead the person to the conclusion you want and the objective you set.

4. *Present strong evidence to support your position*. You need to explain *why* what you want is important. Merely saying your viewpoint is important is not enough.

5. *Tailor your argument to the listener*. Effective persuasion demands flexibility. You have to select your argument for your specific target. Whom are you talking to? What are his or her goals, needs, interests, fears, and aspirations? How much does the target know about the subject you're discussing? What are his or her preconceived attitudes on this subject? How entrenched are those attitudes?

6. *Use logic*. While a logical, reasoned argument is not guaranteed to change another's attitudes, if you lack facts and reasons to support your argument, your persuasiveness will almost certainly be undermined.

7. *Use emotional appeals*. Presenting clear, rational, and objective evidence in support of your view is often not enough. You should also appeal to a person's emotions. Try to reach inside the subject and understand his or her loves, hates, fears, and frustrations. Then use that information to mold what you say and how you say it.

Another meta-analysis, this one covering 207 interventions, has proven more beneficial in helping us assess effectiveness because it emphasized a wider range of interventions and looked at more dependent variables.[24] In this

TABLE 20–4   Effectiveness of Eleven Intervention Programs

Program	Percent Indicating Positive Effect On		
	Productivity	Absenteeism and Turnover	Attitudes
Recruitment and selection	NS	50	100
Training and instruction	92	71	78
Appraisal and feedback	93	60	67
Goal setting	95	67	70
Financial compensation	90	78	75
Work redesign	88	80	70
Supervisory methods	92	92	100
Organization structure	100	100	NS
Decision making techniques	100	NS	0
Work schedules	61	73	78
Sociotechnical systems redesign	95	70	100

NS = No studies identified

Adapted from R. A. Katzell and R. A. Guzzo, "Psychological Approaches to Productivity Improvement," *American Psychologist,* April 1983, p. 469.

meta-analysis, the reviewers placed studies into eleven program categories. (See Table 20–4.) The common denominator among these categories is that they all were concerned with introducing change. But as Table 20–4 illustrates, many of the interventions were programs consistent with OD values. This would include appraisal and feedback, goal setting, work redesign, organization structure, work schedules, and sociotechnical systems.

The results, in aggregate, are impressive. While some of the results are distorted because of the small number of studies identified, you can't ignore the general direction of the findings: eighty-six percent of the measures of productivity showed improvement, seventy-five percent of the measures of withdrawal showed positive effects, and seventy-five percent noted more favorable attitudes toward work. So although the strength of effects vary by type of intervention and choice of dependent variable, change intervention programs overall appear generally to have a positive impact on employee behavior and attitudes.

Maybe one of the strongest cases for the effectiveness of OD values is a review of more than 500 studies, covering tens of thousands of employees, where change agents moved organizations from having authoritarian to participative climates.[25] One to two years after the change, productivity and earnings in the organizations improved fifteen to forty percent, while control organizations that didn't undergo the change interventions failed to generate such improvements.

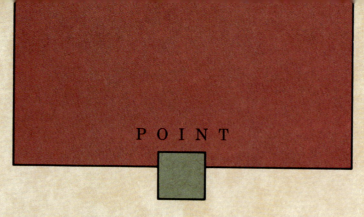

POINT

OD Is Culture-Bound

Few topics in organizational behavior are as culture-bound—that is to say, have as little application in many parts of the world—as is organizational development. We discussed this issue within the chapter, but its importance justifies amplification.

The case for OD being culture-bound is quite clear. It was developed by researchers and consultants essentially from North America, the United Kingdom, and Australia in the post-World War II period. While these societies are not perfect laboratories for OD, their underlying values support participation, autonomy, and many other OD values. It is also not a coincidence that successful major OD experiments in recent years, such as those at Volvo in Sweden, occur in countries whose values are congruent with those of OD.

We should also consider the state of a country's economic development. OD fits well in societies that are relatively wealthy, that make extensive use of sophisticated technologies, and where the labor force is well trained and educated. Again, this suggests that OD fits well into North American and western European countries. But workers in places like Venezuela and Ethiopia don't have the skills or interests to be involved in OD interventions. In terms of Maslow's needs hierarchy, these people are concerned with meeting their lower-order needs, while OD focuses on higher-order needs. Political democracy, by definition, requires that people have both the ability and the willingness to participate in a country's decision-making process. The same logic applies at the organizational level. OD interventions seek to bring humanistic-democratic values to the workplace. If the skills and education levels of workers are so rudimentary as to preclude their active involvement in organizational decision making, how appropriate can OD interventions be?

Finally, many OD interventions have definite orientations to cultural artifacts. For instance, sensitivity training and team building presume at least a moderate or even a small social distance. In many societies, demonstrating the socioemotional closeness that is necessary to succeed with these interventions is as inappropriate as it would be for executives in North America to come to work in their underwear. Social customs make it impossible for most people to do it.

Ideas in this argument were influenced by R. T. Golembiewski, *Organization Development: Ideas and Issues* (New Brunswick, NJ: Transaction Publishers, 1989), p. 71.

OD Is *Not* Culture-Bound

OD is *not* culture-bound. Four points need to be made in rebutting the previous argument.

First, it might just be that highly variable cultural features can coexist with relatively homogeneous personal features. There may, in fact, be some common set of needs that all or almost all people seek to fulfill. Recent transitions in Eastern European countries from totalitarian to democratic systems would attest to the strong need that *all* people have for humanistic-democratic values.

Second, there is no reason why OD interventions can't be implemented and thrive in incongruent cultures. People may need what their culture does *not* favor. In the extreme, the survival of a culture may require precisely what that culture rejects.

Third, some OD interventions seem to have a broad spectrum of applicability. For instance, research finds that survey feedback is effective in almost all cultures. This may be because it permits anonymity and entails limited direct confrontation.

Finally, the full range of OD interventions have in fact been applied in a number of diverse cultures. Estimates of success rates appear to be somewhat lower in nonaffluent countries than in wealthy cultures, but they are still substantial. This final point suggests in a global sense that OD interventions are widely applicable across cultures and that attention needs to be paid only to those unusual cases where OD interventions aren't likely to work. OD should be viewed as innocent until proven guilty; its interventions should be treated as universally applicable until that time that they are specifically proven otherwise.

This is based on R. T. Golembiewski, *Organization Development: Ideas and Issues* (New Brunswick, NJ: Transaction Publishers, 1989), pp. 72–75.

FOR DISCUSSION

1. "OD is built on humanistic-democratic values." Explain what this means.

2. What impact does an organization's culture have on determining whether OD will be successful?

3. What can the politically astute change agent do to increase the probability that an intervention will succeed?

4. What potential ethical issues are involved in OD interventions?

5. Why would OD change agents look with disfavor at mechanistic organization structures?

6. Why do OD change agents favor flat organizations?

7. What type of reward systems are congruent with OD values?

8. Based on job redesign preferences of OD change agents, describe the characteristics of jobs they would like to see people have.

9. Give six examples of quality-of-worklife interventions.

10. What is sensitivity training? What positive outcomes does it provide? Can you think of any negative outcomes?

11. Give an example of an intergroup development intervention.

12. What relationship, if any, is there between OD and organizational adaptability?

FOR FURTHER READING

FRENCH, W. L., and C. H. BELL, JR., *Organizational Development: Behavioral Science Interventions for Organization Improvement,* 4th edition. Englewood Cliffs, NJ: Prentice Hall, 1990. Reviews the major OD interventions.

GOLEMBIEWSKI, R. T., *Organization Development: Ideas and Issues.* New Brunswick, NJ: Transaction Publishers, 1989. Presents 34 OD ideas and issues by one of the leading figures in the field.

KIRP, D., and D. RICE, "Fast Forward—Styles of California Management," *Harvard Business Review,* January–February 1988, pp. 74–85. Explores how California management style is different from traditional styles and how California management is on the forefront of change.

PETERS, T., *Thriving on Chaos.* New York: Knopf, 1988. A provocative prescription of what managers must do if the organizations they lead are to survive. Advocates creating highly adaptive, constantly learning organizations.

PRITCHARD, R. D.; S. D. JONES; P. L. ROTH; K. K. STUEBING; and S. E. EKEBERG, "Effects of Group Feedback, Goal Setting, and Incentives on Organizational Productivity," *Journal of Applied Psychology,* May 1988, pp. 337–58. Demonstrates the value of group-level feedback, group goal-setting, and group incentives as QWL interventions.

TENNIS, C. N., "Responses to the Alpha, Beta, Gamma Change Typology," *Group & Organization Studies,* June 1989, pp. 134–49. Examines the manner in which OD has responded to three types of change.

The Beacon Aircraft Company

Objectives

1. To illustrate how forces for change and stability must be managed in organizational development programs.
2. To illustrate the effects of alternative change techniques on the relative strength of forces for change and forces for stability.

THE SITUATION

The marketing division of the Beacon Aircraft Company has gone through two reorganizations in the past two years. Initially, its structure changed from a functional to a matrix form. But the matrix structure did not satisfy some functional managers. They complained that the structure confused the authority and responsibility relationships.

In reaction to these complaints, the marketing manager revised the structure back to the functional form. This new structure maintained market and project groups, which were managed by project managers with a few general staff personnel. But no functional specialists were assigned to these groups.

After the change, some problems began to surface. Project managers complained that they could not obtain adequate assistance from functional staffs. It not only took more time to obtain necessary assistance, but it also created problems in establishing stable relationships with functional staff members. Since these problems affected their services to customers, project managers demanded a change in the organizational structure—probably again toward a matrix structure. Faced with these complaints and demands from project managers, the vice-president is pondering another reorganization plan. He has requested an outside consultant to help him in the reorganization plan.

THE PROCEDURE

1. Divide yourselves into groups of five to seven and take the role of consultants.
2. Each group identifies the driving and resisting forces found in the firm. List these forces below.

The Driving Forces	The Resisting Forces
_____	_____
_____	_____
_____	_____
_____	_____
_____	_____
_____	_____

3. Each group develops a set of strategies for increasing the driving forces and another set for reducing the resisting forces.

4. Each group prepares a list of changes it wants to introduce.

5. The class reassembles and hears each group's recommendations.

Source: Adapted from K. H. Chung and L. C. Megginson, *Organizational Behavior* (New York: Harper & Row, 1981), pp. 498–99. With permission.

Leadership Development at Pacific Bell

Following its diverstiture from AT&T in 1983, Pacific Bell's management decided its company needed to transform its traditional, risk-aversive culture into a less hierarchical, more entrepreneurial one. To help change the culture and give employees a common purpose and common approach to their work, management implemented a leadership development program. The program, which involved more than 23,000 of Pac Bell's 67,000 employees, consisted of a series of 10 two-day work sessions during which participants learned about running effective meetings, resolving conflicts, cutting costs, evaluating current situations, and implementing new ideas. The emphasis, however, was on communication—to provide employees with common "frameworks" and vocabulary for communicating with each other.

Almost from the beginning, the program was controversial. It used unusual training methods and introduced a language that employees were expected to use that was full of buzzphrases. For instance, employees were taught to be attentive to the needs of "multiple stakeholders" and that the organization and its members were "a nested set of open, living systems and subsystems dependent on the larger environment for survival." A number of participants described the program with terms like "brainwashing," "mind control," "Eastern mysticism," and "coercion."

An evaluation of the program by the California Public Utilities Commission identified several positive results of the program including better and more productive meetings, more participation by union members in problem solving and a feeling that the company is trying something new. But the PUC couldn't ignore the negative comments. A large proportion of the participants disliked the non-optional aspect of the program, the way that it intimidated dissenters, and believed that it was damaging productivity and morale.

In 1987, Pac Bell decided to put the program—which had already cost the company in excess of $39 million—on hold. Management said it would actively solicit employee opinions of the program and make improvements based on those responses.

QUESTIONS

1. What type of intervention does this Pac Bell program use?

2. Relate employee response to this program with the discussion of the ethics of control.

3. How might Pac Bell's management have improved its evaluation of this program's effectiveness?

Source: Based on "Pacific Bell's Management Plan Draws PUC Fire," *Telephony,* June 22, 1987, pp. 14-15; and P. Waldman, "Motivate or Alienate? Firms Hire Gurus to Change Their 'Cultures,'" *Wall Street Journal,* July 24, 1987, p. 19.

NOTES

[1]Based on J. Hyatt, "Surviving on Chaos," *INC.*, May 1990, pp. 60–71.

[2]L. D. Brown and J. G. Covey, "Development Organizations and Organization Development: Toward an Expanded Paradigm for Organization Development," in R. W. Woodman and W. A. Pasmore (eds.), *Research in Organizational Change and Development*, Vol. 1 (Greenwich, Conn.: JAI Press, 1987), p. 63.

[3]V. E. Schein, "Organizational Realities: The Politics of Change," *Training and Development Journal*, February 1985, pp. 37–41; and G. K. Kenny, P. Morgan, and B. Hinings, "The Protection of Interests: Organizational Change in the Australian Services Canteens Organization," *Asian Pacific Journal of Management*, September 1986, pp. 11–23.

[4]V. E. Schein, "Organizational Realities."

[5]D. A. Nadler, "The Effective Management of Organizational Change," in J. W. Lorsch (ed.), *Handbook of Organizational Behavior* (Englewood Cliffs, NJ: Prentice Hall, 1987), p. 362.

[6]See, for example, C. R. Rogers, "Some Issues Concerning the Control of Human Behavior: A Symposium," *Science*, November 30, 1956, pp. 1060–64; and G. A. Walter, "Organizational Development and Individual Rights," *Journal of Applied Behavioral Science*, November 1984, pp. 423–39.

[7]See R. Tainio and T. Santalainen, "Some Evidence for the Cultural Relativity of Organizational Development Programs," *Journal of Applied Behavioral Science*, May 1984, pp. 93–111; N. J. Adler, "The Future of Organization Development in Canada," *Canadian Journal of Administrative Sciences*, June 1984, pp. 122–32; A. M. Jaeger, "Organization Development and National Culture: Where's the Fit?," *Academy of Management Review*, January 1986, pp. 178–90; R. W. Boss and M. V. Mariono, "Organization Development in Italy," *Group & Organization Studies*, September 1987, pp. 245–56; and J. M. Putti, "Organization Development Scene in Asia," *Group & Organization Studies*, September 1989, pp. 262–70.

[8]The following discussion is based on A. M. Jaeger, "Organization Development and National Culture."

[9]*Ibid.*, p. 189.

[10]G. W. Bohlander, "Implementing Quality-of-Work Programs: Recognizing the Barriers," *MSU Business Topics*, Spring 1979, pp. 33–40; and G. R. Oldham and J. R. Hackman, "Work Design in the Organizational Context," in *Research in Organizational Behavior*, Vol. 2, eds., B. M. Staw and L. L. Cummings (Greenwich, Conn.: JAI Press, 1980), pp. 251–58.

[11]E. L. Trist and K. W. Bamforth, "Some Social and Psychological Consequences of the Longwall Method of Coal-Getting," *Human Relations*, January 1951, pp. 3–38.

[12]See, for instance, R. E. Walton, "Quality of Working Life: What Is It?," *Sloan Management Review*, Fall 1973, pp. 11–21; D. A. Ondrack and M. G. Evans, "Job Enrichment and Job Satisfaction in Quality of Working Life and Nonquality of Working Life Sites," *Human Relations*, September 1986, pp. 871–89; and D. Buchanan, "Job Enrichment is Dead: Long Live High-Performance Work Design," *Personnel Management*, May 1987, pp. 40–43.

[13]R. E. Walton, "Improving the Quality of Work Life," *Harvard Business Review*, May–June 1974, p. 12.

[14]E. H. Schein, *Process Consultation: Its Role in Organizational Development* (Reading, MA: Addison-Wesley, 1969), p. 9.

[15]Ibid.

[16]See, for instance, K. P. DeMeuse and S. J. Liebowitz, "An Empirical Analysis of Team-Building Research," *Group and Organization Studies*, September 1981, pp. 357–78; S. J. Leibowitz and K. P. DeMeuse, "The Application of Team-Building," *Human Relations*, January 1982, pp. 1–18; and D. Eden, "Team Development: A True Field Experiment at 3 levels of Rigor," *Journal of Applied Psychology*, February 1985, pp. 94–100.

[17]N. Margulies and J. Wallace, *Organizational Change: Techniques and Applications* (Glenview, IL: Scott, Foresman, 1973), pp. 99–100.

[18]See, for example, E. H. Neilsen, "Understanding and Managing Intergroup Conflict," in J. W. Lorsch and P. R. Lawrence (eds.), *Managing Group and Intergroup Relations* (Homewood, IL: Irwin-Dorsey, 1972), pp. 329–43.

[19]R. R. Blake, J. S. Mouton, and R. L. Sloma, "The Union-Management Intergroup Laboratory: Strategy for Resolving Intergroup Conflict," *Journal of Applied Behavioral Science*, No. 1 (1965), pp. 25–57.

[20]See S. P. Robbins, *Training in InterPersonal Skills: TIPS for Managing People at Work* (Englewood Cliffs, NJ: Prentice Hall, 1989), pp. 149–56.

[21]See, for instance, D. E. Terpstra, "Relationship Between Methodological Rigor and Reported Outcomes in Organization Development Evaluation Research," *Journal of Applied Psychology*, October 1981, pp. 541–43; and J. M. Nicholas and M. Katz, "Research Methods and Reporting Practices in Organization Development: A Review and Some Guidelines," *Academy of Management Review*, October 1985, pp. 737–49.

[22]See R. W. Woodman and S. J. Wayne, "An Investigation of Positive-Finding Bias in the Evaluation of Organization Development Intervention," *Academy of Management Journal*, December 1985, pp. 889–913; and W. M. Vicars and D. D. Hartke, "Evaluating OD Evaluations: A Status Report," *Group & Organization Studies*, June 1984, pp. 177–88.

[23]G. A. Neuman, J. E. Edwards, and N. S. Raju, "Organizational Development Interventions: A Meta-Analysis of Their Effects on Satisfaction and Other Attitudes," *Personnel Psychology,* Autumn 1989, pp. 461–89.

[24]R. A. Katzell and R. A. Guzzo, "Psychological Approaches to Productivity Improvement," *American Psychologist,* April 1983, pp. 468–72; and R. A. Guzzo, R. D. Jette, and R. A. Katzell, "The Effects of Psychologically Based Intervention Programs on Worker Productivity: A Meta-Analysis," *Personnel Psychology,* Summer 1985, pp. 275–92.

[25]R. Likert, "Past and Future Perspectives on System 4," *Proceedings of the Academy of Management,* Orlando, Florida, 1977.

APPENDIX: SCORING KEYS FOR EXERCISES

Exercise 1. What Do You Know About Human Behavior?

The correct answers to this exercise are as follows:

1. T	6. F	11. F	16. T
2. F	7. T	12. T	17. T
3. F	8. F	13. F	18. F
4. F	9. F	14. F	19. F
5. F	10. T	15. F	20. F

How well did you do? Most people get between twelve and sixteen right. Did you beat the average?

The value of this exercise is to dramatize that some of what you know about human behavior is erroneous. The systematic study of OB will help you to sort out fact from fiction regarding the behavior of people at work.

Exercise 2. How Do You Feel About Your Present Job?

For questions 1, 2, 5, 7, 9, 12, 13, 15, and 17, score your answers as follows: Strongly agree = 5; Agree = 4; Undecided = 3; Disagree = 2; Strongly disagree = 1. The remaining questions are scored in the reverse manner: Strongly agree = 1; Agree = 2, and so forth. Now sum up your scores for the eighteen items on the questionnaire. The larger your total score, the higher your job satisfaction. For comparative purposes, you might be interested to know that this questionnaire has been administered to individuals in a wide variety of jobs, including managers, civil service office employees, clerical workers, taxi drivers, nurses, and part-time graduate students. Eleven different studies found the range of mean scores to be between 56.79 and 76.51, with the mean of the means at 64.32. How did your score compare?

Exercise 3. Are You Keeping Up on the Changing Global Economy?

The correct answers are as follows:

1. Great Britain
2. Switzerland
3. Japan
4. United States
5. Great Britain
6. Japan
7. Italy
8. United States
9. United States
10. Germany
11. France
12. Venezuela
13. Japan
14. Finland

Exercise 4. Who Controls Your Life?

This exercise is designed to measure your locus of control. Give yourself 1 point for each of the following selections: 1B, 2A, 3A, 4B, 5B, 6A, 7A, 8A, 9B, and 10A. Scores can be interpreted as follows:

8–10 = High internal locus of control
6–7 = Moderate internal locus of control
5 = Mixed
3–4 = Moderate external locus of control
1–2 = High external locus of control

The higher your internal score, the more you believe that you control your own destiny. The higher your external score, the more you believe that what happens to you in your life is due to luck or chance.

Exercise 6. The Job Feelings Scale

This scale measures five different aspects of job satisfaction. To arrive at your score, sum the items within each category and divide by the number of items within that category.

For comparative purposes, the following mean scores were based on responses given by 35 school principals and 90 public health nurses:

	Principals	Nurses
Work	4.06	3.48
Supervisor	4.04	3.59

Co-workers	3.00	3.66
Promotion	2.93	2.35
Pay	3.16	2.92

Exercise 7. Needs Test

- Growth needs are items 2, 5, 8, 11.
- Relatedness needs are items 1, 4, 7, 10.
- Existence needs are items 3, 6, 9, 12.

Add the scores for each need set (for example, the summation of your scores on items 2, 5, 8, and 11 represent your growth need total). If you considered all four items within a need category to be very important, you would obtain the maximum total of twenty points.

College students typically rate growth needs highest. However, you may currently have little income and consider existence needs as most important. For instance, one student of mine scored 20, 10, and 15 for growth, relatedness, and existence needs, respectively. This should be interpreted to mean that her relatedness needs are already substantially satisfied. Her growth needs, on the other hand, are substantially unsatisfied.

Note that a low score may imply that a need is unimportant to you or that it is substantially satisfied. The implication, however, is that *everyone* has these needs. So a low score is usually taken to mean that this need is substantially satisfied.

Exercise 11. Compute Your LPC Score

Your score on the LPC scale is a measure of your leadership style. More specifically, it indicates your primary motivation or goal in a work setting.

To determine your LPC score, add up the points (1 through 8) for each of the sixteen items. If your score is 64 or above, you're a *high* LPC person or *relationship*-oriented. If your score is 57 or below, you're a *low* LPC person or *task*-oriented. If your score falls between 58 and 63, you'll need to determine for yourself in which category you belong.

According to Fiedler, knowing your LPC score can allow you to find a situational match and, therefore, help you to be a more effective leader.

Exercise 12. Power Orientation Test

This test is designed to compute your Machiavellianism (Mach) score. To obtain your score, add the number you have checked on questions 1, 3, 4, 5, 9, and 10. For the other four questions, reverse the numbers you have checked: 5 becomes 1, 4 is 2, 2 is 4, 1 is 5. Total your ten numbers to find your score. The National Opinion Research Center, which used this short form of the scale in a random sample of American adults, found that the national average was 25.

The results of research using the Mach test have found that (1) men are generally more Machiavellian than women, (2) older adults tend to have lower Mach scores than younger adults, (3) there is no significant difference between high Machs and low Machs on measures of intelligence or ability, (4) Machiavellianism is not significantly related to demographic characteristics such as educational level or marital status, and (5) high Machs tend to be in professions that emphasize the control and manipulation of individuals—for example, managers, lawyers, psychiatrists, and behavioral scientists.

Exercise 13. How Do You Handle Conflict?

Putnam and Wilson's research found that the five conflict-handling approaches described in Chapter 13 collapsed into three conflict strategies: nonconfrontational (which includes avoidance and accommodation), solution-oriented (collaboration and compromise), and control (synonymous with competition).

To calculate your mean score, sum up the total score you made in each of the three categories and divide by the number of items measuring the strategy. Then subtract each score from seven.

Items 1, 4, 6, 8, 9, 11, 13, 16, 19, 20, 21 = Solution-oriented

Items 2, 5, 7, 12, 14, 15, 23, 24, 25, 27, 28, 29 = Nonconfrontational

Items 3, 10, 17, 18, 22, 26, 30 = Control

From a study conducted by Putnam and Wilson, 360 participants scored as follows:

Solution-orientation = 3.73

Nonconfrontational = 2.42

Control = 2.43

You may want to break into small groups and compare your score patterns. Discuss issues such as: Did individual scores align with previous images that each had of his or her conflict-handling style? Is there a common pattern among group members' scores? If so, why? If not, why not? Do you think your group's results are generalizable to all students? How about successful managers?

Exercise 15. Bureaucratic Orientation Test

Give yourself one point for each statement for which you responded in the bureaucratic direction:

1. Mostly agree	11. Mostly agree
2. Mostly agree	12. Mostly disagree
3. Mostly disagree	13. Mostly disagree
4. Mostly agree	14. Mostly agree
5. Mostly disagree	15. Mostly disagree
6. Mostly disagree	16. Mostly agree
7. Mostly agree	17. Mostly disagree
8. Mostly agree	18. Mostly agree
9. Mostly disagree	19. Mostly agree
10. Mostly agree	20. Mostly disagree

A very high score (15 or over) would suggest that you would enjoy working in a bureaucracy. A very low score (5 or lower) would suggest that you would be frustrated by working in a bureaucracy, especially a large one.

Do you think your score is representative of most college students in your major? Discuss.

Exercise 16. Career Assessment Test

This instrument is an expanded version of Schein's five career anchors. It adds service, identity, and variety anchors. Score your responses by writing the number that corresponds to your response (SA = 4, A = 3, D = 2, SD = 1) to each question in the space next to the item number.

1 ___	2 ___	3 ___	4 ___	5 ___	6 ___
7 ___	8 ___	9 ___	10 ___	11 ___	12 ___
13 ___	14 ___	15 ___	16 ___	17 ___	18 ___
19 ___	20 ___	21 ___	22 ___	23 ___	24 ___
25 ___	26 ___	27 ___	28 ___	29 ___	30 ___
31 ___	32 ___	33 ___	34 ___	35 ___	36 ___
37 ___	38 ___	39 ___	40 ___	41 ___	42 ___
43 ___	44 ___				

Now obtain subscale scores by adding your scores on the items indicated and then divide by the number of items in the scale, as shown:

Technical Competence	_____	÷ 6 = _____
	#1, 2, 27, 35, 38, 41	
Autonomy	_____	÷ 6 = _____
	#3, 18, 23, 36, 39, 40	
Service	_____	÷ 6 = _____
	#4, 21, 37, 42, 43, 44	
Identity	_____	÷ 5 = _____
	#7, 13, 20, 22, 26	
Variety	_____	÷ 6 = _____
	#5, 12, 14, 24, 31, 32	
Managerial Competence	_____	÷ 6 = _____
	#6, 10, 11, 15, 25, 30	
Security	_____	÷ 5 = _____
	#8, 16, 17, 28, 33	
Creativity	_____	÷ 4 = _____
	#9, 19, 29, 34	

Briefly, the eight career anchors mean the following:

- *Technical competence.* You organize your career around the challenge of the actual work you're doing.
- *Autonomy.* You value freedom and independence.
- *Service.* You're concerned with helping others or working on an important cause.

- *Identity.* You're concerned with status, prestige, and titles in your work.
- *Variety.* You seek an endless variety of new and different challenges.
- *Managerial competence.* You like to solve problems and want to lead and control others.
- *Security.* You want stability and career security.
- *Creativity.* You have a strong need to create something of your own.

The higher your score on a given anchor, the stronger your emphasis. You'll function best when your job fits with your career anchor. Lack of fit between anchor and a job can cause you to leave the organization or suffer excessive stress.

Ask yourself now: On which anchor did I receive the highest score? What jobs fit best with this anchor? You can use your analysis to help you select the right job and career for you.

Exercise 17. Rate Your Classroom Culture

Add up your score on the eight items. Your score will lie somewhere between 8 and 40.

A high score (30 or above) describes an open, warm, human, trusting, and supportive culture. A low score (20 or below) describes a closed, cold, task-oriented, autocratic, and tense culture.

Compare your score against the ones tabulated by your classmates. How close do they align? Discuss perceived discrepancies.

Exercise 18. The Type A–Type B Exercise

To calculate your Type A/B rating, total your score on the seven questions. Now multiple it by 3. A total of 120 or more indicates you're a hard-core Type A. Scores below 90 indicate you're a hard-core Type B. The following gives you more specifics:

Points	Personality Type
120 or more	A+
106–119	A
100–105	A–
90–99	B+
Less than 90	B

Exercise 19. Managing-in-a-Turbulent-World Tolerance Test

Score four points for each A, three for each B, two for each C, one for each D, and zero for each E. Compute the total, divide by 24, and round to one decimal place.

While the results are not intended to be more than suggestive, the higher your score, the more comfortable you seem to be with change. The test's author suggests analyzing scores as if they were grade point averages. In this way, a 4.0 average is an A, a 2.0 is a C, and scores below 1.0 flunk.

Using replies from nearly 500 MBA students and young managers, the range of scores was found to be narrow—between 1.0 and 2.2. The average score was between 1.5 and 1.6—equivalent to a D+/C− grade! If these scores are generalizable to the work population, clearly people are not very tolerant of the kind of changes that come with a turbulent environment.

GLOSSARY

The number in parentheses following each term indicates the chapter in which the term was defined.

Ability (4). An individual's capacity to perform the various tasks in a job.

Absenteeism (2). Failure to report to work.

Accommodation (13). The willingness of one party in a conflict to place his or her opponent's interests above his or her own.

Action research (19). A change process based on systematic collection of data and then selection of a change action based on what the analyzed data indicates.

Active listening (10). The active search for meaning when one listens.

Adhocracy (15). A structure characterized as low in complexity, formalization, and centralization.

Adjourning (9). The final stage in group development for temporary groups, characterized by concern with wrapping-up activities rather than task performance.

Affiliation need (7). The desire for friendly and close interpersonal relationships.

Assessment centers (16). A set of performance simulation tests designed to evaluate a candidate's managerial potential.

Attitudes (6). Evaluative statements or judgments concerning objects, people, or events.

Attitude surveys (6). Eliciting responses from employees through questionnaires about how they feel about their jobs, work groups, supervisors, and/or the organization.

Attribution theory (5). When individuals observe behavior, they attempt to determine whether it is internally or externally caused.

Attribution theory of leadership (11). Proposes that leadership is merely an attribution that people make about other individuals.

Authoritarianism (4). The belief that there should be status and power differences among people in organizations.

Authority (14). The rights inherent in a managerial position to give orders and expect the orders to be obeyed.

Autocratic leader (11). One who dictates decisions down to subordinates.

Autonomous work teams (8). Groups that are free to determine how the goals assigned to them are to be accomplished and how tasks are to be allocated.

Autonomy (7). The degree to which the job provides substantial freedom and discretion to the individual in scheduling the work and in determining the procedures to be used in carrying it out.

Avoidance (13). Withdrawing from or suppressing conflict.

Bases of power (12). What powerholders control that allow them to manipulate the behavior of others.

Behaviorally anchored rating scales (16). An evaluation method where actual job-related behaviors are rated along a continuum.

Behavioral symptoms of stress (18). Changes in an individual's behavior—including productivity, absence, and turnover—as a result of stress.

Behavioral theories of leadership (11). Theories proposing that specific behaviors differentiate leaders from nonleaders.

Biographical characteristics (4). Personal characteristics—such as age, sex, and marital status—that are objective and easily obtained from personnel records.

Bounded rationality (5). Individuals make decisions by constructing simplified models that extract the essential features from problems without capturing all their complexity.

Brainstorming (10). An idea-generation process that specifically encourages any and all alternatives, while withholding any criticism of those alternatives.

Career (16). A sequence of positions occupied by a person during the course of a lifetime.

Career anchors (16). Distinct patterns of self-perceived talents and abilities, motives and needs, and attitudes and values that guide and stabilize a person's career after several years of real-world experience and feedback.

Career stages (16). The four steps most people go through in their careers: exploration, establishment, midcareer, and late career.

Case study (2). An in-depth analysis of one setting.

Causality (2). The implication that the independent variable causes the dependent variable.

Caused behavior (1). Behavior that is directed toward some end; not random.

Centralization (14). The degree to which decision making is concentrated at a single point in the organization.

Chain of command (14). The superior-subordinate authority relationship that extends from the top of the organization to the lowest echelon.

Change (19). Making things different.

Change agents (19). Persons who act as catalysts and assume the responsibility for managing change activities.

Channel (10). The medium through which a communication message travels.

Charismatic leadership (11). Followers make attributions of heroic or extraordinary leadership abilities when they observe certain behaviors.

Classical conditioning (4). A type of conditioning where an individual responds to some stimulus that would not invariably produce such a response.

Coalition (12). Two or more individuals who combine their power to push for or support their demands.

Coercive power (12). Power that is based on fear.

Cognitive dissonance (6). Any incompatibility between two or more attitudes or between behavior and attitudes.

Cognitive evaluation theory (7). Extrinsic rewards allocated for behavior that had been previously intrinsically rewarded tends to decrease the overall level of motivation.

Cohesiveness (9). Degree to which group members are attracted to each other and share common goals.

Cohorts (9). Individuals who, as part of a group, hold a common attribute.

Collaboration (13). A situation where the parties to a conflict each desire to satisfy fully the concern of all parties.

Collectivism (3). A national culture attribute that describes a tight social framework in which people expect others in groups of which they are a part to look after them and protect them.

Command group (9). A manager and his or her immediate subordinates.

Communication (10). The transference and understanding of meaning.

Communication networks (10). Channels by which information flows.

Communication process (10). The steps between a source and a receiver that result in the transference of meaning.

Competition (13). Rule-regulated efforts to obtain a goal without interference from another party.

Complexity (14). The degree of vertical, horizontal, and spatial differentiation in an organization.

Compressed workweek (8). A four-day week, with employees working ten hours a day.

Compromise (13). A situation in which each party to a conflict must give up something.

Conceptual skills (1). The mental abilities to analyze and diagnose complex situations.

Conflict (13). A process in which an effort is purposely made by A to offset the efforts of B by some form of blocking that will result in frustrating B in attaining his or her goals or furthering his or her interests.

Conflict paradox (13). Conflict contributes to a group's performance but most groups and organizations try to eliminate it.

Conformity (9). Adjusting one's behavior to align with the norms of the group.

Conformity values (6). A low tolerance for ambiguity, having difficulty in accepting people with different values, and a desire that others accept one's values.

Consideration (11). The extent to which a leader is likely to have job relationships characterized by mutual trust, respect for subordinates' ideas, and regard for their feelings.

Constraints of stress (18). Forces that prevent individuals from doing what they desire.

Contingency variables (1). Those variables that moderate the relationship between the independent and dependent variables and improve the correlation.

Continuous reinforcement (4). A desired behavior is reinforced each and every time it is demonstrated.

Controlling (1). Monitoring activities to ensure they are being accomplished as planned and correcting any significant deviations.

Core values (17). The primary or dominant values that are accepted throughout the organization.

Correlation coefficient (2). Indicates the strength of a relationship between two or more variables.

Cost-minimization strategy (15). Strategies that emphasize tight cost controls, avoidance of unnecessary innovation or marketing expenses, and price cutting.

Critical incidents (16). Evaluating those behaviors that are key in making the difference between executing a job effectively or ineffectively.

Culture shock (3). Confusion, disorientation, and emotional upheaval caused by being immersed in a new culture.

Customer departmentalization (14). Grouping activities on the basis of common customers.

Decisional roles (1). Roles that include those of entrepreneur, disturbance handler, resource allocator, and negotiator.

Decoding (10). Retranslating a sender's communication message.

Deep relaxation (18). A state of physical relaxation, where the individual is somewhat detached from the immediate environment and detached from body sensations.

Delphi technique (10). A group decision method in which individual members, acting separately, pool their judgment in a systematic and independent fashion.

Demands of stress (18). The loss of something desired.

Democratic leader (11). One who shares decision making with subordinates.

Dependency (12). B's relationship to A when A possesses something that B requires.

Dependent variable (2). A response that is affected by an independent variable.

Differentiation (15). The degree to which individuals in different functional departments vary in their goal and value orientations.

Disturbed-reactive environment (15). An environment dominated by one or more large organizations.

Division of labor (14). The breakdown of jobs into narrow, repetitive tasks.

Divisional structure (15). A set of autonomous units coordinated by a central headquarters.

Dominant culture (17). Expresses the core values that are shared by a majority of the organization's members.

Driving forces (19). Change forces that direct behavior away from the status quo.

Dysfunctional conflict (13). Conflict that hinders group performance.

Effectiveness (2). Achievement of goal.

Efficiency (2). The ratio of effective output to the input required to achieve it.

Egocentrism values (6). The belief in rugged individualism and selfishness.

Elasticity of power (12). The relative responsiveness of power to changes in available alternatives.

Employee-oriented leader (11). One who emphasizes interpersonal relations.

Encoding (10). Converting a communication message to symbolic form.

Encounter stage (17). The stage in the socialization process in which a new employee sees what the organization is really like and confronts the likelihood that expectations and reality may diverge.

Environment (15). Anything outside the organization itself.

Equity theory (7). Individuals compare their job inputs and outcomes with those of others and then respond so as to eliminate any inequities.

ERG theory (7). There are three groups of core needs: existence, relatedness, and growth.

Ethnocentric views (3). The belief that ones cultural values and customs are superior to all others.

Existential values (6). A high tolerance for ambiguity and individuals with differing values.

Exit (6). Dissatisfaction expressed through behavior directed toward leaving the organization.

Expectancy theory (7). The strength of a tendency to act in a certain way depends on the strength of an expectation that the act will be followed by a given outcome and on the attractiveness of that outcome to the individual.

Expert power (12). Influence based on special skills or knowledge.

Externals (4). Individuals who believe that what happens to them is controlled by outside forces such as luck or chance.

Extrinsic rewards (16). Rewards received from the environment surrounding the context of the work.

Feedback (7). The degree to which carrying out the work activities required by a job results in the individual obtaining direct and clear information about the effectiveness of his or her performance.

Feedback loop (10). The final link in the communication process; puts the message back into the system as a check against misunderstandings.

Felt conflict (13). Emotional involvement in a conflict creating anxiety, tenseness, frustration, or hostility.

Femininity (3). A national culture attribute that emphasizes relationships, concern for others, and the overall quality of life.

Fiedler contingency model (11). The theory that effective groups depend upon a proper match between a leader's style of interacting with subordinates and the degree to which the

situation gives control and influence to the leader.

Field experiment (2). A controlled experiment conducted in a real organization.

Field survey (2). Questionnaire or interview responses are collected from a sample, analyzed, and then inferences are made about the larger population from which the sample is representative.

Filtering (10). A sender's manipulation of information so that it will be seen more favorably by the receiver.

Fixed-interval schedule (4). Rewards are spaced at uniform time intervals.

Fixed-ratio schedule (4). Rewards are initiated after a fixed or constant number of responses.

Flexible benefits (8). Employees tailor their benefit program to meet their personal needs by picking and choosing from among a menu of benefit options.

Flextime (8). Employees work during a common core time period each day but have discretion in forming their total workday from a flexible set of hours outside the core.

Formal group (9). A designated work group defined by the organization's structure.

Formal networks (10). Task-related communications that follow the authority chain.

Formalization (14). The degree to which jobs within the organization are standardized.

Forming (9). The first stage in group development, characterized by much uncertainty.

Friendship group (9). Those brought together because they share one or more common characteristics.

Functional conflict (13). Conflict that supports the goals of the group and improves its performance.

Functional departmentalization (14). Grouping activities by functions performed.

Fundamental attribution error (5). The tendency to underestimate the influence of external factors and overestimate the influence of internal factors when making judgments about the behavior of others.

Generalizability (2). The degree to which results of a research study are applicable to groups of individuals other than those who participate in the original study.

Geographic departmentalization (14). Grouping activities on the basis of territory.

Goal-setting theory (7). The theory that specific and difficult goals lead to higher performance.

Grapevine (10). The informal communication channel.

Graphic rating scales (16). An evaluation method where the evaluator rates performance factors on an incremental scale.

Group (9). Two or more individuals, interacting and interdependent, who come together to achieve particular objectives.

Group demography (9). The degree to which members of a group share a common demographic attribute such as age, sex, race, educational level, or length of service in the organization, and the impact of these attributes on turnover.

Group order ranking (16). An evaluation method that places employees into a particular classification such as quartiles.

Groupshift (10). A change in decision risk between the group's decision and the individual decision that members within the group would make; can be either toward conservatism or greater risk.

Groupthink (10). Phenomenon in which the norm for consensus overrides the realistic appraisal of alternative courses of action.

Groupware (9). Computer software programs that allow employees to collaborate across barriers of space and time.

Halo effect (5). Drawing a general impression about an individual based on a single characteristic.

Hierarchy of needs theory (7). There is a hierarchy of five needs—physiological, safety, love, esteem, and self-actualization—and as each need is sequentially satisfied, the next need becomes dominant.

Higher-order needs (7). Needs that are satisfied internally; needs for love, esteem, and self-actualization.

Horizontal differentiation (14). The degree of differentiation between units based on the orientation of members, the nature of the tasks they perform, and their education and training.

Human relations view of conflict (13). The belief that conflict is a natural and inevitable outcome in any group.

Human skills (1). The ability to work with, understand, and motivate other people, both individually and in groups.

Hygiene factors (7). Those factors —such as company policy and administration, supervision, and salary— that, when present in a job, placate workers. When these factors are present, people will not be dissatisfied.

Hypothesis (2). A tentative explanation about the relationship between two or more variables.

Illegitimate political behavior (12). Extreme political behavior that violates the implied rules of the game.

Imitation strategy (15). Strategies that seek to move into new products or new markets only after their viability has already been proven.

Implicit favorite model (5). A decision making model where the decision maker implicitly selects a preferred alternative early in the decision process and biases the evaluation of all other choices.

Impression management (12). The process by which individuals attempt to control the impression others form of them.

Independent variable (2). The presumed cause of some change in the dependent variable.

Individual ranking (16). An evaluation method that rank orders employees from best to worst.

Individualism (3). A national culture attribute describing a loosely knit social framework in which people emphasize only the care of themselves and their immediate family.

Informal group (9). A group that is neither structured nor organizationally determined; appears in response to the need for social contact.

Informal network (10). The communication grapevine.

Informational roles (1). Roles that include monitoring, disseminating, and spokesperson activities.

Initiating structure (11). The extent to which a leader is likely to define and structure his or her role and those of subordinates in the search for goal attainment.

Innovation strategy (15). Strategies that emphasize the introduction of major new products and services.

Institutionalization (17). When an organization takes on a life of its own, apart from any of its members, and acquires immortality.

Integration (15). The degree to which members of various departments achieve unity of effort.

Intellectual ability (4). That required to do mental activities.

Intensive technology (15). A customized response to a diverse set of contingencies.

Interacting groups (10). Typical groups, where members interact with each other face to face.

Interactionist view of conflict (13). The belief that conflict is not only a positive force in a group but that it is absolutely necessary for a group to perform effectively.

Interest group (9). Those working together to attain a specific objective with which each is concerned.

Intergroup development (20). OD efforts to improve interactions between groups.

Interpersonal roles (1). Roles that include figurehead, leadership, and liaison activities.

Intermittent reinforcement (4). A desired behavior is reinforced often enough to make the behavior worth repeating, but not every time it is demonstrated.

Internals (4). Individuals who believe that they control what happens to them.

Intrinsic rewards (16). The pleasure or value one receives from the content of a work task.

Intuition (1). A feeling not necessarily supported by research.

Job analysis (16). Developing a detailed description of the tasks involved in a job, determining the relationship of a given job to other jobs, and ascertaining the knowledge, skills, and abilities necessary for an employee to perform the job successfully.

Job characteristics model (7). Identifies five job characteristics and their relationship to personal and work outcomes.

Job description (16). A written statement of what a jobholder does, how it is done, and why it is done.

Job design (8). The way that tasks are combined to form complete jobs.

Job enlargement (8). The horizontal expansion of jobs.

Job enrichment (8). The vertical expansion of jobs.

Job involvement (6). The degree to which a person identifies with his or her job, actively participates in it, and considers his or her performance important to his or her sense of self-worth.

Job rotation (8). The periodic shifting of a worker from one task to another.

Job satisfaction (2). A general attitude toward one's job; the difference between the amount of rewards workers receive and the amount they believe they should receive.

Job sharing (8). The practice of having two or more people split a forty-hour-a-week job.

Job specification (16). States the minimum acceptable qualifications that an employee must possess to perform a given job successfully.

Kinesics (10). The study of body motions.

Knowledge power (12). The ability to control unique and valuable information.

Labor unions (16). A formal group of employees that acts collectively to protect and promote employee interests.

Laboratory experiment (2). In an artificial environment, the researcher manipulates an independent variable under controlled conditions, and then concludes that any change in the dependent variable is due to the ma-

nipulation or change imposed on the independent variable.

Leader-member-exchange theory (11). Leaders create in-groups and out-groups, and subordinates with in-group status will have higher performance ratings, less turnover, and greater satisfaction with their superior.

Leader-member relations (11). The degree of confidence, trust, and respect subordinates have in their leader.

Leader-participation model (11). A leadership theory that provides a set of rules to determine the form and amount of participative decision making in different situations.

Leading (1). Includes motivating subordinates, directing others, selecting the most effective communication channels, and resolving conflicts.

Leadership (11). The ability to influence a group toward the achievement of goals.

Learning (4). Any relatively permanent change in behavior that occurs as a result of experience.

Legitimate political behavior (12). Normal everyday politics.

Leniency error (16). The tendency to evaluate a set of employees too high (positive) or too low (negative).

Line authority (14). Authority that entitles a manager to direct the work of a subordinate.

Locus of control (4). The degree to which people believe they are masters of their own fate.

Long-linked technology (15). Tasks or operations that are sequentially interdependent.

Lower-order needs (7). Needs that are satisfied externally; physiological and safety needs.

Loyalty (6). Dissatisfaction expressed by passively waiting for conditions to improve.

LPC (11). Least preferred co-worker questionnaire that measures task or relationship-oriented leadership style.

Machiavellianism (4). Degree to which an individual is pragmatic, maintains emotional distance, and believes that ends can justify means.

Machine bureaucracy (15). A

structure that rates high in complexity, formalization, and centralization.

Management by objectives (MBO) (8). A program that encompasses specific goals, participatively set, for an explicit time period, with feedback on goal progress.

Managerial Grid (11). A nine-by-nine matrix outlining eighty-one different leadership styles.

Managers (1). Individuals who achieve goals through other people.

Manipulative values (6). Individuals who value striving to achieve their goals by manipulating things and people.

Maquiladoras (3). Assembly plants operating along the Mexican side of the border from Texas to California.

Masculinity (3). A national culture attribute describing the extent to which the dominant societal values are characterized by assertiveness, acquisition of money and things, and not caring for others or for the quality of life.

Mass production (15). Large-batch manufacturing.

Matrix structure (15). A structure that creates dual lines of authority; combines functional and product departmentalization.

Maturity (11). The ability and willingness of people to take responsibility for directing their own behavior.

Mechanistic structure (15). A structure characterized by high complexity, high formalization, and centralization.

Mediating technology (15). Linking of independent units.

Message (10). What is communicated.

Meta-analysis (2). A quantitative form of literature review that enables researchers to look at validity findings from a comprehensive set of individual studies, and then apply a formula to them to determine if they consistently produced similar results.

Metamorphosis stage (17). The stage in the socialization process in which a new employee adjusts to his or her work group's values and norms.

Middle line (15). Managers who connect the operating core to the strategic apex.

Model (2). Abstraction of reality;

simplified representation of some real-world phenomenon.

Moderating variable (2). Abates the effect of the independent variable on the dependent variable; also known as contingency variable.

Motivating potential score (7). A predictive index suggesting the motivation potential in a job.

Motivation (7). The willingness to exert high levels of effort toward organizational goals, conditioned by the effort's ability to satisfy some individual needs.

Motivation-hygiene theory (7). Intrinsic factors are related to job satisfaction, while extrinsic factors are associated with dissatisfaction.

Multinational corporations (3). Companies that maintain significant operations in two or more countries simultaneously.

N ach (4). Need to achieve or strive continually to do things better.

National culture (3). The primary values and practices that characterize a particular country.

Need (7). Some internal state that makes certain outcomes appear attractive.

Neglect (6). Dissatisfaction expressed through allowing conditions to worsen.

Nominal group technique (10). A group decision method in which individual members meet face to face to pool their judgments in a systematic but independent fashion.

Nonverbal communication (10). Messages conveyed through body movements, the intonations or emphasis we give to words, facial expressions, and the physical distance between the sender and receiver.

Norming (9). The third stage of group development, characterized by close relationships and cohesiveness.

Norms (9). Acceptable standards of behavior within a group that are shared by the group's members.

OB Mod (8). A program where managers identify performance-related employee behaviors and then implement an intervention strategy to strengthen desirable performance behaviors and weaken undesirable behaviors.

Operant conditioning (4). A type of conditioning in which desired voluntary behavior leads to a reward or prevents a punishment.

Operating core (15). Employees who perform the basic work related to the production of products and services.

Opportunity power (12). Influence obtained as a result of being in the right place at the right time.

Opportunity to perform (7). High levels of performance are partially a function of an absence of obstacles that constrain the employee.

Optimizing model (5). A decision making model that describes how individuals should behave in order to maximize some outcome.

Organic structure (15). A structure characterized by low complexity, low formalization, and decentralization.

Organization size (14). The number of people employed in an organization.

Organization (1). A consciously coordinated social unit, composed of two or more people, that functions on a relatively continuous basis to achieve a common goal or set of goals.

Organizational behavior (OB) (1). A field of study that investigates the impact that individuals, groups, and structure have on behavior within organizations, for the purpose of applying such knowledge toward improving an organization's effectiveness.

Organizational commitment (6). An individual's orientation toward the organization in terms of loyalty, identification, and involvement.

Organizational culture (17). A common perception held by the organization's members; a system of shared meaning.

Organizational development (OD) (19). A collection of techniques that attempt to effect systematic planned change.

Organization structure (14). The degree of complexity, formalization, and centralization in the organization.

Organizing (1). Determining what tasks are to be done, who is to do them, how the tasks are to be grouped, who reports to whom, and where decisions are to be made.

Paired comparison (16). An evaluation method that compares each employee with every other employee and assigns a summary ranking based on the number of superior scores that the employee achieves.

Paraphrasing (10). Restating what a speaker has said in your own words.

Parochialism (3). A narrow view of the world; an inability to recognize differences between people.

Participative management (8). A process where subordinates share a significant degree of decision making power with their immediate superiors.

Path-goal theory (11). The theory that a leader's behavior is acceptable to subordinates insofar as they view it as a source of either immediate or future satisfaction.

Perceived conflict (13). Awareness by one or more parties of the existence of conditions that create opportunities for conflict to arise.

Perception (5). A process by which individuals organize and interpret their sensory impressions in order to give meaning to their environment.

Performance-based compensation (8). Paying employees based on some performance measure.

Performing (9). The fourth stage in group development, when the group is fully functional.

Personal power (12). Influence attributed to one's personal characteristics.

Personality (4). The sum total of ways in which an individual reacts and interacts with others.

Personality traits (4). Enduring characteristics that describe an individual's behavior.

Persuasive power (12). The ability to allocate and manipulate symbolic rewards.

Physical ability (4). That required to do tasks demanding stamina, dexterity, strength, and similar skills.

Physiological symptoms of

stress (18). Changes in an individual's health as a result of stress.

Piece-rate pay plans (8). Workers are paid a fixed sum for each unit of production completed.

Placid-clustered environment (15). An environment in which change occurs slowly, but threats occur in clusters.

Placid-randomized environment (15). An environment in which demands are randomly distributed and change occurs slowly.

Planned change (19). Change activities that are intentional and goal-oriented.

Planning (1). Includes defining goals, establishing strategy, and developing plans to coordinate activities.

Political behavior (12). Those activities that are not required as part of one's formal role in the organization but that influence, or attempt to influence, the distribution of advantages and disadvantages within the organization.

Pooled interdependence (13). Where two groups function with relative independence but their combined output contributes to the organization's overall goals.

Position power (11). Influence derived from one's formal structural position in the organization: includes power to hire, fire, discipline, promote, and give salary increases.

Power (12). A capacity that A has to influence the behavior of B so that B does things he or she would not otherwise do.

Power-control view of structure (15). An organization's structure is the result of a power struggle by internal constituencies who are seeking to further their interests.

Power distance (3). A national culture attribute describing the extent to which a society accepts that power in institutions and organizations is distributed unequally.

Power need (7). The desire to make others behave in a way that they would not otherwise have behaved in.

Power tactics (12). Identifies how individuals manipulate the power bases.

Prearrival stage (17). The period of learning in the socialization process that occurs before a new employee joins the organization.

Problem analyzability (15). The type of search procedure employees follow in responding to exceptions.

Process consultation (20). Consultant gives a client insights into what is going on around him or her, within him or her, and between him or her and other people; identifies processes that need improvement.

Process departmentalization (14). Grouping activities on the basis of product or customer flow.

Process production (15). Continuous-process production.

Product departmentalization (14). Grouping activities by product line.

Production-oriented leader (11). One who emphasizes technical or task aspects of the job.

Productivity (2). A performance measure including effectiveness and efficiency.

Professional bureaucracy (15). A structure that rates high in complexity and formalization, and low in centralization.

Projection (5). Attributing one's own characteristics to other people.

Psychological contract (9). An unwritten agreement that sets out what management expects from the employee, and vice versa.

Psychological symptoms of stress (18). Changes in an individual's attitudes and disposition due to stress.

Quality circle (8). A voluntary work group of employees who meet regularly to discuss their quality problems, investigate causes, recommend solutions, and take corrective actions.

Quality of worklife (QWL) (20). A process by which an organization responds to employee needs by developing mechanisms to allow them to share fully in making the decisions that affect their lives at work.

Rationality (5). Actions that are consistent and value maximizing.

Reactive values (6). Individuals who value basic physiological needs and are unaware of themselves or others as human beings.

Reciprocal interdependence (13). Where groups exchange inputs and outputs.

Referent power (12). Influence held by A based on B's admiration and desire to model himself or herself after A.

Refreezing (19). Stabilizing a change intervention by balancing driving and restraining forces.

Reinforcement theory (7). Behavior is a function of its consequences.

Reliability (2). Consistency of measurement.

Research (2). The systematic gathering of information.

Responsibility (14). An obligation to perform.

Restraining forces (19). Forces that hinder movement from the status quo.

Rituals (17). Repetitive sequences of activities that express and reinforce the key values of the organization, what goals are most important, which people are important and which are expendable.

Role (9). A set of expected behavior patterns attributed to someone occupying a given position in a social unit.

Role conflict (9). A situation in which an individual is confronted by divergent role expectations.

Role expectations (9). How others believe a person should act in a given situation.

Role identity (9). Certain attitudes and behavior consistent with a role.

Role perception (9). An individual's view of how he or she is supposed to act in a given situation.

Satisficing model (5). A decision making model where a decision maker chooses the first solution that is "good enough"; that is, satisfactory and sufficient.

Selective perception (5). People interpret what they see based on their interests, background, experience, and attitudes.

Self-actualization (7). The drive to become what one is capable of becoming.

Self-efficacy (16). A person's expectation that he or she can successfully execute behaviors required to produce an outcome.

Self-esteem (4). Individuals' degree of liking or disliking for themselves.

Self-management (4). Learning techniques that allow individuals to manage their own behavior so that less external management control is necessary.

Self-monitoring (4). A personality trait that measures an individual's ability to adjust his or her behavior to external, situational factors.

Self-perception theory (6). Attitudes are used, after the fact, to make sense out of action (behavior) that has already occurred.

Self-serving bias (5). The tendency for individuals to attribute their successes to internal factors while putting the blame for failures on external factors.

Sensitivity training (20). Training groups that seek to change behavior through unstructured group interaction.

Sequential interdependence (13). One group depends on another for its input but the dependency is only one way.

Shaping behavior (4). Systematically reinforcing each successive step that moves an individual closer to the desired response.

Similarity error (16). Giving special consideration when rating others to those qualities that the evaluator perceives in himself or herself.

Simple structure (15). A structure characterized by low complexity, low formalization, and authority centralized in a single person.

Situational leadership theory (11). A contingency theory that focuses on followers' maturity.

Skill variety (7). The degree to which the job requires a variety of different activities.

Socialization (17). The process that adapts employees to the organization's culture.

Social learning theory (4). People can learn through observation and direct experience.

Social loafing (9). Group size and individual performance are inversely related.

Sociocentric values (6). The belief that it is more important to be liked and to get along with others than to get ahead.

Sociotechnical systems (20). Work redesign must jointly optimize both the social and technological demands in the job.

Sources of power (12). How powerholders come to control the bases of power.

Span of control (14). The number of subordinates a manager can direct efficiently and effectively.

Spatial differentiation (14). The degree to which the location of an organization's offices, plants, and personnel are geographically dispersed.

Staff authority (14). Authority that supports, assists, and advises.

Stereotyping (5). Judging someone on the basis of the perception of the group to which that person belongs.

Storming (9). The second stage of group development, characterized by intragroup conflict.

Strategic apex (15). Top-level managers who are charged with the overall responsibility for the organization.

Stress (18). A dynamic condition in which an individual is confronted with an opportunity, constraint, or demand related to what he or she desires and for which the outcome is perceived to be both uncertain and important.

Strong cultures (17). Cultures where the core values are intensely held and widely shared.

Subcultures (17). Minicultures within an organization, typically defined by department designations and geographical separation.

Support staff (15). People who fill the staff units that provide indirect support services for the organization.

Survey feedback (20). The use of questionnaires to identify discrepancies among member perceptions; discussion follows and remedies are suggested.

Synergy (9). An action of two or more substances which results in an effect that is different from the individual summation of the substances.

Systematic study (1). Looking at relationships, attempting to attribute causes and effects, and drawing conclusions based on scientific evidence.

Task characteristic theories (7). Seek to identify specific task characteristics of jobs, how these characteristics are combined to form different jobs, and their relationship to employee motivation, satisfaction, and performance.

Task group (9). Those working together to complete a job task.

Task identity (7). The degree to which the job requires completion of a whole and identifiable piece of work.

Task significance (7). The degree to which the job has a substantial impact on the lives or work of other people.

Task structure (11). The degree to which job assignments are procedurized.

Task uncertainty (13). The greater the uncertainty in a task, the more custom the response. Conversely, low uncertainty encompasses routine tasks with standardized activities.

Task variability (15). The number of exceptions individuals encounter in their work.

Team building (20). High interaction among group members to increase trust and openness.

Technical skills (1). The ability to apply specialized knowledge or expertise.

Technology (15). How an organization transfers its inputs into outputs.

Technostructure (15). Analysts, who have the responsibility for effecting certain forms of standardization in the organization.

Telecommuting (8). Employees do their work at home on a computer that is linked to their office.

Theory (2). A set of systematically interrelated concepts or hypotheses that purport to explain and predict phenomena.

Theory X (7). The assumption that employees dislike work, are lazy, dislike responsibility, and must be coerced to perform.

Theory Y (7). The assumption that employees like work, are creative, seek responsibility, and can exercise self-direction.

Three needs theory (7). Achievement, power, and affiliation are three important needs that help to understand motivation.

Traditional view of conflict (13). The belief that all conflict must be avoided.

Trait theories of leadership (11). Theories that sought personality, social, physical, or intellectual traits that differentiated leaders from nonleaders.

Transactional leadership (11). Leaders who guide or motivate their followers in the direction of established goals by clarifying role and task requirements.

Transformational leaders (11). Leaders who give individualized consideration, intellectual stimulation, and possess charisma.

Tribalistic values (6). The belief in tradition and power exerted by authority figures.

Turbulent-field environment (15). An environment that changes constantly and that contains interrelated elements.

Turnover (2). Voluntary and involuntary permanent withdrawal from the organization.

Two-tier pay system (8). New employees are hired at significantly lower wage rates than those already employed and performing the same jobs.

Type A behavior (18). Aggressive involvement in a chronic, incessant struggle to achieve more and more in less and less time and, if necessary, against the opposing efforts of other things or other persons.

Type B behavior (18). Rarely harried by the desire to obtain a wildly increasing number of things or participate in an endlessly growing series of events in an ever-decreasing amount of time.

Uncertainty avoidance (3). A national culture attribute describing the extent to which a society feels threatened by uncertain and ambiguous situations and tries to avoid them.

Unfreezing (19). Change efforts to overcome the pressures of both individual resistance and group conformity.

Unit production (15). The production of items in units or small batches.

Unity of command (14). A subordinate should have only one superior to whom he or she is directly responsible.

Validity (2). The degree to which a research study is actually measuring what it claims to be measuring.

Values (6). Basic convictions that a specific mode of conduct or end state of existence is personally or socially preferable to an opposite or converse mode of conduct or end state of existence.

Value system (6). A ranking of individual values according to their relative importance.

Variable (2). Any general characteristic that can be measured and that changes in either amplitude, intensity, or both.

Variable-interval schedule (4). Rewards are distributed in time so that reinforcements are unpredictable.

Variable-ratio schedule (4). The reward varies relative to the behavior of the individual.

Vertical differentiation (14). The number of hierarchical levels in the organization.

Voice (6). Dissatisfaction expressed through active and constructive attempts to improve conditions.

Wellness programs (18). Organizationally-supported programs that focus on the employee's total physical and mental condition.

Work sampling (16). Creating a miniature replica of a job to evaluate the performance abilities of job candidates.

NAME INDEX

ORGANIZATION INDEX

Mitsubishi, 56
Mobil Oil, 365
Montgomery Ward, 635
Morgan Guaranty Trust, 582
Mormon Tabernacle Choir, 356
Motel 6, 76
Motorola, Inc., 8, 108, 195, 633

NASA, 494
National Broadcasting Co., 650
National Institute of Health, 18
National Opinion Research Center, 199
Nestlé, 56
New York City Public Library, 509
New York Life Insurance Co., 107
Nordstrom, 595
Northrop, 499

Ohio State University, 357–58, 368, 369, 376
Olympia & York Development Ltd., 63

Pacific Bell, 253, 683
Paramount Communications, 212, 400
Penn Central Railroad, 438
PepsiCo., 248
Peugeot, 249
Pillsbury, 56, 619
Pittston Coal, 178
Planned Parenthood, 505
Procter & Gamble, 27, 401, 577, 579, 580–81

Quaker Oats, 619

RCA, 81
Reader's Digest, 489
Reynolds Metals Co., 469
Roman Catholic Church, 431
Royal Dutch-Shell Group, 439

Safeway Stores, 600, 601
San Diego Padres, 215
Sanford Co., 206
San Francisco Forty-Niners, 383
Sanyo, 57
Schering-Plough, 201
Schlumberger, 577
Schwab, Charles & Co., 589
Scott Paper, 668
Seagrams, 56, 63
Sears, Roebuck, 175, 468, 489, 635
Seiko Epson, 620
Sheraton Hotels, 461
Simon & Schuster, 125
Sony, 56, 340, 576
Southwest Airlines, 650
Southwestern Texas State Teachers College, 398
Spalding, 76
Standard Oil of New Jersey, 489
Stride Rite Corp., 261
Sun Petroleum Products, 470
SuperValu, 534

Tandem Computers, 586
TGI Friday's, 157
Thermos, 76
3M Co., 95, 489, 490, 577
Times Mirror Co., 400
Timex Corp., 572
Toshiba, 573
Toyota Motor Co., 259, 352, 353, 518, 634
Toys R Us, 247, 635
TWA, 650

Union Bank of California, 261
United Airlines, 273
United Auto Workers, 674

United Parcel Service, 434, 579
U.S. Army, 357, 475, 551
U.S. Department of Defense, 460
U.S. Internal Revenue Service, 474, 507, 572
U.S. Marines, 581
U.S. Postal Service, 490, 608
U.S. Shoe Co., 257
Universal Pictures, 393
University of Michigan, 358, 376
University of Oregon, 300
University of Virginia, 580
USAA, 243
USX Corp., 8, 277

Victoria's Secret, 635
Volvo, 255–56

Waldenbooks, 635
Wal-Mart, 468, 489, 580, 635
Walt Disney Co., 54, 55, 56, 212, 571, 578, 580, 587, 588, 589
Wang Laboratories, 577
Warner Communications, 393
Weaver Popcorn, 660, 661, 662, 668
Western Electric, 288, 289
Westinghouse Electric, 446
Weyerhaeuser, 242
Wilson, Lynn Associates, 542
Wilson Sporting Goods, 76
Winnebago Industries, 634
Woolworth, F.W., 635

XA Systems Corp., 319
Xerox, 365, 511, 544, 578, 581, 668

Zenith, 57

SUBJECT INDEX